Marylanders in the Confederacy

Daniel D. Hartzler

Willow Bend Books
Westminster, Maryland
2001

Willow Bend Books
65 East Main Street
Westminster, Maryland 21157-5026
1-800-876-6103

WB0426

Source books, early maps, CDs—Worldwide

For our listing of thousands of titles offered

by hundreds of publishers see our website

www.WillowBendBooks.com

Visit our retail store

Fourth Printing, 2001

International Standard Book Number: 1-940907-00-3

Printed in the United States of America

The author has been a student of Maryland history since his college days. He has been a collector of Marylandia from the colonial period through the War Between the States. He has written four books, several journal reports, numerous magazine articles and lectured on the subject of antique arms, history and hunting.

Dedicated to:

HARRY D. BERRY, Jr.

A third generation dealer and restorer of antique decorative art, unsurpassed in his knowledge of martial and civilian arms.

FORWARD

The number of Marylanders in the Confederate service has long been a subject of conjecture, even during the war itself and the years immediately following. Most historians use the figure referred to by General Isaac R. Trimble of over 21,000 men. However, the question remains how Adjutant General Cooper arrived at this figure and whether it only included the vast majority in the Army of Northern Virginia. Many Marylanders served in more than one unit during the course of the war and therefore could have been counted more than once, making the total number somewhat less.

When I first met Dan Hartzler in the early 1970's he had already been diligently at work on this roster of Maryland Confederates. Over the years I have seen it grow from a few thousand names to the number contained in this publication. Although the roster is still far from complete, it is truly amazing that Mr. Hartzler has compiled as many names as he has. At various intervals, as I would leaf through the results of his countless hours of research, I was excited by the impressive names. The fragmentary state of Confederate records and the fact that many native Marylanders migrated to other southern states and the west during the decades prior to the war, and served in units from other states, make the task all but impossible. Still, Mr. Hartzler has drawn on 1,690 separate sources in compiling this roster, many never before available to historians.

There were several attempts during the 19th century to reconstruct the names of those from Maryland who wore the gray, but the scope of all was very meager. Finally, through years of earnest research, a significant number of documented names has been amassed. This is preceded by an enlightening chronicle depicting the important role played by Marylanders in the Confederacy.

Erick Davis

PREFACE

When Fort Sumter fell there were no deaths on either side. Those who first lost their lives on the altar of the Confederacy were Marylanders. The date was April 19, 1861. The 6th Massachusetts Regiment, first to march in obedience to the call of President Lincoln to bring the seceded states back in to the Union, was on its way to Washington. They had progressed down Broadway in New York through New Jersey and Philadelphia amidst enthusiastic demonstrations. Expecting trouble as they approached Baltimore, ammunition was distributed and weapons loaded. As the troops went from President Street Station to Camden Station, thousands of excited Baltimoreans rushed to Pratt Street where the troops were met with jeers and groans. The National flags had been hauled down, substituted by the South Carolina palmetto and Maryland black and gold flags. Cheers for Jeff Davis and the Confederacy grew louder as the troops progressed. Near the Pratt Street Bridge where the street was being repaired, cobblestones flew thick and fast at the troops. Shots rang out as the untrained soldiers began to fire at the unarmed civilians. Muskets were wrestled from the hands of soldiers and turned on the troops. Thus the first lives to be lost in the War Between the States were those of Marylanders.

Not being able to decide her own fate because of the arrest of her legislators, the state was shackled to the Union. It is remarkable that so many Marylanders were able to make their way out of the state during a period of military occupation. There was no area within the Confederacy that gave so many volunteers while under control of the enemy. The number of volunteers under such conditions was astonishing - and they stayed until the bitter end at Appomattox. Freestaters remained steadfast in their support of the Confederacy into the spring of 1865 when the consecrated banner was furled for the last time.

I regret that at the beginning of this work I did not record all those who made the supreme sacrifice. Approximately twenty-four percent of the listed partriots did not survive the war because of disease and combat. They fought without personal reward and died nobly, buried without ceremony. It was enough for them to answer the call of duty and follow a rugged path even if it led to a bloody grave. William Norris wrote in his publicaiton, The Story of the Confederate States Ship Virginia, Once Merrimack, "Being forced to struggle through the enemy's lines, to reach the Confederate colors, we were in a particular degree isolated from our homes and friends. But for the infamous arrest of her legislature, the state, by the absolute unanimous voice of her people on that day, would in a few hours, have been wielded into line with her sister states. The southern brothers tell us that wherever confederate bugles blew, the notes reached the ears of Marylanders; that wherever it adorned and hallowed the landscape, our beautiful flag looked down upon Marylanders, who, in turn, looked up to it, their eyes beaming with love and devotion; that wherever the daylight air was startled with a crash and a roar of battle, and thickest of the smoke and close to the colors, were men who were then illustrating the glories of the 'Old Maryland Line,' and when the bugles sang truce, for the night clouds had lowered and the sentinel stars sent their watch in the sky they looked down upon Maryland's dead and dying; we take no pride in these flattering works, none whatsoever. The cause was ours as much as theirs, and called for the same sacrifice even to the going down into the grave."

With the outcome of the War, the destruction of the records, and the lapse of time, this project of finding all the patriots from Maryland who served in the Confederacy can never be completed. After exhausting all known possibilities in writing *Medical Doctors of Maryland in the C.S.A.*, I immediately received two letters from ladies upset as to why I had not included their great-grandfathers. This project also falls short of what was desired. Dorchester County history states that no less than twenty members of the Lake family of Lake's District served in the Southern Army and I have only located two-thirds of this number. Records of the United Daughters of the Confederacy reveal that John Ker left Baltimore early in 1864 to join his six brothers, unnamed, in the Confederate Army; yet I have no other references to Ker or his brothers. If you have information on any veterans not listed in this work please write to me at 310 Church Street, New Windsor, Maryland 21776, so that I may add them to the list of our gallant forefathers.

In this work I have described some groups of interesting Marylanders about whom information came to light during the course of my research. The categories covered by the various chapters were somewhat arbitarily selected based on available material and by no means suggest a complete coverage of Maryland's support of the Confederacy. Hopefully this portion of the book will contribute to understanding the roles played by Marylanders in certain aspects of the War.

The heart of this book is a listing of the veterans and is contained in Appendix A: Roster. The format is composed of five sections: name, rank, command, residence and references.

Name - The surname is given in all capital letters, consistent with my use of capital letters throughout the book to indicate Marylanders who served in the Confederate forces. The roster lists last name, first name and middle name. Nicknames, often a source of confusion to researchers, are included in quotes. In the 4th Maryland Artillery material, "Dr. Jack" was Andrew Bryan and "Dad Baker" was Henry Baker. Dr. Frederick Garretson Van Bibber, after resigning from the old Navy and entering the Southern Navy, dropped his last name and used his middle name that was his mother's maiden name. Some appear to be duplications such as James Roberdeau Annan and Roberdeau Annan, both of Company G, 2nd Virginia Infantry. Upon further examination, it is revealed that James Roberdeau Annan later served in the 3rd Virginia Local Defense Infantry, Company E, while Roberdeau Annan remained with Company G. They were probably father and son. In-depth research reveals that Company B, 9th Virginia Infantry, contained two men named William J. Fisher, senior and junior. H. Bowie Dusenberry was in Stuart's Horse Artillery, after first serving in Company B, 21st Virginia Infantry, at this same early period as B. Dusenberry was in Company K, 1st Virginia Cavalry, so they are not considered to be the same. Names were spelled differently in various sources of material. Only one spelling is used herein. T. S. Brown of the 1st Virginia Infantry is considered to be the same as Thaddeous T. Brown of Company E and is listed under the latter name. William H. Guyther and W.H. W. Guyther, both of Great Mills in St. Mary's County, are considered to be two different veterans, one born in 1840, the other in 1843. Birth and death dates are not shown but were often used in determining identification and may be supplied upon request.

Rank - The highest grade of a verteran's military record was used. The few surviving Confederate documents do not always reveal their status, particularly in the scarce Naval records.

PREFACE

Command - The majority of men were in the line of the army and are indicated by regiment and company. Designation is made for local defense, reserve, staff, special corps and militia as well as navy and marine. Veterans typically served in several commands during the course of the War, but because of space limitations, only one unit is given. George Pielert served in the Tredagor Iron Works Artillery, 3rd Virginia Artillery, 2nd Maryland Artillery and the Navy. By examining the references shown with each entry a fairly complete listing of commands can be compiled. Some Marylanders could not be linked to a specific unit. For example, in the Confederate military records collection of the National Archives there are forty-two veterans by the name of William Short listed in the general index of microfilm rolls. There is no way to determine which one is the Marylander without examining each service record. Even so, there is only a chance that the record will reveal the state of residence or birth. A reference to a Major Charles Wallach could not be determined because a Major Charles S. and a Major Charles T. are found in the Confederate records with no designation as to their origin. Charles Kephart was killed early in the conflict just after joining the army and no unit has been located; thus it is not shown.

Residence - When more than one address was found, the latest address prior to the conflict is given. The name of the town is normally used; however, many lived in rural areas, and the name of a district or plantation is sometimes included. Following this is the county of residence. The fact that a veteran was residing in Maryland following the War did not necessarily meet my criterion for inclusion in the listing; depending on their known expressions of allegiance to other states they may have been excluded. For example, John Wilkinson, a conspicious naval captain, returned to Maryland after the war to reside with his Maryland-born wife. He was a member of the Society of the Army and the Navy in the State of Maryland but considered himself a Virginian by reason of birth.

Reference - The credentials of a veteran could refer to single mention in a diary or a biography of exciting sagas which would provide days of enjoyable reading - not to be confused with fictional books that use some real names, such as *The Gray Captains* by Jere Wheelwright and *For Maryland's Honor* by Lloyd T. Everett. If the reference is not a book, pamphlet or published item, the designation of the location is given when possible. Some owners of these valuable documents prefer to remain anonymous. If you contact me, I will forward your written request.

Abbreviations have been used for rank, command and residence. The rank of officers is capitalized, while enlisted rank is given in lower case. A complete listing of abbreviations is given below.

Army titles:

- Maj Gen - Major General
- Brig Gen - Brigadier General
- Col - Colonel
- Lt Col - Lieutenant Colonel
- Maj - Major
- Capt - Captain
- Lt - 1st Licutenant or 2nd Lieutenant
- sgt - Sergeant
- cpl - Corporal
- pvt - Private
- Asst A.G. - Assistant Adjutant General
- C.C.S. - Chief Commissary of Supply
- A.C.S. - Assistant Commissary of Supply
- A.I.G. - Assistant Inspector General
- Adj & I.G. - Adjutant & Inspector General

Q.M. - Quartermaster
Asst Q.M. - Assistant Quartermaster
Adj - Adjutant
Engr - Engineer
Surg - Surgeon
Asst - Assistant
P.M. - Provost Marshall
Hdqrtrs - Headquarters

Navy titles:
Adm - Admiral
R. Adm - Rear Admiral
Com - Commodore
Capt - Captain
Cmdr - Commander
Lt. Commanding - Lieutenant Commanding
Lt - 1st or 2nd Lieutentant
Mast - Master
Midn - Midshipman
bsn - Boatswain
gun - Gunner
mast. m. - Mastermate
p.m. - Paymaster
C. Engr - Chief Engineer
N.C. - Naval Constructor
ymn - Yeoman
cptr - Carpenter
sm - sailmaker
mast. a - Master of Arms
amr - Armorer
mach - Machinist
lmn - Landsman
smn - seaman
fmn - Fireman
g.c. - Gunboat Crew
d.h. - Deckhand
c.h. - Craftholder
c.hr. - Coal Heaver
std - Steward

Units:
Inf - Infantry
Cav - Cavalry
Arty - Artillery
Div - Division
Brig - Brigade
Leg - Legion
Regt - Regiment
Bn - Battalion
Vol - Volunteer
Co - Company
MLCSH - Maryland Line Confederate Soldiers Home

Abbreviations of states: Standard postal abbreviations

Counties:
All - Allegany County
AA - Anne Arundel County
Balt - Baltimore City
Bt - Baltimore County
Cal - Calvert County
Caro - Caroline County
Carr - Carroll County
Cec - Cecil County
Cha - Charles County
Dor - Dorchester County
Frd - Frederick County
Gar - Garrett County
Har - Harford County
How - Howard County
Kt - Kent County
Mont - Montgomery County
PG - Prince George's County
QA - Queen Anne's County
St. M - St. Mary's County
Som - Somerset County
Tal - Talbot County
Wash - Washington County
Wic - Wicomico County
Wor - Worcester County

PREFACE

This publication has been in preparation for fourteen years and I am indebted to staff personnel of many institutions and private individuals. Those listed in the references have been especially gracious in sharing information. Following is a partial list of those to whom I am indebted: William A. Albaugh, III; Edwin W. Beitell; Hugh Benet, Jr.; Harry D. Berry, Jr.; Carroll Brice; Howard E. Brown; William L. Brown, III; Edward St. C. Buckler, Jr.; Ronald Byrnes; Janet R. Colburn; Erick Davis; Ralph W. Donnelly; William Duffin; Richard Eichman; David W. Gaddy; Charles Haislip; Jeb Hartzler; Kit Hartzler; Sandy Hartzler; Judge George Henderson; Pat Hinkle; Kevin Kendrick; Robert K. Krich; Dave Mark; Marie Melchiori; Robert Melchiori; Roger Melchiori; Cy Nelson; Harry W. Newman; Edward Schlotzhauer; Frederick Schroyer; Clyde Smith; Daniel C. Toomey; Miss Mary R. Trippe; F. Edward Wright.

If I have overlooked anyone please accept my apology. Let me simply thank all those who have helped to perpetuate the remembrance of our gallant forefathers who bore the bottony cross for the Confederacy.

Daniel D. Hartzler
New Windsor, Maryland

CONTENTS

Chapter One

COMPARATIVE STRENGTHS

This work identifies and discusses a major portion of those citizens of Maryland who voluntarily left their families and loved ones to take up the cause of the Southern Confederacy. They crossed the Potomac simply as patriotic volunteers, desiring to serve a cause in which they deeply believed and for which they were willing to endure hardship and sacrifice their lives. There were other Marylanders, tens of thousands, who desired to join with the South but were prevented by censorship, intimidation, coercion, seizures, fines, confiscations, arrest and imprisonment.

The exact number of Marylanders who served for the Confederate States of America (C.S.A.) may never be known due to the destruction of the repositories and records of the Confederate government. About 4,580 Marylanders served in Maryland designated commands.[1] Thousands of additional Marylanders joined already existing commands throughout the South. Johnson says, "Men of Maryland descent were scattered all over the Confederacy, and thousands of young men who got through the line sought out their relations or kinsmen in nearly every regiment of the army."[2]

During the War, and even today, estimates of the number of Marylanders who volunteered for service in the Confederacy have varied greatly. Estimates by historians and others generally range between 20,000 and 25,000. Major General Isaac R. TRIMBLE, in a prepared address delivered to the Society of the Army and Navy of the Confederate States in Maryland on February 22, 1883, said "General S. Cooper, Adjutant-General of our government, told me in Richmond that over 21,000 Marylanders had entered the Southern armies."[3] William Wilkins Glenn stated that, "John T. B. DORSEY tells me that there were 22,000 enrolled in Richmond. Of course, the actual number must have been larger."[4] L. Nathan WOODHOUSE wrote, "Far more than 25,000 of the flower of her youth and manhood, the staunch and true, the brave and gallant of her sons from before Manassas, up almost to Appomattox, braved the dangers, underwent the hardships and crossed the Potomac to enter the service of the South and wore the Confederate gray, in the red-dyed field of many a hard fought battle."[5]

There are different ways in which one might attempt to construct an estimate of Marylanders serving in the Confederate forces. One might begin with the number of Marylanders who returned to the state immediately after the War and increase that figure by the estimated number who died, returned later and never returned. A reasonable starting figure might be that given by Glenn, namely, 11,770 paroled prisoners, having reported to the Baltimore provost marshal's office by June 29, 1865.[6] To this figure one would have to add those who reported to other provost marshals within the state, and the many Maryland veterans who settled in Dixie, went west, or went to Euorpe before returning. Finally, one would have to include those who never returned at all.

From the outset, those who did return were treated harshly and unfairly. When they reported to one of the area provost marshal offices they were sometimes arrested and confined for several weeks, despite the fact that this was a violation of the agreement stated in their paroles. In view of this practice, many families urged their loved ones not to return, at least not immediately.

MARYLANDERS IN THE CONFEDERACY

Examination of surviving documents of southern states reveals that some Marylanders were recorded as natives of other Confederate states. This resulted from the difficulty Marylanders experienced in securing upper level positions, since Maryland had no voice in the Confederate government. This author was amazed, while perusing the records of appointed staff officers, to find that approximately half of all the successful Maryland applicants claimed to be from other states of the South. Elias GRISWOLD was appointed on November 15, 1861, not from his home state of Maryland, but from Alabama - as a captain and assistant quartermaster. After being reappointed on April 17, 1862, with his position secure as Assistant Adjutant General, his subsequent records indicated Maryland as his home state. John Taylor WOOD resigned from the U.S. Navy on April 21, 1861. Awaiting to see what course Maryland would take, he harvested his crops on his Anne Arundel County farm. Then on September 3, he buried his silver and departed with his family to join the Confederate forces. On his arrival he began signing his name as J. Taylor Wood, and claimed Louisiana, birthplace of his mother, as his home state.[7]

In attempting to ascertain the number of Marylanders who fought for the Blue one can be easily deceived. For example, *The History and Roster of Maryland Volunteers* which has been widely used as a reference in historical works, lists members of all commands by unit.[8] Since the same person could appear in several units over the course of time (due to promotion, reenlistment, reorganization and other factors,) an exaggerated number of Marylanders who served in the Union Army has often been presented. In compiling an index to the *Roster*, Daniel C. Toomey revealed the extent of duplication in this work.[9] This author has identified over 6,272 multiple listings attributable to transfers alone. It is clear that the total strength of Marylanders fighting for the Union was far less than the grand total of 62,959 given in Volume I of the *Roster*. Volume II of the *Roster* shows 3,925 naval personnel and 8,718 colored troops who were state residents. Easily overlooked in using these figures is the duplication of entries for 550 black men who were transferred from the Army to the Navy.

Whereas the Marylanders who served in the Confederacy were true volunteers in the finest sense, there were a number of Marylanders serving in the Union Army with far less conviction and dedication. Many were drafted; others were motivated by the promise of bounty for themselves and their slaves; and still others (not always Marylanders) were paid as substitutes. It is not surprising that a large number soon deserted. In Volume I of the *Roster*, 4,808 soldiers are listed as deserters.

The story of John HENRY and his company illustrates the misgivings of many Marylanders who initially enrolled on the side of the Union. At the outbreak of the War John Campbell HENRY raised a company of volunteers for the Federal Army, known as Company A, of which he was captain, in the 1st Eastern Shore Infantry Regiment. Captain HENRY soon shifted his allegiance and decided to cast his lot with the South in the Battle for Independence. He resigned his command in the Federal Army on August 16, 1862, and went south. HENRY enlisted in Richmond on March 19, 1863, as a private in Company A, 2nd Maryland Infantry, for three years or the duration of the war. Four months later, Private HENRY stood in the ranks of the 2nd Maryland on Culp's Hill opposed by his former comrades of the 1st Regiment Eastern Shore Infantry. As these Federal Eastern Shoremen marched toward Gettysburg, there was much dissension within their ranks. On July 2 at Gettysburg, 49 men out of 92 in Company K refused to go into action and were immediately dishonorably discharged. HENRY, on the other hand, continued to serve with distinction with the Confederacy.[10]

Of those listed as Marylanders who served with the Union forces, many were recent immigrants. According to the 1860 census, there were some 77,000 foreign-born persons living in Maryland. For the most part, they proved to be loyal to their newly adopted government. Even with this large pool of immigrants, Maryland never filled more than 61 percent of its conscription quota, the lowest rate of all states who remained in the Union.

Bradley T. JOHNSON contrasts the enrollments of Marylanders, Blue and Gray, in his *Confederate Military History, Volume II*. In it he says:

"Recruiting was at once begun in Baltimore by J.C. McConnell, and other companies were raised in different parts of the state, and before the first of June 1861, the 1st Regiment Maryland Volunteers was mustered into service of the United States, and John R. Kenley commissioned colonel, and Nathaniel T. Dushane lieutenant colonel. The 2nd Regiment was mustered in about the middle of September under Colonel Summers and Lieutenant Colonel Duryea. The 3rd Maryland was recruiting foreigners in Baltimore City and Western Maryland and was commanded by Colonel DeWitt. The 4th Regiment, commanded by Colonel Sudburgh, was composed of Germans. The 1st and 2nd Maryland Artillery Companies were commanded by Captains Hampton and Thompson and the 1st Maryland Cavalry by Lieutenant Colonel Miller.

"These first forces raised for the Union in Maryland were, with the exception of the 1st Regiment, mainly composed of foreigners, alien by birth and alien to the institution, ideals and motives that for nine generations had formed the character of Marylanders. They were good men, but they were not Marylanders. They were devoted to the Union, but they had no concept of the force and duty of courage and chivalry.

"The 1st Maryland under Kenley was the only Maryland regiment on the Union side. The Confederate Marylanders on the other hand, embodied faith and pride of the state. Not a historic family of Maryland was not represented in the Maryland Line. Five grandsons of John Eager Howard, of Cowpens carried sword or muskets in the 1st Maryland Regiment. A grandson of Charles Carroll of Carrollton rode as a private in Company K, 1st Virginia Cavalry. Colonel JOHNSON of the Maryland Line, rode at the head of 72 kinsmen, descendants of soldiers of the Revolution, his own flesh and blood."[11]

Chapter 2

SENIOR GRADE AND FLAG RANKED OFFICERS

Before the war ended, twelve men from Maryland had attained the rank of general or admiral in the Union forces. Of these twelve top commanders, only five were born in Maryland. To the Southern cause, Maryland gave seventeen officers who would rise to general or flag rank.

Brigadier General James Jay ARCHER (1817-1864) was born in Harford County of a distinguished Maryland family. He graduated from West Point in 1826 and was assigned to the 3rd Infantry. Serving on the frontier in the West, he was promoted to first lieutenant in October, 1833. On March 31, 1834,

ARCHER resigned to enter the lumber business at Havre-de-Grace. A number of the Harford County Archers migrated to Texas. In 1847 ARCHER moved to San Patricio, Texas where he practiced law. On March 16, 1861, he was commissioned a captain in the regular Confederate Army. In a matter of weeks, he became colonel of the 5th Texas Regiment, and in May he was made commander of the Texas brigade. After the Battle of Seven Pines he was promoted to brigadier general and commanded a brigade in A.P. Hill's division. At Mechanicsville, Gaine's Mill, Manassas, Cedar Mountain and Second Manassas, his brigade won many laurels, rising to prominence in the famous Light Division. He participated in the capture of Harper's Ferry and then proceeded to Antietam. At Chancellorsville his brigade participated in Jackson's flank movement.

General ARCHER's troops led the advance into Gettysburg and fired the first shots of that memorable struggle. While occupying McPherson's woods, he was wounded shortly after his men had killed Major General Reynolds. ARCHER's brigade was almost surrounded by superior forces in front and on both flanks, forcing them back when General ARCHER, with sixty or seventy men, was captured.

Every flag in the brigade except one was captured and General ARCHER was imprisoned on Johnson's Island. In the summer of 1864, he was among six hundred Confederate officers sent from Fort Delaware and placed under fire of their own guns in Charleston harbor. Subsequently exchanged, he was assigned to command his old brigade and Welker's brigade on August 19, 1864, just after his rigorous confinement. He died from the effects of his wounds on October 24, 1864, as he was about to be promoted to major-general.

Brigadier General Joseph Lancaster BRENT (1826-1905) was born and reared in Charles County. He graduated from Georgetown University in the class of 1840, became an attorney in Baltimore, and later migrated to California. When the war broke out he took passage on a ship for the South with William M. Gwyn, ex-United States Senator, and Calhoun Benham, United States District Attorney. They were arrested on the high seas, sent to Fort Lafayette, held for three weeks and finally released with the help of political influence.

In the winter of 1861 and 1862 BRENT proceeded to Richmond and was commissioned as a captain on the staff of General J.B. Magruder. After the Yorktown campaign, he was promoted to Major of Artillery as Chief Ordnance Officer. In 1862, he was assigned as an aide-de-camp to the staff of General R. Taylor in Western Louisiana.

BRENT later commanded the First Louisiana Brigade of Cavalry and in October, 1864, was promoted to brigadier general. He commanded a department in the West that extended from Arkansas to the Gulf of Mexico, and was the last line held by the Confederate Army. General BRENT was paroled at Alexandria, Louisiana in May, 1865. After returning to Baltimore, he resumed his law practice.

Admiral Franklin BUCHANAN (1800-1874) was born in the Druid Hill section of Baltimore of a prominent Maryland family. He became a midshipman in the United States Navy at the age of fifteen on board the man-of-war *Java*. In February , 1821, he became second officer on board the *Dorothea*., and on January 13, 1825, a lieutenant. On September 3, 1841, BUCHANAN was commissioned a commander, and in August, 1846, he was chosen as the first superintendent of the Naval Academy at Annapolis which he assisted in founding. With the beginning of the Mexican War, he immediately requested sea service, and was turned down. His request was renewed several times until March 9, 1847, when he took command of the newly completed sloop *Germantown* and sailed for the Gulf of Mexico. He was honored for his gallant service in the war by the state legislature and given one hundred and sixty acres in Iowa by the United States Congress. He served on several Naval Boards along with the Lighthouse Committee, and commanded the *Baltimore Rendezvous* after the war. In 1852, he commanded Commodore Perry's flag ship in the expedition to Japan. In 1855, BUCHANAN was promoted to captain, and had more sea service than any other commander. On May 26, 1859, he was ordered to the Washington Navy Yard. On April 22, 1861, feeling that Maryland would secede, he resigned his commission and retired with his family to his home on Miles River in Talbot County. On May 4, realizing that Maryland would not secede, he wrote to the Secretary of the Navy in an attempt to recall his resignation, but he was informed that it had been accepted. On August 31, 1861, he appeared before a Justice of the Peace in Easton to legally acknowledge bills of all his personal and real property to his family. On September 5, 1861, BUCHANAN was commissioned a captain in the Confederate Navy as Chief of Orders and Details. On February 24, 1862, he was placed in command of the naval defenses of the James River. BUCHANAN commanded the ironclad *Virginia* in its near-destruction of the Federal fleet at Hampton Roads, and was wounded in the first day's action. On August 19, 1862, he was promoted to the rank of admiral. After recovering from his wound, he commanded the Naval forces in the battle of Mobile Bay in August, 1864, and was again seriously wounded in the leg and captured. Exchanged on March 4, 1865, he reported to Mobile where he was paroled on May 14th. Returning to his home he served as President of the Maryland Agricultural College in 1868, and in 1879 he accepted a position as secretary and state manager of the Alabama Life Association in Mobile. He remained there a year and a half and then returned to Miles River.

Major General Arnold ELZEY (1816-1870) was born at Elmwood on the Manokin River in Somerset County. His ancestors were among Maryland's earliest and most prominent. He graduated from West Point in 1837 and, noticing that a number of officers in the army bore his paternal last name of Jones, he adopted his grandmother's maiden name of Elzey. He served with distinction during the Seminole Indian outbreak in Florida, and he had the honor of firing the first gun of the Mexican War. From the opening gun until the surrender of Mexico City he participated in nearly every battle, and was twice brevetted for gallantry and meritorious conduct. ELZEY was promoted to captain in 1860 and placed in command of the United States arsenal at Augusta. After the fall of Fort Sumter, the arsenal was surrounded by state troops and he was compelled to surrender. Having already decided that his place must be with the South, he subdued his passion to resign immediately, escorted his command to Washington and then resigned his commission.

After crossing the Potomac, ELZEY became colonel of the First Maryland Infantry on June 16, 1861. At Manassas, after the wounding of General K. Smith, the command of the brigade devolved upon ELZEY, the senior colonel, who successfully continued its movements. He assailed the enemy by leading the charge which turned the tide of the battle, broke the Federal forces, and started the rout of the almost victorious Union forces under McDowell.

For his gallant service ELZEY was proclaimed the "Blucher" of the day and promoted to brigadier general on the field by President Davis who had witnessed ELZEY'S decisive charge.

Commanding a brigade under Stonewall Jackson all through the celebrated Valley campaign, ELZEY was slightly wounded in the leg at Port Republic and then severely wounded through the head at Cold Harbor. Twice in early 1862 General R.E. Lee requested that ELZEY be made a major general, and after a miraculous recovery and promotion, Major General ELZEY assumed command of the Richmond defenses. On April 25, 1864, he established headquarters in Staunton as commander of the Maryland Line, but on June 17 was sent to Breckinridge. On September 8, 1864, he was assigned to the Army of Tennessee as Chief of Artillery.

General ELZEY was captured on April 19, 1865, in Macon, Georgia, and paroled on May 8, 1865. ELZEY went to Baltimore, and then settled on a farm in Anne Arundel County.

Commodore George Nicholas HOLLINS Sr. (1799-1878) was born in Baltimore, and in 1814 became a midshipman in the United States Navy, serving on the *Erie* against the British during their blockade of the Chesapeake Bay. He transferred to the *President*, under the command of Stephen Decatur, and was captured in Bermuda where he was held for the duration of the war.

In the Algerian war of 1815, HOLLINS again served under Decatur and was presented a sword in recognition of his meritorious conduct. He was promoted to lieutenant in 1829, commander in 1841, and captain in 1855.

Hollins resigned his commission in the spring of 1861 while on a cruise in the Mediterranean. After returning to Baltimore he crossed the Potomac on June 18, 1861 in an open boat. Proceeding to Richmond, he was commissioned a captain in the Confederate Navy on June 22,1861. HOLLINS was introduced to Richard THOMAS and the two entered into a plan to capture the *Saint Nicholas*. That same afternoon, the two recrossed into Maryland and THOMAS proceeded north to purchase arms.

On June 29, 1861, HOLLINS, THOMAS and a detail of ZARVONA's Maryland Zouaves captured the *Saint Nicholas* on the Potomac. At Richmond, HOLLINS strengthened longshore fortifications on the James River, and was then sent to New Orleans on July 31, 1861, to command the naval station with the rank of commander. Appointed flag officer in December, he took a fleet up the Mississippi to Columbus, Kentucky. During the war, he commanded naval stations on the Mississippi River, the coast of Louisiana, Richmond and Wilmington. He outfitted many ships, tugs and fireboats; skippered the CSS *Florida* and the cutter *Harriet Lane*; and then was sent to Europe on special duty. At the conclusion of hostilities, Commodore HOLLINS returned to his native Baltimore.

Brigadier General Bradley Tyler JOHNSON (1829-1903) was born in Frederick of an old prominent family. After graduating from Princeton, he practiced law and became prominent in state politics. He represented the Maryland Democratic party in the 1860 National Convention.

In December 1860, JOHNSON organized a company of militia, the Frederick Mounted Dragoons, who became known as the Frederick Volunteers. They were among the first to fly to the defense of their state after secessionists clashed with Federal troops on April 19 that same year. When the futility of opposition to the Federal government became apparent, he marched his company of sixty men to Point of Rocks, Frederick County, Maryland. He declined a commission as lieutenant colonel in the Virginia service and undertook to organize a distinctive Maryland command. His hopes were realized in the organization of the 1st Maryland Regiment, of which his unit was the senior company. He became major in June, 1861, lieutenant colonel in July, and colonel in March, 1862. The regiment was mustered out in August of 1862, because of the expiration of their term.

General T.J. Jackson had been so impressed with JOHNSON that he was placed in command of a brigade. So ably and fully did he discharge his duties that Jackson recommended him for brigadier general. This was not acted upon for the reason that so many generals had already been appointed from Maryland.

During the Maryland campaign, JOHNSON was appointed provost marshal of his native city, and then served in Richmond on a military court. On February 4, 1863, General Jackson renewed the recommendation for JOHNSON's promotion and a week later again urged action upon the request. JOHNSON secured his relief from the court, and in November, 1863 brought together Maryland infantry, cavalry and artillery, established the Maryland Line and was elected its commander.

Towards the close of February, 1864 JOHNSON intercepted a dispatch from Dahlgren to Kilpatrick during their Richmond raid. JOHNSON, with a handful of Maryland cavaliers, harrassed the column's rear, striking them continually and never losing contact with them until their opportunity to seize Richmond was lost. He was proclaimed to be the savior of Richmond and on June 25, 1864, received his commission as brigadier general.

General JOHNSON preceded Jubal Early's command on the Baltimore and Washington Campaign, and led the cavalry on its raid around Baltimore. In July, 1864 he was recalled and disallowed his plan to release the Confederate prisoners at Point Lookout because of the massing of Union forces around Washington at that time. He accompanied General McCausland on the Chambersburg expedition.

General JOHNSON, being junior in rank and commanding only a few troops from Maryland, was forced to give way to others in the field. In the latter part of November, 1864 he was given command of the military prison at Salisbury, North Carolina. After his surrender, during the investigation of the prison by a Federal military court, the voluntary testimony of his former prisoners so eloquently attested to his humanity that General JOHNSON was promptly cleared of any wrongdoing. Broken in fortune, he made his home in Richmond and as soon as the restrictive legislation of the reconstruction period permitted he served in the Virginia Senate. He still yearned for his native state, however, and in 1878 he returned to Baltimore and resumed his law practice. He assisted in organizing the Society of the Army and Navy of the Confederate States in Maryland, the Association of the Maryland Line, and the establishment of the Maryland Line Confederate Soldiers Home.

Brigadier General Lewis Henry LITTLE (1817-1862) was a native Baltimorean, the son of a colonel and a congressman of eighteen years. In 1839 he graduated from St. Mary's College and received a commission as 2nd lieutenant, becoming one of the few regular army officers of that time who was not a West Point graduate. In 1845 he was promoted to 1st lieutenant in the 5th United States Infantry. For gallant and meritorious conduct on August 20, 1847, at the Battle of Monterey during the Mexican War, LITTLE was commissioned a captain. On April 25, 1861, he was in St. Louis when he resigned his commission and prepared to return to Maryland. While waiting for his resignation to be officially accepted, he became Adjutant General to Sterling Price in organizing the Missouri State Guard with the rank of major. He was subsequently promoted to colonel, and commanded a brigade at the battle of Pea Ridge. Special commendations were bestowed upon him, and he was promoted to brigadier general on April 16, 1862. In May, General Van Dorn requested that he be made a major general. General LITTLE led the Army of the West to the aid of Albert Sidney Johnston east of the Mississippi to Corinth where he began to suffer severely from malaria. He was placed in charge of a division which consisted of four brigades and on August 25, Price urged LITTLE's promotion to major general.

On September 19, 1862, at Iuka, Mississippi, while commanding the left wing, Generals Price and LITTLE were conferring on horseback when a Minie-ball struck him above the left eye. Falling into the arms of a comrade, he died without speaking a word.

General LITTLE was buried in a small garden behind his headquarters at midnight by torchlight. After the war his remains were exhumed and reinterred in Greenmount Cemetery, Baltimore, where six other Confederate generals were later buried.

Major General Mansfield LOVELL (1822-1884) was born in Washington, D.C., the son of a distinguished Marylander who served as surgeon general of the United States Army. He graduated ninth in his class from the United States Military Academy in 1842 and received a second lieutenancy in the Fourth Artillery. LOVELL was wounded during the Mexican War at Monterey in 1846. He became a first lieutenant in 1847. He participated in all actions from Vera Cruz to Mexico City and was wounded again at Belasco gate. He was brevetted captain for bravery at Chapultepec.

After the war he commanded several garrison batteries. He resigned on September 18, 1854 in New York. There he drilled the Old City Guard and was deputy street commissioner from 1858 until the Civil War. He was bitterly opposed to the election of Lincoln because he felt that his election would completely divide the country.

Tendering his services to the Confederacy, LOVELL was commissioned a brigadier general, and on October 7, 1861, promoted to major general and assigned to command Department Number One at New Orleans. His advice to combine naval and military operations was turned down. With less than 3000 short-term enlisted men, of whom only twelve hundred were armed, he prevented the destruction of New Orleans by evacuating the city.

In December of 1862, LOVELL was superseded by Van Dorn at Corinth, where he commanded the rear guard during the retreat. In 1864, J.E. Johnston applied for him to command a corps, but his recommendation was not acted upon. Desiring field duty he served as a volunteer on the staff of General Johnston. After the war, LOVELL remained in the South for several years and then returned to New York, where he was subsequently employed as a civil engineer.

Brigadier General William Whann MACKALL (1816-1891) was born and educated in Cecil County. He graduated from West Point in 1837 and was assigned to the First Artillery as a second lieutenant. In the Seminole Indian War he was promoted to first lieutenant and was severely wounded in an ambush in

February, 1839, at New Inlet. He served at Plattsburg, New York during the Canadian border disturbances in 1840 and for the next two years on the Maine frontier. In the Mexican War he was brevetted captain at Monterey, and again wounded at Chapultepec. MACKALL served on the staff of Generals Butler and Worth in 1846-48 and subsequently as adjutant general of the Western Division and the Third Military Department. In 1853 he was made a brevet major as adjutant general of the Eastern Division.

MACKALL declined promotion to lieutenant colonel and resigned on July 3, 1861. Disguised as a cattle buyer, he made his way through the Southern counties of Maryland to Richmond where he accepted a commission as lieutenant colonel and assistant adjutant general on the staff of Albert Sidney Johnston. In January, 1862, he was promoted to the rank of colonel and by March he had become a brigadier. He commanded the forces at Madrid Bend and Island Number 10 where he was captured on April 8. General MACKALL was exchanged in August of 1862, and General Beauregard immediately requested that MACKALL be assigned to him as a division commander, but MACKALL was placed in charge of the district of the Gulf in the Department of Tennessee. In February 1863, he took charge of the Western Division until April when he was appointed as chief of staff by Braxton Bragg. Returning to General Johnston's department, he commanded General Hebert's brigade in Mississippi and East Louisiana.

General MACKALL was paroled on April 20, 1865, at Macon, Georgia. His postwar years were spent near Fairfax, Virginia where he owned several farms.

Raphael SEMMES (1809-1877) was born in Charles County of an old colonial family. He was raised by his uncle and secured an appointment as a naval midshipman in 1826. SEMMES spent several years in naval study at Norfolk. Not receiving a commission as lieutenant until 1837, he went to Hagerstown, studied law with his brother, and was admitted to the bar in 1834. He served on routine surveys of the southern and Gulf coasts, and became known as a maverick sea lawyer.

With the beginning of the Mexican War he was given command of the brig *Somers*, to aid in the blockage of Vera Cruz. His ship foundered in a gale. He dispatched all his available boats, and stayed with the sinking ship on which thirty-nine of the crew drowned. Upon the return of a courageous midshipman, SEMMES and the only two others who had survived were plucked from the water.

SEMMES then served as flag lieutenant to Commodore David Conner, and also served on various land assignments. He was promoted to commander in 1855 and served on various boards. On February 15, 1861, while serving in Washington, he tendered his resignation. The next day he departed for Montgomery where he was commissioned a commander in the Southern service and then he was sent north to purchase needed military supplies. Desiring sea duty, he persuaded the Secretary of the Confederate Navy to assign him a ship and on April 18, 1861, he began to outfit the steamer *Sumter*, which would become the first warship of the Confederacy. This commercial raider cruised for six months and was used in the capture of seventeen United States merchant ships, burning eight and releasing the others in ransom bond. In June 1862, SEMMES was promoted to captain and ordered to take command of the CSS *Alabama*, a newly completed English raider. In the next 22 months, while continuously at sea, he captured, ransomed, sank or burned

82 Federal vessels, literally obliterating United States commerce. On June 19, 1864, off Cherbourg, France, the *Alabama* was sunk by the USS *Kearsarge*. Upon returning to Richmond, SEMMES was appointed rear admiral on February 10, 1865, and assumed command of the James River Squadron. After the evacuation of Richmond, Rear Admiral SEMMES with the rank of brigadier general, organized a brigade of artillery known as SEMMES Brigade.

SEMMES was paroled on May 1, 1865 at Greensboro, North Carolina and retired to Mobile, Alabama as an attorney. While living in Mobile he was arrested by federal authorities (Dec. 15, 1865) in response to the continuing outcry for vengeance. After four months confinement, he was released. He returned to Mobile and was later elected judge, but by order of President Johnson he was forbidden to be inducted, and so turned to journalism along with his law practice.

Brigadier General George Hume STEUART Jr. (1828-1903) was born in Baltimore, son of a prominent militia general. Graduating from the United States Military Academy in 1848 with a lieutenancy in the Second Dragoons, he served on the Texas western frontier. On March 3, 1855, he was promoted to first lieutenant and on December 20, to captain.

While engaged in garrison duty in Kansas, Nebraska, and Colorado, STEUART participated in the Cheyenne expedition of 1848, and fought against the Comanche in 1860. Immediately after the April 19th clash of Federal forces and Southern sympathizers in Baltimore he resigned, and was commissioned a captain of cavalry in the regular army of the Confederate states. Upon the formation of the First Maryland Infantry, STEUART was appointed lieutenant colonel. At Manassas he was taken prisoner but was recaptured after several hours. Upon the promotion of ELZEY, STEUART became colonel, and in March of 1862, he became a brigadier general. On May 17, 1862 STEUART was ordered by T.J. Jackson to proceed to organize Marylanders into the Maryland Line. With the coming of the spring campaign he was obliged to postpone his recruiting and was given command of a brigade in Ewell's division to which the First Maryland Infantry was attached. He commanded a brigade in which he and the Second Maryland Infantry distinguished themselves on Culps' Hill. On May 12, 1864 at the salient at Spottsylvania, known as Bloody Angle, his division was overwhelmed and he was captured. While imprisoned at Fort Delaware he was among the Southern officers placed under Confederate artillery fire at Hilton Head. Exchanged in August of 1864, General STEUART was assigned to command Barton's Brigade in Lee's Second Army Corps. This brigade fought at the center of Pickett's line at Five Forks, and after the evacuation of Richmond and Petersburg he was paroled at Appomattox. After the war STEUART resided on a farm in Anne Arundel County and commanded the Maryland United Confederate Veterans.

Brigadier General Allen E. THOMAS (1830-1907) was born and reared in Howard County. He graduated from Princeton in 1850, passed the bar and became an attorney. THOMAS married a sister of Richard Taylor, who later became a Confederate lieutenant general. THOMAS and his wife moved to Louisiana where they were residing when hostilities opened. At this point, as a major, he organized the 28th Louisiana Infantry. At Chickasaw, in command of a brigade, he defeated the Union attempt to complete a pontoon bridge. The next day, commanding his regiment on the Federal side of the bayou, THOMAS fought against Blair's brigade with only his regiment for six and one-half hours, inflicting a loss of four hundred. The next day, while holding the bluffs against Sherman, he again distinguished himself. At Vicksburg in June, 1863, he was captured and imprisoned. After being exchanged, THOMAS was promoted to brigadier general on February 4, 1864, but he and his brigade were under parole and did not participate in the spring campaign. General THOMAS gallantly commanded Polignac's division under Kirby Smith until the conflict ended. After the War he made his home in Florida. He was appointed as United States minister to Venezuela before retiring to Mississippi.

Brigadier General Lloyd TILGHMAN, Sr. (1816-1863) was born in Talbot County of a distinguished colonial Maryland heritage. He graduated from West Point in 1836 and was commissioned a second lieutanant in the First Dragoons. Resigning on September 30, 1836, he followed the profession of civil engineering, becoming division engineer of the Baltimore and Susquehanna Railroad (1836-38), Maryland Eastern Shore Railroad (1838-39), and the Baltimore and Ohio Railroad (1839-40). During the Mexican War he was a volunteer aide to General Twiggs in the battles of Palo Alto and Resaca de la Palma. In 1847 he was commissioned a captain of the Maryland and District of Columbia battalion. Returning to his profession, TILGHMAN became assistant principal engineer of the Panama division of the Isthmus. Offering his services in the Southern War For Independence, he was commissioned a colonel at Cairo, then called Hopkinsville, Kentucky, and soon became a brigadier general. On February 6, 1862, he surrendered Fort Henry before Grant's overwhelming forces of 12,000 men. General TILGHMAN retired his main body of 2,600 poorly armed soldiers toward Fort Donelson but stayed with his staff and sixty men to hold the Union army as long as possible. At one point, General TILGHMAN took the place of an exhausted gunner, working the 32 pounder until captured. He was exchanged in August, 1862, whereupon he was placed in command of the 1st brigade of Loring's division. On the retreat from Holly Springs on May 15, 1863, while handling the rear guard at Champion's Hill, Mississippi, he dismounted to give directions for sighting a piece of artillery when he was severely wounded by fragments of an exploding shell and died. His body was escorted by his personal staff and his son to Vicksburg for burial. Within a year his only son, young Lieutenant Lloyd TILGHMAN, Jr., was also killed while serving with the western army.

Major General Isaac Ridgeway TRIMBLE (1802-1888) was born in Culpeper County, Virginia and graduated from West Point in 1822 where he had a distinguished record in engineering. As a second lieutenant in the first artillery he was detailed to survey the military road from Washington to the Ohio River. TRIMBLE resigned in 1832 and settled in the Free State. He became chief engineer of the Baltimore and Susquehanna Railroad. He was subsequently chief engineer of the Philadelphia, Wilmington, and Baltimore Railroads, Boston and Providence Railroads and the West Indies Railroad. In April, 1861, he was appointed to command the volunteer un-uniformed corps of Baltimore. A month later he crossed the Potomac and was appointed a colonel of engineers in the Virginia service, and was assigned to construct the defenses around Norfolk. In August he was commissioned a brigadier general amd commanded a brigade at Evansport, erecting batteries along the river. In November he was assigned to command the Fourth Brigade, Second Division supporting Stonewall Jackson in the glorious valley campaign of 1862.

TRIMBLE played a conspicuous part at Cross Keys in commanding two brigades which repulsed the attack of Fremont. With reinforcements, General TRIMBLE took the offensive and routed the enemy. Before Richmond at the Seven Days battle he continued to distinguish himself, and at Cold Harbor he personally led a successful charge against the Union defenses. At Second Manassas, after marching his weary men by night, he crushed the Federal resistance at the point of the bayonet without a fatality, and captured 300 prisoners, eight guns and immense stores. He was recommended for promotion by Jackson on October 26, 1862; Lee also recommended that he be made a major general. General TRIMBLE was seriously wounded at Groveton and on January 19, 1863, he commanded the Shenandoah Valley, forming the left wing of the army. He had been ordered to form all the Maryland troops into brigades, but at Gettysburg on July 3, General TRIMBLE led Pender's division against the Federal center in Pickett's charge and was severely wounded, resulting in his capture and the amputation of his right leg. Held as a prisoner of war at Johnson's Island and Fort Warren, he was subsequently exchanged in April 1865, for Major Generals Crook and Kelly, who had been captured by McNeill's men of GILMOR's command. When he reached Lynchburg he found that the army had surrendered, and so he returned to his residence in Baltimore.

Brigadier General Robert Charles TYLER (1833-1865) was born and reared in Baltimore. In 1856 he embarked in the first expedition in Nicaragua under William Walker. After returning he was employed in Baltimore until 1860 when he moved to Memphis. On April 18, 1861, he enlisted as a private in Company D 15th Tennessee Infantry and was soon promoted to regimental quartermaster. That autumn TYLER was made a major on the staff of Cheatham, and in a few months was promoted to lieutenant colonel of the 15th regiment which he commanded at the battles of Belmont and Shiloh where he was wounded. The regiment was reorganized at Corinth, and TYLER was promoted to colonel. He was appointed provost marshal during the invasion of Kentucky in the fall of 1862. While leading his regiment with distinction during the subsequent campaigns of the Tennessee Army, he was dangerously wounded at Missionary Ridge where his leg was amputated. On February 23, 1864 he was commissioned a brigadier general but he was still disabled and could not take the field. While recuperating near West Point, Georgia, General TYLER organized convalescents and Georgia militia against Wilson's cavalry raid. On April 16, 1865, he defended an earthwork fort called Fort Tyler, on the west side of town, with two field pieces, a 32 pounder and 265 desperate men. The southerners had no trained gunners and General TYLER was on crutches, but the little garrison refused to surrender and maintained the defense of the earthwork until they were completely overrun and captured. There were casualties of 48 killed or wounded including General TYLER, who was killed instantly by a sharpshooter's ball in the head. He was buried at Fort Tyler.

Brigadier General Charles Sidney WINDER (1829-1862) was born in Talbot County. He graduated from the U.S. Military Academy in 1850, was appointed to the 3rd United States Artillery, and was advanced to first lieutenant in 1854. He was ordered to the west coast on board the steamer *San Francisco* which went down in a hurricane off the Atlantic coast. Rescued after several days, WINDER, for coolness in survival efforts and devotion to his men, was promoted to captain on March 3, 1855, which made him the youngest captain in the army. In Washington territory he saw combat with the Columbia River Indians in 1856 and in Spokane country in 1858.

Early in 1861, WINDER resigned his commission and became a major of artillery in the Southern army on March 16, 1861. He served at Charleston during the reduction of Sumter, commanding the South Carolina arsenal until commissioned colonel of the 6th regiment of South Carolina Infantry on July 8, 1861. He was promoted to brigadier general in March, 1862, and took command of the Stonewall Brigade. General WINDER led the advance and opened the battle of Port Republic, and later in the campaign on the Chickahominy, he brilliantly led his brigade in the desperate and memorable charge which broke the Federal Lines at Cold Harbor, winning commendations for himself and the First Maryland Infantry of his brigade. At Cedar Mountain on August 9, 1862, General WINDER was ill but went into action in an ambulance. While directing the movements of his artillery batteries, he was wounded by an artillery shell and died a few hours later.

Brigadier General John Henry WINDER (1800-1865) was born, reared, and educated in Somerset County, son of General W. H. Winder of War of 1812 fame.

After graduating from the United States Military Academy in 1820, he served at Fort McHenry and on the Florida frontier. He resigned in August, 1823, but was reappointed a second lieutenant in the First Artillery in 1827. Promoted to first lieutenant in 1833, WINDER served in the Florida Indian War. In 1842 he became a captain. During the Mexican War he was breveted major and lieutenant colonel for gallantry at La Hoya, Ocolaca, Contreras, Churubusco, Chapultepec, and Mexico City. He resigned on April 27, 1861, and offered his services to the Confederacy. He accepted a brigadier generalship as commander of the Department of Henrico. In May, 1862, he was in charge of military prisons at Libby, Belle Isle, and Danville. In May of 1864, General WINDER was assigned to the Second District of North Carolina and Southern Virginia, with headquarters at Goldsboro. In June of 1864, he was commander of Andersonville Prison, and by fall was in charge of all prisoners of war in Alabama and Georgia. By November, 1864, he had been appointed commissary general for all prisoners east of the Mississipppi. Before the conclusion of hostilities, General WINDER was broken in health and fortune. He died of diabetes in Columbia, South Carolina on February 7, 1865.

There were various high ranking Maryland officers who were capable and deserving, many of whom were repeatedly recommended for promotion to the rank of general. But since the majority of Marylanders were absorbed into commands of other states, there were no Maryland divisions for those of military merit to command. The seceded states' authorities desired to have their native sons heading their own troops.

Notable among those Marylanders who were almost promoted to general rank were the following:

Richard H. BREWER recruited his cavalry battalion up to a regiment after the battle of Shiloh, and so ably commanded that he was recommended for promotion by five superiors.

Thomas Smith RHETT was recommended to brigadier general by Major General ELZEY on October 31, 1863.

MARYLANDERS IN THE CONFEDERACY

Dr. Lucius Bellinger NORTHROP held the position of Commissary General of the Confederacy, and was bitterly criticized because of the shortage of food. The president had appointed him as brigadier, to rank from November 26, 1864, but never forwarded his nomination to the senate in fear that it might not pass.

Towards the end of the war, motions were made for three Marylanders to become senior grade men:

Henry Kyd DOUGLAS, who was assigned to command the Light Brigade and, David Gregg McINTOSH of Walker's Corps, were recommended by Secretary of War Breckinridge to general rank.

Clement SULLIVAN was ordered by President Davis to head G.W.C. Lee's Brigade as a brigadier.

Richard Snowden ANDREWS was highly regarded by General Bradley T. JOHNSON who said, "Taking him all in all, I think he was the best artillery commander in the Army of Northern Virginia; not courage so much but sense of battle and genius of war. Under Napolean 1st, he would have been a field marshall; and under other than Davis's would have been a brigadier general of artillery. But he came from Maryland, and Maryland had more than her share of general officers." [12]

There were a number of southerners who had been educated in Maryland who received their general's wreath. Others were educators within the state: Rev. William N. Pendleton, after he was rector in 1853 at Frederick, and John R. Jones of the same county until 1861. Roswell S. Ripley was made a Captain of the Independent Grays in the Baltimore Militia on July 18, 1853. Benjamin Huger commanded the 53rd Militia Regiment in the Baltimore Militia's 1861 build-up under General TRIMBLE. He resigned on May 10, and four days later enlisted in Richmond. He was buried in Maryland. Joseph E. Johnston and his Maryland-born wife resided in the state before the war and are also buried there, but they did not consider themselves residents.

Chapter Three

MARYLANDERS OF THE U.S. MILITARY ACADEMY

The Military Academy was established by Congress in 1801 at West Point, New York. There were twenty-six West Point graduates serving in the C.S.A. who were born in Maryland or were appointed from Maryland.

Graduates

John Henry WINDER (Class of 1820); 2nd Lieut., Arty Corps (1820); resigned (1823); 2nd Lieut., 1st Arty (1827); 1st Lieut., 1st Arty (1833); Capt., 1st Arty (1842); Major, 3rd Arty (1860); resigned (April 27, 1861) ---
C.S.A.: Col., Inf. Corps (Oct. 1861); Brig. Gen., Dept. of Henrico (Aug. 1861); Brig. Gen., Prison Dept. (May 1862); Brig. Gen., Prison Dept. Commmander (May 1864); Brig. Gen., Commissary Gen. (Nov. 1864)

Isaac Ridgeway TRIMBLE (Class of 1822); 2nd Lieut., 1st Arty (1822); resigned (1832) ---

C.S.A.: Col., Engineers Corps (May 1861); Brig. Gen., brigade command (Aug. 1861); Major Gen., Div. Commander (Dec. 1862); Major Gen., Maryland Line (June 1863); Major Gen., Div. Commander (July 1863)

James Jay ARCHER (Class of 1826); 2nd Lieut., 3rd Inf. (1826); 1st Lieut., 3rd Inf. (1833); resigned (1834) ---
C.S.A.: Col., 5th TX Inf. (March 1861); Brig. Gen., Light Div. (May 1861); died from wounds (Oct. 24, 1864)

Lloyd James BEALL (Class of 1830); 2nd Lieut., 1st Inf. (1830); 1st Lt, 2nd Dragoons (1836); Capt. 2nd Dragoons (1836); Board of vistors, West Point (1843); Major, staff paymaster (1844); resigned (April 22, 1861) ---
C.S.A.: Col. Marine Corps (May 1861)

Robert Harris ARCHER, Jr. (Class of 1832); Brevet Lieut., 3rd Inf. (1832); 2nd Lieut., 4th Arty (1835); resigned (1837) ---
C.S.A.: Lieut. Col., 55th VA Inf. (Oct. 1861); Asst. Adj. Gen Archer's Brigade (June 1862)

Robert T. P. ALLEN (Class of 1834); 2nd Lieut., 1st Inf. (1834); resigned (1836); established KY Military Institute, Frankfort, KY (1838); Bastrop Military Institute, Bastrop, TX (1858) ---
C.S.A.: Col., 17th TX Inf. (June 1862); resigned (June 17, 1864)

James M. WELLS (Class of 1835); 2nd Lieut., 7th Inf. (1836); 1st. Lt, 7th Inf. (1838); resigned (1839); Major, TX Rifles (1846); Capt., 12th Inf. (1847); resigned (1848) ---
C.S.A.: Col., 23rd MS Inf. (Aug. 1861)

Lloyd TILGHMAN, Sr. (Class of 1836); 1st Lieut., 1st Dragoons (1836); resigned (1836) ---
C.S.A.: Col., KY Inf. (June 1861); Brig. Gen., Army of the West (Oct. 1861); killed at Champion's Hill (May 16, 1863)

Arnold ELZEY (Class of 1837) 2nd Lieut., 2nd Arty (1837); 1st Lieut., 2nd Arty (1839); Capt., 2nd Arty (1843); resigned (April 20, 1861) ---
C.S.A.: Lieut. Col., 1st MD Inf. (May 1861); Col., 1st MD Inf. (June 1861); Brig. Gen., Commander of Brigade (Aug. 1861); Maj. Gen., Richmond Dept (Dec. 1862); Maj. Gen., Richond Dept. (Dec. 1862); Maj. Gen., Commander of Maryland Line (April 1864); Maj. Gen., Chief of Arty, Army of TN (Sept. 1864)

William Whann MACKALL (Class of 1837); 2nd Lieut., 1st Arty (1837); 1st Lieut., 1st Arty (1838); Brevet Capt., Asst. Adj. Gen. (1846); Brevet Major, Asst. Adj. Gen. (1853); resigned (July 3, 1861) ---
C.S.A.: Lieut. Col., Gen. J.E. Johnston's staff (July 1861); Col., Gen. J.E. Johnston's staff (Jan 1862); Brig. Gen., 1st Grand Div. (March 1862); Brig. Gen., Chief of Staff, Army of TN (Oct. 1863)

Edward MURRAY (Class of 1841); 2nd Lieut., 2nd Inf. (1842); 1st Lieut., 2nd Inf., (1847); Capt., 2nd Inf. (1853); resigned (1855) ---
C.S.A.: Lieut. Col., 49th VA Inf. (July 1861); Lieut. Col., Gen. Inspection Dept. (Dec. 1864)

Smith STANSBURG (Class of 1841); 2nd Lieut., Ordnance (1842); resigned (1844) ---
C.S.A.: Major, Ordnance Dept. (May 1861); Major, Board of Applicants for Arty; Lieut. Col., enrolling conscripts (Dec. 1862); Lieut. Col., Ordnance Dept. (June 1863); died of wounds (April 25, 1864)

Mansfield LOVELL (Class of 1842); 2nd Lieut., 4th Arty (1842); 1st Lieut., 4th Arty (1847); resigned (1854) ---
C.S.A.: Brig. Gen. (June 1861); Maj. Gen., commanded Dept. #1, New Orleans (Oct. 1861); Maj. Gen., Gen. J.E. Johnston's staff (April 1864)

Eugene Eckcl McLEAN (Class of 1842); 2nd Lieut., 1st Inf. (1844); 1st Lieut., 1st Inf. (1850); Capt., Asst. Quartermaster (1855); resigned (April 25, 1861) --
C.S.A: Capt., Quartermaster, Harper's Ferry (April 1861); Major, Chief Quartermaster, Army of Virginia (May 1861); Major, Chief Quartermaster, Army of MS (March 1862); Lieut. Col., Asst. Quartermaster General (Aug. 1862)

Francis J. THOMAS (Class of 1844); 2nd Lieut., 2nd Arty (1846); 1st Lieut., 3rd Arty (1847); resigned (1852) ---
C.S.A.: Col., Virginia Adj. Gen. of MD Vols. (May 1861); Col., Gen. J. E. Johnston's staff (June 1861); killed Manassas (July 21, 1861)

Thomas Grimke RHETT (Class of 1845); 2nd Lieut., Mounted Rifles (1846); 1st Lieut., Mounted Rifles (1847); Capt., Mounted Rifles (1853); Major, Paymaster (1858); resigned (April 21, 1861) ---
C.S.A.: Gen., SC Militia (March 1861); Major, Arty Corps (May 1861); Major, Gen. J.E. Johnston's staff (July 1861); Major, Chief of Arty to Gen. Holmes (Oct. 1862); Major, Chief of Arty, Trans-MS Dept (April 1863); Major, Chief of Arty to Gen. K. Smith (Jan. 1864)

John A. BROWN (Class of 1846); 2nd Lieut., 4th Arty (1847); 1st Lieut., 4th Arty (1848); Capt., 4th Arty (1856); resigned (July 3, 1861) ---
C.S.A.: Capt., Arty Dept. of NC (July 1861); Major, Chief of Arty, Dept. of Eastern TN (Jan. 1862); Lieut. Col., Gen. K. Smith's staff (Feb. 1863); Lieut. Col., commanded City Redoubts, Mobile (Aug. 1864); Col., Chief of Arty, Gen. Maury's staff (March 1865)

Thomas Smith RHETT (Class of 1848); 2nd Lieut., 2nd Arty (1849); 1st Lieut., 2nd Arty (1853); resigned (1855) ---
C.S.A.: Capt., Arty Corps Charleston (Nov. 1861); Col., Dept. of Rifled Cannon (July 1861); Col., Chief of Arty (Aug. 1861); Col., Ordnance Dept. (Oct. 1864)

George Hume STEUART, Jr. (Class of 1848); 2nd Lieut., 2nd Dragoons (1849); 1st Lieut., 1st Cav. (1855); Capt., 1st Cav. (1855); resigned (April 22, 1861) ---
C.S.A.: Capt., Cav. (May 1861); Lieut. Col., 1st MD Inf. (June 1861); Col., 1st MD Inf. (July 1861); Brig. Gen., commanding a brigade (March 1862); Brig. Gen., Maryland Line (May 1862); Brig. Gen., commanding a brigade (June 1862)

MARYLANDERS OF THE U.S. MILITARY ACADEMY

Donald C. STITH (Class of 1850); 2nd Lieut., 5th Inf. (1853); 1st Lieut., 5th Inf. (1855); Capt., 5th Inf. (1861); resigned (Sept. 25, 1861) ---
C.S.A.: Capt., Inf. Dept. of TX (Sep. 1861); Major, Asst. Adj. Gen., Gen. Van Dorn's staff (Nov. 1861); Col., 1st MS Rangers (Feb. 1863); Col., Gen. S. D. Lee's staff(Nov. 1863); Capt., Maryland Line (April 1864); Col., Gen. S. D. Lee's staff (Oct. 1864)

William Thomas MAGRUDER (Class of 1850); 2nd Lieut., 1st Dragoons (1851); 1st Lieut., 1st Dragoons (1855); Capt., 1st Cav. (1861); resigned (Oct. 1, 1862) ---
C.S.A.: Capt., Asst. Adj. Gen., David's Brigade (Nov. 1862); killed at Gettysburg (July 3, 1863)

Charles Sidney WINDER (Class of 1850); 2nd Lieut., 3rd Arty (1851); 1st Lieut., 3rd Arty (1854); Capt., 9th Inf. (1855); resigned (April 1, 1861) ---
C.S.A.: Major, Arty Corps (April 1861); Col., 6th SC Inf. (July 1861); Brig. Gen., Stonewall Brigade (March 1861); killed at Cedar Mountain (Aug. 9, 1862)

Richard H. BREWER (Class of 1858); 2nd Lieut., 1st Dragoons (1859); 1st Lieut., 1st Dragoons (1861); resigned (May 13, 1861) ---
C.S.A.: 1st Lieut., Cav. Corps (Sept. 1861); Lieut. Col., 2nd MS Cav (Dec. 1861); Col. 2nd MS Cav. (June 1862); Col., Asst. Adj. Gen, Gen. Polk's staff (March 1863); Col., Asst. Adj. Gen., Gen. Ramson's staff (April 1864); died from wounds, Piedmont (June 25, 1864)

John Selden SAUNDERS (Class of 1858); 2nd Lieut., ordnance (1861); resigned (April 22, 1861) ---
C.S.A.: 1st Lieut., Richmond Armory (May 1861); Major, Judge Advocate, General G.W. Smith's staff (Jan. 1862); Lieut. Col., Ordnance Dept. (Feb. 1863)

Clarence DERRICK (Class of 1861); 2nd Lieut., Engineer Corps (1861); resigned (July 16, 1861) ---
C.S.A.: 2nd Lieut., Arty Corps (July 1861); Capt., Asst. Adj. Gen., Gen. Floyd's staff (Dec. 1861); Lieut. Col., 23rd VA Inf. (May 1862);

Lywellyn Griffith HOXTON (Class of 1861); 2nd Lieut. (May 6, 1861); dismissed (May 25, 1861) ---
C.S.A.: 1st Lieut., VA Inf. (June 26, 1861; Capt., Tobin's Co. (March, 1862); Major, Chief of Arty, Hardee's staff (Dec. 1862); Lieut. Col. (April 1864)

- - - - -

Cadets

Southern sympathy was strong within the walls of West Point. There were six Marylanders in the corps of cadets in the spring of 1861, of whom four resigned and joined the Confederacy. A potential cadet, Edward C. Murray, received an appointment to report to the Academy in the summer of 1861, but instead, went south and enlisted in Dea's Maryland Artillery.

David G. WHITE, 2nd Class; admitted July 1, 1857, at age 19; resigned. He left the Academy April 23, 1861, returning to his home in Cecil County. On May 24 he was commissioned 1st lieutenant on General W. J. Hardee's staff; he became a captain August 1. In the fall of 1862, WHITE was acting Major of the 6th Arkansas Cavalry; on December 31 he was promoted. He remained with the battalion until April 15, 1863. Returning to Hardee's staff, he was promoted to colonel. WHITE commanded the 5th Georgia Cavalry Regiment until February 11, 1865, when he was assigned as acting Assistant Inspector General. He was paroled at Greensboro, May 1.

Robert E. NOONAN, 3rd Class; admitted July 1, 1858 at age 17; resigned. After submitting his resignation he returned to his home near Libertytown. He was commissioned 1st lieutenant on the staff of General J. H. WINDER in the fall of 1861. He was assigned to the 21st Virginia Regiment and on Sunday, March 23, 1862, NOONAN was killed advancing on Winchester while gallantly cheering on his brother Marylanders of Company B.

William Thomas BLACKISTON, 3rd Class; admitted Sept. 1, 1858 at age 16; resigned April 25, 1861. After leaving the Academy he went home to St. Mary's County to raise a militia company. When he realized that his home state could not secede, he enlisted as a private in company H, 1st Maryland Infantry, later serving as sergeant in company A, 2nd Maryland Infantry. On August 18, 1863, BLACKISTON was commissioned 2nd lieutenant of ordnance. He died of wounds on October 5, 1863.

Joseph H. STEWART, 5th Class; admitted July 1, 1860; resigned March 1861. He returned home to Cambridge, then went to Richmond where he became sergeant of Company D., WESTON's Battalion. Subsequently he was elected 3rd lieutenant of Company F, 1st Maryland Infantry. He was wounded in March 1862, near Manassas. On June 18, 1864, 2nd Lieutenant STEWART was ordered to West Point, Georgia. He was paroled on May 4, 1865, at Macon.

Chapter Four

MARYLANDERS OF THE U.S. NAVAL ACADEMY

At the outbreak of the War those of highest naval rank had not had the opportunity to attend the Naval Academy. Establishment of a naval school had long been a major goal of the Navy, but it was not until 1845 that Fort Severn at Annapolis was transferred from the War Department to the Navy for the specific purpose of training naval officers. As hostilities became imminent, Maryland graduates of the Naval Academy were compelled to make painful decisions. Of the seventeen graduates still in naval service, seven continued to serve the Union while ten of their number, listed below, resigned to follow the cause of the Confederacy. They were subsequently listed in the Naval Register as "dismissed."[13]

MARYLANDERS OF THE U.S. NAVAL ACADEMY

Augustus McLAUGHLIN (Class of 1846); sea duty: 8 yrs., 9 mos.; shore duty: 2 yrs., 2 mos.; unemployed: 10 yrs.; total: 20 yrs., 11 mos.; "dismissed" as Lieut. (April 23, 1861) ---
C.S.A.: apptd 1st Lieut. (June 15, 1861); C.S.R.S. United States Apalechicola Naval Station; Columbia Naval Station

John W. BENNETT (Class of 1847); sea duty: 15 yrs., 2 mos.; shore duty: 3 yrs., 4 mos.; unemployed: 2 yrs., 4 mos.; total: 20 yrs., 10 mos.; Naval Observatory, Washington, D. C.; "dismissed" as Lieut. (April 19, 1861) ---
C.S.A.: apptd 1st Lieut. (June 20, 1861); Naval guns at Manassas; C.S. cruiser *Nashville;* Lieut. Commanding, C.S. steamer *Gaines*; Battery "Buchanan" Mobile; Captain, C.S. ironclad *Nashville*

George Henry BIER (Class of 1847); sea duty: 14 yrs., 3 mos.; shore duty: 2 yrs., 11 mos.; unemployed: 2 yrs.; total: 19 yrs., 2 mos.; receiving ship *Baltimore*; "dismissed" as Lieut. (April 23, 1861) ---
C.S.A.: apptd 1st Lieut. (Nov. 13, 1861); C.S.R.S. *St. Phillip*; New Orleans Naval Station; Jackson Naval Station; Richmond Naval Station; C.S. ram *Chicorn*

Dulany A. FORREST (Class of 1847); sea duty: 13 yrs., 4 mos.; shore duty: 4 yrs., 4 mos.; unemployed: 2 yrs., 1 mos.; total: 19 yrs., 9 mos.; "dismissed" as Lieut. (Dec. 1, 1861) ---
C.S.A.: taken prisoner, Fort Warren (Dec. 4, 1861); exchanged as prisoner (Jan. 28, 1862); appted 1st Lieut. (Feb. 8, 1862); Richmond Naval Station; C.S. ram *Palmetto States*; C.S. cruiser *Florida*; died at Wilmington Naval Station (Aug. 10, 1863)

Charles P. McGARY (Class of 1847); sea duty: 14 yrs., 3 mos.; shore duty: 1 yr, 8 mos.; unemployed: 3 yrs., 3 mos.; total: 19 yrs., 2 mos.; Store ship *Relief*; "dismissed" as Lieut. (April 25, 1861) ---
C.S.A.: apptd 1st Lieut. (June 27, 1861); C.S. gunboat *Jackson*; Lieut. Commanding, C.S. cruiser *Tuscarora*; C.S. steamer *Spray*; C.S. steamer *Stono*; C.S. gunboat *Tuscaloosa*

William Harar PARKER (Class of 1847); sea duty: 11 yrs., 4 mos.; shore duty: 5 yrs., 10 mos.; unemployed: 2 yrs.; total: 19 yrs., 2 mos.; Naval Academy, "dismissed" as Lieut. (April 20, 1861) ---
C.S.A.: apptd 1st Lieut. (June 10, 1861); North Carolina Sound; C.S. gunboat *Beaufort*; Executive Officer, C.S. ironclad *Palmetto States*; Capt., Commandant of the C.S. Naval Academy

James Iredall WADDELL (Class of 1847); sea duty: 10 yrs., 4 mos.; shore duty: 4 yrs., 11 mos.; unemployed: 4 yrs.; total: 19 yrs., 3 mos.; "dismissed" as 1st Lieut. (Jan. 19, 1862) ---
C.S.A.: apptd 1st Lieut (March 27, 1862); New Orleans Naval Station; Drury's Bluff; Lieut. Commanding, C.S.S. *Shanandoah*

Beverly KENNON (Class of 1852); sea duty: 11 yrs., 2 mos; shore duty: 1 yr, 7 mos.; unemployed: 1 yr, 7 mos.; total: 14 yrs., 4 mos.; Washington Naval Yard, "dismissed" as 1st Lieut. (April 23, 1861) ---

C.S.A.: apptd 1st Lieut. (April 30, 1861); Chief of Ordnance, New Orleans; Lieut. Commander, C.S. cruiser *Tuscarora*; C.S. gunboat *Louisiana State*; C.S. gunboat *Gov. Moore*; Executive Officer, C.S. *Charles Morgan*

John Taylor WOOD (Class of 1852); sea duty: 14 yrs., 6 mos.; shore duty: 2 yrs., 10 mos.; unemployed: 2 yrs., 3 mos.; total: 19 yrs., 7 mos.; Naval Academy, "dismissed" as Lieut. (April 21, 1861) ---
C.S.A.: apptd 2nd Lieut. (Oct. 4, 1861); 1st Lieut., Evansport Batteries, Virginia; Col., Pres. Jefferson Davis's staff; Commander, boat raiding expedition; Capt., C.S. ship of war *Tallahassee*; James River Squadron

Wilburn Briggs HALL (Class of 1859); sea duty: 1 yr, 10 mos.; shore duty: 3 yrs., 2 mos.; unemployed: 3 mos.; total: 5 yrs., 3 mos.; "dismissed" as Midn. (March 7, 1861 ---
C.S.A.: apptd 1st Lieut. (July 24, 1861); Charleston Naval Station; prize *Harriet Lane*: C.S. steamer *Webb*; C.S. gunboat *Savannah*; C.S. gunboat *Drewry*; C.S. gunboat *Resolute*

- - - - -

Acting Midshipmen

Of the thirteen Maryland midshipmen attending the U.S. Naval Academy designated as born, appointed, or resident Marylanders, seven resigned. Of those whe remained loyal to the Union, five completed their course of study, graduated and received commissions in the U.S. Navy. One became a seaman in the U.S. Navy.

William Pinckney MASON, 1st Class, acting Midn; entered Sept. 26, 1865; resigned April 22, 1861. He received his warrant as a midshipman in the Virginia Navy. He served at Fort Caswell, Hardy's Bluff, and Drewry's Bluff before being ordered to Charleston where he was sent to England and France. Returning to Wilmington on the blockade runner *Helen* on September 7,1864, 2nd Lieutenant MASON reported for duty aboard the steamer *Virginia*. He was wounded on the morning of January 24, 1865, in the left thigh and right foot.

Thomas Lardner DORNIN, 1st class, acting Midn; entered Sept. 22, 1856; resigned from Annapolis, but his resignation was not accepted, and he was listed as dismissed on June 4, 1861. That same month, DORNIN was listed as a captain's clerk in the Confederate Navy at which position he remained until March 8, when he became a midshipman serving aboard the steamer *Jamestown* and the ironclad *Virginia*. During the next two years, he was stationed on the ram *Baltic* of the Mobile Squadron. Midshipman DORNIN then was stationed aboard the steamer *Patrick Henry* and the gunboat *Roanoke* of the James River Squadron. In 1864 he was promoted to 1st lieutenant on the gunboat *Gaines* and was severely wounded at the bombardment of Fort Fisher. He was paroled May 10, 1865.

Julian Murray SPENCER, 1st class, acting Midn; entered Sept. 26, 1856; resigned May 16, 1861. He became a midshipman in the Southern Navy. Serving in the James River Squadron and at Drewry's Bluff he was promoted to 2nd lieutenant on June 1, 1862. Ordered to the Mobile Suadron in 1863, Spencer was on the ram *Baltic* and gunboat *Morgan*. He surrendered at Mobile on May 4, 1865 and was paroled on May 10.

Henry Hungerford MARMADUKE, 2nd class, acting Midn; entered Sept. 21, 1858; resigned April 24, 1861 and on May 8, he enlisted in the Confederate Navy as an acting Midshipman. By 1863, he was a 2nd lieutenant and the following year advanced to 1st lieutenant on special duty in the torpedo service. He was at the Charleston Naval Station when it was evacuated and was assigned to the big gun batteries near Drewry's Bluff. While commanding a company in the Naval brigade, he was captured at Sailor's Creek and released from Johnson's Island on June 20, 1865.

Daniel CARROLL, 3rd class, acting Midn; entered Nov. 29, 1859; resigned, vacated the Naval Academy on April 20, 1861, and proceeded to his home in Baltimore. He travelled to Richmond and upon tendering his services to the Confederacy was appointed a midshipman on July 23, 1861. While serving aboard the steamer *Patrick Henry* as a signal officer, CARROLL was killed in action on May 15, 1862, off Drewry's Bluff.

William Joseph CARROLL, 4th class, acting Midn; entered Sept. 21, 1860; resigned on April 25, 1861. Accepting the rank of Midshipman in the Southern Navy, he was ordered to the New Orlean's Station and sailed aboard the C.S.R.S. *St. Phillips* and the gunboat *Pamlico*. Next assigned to the Jackson Station, CARROLL saw service on the cruiser *Tuscaloosa*. In the spring of 1863, he was aboard the steamer *Patrick Henry* and a year later was ordered to the cruiser *Nashville* until the flag was tearfully saluted for the last time on May 10, 1865, in the Tombigbee River when Passed Midshipman CARROLL surrendered.

James Morris MORGAN, 4th class, acting Midn.; entered Sept. 20, 1860; resigned April 16, 1861, and returned to his home in Montgomery County. Choosing to follow the Southern banner at the age of fifteen, he became a steward to George N. HOLLINS. In the early spring of 1862, young MORGAN accompanied Hollins to the Mississippi, then served aboard the cruiser *Georgia* and gunboat *McRae*. Aide-de camp MORGAN was captured at Ship Island and due to his youth was exchanged on March 2, 1865. He was one of the officers detailed to accompany Mrs. Jefferson Davis when she left Richmond. He later left for Egypt and became a member of the Khedive staff.

Chapter 5

COLLEGES

During the 1800's higher education made significant progress. There were numerous burgeoning professions which required more extensive education, and new colleges sprang up throughout the state of Maryland. Many of the newer schools were small, private organizations, while the larger schools normally had church affiliation.

St. James College of Hagerstown, a diocesan school of the Episcopal Church of Maryland, was remarkable in that most of its southern boys were first opposed to secession. However, this did not in any way diminish their loyalty as events unfolded. Reverend Dr. John B. Kerfoot, the president, and nearly all the teachers, were from the north and remained loyal. He declared that the most extreme secessionists among the students were the native Marylanders.

In 1861 there were one hundred and ninety-five students at St. James College. By the close of the academic year, eighty-seven were volunteers in the C.S.A., while seventy-eight were serving in the Union Army.[14] Only sixteen students returned to the next session which began in October of 1861. Later, the number increased to between forty and fifty.

Early in 1862 Bishop Whittingham ordered the Prayer of Thanksgiving for Federal victory to be said in churches. When Dr. Kerfoot read the prayer in the college chapel, eighteen of the young men arose and left the chapel in a body. In a letter to the president they disclaimed any disrespect to him or the other college authorities. Thereafter political prayers were discontinued.[15]

In 1861 Georgetown College was seventy-two years old. It had taken on a feverish military spirit and had an active corps of cadets even though it was under the auspices of the Roman Catholic Church. The college cadets were trained by father James Clark who had intensified their program of drill and exhibitions. Father Clark had graduated from West Point before entering the priesthood, and had been a classmate of Robert E. Lee and Joseph E. Johnston. The approaching conflict was very evident to the young scholars on campus who felt that this border state would soon join the seceded states. By January 2, the first southern students had departed for their homes. Students continued to drop out in small numbers until the Pratt Street Massacre, when more than a hundred left within a day or two. One afternoon the student body, to display their dislike for the war proceedings against the South, burned President Lincoln in effigy at the west end of the Tower Building. Quite a stir was created among the people in Washington, particularly among government officials.

By May 4, the student body had dropped to fifty, shortly after Secretary Staunton ordered the College to prepare to house the 69th New York National Guard. During the War, the student body never numbered over sixty. News from various fronts brought sad tales of death, wounds and imprisonment for so many who just a short time before had been happy collegians. Of some 1500 students and alumni of military age when the war began, 1141 actually donned uniforms; 216 in blue, 925 in gray.[16] Of this number, two alumni served in the Federal Army who would reach the rank of general, and eight in the Confederate Army would attain flag rank, one being Marylander Joseph Lancaster BRENT.

St. John's College of Annapolis was closed in 1861, and the college buildings were utilized as a military hospital by the U.S. Army. The school was reopened in September 1866, but it was a year before the buildings could be completely repaired. The school was reorganized in 1867. In 1870, under President James Mercer GARNETT, the college was again flourishing, producing some of the state's most distinguished leaders. Dr. GARNETT was a former graduate of St. John's and was taking post-graduate courses at the University of Virginia when hostilities broke out and he joined one of the two companies of students. He entered the Confederate Army as a private in the Rockbridge Artillery and rose to the rank of captain of ordnance under General Charles S. WINDER.

COLLEGES

Many colleges could not retain their students during this period and had to close. In northeast Carroll County just four miles from Pennsylvania, in the small town of Manchester, there were two schools, the Manchester United Academy and Irving College. Both shut their doors because of the bitterly divided sentiment among the student body. Even this area, so close to the Mason-Dixon Line, suffered from clashing opinions. In 1861 Manchester United Academy was under the direction of Reverend Henry Wissler and closed because of the division among the trustees concerning the war. Irving College, originally opened as the Independent Academy, was founded by Dr. F. Dieffenbach. Dr. Jacob Showers was elected Captain of the Manchester Militia in 1855, and organized the military program at the school. Also included in the faculty of seven was Colonel Samuel S. Mills of the state militia, who was listed as military inspector. After the semester ending in the spring of 1861 the doors were closed until 1886. Among the cadets was Dr. Showers' son, George Theodore SHOWERS, who with several other companions left Manchester on June 29, 1863, and joined the Confederate Army at York.[17]

Some schools were shut down entirely for their strong Confederate sentiment. The Union Academy of Snow Hill, for example, was seized by Union forces.

St. Timothy's Hall - also known as Catonsville Military Institute - was a military preparatory school located at Catonsville which had been established in 1845 by Reverend Libertus Van Bokkelen of New York. The first military instructor was a young lieutenant in the state militia, George W. Brown, who during the trying pre-war period was elected mayor of Baltimore. The school's infantry battalion was composed of five companies and known as the Taylor Light Infantry. The entire corps of cadets was under the command of Frederick M. Crandal of Pennsylvania, who would become colonel of the 48th U.S. Colored Infantry during the War.[18]

As news of the Southern States' secession reached the campus of St. Timothy's, the pro-Southern student body of the state's largest military school began greeting the sunrise with an unauthorized artillery salute. Rev. Van Bokkelen and his staff were strong Union supporters and eagerly sought to put an end to displays of secessionist sentiment. When seven states had seceded, the occasion was marked by the firing of a salute for the whole seven, resulting in the arrest of half of the school and the expulsion of ring-leaders. The students then secretly organized themselves into two companies of infantry, elected officers and drilled. Following the Pratt Street upheaval, civilians broke into the armory of the school and stole about seventy of the muskets. Later that same day, Bradley T. JOHNSON and his Frederick Volunteers, under orders of city authorities, removed the school's muskets and the six field pieces to Holliday Square in Baltimore.[19]

"Many of the former students of St. Timothy's Hall served with distinction in the Confederate Army. General Fitzhugh Lee of Virginia had attended the school, as had General Steven Eliott of South Carolina." General Joseph Finegan of Florida had been military instructor at the school prior to the war. On the Union side, General Charles Phelps of Maryland was educated at the school.[20]

The school did not prosper during the war years, but managed to stay open. In 1864 Reverend Van Bokkelen was appointed by Governor Bradford as the first superintendent of public education in the state of Maryland. The school continued under the direction of Professor E. Parsons. It closed in 1868.[21]

Tench Tilghman was a general of the militia and an ardent advocate of education. It was through his personal efforts that the Maryland Military Academy was established at Oxford in 1849. Professor John H. Allen of Ohio, a graduate of the U. S. Military Academy and a classmate of General Tilghman, became its first superintendent. The faculty consisted of two other military men, Joseph Strong, who was also at West Point in 1818, and General Tilghman. Franklin BUCHANAN was a trustee of the school along with a number of distinguished citizens on the Board of Visitors. The sons of the leading citizens of Maryland and Delaware were educated there.[22]

Six years after the college's founding, the principal academic building was accidentally destroyed by fire and this military institution which had infused new life into the quiet town of Oxford was brought to a close. Three of the four sons of General Tilghman who attended this school would later join the southern ranks: Tench F., John Leeds and Oswald. The school was again established in the early 1880's, this time as the Maryland Military and Naval Academy. During this period the school showed a student enrollment of over 150. At the head of the Board of Visitors was Colonel Oswald TILGHMAN. The faculty was composed of sixteen members who, with the exception of one, had received their prior schooling south of the Mason-Dixon Line.

Charlotte Hall Academy, later named Charlotte Hall Military Academy, was founded in 1774 in St. Mary's County. Two of the military department heads gained prominence during the Civil War: Colonel Simeon B. GIBBONS of the 10th Virginia Infantry and Major James Parran CRANE of the 2nd Maryland Infantry. During the War, Union soldiers visited Charlotte Hall and carried off all its weapons and accouterments. The arms were not recovered until 1868.

Some schools were closed because the military instructors felt that they had to become directly involved in the conflict. The Urbana Military Academy was formed in 1846 in a structure that had been used as a female academy. It became known as the Landon Academy and Military Institute for Boys. The institute was managed by Principal John R. Jones who taught military tactics, mathematics and modern language. There were only a few students from above the Mason-Dixon Line. In April of 1861, Jones dismissed the student body and returned to his native Virginia, where he enlisted in the Southern Army. He rose to the rank of brigadier general. The majority of the former students went into the southern ranks, and the institute was sold and once again became a female academy.[23]

When the guns of the Civil War began to rumble, the college students and faculty of the University of Maryland had strong Confederate sympathies. The five schools which composed the University of Maryland were: the Medical College, Dental College, Pharmaceutical College and Undergraduate College, all of Baltimore, and the Agricultural College. Statistics of the alumni of the 1860 class show that at least thirty percent fought for the Confederacy and about ten percent for the Union:

COLLEGES

Class of 1860, University of Maryland[24]

College	Number of graduates	Confederacy	Union
Medical	52	17	5
Dental	35	11	3
Pharmacy	6	1	0
Undergraduate	4	2	1
Total	97	30	9

During the War "The medical faculty delighted in flaunting their sympathies one step short of treason. Each year the professors ostentatiously refused to fly the United States flag at commencement and each year the Union troops in Baltimore ordered them to do so. ... Graduates known to have been Southern sympathizers received great applause and many bouquets at commencement but the Unionists were roundly hissed. When the rumor spread that Unionists always seemed to fail their examinations, the faculty announced proudly that the 1862 class included two known Union sympathizers."[25] So blatant was faculty disloyalty that one of the newspapers demanded that the General Assembly require the officers of the institution to take the Oath of Allegiance. The newspapers specifically accused the faculty of keeping open vacancies in the staff to be filled after the War by southern men. Enrollments in the Medical school had been about 150, but during the course of the War fell to about 100. The College of Dental Surgery saw its enrollment fall from over 100 to less than thirty students during the War. "The alumni of the Dental Department of the University of Maryland were certainly allied to the South. Of the sixty-seven dentists who were soldiers during the conflicts, eight saluted Old Glory while fifty-nine saluted the Stars and Bars."[26] The College of Pharmacy seemed to have suffered the least and maintained its ante-bellum enrollment of between twenty and thirty students annually. The Undergraduate College of the University suffered the fate of most classical schools, barely struggling through the war and finally closing. It produced four graduates in 1860, three in 1861, one in 1863 and one in 1866. At the Maryland Agricultural College, practically all of the trustees sympathized with the South and secession. At least five of the trustees were arrested, while others fled the state to escape arrest during the War. Twelve of the students were from seceded states, and most of them left about Christmas of 1860. The preceding fall term had begun with seventy-eight students and six professors; only seventeen students and three professors remained until commencement day in July. Of the seventy-eight students, twenty fought for the Confederacy and nine for the Union.

It was not easy to make the decision to fight against one's friends and classmates. No doubt, it was more difficult in Maryland to go to war for one's conviction than in the deep South or in most Northern states. From the Medical School faculty, Edward WARREN became Surgeon General of North Carolina in the Confederate Army, and William A. Hammond, Surgeon General of the U.S.A. From the Dental College two professors fought for the Confederacy; from the Pharmaceutical College two professors fought for the Union; from the Undergraduate College one professor fought for the Confederacy, and from the Agricultural College one professor fought in the Union Army and two for the Confederacy.

MARYLANDERS IN THE CONFEDERACY

The Maryland Military Instititute was founded in 1862 by Thomas P. Chiffelle of South Carolina, a graduate of the U.S. Military Academy, class of 1836. After his military service he settled in Baltimore County where he became a civil engineer. Like several of his former military colleagues, his emotions were so split over the secession issue, that he did not participate, but established this school at Saint Dennis. It is surprising that a military school could have been founded during the war and survived, but apparently parents were still interested in this type of training for their sons who were too young for the Army.[27] The school was moved to what had been the Paradise Hotel on the Frederick turnpike in Catonsville in 1864. Throughout the War, as in all other schools, young men ran away from their educational training to join the Confederate Army. During the rebellion the staff consisted of eight. Afterwards there were two positions made open for Lieutenant Colonel Lywellyn G. HOXTON, a graduate of West Point in 1861, and Dr. Charles G. W. MACGILL.

In 1839 the Virginia Military Institute was created and was one of the foremost of all state military schools. Although Marylanders were not numerous, Dr. Thomas Henry CARTER, Joseph Hart CHINOWETH, Dr. Thomas Hall EMORY, Sr. and John GRAYSON were graduates. William Stewart POLK, formerly of the Old Navy, was treasurer and in charge of the quartermaster's department before joining the Confederate Engineer Corps. Among the two hundred cadets in April of 1861, the following Marylanders were among the many who relinquished their books for Army service in the C.S.A.: Archie H. AISQUITH, John DENEGRE, Henry Clay HEWITT, Jr., John Monroe RODGERS, John TAYLOE and Henry Alexander WISE, while Daniel Murray LEE entered the Confederate Navy. The Corps of cadets had long desired combat, and on May 15, 1864 the anticipated day arrived at New Market. Among the young Maryland men in the cadet battalion were Robert Montague BLUNDON, Thomas Rufus CLENDINEN, Thomas Gordon HAYES, Thomas Herbert SHRIVER, John TABB, Anderson Clay TOMS and Wilberforce VEITCH. Three of these young cadets had seen prior military service.

Thomas Rufus CLENDINEN "was merely a spirited boy of fourteen years when in June of 1861 he went to St. Andrew's Bay and joined the Alabama State Forces, who were stationed there to protect the important salt works from being taken and destroyed. Here he remained on duty as a private, until, during the winter of 1862, he was captured by federal forces who were on a Naval expedition, and was kept on the frigate as a prisoner for several days. Observing his extreme youth the captors released him on the condition that he would go to school, and accordingly he proceeded to Lexington, Virginia."[28] He entered the institute on May 6, 1864 and took part as a cadet private in Company D in the Battle of New Market.

Thomas Gordon HAYES "was at school in Alexandria when the War broke out but enlisted in the Alexandria Riflemen which company subsequently became famous as a component part of the 17th Virginia Regiment. He was later transferred to the 10th Virginia Cavalry commanded by Colonel J. Lucius Davis. He then served with the Wise Legion until it returned to the East, when he left the Army and on January 1, 1862 matriculated at VMI."[29] During the battle of New Market he served as 1st Cadet Corporal in Company B.

Thomas Herbert SHRIVER's home at Union Mills was used by J.E.B. Stuart while he searched for the Army of Northern Virginia. "Just a lad of sixteen, my father, T. Herbert SHRIVER, was taken by General J.E.B. Stuart to

Gettysburg June 30, 1863, as his personal guide at Stuart's request, with positive assurance to keep him by his side, and stated, that he (Stuart) would send him to the Virginia Military Institute when things adjusted, and that when he (father) graduated he would be put on his staff."[30] He rode with Company K, 1st Virginia Cavalry, through the summer engagements and on September 1, 1863, with J.E.B. Stuart as his sponsor, entered the Institute. He was a private in Company C at New Market and was detailed with the artillery.

Chapter 6

GROUPS OF MEN WHO LEFT MARYLAND

In December, 1860, South Carolina sent recruiting officers to Baltimore. They enlisted and sent to Charleston 500 men who were placed in South Carolina units in the Charleston area. "They served with fidelity, gallantry and distinction in the defense of Fort Sumter, for a large part of the garrison of that fortress during its bombardment were Marylanders."[31] Captains W. D. Pender and Charles L. Haskett were the enrolling officers in Baltimore, and over a period of time used three different ships to convey men. On March 21, Louis T. Wigfall in Washington wrote, "Large numbers of men in Baltimore cannot be kept together much longer."[32] On March 25th, General Beauregard informed the adjutant general of the arrival of another ship with Baltimore men. They were under the care of Robert E. HASLETT, a former officer during the Mexican War in the Baltimore-Washington Battalion, now recruiting for the Wise Legion. The muster dates of these volunteers were February, March and April of 1861. Some are listed as having been enrolled in Baltimore, while others were not enlisted until they reached Charleston. "Recruiting for the armies the parties who for nearly a month had been keeping an office near Centre Market for the purpose of sending off men to enlist in the forces of the Confederate States had for the present suspended their services, alleging that the recruiting officers at Charleston were not prepared to enlist amy more for a few weeks. ... The enlistment of men here for the U.S. Army is progressing very slowly, the headquarters are on Camden Street near Charles and only about 20 men had been received during the past weeks."[33] These men were referred to as the Baltimore Rebels, and were enlisted in Alfred Rhett's First Regular Heavy Artillery Battalion, J.J. Lucas' 15th Battalion, Heavy Artillery, and the First South Carolina Infantry, Company G. South Carolina officers were appointed to these units and it was not until the fall of 1862 that Charles Harrison CLAIBORNE, and soon other Marylanders, were able to attain officer rank. In 1863 the Baltimore Rebels were still on garrison duty with the big guns in defense of Charleston Harbor. Rhett's artillery was still in Fort Sumter. Lucas' Artillery Battalion was on James Island in Fort Pemberton and Company G of the First South Carolina Infantry was in Fort Moultrie as foot soldiers on the bunkers and in the rifle pits, then later as artillerists working a battery. The Baltimore Rebels in 1861 and again in 1863 were under the command of General States Rights Gist, who was son of the famed revolutionary Free Stater General Mordecai Gist. A number of the Baltimore Rebels were organized in a heavy battery in Castle Pinckney.

On May 8, 1861, the Frederick Volunteers joined the Confederacy and mustered in 60 Frederick men. On the following day, a body of 37 men under Captain Henry WILLMORE, a body of 19 under Captain (Frank S.) PRICE, and another body of about 80 men under Captain C. C. EDELIN, passed through Frederick on their way to join the southern forces at Harper's Ferry. This was the nucleus from which the first Maryland Infantry Battalion would later be organized.[34]

The First Maryland Artillery was formed by several groups coming from the state. William Fendlay DEMENT on May 10, 1861, with 25 men from a Charles County militia cavalry company "crossed the river at Mathias Point for the purpose of riding to Richmond where their services would be gallantly offered to the Confederacy. In about five days he reached the city, and gathering authority went to Fredericksburg in the department commanded by General Holmes, to establish a recruiting office for the purpose of organizing artillery companies. In executing this mission he made a visit to Maryland and brought back with him into Virginia another detachment of the cavalry company, with whom, added to the first squad and making a body of about fifty good and true men."[35] Nichols Snowden HILL "organized a party of twenty (Prince George's County) cavalrymen to cross into Virginia but on account of the vigilance of the Federal patrol all of his men were compelled to cross the Potomac without their horses. Major HILL, having been presented with a thoroughbred stallion named Wicomico by the ladies of Prince George's County, determined not to abandon this gift, he succeeded in crossing in a skiff with the horse behind."[36]

Many of the men who came south in groups were from militia companies forced to disband when the Federals took over the state. Captain George Ridgely GAITHER with 23 men from the Howard County Dragoons early in May "mounted and equipped, crossed at Point of Rocks and rendezvoused at Leesburg with other Montgomery Countians."[37] This troop of horsemen did picket duty at Edward's Ferry for some weeks before being mustered in as Company M, 1st Virginia Cavalry.

On May 28, 1861, the Lanier Guards were mustered into the 13th Virginia Infantry as Company G. "George Lanier of Lanier Brothers, Wholesale Dry Goods Merchants in Baltimore, equipped and sent off this company to join us at Harper's Ferry; times were exciting there then. This scheme was adopted to get out of the city in a body, a funeral procession was planned. Loading a coffin with guns, and making preparations for a decent burial, they took carriages and followed the hearse to Louden Park Cemetery, a few miles west on the Catonsville Road. When a safe distance from the city the coffin was opened, and quickly each man was armed and on his way to join the young Confederacy. Many of the Lanier Guards were engaged in the attachment of Federal soldiers when they made their memorial march up Pratt Street in Baltimore."[38]

This company was joined by two other groups. Matthew CLARK, "took with him twenty Baltimoreans who formed the nucleus of a company which he subsequently organized at Harper's Ferry; this company entered and completed the 13th Virginia Infantry."[39] John Ignatius McWILLIAMS "left Baltimore on or about May 8, 1861, with thirty young men to proceed to Richmond, went through Washington City, put up at James Jackson's Marshall House, Alexandria, Virginia. I was delayed here five days in procuring transportation when I proceeded to Richmond with my men and put them in the Columbia Hotel and returned myself to Baltimore for more men. Upon arriving in Baltimore I found it too hot for me. I left with five men for Harper's Ferry, Virginia, at the latter place I met for the first time Colonel T.J. Jackson, after a short interview he gave me a pass and transportation to Richmond for the purpose of bringing my men to Harper's Ferry then being joined by thirty other young men from Baltimore we formed Company G, 13th Virginia Infantry."[40]

The Maryland Guard Battalion was the elite military organization of the day and many members were young men of prominent Baltimore families. The roster of Company G shows that no less than fifty-six of its sixty-eight men joined the C.S.A.[41] Richard Curzon HOFFMAN, Lieutenant of Company F of the Maryland Guard, did not hesitate in deciding on which side his sword should be drawn. Early in 1861 he moved his command to Harper's Ferry and crossed into Virginia. His company was mustered on May 24, 1861, as Company B, 21st Virginia Infantry."[42]

Wilson Carey NICHOLAS had been a second lieutenant in the Forest Rangers of Garrison in Baltimore County. He was among the foremost to bring a large number of the Forest Rangers to Harper's Ferry where they mustered in as Company G, 1st Maryland Battalion.[43]

Charles Worthington DORSEY, a member of the Howard County Dragoons, "crossed the Maryland border at Leesburg with about seventy-five members of the Company, in the first of June 1861, where they did patrol duty without being mustered into service for about two weeks then becoming members of Company G, 7th Virginia Cavalry."[44]

Richard THOMAS, a soldier of fortune, had just returned to America before the outbreak of hostilities and saw his two younger brothers go South. He was expected to stay home to take care of his mother. On April 26, 1861 he wrote, "if Maryland raises no Navy will not someone be willing to fit out a small, strong, swift propeller carrying two or even one ten or eleven inch guns mounted upon a patent carriage boat guns ammunition? As for men I believe I can get one hundred and fifty in one day."[45] After going South Richard THOMAS returned to St. Mary's County and organized Zarvona's Maryland Zouaves. Proceeding to Baltimore with sixteen of his men, they boarded the *St. Nicholas*. One of the Zouaves was George W. WATTS who had been a sailor on a merchant ship before resigning from the U.S. Navy and who wrote, "there were about sixty passengers aboard, and among them I counted my fifteen comrades. We all kept separated, however, and didn't let anyone know we knew each other. But what worried me a lot was I couldn't find the colonel or anyone who looked like him. I could see the future of the whole expedition, and also I could see myself behind bars in Fort McHenry, and the picture didn't look a bit good to me. So after the boat started I couldn't help noticing a mighty pretty young woman, stylishly dressed, flirting outrageously with some of the young officers. She talked with a strong French accent and carried a fan which she used like a Spanish dancer. That young woman behaved so scandalously that all the other women on the boat were in a terrible state over it. Just about dark I was up on deck and wondered where it was all going to end, whether I'd be hung as a rebel spy when someone touched me on the arm. I wheeled around like somebody had stuck a knife in me and saw ALEXANDER. He grinned at the fact that he had scared me and said, 'you are wanted in the second cabin.' I hurried below and nearly had a fit when I found all the boys gathered around the frisky French lady. She looked at me when I came in and Lordy, I knew those French eyes in a minute. It was the colonel; he had shed his bonnet, wig and dress and stepped forth clad in a brilliant new Zouave uniform. In a jiffy the French lady's three big trunks were dragged out and opened. One was fitted with cutlasses, another with Colt revolvers and a third with carbines. Each man buckled on a sword and pistol and grabbed a gun, and then the Colonel told us what to do."[46]

Major J. Alden WESTON had organized four companies, Company A of the Weston Guard, Company B of the Maryland Guard, Company C of the Old Line and Company D of the Maryland Guards. After the company returned from Suffolk to Richmond the Secretary of War began to shift companies into existing regiments where they were needed. Each man of WESTON's Battalion signed an individual petition which was sent to Jefferson Davis requesting that the battalion not be separated. On June 21, Captain Edward R. DORSEY's Weston Guards were ordered to the 1st Maryland Infantry and became Company C. Captain J. Lyle CLARKE's Maryland Guard was ordered to the 21st Virginia where they became Company B. Captain Michael Stone ROBERTSON's Southern Marylanders were not completely equipped or uniformed and were used to guard prisoners at Richmond until August 1, when they became Company I of the 1st Maryland Regiment and Captain William H. MURRAY's Maryland Guards were also sent to the 1st Maryland as Company H on June 21.

The National Rifles of Washington was a District of Columbia Militia Company. Captain Francis B. SCHAEFFER led the majority of his hundred-man company across the river into Virginia service. They became Company F, 1st Virginia Infantry, called the Beauregard Rifles. The National Rifles had fallen out of favor with the Federal Government early when Charles P. Stone wrote, "On April 2 (1861) I met, at the entrance of the Metropolitan Hotel, Captain SCHAEFFER, of the National Rifles of Washington, and I spoke to him about his company, which was remarkable for drill. SCHAEFFER had been a lieutenant in the 3rd U.S. Artillery, and was an excellent drillmaster. He had evidently not heard of my appointment as Inspector General, and he replied to my complimentary remarks on his company; 'yes, it is a good company and I suppose I will have to lead them to the banks of the Susquehannah.' 'Why so?,' I asked. 'Why to guard the frontier of Maryland and to help keep the Yankees from coming down to coerce the South.' I said to him quietly that I thought it was very imprudent in him, an employee of the Department of the Interior and captain of a company of District of Columbia volunteers, to use such expressions. He replied that most of his men were Marylanders, and would have to defend Maryland."[47]

Another D.C. Militia Company was the National Volunteers which was composed of ardent Southern sympathizers, many of whom were Marylanders. Charles K. SHERMAN wrote L.T. Wigfall on March 16, 1861, that they could muster from sixty-four to a hundred rank and file men to go into the service of the Confederacy. After offering their services to the city of Baltimore, following the Pratt Street melee, they went into Virginia and became Company E, 1st Virginia Infantry, known as the Washington Volunteers. "Company E, Washington Volunteers, District of Columbia records show that this company was formed in Washington in December 1860, for the purpose of enforcing the surrender of the District of Columbia to Maryland or Virginia when either seceded; enrolled into active service of the state of Alexandria on April 22, 1861, for one year; mustering into service on May 6, 1861; after temporarily attached to the 1st Regiment Virginia Volunteers; regimental return states the company being composed of Marylanders, was mustered out of service April 26, 1862."[48]

GROUPS OF MEN WHO LEFT MARYLAND

Colonel Francis J. THOMAS was appointed Adjutant General of the Maryland Volunteers in Virginia service and assumed command of the troops on May 17, 1861. In a letter of May 22 he writes to Colonel R. S. Garnett, "Many of these men are well drilled, about three hundred of them being of the 53rd Regiment, Maryland Guard. There are in all about two thousand eight hundred reported to me, but only fourteen companies organized. I have been unwilling to bring more into Virginia until steps are taken to properly organize and arm them as they come."[49] Colonel THOMAS proposed that three infantry regiments of Free Staters be formed, one under Major WESTON at Richmond, one at Point of Rocks, and another at Harper's Ferry, consisting of three thousand two hundred men and that cavalry and artillery battalions be organized to be filled by the numerous new arrivals. The officers of the companies at Point of Rocks didn't want to serve in the Provisional Army of the State of Virginia which Colonel THOMAS represented. They wanted to enlist in the Army of the Confederacy and desired that their state affiliation be recognized, feeling that Maryland must not lose her own sons, but that they should bear the Maryland flag in defense of the Confederate States. They were opposed to Colonel THOMAS who was responsible for accepting adopted Marylanders into the Virginia State Service. On June 8, Governor Letcher transferred the forces of the State of Virginia to the Confederate Government which relieved THOMAS of his post. He was killed while serving on the staff of General J. E. Johnston at Manassas while gallantly leading four companies. Had Colonel THOMAS' original proposal of organizing several regiments of the three branches of service materialized, thousands of newly arriving Maryland patriots could have easily been funneled into these commands, instead of being scattered throughout the entire Southern Army.

Upon the first major advancement by Confederate forces into the Free State in 1862, thousands wished to enlist. They asked, "where is the 1st Maryland?" The disappointment was great. They had no Maryland organization to rally to. "Colonel (Bradley T.) JOHNSON tried to organize a force in Frederick, but before a skeleton unit could be formed the Army marched, Sharpsburg was fought, Maryland evacuated, and the whole Confederacy filled with complaints that Maryland did not [come to the aid of the Confederate forces]; that no men joined our army and that she was untrue to the South. Had the 1st Maryland Regiment been with JOHNSON in Frederick during the three days he was there it would have filled up to two thousand men. Eight hundred, at least joined the cavalry and artillery companies as it was, but with that regiment as a nucleus, two thousand men would certainly have been obtained in the three days."[50] The former editor of The Frederick Herald, John William HEARD, issued a proclamation calling for enlistment in a company he was raising on September 9, 1862. Captain George W. CHISWELL had organized a group of Poolesville men, and for the past two months had been waiting for an opportunity to join the Southern Army. They proceeded to Frederick and joined Elijah Veirs WHITE's Battalion, where they became Company B; Robert Marion CHAMBERS II, after his enlistment with the 13th Virginia Infantry expired, received a commission as lieutenant colonel to organize an independent artillery organization. It was organized at Frederick with his father, Robert M. CHAMBERS I, who had been a private in the 1st Maryland Infantry, Company A, becoming senior captain. Charles E. TARR was captain of Company B; Robert H. GOLDSBOROUGH captain of company C; and John WILLIAMS captain of company D. CHAMBERS' Independent Artillery Battalion proceeded to Sharpsburg and participated in the engagement. Unfortunately,

Lieutenant Colonel CHAMBERS fell into the hands of the enemy, and his father became one of the martyrs of the Confederacy on the battle field. With the severe loss of so many members of the battalion during this campaign, the men apparently were absorbed into other artillery units.

Another group also joined the Confederate forces during the Southern invasion of Maryland. On February 21, 1863, General Isaac R. TRIMBLE wrote to the Secretary of War, "I respectfully apply for the appointment of Mr. W. W. DALLAS a citizen of Maryland as my aide-de-camp with the rank of Lieut. Mr. DALLAS joined the Army when in Maryland and brought into the services from that state sixty-two mounted cavalry, equipped at his own expense, who are now in the Army."[51]

Chapter 7

MARYLAND DESIGNATED COMMANDS

The 1st Maryland Infantry Regiment was organized on June 16, 1861, and elected Arnold ELZEY as colonel, George H. STEUART, Jr. as lieutenant colonel, and Bradley T. JOHNSON as major. Two of the three companies of WESTON reached Winchester on June 25 and united with the Harper's Ferry companies and the Point of Rock companies. Company A was commanded by William Worthington GOLDSBOROUGH, Company B by Charles C. EDELIN, Company C by Edward R. DORSEY, Company D by James R. HERBERT, Company E by Harry McCOY, company F by J. Louis SMITH, Company G by Wilson Carey NICHOLAS, Company H by William H. MURRAY and Company I, which soon joined them, by Michael Stone ROBERTSON. After twelve months of service the 1st Maryland was disbanded.

The 2nd Maryland Infantry Regiment was composed of many veterans of the former 1st Maryland, who made their way to Richmond, and under veteran officers formed into the following companies: Company A under William H. MURRAY, Company B under J. Parran CRANE, Company C under Ferdinand C. DUVALL, Company D under Joseph L. McALEER, Company E under John W. TORSCH, Company F under Andrew Jackson GWYNN, Company G under William Worthington GOLDSBOROUGH and Company H under James Thomas BUSSEY. They served with the Army of Northern Virginia until Appomattox, where on April 9, 1865, the 2nd Maryland Infantry had only sixty-three men left to surrender.

Richard Snowden ANDREWS had returned to Maryland to notify Thomas Smith RHETT that he had received a commission as colonel to organize the Maryland Artillery, but RHETT informed him that he could not leave Baltimore for several months. Returning with eighteen recruits, ANDREWS opened a recruiting office in Richmond for Marylanders. He commonly referred to his recruits as orphans, born under the black and gold flag. His cousin, Charles Snowden CONTEE, opened a branch in Fredericksburg. Colonel Walter Hanson JENIFER had received a colonel's commission of cavalry, but his men grew restless at his nonappearance, and agreed to transportation to Richmond, where they joined the 1st Maryland Light Artillery. ANDREWS had proceeded to Tredegar Iron Works, which was making Napoleon cannons for the battery. The first two guns were completed in August, but were given to the Washington Artillery who were short two guns. ANDREWS was elected captain and soon they were supplied with four Napoleons and four Parrots. In June of 1862, Company B was attached to the Hampton Legion, South Carolina Artillery. No battery in the Confederacy won more distinction than did the 1st Maryland

Artillery, who, after the Battle of Seven Pines, were referred to as the Maryland Flying Artillery. They were one of the very few batteries in the Army of Northern Virginia that never lost a gun, and no battery in the Army saw harder fighting or lost more men.

At Richmond on September 17, 1861, a unit of young men was mustered into service as the Baltimore Light Artillery. They chose for their commander John Bowyer BROCKENBOROUGH, and proceeded to camp near Centerville. Armed with loud-mouthed Blakeleys they became the 2nd Maryland Artillery. The accuracy of their guns attracted much attention throughout the war.

Henry B. LATROBE was one of three brothers who fought under the Southern Cross. He was authorized on September 9, 1861 to organize an artillery company. Recruiting began at Ashland, and by November 4th the 3rd Maryland Light Artillery had been established and was ordered to Camp Dimmock for instruction.

On November 15, Lieutenant Harry A. STEUART and Sergeant J.N.L. McREARY started for their native state to procure medical supplies and raise additional recruits. STEUART went to his home in Baltimore to see his mother who was the only family member residing there, his father and brother having already entered Southern service. On the return route, STEUART was captured. McREARY returned with the additional recruits and enrolled them in the Richmond Howitzers, since the 3rd Maryland Artillery had already been mustered and ordered to Knoxville, Tennessee. The 3rd Maryland Artillery arrived on February 11, destined to serve with distinction west of the Alleghenies, and was one of nine Maryland units that never fired their guns in their home state. The 3rd Maryland Artillery was the largest artillery unit from the state. They became a six-gun battery with the acquisition of two three-inch iron rifles received from Richmond. By the winter of 1865 the 3rd Maryland Artillery was in Battery D in Mobile, Alabama, where they were working siege pieces. Upon their evacuation on April 11, they were moved to Meridian, Mississippi, and surrendered with General R. Taylor's command which was paroled on May 10.

Joseph FORREST and William Dawson BROWN recruited a number of men from the state in December of 1861 for infantry service, but rather than infantry they became the 2nd Company of McINTOSH's Artillery Battalion. They enlisted on January 1, 1852 for three years or the duration of the War as FORREST Company, Chesapeake Battery. After being sent to Camp Lee for instructions, they were equipped with four inferior caliber, smooth-bore guns. By the coming spring, the Chesapeake Battery was increased with new recruits from the state and fully organized as the Chesapeake Artillery, subsequently known as the 4th Maryland Light Artillery under Captain William BROWN. They won distinction at Cedar Run in August of 1862, literally cutting the enemy to pieces while attached to Snowden ANDREWS' Battalion. General Early complimented the 4th Maryland by presenting them with four ten-pound Parrot guns which enabled them to discard their old smooth-bores. In January, 1864, Colonel ANDREWS and Thomas Smith RHETT were requested by General Lee to go to Europe and purchase cannon. On June 22, 1864, the 1st and 4th Maryland Artillery Battalions were transferred to David Gregg McINTOSH's Battalion.

Eighteen young Marylanders who had signed for one year's service in Company K, 1st Virginia Cavalry, refused to reenlist. Believing a Maryland

Regiment could be formed, they met in Richmond on May 15, 1862, and began to organize what would become Company A. The Company was known as BROWN's Company, and was ordered to the Shenandoah Valley attached to the 2nd Virginia Cavalry. When BROWN's troopers returned from the Sharpsburg campaign they were joined by a company of young men who would become Company B under George W. EMACK, organized in September at Orange Courthouse. Robert Carter SMITH, a former captain in the 1st Maryland Infantry, recruited many men from his former command into Company C. Warner Griffith WELSH resigned his commission from Company F, 12th Virginia Cavalry, when he and his brother raised a unit of men from Carroll and Frederick counties that became Company D. These companies formed the 1st Maryland Cavalry Battalion, which was officially organized on November 25, 1862, at Winchester. At Camp Lee, William Independence RASIN was recruiting a company to be exclusively Marylanders. They were known as WINDER's Cavalry and became Company E. Company F was organized under three rich, young Baltimoreans who ran the blockade for all their arms and accouterments. In July 1864, Company K of the 1st Virginia Cavalry was finally transferred to the 1st Maryland Battalion.

After going to Richmond and obtaining authority from the Secretary of War to raise a battalion to act independently near or within enemy lines, Harry W. GILMOR resigned his commission in the 12th Virginia Cavalry and on May 7, 1863 began to recruit. The recruiting was very rapid, for within a month five new Maryland companies were ordered up the Valley. Company A was commanded by Nicholas BURKE and contained mainly new recruits; Company B under Eugene DIGGS contained a number of men who had seen service in the 1st Maryland Infantry; Company C under James P. BAYLY contained a number of men from the Maryland Guard of the Virginia Infantry; Company D under John Redmond BURKE, who was a personal scout for J.E.B. Stuart, drew many Marylanders from the 1st Virginia Cavalry; Company E under John E. SUDLER contained mainly new recruits. On May 22, 1863, fifty-eight Maryland members of GILMOR's old company (company F, 12th Virginia Cavalry) signed a petition and forwarded it to the Adjutant General that they might be attached to his command. The Company was ordered to GILMOR's Battalion, but in August was recalled to the 12th Virginia due to the protest of Colonel Harman who felt that, although they were Marylanders, they were more critically needed in his command. Not until the spring of 1864 were they finally added to GILMOR's command. As their reputation grew through their bold, courageous riding they became known as "The Band." Not until they were ordered to the Maryland Line were they known officially as the 2nd Maryland Cavalry Battalion.

Chapter 8

MARYLAND UNITS

At Canary Island, a group of Free Staters was endeavoring to enroll transient fellow Marylanders into an artillery company known as the Baltimore Artillery. They enlisted on June 5, 1861. There being a scarcity of guns, they were assigned to the 9th Virginia Infantry as Company B, under Captain John D. MYRICK. After their twelve-month enlistment had expired, they were reorganized on May 8, 1862, with a great majority continuing to serve with the Virginia Infantry.

MARYLAND UNITS

The 1st Company of Maryland Zouaves, 1st Zarvona Regiment held a meeting on the 4th of July in Richmond to elect officers. It was commanded by William C. WALTERS. After the capture of Colonel ZARVONA, the Zouave Regiment was dissolved. The Zouave 1st Company was ordered to Tappahannock, Virginia, on November 1, and absorbed into the 47th Virginia Infantry as Company H. In March of 1862 they were transferred to the 2nd Battalion Arkansas Infantry. The 2nd Company of ZARVONA's Maryland Zouaves was under the command of Thomas BLACKISTONE. It has not been established where the 2nd Company was sent, but a number of the men can be found with two line officers who received promotions to captains, George W. ALEXANDER at Castle Thunder Prison and John W. TORSCH of the 2nd Maryland Infantry.

Company M, 1st Virginia Cavalry, after being reorganized and regularly mustered, on August 1, 1861, became part of Stuart's Cavalry and by order of Fitzhugh Lee the initial of the company was changed to K, which placed them on the right flank of the column, signifying his respect for their skill and reliability. The Marylanders of Company K served the entire period of the War, and after General Stuart's death were transferred to the 1st Maryland Cavalry and continued as Company K.

In January 1862, a large portion of Company B, 1st Maryland Infantry reenlisted. After receiving a furlough they offered to forego their well-deserved leave, and consequently were ordered by the War Department from Gordonsville to detached service at Goldsboro, North Carolina. They served as infantry at the Battle of Newbern, then in scouting service, and at Brunswick Point as heavy artillerists. About to return to their regiment, Captain Charles C. EDELIN wrote on March 12 to General L.O. Brandt, "Believing an engagement with the enemy is imminent, I am desirous to remain with my command for inasmuch as I have remained this long I would like not to leave until I have struck another blow at the would be dispoilers of the Old North State, our furlough expires on the 15th approximately and we are to leave that day, should the enemy advance on the next it would cause much malicious speculation. Hoping you will take immediate actions in the premise."[52] Soon the patriots of old Company B learned that their regiment was not to be reestablished and remained in service of North Carolina. They made several requests for infantry arms but served as heavy artillerists and were known as EDELIN's Maryland Battalion of Heavy Artillery. They were soon recruiting other Marylanders who were serving in North Carolina units. By the summer of 1864, Captain EDELIN and his men were with WINDER's Legion in defense of Richmond.

George S. LEMMON was dispatched from Company H, 1st Maryland Infantry, in February of 1862 and sent to Charleston, South Carolina to bring Maryland men from Fort Sumter to the Maryland Line. The number of men that he brought back has not been established, but it probably was not a full company allotment since he accepted a staff appointment while they served in ARCHER's Brigade as artillerymen until September of 1864, when they were placed on arsenal duty in Richmond.

Elijah Viers WHITE, after his meritorious conduct at the Battle of Ball's Bluff, was sent to Richmond and commissioned to raise a company of independent cavalry. In the last days of December, 1861 he and fifteen men became couriers between Leesburg and Winchester. The first company was completely organized by March 19, 1862 and by October, Bradley T. JOHNSON had organized and mustered "Lige WHITE's Battalion" into regular service as the 35th Virginia Cavalry. This Battalion contained a large number of men from the Old

Line State, and of the line officers eleven were Marylanders. Immediately after the surrender of the Army in '65, only those Marylanders who had been previous residents were allowed to cross back into the state. By checking the paroles of members of the 35th, the author has been able to identify at least two hundred and seventy-two Marylanders.

On March 10, 1862, Webster H. SOTHORN was ordered by General George Hume STEUART, Jr. to enlist Maryland soldiers at Suffolk and Petersburg into the Maryland Line. On May 17, STEUART was officially ordered to organize those of the Old Line State into the Maryland Line. Unfortunately, General T. J. Jackson needed the services of STEUART as a brigade commander in the spring campaign, so the consolidation of the Marylanders was postponed. These new recruits of SOTHORN's followed him into the Virginia Light Artillery where he was commissioned a lieutenant.

Harry W. GILMOR obtained permission to organize a cavalry company for the 7th Virginia Regiment. This was also a complete Maryland unit, but instead of being affiliated with their state kinsmen of Company G, they were sent to the 12th Virginia Cavalry where they became Company F on April 10, 1862.

On May 3, 1862, a unit of men from the Old Line State enlisted for the duration of the War as light artillerists for the Maryland Line under Captain J. Norris MONTGOMERY. Through the summer of 1862 they served as light artillerymen and became known as Dea's Maryland Artillery. At the approach of winter, and with the dwindling of combat, they expected to join the Maryland Line, but on November 3, Dea's Maryland Artillery was ordered to Battery 8, Richmond Defenses, and became Company C, 19th Virginia Heavy Artillery.

After gaining his release from Fort McHenry, Ogle S. TILGHMAN proceeded to Richmond where he advertised that he was forming a company of riflemen from his native Talbot County. In the same newspaper where this advertisement appeared, Captain William J. MADDOX announced recruitment of a company which would be known as the Maryland American Rifles.

On May 24, 1862, the Maryland Guard, Company B, 21st Virginia Infantry was mustered out with the expiration of their term of service. Richard Curzon HOFFMAN received a captain's commission and was ordered to recruit a company of sharpshooters. Many of Company B, along with a group of Free Staters brought together by James P. ADAMS, were mustered in for three years or the duration of the War, on September 1, 1862, as Company E, 30th Virginia Sharpshooters. Much to their joy, their former commander, J. Lyle CLARKE, was promoted to major and appointed to command the six companies of sharpshooters.

Captain Philip Henry LEE organized a company of horsemen in 1862 who were known as Lee's Maryland Cavalry. They were established to become part of the Maryland Line but acted as scouts, guides and couriers for the Army of Northern Virginia.

William H. JACOBS recruited Marylanders into his company of mounted riflemen. Before their ranks could be completely filled, they were ordered to consolidate with the Radford Rangers, and pressed into service with the 30th Virginia Volunteers, later becoming Company I of the 2nd Virginia Cavalry.

James BREATHED went to Missouri to practice medicine but returned to Maryland at the outbreak of war. On his journey east, his traveling companion was J.E.B. Stuart. Finding the legislature very hesitant about the future course of the state, he departed for the South and joined Company B of Stuart's 1st Virginia Cavalry. Stuart recognized young BREATHED and in a few weeks he was detached to serve as a scout. On March 23, 1862, he was elected as first lieutenant in Stuart's Horse Artillery, and by August 9, he had received a captain's commission and was recruiting a number of veterans who had previously served in the 1st Maryland Infantry. BREATHED's Battery of Stuart's Horse Artillery would soon include ten Maryland commissioned officers along with many enlisted men.

Thomas H. HOLBROOK, formerly of the 1st Maryland Infantry, had served in Gorham's Artillery until he was authorized to organize an artillery battery which became known as HOLBROOK's Independent Maryland Light Artillery. They were sent to the Army of the West and served gallantly at Shiloh, Farrington and Memphis. HOLBROOK's Independent Maryland Artillery retreated to Vicksburg where, during the siege, they were wiped out by casualties. Lieutenant Thomas A. TORMEY took a portion of the battery into the 42nd Tennessee Cavalry where he became captain. Lieutenant Thomas F. McCARDELL returned with some of the men to the Army of Northern Virginia, where they desired to serve with the Maryland Line under General ELZEY at Staunton, but due to ELZEY's reassignment, McCARDELL and his men were absorbed into the 64th Virginia Infantry.

James Louis CLARK, a former quartermaster of the 1st Maryland Infantry, requested an appointment on September 29, 1862, to the regular cavalry. He had been in service for ten months and at the time of the advance into Maryland had raised a cavalry company of one hundred men, but was prevented from carrying them into the field because the government could not furnish horses which had been promised. He did not receive an appointment and carried his men into Stuart's Horse Artillery.

After leaving the Quartermaster Corps, T. Sturgis DAVIS organized a company in the summer of 1863 for the 1st Maryland Cavalry. They were not, however, assigned to this battalion. Instead, they acted independently. By August 13, six companies of Marylanders were mustered into DAVIS's Battalion of cavalry as partisan rangers, and he was commissioned a major with the following company commanders: Company A, Thomas Benton GATCH; Company B, Charles E. BISHOP; Company C, John G. PHILLIPS; Company D, George M.E. SHEARER; Company E, W.C. NICHOLAS; Company F, A.D. ERWIN. At Winchester on September 19, 1864, then Lieutenant Colonel DAVIS was captured and his battalion, being diminished by combat, was dismantled, with Captain GATCH of Company A transferring his company to the 23rd Virginia Cavalry as Company M, Captain BISHOP with Company B to the 1st Maryland Cavalry as Company G, Captain PHILLIPS with Company C to the 41st Virginia Cavalry as Company G, George T. SNOWDEN and his Company D to the 2nd Maryland Cavalry as Company G, Captain NICHOLAS with Company E and Captain ERWIN with Company F to the 1st Maryland Cavalry as companies H and I. BISHOP and his men were ultimately sent to the 2nd Maryland Cavalry, where they merged with SNOWDEN's Company G. NICHOLAS' and ERWIN's companies, apparently unable to fill their depleted ranks, were combined and designated as Company G, 1st Maryland Cavalry.

John Donnell SMITH resigned as an aide-de-camp on General Magruder's staff, and on October 4, 1862 with forty-six men, organized an independent battery known as Lee's Baltimore Light Artillery. They served with the Bedford Light Artillery, which later transferred to Jordan's Artillery. The Baltimore Artillery many times was officially mentioned as J.D. SMITH's Artillery. In the summer of 1864 this battery served in Huger's Battalion, and later Alexander's Battalion. At Appomattox, Captain SMITH surrendered the remains of Lee's Baltimore Artillery which consisted of two pieces and sixty-four men.

Louis KEEPERS was elected commander of a company called the Maryland Guerrilla Zouaves, which was organized in Richmond. They were assigned to Louisiana troops by the Secretary of War and became the 2nd Company C of Velligan's Louisiana Infantry.

In the late fall of 1862, Edmund BARRY was recruiting a company at Camp Maryland. BARRY's Maryland Volunteers were to become Company C when the 1st Maryland Regiment was reorganized. When this did not occur, Barry was ordered to report to General ELZEY who placed him in command of the detectives on the Rappahannock transporting prisoners and goods across the lines. BARRY's Maryland Volunteers continued on independent service until October 29, when they were ordered to Major Elias GRISWOLD with their headquarters at Hedgesville. By the fall of 1864 they were assigned to duty at Andersonville Prison under General John H. WINDER.

On April 6, 1863, General George H. Stuart, Jr., wrote to the Secretary of War stating that Lieutenant D.M. SNOVELL had been authorized to raise a company for local defense and already had sixty-four men, and that he desired to go into the field. Fifty of these were Marylanders and he thought that he could get additional Marylanders to raise a company for the Maryland Line.

The largest number of government clerks in pre-war Washington government were Marylanders or Virginians. The majority left the new Republican administration, and many of them went south. The Confederate government in Richmond contained a number of Marylanders. On June 4, 1863, Albert ELLERY was elected captain of the 2nd Company D, 3rd Battalion Virginia Infantry, Local Defense Troops. This company was composed of Marylanders who worked in various departments as clerks for the Confederate War Department, and were known as the Treasury Guards. At various times they were called out in defense of Richmond. Captain ELLERY was killed at the age of fifty, on March 1, 1864, at Glen Burnie. Three days later a collection was taken up by his fellow clerks for his wife and children.

There were units not commanded by Marylanders that contained significant numbers of Marylanders, such as McNeill's Rangers, which contained twenty-three. John Singleton Mosby's detail of fifteen men included three Marylanders: Edward S. HURST from CLARK's Independent Cavalry; Daniel L. THOMAS, Jr., formerly of the 1st Maryland Infantry, Company C; and Thomas TURNER, Company K, 1st Virginia Cavalry. These original fifteen men were selected to report to Mosby and became a part of the core of these famous partisan rangers. The author has been able to document two hundred and fifty-one Marylanders within their ranks.

Chapter 9

THE MARYLAND LINE

The original Maryland Line was born during the Revolutionary War, and the reestablishment of the Line in the service of the South was a dream of many Marylanders who were in the Confederacy. Maryland units were dispersed throughout various companies in the Confederacy and Maryland men were everywhere to be found, but the thought of bringing together Marylanders in one joint command of infantry, artillery and cavalry was desired by many. The first effort to organize the Maryland Line in Confederate service was held at Leesburg, Virginia on August 6, 1861. A constitution was unanimously adopted and printed for distribution among the influx of Southern patriots crossing the Potomac. An election was held two days later and the following were chosen: President, Coleman Yellott; Vice President, Dr. Charles A. HARDING; Secretary, Horace Edwin HAYDEN; Treasurer, Benjamin S. WHITE; Executive Council, Robert Harris ARCHER, Jr., T. Sturgis DAVIS, Frank A. BOND, George Ridgely GAITHER, Jr., and James A. KEMER. Their constitution called this the Association of the Independent Maryland Line of 1861. The object of the association was to protect the freedom and property of the people of Maryland. One of its goals was to organize the membership into copmanies, regiments and brigades. With the coming of the summer campaigns, the Association faded, and plans for the Maryland Line were further delayed.

In response to efforts by George Hume STEUART, Jr., the Confederate Congress passed an act authorizing the organization of the Maryland Line. All native or adopted citizens of Maryland who were or should become volunteers in Confederate States service might, at their option, be enlisted in the Maryland Line. This General Order No. 8 from the War Department was issued on February 26, 1862. On May 17, General STEUART was ordered by T.J. Jackson to organize the Maryland command. Other events interrupted, however. With the opening of the spring campaign he was given command of a brigade in Ewell's Division and severely wounded at Cross Keys.

In June of 1863, James A. Seldon, Secretary of War, directed Major General Isaac R. TRIMBLE to organize the Line. The order caught up with him while he was with the army at Gettysburg. On the first day General Pender fell and TRIMBLE was assigned to command his division. During Pickett's charge at Gettysburg, General TRIMBLE was severely wounded, captured, and had his right leg amputated. And again the organization of the Maryland Line was foiled.

On November 1, 1863, General R.E. Lee assigned Bradley T. JOHNSON to the Maryland Line, which was finally established. At the time, Marylanders were dispersed more than ever, with only a few in consoldated units, but at last after more than two year's effort and struggle, the Maryland Line came into being. Fifteen hundred Marylanders were collected. The command of the Maryland Line consisted of the 1st Maryland Cavalry, the 2nd Maryland Infantry, the Flying Artillery (then designated as the 1st Maryland Artillery), the Baltimore Artillery (then termed the 2nd Maryland Artillery), and the Chesapeake Artillery, which became known as the 4th Maryland Artillery. The field officers elected on February 6, 1864 were Bradley T. JOHNSON, Colonel, commanding; George Wilson BOOTH, Captain and Assistant General; Wilson Carey NICHOLAS, Captain and Assistant Inspector General; George H. KYLE, Major and Commissary of Supply; Charles R. HARDING, Major and Quartermaster; Richard Potts JOHNSON, Surgeon and Medical Director; Thomas Sargent LATIMER, Assistant Surgeon; Reverend Thomas DUNCAN, Chaplain; and Andrew Cross TRIPPE, Lieutenant and Ordnance Officer.

To rally Marylanders from other commands, George P. KANE prepared a brochure which read, in part: "I call upon you, then, one and all, whether now in military service or civil life, to come forward at once, and repair to the flag of our own beloved State, oppressed though she has been for years, her worthiest citizens languishing in dungeons, or exiles from her soil; her fair daughters insulted by ruffians and mourning in tears the fate of their country. We will know that there is yet for Maryland a future, and a hope. I appeal to you by all the wrongs heaped upon our people, by the noble blood poured out in the battles of the war, by the memories of your ancestors to rally as a band of brothers, and unite in a common effort for the rescue of our State from the hands of the spoilers and the despot."[53]

On the second page of Colonel KANE's plea is a copy of General Order No. 38 (authorizing enlisted Marylanders the right to transfer), and on page three a form of transfer that could be filled out by the Free Staters. By this time, however, many Maryland veterans were comfortably entrenched in commands with friends and relatives. There were others who desired to transfer but their commanders stated that they were essential and would not release them. On June 13, General ELZEY wrote to the Secretary of War, "I have the honor to report that up to this time my efforts to organize the Maryland Line have been fruitless. I found about fifty of GILMOR's dismounted men at Staunton, and only about thirty transferred men reported to me at Camp Maryland. They were sent from Charleston, and were men who had been confined in jail. When General Imboden was pressed in the Valley, I sent this detachment of about eighty men, under Captain (Donald C.) STITH to join his forces." Four days later ELZEY was ordered to Lynchburg for other duty.[54]

With the evacuation of the capital of the Confederacy, the gallant Maryland Line was reduced to less than one hundred. It had fired the first gun in the Seven Days' Battle; it had fired the first gun in Early's advance into Maryland in 1864 and the last when he recrossed at Poolesville; and it would make the last cavalry charge at Appomattox on April 9, 1865.

Chapter 10

DIVIDED FAMILIES

The issues leading to the greatest American tragedy divided familes in Maryland as much as in any of the other border states. Families were torn apart in every sector of Maryland. Compelled to take sides were Foxhall and William PARKER, brothers who carried on the naval tradition of their father. They met in Washington just prior to the secession crises and discussed what they would do if it came to a fight. Foxhall PARKER stressed the importance of the family's southern heritage while William PARKER argued for loyalty to the old flag. "So persistent did each put their case that when it came time to decide, each followed the others advice." Foxhall remained in the Federal Navy while William entered that of the Confederacy.[55]

There were family members who were compelled to be completely neutral. They were bewildered, and cringed as news of each engagement reached their ears, for brothers were fighting against brothers. From New Windsor, R.S.

EASTON was a private in Stuart's Horse Artillery, C.S.A., and his brother James Easton a Sergeant in the 4th Maryland Infantry, U.S.A. Letters from the family show the confusion and doubt which persisted during the war years.

During the course of the war many opposing family members met on the battlefield. "Joseph HURD of Washington County owned some property in Alabama, where he was during part of the Civil War. He was a member of the Confederate Army (1st Alabama Infantry) and while at Vicksburg, Mississippi, he was captured by Union soldiers among whom was his brother, Bryan Pitney Hurd. The brothers were fighting in armies hostile to each other, and they were not aware of each other's enlistment until they met as foes at Vicksburg."[56]

In June of 1863 at Winchester, the 2nd Maryland captured some of Milroy's Force. Among the prisoners was "My cousin Dr. Lloyd Goldsborough, Surgeon of the 5th Maryland Federal Infantry, a brother of our own Major William W. GOLDSBOROUGH. The doctor was sure surprised to see me, and the first thing he said was, 'Where in the hell is Captain Bill GOLDSBOROUGH?' and Captain DUVALL said, 'He's a Major now - and God only knows what he's liable to do with you'."[57] Michael Aloysious QUINN, Chief Musician of the 2nd Maryland Infantry, wrote, "In front of Petersburg, Virginia I met and talked to my father (Private Thomas Quinn, company I) who was a member of the 2nd Infantry in the Federal Army, this occurred on the lines at the front."[58]

This division of families was not limited to one geographical area or social class. Wilson Carey NICHOLAS left his home and was elected captain of Company G, 1st Maryland Infantry, C.S.A., while his father continued to serve as a captain in the U.S. Navy.

Even those in high Federal and state offices were affected by opposing family feelings and bitterness. Edmund P. and John Francis HICKEY were sons of General William Hickey, Secretary of the U.S. Senate. Their political feelings were opposite that of their father. They were sent to Georgetown College but instead went to Charlottesville where they enlisted in the 1st Maryland Cavalry. Edmund was captured at Raccoon Ford in August of 1863 and confined in Fort Delaware. John was wounded, lost a leg, and was sent to Camp Chase. On March 6, 1865, both were released without taking the oath of allegiance, by order of President Lincoln, and taken to Washington where they were placed in the custody of their father.

George Vickers advised Governor Hicks to recruit an Eastern Shore regiment to combat secession. Vickers was commissioned a major general of the Eastern Shore Militia. Two of his sons remained and fought in defense of the Union, while a third, Benjamin Clothier VICKERS, joined the Southern army. A few days before his death, suffering from mortal wounds at Shiloh, Benjamin Vickers married the niece of Sam Houston.[59]

In a letter dated April 8, 1861, William K. BRADFORD wrote his father that he would abandon his ideas of going south. However, within two months he cast his future with the Confederacy and became a captain of staff, while his father, A.W. Bradford, was elected the Unionist Governor of the state. Near the end of the War a friend inquired to the Governor if his son would be welcome, and he replied, "My son has always been and would continue to be welcome to a home in my home."[60] A letter of January 24, 1865, from Captain BRADFORD to his father, stated, "I had the honor to apply to you for a pass for myself to come North and see my lame and afflicted wife. The circumstances are well known to you and my own health is very bad and if granted permission to go and return I will give proper parole under the circumstances."[61]

Southern families in Maryland frequently suffered heartbreak and grief at the fate of their loved ones. Two brothers from Frederick County, Joseph Thomas REID and James Henry REID, were both killed at Shiloh. Divided familes were in a position to experience devastation. Napoleon B. HULL resided at Funkstown, served in the Confederate Army under General Stonewall Jackson, and was in the engagement at Chancellorsville, where his son and namesake, Napoleon B. Hull, Jr., was among those killed in the Union ranks.[62]

Chapter 11

FIELD GRADE OFFICERS

Besides the seventeen generals and admirals which Maryland gave the Confederacy, the author's research has brought to light 221 field grade officers. No doubt there were more. Some rose to high rank through immediate popularity - such as Aaron Bascom HARDCASTLE who recruited a battalion of Mississippians and Alabamians and - Paul Francis DeGOURNAY, who recruited a Louisiana battalion. There were others, such as Thomas Balch BEALL, who enlisted as a private in Company I, 10th Mississippi Infantry, and through field promotions became a major on Early's staff. Thomas Hewlings Stockton BOYD advanced from a private in the 1st Louisiana Infantry to lieutenant colonel of the 47th Virginia Cavalry. These four were among the many Marylanders who departed for the deep South early in the struggle.

Frank H. JONES experienced the complete gamut of a military man, rising from the enlisted ranks to become a field grade officer. He joined the Confederacy in November, 1862, as an enlisted man, and was wounded at Fredericksburg by a shell fragment in December of 1862. He was hospitalized for several months. He then was detailed as clerk in a quartermaster department at Hanover Court House. In 1863 he was sent to Richmond for telegraphing duties, and was dangerously exposed in numerous engagements. In 1864 he reenlisted and recruited the 2nd regiment of Alabama and Tennessee Border Rangers, of which he was subsequently elected colonel.[63]

In March of 1863 the Niter and Mining Bureau was established under Superintendent I.M. St. John. Prior to the war, he had studied law and had been a newspaper editor in Baltimore before giving up journalism to become a civil engineer. Colonel Richard MORTON would become chief of the Bureau, and along with Major John ELLICOTT, drew many Marylanders into the bureau.

William NORRIS left his family of six and went to Virginia as a civilian aide on the staff of J.B. Magruder, where on July 18, 1861, he was authorized to establish a system of signals. After taking command as chief of the Signal Corps in 1862, he surrounded himself with other Marylanders. They were in the field as telegraph operators, wire tappers, flagmen and couriers. NORRIS organized a systematic network across the Potomac known as the Secret Line. As head of the Secret Service Bureau, his wartime exiles from Maryland again were invaluable to him, establishing a line of boatsmen, way stations and safe houses with agents and Southern sympathizers that reached as far north as Canada. The Secret Line reported many of the enemy's movements in dispatches using secret codes and ciphers. Colonel NORRIS was also made commisssioner of prison exchange, and in all three of the departments he headed, Marylanders were conspicuously present.

The loyalty of some of the field grade officers who lost their positions after reorganization of their commands is amazing. William MUNFORD was lieutenant colonel of the 17th and 24th Virginia Regiments. When it was reorganized, he was not reelected and was sent to Canada by the governor of Virginia. In 1863 he was unsuccessful in recruiting a battalion, and, realizing the need for fighting men, he joined the Otey Virginia Battery as a private. After being exchanged from Fort Delaware, Lieutenant Colonel Robert Marion CHAMBERS II had no battalion to command, and found a hearty welcome among the cavaliers of the 1st Maryland. St. Clair F. SUTHERLAND was lieutenant colonel of the Quartermaster Department in Richmond, and was "cashiered, December 20, 1864, and returned to the ranks as a pvt., Co. E."[64]

Other noteworthy field grade officers from Maryland are Colonels Jeremiah Yellott DASHIELL and James Calvert WISE who became adjutant generals of Texas and Louisiana respectively and George PETERS, commander of the Ambulance Corps in the Army of Northern Virginia.

Chapter 12

ENLISTMENTS

While the leaders of the Southern movement in Maryland bided their time to wait for state action, many young men were fervent in their willingness to pursue that which they knew was going to burst upon the land. Parents tried to calm the impatient desires of their youth, but many ran away from school only to inform their parents later of what they had done. Noah Dixon WALKER went to Richmond, notifying the family of his determination to espouse the Confederate cause. In reply he received a letter "frought with love and despair, in which his father appealed to him to relinquish his purpose, and promised him, if he would, through the firm of Brown, Shipley and Co. send him a letter of credit for two hundred thousand dollars. This offer his son would not consider for a moment. The South was dearer to him than money, dearer even than life."[65] John Chapman SPENCER was killed in his first charge in his first engagement. He penned, "I shall be very sorry if my departure South causes any pain to my father, and I hope he will not be vexed at my saying that I consider all my duties subordinate to the great duty of fighting for the liberties which have been handed down to us by our fathers. I have long desired to help the South, and when the opportunity presented I embraced it."[66]

Joining the Confederate army from Maryland was difficult and dangerous. "But they braved the danger, ran the risks, and went over singly and in squads, and joined the first gray-jacket soldiers they met, or hunted up some friends from Maryland already there to share his mess. Some of these would-be recruits never reached there, they were either drowned in the attempt, or captured, and dragged off to some loathsome den to pine away and die, under the humane treatment of Northern Christian humanity --- wartime edition."[67] The last time anyone heard of young J. Gabby Duckett of Washington County he was attempting to cross the river and join the Confederates. Several weeks passed and his body came ashore at Shepherdstown with a bullet hole in his breast. Thomas A. Cross was captured in the winter of

1861 on his way to join the Confederate men in arms and was imprisoned until the end of the war and never had an opportunity to enlist.

In the secluded parlors of many homes, women of Confederate loved ones thought of their men proudly and hoped for their safe return. William Kennedy JENKINS wrote, "When I left my dear mother, her last words to me were sooner should she see me dead on the field of battle than to know that I had shirked my duties to the cause so dear to our hearts. 'Yes had I seven sons to give to the Cause gladly would I do that than that you should be false to the colors that you now go to defend.'"[68]

The age of the 1st Maryland Infantry rank and file averaged less than nineteen. They were generally beardless boys with the spirit, the enthusiasm, and the dedication of their forefathers. Most of these volunteers were in the flower of their youth. Henry S. POLE was only fourteen years old when he ran away from home to enlist in the confederate army. Albert B. CUNNINGHAM was only fourteen years of age when he enlisted in June, 1861, in the 18th Louisiana Infantry. There were many such as these two who were discharged under the Acts of Congress regarding boys under eighteen. CUNNINGHAM was released from the army, but after only two months he was actively campaigning again as a scout with the 5th Texas Cavalry. Others, such as William S. GAVIN, who was fifteen years of age serving in Company F, 54th Georgia Infantry, served admirably, and surrendered in Greensboro. John Bailey TYLER was the youngest soldier in his command and was a favorite of all the officers and men. He enlisted as a cavalryman when he was twelve years old, served throughout the war in B Troop of the 1st Maryland Confederate Cavalry, and was called "The Boy."[69]

There were also those at the other end of the age scale who were likewise devoted and could not stand idly by. Dr. Samuel ANNAN, former professor at the Washington Medical College in Baltimore, in 1862, at the age of sixty-two, joined the Confederate Medical Corps. Charles Tiberghein JONES enlisted in 1861 at the age of fifty-two. Thomas W. DAWSON entered the service at the age of sixty. In the 3rd Maryland Artillery there were four men over the age of fifty. Frederick William Nicholls CROUCH was a doctor of music who became a private in the Richmond Howitzers at the age of fifty-three. Despite his age, with the spirit and endurance of a youth, he never lost a day from sickness, though he was several times wounded. The crippled old gunner stayed to the last bitter day and was always proud of his state. Dr. CROUCH would take great satisfaction in telling that he was the number one man at the number one gun of the 1st Howitzers, 1st Battalion, 1st Regiment Light Artillery, 1st Army Corps of the Army of Northern Virginia.

There was a father-son duo, James Aloysius RYAN, Sr. and Jr., in Stuart's Horse Artillery. The 3rd Maryland Artillery had two such pairs, John SULLIVAN I and II and W. HATTAWAY, Sr. and Jr.

Throughout the War the citizens of Maryland were greatly oppressed by the occupying northern troops. The harshness of the Federals made many Marylanders submissive for fear of worse things. Ezra Mantz enlisted under the name G. Wiskee WALTON when he joined the 4th Kentucky Infantry, because he was under age and did not want to bring harsh treatment upon his parents. Campbell Pinkey White, to lessen the possibility of pressure upon his father and brother who, like himself, were Baltimore attorneys, changed his name to Campbell W. PINKEY when he enlisted.

Chapter 13

NAVAL

As a result of Marylanders' participation in the Revolutionary War and the War of 1812, the Old Line State was justly able to boast of its Naval heroes. In the War Between the States her sons again played an heroic leading part in the Navy of the Confederacy. There were three admirals from Maryland who served in the Civil War, one in Federal service and two in Southern service. At Hampton Roads Franklin BUCHANAN was the flag officer of the ironclad *Virginia*, commonly referred to as the *Merrimac*. He continued his distinguished service in the Confederacy and came to be the top ranking officer in the Confederate Navy. In the last years of the War, Raphael SEMMES, who had become renowned on the cruiser *Alabama*, became a rear admiral. Thus the only two admirals in the Confederacy were Marylanders. In fact the Confederate Navy was top heavy with Marylanders. Besides the two admirals there were Marylanders in the rank of commodore (1), captain (7), commander (4), lieutenants commanding (7) and lieutenant (15). The career prospects for Naval personnel in the new Confederacy were not good, for there were few ships. Those former captains and commanders who commanded squadrons could only aspire to command a few converted river steamers. The first and second lieutenants of many years' service were relegated to command of canal boats. However, "The largest percentage of Marylanders resigned from the Army and Navy of the United States and gave their services to the South; they made greater sacrifices than any others. War was their profession in life, but it was not as soldiers and sailors of fortune that they went, following the trumpet's call and the rolling of the drums, but as patriotic soldiers and sailors."[70] Resignations from the Union Navy were not accepted, but instead, the names of those asking to resign to go south were stricken from the rolls, as having been dismissed - an apparent display of bureaucratic vindictiveness. Eventually 163 Marylanders would serve as officers in the relatively small Southern Provisional Navy.

Franklin BUCHANAN resigned from the U.S. Navy on April 20, the day after the Federal attack in Baltimore and spent the next four months at his home in Talbot County, anxiously watching the course of the War. "I am as strong a Union man as any in the country, Union under the Constitution and laws and as to the stars and stripes I have as strong a loyal feeling for them as anyone who was ever born; I have fought my country's enemies under the glorious stripes, and will do so again when occasion calls for my services, but as to fight my own countrymen and relatives under it I never can. I am no secessionist, do not admit to the right of secession, but at the same time I admit the right of revolution."[71] Franklin BUCHANAN, on August 31, 1861, appeared before a Justice of the Peace in Easton and conveyed all his real estate and personal property to his wife and children, thereby escaping the confiscation of property by the Federal Government that plagued many Free Staters who went into Confederate service.

Many sailors on foreign seas had to delay their resignations until they returned to U.S. ports. Daniel Smith GREEN, a surgeon in the Pacific squadron - hearing about the invasion of Maryland and the loss of life on Pratt Street - resigned, jumped ship at Panama, and returned to Baltimore. James I. WADDELL handed his resignation to the commander of the *John Adams* on the high seas on November 20, 1861, after reading a newspaper account of the conflict. Upon landing at the New York Naval Yard in early January, 1862, he proceeded to his home in Annapolis. There he received notice that his name had been stricken from the naval rolls. He endeavored to collect his back pay, but when this failed WADDELL departed for Richmond in late February.

John HIPKINS, a master mate on board the U.S.S. *Vincenes*, wrote, "We were stationed in the Gulf of Mexico. I then tendered my resignation stating that it was impossible for me to fight against my own people and principles, respectfully request to be sent home on the first passing vessel, in about an hour after I had sent in my resignation I was ordered to consider myself under arrest, and confined to my quarters, spoken to by none and scorned by all. On the fourth or fifth day of my confinement the transport, *Rhode Island* came to anchor near us, and I was sent aboard and stowed away below, a hammock was assigned to me. After a voyage of days we arrived in New York Harbor. I was then moved and taken to Fort Lafayette where I remained twenty months."[72]

Dulany A. FORREST returned to America from sea duty, resigned on December 1, 1861, and was immediately imprisoned at Fort Warren until January 28, 1862. He was then traded for a Federal naval prisoner, not yet having entered into Confederate service.

Over a dozen Marylanders saw service aboard the ships, *Florida*, *Patrick Henry, Richmond* and *United States*. Charles L. HOWELL entered the service on November 3, 1861 at the age of thirteen and served as second class boy on the gunboat *Simpson*.[73] After serving aboard three other ships he received the rating of landsman. The Confederate Navy was small and much less accessible for Marylanders to join than one of the many army units who sought their enlistment. To join the Navy one had to go through the Richmond Naval Bureau. James R. HERBERT, who was an accomplished seaman, was anxious for combat and was lured into the infantry.

The commissioned and warrant officers employed by the Naval Department in the Provisional Navy were nominated as in line for promotion or not in line for promotion. Those who could be advanced in rank had little opportunity because of the scarcity of ships. Senior officers were fortunate if they were raised one grade during the entire four years of the War. Among those who were not in line for promotion were Lieutenants John G. BLACKWOOD and Thomas W. BENTHALL.

Former naval captains of private enterprise entered the Southern Navy with the rank of master. Richard Fleming FOLEY and Richard Bayley WINDER were masters in line for promotion. William D. PORTER, A. ROBINSON and John WILLIAMS were not. They had come into Confederate naval service with their ships after the Federal Government began confiscating ships to be used in federal service, particularly those of owners unfaithful to the Union cause. John WILLIAMS was the owner and master of the schooner *Mary Virginia* that had shipped out of the port of Baltimore. Captain Jack, as he was called, offered the services of the *Mary Virginia*, with a crew of twenty-four, and was ordered to Mobile Bay. There she was used as a tender to the ironclad *Tennessee*, for which Captain Jack received three hundred and twenty dollars a day.

Richard THOMAS, who had attended the U.S. Military Academy, planned and executed one of the first actions on the Chesapeake Bay. Returning from Baltimore where he had purchased arms, he had on the dress of a French lady over his Zouave uniform. With a few of his Zarvona's Maryland Zouaves, he seized the side-wheeled steamboat, *St. Nicholas*. He turned it over to

George Nicholas HOLLINS, Sr., who had returned to Maryland also to purchase arms and get his two sons. They captured three other vessels and went to Fredericksburg. The raiding party was honored and Richard THOMAS - "Zarvona," as he was known - was commissioned a colonel in the Virginia state forces.

On May 6, 1861, when the new congress of the Southern Confederacy by special session sought the commissioning of private vessels by letters of marque, Marylanders answered the call. The two most famous Baltimore-built privateers were the brig, *Jefferson Davis*, and a two-hundred and thirty ton fully-rigged ship carrying four waist guns, two eighteen pounders, two twelve pounders and one long eighteen pounder, and the *York*, a large pilot boat with one large rifled cannon. In June of 1861, there were two privateers fitted out in Baltimore. "One was the *Lorton*, a schooner of ninety five tons managed by a crew of twenty-five. The other was a brig of a hundred and seventy-nine ton burden called the *Sealine* and carried a ship's company of thirty-five men. Both vessels were armed with one pivot gun, and were owned by W. T. Kendall, a Baltimorean."[74] Thomas Smith, owner of the *Chesapeake*, was a Baltimorean who had suffered loss at the hands of the United States officials and wishing to send out his armed schooner to effect reprisals, requested letters of marque for his ship. This vessel was reported to be a fast sailer; it was mounted with four guns and carried fifty men.

Due to the early containment of Maryland waters by Federal authorities and the early blockade of all Southern ports, the lives of these privateer vessels were brief. Acting master John W. HEBB of the Navy was on the Eastern shore of Maryland securing arms and equipment for a privateer when he was captured on November 8, 1863.

Thomas Francis HOGG, a citizen of Maryland, was on the Mexican frontier in 1863. He had a plan to capture one or more of the merchant vessels of the United States and he obtained from General Hampton P. Bee, commanding the Confederate troops in Brownsville, Texas, a paper sanctioning the undertaking. HOGG and a party of six captured the schooner *Joseph L. Gerrity* on November 16, 1863 which was laden with one hundred and twenty-two bales of cotton bound for New York, and ran her to Cedar Keys, Florida.[75]

Several Marylanders took leading roles in ship construction. George Nicholas HOLLINS fitted out many ships of the line during the war along with numerous tugs and fireboats. Captain Frederick CHATARD and master Robert H. MAURY, Jr., in late 1862, were on special duty constructing and converting gunboats. French FORREST held the position of Chief of the Bureau of Ordnance and Detail while Commandant of the Norfolk Naval Yard.

Marylanders also shared in harbor defenses. Charles Henry McBLAIR established the defenses of Fernandina, Florida, in 1861, while a colonel and later received his previous grade of a commander in the Confederate Navy. Henry Ashton RAMSAY was in command of naval defense construction in Charlotte, North Carolina and was appointed lieutenant colonel in the Provisional Army to continue defense of the city from raids.

Highly significant is the amount of destruction effected by three Maryland navy men of the Confederacy. Admiral SEMMES destroyed more vessels than any other in naval history. Second in the amount of naval commerce destroyed and captured during the Civil War was Marylander John Taylor WOOD who captured over forty prizes. Third in this latter category was James Iredell WADDELL who destroyed thirty-four ships and ransomed four.

The Confederate States Naval Academy was established on March 23, 1863 under Commandant William Harwar PARKER of the Old Line State. The steamship *Patrick Henry* of the James River Squadron was chosen as the school ship for the 106 acting midshipmen. The Patrick Henry was usually stationed near Drewry's Bluff, the scene of desperate fighting. Confederate cadets were frequently called from their studies into combat.[76]

Chapter 14

MARINES

"The U.S. Marine Corps was handicapped during the War by the loss of so many of its better officers to the Confederacy. The few active ones remaining were not sufficiently numerous to cope with the dual problem of training new replacement officers properly and with providing an expanded corps."[77] Four Maryland officers relinquished their commissions and joined the newly established Confederate Marine Corps. This left only two Maryland Marine Officers to continue in Federal service. One of the four who resigned was Richard Taylor ALLISON, who, on April 20, 1861, "tendered his resignation to Secretary Wells, being moved to that action by the occurrences of the previous day in Baltimore, and wrote to General George H. Stewart (Sr.), commanding the Maryland troops in Baltimore offering his services. At the same time he informed President Davis what he had done. Owing to the interruption of railroad traffic north of Baltimore, no officer could be immediately obtained to relieve him at the Washington Naval yard; and, in compliance with the request of Secretary Wells, he remained on duty as paymaster until May 1."[78]

The corps was organized under Lloyd James BEALL as commandant with the rank of colonel. The organization also called for a lieutenant colonel and four majors. Two Marylanders were appointed as majors: Richard T. ALLISON and Algernon S. TAYLOR. Each of these three Marylanders held his staff appointment from 1861 until the war's end, elevated as far as they could go in a corps that was never enlarged.

Besides the headquarters in Richmond there were three other Marine stations: Drewry's Bluff, Savannah and Mobile. On April 3, 1862, Julius Ernest MEIERE was ordered to Mobile to command its marine station. He was a marine lieutenant and had married Franklin BUCHANAN's daughter, Nannie, on April 3, 1861. President Lincoln had attended the ceremony and had cut the wedding cake. "BUCHANAN's daughter, Elizabeth Taylor, then fifteen years old, refused to shake hands with Mr. Lincoln, at first who called her a little rebel and finally won her over with bonbons and the charm of his personality."[79]

An attorney, Thomas St. George PRATT, son of former governor Thomas George Pratt, served as a private in the 2nd Maryland Infantry, and James Campbell MURDOCH, a private in Company K, 1st Virginia Cavalry. Both were confirmed by the Senate as second lieutenants in late 1863.

Efforts were made to include one drummer and one fifer in every marine guard. Demand for musicians was so great that Lawrence CLEMENTS was detailed twice because of the need for a bugler.

Even at the end of the War, when there were few ships, the Marines were still active. James THURSTON, with his Marine detail, accompanied C.W.

Read's unsuccessful torpedo boat expedition behind Federal lines in February 1865. James Campbell MURDOCH led marines in the capture of the schooners *St. Mary's* and *J. B. Spafford* on March 31, 1865 in the last Confederate privateering exploit on the Chesapeake Bay.

Chapter 15

PHYSICIANS

Maryland contributed far more medical men to the Confederacy in proportion to its enlisted men than any other Confederate state. Maryland gave two hundred and ten licensed physicians to the Southern cause. These were supplied mainly by the three large medical schools of the state: The University of Maryland Medical College and Washington Medical College, both of Baltimore, and the Georgetown University Medical College. (An exception was Easternshoreman Jerome Humphrey HARDCASTLE who graduated in early 1865 from the only college in Richmond that was able to withstand the impact of war.) Allegany County, a Union stronghold, gave three doctors to the cause, while Washington contibuted eight and Frederick an unbelievable eighteen.[80]

Attitudes of the doctors serving in the military regarding the North-South conflict were similar to those of their officer colleagues. Eight career military physicians resigned from the U.S. Army to go to the aid of the South and eight Naval doctors resigned to enter the Confederate Medical Corps. Five who had seen previous service, reentered military life, this time against their former government. Twelve served previously in the Maryland Militia, one of whom, Dr. Charles MACGILL had been a major general. Dr. Lucius Bellinger NORTHROP of Maryland, who graduated from West Point in the class of 1829 with Jefferson Davis, became a brigadier general as commissary general of South Carolina. Dr. Cary Breckinridge GAMBLE became surgeon general of Florida, Dr. Edward WARREN, surgeon general of South Carolina and Dr. Charles Bell GIBSON, surgeon general of Virginia.

Of those absorbed into the medical services of the Confederacy, sixty-five Marylanders attained the position of army surgeon. Of the eighteen Naval physicians, two were surgeons, four passed assistant surgeons, eleven assistant surgeons and one acting assistant surgeon.[81]

The great majority of physicians entered the Confederate forces as privates in the enlisted ranks. Two of the four licensed doctors in the 1st Maryland Artillery were killed while fighting as cannoneers. Fifteen Maryland doctors continued to wear everything from the butternut of the enlisted man to the wreath of a brigadier general. Seven medical practitioners from WESTON's Infantry Battalion received commissions to the medical corps from the enlisted ranks.

There were numerous complaints about the incompetency, drunkenness and knife-happy butchery of the Surgical Corps. The surgeon general was requested to have the medical board reexamine all doctors. On May 19, 1862, Dr. J.W.F. BEST was appointed surgeon of his regiment. Later he became senior medical officer of the 40th Georgia. On May 30, 1864, Surgeon BEST was dismissed and dropped from the rolls for failure to pass the board."[82]

Many of these doctors had brothers and sons who had made the great sacrifice to the Southland and some were father and son medical teams. Dr.

Daniel Smith GREEN and his son Dr. William GREEN were both surgeons in the Army. Dr. Charles MACGILL and his son Dr. Charles G.W. MACGILL established a hospital at their home to give aid to Confederate soldiers when Lee's Army crossed into the black and gold state during the Gettysburg campaign. After the battle, they continued with their infirmary and upon the evacuation of Hagerstown on July 12, 1863, both received commissions in the medical department and went south with Lee's army.

The strain of division was felt in all occupations in Maryland, "Every member of the Jarrett family, parents, five sons and one daughter were advocates of the Confederacy except James. When he announced that he was in favor of the Union and intended to enter the U.S. Army his course was bitterly opposed by the family and caused a sensation in the community, but he joined the Purnell Legion as assistant surgeon. Young Martin L. JARRETT departed from Harford County upon hearing that the Army of Northern Virginia was near the Potomac in 1863 and became acting assistant surgeon of the 1st Maryland Cavalry."[83]

Doctors Caleb Dorsey BAER and James J. BAER were sons of Dr. Jacob Baer. The trio practiced together in Middletown Valley between the Catoctin and Blue Ridge Mountains. The father deplored the unconstitutional conduct of the Federal Government and beseeched the immediate recognition of the new Confederacy, yet he could not forsake his nation and on July 28, 1861 became the examining doctor of his Congressional district. He was soon appointed as surgeon of the 1st Regiment, Potomac Home Brigade Infantry. In the meantime, Caleb reversed his allegiance and tendered his abilities to the C.S.A. He became senior surgeon of the 4th Brigade of Forrest's Division and died of illness on August 30, 1863. Surgeon BAER was one of seven physicians in the medical corps who gave their lives on the altar of the Confederacy.

Many attained prominence from the conflict. Surgeon Aaron Snowden PIGGOTT built and supervised the pharmaceutical laboratories near Lincolnton, North Carolina. Surgeon Julian J. CHISOLM, as an inventor and author of the official text for the Confederate Medical Corps, guided medical and surgical studies.

Up to this time nurses were male only. Maryland women were not allowed by the Federal authorities to treat or even give comfort to Confederate soldiers. After the large battles the need for nurses was so great that Southern women were given the opportunity. Miss Elizabeth H. Murray, along with several other ladies from West River, drove to Gettysburg to attend the wounded Southerners. There she found that her brother, Captain William H. MURRAY, had been killed. She and those like her were the forerunners of female nurses who brought forth a major improvement in standards of cleanliness in paramedical treatment.

It became apparent during the war that soldiers stood greatly in need of dental work. A plan to contract with dentists engaged in private practice was discussed, but instead, Confederate medical authorities adopted the nation's first dental corps in the summer of 1864. The Medical Bureau recognized that Dr. James Baxter BEAN had a phenomenal rate of recoveries in maxilo-facial surgery. Medical Doctor Alexander Mills CAMPBELL, who was also a graduate of the University of Maryland College of Dental Surgery, devoted himself to specializing in facial wounds suffered from behind breast works. Private James Howard HARRIS, who was an M.D. and a D.D.S., was in Company I, 4th Virginia Cavalry and on November 3, 1864 was assigned to the

Dental Corps at Harrisonburg General Hospital. There were five other enlisted men with the degree D.D.S. who were commissioned into the Corps. They held the rank of a hospital steward which was comparable to second lieutenant.

Casualty rates were high, and Marylanders who became unfit for duty had peculiar problems. Their homes were within enemy lines, and they could not go to their familes to be nursed back to health. After their convalescence and discharge, a few sought work in public or private enterprises, but most found government or military work as noncombatants in voluntary service to the Confederacy, many as hospital stewards or clerks.

Dr. Edwin Samuel GAILLARD was assistant surgeon of the 1st Maryland Infantry, but because there was an overabundance of medical personnel he resigned on June 24, 1861 and accepted another position. At Fair Oakes, shortly after attending the wound of General Wade Hampton, he was wounded by a piece of shell and his right arm had to be amputated. By April 29, 1863, he was Surgical and Medical Inspector of Richmond.

Dr. J. Penbroke THOM was wounded at Kernstown on March 23, 1862, in the right hand, right leg and over the heart by a ball that penetrated through a Testiment in his pocket. Upon being sufficiently recovered, he was detailed to Richmond, forwarding troops and supplies down the James River.

Chapter 16

CLERGYMEN

The storm clouds which covered the land in 1860 also darkened the churches. Some were able to weather the conflicting attitudes, while other flocks were split. The Lutheran, Unitarian and Jewish clergymen appear to have remained loyal while many pastors of the Methodist, Episcopal and Presbyterian denominations leaned toward a Southern conviction. There were twenty-four ordained clergymen of the Maryland deaconcy who sought service in the Confederate Army.

Methodism was the predominant Christian denomination of Maryland. In 1818, the Methodist Episcopal Church had a group withdraw, calling themselves the Methodist Protestant Church. In 1843 a group opposing slavery founded the Wesleyan Methodist Church while the following year another group split over the same slavery issue becoming the Methodist Episcopal Church South. The Maryland Methodist churches, with the exception of a relatively small number of Wesleyans, held to the view that slaveholding, if necessary and merciful, was not a sin in itself. Many new Methodist assemblies were established and new churches sprang up as worshipers endeavored to commune with those of more amicable sentiments. It should not be surprising that, over a hundred years later the state is saturated with Methodist churches.

In the Roman Catholic churches, priests, like their protestant counterparts, were not able to express themselves in conformity with their beliefs. They were threatened with arrest if they spoke against the glorification of the Union or supported the alleged crimes of the Southern states. The Catholic Church as a whole was quietly supportive of the South. When St. John's Church in Frederick was remodeled a few years ago, the wall housing the organ pipes was completely covered with names, rank and regiments of many Confederates who apparently sought refuge there. The archives for the

Visitation Convent in Georgetown where there were eighty-three nuns during this period are blank, except for a single entry of a sister who wrote, "There was a great deal of tension in the community of the Convent because sisters from both sides were living together. The strains that these women endured in such constricted circumstances was severe. Roughly half of the sisters were born in Ireland and may not have taken sides. The remaining residents were equally divided between the North and the South. All agreed that whenever a foot-weary soldier came to the door for refreshment or water, he should be cared for. So according to convent lore they worked out this solution: Nuns of Southern sympathy would feed Johnny Rebs, and Northern nuns would take care of Billy Yanks. Whenever all were together, it was understood they would never discuss the War."[84]

With the heavy concentration of Federal troops in and around Baltimore churches and congregations with Southern sympathies suffered unduly. Reverend John H. DASHIELL of the Angelic Parish was arrested and endured days of imprisonment when it was reported that he had removed the national flag from his church. Dr. Bullock, a Presbyterian minister, was taken into custody for harboring a Southern officer in his home. Late in the War many churches that no longer displayed the national flag were closed by military order. As late as April 19, 1865, four Methodist churches in Baltimore were closed by military authorities because of their sympathetic feeling toward the suffering of the South.

Rev. Dr. John BOCOCK, paster of the Bridge Street Presbyterian Church of Georgetown since 1856, left with his family on May 4, 1861, for the South where he became chaplain of the 7th Virginia Infantry.

Rev. William NORWOOD, minister of Christ Episcopal Church since 1854, received from the Episcopal Bishop of Maryland in April of 1861 a letter instructing the clergy not to omit from the services the usual prayer for the President of the United States. Rev. NORWOOD refused to obey the circulated letter and the standing committee of the deaconcy placed him under restraint, causing him to leave town for the South. They had no permanent clergyman until March 19, 1862 when Rev. William Harris of Washington came to the church for services. The Washington Evening Star, dated March 20, 1862, reported, "when he commenced to read the Bishop's prayer many of the irrate, weakminded brethren arose to leave. There was a terrible rush of turned-up pretty noses who crushed through the pews and aisles to reach the outer doors. The clergyman, we understand, announced in an apologetic way that a sense of duty obligated him to comply with the directions of his Bishop."[85]

Rev. William Francis BRAND, a native of Anne Arundel County, went to Emmorton, Harford County, in 1850, and built St. Mary's Episcopal Church. As a consequence of the War, Rev. BRAND moved to the South. During the War he was placed in charge of the education of two of Jefferson Davis's sons. After his return to Maryland, at the end of the struggle, he was visited by the Confederate President. Another Episcopal minister, Rev. John C. TENNENT, wrote on October 26, 1861, "I am a refugee from my known sympathies and activities, cooperating with the holy cause of the South."[86]

In 1850 Rev. Thomas Nelson CONRAD was preaching at Dunbarton Methodist Episcopal in Georgetown and operating a private boys' school, The Georgetown Institute, next to the church. "Certainly nobody knew that he was actually a Rebel spy feeding information to the Confederates through a doctor's line from the Navy Yard past Federal gunboats which patrolled the Potomac River to a Rebel camp near Aquia Creek on the Virginia Shore. Evidently, he was given access to the church for commencement exercises and at these times he encouraged his students to stage secession demonstrations. Bands played Dixie, the audience cheered wildly for the South and the boys sported palmetto badges."[87] CONRAD was arrested on August 4, 1862, and placed in chains and held in the Old Capitol Prison. His claims of being a man of God and an educator soon brought his release. He then crossed the lines and became chaplain of the 3rd Virginia Cavalry. Several times Rev. CONRAD scouted the Washington area for General J.E.B. Stuart. Using Madam Surratt's house near Port Tobacco as his rendezvous and wearing various disguises, he smuggled out information in the hollow heel of his English-made shoes. After the Battle of South Mountain, the Dunbarton Church was confiscated for a Union hospital; the pews were removed, the basement arranged for horses and the church was not returned to the congregation until January, 1863.

Many ministers enlisted as regular soldiers in the field. Rev. John Thomas MAXWELL of Park Mills in Frederick County was the shepherd of Flint Hill Methodist Episcopal Church North, but left his congregation to become a trooper in Company B, 35th Virginia Cavalry. Rev. John Poisal HYDE fell back on his military training at St. John's as did Rev. Horace Edwin HAYDEN, a graduate of St. Timothy's Hall. Many ministers such as the Rev. James D. THOMAS, joined the rank and file to fight, and later became chaplains. Some were chaplains and fighting soldiers. In August, 1861, near Fairfax, the 1st Maryland Infantry Chaplain was also a warrior; "Chaplain (Stephen J. CAMERON) who had accompanied us took a gun and fired once and was assured that he had killed his man through or around a haystack and not doubting it, was filled with mixed feelings of triumph and remorse. It was not the last of his uncanonical acts."[88]

Clergymen gave emphasis to the care and needs of the wounded. Rev. Matthew O'KEEFE served the hospitals of Richmond, and later transferred to Mahon's Brigade on April 16, 1862.[89]

Rev. Alfred Magill RANDOLPH of the Baptist fold preached to barefoot, devoted worshippers who stood in snow several inches deep. They did not allow failing weather to interrupt their religious activities. After a long march, many bivouacs were started by someone striking up a dear old hymn which recalled hallowed memories of home and loved ones and of a far away congregation that was praying for them.

Surprisingly, there were a number of Marylanders serving in the Army of the West. Abram Joseph RYAN, better known as Father RYAN, was a native son who is best remembered as "the poet of the lost cause." He was ordained into the priesthood of the Roman Catholic Church and became chaplain of the 8th Tennessee Infantry. Rev. Wilbur Fisk MISTER, after being a private for three months, was appointed chaplain of the 15th Infantry and William C. MALOY, after eighteen months became chaplain of the 44th Mississippi. Rev. John SCHWARAR was appointed on September 26, 1863 in the 4th Tennessee Infantry and was confirmed by the War Department on October 13.[90]

A chaplain usually held the rank and pay of captain. Rev. Dabney BALL, pastor of the Columbia Street Episcopal Church in Baltimore, departed from his church to go to the South. It was reported in the Baltimore paper that a week later he was seen in Richmond in a lieutenant's uniform wearing a brace of pistols. He requested the rank of major but resigned in July of

1863 noting, "My reason for resigning is that my salary is utterly inadequate to support myself and my dependent family."[91]

During the winter of 1863-64, the Maryland Line, about fifteen hundred strong, was quartered near Hanover Junction at Camp Howard. Recognizing the spiritual needs of these men, Mrs. Claudia Johnson, wife of General Johnson, proposed the construction of a church. A major stucture was completed, capable of accommodating 500 worshipers, a choir and a library.[92]

There were veterans who felt justified in leaving the ranks to follow their convictions to become ministers of the gospel. In 1863-64 in the temporary Theological Seminary of Virginia in Staunton, there were four soldiers who were candidates for orders in the Protestant Episcopal Church three of which were Marylanders. Randolph Harrison McKIM resigned his commission and was accepted into the Staunton Seminary on September 1, 1863. He had been preparing for his Christian calling for the previous five years. On May 11, 1864, after eight months, he passed his examination for the deaconcy order and became chaplain of Chew's Artillery, then of the 2nd Virginia Cavalry. William F. GARDNER, who had enlisted in Company H, 17th Virginia Infantry as a private, had had some seminary training in preparation for ordination before leaving his home in Howard County. After being licensed as a clergyman, he turned to the pressing need in the Army for chaplains and became spiritual leader in Pickett's Division. Horace Edwin HAYDEN had enlisted as a private on May 14, 1861, in Company K, 1st Virginia Cavalry. Not fully recovered from an illness, he was detailed to the General Hospital of Charlottesville as a steward and wardmaster. By the spring of 1864, he was studying to be a theologian and was soon to be carrying out his chaplaincy duties in hospitals among the suffering, sick and wounded. Rev. George H. ZIMMERMAN of BREATHED's Battery Stuart's Horse Artillery, after being confirmed in the Methodist Episcopal Church on March 18, 1864, became chaplain of the 12th Virginia Cavalry.

Charles Frederick LINTHICUM, who was reared in the shadow of Sugar Loaf Mountain, entered the Confederate service in the 8th Virginia Infantry. He was later detailed by Colonel Hunton as chaplain of the Regiment, "and being commissioned as such in this capacity he followed its fortune but always with a musket in the front ranks. Captain LINTHICUM was President of the Brigade Christian Association. He raised considerable sums of money from his Maryland friends for relief of widows and orphans of his fellow comrades."[93] He was killed at Second Cold Harbor June 3, 1864.

Many veterans entered the ministry after the War. George William PETERKIN who was studying theology from his father in the Episcopal Church, went into the Army first as an enlisted man in the 21st Virginia Infantry, and then as an officer on General W.N. Pendleton's staff. After the War he resumed his studies and became a bishop.[94]

Chapter 17

LEGISLATORS AND CONGRESSMEN

There were prominent men who were native sons of Maryland but did not participate in the state's history. Thomas Jenkins Semmes became attorney general of Louisiana in 1859. He helped frame the Ordinances of Secession in Louisiana and was a member of the Confederate Senate. William Smith practiced law in Baltimore, and after returning to Virginia became governor from 1846-49. He was also a member of the Confederate Congress at the outbreak of the War. William Sydney WILSON had been a practicing attorney in Fort Gibson, Mississippi, and served in the Mississippi legislature and the Confederate Congress for a short period before going into the field as a lieutenant colonel. He was mortally wounded in his native Maryland, at Antietam. Dr. Alfred Hughes, a correspondent of the Baltimore Exchange left Baltimore after his imprisonment by Union forces and was elected to the Virginia legislature. Dr. William H. Cole went to Kansas to take part in the fierce struggle of 1857 and was chosen a member of the territorial legislature. Franklin P. TURNER of Charles County, who moved to Sharpsburg, was admitted to the bar. In 1855 he moved to Ripley, Virginia where he spent four terms in the legislature. "He was a member of the Secession Convention of Virginia. Returning from the convention, he organized two companies of militia. He rose to the rank of major and at Antietam, fought on the ground where he had resided and where he would later be interred in the family plot."[95]

Military rule bred further secession sympathies, so when the legislature was finally called together many thought that the state should be declared out of the Union. Lincoln ordered Secretary of War Cameron to tell General Scott to see that this did not occur. "The passage of an act of secession by the legislature of Maryland must be prevented if necessary, all or part of its members must be arrested."[96] On September 17, 1861, thirty-two members of the Maryland House and Senate were arrested. The oath of allegiance was offered to all, and the few who took it were released, while twenty-nine legislators were taken to prison. Others, such as Senator Colleman Yellott, departed for the South. Delegate John C. Brune left for Canada and eventually made his way to the South. John B. BROOKE, who had been president of the Senate, after learning of the arrest, fled and lost all of his holdings in the state; he became a colonel serving as provost marshal of Winchester. Delegate George FREAMER entered the Southern army in the autumn of 1861 as adjutant of the 1st Virginia Cavalry. He became a member of the staffs of Generals Wade Hampton, J.E.B. Stuart and Fitzhugh Lee and attained the rank of a major. Dr. James Thomas JOHNSON, Jr. a former member of the house and a delegate from Frederick County to the State Convention, was one of three brothers who wore gray. E. Pliny BRYAN was one of the early secessionists and a member of the legislature. He was a volunteer private in the 1st Virginia and offered his service to Alexander's Signal Corps. "With the approval of General Beauregard (Bryan), was trained in the signal system and sent into Washington to live, equipped to transmit back whatever information he obtained. Another of Alexander's volunteers, Charles H. Cawood, showed a talent for getting back and forth across the Potomac in the beginning of the secret line."[97]

1864 the legislature had passed bills which laid down detailed qualifications for voting. Adopted was a set of questions to be asked of voters: "Have you served in the Rebel Army? Have you aided the Rebellion? Have you given any aid to those intending to join the Rebel cause? Have you sent money to those in the Rebel areas? Have you given comfort and encouragement? Have you wished for the success of the Rebellion? Have you disengaged the Federal cause? Are you a loyal citizen of the United States? Did you rejoice over the downfall of Fort Sumter? Did you rejoice over the success of the Rebels and in the defeat of the Union Army? When the Rebel army (meets) the Union army in battle who do you wish would gain victory?" Only 35,000 out of 95,000 in the state were allowed to vote. Two-thirds of the voters were disenfranchised while troops from the Union states who were policing Maryland were permitted to vote in its elections.[98]

Benjamin Gwinn Harris, who had served two terms in the State legislature, was elected from the 5th District to the 38th Congress of the U.S. He spoke out fearlessly and boldly against waging an unconstitutional war on the seceded states. On April 26, 1865, Congressman Harris was arrested by the military at his farm, accused of treason and imprisoned in Old Capitol Prison without specific charges. At a court martial held in May he was charged with violation of the 56th Article of war, found guilty and sentenced to three years in prison.

Chapter 18

MARYLANDERS AT HOME

When Southern troops arrived in Maryland, doors were opened to them and the troops were fed and clothed. The Southern sympathizers had been at the cruel hands of the Federalists and now the tide was turned. The Confederate troops were told where to take horses from loyalists. In the process of stealing these horses, some barns were burned. When the Southern troops retreated and the state was retaken by the Union forces, Confederate sympathizers were made to pay for the reconstruction of the Unionists' barns in Anne Arundel, Frederick, and Harford counties.

John Henry Cramer lived between Libertytown and Woodsboro and had acted as a guide for the Confederate Army during the Antietam Campaign, the return of J.E.B. Stuart from Chambersburg and the Gettysburg campaign. Three times he had been drafted by the Union administration compelling him to hire a substitute. Cramer's two young sons were named Bradley Johnson Cramer and Robert E. Lee Cramer.

There were many Confederate agents who were never suspected or discovered operating in Maryland and the national capital. These agents organized a network of linked safe houses which stretched throughout the state to provide food, shelter and transportation to compatriots. These secret lines were begun early in the war and many remained undetected throughout the war.

Recruiting for the Southern Army was done by some who remained at home to help the young men find the secret routes into the Confederacy. Thomas C. Fitzpatrick and R.H. Rogers were among these recruiters. Christian Emmerich had two sons, George W. and John W., who were in the army. He was arrested several times for recruiting and finally imprisoned from June, 1864, until the close of the War. Colonel John H. Waring, who had been in the state militia, also had two sons, Robert Bowie WARING and William Worthington WARING, serving in the Southern Army. For acting as a recruiter, Colonel Waring was arrested and imprisoned. His wife and two daughters were sent through the lines, and then their property was confiscated. Only the land was returned to them in December, 1865.[99]

The Southern Relief Organization, which gave only monetary relief, was tolerated by the Federal Government. Israel M. Parr, a wholesale grocer in Baltimore, was president of another organization, the Maryland Prisoner's Aid Society, which gave relief to those who were captured. There were other organizations that were constantly being penetrated by Federal spies. The largest Southern secret organization was the Knights of Liberty.

Through trustworthy sympathizers and stations on both sides of the river, large quantities of mail were sent to and from the boys in the Southern army. Thomas M. Webb was known as the Confederate postmaster of Maryland. "Before the war when General Lee, as colonel of engineers in the old army, was engaged in building Fort Carroll in Baltimore Harbor he lived on 908 Madison Avenue. Webb had a cigar store at Madison and Gardner Streets, and General Lee often went into his store for a chat. The friendship lasted until Lee's death. Webb said that he sent General Lee all the hats the General wore from the outbreak of the war until his death."[100]

Two of the frequent routes used for letters and parcels was by crossing at Potomac ferry in St. Mary's and the roundabout way via Frederick, Hagerstown, and Charlestown. Two uniforms were sent to General Lee during the War, one made by the ladies of Baltimore via the St. Mary's County route and one by the women of Carroll and Frederick Counties via the Charlestown route. Gifts such as horses and weapons were presented to the Southern leaders when they were within the state. The ladies of Baltimore sent General J.E.B. Steuart a pair of gold spurs and received private letters from him signed "Knight of the Golden Spurs." Richard O. Mullikins was selected by the gentlemen of Prince George's County to order from G.W. Webb and Company a pair of gold spurs which were sent to General Lee by one of the Patuxent Bay routes. The immaculate presentation sword, worn by General Lee and bearing inscription of "1863 from a Marylander," also secretly passed through one of these routes. After the Battle of Manassas,P.M. Sowden, at his own expense, sent his friend, Captain Francis THOMAS, over fifty overcoats for his men, who were Marylanders. John A. Barry transferred rifles and arms from the secret hiding place in his house to the Southern army.

William NORRIS became the head of the Confederate secret service bureau while General John H. WINDER became the head of the department at Richmond. Both of these men had a number of Marylanders on their staff. They had many connections in the state and apparently recruited agents for all types of intelligence work without much difficulty. Thomas A. Jones of Pope's Creek near La Plata became one of NORRIS' chief agents. His plantation overlooked the Potomac on a high knoll and he could see several miles in both directions. "Mr. Jones served as chief signal officer for the duration of the war, and he boasts that in all that time not one letter or paper was lost."[101] Passes to cross the lines were obtained from General John Henry WINDER. His detectives were notorious for accepting a dollar and fifty cents per letter for guaranteeing their passage into the state. Around him in the detective bureau were a large group of Marylanders who freely passed back and forth across the Potomac.

Thomas I. Chew of Upper Bennet in Calvert County purchased arms and assisted soldiers who returned to Maryland to get supplies, such as Joseph L. McALEER who purchased a vessel in Baltimore in the winter of 1862 for returning to the South. Other soldiers followed the same routes into Maryland to make dare-devil raids. Some Marylanders participating in these raids were Walter BOWIE, John H. BOYLE, Jr., and L. H. SCHOOLFIELD. The latter was a member of the Confederate Naval Secret Service (discharged October, 1864).

Joseph F. TORRENT ran aground with the ship *Elizabeth*. "We had on board twenty thousand dollars in gold for the government of which the crew was ignorant so we lowered our boats and took the crew with some provisions ashore and the captain directed them to make their way to land to Wilmington. The captain and I then returned to our ship, secured the gold and put it with our wearing apparel and the small quantity of provisions in a boat, set the Elizabeth on fire in several places and left by the light."[102]

Levi S. WHITE also burned one of his own boats when captured in a cove on the Potomac during the night after unloading his provisions. He was commissioned an acting master in the Navy as purchasing agent for the Confederacy in Baltimore. His travels took him from Richmond to Nova Scotia to secure ordnance stores. He obtained everything from caps and potassium to buttons. An engraver in Baltimore produced Virginia military buttons which White delivered to Mitchell and Tyler of Richmond. He also purchased military buttons from New York with insignia of Southern states. Contraband goods could be purchased in New York almost as readily from a Union man as from a sympathizer; no questions were asked if you had the cash. One of White's secrets in avoiding the strict line between Maryland and Virginia was to use small sloops or large schooners. With the stores on the water, there could be no trail for detectives to follow. When one point became dangerous, they moved to another one of the many inlets on the river. "I had purchased a good schooner and placed her under command of Captain Bennett, a nervy old Chesapeake pilot. On this schooner Mr. John Forester had constructed for me a roomy false bulkhead entered from the cabin. Bennett would get a cargo of coal from Havre de Grace to Washington and on his way would stop at Middle River and receive me and the goods on board. The goods would be securely placed inside the false bulkhead and then we would sail for Washington. Whenever we were boarded or there was a danger of being boarded, I would slip inside the bulkhead and sit there until the danger passed. It would imperil the expedition for me to be seen. Whenever we arrived at the guard boat on the Potomac we were of course boarded. I always had some prime whiskey on board, and when the boarding officer came, Bennett would meet him courteously, take him into the cabin and ask him to take something which of course he did. From my concealment, I could hear the boarding officer praising the quality of the whiskey. It was really a good quality on board for that very reason our papers being declared alright, the boarding officer would take another and then depart for the guard ship."[103] WHITE also had a false bulkhead constructed in a back room of his Baltimore home where he eluded searching detectives.

A.S. Goodwin was master of the schooner *Nanjemey* from Queen Anne's County. John N. Hall from Baltimore had three vessels sunk during the war. William H. Hayden was master of a blockade runner. The schooner *William H. Travers* was owned by R.P. Blackistone of St. Mary's County and was sailed by

Captain Rice. The schooner *Trifle* was owned by E.R. Quine, T.R. Quine and George N. Nellis, and was commanded by Captain Steward.

Two Tucker brothers of Kent Island commanded the schooner *Hard Times*. She was seized in January, 1863, by Federal authorities for conveying men and supplies to the South. The *Hard Times* was placed under guard at Clash's Wharf at Centreville to be used by the Federal Government. "The watchman having gone down to take a drink, a band of Southern sympathizers, disguised, got on board and having fastened the guard down in the hole, set fire to the vessel. It was generally known that it was to be done and one hundred persons assembled on the Corsica side to see it. The guard was terribly frightened but released in time."[104]

James Edward Moss and Robert Levingston Moss of the blockade running sloop Mederia stated that the abundant number of Federal detectives seemed more anxious to capture farm produce, tea, salt, and whiskey, which when confiscated could be sold with the proceeds going into their pockets. On the other hand, captured military stores had to be turned in. For some of the blockade runners, the Chesapeake Bay became too dangerous and William SMITH and William P. ZOLLINGER quit the trade to join the Southern service. Master Jesse Taylor of Worcester County, after running the blockade, was killed in Charleston Harbor by gunfire from Federal boats. The author has obtained a large list of blockade runners from all counties that border Virginia and many from the counties which possess many of the tributaries that empty into the Potomac or Chesapeake.

There were many who simply ferried men and supplies in small craft to the Virginia shore - not serious blockade runners, but merely local residents ready to assist in a noble cause. There were also those few such as Nicholas G. Penniman who was a blockade runner paid from the Confederate treasury, while there were still others who dealt in contraband material. From St. Mary's County smugglers like Robert Clarke and B. Jackson Bell were dealing in material of warfare for their own benefit. Three contraband-laden vessels out of Worcester County were the *Monticello*, *Mary Pierce* and *The Margaret*.

There are wonderful stories of those Maryland women who suffered and who bravely labored for the Confederate cause.

§ Rose O'Neal Greenhow maintained her indisputable social position with the Federal capital administrators.

§ Annie Lamb Kimball was the youngest female arrested as a spy, a child of six years.

§ Miss Matilinda Saunders, a volunteer nurse, operated several war hospitals for Confederate soldiers, ran the blockade several times and was taken prisoner more than once.

§ Mrs. Ridgely Duvall, on a winter's night, in a blinding snowstorm, walked eight miles while pregnant with her first son, to advise Confederates that the Federals were only a few miles from their garrison.

§ Mistress Olivia Floyd of Rose Hill Plantation in Charles County, who had been crippled since birth, took messages from Canada, rolled them up in her hair and with troops surrounding her house, carried the messages to the signal post at Pope's Creek for further transmission to Intelligence Headquarters in Richmond.

Chapter 19

FORMER GOVERNORS

During the War there were seven surviving ex-governors, all attorneys, who had served the state prior to the war. Four actively supported secession of the state, one supported the Union and two took no active part.

Thomas Watkins Ligon, 1854-1858, of Baltimore, was completely inactive, not unexpected in view of his unpopular administration.

Enoch Louis Lowe, 1851-1854, of Frederick County, advocated secession. After the state was under marshal law, he went into voluntary exile in the South until the war was over.

Philip Francis Thomas, 1848-1851, of Easton, occupied a cabinet position under President Buchanan. A strong secessionist, he was forced into seclusion and retirement. His only son, John Roger THOMAS went to the South at the age of eighteen and joined the 1st Maryland Artillery.

Thomas G. Pratt, 1845-1848, of Annapolis, a leader of the Southern movement in Maryland, was arrested and confined in Fort Monroe for several weeks. On November 30, 1863, he and Col. Nicholson, his private secretary, were sent to the South for refusing to take the oath of allegiance. His son, Thomas St. George PRATT, a law graduate, served as a private in Company A, 2nd Maryland Infantry until February 9, 1864, when he became a 2nd lieutenant in the Confederate Marine Corps.

Francis Thomas, 1842-1845, of Frederick County, espoused the Union cause, assisted in raising a Federal regiment and served in Congress.

William Grason, 1839-1842, of Queen Anne's County, was an advocate of secession and was chosen to represent his county in the Baltimore conference to determine Maryland's course. Succumbing to the Federal takeover and his failing health, he retired from public life. His son, John GRASON was a lieutenant in the 4th Maryland Artillery.

Thomas King Carroll, 1830-1831, of Dorchester County, at the age of 73, took no active part.

Ex-governor Enoch Lowe, after going to the South, addressed the Virginia Legislature in December of 1861. Lowe said that he hoped that Maryland would secede, believing that the state would eventually join the Confederacy. "God knows," he declared, "Marylanders love the Sunny South as dearly as any sons of the Palmetto State. They idolize the chivalrous honor, the stern and refined idea of free government, the social dignity and conservatism which characterize the Southern brethren who were born where the snow never falls." He was bitter in his denunciations of Thomas H. Hicks whom he characterized as "a false hearted" governor.[105]

Former governors Pratt and Thomas were refused admission to the U.S. Senate on the grounds of disloyalty during the war.

Chapter 20

ADJUTANT GENERALS

During the War between the States, Maryland had two adjutant generals, Nicholas Brewer of John (1858-1864) and John Summerfield Berry (1864-1869) who, of course, supported the Northern cause. Beyond equipping and reviewing the government troops sent from this state into the Federal army, they had no other functions to perform since the state militia was non-existent. As one looks at the military biographical sketches of those appointed after the rebellion, it is interesting to note that none of these men was a Federalist.

Major General George Henry BIER, a Baltimorean, was the tenth adjutant general. He entered the Naval Academy in October, 1841, as a midshipman, promoted to passed midshipman August 10, 1848, and became a lieutenant on September 15, 1855, resigned April 23, 1861, and commissioned a lieutenant in the Confederate Navy. He was appointed a major and became Chief of Ordnance under General T.J. Jackson. He resigned the position on June 24, 1863 and subsequently he commanded the blockade runner *Dee* until captured on May 10, 1864. BIER was again living in Baltimore when he was appointed as Maryland adjutant general on April 6, 1869. He resigned on February 3, 1871.

Major General Charles Henry McBLAIR of Baltimore was the eleventh adjutant general. He entered the U.S. Navy as a midshipman on March 4, 1823, passed midshipman November 23, 1829, lieutenant July 12,1831, and commander April 18, 1855. He resigned on April 22, 1861 and entered the Confederate Navy as a commander. He transferred temporarily to the army with the rank of captain and soon became colonel as Chief of Artillery Department of Middle and East Florida. By March 1862, he was again a commander and served as commanding officer of the following C.S.S. ships: *Morgan*, *Gaines*, *Tuscaloosa* and the *Huntsville*. He surrendered at Greensboro and was paroled April 28, 1865. Residing in Baltimore County, McBlair was appointed colonel and aide-de-camp to Governor Oden Bowie on April 20, 1869, and state adjutant general on February 9, 1871, for three years.

Major General Frank A. BOND of Harford and Anne Arundel Counties, was the twelfth adjutant general. He raised a militia company, the United Rifles, 1859. Being disarmed, in the spring of 1861 it was disbanded. Going to the South, he was appointed captain and drill-master of the 8th Virginia Infantry by Governor Letcher. He resigned and became a corporal in Company M, 1st Virginia Cavalry. In May 1862, BOND was elected 1st lieutenant in Company A, 1st Maryland Cavalry, amd promoted to captain November 12th. He was wounded and captured at Hagerstown whereupon he was confined at Fort McHenry and Point Lookout. After being exchanged in May, 1864, he accepted a position as adjutant general with the rank of major on the staff of General C. Leventhorpe. He was paroled at Greensboro on May 1, 1865, and returned to Jessup where he organized Company G, 3rd Maryland Militia Cavalry. BOND was elected colonel of the 3rd Battalion Cavalry on November 22, 1867. On May 25, 1869, he was brigadier general of the 2nd Brigade, 3rd Division, and on May 14, 1870, major general 3rd Division, Maryland National Guard. He held the position of adjutant general from April 4, 1874, until 1880.

Major General James HOWARD, a Baltimorean, was the fourteenth adjutant general. He was commissioned 2nd lieutenant in Company B, 3rd U.S. Artillery, on February 27, 1857, and resigned on April 3, 1861. Entering the C.S.A. at Montgomery he was appointed a 1st lieutenant on April 13 of the same year. As instructor of artillery at Pensacola he became a lieutenant colonel on August 30, 1862. HOWARD commanded the heavy artillery in the defense of Richmond. As commander of the 18th and 20th battalions of Virginia artillery he was captured at Sailor's Creek and sent to Johnson's Island for six weeks. Returning home, HOWARD was commissioned colonel and aide-de-camp on the staff of Governor Oden Bowie on February 8, 1871. In 1872, he was assistant adjutant general and became a brigadier general and chief of militia artillery in 1873. During the railroad riots of 1877 HOWARD commanded the 7th regiment of the Maryland National Guard. While a major general he was appointed adjutant general on April 8, 1884, at which post he served for eight years.

Major General Henry Kyd DOUGLAS of Hagerstown was the fifteenth adjutant general. A law graduate from Franklin-Marshall College in 1860, he enlisted as a private in Company B, 2nd Virginia C.S.A. on April 18, 1861. He was promoted to 1st sergeant June 5, 2nd lieutenant September 14, and captain in 1862. On June 13, 1863, as an assistant adjutant general with the rank of major, he served as adjutant of the Stonewall Brigade. After Jackson's death DOUGLAS served on various staffs until he was promoted to colonel of the 13th and 14th Virginia Regiments. He was commander of the Light Brigade when he surrendered at Appomattox; his commission as brigadier general was signed in Richmond but not effected. After returning to Maryland he served as colonel of militia on the staff of Governor Carroll. During the railroad strikes, he commanded the Department of Western Maryland. On November 22, 1880, DOUGLAS was captain of the Hagerstown Light Infantry, promoted to lieutenant colonel on September 29, 1881, 1st Battalion Infantry, and to colonel May 29, 1886, 1st Infantry Brigade. On March 3, 1892, he became adjutant general of this state, a position he held for four years.

Major General John Selden SAUNDERS of Baltimore and Annapolis was the seventeenth adjutant general. He was educated at St. James' College followed by an appointment to West Point on July 1, 1854. Graduating fifth in his class, he was appointed to a 2nd lieutenant in the 2nd U.S. Artillery. He resigned on April 22, 1861. He was commissioned a 1st lieutenant in the Confederate Artillery on May 18 and promoted to captain on May 8, 1862. On November 14 of the same year SAUNDERS was promoted to lieutenant colonel as commander of six batteries at Norfolk. He was later ordered to Vicksburg and placed in charge of fortifications where he was captured but promptly exchanged. He was chief of artillery in the inspector general's office when he was paroled at Appomattox. On May 7, 1887, he became a colonel of the Maryland National Guard as brigade inspector on May 7, 1887. Appointed Maryland adjutant general on February 7, 1900, he served until his death in 1904.

Chapter 23

POST WAR ORGANIZATIONS

The preponderance of public opinion in Maryland supporting the South was reflected in an outpouring of public sentiment and contributions following the War. In a collective venture, a Southern bazaar was held at Baltimore in April of 1866, which yielded over two hundred thousand dollars for the relief of suffering Southern people. During the following year the legislature of Maryland appropriated one hundred thousand dollars for the same purpose.

As time passed sentiment increased to pay greater tribute to those who had made the ultimate sacrifice. In 1870 a section of Mt. Olivet Cemetery was purchased for those Confederate soldiers who fell at the battles of South Mountain, Crampton's Gap and Monocacy. In that year at Point Lookout, two acres of land were purchased as a cemetery site for prisoners who died during the war. The following year, the Society of the Army and Navy of the Confederate States in the state of Maryland was organized. An immediate program was undertaken to locate and return to Maryland the remains of the fallen soldiers who had been buried in unconsecrated ground. This endeavor was headed by James Henry SMITH and continued until June of 1896. In 1879, chapters of the Confederate Monumental and Memorial Assoiation were organized by veterans in various counties. Within a year after the formation of most of these associations, a ladies Confederate Monumental Association was also established by the wives, widows and friends to honor fallen Southern soldiers. In 1878 in Hagerstown at Rose Hill Cemetery, ten acres were purchased by a board of trustees for reinterment of those Confederates who died during the battles around Sharpsburg and enroute to and from Gettysburg. As the Old Gray Line became thinner a number of monuments sprang up in their remembrance. Besides the individual cemetery headstones and monuments to Confederate Marylanders found in other states and on the battlefields within our state, eleven Confederate monuments can be found in various areas of the state (only one Federal monument is in existence). In front of the Kent County courthouse there is a monument which on one side names the Confederate men of the area, and the other names the Union men.

Eventually the needs of aging and indigent Confederate veterans were given attention. The association of the Maryland Line was formed in 1880. The main focus of this new organization was the relief of old soldiers, who until then, were finding refuge in the alms houses of the state. After much deliberation it was determined to make an effort to establish a Confederate Soldiers Home in Maryland. The old Federal Arsenal at Pikesville had been transferred to the state in 1823. This was later secured from the state of Maryland and in June of 1888 the Maryland Confederate Soldiers Home came to fruition. The home was managed by a president, secretary, corresponding secretary, treasurer, board of governors, board of managers, board of visitors and an executive committee all composed of Southern soldiers. The home soon housed over a hundred men. Bazaars were again held in 1885 and 1889. The proceeds of fifty thousand dollars were devoted to the care of these indigent Confederates.

Confederate societies began to spring up all over the state. There was an auxiliary of the Association of the Maryland Line which was composed of males who were non-veterans, as well as the board of visitors of the Association of the Maryland Line composed of women. William Henry POPE who was superintendent of the home, wrote in the first volume of the Confederate Veteran Magazine in 1893, "Now a little insight into the way we do in Maryland; we have no ex-Confederate societies, but several large, strong and active Confederate societies. We have never mixed in any manner with the other side - have no joint reunions, no joint banquets, no decorations or memorial days in common. In fact, we do not mix, we go our way and they go theirs, and we find that we gain more respect by doing so. We do not belong to that class of Confederates who believe that they were right. We know we were right in 1861. We know we were right when the war closed and we know today that we were right."[106]

The strength of many of the Confederate veterans groups varied from thirty members in Company A 1st Maryland Cavalry camp to 1,100 men in the Society of the Army and Navy of the Confederate States in Maryland. In 1917 there were 629 Confederate Veterans Camps in seventeen states and the District of Columbia. Maryland had 31 camps; the District of Columbia had two.[10] There were also Confederate Veterans Camps in other states which bore Marylanders' names: Lloyd TILGHMAN Camp of United Confederate Veterans in Twigg County, Tennessee; James BREATHED Camp in Pulaski, Virginia; and Raphael SEMMES Camp in Mobile, Alabama. Women of the South also began to organize. The Baltimore Chapter, United Daughters of the Confederacy No. 8, was organized on May 10, 1895. Its membership reached over a thousand, making it the largest chapter of United Daughters of the Confederacy in the country. The author has been able to locate twenty U.D.C. chapters. There were also Sons of Confederate Veterans Camps (S.C.V.) which were located in Frederick, Riverdale, Rockville, Hagerstown, Williamsport, Easton and Wheaton. There were two chapters of Children of the Confederates established, one in Baltimore and one in Hagerstown. The Society of Confederate Mothers and Widows of Baltimore was formed and a Confederate Women's Home was established at 1020 Linder Avenue. In 1925 the home was moved from Baltimore to Catonsville. Today in our state, there are eight active U.D.C. chapters, and five flourishing S.C.V. camps. In contrast, no Union societies of the Civil War have survived.

Notes

1. Randolph MCKIM, *The Numerical Strength of the Confederate Army*. (New York: The Neale Publishing Co., 1912), pp. 64f. McKim disputes a figure of 20,000 credited to Maryland and cites a grand total of 4,580 who served in Maryland organizations.

2. Bradley T. JOHNSON, *Confederate Military History, Vol II* (Atlanta, Georgia: Confederate Publishing Company: 1899), p. 43.

3. "Marylanders in the Confederate Army ," *Confederate Veteran Magazine*, June 1909, XVIII, p. 235.

4. William Wilkins Glenn, *Between the North and South: The Narrative of William Wilkins Glenn, 1861-1869* (London, England: Associated University Press, 1976), p. 228.

5. L. Nathan WOODHOUSE, *The Cause That Was Lost and the Home That Was Found*, p. 2.

6. Glenn, *Between the North and South*, p. 228.

7. John Taylor WOOD, *Sea Ghost of the Confederacy* (Athens, Georgia: The University of Georgia Press, n.d.), pp. 4-19. Wood was born on Fort Snelling, an army post, then in Iowa territory; his father was from Rhode Island, and his mother from Louisiana, and Wood himself made his home in the border state of Maryland.

8. Wilmer, Jarrett, and Vernon, *The History and Roster of Maryland Volunteers, War of 1861-65*. In 1896 the State Legislature commissioned three Union veterans to compile this listing. The project was finished two years later, showing 50,316 white volunteers, 7,718 colored volunteers and 3,925 sailors and marines as serving the federal government, a grand total of 62,959.

9. Daniel C. Toomey, *Index to the Roster of the Maryland Volunteers* (Harmans, Maryland: Toomey Publishing Company, n.d.). Many changes in organization occurred. The 11th Regiment Infantry was consolidated with the 2nd Regiment; the 12th Regiment was assigned to the 1st Eastern Shore Regiment; in 1864 the 1st Regiment, Potomac Home Brigade was recruited up to a full regiment and its name changed to the 13th regiment; in 1864, the cavalry units of Purnell's Legion were transferred to the 8th Regiment to serve as infantry. Another regiment was not completed until March 1, 1865.

10. Elias Jones, *Revised History of Dorchester County, Maryland* (Baltimore: Read-Taylor Press, 1925), pp. 337f.

11. Bradley T. JOHNSON, *Confederate Military History* (Atlanta, Georgia: Confederate Publishing Company, 1899), pp. 97f.

12. Bradley T. JOHNSON, Letter to Tunstall Smith, November 30, 1897.

13. Fifteen former graduates of the U.S. Naval Academy were no longer in naval service. Their whereabouts at the time of the War were not determined.

14. Thomas J.C. Williams, *History of Washington County* (Hagerstown, Maryland, 1906), I, p. 362.

15. J. Thomas SCHARF, *History of Western Maryland* (Philadelphia, Pennsylvania: Everts, 1882), Vol. I, p. 362. "At every Confederate invasion all through the War the college had been visited by former pupils who were officers or soldiers in the Southern Army. All came to pay their respects to Dr. Kerfoot who never seemed to lose their love or respect despite his firm stand for the Union. On the last day of the year Dr. Kerfoot read in chapel a list of twelve of the former college boys of whose deaths in the Southern Army he had received information."

16. *Blue and Gray at Georgetown University and the Civil War* (n.p.: Georgetown University Alumni, 1904), p. XIV. A copy is held by the Georgetown University Library.

17. A photograph (held by Carroll County Historical Society) of the corps of Irving College shows thirty cadets in dark blue uniforms parading in front of the college.

18. The students were furnished with dress uniforms and were required to wear daily fatigue uniforms. In the winter the suit was a gray cloth frock coat or single-breasted jacket with standing collars and gilt buttons. The cap was made of blue cloth with a silver star in the front surrounded by a gilt wreath. For summer the dress was white pantaloons and a brown linen single-breasted jacket with standing collar.

19. John Goldsborough WHITE, a student of seventeen at the time, remembers, "Finding themselves without arms, the students in St. Timothy's Hall were forced to disband their military companies. My next step was a letter to my father in which I frankly told him that myself and a considerable number of the other boys were determined to leave for Virginia where we could join the Southern Army, asking him for some money to defray the expenses. The answer to this was in the shape of my father in person, who came in a hurry. I was immediately packed up and checked out of school. I bid farewell to Major Van Bokkelen, who I never was to see again, farewell to my classmates, many of whom I would meet again around the campfires or the long marches with the Army in Northern Virginia." John Goldsborough WHITE, "A Rebel's Memories of the Civil War," *The Baltimore Sun* Newspaper, 19 May 1929.

20. Erick Davis, "St. Timothy's Hall," *History Trails*, Baltimore County Historical Society, Vol. 11, No. 3, Spring, 1977, p. 14.

21. On April 19, 1865, Major General Lew Wallace issued General Order No. 86, "The gray uniform worn by certain young men said to be students has become so offensive to the loyal soldiers and citizens that it is prohibited in this department." See George C. Keidel, *Reverend Libertus Van Bokkelen.*

Typescript held by Enoch Pratt Free Library, p. 5. The school then adopted a black cloth uniform, trimmed with gilt, styled after the French corps d'Afrique.

22. A school catalog (held by Enoch Pratt Free Library, Baltimore) indicates an enrollment of about fifty cadets. They were uniformed in winter and summer gray cloth pantaloons (of different weight material depending on the season).

According to the school's catalog, the founders adopted a course of study which combined "the systems of instruction of West Point and Annapolis," providing naval drill, mathematical, engineering, practical and gymnastic experiences - proclaiming, that the academy was unique in this regard. Catalog Maryland Military and Naval Academy (New York: Liberty Printing Company, 1885), page intro.

23. An 1856 catalog shows the tuition and boarding at $180 for ten months plus $20 for the institute's uniform, which consisted of a "single-breasted frock of navy blue standing collar with a star on each side (and) pants of skyblue cassimere with black stripe and a cap of navy blue." *The Frederick News* newspaper, October 30, 1862.

24. George H. Callcott, "A History of the University of Maryland," *Maryland Historical Society Magazine*, Baltimore, Maryland, 1966, p. 157.

25. *Baltimore American* Newspaper, March 10, 1863, March 13, 1863.

26. Daniel C. Hartzler, *Medical Doctors of Maryland in the C.S.A.* (Funkstown, Maryland: Tristate Printing, 1979), p. 24.

27. "The course of study at the institute was molded after that in use at West Point and at Yale. The annual tuition and board per student was $350. The cadets were requried to wear military uniforms at all times. They were made of gray cloth and were adorned with gilt buttons bearing the seal of the institution." Erick F. Davis, "The Maryland Military Institute," *History Trails*, Vol. II, No. 3, Baltimore County Historical Society, p.16.

28. JOHNSON, Vol. II, p. 236.

29. William Couper, *The VMI New Market Cadets* (Charlottesville, Virginia: The Michie Company, 1933), p. 92.

30. Frederick Shriver Klein, *Just South of Gettysburg, Carroll County, Maryland in the Civil War* (Westminster, Maryland: The Newman Press, 1963), p. 200.

31. JOHNSON, Vol. II, p. 48.

32. *War of the Rebellion, Official Records of the Union and Confederate Armies*, Series I, Vol. I (U.S. War Department, Washington, D.C.), p. 278.

33. *Baltimore American and Commercial Advertiser:* Newspaper, April 18, 1861.

34. SCHARF, p. 212.

35. JOHNSON, Vol. II, p. 258.

36. JOHNSON, Vol. II, p. 301.

37. Reverend Horace Edwin HAYDEN, The 1st Maryland Cavalry CSA (*Southern Historical Society Papers,* 1879), Vol. VI, p. 251.

38. F.M. Burrows, "Harper's Ferry in 1861," *Confederate Veteran Magazine,* Vol. I, Apr. 1893, p. 103f.

39. *Biographical Encyclopedia of Representative Men of Maryland* (Baltimore, Maryland: National Biographical Company, 1879), p. 538.

40. *Biographical Sketches of the Members of Maryland Line Confederate Soldiers Home, January 1900,* written in long hand p. 150f. Held in Erick Davis Collection, Baltimore, MD.

41. Hartzler, p. 35.

42. JOHNSON, p. 304.

43. Scrapbook of James Innis RANDOLPH. Held by White House of the Confederacy, Richmond, Virginia

44. *Biographical Sketches of the Members of Maryland Line Confederate Soldiers Home, January 1900,* written in long hand, p. 47. Held in Erick Davis Collection, Baltimore, MD.

45. Armstrong THOMAS, *The THOMAS Brothers of Mattapany,* 1963, p. 218.

46. *Baltimore Evening Sun* Newspaper, Aug.27, 1910.

47. *Battles of Leaders of the Civil War* (New York: The Century Company, 1888), p. 11.

48. Lee A. Wallace, Jr. *A Guide to the Virginia Military Organization, 1861-1865* (Richmond, Virgina: Virginia Civil War Commission, 1964), p.105.

49. *War of the Rebellion, Official Records of the Union and Confederate Armies,* Series I, Vol. LI, Part II, (U.S. War Department, Washington, D.C.), p. 101.

50. Bradley T. JOHNSON, Memories of the 1st Maryland (*Southern Historical Society Papers*, 1881), Vol. IX, p. 221.

51. National Archives, General and Staff Officers, Record Group 109, Series 818, Roll 9, under the heading of "DALLAS, W.W."

NOTES

52. National Archives, Record Group 109, Series 321, Roll 15, under the heading of "EDELIN, Charles C."

53. George Proctor KANE, *To All Marylanders in the Confederate States.* A broadside issued during the War. A copy is held by Daniel D. Hartzler, New Windsor, MD.

54. *War of the Rebellion,* Series I, Vol. XL, Part II, p. 650.

55. William Harwar PARKER, *Recollections of a Naval Officer* 1841-1865 (Annapolis, Maryland: Naval Institute Press, 1985), p. XVI.

56. Thomas J.C. Williams, *History of Washington County* (Hagerstown, Maryland: n.p., 1906), Vol II, p. 1246.

57. John G. White, "From a Rebel's Memories of the Confederate States," *Baltimore Sun* Newspaper, May 1929.

58. *Biographical Sketches of the Members of Maryland Line Confederate Soldiers Home, January 1900*, written in long hand, p. 197. Held in Erick Davis Collection, Baltimore, MD.

59. "The young lady, even though she knew he was about to die, insisted upon their marriage, which was solemnized ten days after the battle and a few days before his death." Walter J. Kirby, *Roll Call - The Civil War in Kent County, Maryland* (Silver Spring, Maryland: Family Line Publications, 1985), p. 107.

60. A.W. BRADFORD Letter, January 17, 1865.

61. Letter from William K. BRADFORD to Governor A.W. Bradford, January 24, 1865.

62. Williams, p. 1023.

63. Elias Jones, *History of Dorchester County, Maryland*, rev. ed. (Baltimore, Maryland: Read-Taylor Press, 1925), p. 267.

64. Robert K. Krick, *Lee's Colonels, A Biographical Register of Field Officers of the A.N.V.* (Dayton, Ohio: Morningside Bookshop, 1979), p. 338.

65. *Genealogical Biography of the Leading Families of the City of Baltimore and Baltimore County* (Chicago, Illinois: n.p., 1897), p. 1049.

66. Kirby, p. 97.

67. L. Nathan WOODHOUSE, *The Cause That Was Lost and the Home That Was Found* (n.p.: n.p., n.d.), p. 2f.

68. William K. JENKINS, *A Memory of Comrades and Campaigns in the 1st Maryland Artillery CSA* (n.p.: n.p., 1903), p. 8.

69. Susan R. Hull, *Boy Soldiers of the Confederacy* (Washington, D.C.: Neal Publishing Company, 1905), p. 180.

70. McHenry HOWARD, *Recollections of a Maryland Confederate Soldier and Staff Officer* (Baltimore, Maryland: Williams and Wilkins Company, 1914), p. 414.

71. Charles Lee Lewis, *Admiral Franklin BUCHANAN: Fearless Man of Action* (Baltimore, Maryland, The Norman Remington Company, 1929), p. 166.

72. *Biographical Sketches of the Members of Maryland Line Confederate Soldiers Home, January 1900,* written in long hand, p. 96. Held in Erick Davis Collection, Baltimore, MD.

73. Charles Fishus, *Maryland in the Confederate Navy*, Maryland Historical Society, p. 4.

74. William Robinson, Jr., *The Confederate Privateers - Letters of*of *Marque* (New Haven, Connecticut: Yale University Press, 1928), p. 241.

75. Robinson, p. 206.

76. Their studies comprised six departments and twenty-two branches. There were four annual courses and the midshipmen were arranged into four classes.

While the Confederate cadets remained at the seat of war the acting midshipmen of the U.S. Naval Academy were transferred to Newport, Rhode Island, far from the scene of combat.

77. Ralph W. Donnelly, *The History of the Confederate States Marine Corps* (New Bern, North Carolina: Owen G. Dunn Company, 1976), p. 175.

78. J Thomas SCHARF, *History of the Confederate States Navy* (New York: Rogers and Sherwood, 1887), p. 771.

79. Lewis, p. 163.

80. Hartzler, p. 5.

81. In the Army, doctors were ranked as surgeons, assistant surgeons, acting assistant surgeons and contract surgeons, while Naval medical officers were similarly ranked as surgeons, passed assistant surgeons, assistant surgeons and acting assistant surgeons. Subordinate to the surgeon general was a surgeon-in-chief who was the administrator of a hospital group or medical board. A surgeon-in-charge was in charge of a hospital or infirmary. A medical director supervised a corps, a division surgeon headed surgery in a division, a regimental surgeon directed a brigade field hospital and a senior surgeon or chief surgeon acted as the ranking physician of a group. Contract surgeons were private doctors who had passed the military boards and were employed by the government at a given institution for a given period of time with the pay of a first lieutenant.

NOTES

82. Hartzler, p. 16f.

83. Hartzler, p. 48.

84. Mary Mitchell, *Divided Town* (n.p: Barre Moss Publishing, 1968), p. 93f.

85. *Washington Evening Star* Newspaper, March 20, 1862.

86. National Archives, Record Group 109, Series M331, Compiled Service Records of Confederate General and Staff Officers and Nonregimental Enlisted Men, Roll 244, under the heading of "TENNANT, John C."

87. *Washington Evening Star* Newspaper, July 28, 1962.

88. HOWARD, p. 53f.

89. In his commentary on "Christ in Camp" J. William Jones describes the message of the chaplain. "They preached the Gospel. He does not discuss the relation of science to religion, or the slavery question, or the causes which led to the war, or the war itself. He does not indulge in abusive epithets of the invader of our soil, or seek to fire his hearers with hatred or vindictiveness toward the enemy. He is looking in the eyes of heroes of many a battle, and knows that the long roll may beat in the midst of his sermon and summon the men to battle, and death, and therefore he speaks as a dying man to dying men, telling with simple earnestness the old, old story of salvation." (J. William Jones, *Confederate Military History, Vol. XII*, Confederate Publishing Co., Atlanta, Georgia, 1899, p. 151.)

90. In his account of war experiences, Chaplain SCHWARAR relates a special concern of the soldier. "The other day I rode to the line of battle to see the soldiers ... To my great joy a young captain whom I had baptized in his infancy approached me and said, 'I wish to join the church, and I wish you to give me a certificate; the Lord has converted me.' I gave him the document with a glad heart. 'Now,' said he, 'if I fall in battle, let my mother know of this transaction. It will afford her great joy.'" (The Southern Christian Advocate, printed in Atlanta Georgia, June 1889, p. 6).

91. National Archives, General and Staff Officers, Record Group 109, Series 324, Roll 49, under the heading of "BALL, Dabney."

92. "The great majority of them had left comfortable Christian homes and had been carefully trained by good Christian parents. Free from the sweet influence of home and under no restraint save that of military discipline, they were indeed growing a little wild and reckless, and no doubt did many things that they would now be ashamed of; but the good seed sown had not been entirely overgrown by weeds of denominational scattering by the red hand of war, and when the proposition was made by the wife of the commanding officer, Mrs. Bradley T. JOHNSON to build a church, there were more workmen than were needed. Everyone set to work to make the project a success ... day after day the building grew till at last, with a shout of triumphant joy, the last log was laid and the last pin driven, and the little church in the wilderness was ready for occupation. It was a long building capable of

seating nearly five hundred men. There were no windows, the light came from above and on each side was a large fireplace, which was filled with blazing logs, giving out a most gentle heat. The roof was made of hospital tent flies, which admitted a soft pleasing light, and turned every drop of rain. At the upper end was a platform to serve as a chancel, and the reading desk and the pulpit was a large round pine post, driven well into the ground and capped with a board to hold with the Bible; while at the back, well up on the end of the wall, was a large cross of evergreen, kept fresh and bright all the time. Opposite the chancel was the door, over which was a gallery where the choir was to sit and from which many a familiar hymn was sung to the prise of God. Outside, over the door, was a large wooden cross, and while our modest little temple could not compare with some of the grand stone churches in the great cities, it was to us a thing of beauty, and became a consecrated spot to many a weary and sin-laden soldier who there found peace and reconcilation and joy ... There were many church boys, and Methodists, Presbyterians, and Romanists and many, alas who own up that they belong only to the big church. Among the latter, a goodly number were brought to the knowledge of Christ, and confessing him before their fellow man in confirmation, took up the cross as a badge and ensign of their life-long battle with sin. The Rev. Thomas DUNCAN, now Dr. DUNCAN of the deaconcy of Easton, became our chaplain and noble, faithful work he did among the men committed to his charge. The church was not, of course consecrated, and its doors were always open to the men who made constant use of it. The choir and the glee club practiced within its walls; the men went there to read - a good library having been provided and to write their letters, and the people of the neighborhood gathered there on Sundays to enjoy with the soldiers the beautiful and inspiring services." (Edward R. RICH, *Comrades Four,* Washington, D.C.: The Neale Publishing Company, 1907) , p. 70-72).

93. JOHNSON, p. 340-342.

94. JOHNSON, p. 416.

95. Williams, p. 1310.

96. William A. Russ, Jr., "Disfranchisement in Maryland in 1861-1865," *Maryland Historical Magazine,* Vol. XXVIII, 1933, p. 310.

97. David Winfred Gaddy, "Williams NORRIS and the Confederate's Signal and Secret Service," *Maryland Historical Magazine,* Vol. 70, No. 2, 1975, p. 177.

98. Russ, p. 317.

99. R.B. WARING, United Daughters of the Confederacy No. 8 Records, Maryland Historical Society, Baltimore.

100. "Confederate Postmaster of Maryland," *Confederate Veteran Magazine,* Vol. XXVIII, May 1920, p. 267.

101. Klaphor, Margaret B. and Paul D. Brown, *History of Charles County, Maryland* (La Plata, Maryland: Tercentenary Inc., 1958), p. 126.

102. Joseph F. TORRENT, "With the Blockade Runners," *Confederate Veteran Magazine*, Vol. XXXIII, June, 1925, p. 208f.

103. Levi S. WHITE, "Running the Blockade on the Chesapeake Bay," *Baltimore Sun* Newspaper, December 15, 1907.

104. Frederic Emory, *History of Queen Anne's County, Maryland*. (Baltimore, Maryland: Maryland Historical Society, 1950), p. 511.

105. Heinrich E. Buchholz, *Governors of Maryland* (Baltimore, Maryland: Williams & Wilkins Company, 1908), p. 143.

106. William Henry POPE, *Confederate Veteran Magazine* , Vol. I, November 1893, p. 326.

107. *Confederate Veteran Magazine,* Vol. XXV, July 1917, p. 298.

ABBOTT, James; cpl; 1st MD Inf, Co A; ref: 1, 2, 19, 23

ABBOTT, William of William; pvt; 1st MD Cav, Co B; res: Cedar Creek, Dor Cty; ref: 1, 19, 1547

ABEL, Charles, pvt; 1st MD Inf, Co B; res: St. Mary's Co; ref: 1, 2, 6, 19, 21

ABELL, Frank, pvt; Zarvona's MD Zoaves; res: Oakville, St. M. Cty; ref: 1, 6, 735, 1509, 1555, 1662

ABRISCH, Jacob; pvt; 40th VA Inf; res: Har Cty; MLCSH; ref: 1, 627, 700, 786

ACKHURST, Charles E.; pvt; 1st MD Inf, Co A; ref: 1, 2, 19, 21

ACKLER, William F.; pvt; 1st MD Inf, Co D; res: Balt; MLCHS; ref: 1, 2, 19, 21, 240, 559, 700, 786, 1511

ACKWORTH, William W.; pvt; 1st MD Cav, Co B; ref: 1, 19

ACRCE, Thomas L.; pvt; 2nd MD Cav, Co A; ref: 1, 19, 1609

ACTON, Samuel; McPherson Pack; res: AA Cty; ref: 1539

ACTON, Washington; pvt; 4th MD Lt Arty; ref: 1, 2, 19, 21

ACWORTH, William W.B.; pvt; 35th VA Cav, Co A; res: Som Cty; ref: 1, 1611, 1677

ADAIR, William R.; pvt; 2nd Md Inf,Co A; res: Balt; ref: 1, 2, 19, 21, 650

ADAMS, Andrew; pvt; Davis's MD Cav, Co A; res: Balt; res: 1, 19, 735, 1540

ADAMS, Clinton; 6th VA Cav, Co A; res: Carrollton Manor; ref: 1, 19, 73, 643, 1548

ADAMS, Edward T. (M.D.); Asst Surg; 25th VA Cav; res: 1, 18, 316, 735, 1534

ADAMS, F. S.; pvt; 1st SC Inf, Co G; ref: 1

ADAMS, Francis; pvt; 17th VA Inf, Co A; res: PG Cty; ref: 1, 133, 142

ADAMS, Franklin; pvt; 2nd MD Inf, Co C; res: Allens Fresh, Cha Cty; ref: 1, 2, 19, 21, 1546

ADAMS, George; pvt; 2nd MD Inf, Co C; ref: 1

ADAMS, Henry S.; pvt; 1st MD Inf, Co E; res: Carr Cty; MLCSH; ref: 1, 2, 19, 21, 93, 700, 786, 791

ADAMS, J. A.; pvt; Stuart's Horse Arty, Breathed's Battery; ref: 1

ADAMS, J. H.; pvt; 3rd MD Lt Arty; ref: 1, 2, 21, 160, 726

ADAMS, J. W.; pvt; 1st SC Inf, Co G; ref: 1

ADAMS, Jacob Thomas; pvt; 24th NC Inf, Co D; res: Lakesville, Dor Cty; ref: 1, 70, 1547

ADAMS, James A.; pvt; 44th NC Inf, Co I; res: Balt; ref: 1, 21, 700

ADAMS, James P.; 2nd Lt; 30th VA Inf, Co E; ref: 1, 20, 64

ADAMS, John; pvt; Davis's MD Cav, Co A; ref: 1, 735

ADAMS, John Grove; pvt; 17th VA Inf, Co A; res: Balt; MLCSH; ref: 1, 92, 93, 133, 627, 700, 786

ADAMS, John Q.; pvt; 2nd MD Inf, Co H; ref: 1, 2, 21

ADAMS, John S.; pvt; 1st MD Inf, Co I; res: Cha Cty; ref: 1, 2, 19, 21

ADAMS, Joseph C.; pvt; 1st SC Inf, Co G; res: Balt; res: 1, 735, 1599

ADAMS, Thomas Jacob; pvt; 56th NC Inf, Co D; res Point of Rocks, Frd Cty; ref: 1, 70, 1548

ADAMS, William; pvt; 11th GA Inf, Co E; res: Frd Cty; ref: 1, 19

ADCOCK, Robert; pvt; 1st MD Lt Arty; ref: 1

ADDISON, E. Saunders; cpl; 17th VA Inf, Co A; ref: 20

ADDISON, John Fagette; sgt; 17th VA Inf, Co A; ref: 1, 12, 20, 133, 142, 251

ADDISON, John W.; sgt; 2nd VA Inf, Co F; res: Balt; ref: 1, 19, 20, 21, 700, 791

ADDISON, W. John (M.D.); Asst Surg; Navy; C.S.S. Maurepas; res: PG Cty; ref: 1, 18, 19, 58, 97, 279, 791, 1564

ADDISON, W. S.; Pvt; 1st SC Inf, Co B; res: PG Cty; ref: 1, 7

APPENDIX A: ROSTER

ADDISON, Walter Dulany; pvt; Stuart's Horse Arty, Breathed's Battery; res: PG Cty; ref: 1, 20, 70, 133, 142, 251, 498

ADIE, Hugh Jr; Lt; 9th VA Cav, Co A; ref: 1, 21, 700

ADKINS, P.; pvt; Stuart's Horse Arty, Breathed's Battery; ref: 1, 498

ADKINS, S. E.; pvt; 2nd MD Inf, Co G; ref: 1, 2, 21, 23

ADRIAN, James Allexander; pvt; 35th VA Cav, Co C; ref: 1677

AFFELDER, William; pvt; Lucas' 15th SC Heavy Arty; ref: 1

AGEN, Peter; pvt; 20th GA Inf, Co D; ref: 1, 2, 19, 21

AHERN, Frank I.; pvt; Cobbs SC Leg, Co A; res: Laurel, PG Cty; ref: 1, 21, 700, 786

AKERN, John A.; pvt; MD Guerrilla Zouaves; ref: 1

AHRENDTS, U. A.; pvt; ref: 700

AIKIN, John E.; pvt; Stuart's Horse Arty, Breathed's Battery; ref: 1

AINSWORTH, Thomas; pvt; 2nd MD Cav, Co A; ref: 1

AINSWORTH, William B.; pvt; 8th GA Inf, Co C; ref: 1, 735

AISQUITH, Archie H.; pvt; 2 VA Inf, Co G; ref: 1, 70, 1687

AISQUITH, Hobart; pvt; 1st Md Cav, Co B; res: AA Cty; MLCSH; ref: 1, 2, 19, 21, 39, 92, 93, 785, 786, 1361, 1379, 1380, 1383, 1387, 1474, 1483

ALBAND, W. H.; 2nd MD Cav, Co D; ref: 1, 93

ALBAUGH, Ira H.; sgt; 1st VA Cav, Co K; res: Carr Cty; ref: 1, 2, 19, 21, 601

ALBAUGH, John W.; pvt; 1st VA Cav, Co K; res: Carr Cty; ref: 1, 2, 19, 21, 602

ALBERT, Augustus James Jr; pvt; 1st Md Lt Arty; res: Balt; ref: 1, 2, 19, 21, 34, 63, 64, 68, 70, 215, 686, 690, 700, 777, 782, 791, 1273

ALBERT, Martin; pvt; Lee's MD Cav; ref: 1, 19

ALBERT, William; pvt; Lucas' 15th SC Heavy Arty; res: Bt Cty; ref: 1, 19, 20

ALBRESCH, Jacob; pvt; 40th VA Inf, Co A; ref: 1, 92, 93

ALCHER, Frank G.; pvt; 2nd MD Cav, Co A; ref: 1

ALCOCK, William C.; pvt; 2nd MD Cav, Co C; res: Balt; ref: 1, 2, 19, 21

ALDERSON, John H.; cpl; 3rd KY Mounted Inf, Co D; res: Balt; MLCSH; ref: 1, 786

ALDRIDGE, George W.; sgt; 1st SC Inf, Co C; res: PG Cty; MLCSH; ref: 1, 21, 93, 672, 700, 735, 781, 786, 791

ALDRIDGE, John H.; pvt; 1st MD Lt Arty; res: Balt; res: 1, 2, 19, 21

ALDRIDGE, Joseph West; pvt; 43rd VA Cav, Mosby's Co D; res: Westminister, Carr Cty; ref: 1, 8, 20, 123, 684

ALDRIDGE, Robert Moses; pvt; 35th VA Cav, Co B; res: East New Market, Dor Cty; ref: 1, 3, 7, 1547, 1611, 1677

ALESEN, James; res St. M. Cty; ref: 6

ALEXANDER, A. B.; Pvt; 2nd AR Inf, Co C; res: Cec Cty; ref: 1, 20

ALEXANDER, George W.; Col; Commander of Castle Thunder Prison; res: PG Cty; ref: 1, 2, 19, 21, 58, 61, 64, 70, 97, 593, 700, 703, 735, 781, 791, 1113, 1520, 1578, 1583

ALEXANDER, Lawrence; pvt; 1st VA Inf, Co E; ref: 1

ALFRED, W.; pvt; MD America Rifles; ref: 1, 19

ALL, S. D.; 2nd MD Cav, Co B; ref: 1, 93

ALLAN, William; Lt Col; Ordnance Dept, 2nd Army Corps; ref: 1, 2, 21, 24, 110, 111, 114, 126, 127, 150, 155, 383, 560, 667, 700, 782, 791, 1569, 1600, 1617, 1642

ALLEN, ---; 35th VA Cav, Co B; ref: 1611

ALLEN, Lt; ref: 141

APPENDIX A: ROSTER

ALLEN, James; pvt; 1st MD Inf, Co F; ref: 1, 2, 19, 21
ALLEN, John; pvt; 2nd MD Cav, Co F; ref: 1, 2, 19, 21
ALLEN, Robert T. P.; Col; 17th TX Inf; ref: 1, 177, 236, 791
ALLEN, Thomas Murphy; Lt; 4th NC Inf, Co E; ref: 1, 21, 700
ALLEN, William L.; pvt; 1st MD Inf, Co C; ref: 1, 19
ALLEN, William N.; Q.M. sgt; 1st MD Cav; res: Carr Cty; ref: 1, 2, 19, 20, 21, 740
ALLHARN, Joseph; pvt; 2nd MD Cav, Co A; ref: 1
ALLISON, Richard Taylor; Maj; Marine Corps; res: Phoenix, Bt Cty; ref: 1, 18, 19, 20, 21, 431, 674, 700, 735, 791, 792, 1349, 1495, 1500, 1501, 1515, 1564, 1593, 1594
ALLISON, W. W. (M.D.); pvt; 10th VA Inf, Co F; res: Hagerstown, Wash Cty; ref: 21, 700
ALLSTON, Joseph Blyth; Capt; 27th SC Inf, Co F; res: St. M. Cty; ref: 1, 21, 631, 700, 1509
ALMOND, J. W.; pvt; 2nd MD Cav, Co A; ref: 1, 19, 1609
ALSTON, Frederick; pvt; 4th MD Lt Arty; St. M. Cty; ref: 2, 6, 19, 21
ALTWATER, J. W.; pvt; 1st MD Cav, Co F; ref: 2, 19, 21
ALVEY, James Perrie; pvt; 2nd MD Inf, Co B; res: Charlotte Hall, St. M. Cty; ref: 1, 2, 6, 19, 21, 72, 1509, 1555
ALVEY, John F.; Maj; 45th VA Inf; ref: 1, 2, 19, 21, 700, 791
AMABLE, James; pvt; 2nd MD Cav, Co D; ref: 1, 1609
AMBLER, James Marshall; res: Balt; ref: 20
AMBLER, William H.; pvt; MD Guerrilla; res: Balt; ref: 1
AMBROSE, Montien; pvt; 26th VA Inf, Co A; res: Millersville, AA Cty; ref: 1, 1539
AMBURGE, Valentine; res: Millersville, AA Cty; ref: 1539
AMEY, Charles; pvt; 1st MD Inf, Co B; res: Balt; ref: 1, 2, 19, 21
AMISS, Edward L.; pvt; 6th VA Cav, Co B; res: Mont Cty; ref: 1, 20, 718, 873, 1574
AMMELL, Charles S.; ref: 1444
AMOS, Franklin Benjamin; cpl; Zarvona's MD Zouaves; res: Balt; ref: 1, 2, 19, 21, 23, 735
ANDERSON, Arthur; pvt; 1st SC Inf, Co G; ref: 1, 735
ANDERSON, Colmore; pvt; 35th VA Cav, Co A; ref: 1, 3, 15, 1611, 1677
ANDERSON, Charles Jefferies; ref: 1620
ANDERSON, Edward T.; Lt; 9th VA Cav, Co H; res: Balt; ref: 70
ANDERSON, Eli S.; pvt; 37th VA Inf, Co E; res: Adamstown, Fred Cty; ref: 1, 933, 1573
ANDERSON; Esli; pvt; 47th VA Inf, Co H; ref: 1
ANDERSON, Frank C.; sgt; 14th TN Inf, Co A; res: Balt; ref: 1, 70
ANDERSON, George; pvt; 1st MD Lt Arty; ref: 1, 19
ANDERSON, Isaac; pvt; 43rd VA Cav, Co H, Mosby's; res: Balt; ref: 1, 8, 1613
ANDERSON, J. H.; smn, Navy; ref: 1, 793
ANDERSON, James; Capt; 35th VA Cav, Co D; res: Rockville, Mont Cty; ref: 1, 3, 15, 19, 20, 64, 73, 371, 557, 1574, 1611
ANDERSON, James; pvt; Davis's MD Cav, Co A; ref: 1, 19, 735
ANDERSON, James M.; pvt; 1st MD Inf, Co C; res: AA Cty; ref: 1, 2, 4, 791
ANDERSON, John; pvt; 13th VA Inf, Co G; ref: 1
ANDERSON, John H.; pvt; Cabell's Howitzers, 1st Battery, Balt; ref: 1, 21, 101, 700, 783
ANDERSON, Joseph; pvt; Davis's MD Cav, Co A; res: Cumberland, All Cty; ref: 1, 19, 735, 1538, 1613
ANDERSON, Leroy; pvt; 1st MD Inf, Co F; ref: 1, 2, 19, 21, 23
ANDERSON, Mac; pvt; 43rd VA Cav, Co H, Mosby's; res: AA Cty; ref: 4, 8

ANDERSON, Minor; pvt; 14th TN Inf, Co E; res: Balt; ref: 1, 70, 1613
ANDERSON, Oscar; pvt; 1st MD Cav, Co C; ref: 1, 2, 19, 21
ANDERSON, Richard T.; pvt; 2nd MD Inf, Co C; res: Crownsville, AA Cty; ref: 1, 2, 19, 21, 72, 90, 1539, 1559
ANDERSON, Samuel Woodward; pvt; 2nd Md Inf, Co C; Crownsville, AA Cty; ref: 1, 2, 19, 21, 72, 79, 1539, 1579
ANDERSON, Thomas; pvt; 2nd MD Lt Arty; res: PG Cty; ref: 1
ANDERSON, William M.; pvt; 1st SC Inf, Co G; ref: 1, 936
ANDRE, John A.; cpl; 2nd MD Cav, Co F; ref: 1, 2, 19, 21
ANDREWS, Bohn; pvt; MD Guerrilla Zouaves; res: Carr Cty; ref: 1, 323, 511
ANDREWS, J.; pvt; Davis's MD Cav, Co B; ref: 1, 19
ANDREWS, Matthew Page; 1272, 1329, 1333, 1344, 1372, 1374, 1392, 1394, 1399, 1402, 1410, 1416, 1427, 1430, 1436, 1441, 1450, 1454, 1456, 1458, 1462, 1468, 1469, 1479
ANDREWS, Richard Snowden; Lt Col; 1st MD Lt Arty; res Balt; ref: 1, 2, 11, 13, 18, 19, 21, 23, 32, 34, 35, 42, 44, 50, 53, 63, 64, 68, 88, 104, 107, 129, 140, 150, 168, 169, 215, 222, 240, 331, 431, 443, 458, 459, 461, 462, 489, 511, 559, 604, 631, 684, 686, 700, 724, 727, 753, 757, 782, 791, 794, 823, 824, 838, 869, 908, 1020, 1104, 1273, 1342, 1400, 1532, 1575, 1578, 1579, 1600, 1644, 1673
ANGEL Henry R.; pvt; 9th VA Inf, Co B; ref: 1
ANGELL Thomas; pvt; 1st MD Inf, Co F; res: Frd Cty; ref: 1, 2, 19, 21, 89
ANNAN, James Roberdeau; pvt; 2nd VA Inf, Co G; res Cumberland, All Cty; ref: 1, 9, 19, 65, 95, 148, 511, 735, 1634
ANNAN, R.; smn, Navy; res: Balt; ref: 1
ANNAN, Roberdeau; pvt; 2nd VA Inf, Co G; res: Cumberland, All Cty; ref: 1, 9, 19, 21, 65, 95, 148, 511, 700, 735, 976, 1610
ANNAN, Roger P.; pvt; 7th VA Cav, Co G; res: Cumberland, All Cty; ref: 1, 3, 9, 19, 65, 95, 148, 511
ANNAN, Samuel; Surg; St. Mary's Hospital West Point, GA; res: Emmitsburg, Frd Cty; ref: 1, 18, 1533, 1536
ANNEN, Henry; pvt; 1st MD Inf, Co D; ref: 1, 2, 19, 21
ANTHON, William E.; pvt; Pollock's Co, VA Lt Arty; res: Balt; ref: 1, 21, 700
APPLEBY, John W.; pvt; 35th VA Cav, Co A; res: Clarksville, Mont Cty; ref: 1, 1574, 1611, 1677
APPLEBY, Wesley; pvt; 35th VA Cav, Co A; res: Clarksville, Mont Cty; res: 1, 1611, 1622, 1677
APPLEGARTH, James B.; pvt; 2nd MD Inf, Co E; Cornersville, Dor Cty; ref: 1, 2, 19, 21, 1547
APPLER, John C.; Capt; 1st MO Inf, Co H; res: Uniontown, Carr Cty; ref: 1, 1307
ARCHER, George Washington (M.D.); Asst Surg; White Sulphur Springs Hospital, Montgomery, AL; res: Belair, Har Cty; ref: 1, 18, 631, 689, 735, 766, 791, 1525, 1528, 1533, 1534, 1596
ARCHER, James; pvt; 11th TX Inf, Co H; res: Har Cty; ref: 1, 689, 766
ARCHER, James Jay; Brig Gen; Army of Tennessee and Army of Northern Virginia; res: Har Cty; ref: 1, 2, 18, 19, 23, 31, 32, 34, 39, 44, 48, 50, 62, 64, 68, 97, 104, 105, 110, 111, 113, 116, 123, 125, 126, 127, 129, 138, 140, 152, 159, 165, 239, 249, 350, 353, 397, 403, 414, 431, 443, 511, 601, 631, 674, 689, 735, 753, 766, 787, 791, 816, 818, 825, 847, 851, 857, 875, 908, 993, 1006, 1121, 1279, 1319, 1331, 1347, 1486, 1523, 1569,

1570, 1577, 1578, 1579, 1588, 1623, 1650, 1674
ARCHER, John; Capt; Asst A.G., Gen C. S. Winder's staff; res Cec Cty; ref: 1, 631, 689 766, 791
ARCHER, John R.; pvt; 1st MD Inf, Co E; ref: 1, 2, 19, 21, 511
ARCHER, Robert Harris Jr; Lt Col; 55th VA Inf; res: Har Cty; ref: 1, 2, 18, 19, 457, 511, 631, 689, 735, 766, 787, 791, 1331, 1600
ARCHER, Thomas J.; pvt; VA Lt Arty, Pegram's Co; res: Belair, Har Cty; ref: 1, 70
ARCHER, William H.; Lt; 2nd MD Cav, Co E; res: Ellicott City, How Cty; ref: 1, 19, 1550, 1609
ARDS, Jeremiah; pvt; 29th GA Cav, Co G; res: St. M. Cty; ref: 1, 1509
ARENDTS, Henry; pvt; 2nd MD Lt Arty, Co E; ref: 1, 2, 19, 21
ARGONE, Joseph; pvt; 2nd MD Cav, Co D; res: West River, AA Cty; ref: 1, 1539
ARGYLE, E. H.; pvt; Stuart's Horse Arty, Breathed's Battery; ref: 1
ARMIGER, William; pvt; Edelin's MD Heavy Arty; res: Johnsons Store, AA Cty; ref: 1, 1539
ARMISTEAD, John Royster; pvt; 12th VA Inf, Co E; ref: 1, 70
ARMOUR, James E.; Lt; MD Guerilla Zouaves; ref: 1, 2, 19, 735
ARMSTRONG, Frank C.; pvt; 23rd VA Cav, Co F; ref: 1, 674, 677
ARMSTRONG, James B.; Asst Engr, Navy; C.S.S. Red Rover; ref: 1, 1564
ARMSTRONG, James F.; pvt; 3rd TX Cav, Co K; res: Johnsons Store, AA Cty; ref: 1, 1539
ARMSTRONG, Joshua; pvt; 1st MD Cav, Co A; res: How Cty; ref: 1, 2, 19, 21
ARMSTRONG, Louis; pvt; 3rd MD Lt Arty; ref: 1, 2, 19, 21, 160, 726
ARMSTRONG, William H.; sgt; 35th VA Cav, Co C; Cumberland, All Cty; ref: 1, 9, 19, 65, 95, 148, 1677
ARMSTRONG, William Johnson; pvt; 43rd VA Cav, Co G, Mosby's; res: Urbana, Frd Cty; ref: 8, 20, 1548
ARNETT, William; pvt; 1st VA Cav, Co K; ref: 1, 2, 19, 21
ARNIE, E. C.; pvt; 6th Va Cav, Co B; res: Gaithersburg, Mont Cty; ref: 1574
ARNOLD, Charles; pvt; 9th Va Inf, Co B; ref: 1, 1576
ARNOLD, Charles A.; cpl; 1st MD Inf, Co C; res: Balt; ref: 1, 2, 19, 21, 23, 700, 1608
ARNOLD, Frank A.; pvt; Stuart's Horse Arty, Breathed's Battery; res: Hookstown, Bt Cty; ref: 1, 2, 19, 21, 498, 1541
ARNOLD, George; Capt; Nitre & Mining Dept; res: AA Cty; ref: 1578
ARNOLD, Harry W.; cpl; 13th VA Inf, Co G; ref: 1, 735
ARNOLD, Samuel B.; pvt; 1st MD Inf,Co C; res: Balt; ref: 1, 2, 19, 21, 316, 700, 1560, 1578, 1607, 1608
ARNOLD, Thomas; pvt; 8th AR Inf,Co H; res: St. Margarett, AA Cty; ref: 1, 1539
ARTHUR, Frank; Midn, Navy; C.S.S. Morgan; res: Bt Co; ref: 1, 19, 58, 97, 1564
ARTIS, Jeremiah; pvt; 2nd MD Cav,Co B; res: Smithville, St. M. Cty; ref: 1, 2, 6, 11, 19, 21, 881, 1563, 1627
ARVIN, Thomas E.; pvt; 2nd MD Cav, Co D; res: Carr Cty; ref: 1,19, 1609
ASBORNE, C.; 13th NC Inf, Co K; ref: 735
ASFOR, W.; pvt; 1st SC Inf, Co G; ref: 1
ASHAM, Cartright; res: St. M. Cty; ref: 6
ASHBURN, A. R.; pvt; 3rd MD Lt Arty; ref: 1, 2, 19, 21, 160
ASHBY, John T.; Capt; 8th VA Inf, Co B; ref: 1, 71
ASHBY, R. W.; pvt; 1st MD Cav, Co F; ref: 1, 2, 19, 21
ASHCOM, John Cartright (M.D.); Jacob's Mounted Riflemen; res: St. M. Cty; ref: 1, 1509, 1670
ASHE, James; pvt; 2nd MD Inf, Co G; ref: 1, 2, 19, 21

ASHE, Jerome C.; pvt; Barry's Co, MD Vols; ref: 1, 19
ASHLEY, Camm, B.; pvt; 34th VA Inf, Co K; res: Balt; ref: 1, 21, 700
ASHTON, Henry; pvt; 15th LA Inf, Co A; ref: 1
ASHTON, J. J.; pvt; 1st MD Inf, Co D; ref: 1, 2, 19, 21
ASHTON, Richard W.; pvt; 1st MD Inf, Co D; ref: 1, 19, 700
ASKEW, William F.; Capt; Asst Q.M., Raleigh, NC; ref: 1, 70, 791
ATHEY, James; pvt; 12th VA Cav, Co D; Cumberland, All Cty; ref: 1578
ATKINS, John; pvt; 43rd VA Cav, Co C, Mosby's; ref: 1, 8, 20
ATKINS, Samuel E.; pvt; 1st MD Inf, Co G; ref: 1, 2, 19, 21
ATKINSON, Archibald Jr (M.D.); Surg; 31st VA Inf; res: Balt; ref: 1, 18, 21, 631, 700, 1534, 1536
ATKINSON, William Griffith; Lt; Nitre & Mining Bureau; res: All Cty; MLCSH; ref: 1, 2, 19, 21, 70, 700, 786
ATWATER, J. W.; pvt; 1st MD Cav, Co F; ref: 1, 2, 19, 21
ATWELL, Ewell B.; pvt; 43rd VA Cav, Co C, Mosby's; ref: 1, 8
ATWELL, Richard M. Johnson; pvt; 6th VA Cav, Co A; res: Buck Lodge, Mont Cty; ref: 1, 73, 133, 677
ATWELL, Thomas; pvt; 6th VA Cav, Co K; res: Traceys Landing, AA Cty; ref: 1, 1539
ATWELL, William H.; pvt; 43rd VA Cav, Co C, Mosby's; res: AA Co; ref: 8, 1539
ATZEORADT, Henry; pvt; 2nd MD Inf,Co F; res: Port Tobacco, Cha Cty; MLCSH; ref: 1, 2, 19, 21, 39, 700, 786, 1544, 1608
AUBERG, Andrew J.; pvt; 1st MS Cav, Co A; res: Balt; ref: 1, 1540
AUBERG, James L.; pvt; 2nd MD Inf,Co E; res: Balt; ref: 1, 2, 19, 21, 488, 700, 848, 849, 906, 923, 1509
AUBREY, Tobias; drummer; 2nd MD Inf; ref: 1, 64
AULD, Charles S.; pvt; 1st MD Inf, Co A; res: Balt; ref: 1, 19
AULD, Thomas Edward; pvt; 1st VA Cav, Co B; res: Balt; ref: 1, 70
AULTMAN, N.; pvt; 3rd MD Lt Arty; ref: 1, 2, 19, 21, 160, 461, 726
AULTMAN, S.; pvt; 3rd MD Lt Arty; ref: 1, 2, 19, 21, 160, 726
AUSTEN, Dempsey; pvt; Davidson's Co, VA Lt Arty; res: West River, AA Cty; ref: 1, 735, 1539
AXTELL, Frederick S.; ref: 20
AYERS, John; pvt; Davis's MD Cav, Co C; ref: 1
AYRES, Henry; pvt; 13th VA Inf, Co G; ref: 1, 735

BADEN, John H.; pvt; 1st MD Cav, Co B; res: Nottingham, PG Cty; ref: 1, 2, 19, 21, 93, 1553
BADEN, Joseph Abell (M.D.); Asst Surg; Winder Hospital Richmond; res: St. M. Cty; ref: 1, 18, 720, 1509, 1534, 1536, 1670
BADEN, Joseph N.; pvt; Signal Corps; res: Nottingham, PG Co; ref: 1, 19, 1553
BADEN, William A. H.; pvt; 1st MD Cav, Co E; res: PG Co; ref: 1, 2, 19, 21, 730
BAER, Caleb Dorsey (M.D.); Senior Surg; 4th Brig, Forrest Div; res: Middletown, Frd Co; ref: 1, 18, 90
BAILEY, ---; 1st MD; 20, 141
BAILEY, Charles L.; pvt; 35th VA Cav, Co F; ref: 1, 19, 1677
BAILEY, Edward; pvt; 8th VA Inf, Co D; ref: 1, 37
BAILEY, F. M.; Pvt; 3rd MD Lt Arty; ref: 1, 2, 19, 21, 160, 726
BAILEY, Henry; pvt; Lucas' 15th SC Heavy Arty; res: Balt; ref: 1
BAILEY, Henry M.; pvt; 1st MD Inf, Co I; res: Cha Cty; ref: 1, 2, 19, 21
BAILEY, James; pvt; 1st MD Lt Arty; ref: 1, 470
BAILEY, James; pvt; McNeals Rangers; ref: 1, 735
BAILEY, James T.; pvt; 2nd MD Inf, Co B; res: Cha Cty; ref: 1, 2, 19, 21, 1509

BAILEY, John; pvt; 8th VA Inf, Co H; ref: 1, 37
BAILEY, Joseph B.; pvt; Hollbrook's Independent MD Lt Arty; ref: 1, 628
BAILEY, Sydnan; sgt maj; 40th VA Inf, Co H; res: Balt; MLCSH; ref: 1, 21, 92, 93, 627, 700, 786
BAILEY, W. H. C.; 1st VA Inf, Co F; ref: 1, 735
BAILEY, William; pvt; 2nd MD Inf, Co A; res: St. M. Cty; ref: 1, 2, 6, 19, 21, 650, 1509, 1665
BAILEY, William L.; Maj; Q.M., Gen J. E. Johnston's staff; MLCSH; ref: 1, 21, 53, 684, 686, 700, 758, 772, 786, 791
BAIRD, William; Capt; Asst A.G., Gen W. Mahone's staff; res All Cty; ref: 1, 2, 19, 735
BAKER, Alexander; pvt; Hankin's Co, VA Lt Arty; res: Balt; ref: 1, 700
BAKER, Andrew J.; pvt; Stuart's Horse Arty, Brown's Co; res: Mt. Airy, Carr Cty; ref: 1, 20, 23
BAKER, Charles; pvt; Castle Pinkney SC Heavy Arty; ref: 1, 735
BAKER, Charles H.; cpl; 13th VA Inf, Co H; ref: 1, 70
BAKER, Francis; pvt; Lucas' 15th SC Heavy Arty; res: Georgetown; ref: 1
BAKER, Frederick D.; sgt; 2nd MD Cav, Co Co; res: Kt Cty; ref: 1, 2, 19, 21, 23, 1609
BAKER, George E.; pvt; 43rd VA Cav, Co A, Mosby's; res: Hyattstown, Mont Cty; ref: 1, 20, 86
BAKER, George H.; pvt; 2nd MD Cav, Co B; ref: 1
BAKER, George W.; pvt; David's MD Cav, Co A; ref: 1, 735
BAKER, Henry "Dad"; Veterinarian; 4th MD Lt Arty; ref: 1, 2, 19, 21, 23
BAKER, Henry W.; pvt; 1st SC Inf, Co G; res: Balt; ref: 1, 2, 19, 21, 700, 735, 1540
BAKER, J.; pvt; 3rd MD Lt Arty; res: Balt; ref: 1
BAKER, James; pvt; 2nd MD Cav, Co B; ref: 1, 800
BAKER, James W.; Lt; 77th VA Militia, Co C; ref: 1, 68, 93
BAKER, L. H.; pvt; 2nd MD Cav, Co C; ref: 1
BAKER, Lewis; pvt; 1st MD Cav, Co E; res: Balt; ref: 1, 19, 730
BAKER, Newton D. (M.D.); pvt; 1st VA Cav, Co F; res: Wash Cty; ref: 1, 2, 18, 21, 23
BAKER, Page M.; acting Mast. M, Navy, C.S. Simpson; ref: 1, 685, 1564, 1579, 1650
BAKER, Robert T.; pvt; 20th LA Inf, Co D; res How Cty; ref: 1, 10, 19
BAKER, Samuel; pvt; Stuart's Horse Arty, Carter's Battery; res: Royers' Forge, Bt Cty; ref: 1, 70
BAKER, Samuel B.; pvt; 2nd MD Cav, Co D; ref: 1, 19
BAKER, W. W.; smn, Navy; res: Balt; ref: 1
BAKER, William H.; pvt; 1st MD Cav, Co A; res: Annapolis; ref: 1, 19, 1539, 1628
BALDWIN, Columbus W.; pvt; 25th VA Inf Bn, Co D; res: Balt; ref: 1, 44
BALDWIN, Daniel Sheffey; pvt; 15th AR Inf, Co C; res: Carr Cty; ref: 1, 70
BALDWIN, John H.; Lt; 1st VA Inf Bn, Co A; ref: 1, 21, 700
BALDWIN, Joseph A. (M.D.); Surg; General Hospital, Lake City, FL; res: St. M. Cty; ref: 1, 6, 18, 1533, 1662
BALDWIN, Joseph S. (M.D.); pvt; 3rd VA Lt Arty, McClanahan's Battery; res: Bt Cty; ref: 1, 21, 700, 1670
BALDWIN, Thomas S. (M.D.); Physician Medical Corps; ref: 1, 18, 700, 1673
BALDWIN William Buckner; pvt; 26th VA Inf, Co I; res: AA Cty; MLCHS; res: 1, 21, 700, 786
BALDWIN, William Wesley; pvt; 11th KY Cav, Co A; res: Elk Ridge Landing, AA Co; ref: 1, 1539

BALES, J. K.; pvt; 2nd KY Cav, Co E; res: Balt; ref: 1, 21, 93, 700
BALL, Benjamin F. (Revd); cpl; 43rd VA Cav (Mosby's), Co C; res: Wash Cty; ref: 1, 8, 21, 73, 700, 906
BALL, Dabney (Rev.); Chaplain; Richmond hospitals; res: Balt; ref: 1
BALL, Dyonysius; pvt; 2nd MD Inf,Co B; ref: 1, 2, 19, 21, 866
BALL, James; pvt; Lee's MD Cav; ref: 1
BALLARD, Edward W.; pvt;1 Barry's Co, MD Vols; ref: 1, 19
BALLARD, William W.; pvt; 1st MD Lt Arty; res: Cambridge, Dor Cty; ref: 1, 2, 19, 21, 470, 1547
BALLANGER, Benjamin F.; pvt; 35th VA Cav, Co A; res: St. M. Cty; ref: 1, 3, 1611, 1670, 1677
BALLMAN, John M.; pvt; Stuart's Horse Arty, Breathed's Battery; ref: 1, 498
BAMBERGER, H.; pvt; 2nd MD Cav, Co B; ref: 1, 19, 1609
BANAGAN, John S.; pvt, Cav; res: St. M. Cty; ref: 1670
BANDS, James O.; 2nd GA Reserve, Co G; ref: 1, 93
BANGS, Frank C.; sgt; 19th VA Heavy Arty, Co C; ref: 1, 1580
BANK, R. T.; Lt; 20th AR Inf, Co I; res: Balt; ref: 1, 20
BANNER, Charles; pvt; 2nd MD Lt Arty; ref: 1, 2, 19, 21
BARBER, Charles (M.D.); Physician; Medical Corps; res: AA Cty; ref: 18, 20
BARBER, Christopher Columbus; pvt; 1st MD Cav, Co C; res: Chaptico, St. M. Cty; ref: 1, 2, 19, 21, 1555, 1670
BARBER, Ewgnn H.; pvt; 30th TX Cav, Co H; res: Cha Cty; ref: 1, 20, 559, 1511
BARBER, Jacob; pvt; Zarvona's MD Zouaves; ref: 1, 735
BARBER, John Gwinn; sgt; 2nd MD Inf, Co B; res: St. M. Co; ref: 1, 2, 6, 19, 21, 23, 1509, 1627, 1670
BARBER, Joseph W.; Lt; 2nd MD Inf, Co C; res: Millersville, AA Cty; ref: 1, 2, 4, 5, 19, 21, 23, 64, 674, 1523, 1539
BARBER, Leonidas; pvt; Stuart's Horse Arty, Breathed's Battery; ref: 1, 498
BARBOUR, Oscar; pvt; 1st MD Cav, Co C; res: Frd Cty; ref: 1, 2, 19, 21
BARCHUSS, William W.; pvt 4th MD Lt Arty; ref: 1, 2, 19, 21
BARCLAY, A. A. E. W.; acting Mast. M, Navy, C.S.S. Sampson; ref: 1, 735, 1564
BARHARD, Edward; pvt; Davis's MD Cav, Co B; ref: 1, 19, 735
BARKER, John R.; pvt; 1st VA Inf, Co E; ref: 1, 735
BARKER, Robert; pvt; 19th VA Heavy Arty, Co C; res: Balt; ref: 1, 1580; 1613
BARKER, William N.; Lt; 1st VA Inf, Co E; ref: 1, 735
BARKHAUS, H.; pvt; 1st SC Inf, Co G; res: Balt; ref: 1, 735
BARNES, George D.; Color Bearer; 9th VA Inf, Co K; res: Balt; ref: 1, 21, 700
BARNES, J. C.; pvt; 1st MS Lt Arty, Co F; res: Broad Creek, QA Cty; ref: 1, 700, 1554
BARNES, Jacob Smallwood; pvt; 7th VA Cav, Co A; res: Balt; ref: 1, 2, 3, 19, 21, 56, 70, 700, 1579
BARNES, James W.; pvt; 35th VA Cav, Co B; res: How Cty; ref: 1, 10, 1611, 1677
BARNES, John; pvt; 1st MD Cav, Co F; 1, 2, 21
BARNES, John T. M.; Maj; 3rd LA Lt Arty; res: Wash Cty; ref: 1, 2, 19, 21, 23, 56, 70, 700, 735, 791, 1087
BARNES, P.; pvt; 2nd MD Cav, Co C; ref: 1, 19, 1609
BARNES, Richard M.; sgt; 21st VA Inf, Co B; res: Wash Cty; ref: 1, 2, 19, 70, 312, 681, 690, 1520
BARNES, Robert B.; pvt; 3rd MD Lt Arty; ref: 1, 2, 19, 21, 160, 461, 726
BARNES, William; cpl; 1st VA Cav, Co K; ref: 1, 2, 19, 21

BARNETT, Creel; pvt; 2nd MD Cav, Co A; ref: 1, 19, 1609
BARNETT, William H.; pvt; 2nd MD Cav, Co B; res: Balt; ref: 1
BARNETTE, Dudley P.; Capt; 26th VA Inf, Co A; res: Catonsville; ref: 1, 21, 70, 133, 700
BARNEY, Joseph Nicholas; Commander, Navy; C.S.S. Florida; res: Balt; ref: 1, 18, 19, 21, 58, 61, 64, 70, 97, 137, 330, 511, 550, 559, 602, 674, 700, 735, 783, 791, 828, 940, 1338, 1520, 1523, 1564, 1571, 1578, 1581, 1583, 1623, 1673
BARRANGER, Victor C.; Master, Navy; ref: 58
BARRETT, Charles Boyd; sgt; 35th VA Cav, Co A; res: Balt; ref: 1, 1540, 1611, 1677
BARRETT, George F.; pvt; 1st VA Inf, Co E; ref: 1
BARRETT, George Washington; pvt; 3rd VA Inf, Co H; res: Balt; MLCSH; ref: 1, 21, 88, 93, 627, 700, 735, 786
BARRETT, J. H.; pvt; 3rd MD Lt Arty; ref: 1, 2, 19, 21, 160, 726
BARRETT, Joseph S.; pvt; 31 LA Inf, Co C; ref: 1, 735
BARRETT Martin P.; Lt; 13th VA Inf, Co G; ref: 1
BARRETT Samuel H.; pvt; 14th VA Cav, Co G; ref: 1, 735
BARRETT Tristan S.; pvt; 1st NC Inf, Co K; ref: 1, 735
BARRETT, William H.; pvt; Lucas' 15th SC Heavy Arty; ref: 1
BARRICK, William; pvt; 1st MD Cav, Co D; res: Frd Cty; ref: 1, 2, 19, 21, 1601
BARRON, Richard H.; pvt; MD Guerrila Zouaves; res: Bt Co; ref: 1, 1575
BARRON, Thomas D.; sgt; 2nd MD Inf, Co C; res: Balt; ref: 1, 2, 21, 23, 1540
BARRY, Alonzo L.; sgt; 1st NC Lt Arty, Co D; res: Emmittsburg, Frd Cty; ref: 1, 70
BARRY, Arthur R. (M.D.); Surg; 9th VA Inf; res: PG Cty; ref: 1, 18, 69, 316, 735, 951, 1369, 1576, 1622
BARRY Daniel R.; pvt; 1st VA Cav, Co K; res: Balt; ref: 1, 2, 19, 21
BARRY, Edmund; Capt; Barry's MD Vols; ref: 1, 2, 21, 456, 559, 1520, 1523, 1563
BARRY, Hugh C.; pvt; 2nd MD Lt Arty; Emmittsburg, Frd Cty; ref: 1, 2, 19, 21, 70
BARRY, James; pvt; 1st VA Inf, Co E; ref: 1, 735
BARRY, McClintock; pvt; 1st MD Lt Arty; ref: 1, 2, 19, 21
BARRY, Michael; pvt; 2nd MD Inf, Co E; ref: 1, 2, 19, 21
BARRY, Philip; pvt; 2nd MD Inf, Co A; res: Balt; MLCSH; ref: 1, 2, 19, 21, 650, 700, 786
BARRY, William; sgt; Barry's Co, MD Vols; ref: 1, 21
BARRY, William D.; pvt; 1st MD Cav, Co B; res: PG Co; ref: 1, 2, 19, 21, 785
BARRY, William J. (M.D.); Surg; Conscript Service 10th Congressional District, TN; res: Balt; MLCSH; ref: 1, 18, 21, 700, 735, 786, 791, 1534, 1536
BARTGIA, Martin L.; res: Frederick, Frd Cty; ref: 89
BARTHOLOMEW, Thomas Jefferson; cpl; 7th TN Inf, Co C; res: Balt; MLCSH; ref: 1, 21, 92, 93, 627, 700, 786
BARTON, Bolling W. (M.D.); Lt; 1st Foreign Bn, Co D; res: Pikesville, Bt Co; ref: 1, 21, 107, 700, 1533
BARTON, Green H.; sgt; 1st MD Inf, Co E; ref: 1, 2, 19, 21, 23
BARTON, Randolph J.; Maj; Asst A.G.; 33rd VA Inf; res Pikesville, Bt Co; ref: 1, 19, 21, 23, 44, 56, 70, 105, 145, 700, 791, 913, 1277, 1295, 1633
BASFORD, George W.; pvt; 1st MD Lt Arty; ref: 1, 2, 19, 21, 700
BASIL Manly Walker (D.D.S.); 8th AL Inf, Co K; res Balt; ref: 1689
BASIL, James; pvt; 10th AL Inf Bn, Co A; res: Cal Cty; ref: 1, 746

BASKIN, C. N.; pvt; Davis's MD Cav, Co A; ref: 1
BASKIN, John; pvt; Davis's MD Cav, Co A; ref: 1
BASTABLE, A. N.; pvt; AR Inf, Co A; res: Balt; ref: 1, 700
BATEMAN, Howard; pvt; 1st MD Cav, Co C; ref: 1, 2, 19, 21
BATES, Frank; pvt; Zarvona's MD Zouaves; ref: 1, 735, 1574
BATES, George; cpl; 1st Md Inf, Co B; ref: 1, 2, 19, 21, 23, 1509
BATES, Julius E.; pvt; Stuart's Horse Arty, Breathed's Battery; ref: 1
BATESWORTH, O. F.; pvt; 1st MD Lt Arty; ref: 1, 93
BATH, ---; res: St. M. Cty; ref: 6
BATT, Moses; pvt; 7th VA Cav, Co G; ref: 1
BATTE, Robert; pvt; Davis's MD Cav, Co C; ref: 1
BATTEN, Samuel; pvt; 3rd VA Inf, Co F; res: Balt; ref: 1, 1540
BATTERY, J. C.; pvt; MD Guerrilla Zuaves; ref: 1
BATTLE, John Moore; Lt; 1st AL Heavy Arty, Co D; res: Mont Cty; ref: 1, 20, 791, 1564
BATTLE, Romulus Riggs; Lt; 63rd AL Inf, Co K; res: Mont Cty; ref: 1, 20
BAUGHER, Isaac A.; pvt; 7th VA Cav, Co G; res: Frd Cty; ref: 1, 88
BAUGHMAN, Louis Victor; pvt; 1st MD Cav, Co D; res: Frederick, Frd Cty; ref: 1, 2, 19, 21, 23, 64, 66, 67, 67, 70, 72, 90, 643, 798, 1573, 1601
BAUGHMAN, William; pvt; 6th KY Cav, Co A; res: Frederick, Frd Cty; ref: 1, 64, 89
BAULDEN, Daniel; pvt; Davis's MD Cav, Co B; ref: 1, 19
BAULER, D. W.; pvt; 34th VA Inf, Co G; ref: 1, 20
BAXLEY, William G. D.; pvt; 2nd MD Inf, Co A; res: How Cty; ref: 1, 2, 19, 21, 23, 93, 259, 650
BAXTER, George O.; pvt; Cooper's Battery, VA Lt Arty; res: Balt; ref: 1, 21, 93, 700
BAXTER, T. W.; Lt; 15th TX Inf, Co D; ref: 1, 21, 119, 700
BAXTER, William; res: Henry; pvt; 17th VA Inf, Co E; res: Woodsboro, Frd Cty; MLCSH; ref: 1, 700, 786
BAYLEY, Charles B.; pvt; Jacob's Mounted Riflemen; res: Balt; ref: 1, 1540
BAYLEY, James P.; pvt; 21st VA Inf, Co H; res: Balt; ref: 1, 2, 312, 690
BAYLEY, William H. C.; pvt; Jacob's Mounted Riflemen; res: Balt; ref: 1, 1540
BAYLOR, H. B.; res: Cumbarland, All Cty; ref: 919, 924
BAYLOR, R. B.; pvt; 6th VA Inf, Co G; res: Balt; ref: 1, 21, 700
BAYLY, Alexander Hamilton; sgt; 4th VA Lt Arty; res: Cambridge, Dor Co; ref: 1, 20, 70, 112, 685, 1579
BAYLY, James P.; Capt 2nd MD Cav, Co B; res: Mont Cty; ref: 1, 11, 19, 21, 233, 614, 693, 700, 1540, 1560, 1562, 1565, 1609, 1631
BAYNE, William H.; sgt; Halbrook's Independent MD ARTY; ref: 2, 19, 21, 700
BEAL, Albert S.; pvt; 9th VA Cav, Co C; res: St. M. Cty; ref: 1670
BEALE, G.S.; pvt; 28th GA Inf, Co C; res: Balt; ref: 1, 7
BEALE, James Shields (M.D.); pvt; 1st MD Lt Arty; ref: 1, 2, 18, 19, 21, 316
BEALE, L. W.; cpl; 3rd VA Inf, Co D; ref: 1, 21, 700
BEALE, Nathaniel L.; pvt; 9th VA Inf, Co B; ref: 1, 1576
BEALE, Robert; pvt; 2nd MD Inf; res: St. M. Cty; ref: 1, 2, 19, 21, 1509
BEALE, Solomon W.; pvt; 9th VA Inf, Co B; ref: 1, 1576
BEALE, Terry; pvt; 9th VA Inf, Co B; ref: 1, 1575, 1576
BEALL, Alexander; pvt; 1st MD Cav; res: St. M.Co; ref: 1, 2, 7, 19, 21, 785

BEALL, Edward Sinclair; sgt maj; 13th VA Lt Arty, Co H; res: Balt; ref: 1, 2, 21, 70, 272, 700
BEALL, Henry D.; pvt; 12th VA Cav, Co B; res: Balt; ref: 1, 21, 36, 255, 700
BEALL, J. W.; fmn, Navy; Naval Brigade; res: Balt; ref: 1
BEALL, Lemuel Thomas; pvt; 35th VA Cav, Co B; res: Licksville, Frd Cty; ref: 1, 3, 19, 90, 1611, 1677
BEALL, Lloyd; pvt; Stuart's Horse Arty, Breathed's Battery; ref: 1, 498
BEALL, Lloyd James; Col, Marine Corps; res: Georgetown; ref: 1, 18, 19, 58, 61, 97, 431, 674, 735, 787, 791, 792, 1349, 1492, 1495, 1500, 1501, 1515, 1564, 1593, 1594
BEALL, Richard M.; sgt; 35th VA Cav, Co B; ref: 1, 1611, 1677
BEALL, Robert; pvt; 2nd MD Inf, Co B; res: St. M. Cty; ref: 1, 2, 6, 19, 21
BEALL, Thomas Balch; Maj; Asst Q.M., Gen J. R. Chalmer's staff; res: Balt; ref: 1, 4, 23, 70, 1368
BEALL, William B.; pvt; 2nd MD Cav, Co F; ref: 1, 2, 11, 19, 21
BEALL, William Cyrus; pvt; 4th TN Inf Co; res: Silversburg, Wash Cty; ref: 1, 90, 1558
BEALL, Willis; pvt; 51st GA Inf, Co C; res: How Cty; ref: 1, 7, 10, 19, 20, 23
BEALL, Zabedee; pvt; 1st MS Cav, Co C; res: Ellicott City, How Cty; ref: 1, 435
BEALMEAR, Claudius; res: Patuxent Forge, AA Cty; ref: 1539
BEAN, Elwood M.; Maj; Bean's Bn, Texas Reserve Corps; res: Wash Cty; ref: 1, 361, 791
BEAN, Elwood; pvt; 5th TX Inf, Co G; ref: 1, 735
BEAN, Hezekiah Henry (M.D.); Lt; 1st MD Inf, Co I; res: Cha Cty; MLCSH; ref: 1, 2, 18, 19, 21, 64, 93, 456, 559, 627, 684, 700, 786, 791, 1511, 1519, 1662
BEAN, James Baxter (D.D.S.); Lt; Dental Corps, Receiving & Way Hospital Richmond; res: Balt; ref: 1, 18, 1529, 1688, 1689
BEAN, Joseph A.; sgt; 2nd MD Lt Arty; res: Great Mills, St. M. Cty; ref: 1, 2, 6, 19, 21, 23, 64, 1509, 1520, 1555, 1627
BEAN, Thomas L.; pvt; 13th VA Inf, Co G; res: St. M. Cty; ref: 1, 2, 6, 19, 21, 57, 70, 785, 1509, 1670
BEAN, William Bennett; Lt; 2nd MD Lt Arty; res: St. Gregors, St. M. Cty; ref: 1, 2, 6, 7, 19, 21, 23, 64, 68, 70, 700, 1509, 1523, 1555
BEAN, William N.; pvt; 1st MD Cav, Co B; res: St. M. Cty; ref: 1, 2, 6, 19, 21, 785, 1690
BEANE, Martin; pvt; 2nd MD Lt Arty; ref: 1, 2, 21
BEAR, Frank Alexander (M.D.); Asst Surg; VA State Line; res: Uniontown, Carr Cty; ref: 1, 18, 40, 806, 1534, 1690
BEARD, Henry; pvt; Lee's MD Cav; ref: 1, 19, 1609
BEARD, Robert Hooper; pvt; Stuart's Horse Arty, Breathed's Battery; ref: 1
BEASLEY, Beverly C.; pvt; 47th VA Inf, Co H; ref: 1
BEASLEY, D.; pvt; 3rd MD Lt Arty; ref: 1, 2, 19, 21, 160, 461, 726
BEASLEY, Joseph; pvt; 3rd MD Lt Arty; ref: 1, 2, 19, 21, 160, 726
BEASLEY, William F.; Lt Col; Anderson's NC Bn; res: Balt; ref: 1, 21, 56, 134, 700
BEASTIN, George M.; smn, Navy; res: Locust Grove, Kt Cty; ref: 1, 2, 19, 21, 700, 783, 1584
BEATTY, Edward W.; Lt; 1st MD Cav, Co A; res: Balt; ref: 1, 2, 19, 21, 23, 50, 64, 68, 86, 240, 559, 791, 1251, 1511, 1577, 1634
BEATY, C.L.; Capt; ref: 1690
BECHTOL, Fred F.; pvt; MD Guerrilla Zouaves; ref: 1
BECK, Samuel (M.D.); Asst Surg; Dept of Henrico, Richmond; res:

Hainesville, Kt Co; ref: 1, 18, 1584, 1690
BECKETT, John M.; pvt; 1st MD Cav, Co A; res: Wash Cty; ref: 1, 2, 19, 21
BECKHAM, Henry; pvt; Davis's MD Cav, Co C; ref: 1
BECKHAM, James M.; pvt; 19th VA Heavy Arty, Co C; ref: 1, 1580
BECKLEY, Laurence S.; res: Frederick, Frd Cty; ref: 89
BECKNELL, Frederick; pvt; 1st MD Inf,Co F; ref: 1, 2, 19, 21
BEHAN, Joseph; pvt; Lee's Balt Lt Arty, Alexander's Bn; ref: 1
BEHELER, S. A.; pvt; 1st VA Inf, Co E; Mont Cty; ref: 1
BEHRENS, Barney; pvt; 1st MD Inf, Co F; ref: 1, 2, 19, 21
BEIRS, H. H.; pvt; 35th VA Cav, Co B; ref: 1, 1611, 1677
BELL, Alexander T. (M.D.); Surg; Stuart's Horse Arty; res: Balt; MLCSH; ref: 1, 18, 21, 56, 57, 513, 700, 786, 891, 916, 1091, 1533, 1534
BELL, Daniel; pvt; 1st MD Inf, Co E; ref: 1, 19
BELL, Douglas; pvt; 6th VA Inf, Co G; res: Balt; ref: 1, 21, 700
BELL, Henry C.; pvt; 1st MD Cav, Co A; res: Hagerstown, Wash Cty; ref: 1, 2, 19, 21, 74, 361, 612, 1540
BELL, Jesse T.; pvt; 7th VA Cav, Co C; res: Cumberland, All Cty; ref: 1
BELL, Richard; pvt; Edelin's MD Heavy Arty; res: Princeland, AA Cty; ref: 1, 1539
BELL, S.; pvt; Lucas' 15th SC Heavy Arty; ref: 1, 735
BELL, Samuel; pvt; 2nd MD Inf, Co G; ref: 1, 2, 19, 21
BELL, Walter; pvt; Holbroo's Independent MD Lt Arty; ref: 1
BELL, William; smn, Navy; res: Balt; ref: 1
BELL, William; pvt; 3rd MD Lt Arty; ref: 1, 2, 19, 21, 160, 726
BELLESON, William K.; pvt; 2nd MD Cav, Co E; res: Balt; ref: 1, 19, 1609
BELLIS, William H.; res: Annapolis, AA Cty; ref: 1539
BELLUM, ---; pvt; Letcker's Lt Arty Battery; ref: 735
BELT, Afford Campbell; pvt; 57th VA av,Co K; Frd Cty; ref: 1, 72
BELTON, Patrick; pvt; 38th VA Lt Arty, Co C; res: Balt; MLCSH; ref: 1, 21, 700, 786
BELVIN, James W.; (M.D.); Asst Surg, Navy; C.S.S. Hampton; ref: 1, 18, 19, 58, 59, 97, 279, 1564
BENCHE, John H.; pvt; 43rd VA Cav, Co G, Mosby's; res: Balt; ref: 1, 8, 1677
BENDER, Edward; res: Frd Cty; ref: 89
BENDER, Francis T.; cpl; 1st MD Inf, Co A; res: Frd Cty; ref: 1, 2, 19, 21, 23, 89, 90
BENEFIELD, Robert; pvt; 2nd MD Inf, Co B; ref: 1
BENENT, William Francis; pvt; 2nd MD Inf, Co F; res: Oxon Hill, PG Cty; ref: 1, 2, 21, 69
BENNETT, Eduard; pvt; 1st MD Inf, Co E; res: Balt; ref: 1, 2, 19, 21
BENNETT, Edward W., Jr; pvt; 1st MD Inf, Co E; res: Balt; ref: 1, 21, 700
BENNETT, J. H.; pvt; 5th KY Cav, Co B; ref: 1, 898
BENNETT, James; pvt; Lee's MD Cav; ref: 1
BENNETT, John H.; pvt; 19th VA Heavy Arty, Co C; res: Princess Ann, Som Cty; ref: 1, 1556, 1580, 1684
BENNETT, John W.; Capt, Navy; C.S.S. Nashville; res: Sykesville, Carr Cty; ref: 1, 19, 21, 23, 58, 61, 70, 97, 279, 594, 645, 700, 735, 783, 791, 946, 975, 999, 1152, 1564, 1577
BENNETT, Livingston Orrich; pvt; Stuart's Horse Arty, Breathed's Battery; res: Balt; ref: 1, 21, 52, 56, 57, 498, 700

BENNETT, Thomas J.; pvt; 34th NC Inf, Co C; res: Balt; ref: 1, 21, 700
BENNETT, William; pvt; 2nd MD Cav, Co F; res: Princeland, AA Cty; ref: 1, 19, 1539
BENNETT, William B.; pvt; 3rd MD Lt Arty; ref: 1, 2, 19, 21, 160, 726
BENNETT, William H.; pvt; 2nd MD Cav, Co A; res: Balt; ref: 1, 19, 1609
BENNETT, William I.; pvt; 35th VA Cav, Co A; res: Frd Cty; ref: 1, 72
BENNETT, William V.; pvt; Stuart's Horse Arty, Breathed's Battery; ref: 1, 498
BENNING, James W.; pvt; 28th GA Inf, Co E; res: Princeland, AA Cty; ref: 1, 1539
BENNING, William T.; pvt; 9th KY, Co D; ref: 1, 55
BENSON, Amos; pvt; 4th VA Cav; res: Bt Cty; ref: 1, 735, 929
BENSON, Samuel M.; pvt; 1st LA, Co G; res: AA Co; ref: 1, 735, 1539
BENTHALL, Robert; Mast. M, Navy; C.S.S. Virginia; res: Balt; ref: 1, 19, 58, 97, 1523, 1564
BENTHALL, Thomas W.; Lt, Navy; C.S.S. Jamestown; ref: 19, 58, 97, 279, 1564
BENTON, Amos; pvt; 4th VA Cav, Co A; ref: 1, 70
BENTON, Henry; pvt; Md Guerrilla Zouaves; ref: 1
BENTON, Hugh; pvt; 1st SC Inf, Co G; ref: 1
BENTON, John; pvt; 3rd MD Lt Arty; ref: 1, 2, 19, 21, 160, 726
BENTZ, William T.; pvt; 7th VA Cav, Co C; ref: 1
BENVIL, John; pvt; Calhoun Battery, SC Lt Arty, Calhoun Battery; res: Weathretsville; ref: 1
BERG, John; pvt; 3rd MD Lt Arty; Tal Cty; ref: 1, 2, 19, 21, 160, 726
BERGER, Joseph W.; pvt; 13th VA Inf, Co G; res: Balt; ref: 1, 2, 21, 559
BERNARD, William R.; 10th VA Cav, Co B; ref: 1, 70
BERNAUGH, G. D.; pvt; 1st VA Inf, Co E; ref: 1, 735
BERNER, August; pvt; 1st MD Cav, Co F; ref: 1, 2, 19, 21
BERNIER, Joseph; cpl; MD Guerilla Zouaves; ref: 1
BERRETT, Joseph W.; pvt; 12th VA Inf, Co B; Sykesville, Carr Cty; ref: 1, 19, 20, 23
BERRITT J. T.; pvt; 2nd MD Cav, Co F; ref: 1, 2, 19, 21, 1609
BERRY, Alexander C.; smn, Navy; C.S. Roanoke; res: Balt; ref: 1, 19, 21, 700, 783
BERRY Enock R.; pvt; 1st MD Lt Arty; ref: 1, 2, 19, 21
BERRY, George W.; Lt; 15th VA Inf, Co H; res: Balt; MLCSH; ref: 1, 21, 93, 700, 786
BERRY, John B. N.; pvt; 22nd TX Cav, Co A; res: Georgetown; ref: 1, 631
BERRY, John P.; pvt; 1st MD Inf, Co C; res: Balt; ref: 1, 2, 19, 21
BERRY, John R.; pvt; 1st MD Inf, Co C; res: Tal Cty; ref: 1, 2, 21
BERRY, M; pvt; 2nd MD Inf, Co E; ref: 1, 93
BERRY, Michael; pvt; 19th VA Heavy Arty, Co C; ref: 1, 1580
BERRY T; pvt; 2nd KY Cav, Co D; ref: 1, 559, 1511
BERRY, Thomas B.; cpl; Gray's VA Cav, Co F; Piscataway, PG Cty; ref: 1, 69, 316
BERRY, Thomas S.; pvt; 1st MD Inf, Co D; ref: 1, 2, 19, 21
BERRY, W. H.; sgt; 30th VA Inf,Co B; res: Balt; ref: 1, 21, 57, 700
BERRY, William; pvt; 1690
BERRYMAN, Frank C.; pvt; 43rd VA Cav, Co A, Mosby's; ref: 1, 8
BERRYMAN, John B.; sgt; 1st MD Inf,Co C; res: Balt; ref: 1, 2, 19, 21, 23, 38, 44, 64, 503, 690, 700, 789, 1519, 1523
BESANT, James; res: Point of Rocks, Frd Cty; ref: 643
BESANT, William T.; pvt; 35th VA Cav, Co B; res: Point of Rocks; ref: 1, 3, 19, 21, 90, 615, 643, 700, 1677

BESSELIEU, Thomas E. (D.D.S.); sgt;
BEST, Emory F.; Lt Col; 23rd GA Inf; ref: 1, 735, 791, 1578, 1600
BEST, H. S.; sgt; 23rd GA Inf, Co H; res: Balt; ref: 1, 21, 700, 735
BEST, J. W. F. (M.D.); Surg; 40th GA Inf; res: AA Cty; ref: 1, 18
BEST, Richard; pvt; 43rd VA Cav, Co D, Mosby's; ref: 8
BESTOR, John Rollin; pvt; 21st VA Inf, Co B; res: Balt; ref: 1, 2, 19, 21, 312, 700, 735, 1540, 1593
BETTS, Samuel C.; pvt; 1st VA Cav, Co K; res: Woodbine, Carr Cty; ref: 1, 2, 19, 80, 90
BEUCKE, Charles L.; pvt; 2nd MD Lt Arty; res: Balt; ref: 1, 19, 21, 700
BEUNEFIELD, Daniel; pvt; Davis's MD Cav, Co C; ref: 1
BEVERIDGE, David; pvt; 9th VA Inf, Co B; res: Balt; ref: 1, 1576, 1598
BEVERLY, N. M.; pvt; 3rd MD Lt Arty; ref: 1, 2, 19, 21, 160, 461, 726
BEYER, Adam; pvt; 1st MD Inf, Co F; ref: 1, 2, 19, 21
BIAS, Philip; pvt; 2nd MD Cav, Co C; 1, 693
BIAYS, George; pvt; 1st MD Cav, Co C; 1, 2, 19, 21, 23, 700
BIAYS, P. A.; pvt; 2nd MD Cav, Co D; res: Balt; ref: 1, 19, 1609
BICKSLER, John F.; pvt; 35th VA Cav, Co A; ref: 1, 3, 15, 1677
BIDDLE, Benjamin S.; pvt; 1st MD Cav, Co F; ref: 1, 19
BIEDLER, Andrew J.; Capt; Signal Officer, Gen C. Lee's staff; res: Balt; ref: 1, 8, 23, 735
BIEDLER, Charles E.; pvt; 43rd VA Cav, Co C, Mosby's; res: Balt; ref: 1, 8, 23, 57, 513, 1382, 1613
BIEDLER, W. T.; sgt; 43rd VA Cav, Co C, Mosby's; res: Balt; ref: 1, 8, 23
BIER, George Henry; Lt, Navy; C.S.S. Chicora; ref: 1, 19, 20, 58, 61, 97, 279, 782, 1564
BIGGER, John; pvt; 1st VA Cav, Co K; ref: 1, 2, 19
BIGGS, Benjamin J.; pvt; 2nd MD, Co C; res: Patuxent Forge, AA Cty; ref: 1, 19, 1539, 1609
BILLINGS, ---; Lt; 2nd MD Cav, Co D; ref: 1, 2, 19, 21, 791
BILLOPP, Christopher; pvt; 1st MD Cav, Co C; res: Balt; ref: 1, 2, 19, 21, 700
BILLOP, Thomas F.; Capt; 29th GA Inf, Co A; ref: 1, 2, 19, 21, 700
BIRCH, J. A.; pvt; 1st MD Cav, Co B; res: St. M. Cty; ref: 1, 2, 6, 19, 21
BIRCH, James H.; pvt; 2nd KY Inf, Co K; ref: 1, 21, 700
BIRCH, Joseph E.; pvt; 1st VA Inf, Co E; ref: 1, 735
BIRCKHEAD, Oliver; pvt; 2nd VA Inf, Co D; res: Owensville, AA Cty; ref: 1, 93, 700, 1539
BIRD, Charles DuPont; pvt; 12th VA Inf, Co C; res: Balt; MLCSH; ref: 1, 92, 93, 786, 1511
BIRD, Charles E.; pvt; 1st MD Inf,Co D; res: Cal Cty; ref: 1, 2, 19, 21, 559
BIRD, Spottswood; pvt; 24th VA Cav, Co F; res: Balt; ref: 1, 57, 495, 513, 916, 994, 1287
BIRD, William Edgewater; Maj; 15th GA Inf; res: Balt; ref: 1, 70, 791
BIRDWELL, D. J.; pvt; 3rd MD Lt Arty; ref: 1, 2, 19, 21, 160, 726
BIRELY, Francis Dorsey Howard; ref: 72
BIRMINGHAM, Frank; pvt; 19th VA Heavy Arty, Co C; ref: 1, 1580
BIRMINGHAM, James; pvt; 1st LA Inf, Co L; ref: 1, 735
BISER, Charles Tilghman; Capt; 2nd MS Cav, Co A; res: Barkettsville, Frd Co; ref: 1, 72, 90, 791
BISER, William Doddrige; Lt; Adj, 2nd MS Cav, Co C; res: Burkettsville, Frd Co; ref: 1, 72, 90
BISHOP, Charles E.; Capt; Davis's MD Cav, Co B; ref: 1, 19, 72, 1609
BISHOP, Elijah; cpl; 25th VA Cav, Co I; res: Bt Cty; ref: 1, 1578

BISHOP, George W.; sgt maj; Lee's MD Cav; res: Balt; ref: 1, 2, 8, 19, 21, 700, 1540
BISPHAM, Stacy B.; sgt; 43rd VA Cav, Co D, Mosby's; res: Balt; ref: 1, 8, 21, 56, 700, 1579
BITCHEL, Frederick F.; pvt; 1st MD Cav, Co F; ref: 1, 2, 19, 21
BITZER, George W.; pvt; 6th VA Cav, Co A; res: Frederick, Frd Cty; ref: 1, 90, 133
BIVAN, John William; pvt; 27th TX Cav, Co I; res: Friendship, AA Co; ref: 1, 1539
BIVEN, William F.; pvt; 1st MD Inf, Co I; res: Cha Cty; ref: 1, 2, 19, 21
BIVEN, Zachariah; pvt; 1st MD Inf, Co I; ref: 1, 2, 19, 21
BIXLEY, J. D.; ref: 92
BLACK, Harry C.; pvt; 17th VA Inf, Co E; Cumberland, All Cty; ref: 1, 9, 19, 65, 95, 148, 1636
BLACK, William J.; pvt; MD Guerrilla Zouaves; ref: 1
BLACKBURN, William; pvt; 3rd MD Lt Arty; ref: 1, 2, 19, 21, 160, 726
BLACKFORD, Eugene; Maj; 5th AL Inf; res: Pikesville, Bt Cty; ref: 1, 23, 44, 70, 126, 127, 280, 385, 468, 684, 699, 791, 1486, 1600
BLACKFORD, John C.; pvt; 2nd MD Cav, Co A; ref: 1, 19
BLACKFORD, William H.; sgt; 2 VA Inf, Co G; res: Bt Cty; ref: 1, 11, 70, 88, 113
BLACKISTON, Henry Curtis; Lt; 1st MD Cav, Co B; res: Sassafras, Kt Cty; ref: 1, 2, 7, 11, 19, 21, 23, 45, 68, 107, 240, 496, 501, 511, 668, 748, 785, 1523, 1560, 1562, 1584, 1609, 1634
BLACKISTONE, George W.; pvt; 1st MD Inf, Co H; res: Chaptico, St. M. Cty; ref: 1, 2, 19, 21, 38, 511, 650, 1555
BLACKISTONE, Samuel Hepbron; pvt; 1st MD Cav, Co B; res: Sassafras, Kt Cty; ref: 1, 2, 19, 21, 511, 612, 700, 785, 1584
BLACKISTONE, Thomas; Capt; Zarvona's MD Zouaves; res: St. M. Cty; ref: 1, 6, 19, 486, 511, 1509, 1520, 1627, 1662
BLACKISTONE, Wellington; sgt; MD American Rifles; res: St. M. Cty; ref: 1, 6, 511, 1509
BLACKISTONE, William J.; sgt; 2nd MD Inf, Co A; ref: 1, 2, 19, 21, 511, 1520
BLACKISTONE, William Thomas; pvt; 1st MD Inf, Co H; res: St. M. Cty; ref: 1, 2, 6, 19, 21, 259, 511, 650, 1520
BLACKWELL Elen; pvt; Lucas' 15th SC Heavy Arty; ref: 1, 19
BLACKWELL, Henry L.; pvt; 7th VA Inf, Co I; res: Balt; ref: 1, 70
BLACKWOOD, John G.; Lt, Navy; C.S. Pickens; ref: 19, 58, 97, 279, 1564
BLAIR, Charles H.; pvt; 51st VA Inf, Co A; res: Cumberland, All Cty; ref 1, 9, 65, 148
BLAIR, Charles W.; Lt; 19th VA Heavy Arty, Co C; ref: 1, 2, 19, 21, 23, 64, 456, 1580
BLAIR, N.; pvt; 1st VA Inf, Co E; ref: 1
BLAKE, Francis T.; pvt; 1st MD Inf, Co E; res: Balt; ref: 1, 2, 21, 700, 906
BLAKE, James; pvt; 1st SC Inf, Co G; ref: 1, 735
BLAKE, John; pvt; 1st MD Inf, Co F; res: Balt; ref: 1, 2, 19, 21
BLAKE, Llewellyn A.; pvt; 1st VA Cav, Co E; res: Balt; MLCSH; ref: 1, 786
BLAKELY, William H.; pvt; 1st VA Cav, Co K; ref: 1, 2, 19
BLAKESLEE, Charles E.; pvt; 3rd MD Lt Arty; ref: 1, 2, 19, 21, 160, 726
BLANCHARD, Harris Chamberlaine; sgt; 43rd VA Cav (Mosby's), Arty Co; res: Bt Cty; MLCSH; ref: 8, 20, 601, 627, 700, 786, 1571, 1578, 1579, 1654
BLANCHARD, Wyatt; smn, Navy; res: Balt; ref: 1, 1540
BLAND, John (D.D.S.); Capt; Dental Corps; ref: 1, 18, 19, 1690

BLANFORD, Samuel H.; pvt; 21st VA Inf, Co B; res: Balt; ref: 1, 2, 19, 312, 681, 1540
BLANKNER, Frederick; pvt; 1st VA Inf, Co C; ref: 1, 70
BLEDSOE, Powhatan (M.D.); Asst Surg; 32nd VA Inf; ref: 1, 18, 1534, 1690
BLENNDON, Robert M.; cpl; ref: 700
BLESSING, John P.; pvt; 23rd Bn GA Lt Arty, Co E; res: Jefferson, Frd Cty; ref: 1, 361, 1573
BLOCK, Meyer J.; sgt; MO Border Guard; res: Balt; ref: 2, 21, 57, 513, 700, 891, 916
BLOCK, Solomon; pvt; 48th AL Militia, Co H; res: Balt; ref: 1, 1540
BLOCKER, Albert B.; pvt; 2nd MD Cav, Co A; res: Balt; ref: 1, 19, 1609
BLODGET, William (M.D.); pvt; Davis's MD Cav, Co A; ref: 1, 18, 735, 791
BLOOM, Fritz; pvt; 9th VA Inf, Co B; ref: 1, 1576, 1598
BLOUNT, Ringold; pvt; 9th FL Inf, Co B; res: Johnsons Store, AA Cty; ref: 1, 1539
BLUMENAUR, John of N.; res: Frederick, Frd Cty; ref: 89, 90, 643
BLUMENAUR, John N.; pvt; 2nd MD Inf, Co Co; res: Balt; ref: 1, 2, 21, 470, 700, 1523
BLUMENAUR, Michael; pvt; 1st MD Lt Arty; res: Frederick; MLCSH; ref: 1, 2, 19, 20, 21, 89, 90, 92, 93, 470, 700, 786
BLUMERAIN, John W.; pvt; 2nd MD Inf, Co F; res: Frederick, Frd Cty; ref: 1, 19
BLUNDON, Robert Montague; cpl; Cadet VMI; res: Balt; ref: 20, 21, 93, 469, 1520, 1687
BLUNT, Isaac James; cpl; 4th MD Lt Arty; Tal Co; ref: 1, 2, 19, 21, 23, 645
BLUNT, Mason M.; sgt; 14th NC Inf, Co E; ref: 1, 735
BLUNT, Robert; pvt; 1st MD Inf, Co G; ref: 1, 2, 19, 21, 700
BLUNT, S. M.; pvt; Stuart's Horse Arty, Breathed's Battery; ref: 1
BLYTHE, A.; pvt; 1st SC Inf, Co G; ref: 1
BOANNAN, Albert J.; pvt; 2nd MD Inf, Co C; ref: 1
BOARMAN, Jerome N.; pvt; 1st MD Cav Co B; res: Cha Cty; ref: 1, 2, 19, 21, 69, 316, 785
BOARMAN, Richard T.; pvt; 1st MD Lt Arty; res: Cha Cty; MLCSH; ref: 1, 2, 19, 21, 700, 786
BOBETH, Charles; pvt; 1st MD Inf, Co A; ref: 1, 2, 19, 21
BODELL, George M.; pvt; 2nd MD Cav, Co C; ref: 1
BODELL, John (Revd.); Chaplain; 7th VA Inf; res: Georgetown; ref: 1, 69, 1492
BOGGS, Gus; pvt; McNeil's Rangers; ref: 1, 504
BOGGS, J. H.; pvt; 1st SC Inf, Co G; ref: 1
BOGUE, Francis; pvt; Lee's MD Cav; ref: 1, 19
BOHRER, C.; pvt; 43rd VA Cav (Mosby's), Co C; res: Georgetown; ref: 1, 8, 261
BOLAND, S. G.; pvt; 1st MD Lt Arty; ref: 1, 2, 21, 34
BOLAND, William F.; pvt; 35th VA Cav, Co C; res: Unionville, Frd Cty; ref: 1, 19, 20, 86, 90, 557, 1677
BOLDEN, Daniel; pvt; Davis's MD Cav; ref: 1, 19, 735
BOLLING, John Minge; pvt; 43rd VA Cav (Mosby's), Co D; ref: Cha Cty; ref: 1, 2, 19, 21, 35, 44, 650, 690, 1578
BOLLING, Robert; MD Guerrilla Zouaves; res: Balt; ref: 1, 20, 35, 70
BOLLING, Thomas B.; pvt; 2nd MD Inf, Co A; ref: 1, 2, 21
BOLLING, William D.; pvt; 35th VA Cav, Co C; res: Germantown, Mont Cty; ref: 1, 3, 1574
BOLLING, William Nickolls; pvt; 43rd VA Cav (Mosby's), Co E; res: Mont Cty; ref: 1,8, 20, 70, 1622

BOLLINGER, Frank W.; cpl; 1st MD Lt Arty; ref: 1, 2, 19, 23, 34, 412
BOLTON, John H.; pvt
BOMAN, Joseph M.; pvt; 1st MD Cav, Co B; ref: 2, 19, 21, 1510
BOND, Arthur W.; sgt Maj; 1st MD Cav; res: AA Cty; ref: 1, 2, 5, 19, 21, 56, 68, 511, 700, 881, 1361
BOND, Benjamin F.; pvt; 2nd MD Inf, Co A; res: Bt Cty; ref: 1, 2, 4, 5, 19, 21, 23, 56, 511, 650, 700, 746
BOND, Beverly W. (Revd); pvt; 2nd MD Cav; ref: 70
BOND, Frank A.; Capt; Asst A.G., Gen C. Liventhrope's staff; res: AA Cty; ref: 1, 2, 4, 5, 10, 18, 19, 21, 23, 64, 68, 88, 93, 240, 445, 456 457, 462, 486, 493, 511, 631, 638, 684, 685, 700, 791, 881, 887, 904, 1001, 1007, 1037, 1096, 1108, 1288, 1321, 1487, 1519, 1523, 1620, 1634
BOND, Frank E.; sgt; 17th TX Inf, Co B; res: Balt; ref: 1, 21, 70, 119, 511, 700, 1540
BOND, George E.; pvt; 1st KY Cav, Co A; res: Balt; ref: 1, 1540
BOND, H.; pvt; 1st MD Cav, Co A; ref: 1, 2, 19, 21, 511
BOND, J. W.; pvt; 1st MD Cav, Co B; res: Bel Air, Har Cty; ref: 1, 2, 21, 511, 785
BOND, James Oliver; pvt; 2nd MD Inf, Co B; res: Great Mills, St. M. Cty; ref: 1, 2, 6, 19, 21, 511, 1509, 1555
BOND, John J.; pvt; 1st MD Inf, Co H; Cal Cty; ref: 1, 2, 19, 21, 511, 650, 746, 1663
BOND, John Thomas of John; pvt; 1st MD Inf, Co H; res: Cal Cty; ref: 1, 19, 650, 1542, 1579, 1663
BOND, Samuel G.; Lt; 1st MD Cav, Co F; ref: 1, 2, 19, 21, 23, 511, 1634
BOND, Wesley W.; pvt; 1st MD Cav, Co A; res: St. M. Cty; ref: 1, 2, 19, 21, 511, 1509, 1634
BOND, William; pvt; 2nd MD Cav, Co A; res: How Cty; ref: 1, 10, 19, 511
BONE, Hugh Phillips (DDS); Surg; ref: 1690
BONE, James; pvt; 10th MS Cav, Co A; res: Balt; ref: 1, 1540
BONIC, Rufus; pvt; Barry's Co, MD Vols; ref: 1, 19
BONN, Henry H.; sgt; 1st VA Inf, Co H; ref: 1, 92
BONN, Henry R.; sgt; 1st VA Inf, Co H; res: Balt; MLCSH; ref: 70, 93, 627, 700, 786
BONN, Joseph; pvt; 1st MD Cav, Co F; res: Ruxton, Bt Cty; ref: 1, 19, 70, 82
BONN, Samuel G.; Lt; 1st MD Cav, Co F; res: Balt; ref: 1, 19, 507, 1039
BONNER, Memory (Surg); ref: 1690
BOOKER, Miers; pvt; MD Guerrilla Zouaves; ref: 1
BOOKER, Thomas; sgt; 43rd VA Cav (Mosby's), Co E; ref: 1, 8, 602
BOOKER, William D. (M.D.); pvt; 3rd VA Cav, Co K; res: Balt; ref: 1, 18, 21, 700
BOOKER, William T.; pvt; 1st MD Cav, Co E; ref: 1, 2, 19, 21, 730
BOONE, Daniel Alexis; pvt; 7th VA Cav, Co C; res: Frederick, Frd Cty; ref: 1, 2, 3, 19, 21, 23, 70, 90, 700, 735, 866
BOONE, John F.; cpl; 1st VA Lt Arty, Co C; res: PG Cty; ref: 1, 69, 316
BOONE, K. B.; Officer, Navy; ref: 58
BOONE, William C.; pvt; 1st MD Cav, Co E; ref: 1, 2, 19, 21, 94, 730
BOOTH, George Wilson; Capt; Asst A.G.; MD Line; res: Balt; ref: 1, 2, 19, 21, 23, 34, 53, 63, 64, 68, 93, 94, 150, 240, 456, 483, 488, 493, 496, 511, 614, 686, 693, 700, 727, 791, 848, 849, 866, 869, 881, 893, 906, 923, 944, 976, 988, 1058, 1251, 1338, 1523, 1560, 1579, 1607, 1608, 1634
BOOTH, John; pvt; 2nd MD Inf, Co H; ref: 1, 2, 19, 21, 511

BOOTH, Joseph Adrian (M.D.); Surg; ref: 18, 20, 511
BOOTH, Richard J.; ref: 20, 511
BORDAREX, Charles A.; pvt; Davis's MD Cav, Co C; ref: 1
BORNER, Charles T.; res: Balt; ref: 1540
BORNER, John H.; res: Balt; ref: 1540
BOSLEY, John R.; sgt; 2nd MD Cav, Co F; res: Bt Cty; ref: 1, 2, 11, 19, 21, 23, 680, 693, 791, 824, 1540
BOSS, Charles W. A.; res: Balt; ref: 1664
BOSS, Robert J.; pvt; 9th VA Cav, Co H; res: Balt; ref: 1, 1664
BOSWELL, James; pvt; 17th VA Inf, Co I; ref: 1, 20
BOSWELL, Josiah T.; pvt; 2nd MD Cav, Co B; ref: 1, 2, 19, 21, 1609
BOSWELL, Lewis A. (M.D.); Asst Surg; 17th VA Inf; ref: 1, 18, 133, 142, 251
BOSWELL, Richard T.; pvt; 1st MD Lt Arty; res: Homonkey, Cha Cty; ref: 1, 2, 19, 21, 1546
BOSWELL, William; pvt; 35th VA Ca, Co B; ref: 1, 3, 1677
BOTELER, Arthur; res: Frederick, Frd Cty; ref: 89
BOTELER, Cyrus; pvt; Lee's Balt Lt Arty, Alexander's Bn; res: Frederick, Frd Cty; ref: 1, 90, 1573
BOTELER, Frank; Gen T. F. Toon's staff; ref: 689
BOTELER, Robert H. E. (M.D.); Contract Physician;' res: Adamstown, Frd Cty; ref: 1, 18, 90
BOTELER, Walter P.; pvt; 1s MD Lt Arty; ref: 1, 2, 19, 21
BOUCHET, John M.; res: Balt; ref: 1540
BOUIC, John Peter; pvt; 7th VA Cav, Co G; res: Old Medley's, Mont Cty; ref: 1, 3, 86, 106, 1611, 1677
BOULDIN, Constantine; pvt; 1st VA Cav, Co K; ref: 1, 2, 19
BOULDRY, George H.; res: Balt; ref: 1540
BOULWARE, George T.; pvt; 3rd MD Lt Arty; ref: 1
BOURKE, John A.; Asst Engr, Navy; C.S.S. Morgan; ref: 1, 1564
BOURNE, John; pvt; 1st MD Inf, Co E; res: Cal Cty; ref: 1, 2, 19, 21
BOURNE, Joseph B.; pvt; 1st MD Cav, Co E; res: PG Cty; ref: 1, 2, 19, 20, 21, 730
BOURNE, Thomas Blake; pvt; Signal Corps; res: Jessup, How Cty; ref: 1, 70
BOUTZ, Ernest; pvt; MD Guerrilla Zouaves; ref: 1
BOUVE, Joseph; pvt; Lee's MD Cav; ref: 1
BOWDOIN, Lloyd; pvt; 2nd MD Inf, Co A; ref: 1, 2, 21, 650
BOWEN, Henry Bell; pvt; 2nd MD Inf, Co G; Wor Cty; ref: 1, 2, 19, 21, 92, 93, 700
BOWEN, John; pvt; 1st SC Inf, Co C; res: Balt; ref: 1, 735
BOWEN, W. H.; pvt; 1st MD Lt Arty; res: AA Cty; ref: 1, 2, 4, 5, 19, 21, 34, 1628
BOWERMAN, Henry; res: Balt; ref: 1540
BOWERMAN, James B.; sgt; 2nd TX Cav, Co Co; res: Balt; ref: 1, 1540
BOWERMAN, William; pvt; 6th TX Inf, Co C; res: Balt; ref: 1, 1540
BOWERS, Cornelius; pvt; 1st MD Inf, Co A; ref: 1, 2, 19, 21
BOWERS, G. R.; pvt; 1st SC Inf, Co G; ref: 1
BOWERSON, David M.; res: Balt; ref: 1540
BOWIE, Albert; pvt; 1st VA Cav, Co K; ref: 1, 2, 19
BOWIE, Allen Thomas Jr; Capt; Gen W. Adams' staff; res: PG Cty; ref: 12, 791, 1574
BOWIE, Clifford Napoleon; smn, Navy; Norfolk Naval Station; res: PG Cty; ref: 1, 12, 70
BOWIE, Frederick Joseph; cpl; 3rd MS, Co F; ref: 1, 12, 20
BOWIE, Harry; pvt; 1st MD Cav, Co C; ref: 1, 2, 21

BOWIE, Harry Brune; pvt; 1st VA Cav, Co K; res: PG Cty; ref: 1, 2, 12, 19, 34, 70, 700, 720, 1523
BOWIE, Henry Clay; pvt; 43rd VA Cav (Mosby's), Co D; res: Gaithersburg, Mont Cty; ref: 1, 2, 19, 1574
BOWIE, Henry Contee; pvt; 1st MD Lt Arty; Upper Marlborough, PG Cty; ref: 1, 2, 12, 21
BOWIE, John Routh; sgt; Signal Corps; res: Mont Cty; ref: 12
BOWIE, John Truman Stoddert; res: Mattaponie, PG Cty; ref: 12
BOWIE, John W.; pvt; 43rd VA Cav (Mosby's), Co A; ref: 1, 8, 74
BOWIE, Robert S.; Lt, 37th VA Inf, Co K; res: AA Cty; ref: 1, 20
BOWIE, Thomas Contee; Lt; Gen J. D. Major's staff; res: PG Cty; ref: 12
BOWIE, Thomas Daniel; pvt; 1st MD Lt Arty; res: Mont Cty; ref: 1, 2, 12, 19, 21, 690
BOWIE, Thomas Fielder Jr; Maj; Asst I.G., Gen. F. Lee's staff; res: Upper Marlborough, PG Cty; ref: 1, 2, 12, 19, 21, 70, 83, 735, 791, 1577, 1578, 1622
BOWIE, Thomas Miller; pvt; 12th MS Inf, Co A; ref: 1, 12
BOWIE, Walter; Lt; 43rd VA Cav, Co F; Mosby's, res: PG Cty; ref: 1, 8, 12, 19, 34, 64, 70, 257, 258, 261, 393, 710, 1492, 1523, 1560, 1564
BOWIE, Watts; pvt; 1st VA Inf, Co F; ref: 1, 735
BOWIN, James L.; pvt; Edelin's MD Heavy Arty; res: Balt; ref: 1, 1540
BOWLAND, S. G.; pvt; 1st MD Lt Arty; res: Som Cty; ref: 1, 2, 19, 21, 70, 470
BOWLER, Thomas; pvt; 3rd MD Lt Arty; ref: 1, 2, 19, 21, 160, 461, 726
BOWLES, Robert; sgt; Davis's MD Cav, Co C; ref: 1
BOWLEY, William Hollins; pvt; 2nd MD Inf, Co A; res: Balt; ref: 1, 2, 19, 21, 501, 685
BOWLING, Alexander; pvt; 1st MD Cav, Co B; res: Bryantown, Cha Cty; ref: 1, 2, 19, 21, 70, 785, 1665
BOWLING, Charles A.; pvt; 1st VA Cav, Co K; ref: 1, 2, 19
BOWLING, Charles Franklin; pvt; 2nd MD Inf, Co A; res: Miles town, St. M. Cty; ref: 1, 2, 19, 21, 69, 316, 650, 1555, 1627, 1665
BOWLING, Daniel; pvt; 1st MD Cav, Co B; res: Cha Cty; ref: 1, 785, 1665
BOWLING, George F.; pvt; res: St. M. Cty; ref: 1670
BOWLING, Henry A.; Maj; Asst Commissary of Supply, Gen J. S. Williams' staff; res: Aquasco, PG Cty; ref: 1, 2, 12, 19, 69, 83, 316, 735, 1553, 1665
BOWLING, Nicholas; pvt; 1st MD Cav, Co B; res: Bryantown, Cha Cty; ref: 1, 2, 19, 21, 785, 1665
BOWLING, Robert; pvt; 3rd GA Inf, Co C; res: Balt; ref: 1, 1540
BOWLING, Thomas Benton; pvt; 2nd MD Inf, Co A; res: Miles Town, St. M. Cty; ref: 1, 2, 19, 21, 650, 1509, 1555, 1665
BOWLING, Wallace; pvt; 2nd MD Inf, Co A; res: Miles Town, St. M. Cty; ref: 1, 2, 19, 21, 650, 784, 1509, 1555, 1665
BOWLING, William; res: St. M. Cty; ref: 1670
BOWLING, William Francis; sgt; 1st MD Lt Arty; res: Cha Cty; ref: 1, 26, 34, 782, 1540, 1665
BOWLMAN, M.; pvt; 1st VA Cav, Co K; res: Balt; ref: 1, 2, 19
BOWLY, W. Hollis; pvt; 2nd MD Inf, Co A; res: Bt Cty; ref: 1, 19, 259
BOWMAN, J. L.; pvt; 1st VA Cav, Co K; ref: 1, 19
BOWMAN, Thomas; pvt; 26th NC Inf, Co K; res: West River, AA Cty; ref: 1, 1539
BOYCE, John C.; pvt; 1st SC Inf, Co G; res: Balt; MLCSH; ref: 1, 93, 627, 693, 700, 735, 786

BOYD, Andrew G.; pvt; 1st MD Cav, Co A; res: Wash Cty; ref: 1, 2, 19, 21
BOYD, Conrod S.; pvt; ref: 1690
BOYD, David; pvt; 21st VA Inf, Co B; res: Frederick, Frd Cty; ref: 1, 2, 19, 312, 681, 735
BOYD, Hamilton; pvt; 43rd VA Cav (Mosby's), Co C; res: Frederick, Frd Cty; ref: 1, 2, 8, 19, 21, 90
BOYD, J. A.; pvt; 37th AR Inf, Co K; ref: 1, 20
BOYD, James; pvt; 9th VA Inf, Co B; ref: 1, 1576
BOYD, John Mason (M.D.); Asst Surg; Tennessee Hospital; ref: 1, 18, 1530
BOYD, Joseph T.; pvt; 42nd GA Inf, Co A; res: Balt; ref: 1, 1540
BOYD, Loche; res: Balt; ref: 1540
BOYD, Thomas Hewlings Stockton; pvt; 38th VA Inf, Co G; res: Mont Cty; MLCSH; ref: 1, 93, 133, 627, 700, 786
BOYD, William; pvt; 2nd MD Cav, Co D; ref: 1
BOYD, William J.; pvt; MD Guerrilla Zouaves; ref: 1
BOYER, F. A.; pvt; 1st MS Lt Arty, Co H; res: Frederick; ref: 1, 784
BOYERS, Lafayette; 2nd LT; Davis's MD Cav, Co B; res: Frd Cty; ref: 1, 19, 1609
BOYKIN, Thomas Jackson (M.D.); Surg; Medical Purveyor,Wilmington NC; res: Balt; ref: 1, 18, 20, 23, 56, 57, 700, 891
BOYLE, Andrew Hunter (Hon.); Stonewall Brigade; res: Cumberland, All Cty; ref: 148
BOYLE, Charles Brooke (M.D.); pvt; 1st MD Cav, Co D; res: Taneytown, Carr Cty; ref: 1, 2, 18, 19, 21, 40,74, 323, 361, 806, 1601
BOYLE, Charles M.; pvt; 35th VA Cav, Co B; res: Frd Cty; ref: 1, 19, 643, 1677
BOYLE, Cornelius (M.D.); Provost Marshall Gordonsville, VA; ref: 1, 18, 735, 791, 1578
BOYLE, D. Jackson; 1st VA Inf, Co E; ref: 1, 735
BOYLE, Daniel; pvt; 19th VA Heavy Arty, Co C; ref: 1, 2, 21, 1580
BOYLE, Dennis W.; pvt; Barry's Co, MD Vols; ref: 1
BOYLE, Henry; res: Carr Cty; ref: 40, 806
BOYLE, Jackson; pvt; 1st VA Inf, Co E; res: PG Cty; ref: 1
BOYLE, James O.; res: Frd Cty; ref: 19
BOYLE, John H., Jr. (M.D.); Capt; Aide de Camp, Gen G. H. Steuart's staff; res: Upper Marlborough; PG Cty; ref: 1, 12, 19, 44, 627
BOYLE, John H.; pvt; 1st VA Lt Arty, Co C; res: Upper Marlborough, PG Cty; ref: 1, 69, 118, 316
BOYLE, Michael; pvt; Lucas' 15th SC Heavy Arty; res: Balt; ref: 1
BOYLE, Peter; sgt; 1st MD Inf, Co B; ref: 1, 2, 19, 21, 23
BOYLE, Philip; pvt; 2nd MD Cav, Co F; ref: 1, 2, 19, 21
BOYLE, Robert; Stuart's Horse Arty; ref: 52
BOYLES, Daniel; pvt; 2nd MD Inf, Co G; res: Point of Rocks, Frd Cty; ref: 1, 2, 19, 21
BRACCO, Edward L.; pvt; 1st MD Cav, Co A; res: Tal Cty; ref: 1, 2, 19, 21, 70, 645, 1612
BRACY, William Hicks; pvt; 14th VA Inf, Co A; ref: 1, 1529
BRADBERY, L. S.; pvt; 3rd MD Lt Arty; ref: 1, 2, 21, 160, 726
BRADDOCK, Charles S.; pvt; 2nd MD Inf, Co A; res: St. M. Cty; ref: 1, 2, 6, 19, 20, 259, 650, 1509, 1520
BRADDOCK, W. H. H.; pvt; 35th VA Cav, Co B; res: Rockville, Mont Cty; ref: 1, 1611, 1621, 1677
BRADEY, Henry; pvt; 1st SC Inf, Co G; ref: 1, 735
BRADFORD, Baldwin; cpl; 3rd MD Lt Arty; MLCSH; ref: 1, 2, 19, 21, 23, 160, 461, 726, 786
BRADFORD, Daniel; pvt; 2nd MD Cav, Co B; ref: 1, 1609
BRADFORD, H.; pvt; 1st VA Inf, Co E; ref: 1, 735

BRADFORD, John; pvt; Zarvona's MD Zouaves; ref: 1, 735
BRADFORD, Thomas G.; pvt; 1st MD Lt Arty; res: Balt; ref: 1, 2, 19, 20, 21, 70, 93
BRADFORD, William K.; Capt; Ordnance Officer, Gen J. B. Gordon's staff; res: Bt Cty; ref: 1, 111, 670, 791
BRADLEY, Alexander; pvt; 8th TN Cav Co H; res: Balt; ref: 1, 1540
BRADLEY, Isaac; pvt; 1st MD Cav, Co B; ref: 1, 2, 19, 21
BRADLEY, James; pvt; 2nd MD Cav, Co B; ref: 1, 2, 21
BRADLEY, Patrick; pvt; 20th LA Inf, Co K; res: Balt; ref: 1, 1540
BRADLEY, Thomas J.; pvt; 2nd MD Lt Arty; ref: 1, 2, 19, 21, 55, 782, 1523
BRADSHAW, T. S.; Lt; Davis's MD Cav, Co E; ref: 1, 19
BRADY, Charles H.; pvt; Davis's MD Cav, Co A; ref: 1, 735
BRADY, Edward Joseph; pvt; Lucas' 15th SC Heavy Arty; res: Balt; ref: 1, 1540
BRADY, Eugene; pvt; 1st VA Cav, Co K; ref: 1, 2, 19
BRADY, John H.; pvt; 21st VA Inf, Co B; res: Balt; ref: 1, 2, 19, 23, 312, 735
BRADY, Michael; pvt; 56th NC Inf, Co H; ref: 1, 735
BRADY, Michael H.; Artificer; 4th MD Lt Arty; ref: 1, 2, 19, 21, 23, 55
BRADY, S. H.; pvt; 2nd MD Cav, Co B; ref: 1, 1609
BRADY, Thomas Blacksmith; pvt; 4th MD Lt Arty; ref: 1, 2, 64
BRADY, William; pvt; 2nd MD Cav, Co B; res: C. Ferry, Dor Cty; ref: 1, 1547
BRAGLY, J.; pvt; 5th VA Cav, Co E; ref: 1, 92
BRAHM, John; pvt; MD American Rifles: ref: 1
BRAMBLE, Robert; res: Dor Cty; ref: 20
BRANCH, Charles; pvt; Stuart's Horse Arty, Breathed's Battery; ref: 1, 498
BRAND, Alexander J.; Jr; pvt; 1st VA Cav, Co K; res: Balt; ref: 1, 2, 19
BRAND, W. F.; Lt Col; ref: 61, 763, 813
BRANDENBURG, Jesse W.; pvt; 2nd MD Cav, Co C; res: Winfield, Carr Cty; ref: 1, 2, 19, 21, 1544, 1577, 1579, 1609
BRANDT, Alexander; pvt; 2nd MD Inf, Co E; ref: 1, 2, 19, 21
BRANDT, William; pvt; 2nd MD Inf, Co E; res: Balt; ref: 1, 2, 19, 21
BRANNOCK, Charles S.; pvt; 2nd MD Inf, Co A; ref: 1, 2, 19, 21, 650
BRANNOCK, Thomas H.; cpl; Barry's Co MD Vols; ref: 1, 2, 19, 21
BRANNOCK Wallis D.; cpl; 2nd MD Inf, Co A; res: Church Creek, Dor Cty; ref: 1, 2, 19, 21, 23, 112, 650
BRANNOCK William J.; pvt; Barry's Co, MD Vols; res: Townpoint, Dor Cty; ref: 1, 2, 21, 112, 1547
BRANNON, Morgan M.; pvt; 31st VA Militia, Co A; res: Balt; ref: 1, 70
BRANTLEY, George S. J.; pvt, 9th VA Inf, Co B; ref: 1, 1576
BRASHEAR, Charles Hall; cpl; 2nd LA Lt Arty, Co E; res: Merryland Tract, Frd Co; ref: 1, 72, 90
BRASHEAR, Thomas Pitts; pvt; 43rd VA Cav (Mosby's); res: Merryland Tract, Frd Cty; ref: 1, 2, 3, 19, 21, 72, 90, 1273, 1601
BRASHEARS, Thomas Benton; Lt; Tallahasee Guards; ref: 1, 2, 21, 700
BRASS, William; pvt; Lucas' 15th sC Heavy Arfty; ref: 1
BRATH, Augustine; pvt; 2nd MD Cav, Co B; ref: 1
BRATTAN, James H.; sgt; 1st NC Inf, Co A; res: Balt; MLCSH; ref: 1, 21, 700, 786
BRATTAN, John L.; Lt; 1st NC Inf, Co A; ref: 1, 21, 92, 93, 700

BRATTON, James G.; Musician; 1st VA Inf; res: Balt; ref: 1, 19, 21, 92, 93, 700
BRAWNER, John J.; sgt; 1st MD Inf, Co I; res: Cha Cty; ref: 1, 2, 19, 21, 23, 1546
BRAWNER, Richard; pvt; 43rd VA Cav (Mosby's), Co H; ref: 1, 8
BRAWNER, Thomas M.; pvt; 1st MD Cav, Co E; res: Port Tobacco, Cha Cty; ref: 1, 2, 19, 21, 94, 730, 1546
BRAWNER, William F.; pvt; 2nd MD Inf, Co F; res: Frd Cty; MLCSH; ref: 1, 2, 19, 21, 92, 93, 470, 786, 1523
BRAXTON, Tomlin (M.D.); Surg; 30th Bn VA Sharpshooters; ref: 1, 18, 70, 1534
BRAXTON, William Armstead; pvt; 43rd VA Cav (Mosby's), Co F; ref: 1, 8, 70
BREADY, C. Edward; pvt; 35th VA Cav, Co B; res: Adamstown, Frd Cty; ref: 1, 3, 19, 90, 1611
BREADY, Daniel Calvin; pvt; 6th VA Cav, Co K; res: Adamstown, Frd Cty; ref: 1, 19, 67, 72, 90
BREATHED, Isaac; res: Wash Cty; ref: 361, 511
BREATHED, James (M.D.); Lt Col; Stuart's Horse Arty; res: Funkstown, Wash Cty; ref: 1, 2, 11, 15, 17, 18, 19, 23, 29, 40, 45, 46, 48, 49, 64, 65, 66, 103, 105, 113, 115, 126, 127, 168, 169, 311, 361, 443, 497, 498, 501, 511, 684, 685, 791, 827, 838, 857, 892, 897, 1016, 1024, 1025, 1027, 1042, 1091, 1150, 1519, 1523, 1558, 1577, 1578, 1579, 1600, 1610, 1650
BREATHED, John W., Jr; pvt; 35th VA Cav, Co B; res: Wash Cty; ref: 1, 361, 511, 1611, 1677
BREED, Lawrence Henry; pvt; 1st MD Cav, Co F; res: PG Cty; ref: 1, 2, 19, 21, 93, 700
BREEDLOVE, John W.; pvt; 55th Inf, Co I; res: Balt; ref: 1, 20, 21, 23, 700, 939
BREERWOOD, Samuel N.; pvt; res: Dor Cty; ref: 19, 112
BREHM, John Philip; pvt; 1st MD Cav, Co C; res: Balt; MLCSH; ref: 1, 2, 19, 20, 21, 93, 627, 700, 786
BREMER, Jonathan L.; pvt; 1st MD Inf, Co B; res: Balt; ref: 1, 2, 19, 21, 1540
BRENGLE, William D. (M.D.); Surg; Medical Director & Inspector A.N.V.; res: Frederick, Frd Cty; ref: 1, 2, 18, 19, 735
BRENNEN, William; pvt; Ward's Cav Bn, Co D; ref: 1, 21, 700
BRENT, George T.; pvt; 1st MD Cav,Co B; res: PG Cty; ref: 1, 2, 19, 21, 700, 785, 1553
BRENT, Hugh; pvt; 7th VA Cav, Co A; res: Balt; ref: 1, 3, 21, 23, 57, 700
BRENT, J. W.; 7th VA Cav, Co A; res: Balt; ref: 1, 70
BRENT, James R.; pvt; 43rd VA Cav (Mosby's), Co A; res: Balt; ref: 1, 8, 23, 70
BRENT, Joseph Lancaster; Brig Gen, Army of the West & Gulf; res: Cha Cty; ref: 1, 2, 18, 21, 23, 50, 53, 56, 57, 70, 97, 103, 118, 118, 129, 130, 133, 150, 316, 388, 401, 426, 430, 431, 443, 461, 474, 511, 628, 674, 700, 763, 783, 791, 798, 813, 839, 896, 1006, 1031, 1523, 1579, 1588, 1623, 1673
BRENT, Vivian K.; pvt 17th VA Inf,Co H; ref: 1, 86
BRENT, William C.; pvt; Davis's MD Cav, Co B; res: Bt Cty; ref: 1, 19
BRENT, William H.; pvt; 9th VA Cav, Co D; res: Balt; ref: 1, 21, 57, 70, 700, 891, 916, 994, 1001, 1540
BREREWOOD, Robert W. J.; 38th VA Lt Arty; res: Dor Cty; ref: 1, 20
BRESLIN, Edward W.; pvt; 19th VA Heavy Arty; ref: 1, 2, 19, 21, 1580
BRESSNER, John; pvt; 1st MD Inf, Co E; ref: 1, 2, 19, 21
BREWER, Charles (M.D.); Surg; Richmond Hospital; res: AA Cty; ref: 1, 13, 18, 19, 1534

BREWER, Henry D.; Lt; 2nd MD Cav, Co E; res: Georgetown; ref: 1, 19, 614, 693, 1609, 1631
BREWER, Richard H.; Col; 2nd MS & AL Cav; ref: 1, 19, 735, 787, 791
BREZENDINE, Arthur; pvt; 35th VA Inf, Co A; MLCSH; res: Latonsville, Mont Cty; MLCSH; ref: 1, 93, 786, 1622
BRIAN, Luke Tiernan; Lt Col; Chief of Staff, Gen J.E.B. Stuart's staff; res: Urbana, Frd Cty; ref: 1, 2, 21, 46, 67, 69, 88, 90, 105, 113, 316, 362, 385, 693, 700, 725, 757, 791, 1090, 1560, 1600
BRICE, Arthur T.; SC Inf; ref: 20
BRICH, James Douglas; sgt; 1st SC Inf, Co G; ref: 1
BRICKHEAD, ---; 2nd MD; ref: 20
BRICKHOUSE, C.F.; Lt; ref: 1690
BRIDDELL, James Edward; cpl; 39th VA Inf, Co B; res: Snow Hill, Wor Cty; MLCSH; ref: 1, 2, 19, 21, 23, 627, 786, 1553
BRIDDLE, James; pvt; 1st MD Inf, Co D; ref: 1, 2, 21
BRIDE, Samuel; pvt; 1st MD Inf, Co A; ref: 1, 2, 19, 21
BRIDGES, William B.; pvt; 3rd MD Lt Arty; ref: 1, 2, 19, 21, 160, 726
BRIEN, John T. O.; Lt; res: Hagerstown, Wash Cty; ref: 361, 1558
BRIEN, Edward N.; pvt; 1st MD Lt Arty; ref: 1, 2, 19, 21
BRIGGMAN, Isaac; pvt; 1st SC Inf, Co G; ref: 1
BRIGGS, J.; pvt; 2nd MD Cav, Co C; 1, 19, 1609
BRIGGS, William; cpl, Marine Corps; Co C, Drewry's Bluff; res: Balt; ref: 1, 1594
BRIGHT, John Henry; Mast. M., Navy; Pensacola Navy Station; ref: 1, 825, 1564
BRIGHTKAUPT, George E.; Lt; 2nd MD Inf, Co G; ref: 1, 2, 19, 21, 23, 93, 735, 1580
BRIGHTWELL, Joseph William; pvt; 2nd MD Cav, Co D; res: Texas, Bt Cty; MLCSH; ref: 1, 19, 20, 92, 93, 627, 786
BRINE, Samuel G.; pvt; 1st MD Inf, Co A; res: Hagerstown, Wash Cty; ref: 1, 2, 19, 21, 1558
BRISCOE, Alexander; res: Cec Cty; ref: 70, 511
BRISCOE, Chapman B.; sgt; 1st MD Inf, Co H; res: St. M. Cty; ref: 1, 2, 4, 6, 19, 21, 44, 650, 1509
BRISCOE, David Stone; Lt; 43rd VA Cav (Mosby's), Co D; res: Leonardtown, St. M. Cty; ref: 1, 2, 6, 8, 21, 56, 64, 70, 257, 258, 261, 393, 503, 650, 710, 791, 1555, 1579, 1564, 1613, 1627
BRISCOE, Enoch; pvt; 2n MD Cav, Co A; res: St. M. Cty; ref: 1, 6, 1509
BRISCOE, Girard; pvt; 1st MD Inf, Co I; res: St. M. Cty; ref: 1, 2, 6, 21
BRISCOE, Henry; pvt; 1st MD Inf, Co H; res: Cec Cty; ref: 1, 2, 19, 21, 70, 511, 650
BRISCOE, Henry H. (M.D.); Asst Surg; 26th VA Inf; res: Chaptico, St. M. Cty; ref: 1, 6, 18, 684, 735, 1509, 1555, 1578
BRISCOE, James; pvt; 1st TN Inf, Co F; res: Cumberland, All Cty; ref: 1, 9, 19, 65, 95, 148
BRISCOE, James N. D.; pvt; Zarvona's MD Zouaves; res: Leonardtown, St. M. Cty; ref: 1, 6, 700, 735, 1509, 1555, 1627
BRISCOE, John Hanson; pvt; Hampton Leg Lt Arty; Balt; ref: 1, 2, 19, 20, 21, 53, 70, 93, 700, 936, 1578, 1579
BRISCOE, John L.; Capt; 12th MS Inf; res: St. M. Cty; MLCSH; ref: 1, 2, 6, 19, 21, 93, 627, 700, 735, 786, 791, 1509
BRISCOE, Joseph Cottsman; res: Homonky, Cha Cty; ref: 700, 1546
BRISCOE, Marshall; pvt; 2nd MD inf, Co F; res: Homonky, Cha Cty; ref: 1, 2, 6, 19, 21, 93, 1546
BRISCOE, Philip T.; pvt; 2nd MD Cav, Co B; res: Cha Cty; ref: 1, 2, 19, 21, 785, 1609, 1677

BRISCOE, Richard Clarke; pvt; 1st SC Lt Arty, Co F; MLCSH; ref: 1, 2, 19, 21, 93, 735, 786
BRISCOE, Washington; pvt; 1st MD Lt Arty; ref: 1, 19
BRITIN, Frank; pvt; Davis's MD Cav, Co A; ref: 1, 735
BRITTON, James E.; pvt; 2nd MD Cav, Co A; ref: 1
BRIZENDINE, Arthur; pvt; 55th VA Inf, Co A; MLCSH; ref: 1, 627, 700
BROADFOOT, William J.; Lt; 1st MD Inf, Co F; res: Balt; ref: 1, 2, 19, 20, 21, 23, 64, 259, 456, 650, 674, 690, 1523
BROADWAY, William; pvt; MD American Rifles; ref: 1
BROCKENBOROUGH, John Bowyer; Maj; Ordnance Officer, Gen W. B. Taliafaro's staff; res: Balt; ref: 1, 2, 19, 21, 23, 50, 55, 63, 64, 68, 92, 93, 105, 127, 222, 309, 443, 450, 456, 462, 493, 722, 791, 1347, 1523, 1600
BROCKENBOROUGH, W. H.; pvt; 2nd MD Lt Arty; ref: 1, 2, 19, 21, 23, 322
BROCKENBOROUGH, W. N.; pvt; 2nd MD Inf, Co F; ref: 1, 1563
BRODERWICK, James; fifer, Marine Corps; C.S.S. Georgia; res: Balt; ref: 1, 1540, 1594
BROGDEN, Arthur (M.D.); Chief Surg; Jackson's MS Cav; res: AA Cty; ref: 4, 18, 20
BROGDEN, Harry Hale; sgt; Signal Corps; Davidsonville; ref: 14, 19, 735, 803, 1489, 1539, 1563, 1583
BROGDEN, Henry; pvt; 2nd Cav, Co B; res: AA Cty; ref: 1, 4, 70, 601, 757
BROGDEN, J. Sellman; pvt; 2nd MD Cav, Co C; res: Davisonville, AA Cty; ref: 1, 2, 4, 5, 19, 20, 21, 44, 70, 650, 700, 1539
BROGDEN, William; pvt; 54th GA Inf; res: AA Cty; ref: 1, 5, 20
BROGIN, Patrick; pvt; 2nd VA Inf, Co E; res: Balt; MLCSH; ref: 700, 786
BROKEY, Peter; res: Frederick, Frd Cty; ref: 89
BROMLEY, George W.; pvt; Hampton Leg Lt Arty; ref: 1, 2, 19, 21
BROMLEY, Oram J.; pvt; 1st MD Inf, Co B; ref: 1, 2, 19, 21
BROMWELL, Henry Hall; pvt; 1st MD Cav, Co D; res: New Market, Frd Cty; ref: 1, 2, 19, 21, 90, 1601
BROMWELL, Josiah R.; pvt; 1st MD Cav, Co D; res: New Market, Frd Cty; ref: 1, 2, 19, 21, 90, 1601
BROMWELL, Thomas C. S.; pvt; 1st MD Cav, Co D; res: New Market, Frd Cty; ref: 1, 2, 19, 21, 90, 1601
BRONAUGH, George D.; pvt; 1st VA Inf, Co E; ref: 1
BROOK, C. B.; sgt; Davis's MD Cav, Co B; ref: 1, 19
BROOKE, Clements; pvt; 1st MD Cav, Co E; res: PG Cty; ref: 1, 2, 19, 21, 730
BROOKE, George W.; sgt; 1st MD Cav, Co E; res: PG Cty; ref: 1, 2, 19, 21, 23, 44, 700, 730
BROOKE, Henry; 1st Lt; Davis's MD Cav, Co E; res: Upper Marlborough, PG Cty; ref: 1, 12, 19, 730
BROOKE, John B., Jr; Col; P.M. of Winchester; res: PG Cty; ref: 1, 2, 20, 316
BROOKE, Robert M.; pvt; McGreggor's Arty Battery; res: Balt; ref: 21, 700
BROOKE, William H.; pvt; 9th VA Cav, Co F; res: Annapolis, AA Cty; ref: 1, 70
BROOKEY, John Peter; pvt; 2nd MD Inf, Co F; res: Frederick, Frd Cty; ref: 1, 2, 19, 21, 55, 90
BROOKS, Boyd; pvt; 1st SC Lt Arty; res: Balt; ref: 735
BROOKS, Charles; pvt; 43rd VA Cav (Mosby's), Co F; ref: 1, 8
BROOKS, Clement; pvt; 1st SC Lt Arty; res: Balt; ref: 735
BROOKS, Edwin; pvt; Zarvona's MD Zouaves; ref: 1, 735
BROOKS, Eugene; pvt; 1st Va Inf, Co E; res: Upper Marlborough, PG Cty; ref: 1, 1553

BROOKS, John; pvt; MD Guerrilla Zouaves; ref: 1
BROOKS, John R.; Lt; 56th VA Inf, Co A; res: Balt; ref: 1, 21, 700
BROOKS, Richard C.; sgt; 47th VA Inf, Co B; res: Balt; MLCSH; ref: 1, 21, 700, 786
BROOKS, Robert S.; pvt; 27th SC Inf, Co B; res: Har Cty; MLCSH; ref: 1, 2, 19, 21, 93, 700, 786
BROOKS, Rodney; 1st SC; res: Balt; ref: 655
BROOKS, Thomas; pvt; 1st MD Lt Arty; res: Bladensburg, PG Cty; ref: 1, 2, 19, 21, 470
BROOKS, Thorndike; Lt; Ashby's Cav; res: Bt Cty; ref: 91, 1541
BROOME, Robert; pvt; 2nd MD Lt Arty; ref: 1
BROTHERTON, David H.; pvt; 1st VA Inf, Co H; ref: 1, 2, 19, 21
BROUGHTON, James W.; cpl; 24th VA Cav, Co C; ref: 1, 1142
BROUGHTON, William Thomas; pvt; 1st MD Lt Arty; Pocomoke City, Wor Cty; ref: 1, 2, 19, 21, 70, 470
BROWN, A. H.; pvt; 3rd MD Lt Arty; ref: 1, 2, 19, 21, 160, 726
BROWN, Albert S.; pvt; Edelin's MD Heavy Arty; ref: 1, 1405
BROWN, C. C.; pvt; 1st MD Cav, Co A; res: How Cty; ref: 1, 2, 19, 21
BROWN, Charles; pvt; 1st SC Inf, Co G; ref: 1
BROWN, Charles; pvt; 1st VA Cav, Co K; ref: 2, 19
BROWN, Charles A.; pvt; 1st MD Inf, Co C; ref: 1, 2, 19, 21
BROWN, Francis; sgt; 2nd MD Cav, Co D; Princess Anne, Som Cty; ref: 1, 19, 1556, 1609
BROWN, George; pvt; 6th VA Cav, Co A; ref: 1
BROWN, George E.; Acting Master, Navy; C.S.S. Tuscarora; ref: 1, 2, 19, 21, 1564
BROWN, George Henry; pvt; Arsenal Bn, Co G; res: Frederick, Frd Cty; MLCSH; ref: 1, 19, 20, 92, 93, 627, 700, 786, 1578
BROWN, George W.; Lt; 2nd MD Inf, Co H; ref: 1
BROWN, George W.; pvt; 9th VA Inf, Co B; ref: 1, 1576
BROWN, George Washington; pvt; 3rd MD Lt Arty; ref: 1, 726
BROWN, Gustavus T.; pvt; 2nd MD Inf, Co B; ref: 1, 2, 19, 21
BROWN, Henry; pvt; 1st VA Cav, Co K; res: Woodstock, How Cty; ref: 1, 2, 10, 19, 748, 1550
BROWN, Henry C.; pvt; MD Guerrilla Zouaves; res: Mont Cty; ref: 1, 8, 1621
BROWN, J. J.; pvt; 1st SC Inf, Co G; ref: 1, 1613
BROWN, J. Thompson; 1mn, Navy; Richmond Naval Yard; res: Balt; ref: 1, 107, 907
BROWN, Jacob; pvt; 13th VA Inf, Co G; ref: 1, 735
BROWN, James; pvt; Davis's MD Cav, Co A; ref: 1
BROWN, James; pvt; 2nd Inf, Co H; res: millersville, AA Cty; ref: 1, 2, 19, 21, 1539
BROWN, James A.; pvt; 2nd MD Inf, Co D; ref: 1, 2, 19, 21, 23
BROWN, James F.; cpl; Stuart's Horse Arty, Breathed's Battery; res: Hagerstown, Wash Cty; MLCSH; ref: 1, 70, 93, 498, 511, 786, 892
BROWN, James T.; cpl; 2nd MD Inf, Co F; res: Queens Town, QA Cty; ref: 1, 2, 7, 19, 21, 23, 700, 1554
BROWN, John; Louisiana Tigers, Co A; ref: 93, 627
BROWN, John; pvt; Stuart's Horse Arty, Breathed's Battery; res: St. Leonards, Cal Cty; ref: 1, 498, 1542
BROWN, John Joseph; pvt; Zarvona's MD Zouaves; res: Laurel, PG Cty; ref: 1, 19, 58, 1553
BROWN, John A.; Col; Chief of Arty, Gen D. H. Maury's staff; res: Eastern Shore of Maryland; ref: 1, 19, 735, 787, 791
BROWN, John B.; pvt; 2nd MD Inf,Co E; res: Balt; MLCSH; 1, 2, 21, 469, 700, 786
BROWN, John Badger; Capt; 3rd NC Inf Co B; res: Balt; ref: 1, 20, 23, 44, 56, 70, 511, 1520

BROWN, John R.; Jr; 1st MD Cav, Co A; res: Woodstock, How Cty; ref: 1, 2, 10, 19, 21, 70, 75, 700, 1550

BROWN, John W.; pvt; 4th MO Cav, Co A; ref: 1, 2, 21, 79

BROWN, John W. (M.D.); Medical Physician; res: AA Cty; ref: 1, 18, 20

BROWN, John Wesley; pvt; 1st VA Cav, Co K; res: Eldersburg, Carr Cty; ref: 1, 2, 1663

BROWN, John Wesley; Lt Col; Ordnance Dept, Army of Northern Virginia; res: Balt; ref: 1, 19, 20, 21, 29, 56, 57, 70, 209, 511, 700, 791

BROWN, Louis; pvt; 1st VA Cav, Co K; ref: 2, 19

BROWN, Martin Bluford; pvt; 4th VA Cav, Co H; res: Balt; MLCSH; ref: 21, 53, 70, 92, 93, 511, 627, 700, 786

BROWN, N. M.; Pvt; 3rd MD Lt Arty; ref: 2, 19, 21, 160, 726

BROWN, Philip S.H.; sgt; 4th MD Lt Arty; res: Darlington, Har Cty; ref: 1, 2, 19, 21, 23, 64, 1523, 1549

BROWN, R.; pvt; 43rd VA Cav (Mosby's), Co E (Mosby's); ref: 1, 8

BROWN, Richard L.; Lt; Gen Jenkins' Cav; res: AA Co; ref: 19, 23, 57, 456, 462, 488, 791

BROWN, Richard L.; sgt; Barry's Co MD Vols; res: Balt; ref: 2, 20, 21, 511, 700, 923

BROWN, Ridgely; Lt Col; 1st MD Cav; res: Mont Cty; ref: 1, 2, 11, 13, 15, 19, 20, 21, 23, 34, 36, 50, 63, 64, 67, 68, 86, 88, 94, 105, 122, 125, 168, 169, 222, 240, 347, 385, 443, 445, 456, 457, 462, 496, 501, 509, 560, 631, 638, 684, 686, 791, 825, 827, 841, 873, 881, 977, 987, 1012, 1037, 1071, 1073, 1096, 1108, 1251, 1279, 1288, 1301, 1321, 1419, 1452, 1463, 1487, 1519, 1523, 1579, 1600, 1634

BROWN, Robert; pvt; 9th VA Inf, Co B; ref: 1, 1576

BROWN, Robert E.; pvt; 1st MD Cav, Co C; res: Balt; ref: 1, 2, 19, 21, 70, 141, 511, 892

BROWN, Samuel Theopolus; pvt; 1st MD Cav, Co F; ref: 1, 2, 19, 21, 64, 68, 461

BROWN, Thaddeus T.; pvt; 1st VA Inf, Co E; ref: 1, 735

BROWN, Thomas Jefferson; cpl; Hamden Arty; res: Balt; MLCSH; ref: 93, 627, 786

BROWN, W. Judson; Lt; Poague's Co, VA Lt Arty; res: Balt; ref: 1, 2, 19, 21, 56, 57, 160, 461, 511, 700, 726

BROWN, Wesley D.; pvt; 43rd VA Cav (Mosby's), Co E; ref: 1, 735

BROWN, William; pvt; 9th VA Inf, Co B; ref: 1, 1576

BROWN, William; pvt; 47th NC Inf, Co H; res: Darlington, Har Cty; ref: 1, 735, 1549

BROWN, William; pvt; Holbrook's Independent MD Lt Arty; res: PG Cty; ref: 1, 2, 19, 21

BROWN, William B.; pvt; 1st MD Lt Arty; res: Balt; ref: 1, 2, 19, 21, 63, 64, 68, 782

BROWN, William Dawson; Capt; 4th MD Lt Arty; res: Bt Cty; ref: 1, 2, 21, 23, 34, 50, 63, 64, 68, 86, 88, 105, 127, 129, 138, 168, 222, 240, 443, 459, 511, 631, 685, 722, 791, 838, 857, 1523

BROWN, William H.; pvt; 17th VA Inf, Co D; res: Darlington, Har Cty; ref: 1, 2, 19, 20, 21, 124, 735, 1549

BROWNE, Bennet Bernard (M.D.); pvt; 7th Cav, Co G; res: How Cty; ref: 1, 3, 18, 21, 631, 700, 748, 1533, 1536, 1597

BROWNE, Eugene H.; Asst Engr, Navy; C.S.S. Richmond; res: Balt; ref: 1, 21, 23, 56, 58, 75, 97, 684, 686, 700, 758, 783, 866, 906, 1564, 1579

BROWNE, Gustavus; pvt; Lee's Balt Lt Arty, Alexander's Bn; ref: 1, 2, 21

BROWNE, Robert Alphonsus; pvt; 7th VA Cav, Co G; res: QA Cty; ref: 1, 3, 631, 1597
BROWNING, Edward R.; pvt; McNeill's Rangers; res: Cumberland, All Cty; ref: 9, 19, 65, 95, 148, 504
BROWNING, J. J.; sgt; 1st MD Cav, Co A; ref: 1
BRUBAKER, R.; pvt; 2nd MD Cav, Co F; ref: 1, 2, 19, 21, 1609
BRUCE, C. P.; pvt; 1st SC Inf, Co G; ref: 1
BRUCE, Charles; pvt; 7th VA Cav, Co A; res: Cumberland, All Cty; ref: 1, 9, 19, 65, 95, 148, 1610
BRUCE, E. C.; pvt; 1st SC Inf, Co G; ref: 1
BRUCE, L. O.; pvt; 1st SC Inf, Co G; ref: 1
BRUCE, Maynadier T.; pvt; McNiell's Rangers; res: Cumberland, All Cty; ref: 145, 148, 519
BRUCE, R. E.; pvt; 2nd MD Cav, Co B; ref: 1, 1609
BRUCE, Robert; cpl; 1st VA Cav, Co K; res: AA Cty; ref: 1, 2, 4, 5, 19, 497, 505, 947, 1025, 1071
BRUCE, Walter M.; pvt; 19th VA Inf, Co H; res: Cumberland, All Cty; ref: 1, 9, 19, 65, 95, 148
BRUCE, William; pvt; 2nd MD Inf, Co A; res: Cha Cty; ref: 1, 2, 19, 21, 23, 259
BRUCE, William S.; pvt; 47th VA Inf, Co H; ref: 1
BRUDER, Valentine; pvt; 1st SC Inf, Co G; ref: 1, 735, 800
BRUDER, William; musician; 1st SC Inf, Co G; ref: 1, 735
BRUMLEY, Oram J.; pvt; 1st MD Inf, Co B; ref: 1, 19
BRUN, James; pvt; Davis's MD Cav, Co B; ref: 1, 19
BRUNER, Hamilton; pvt; 1st MD Inf, Co B; ref: 1, 2, 21
BRUSMAN, John A.; pvt; 35th VA Cav, Co B; res: Balt; ref: 1, 3, 1677
BRYAN, Andrew Jack, "Dr."; pvt; 4th MD Lt Arty; ref: 1, 2, 21, 34
BRYAN, Charles; pvt; 1st MD Cav, Co B; res: Chesapeake City, Cec Cty; ref: 1, 2, 19, 21
BRYAN, E. Pliny; Capt; Signal Officer, Gen D. G. T. Beauregard's staff; res: Piscataway, PG Cty; ref: 1, 14, 431, 735, 803, 1553
BRYAN, Edward; pvt; 20th VA Heavy Arty, Co E; res: Cumberland, All Cty; ref: 1, 9, 19, 65, 95, 148, 1610
BRYAN, George; Castle Pinkney's Heavy SC Lt Arty; ref: 735
BRYAN, George; pvt; 9th VA Inf, Co B; res: Balt; ref: 1, 1576
BRYAN, Henry B.; pvt; 2nd MD Inf, Co G; ref: 2, 19, 21
BRYAN, James; smn, Navy; C.S.S. Tennessee; res: Tal Cty; ref: 1, 19, 20, 1540
BRYAN, Robert S.; pvt; 1st MD Lt Arty; res: PG Cty; ref: 1, 2, 19, 21
BRYAN, Samuel; pvt; 25th VA Inf, Co E; ref: 1, 2, 19, 21
BRYAN, Thomas Andrew; Capt; Bryan's Co, VA Lt Arty; res: Balt; ref: 1, 20, 21, 23, 105, 700, 791
BRYAN, William; pvt; Davis's MD Cav, Co C; res: Balt; ref: 1, 1540, 1609
BRYAN, William C.; pvt; 1st MD Cav, Co E; ref: 1, 2, 19, 21, 730
BRYAN, Wrightson L.; pvt; 1st MD Cav, Co B; res: QA Cty; ref: 1, 2, 21, 785
BRYAN, Wrightson H. P.; pvt; 2nd MD Inf, Co C; res: Queenstown, QA Cty; ref: 2, 20, 21, 23, 1554
BRYANT, George H.; pvt; 1st MD Cav, Co E; res: Havre de Grace, Harf cty; MLCSH; ref: 1, 2, 19, 21, 350, 730, 786
BRYANT, Jack; pvt; Rhett's 1st SC Heavy Arty; res: Balt; ref: 735
BRYCE, John C.; cpl; 7th SC Cav, Co D; ref: 1, 21
BRYDE, Arthur; Lt; 5th LA Inf, Co E; res: Woodlawn, Bt Cty; ref: 1, 983
BRYSON, Charles; pvt; 1st SC State Troops, Co A; res: Balt; ref: 1, 1540

BUCHANAN, E. Key; pvt; Lee's MD Cav; res: St. M. Cty; ref: 1, 1627
BUCHANAN, Franklin; Adm, Navy; res: Tal Cty; ref: 1, 2, 17, 18, 23, 30, 31, 39, 44, 50, 58, 59, 61, 62, 64, 68, 70, 82, 97, 109, 110, 111, 125, 127, 129, 130, 135, 137, 165, 166, 270, 274, 275, 276, 277, 279, 330, 372, 429, 431, 446, 472, 511, 543, 559, 601, 602, 645, 674, 684, 686, 716, 735, 790, 791, 792, 816, 828, 839, 857, 860, 862, 867, 873, 909, 944, 999, 1118, 1127, 1152, 1157, 1279, 1297, 1338, 1441, 1442, 1451, 1453, 1464, 1486, 1495, 1499, 1510, 1523, 1533, 1564, 1570, 1572, 1577, 1578, 1579, 1581, 1583, 1588, 1620, 1623, 1632, 1636, 1639, 1646, 1673, 1674, 1676, 1685
BUCHANAN, James M., Jr; sgt; 3rd MD Lt Arty; res: Balt Cty; ref: 1, 2, 19, 21, 23, 64, 160, 461, 559, 726
BUCHANAN, John Rowan; pvt; 1st MD Lt Arty; ref: 1, 2, 19, 21, 34, 69, 215, 316, 700, 791
BUCHANAN, Thomas E.; Acting Chief Clark, Navy, Richmond Naval Station; ref: 2, 19, 21
BUCHANAN, William Jefferson; Lt; Quartermaster Corps; res: Balt; ref: 1, 2, 21, 782
BUCK, A. Kirkland; pvt; 21st VA Inf, Co B; res: Balt; ref: 1, 2, 20, 312, 592, 750
BUCK, Edward G.; pvt; 16th TN Cav, Co K; ref: 1, 700
BUCK, Irving A.; Capt; Asst A.G., Gen P. Cleburne's staff; res: Balt; ref: 1, 21, 53, 57, 700, 791, 1633
BUCK, James H.; sgt; 7th VA Cav, Co G; ref: 1, 3, 11
BUCK, Richard B.; Lt; 17th VA Inf, Co B; res: Balt; ref: 1, 2, 21, 23, 70, 133, 142, 251, 700
BUCK, Samuel D.; Capt;o 13th VA Inf, Co H; res: Balt; ref: 1, 21, 56, 70, 700, 791, 837, 845, 865, 853, 925, 927, 953, 967, 979, 1001, 1171, 1266, 1338, 1599, 1633
BUCK, Samuel H.; Capt; Asst Commissary of Supply, Gen J. B. Magruder's staff; ref: 1, 56, 70, 791
BUCKINGHAM, George W.; sgt; 1st VA Cav, Co K; res: Elk Landing, Cec Cty; ref: 1, 2, 10, 19, 735, 1550
BUCKLEY, John; pvt; Davis's MD Cav, Co C; ref: 1, 19, 693, 1609
BUCKLEY, John; pvt; 19th VA Inf, Co F; res: Balt; ref: 1, 21, 700
BUCKMASTER, Henry C.; sgt; 4th MD Lt Arty; ref: 1, 2, 19, 21, 23, 64
BUCKNER, C. C.; pvt; 7th VA Cav, Co G; ref: 1
BUCKNER, Magill Randolph; Capt; 49th VA; ref: 70
BUCKNER, Richard P.; sgt; 43rd VA Cav (Mosby's), Co B; ref: 1, 8
BUCKNER, William; cpl; 3rd MD Lt Arty; 1, 2, 19, 21, 23, 160, 726
BUEKE, C. L.; pvt; 2nd MD Lt Arty; ref: 2, 19, 21
BUEL, G. W.; pvt; 1st MD inf, Co G; ref: 1, 19
BUKEY, J.; pvt; 2nd MD Lt Arty; ref: 1
BULAH, ---; pvt; MD Linke, Co C; ref: 1
BULL, Elijah; pvt; 1st MD Cav,Co C; ref: 2, 19, 21
BULL, J. Wesley (Revd); ref: 70
BULL, James H.; 13th VA Inf, Co E; res: Balt; ref: 720
BULL, John E.; pvt; 1st MD Inf; res: Har Cty; ref: 1, 2, 19, 21
BULLEN, Rhoderick B.; pvt; 1st MD Cav, Co B; res: Broad Creek, QA Cty; ref: 1, 2, 19, 21, 785, 1554
BULLOCK, Walter; Lt; Aid de Camp, Gen R. C. Tyler's staff; res: Balt; ref: 1, 70
BUMP, George C.; pvt; 1st VA Cav, Co K; res: Balt; ref: 1, 2, 19
BUNION, R. W.; pvt; Davis's MD Cav, Co A; ref: 1
BUNTING, John; pvt; 2nd MD Lt Arty; res: Balt; ref: 1, 2, 19, 21

BUNTING, John H.; pvt; 1st SC Inf, Co I; res: Balt; MLCSH; ref: 1, 21, 700, 786
BURCH, Francis E.; pvt; Jacob's Mounted Riflemen; res: Old Medley's, Mont Cty; ref: 1, 106
BURCH, Francis M.; pvt; 62nd NC Inf, Co B; ref: 1, 20
BURCH, James Alton; pvt; 1st MD Cav, Co B; res: Cha Cty; ref: 1, 2, 19, 21, 785
BURCH, John H.; pvt; 2nd Inf, Co A; ref: 1, 19, 650
BURCHELL, John; pvt; 2nd MD Cav, Co B; ref: 1
BURDETT, E. P.; pvt; 1st SC Inf, Co G; ref: 1
BURDETT, Z. B.; pvt; 1st SC Inf, Co G; ref: 1
BURGER, ---; pvt; MD Line Arty; ref: 1
BURGER, Charles; 8th VA Inf; ref: 735
BURGESS, James; sgt; 9th VA Inf, Co B; res: Balt; ref: 1, 735, 1576
BURGESS, John W.; pvt; 2nd MD Lt Arty; res: Hancock, Wash Cty; ref: 1, 2, 19, 21, 55, 361, 700
BURGESS, Newbold, smn, Navy; ref: 1, 58
BURGESS, Thomas; pvt; Stuart Horse Arty, Breathed's Battery; ref: 1
BURGESS, William W.; pvt, 1st VA Cav, Co K; res: How Cty; ref: 1, 2, 10, 19, 46, 93, 505, 748
BURGWYN, William H. S.; Capt; Asst A.G., Gen T. L. Clingman's staff; ref: 1, 21, 700, 791
BURKE, C. L.; pvt; 2nd MD Lt Arty; res: Carr Cty; ref: 2, 21, 40, 806
BURKE, F. W. "Polk"; Lt; 2nd MD Cav, Co D; ref: 1, 2, 19, 21, 23, 614, 1609
BURKE, Hugh; pvt; Stuart Horse Arty, Breathed's Battery; ref: 1, 498
BURKE, John; pvt; 43rd VA Cav (Mosby's), Co E; ref: 1, 8, 20
BURKE, John M.; pvt; 2nd MD Cav, Co A; res: Balt; ref: 1, 2, 19, 21, 44, 259, 650, 700
BURKE, John Redmond; Capt; 2nd MD Cav, Co D; ref: 1, 2, 19, 21, 23, 614, 693, 1486, 1609
BURKE, Martin; bugler; 1st SC INf, Co G; ref: 1, 498
BURKE, Michael; pvt; 1st MD Inf, Co E; ref: 1, 2, 19, 21
BURKE, Nicholas; Capt; 2nd MD Cav, Co A; ref: 1, 2, 11, 19, 21, 23, 88, 349, 614, 1609
BURKE, W. L.; pvt; 4th MD Lt Arty; ref: 1, 2, 19, 21'
BURKHALTER, James; pvt; 35th VA Cav; res: Barnesville, Mont Cty; ref: 1, 7, 1611, 1622
BURLING, D.; pvt; 1st MD CAv, Co B; ref: 2, 19, 21
BURMAN, James; pvt; Davis's MD Cav, Co C; ref: 1
BURNETT, Charles Chester; pvt; 2nd MD Lt Arty; ref: 1, 2, 19, 21
BURNETT, H. J.; cpl; Callan's Cav; ref: 1
BURNETT, Robert Sidney; teamster, Army of Northern Virginia; res: Frd Cty; ref: 72
BURNHAM, James Henry; pvt; 1st KY Inf, Co I; res: Balt; MLCSH; ref: 21, 93, 627, 700, 786, 1677
BURNS, Arthur P. (M.D.); Chief Surg; 8th District Virginia Medical Board; ref: 1, 18, 517, 1534
BURNS, Daniel; pvt; 2nd MD Cav, Co D; ref: 1
BURNS, Edward; pvt; 13th VA Inf, Co G; ref: 1, 735
BURNS, Ignatius; pvt; 2nd MD Cav, Co F; ref: 1, 2, 19, 21
BURNS, James; pvt; 2nd MD Cav, Co B; ref: 1
BURNS, John; pvt; 2nd MD Cav, Co D; ref: 1, 19, 1609
BURNS, John Dickson (M.D.); Surg; Roper Hospital, Charleston; res: Balt; ref: 1, 18, 70,936, 1532
BURNS, John S.; pvt; 1st SC Inf, Co G; res: Balt; ref: 1, 1540
BURNS, Patrick; pvt; 2nd MD Cav, Co D; ref: 1, 19, 1609
BURNS, Patrick J.; pvt; 2nd MD Cav, Co A; ref: 1

BURNS, Robert K.; smn; Schooner General Taylor; res: Balt; ref: 1, 70, 1540
BURNS, William; pvt; 7th VA Cav, Co G; res: Merryland Tract, Frd Cty; ref: 1, 3, 90, 1278
BURRELL, James; cpl; Davis's MD Cav, Co C; ref: 1
BURROUGH, Somersett B.; Lt; 1st MD Cav, Co E; res: PG Cty; ref: 1, 2, 19, 21, 23, 64, 68, 730
BURROUGHS, Chapman; pvt; 9th VA Inf, Co B; res: Charlotte Hall, St. M. Cty; ref: 1, 1555, 1576, 1670
BURROUGHS, Dent (M.D.); Lt; Moody's Co, LA Lt Arty; ref: 1, 2, 19, 69, 316, 791, 1665
BURRESS, Thomas L.; pvt; 35th VA Cav, Co F; res: Beallsville, Mont Cty; ref: 1, 3
BURST, George T.; pvt; 1st MD CAv, Co B; ref: 2, 19, 21
BURTLES, Charles H.; pvt; 1st MD Lt Arty; ref: 1, 2, 19, 21
BURTLES, Thomas W.; pvt; 1st MD Inf, Co I; ref: 1, 2, 19, 21
BURTON, Highly; pvt; 43rd VA Cav (Mosby's), Co F; res: Tal Cty; ref: 8
BURTON, James W.; sgt; 2nd MD Cav, Co B; res: Golden Hill, Dor Cty; ref: 1, 1547
BURTON, Michael; pvt; 3rd MD Lt Arty; ref: 1, 2, 19,m 21, 160, 726
BURTON, Robert C.; pvt; 13th VA Lt Arty, Co A; res: Balt; ref: 1, 21, 70, 700, 1598
BURWELL, Philip Lewis; Capt; Aid de Camp, Gen J. A. Early's staff; res: Mt. Savage, All Cty; ref: 1, 21, 70, 129, 700, 791
BURWELL, Robert; pvt; res: Mt. Savage; All Cty; ref: 70
BUSH, George W.; pvt; 1st MD Inf, Co A; ref: 1, 2, 19, 21
BUSH, William P.; pvt; 2nd MD Inf, Co H; ref: 1, 2, 19, 21
BUSHBAUM, Henry; cpl; 2nd MD Cav, Co C; ref: 2, 19, 21, 23, 628
BUSHONG, J. Andrews; pvt; 3rd MD Lt Arty; res: Bt Cty; ref: 1, 2, 21, 160, 461, 726, 1460
BUSK, Jerome; pvt; 1st MD Lt Arty; ref: 1, 2, 19, 21
BUSSEY, Bennett F. (M.D.); sgt; Gen J. W. Winder's Detectives; ref: 1, 18, 735
BUSSEY, C. F.; pvt; 1st MD Cav, Co C; res: Balt; ref: 1, 19
BUSSEY, James Thomas; Capt; 2nd MD Inf, Co H; res: Cec Cty; ref: 1, 2, 19, 21, 23, 64, 68, 674, 700, 1577, 1578, 1579
BUTCHER, James; pvt; 8th NC Inf, Co C; ref: 1, 735
BUTLER, Charles Martin, Jr; pvt; 35th VA Cav, Co B; res: Old Medley's, Mont Cty; ref: 1, 3, 20, 73, 86, 106, 1552, 1611, 1677
BUTLER, Cyrus Sidney; pvt; 1st MD Cav, Co D; res: Frd Cty; ref: 1, 2, 19, 21, 89, 1601
BUTLER, Elisha; pvt; 14th VA Inf, Co A; ref: 1, 2, 19, 21
BUTLER, George William; pvt, 35th VA Cav, Co B; res: Old Medley's Mont Cty; ref: 1, 3, 20, 86, 106, 1552, 1611, 1677
BUTLER, H. C.; pvt; 3rd MD Lt Arty; ref: 1, 2, 19, 21, 160, 726
BUTLER, James R.; pvt; 15th VA Cav, Co E; res: Balt; ref: 1, 21, 700
BUTLER, Oliver Nathaniel; Lt; Ordnance Officer, Gen C. Butler's staff; res: Balt; ref: 1, 70
BUTLER, Reuben M.; cpl; Norfolk Lt Arty Blues; res: Bel Air, Har Cty; ref: 1, 122, 791
BUTLER, Samuel; pvt; 43rd VA Cav (Mosby's), Co E; res: Bt Cty; ref: 1, 720
BUTLER, Thomas C.; sgt; 1st MD Inf, Co D; ref: 1, 2, 19, 21, 23, 73, 74, 1523, 1578
BUTLER, William H.; pvt; MD Guerrilla Zoauaves; ref: 1
BUTTS, Shannon Fletcher (Revd); Chaplain; 12th VA Cav; res: Balt; MLCSH; ref: 1, 93, 627, 700, 786
BVIAN, D. O.; SC; ref: 693

BYAN, Edmund; pvt; 2nd MD Inf, Co A; ref: 1, 2, 21, 650
BYAS, Phillip; pvt; 2nd MD Cav, Co A; ref: 1, 2, 19, 21
BYERS, James Davis; sgt; 8th VA Inf, Co I; res: How Cty; ref: 1, 71
BYERS, William; pvt; 1st MD Inf, Co G; res: Balt; MLCSH; ref: 1, 2, 19, 20, 21, 93, 627, 700, 786
BYERS, William Robert; Lt; 47th VA Inf, Co H; res: Cambridge, Dor Cty; ref: 1, 627, 1057
BYRAN, W. H.; pvt; 2nd MD Cav; res: Carr Co; ref: 1
BYRD, Harvey Leonidas (M.D.); Surg; 10th GA Cav; res: Balt; ref: 1, 18, 21, 631, 700, 1533, 1536
BYRNE, Andrew J.; sgt; Davis's MD Cav, Co A; ref: 1, 2, 19, 21, 23, 735
BYRNE, Charles K.; pvt; 1st MD Cav, Co C; res: Frederick, Frd Cty; ref: 1, 2, 19, 21
BYRNE, O.; ref: 20
BYRNE, Samuel E.; pvt; 1st TX Inf, Co A; res: Balt; ref: 1, 2, 19, 21
BYRNE, William E.; 7th VA Cav, Co G; res: Maryland Heights, Wash Cty; ref: 1, 72
BYRNES, William; pvt; Davis's MD Cav, Co B; ref: 1, 19, 1563
BYRON, Timothy; pvt; 3rd MD Lt Arty; ref: 1, 2, 19, 21, 160, 726
BYRONS, Terence J.; pvt; 13th VA Inf, Co G; ref: 1, 735
BYUS, Charles E.; pvt; Zarvona's MD Zouaves; res: Tal Cty; ref: 1, 2, 19, 21, 23, 645, 735
BYUS, Stanley M.; pvt; 2nd MD Inf, Co E; res: Tal Cty; ref: 1, 2, 19, 21, 645
BYUS, William R.; Lt; 2nd MD Inf, Co E; res: Easton, Tal Cty; MLCSH; ref: 1, 2, 19, 20, 21, 23, 64, 68, 674, 700, 735, 786, 1152

CABELL, George Craighead; Lt Col; 18th VA Inf; res: Balt; ref: 1, 1600
CACEY, G. W. N; Capt; Co D, MD Line; ref: 1
CADLE, James R.; pvt; 19th VA Heavy Arty, Co C; res: PG Cty; ref: 1, 2, 19, 21, 133, 142, 730, 1580, 1622
CADLE, John H.; res: Annapolis, AA Cty; ref: 1539
CAGITT, Robert; pvt; 1st MD Cav, Co C; ref: 1, 2, 21
CAHILL, John J.; pvt; 43rd VA Cav (Mosby's), Co F; ref: 1, 8
CAHILL, Joseph A.; 7th VA Cav, Co F; Cumberland, All Cty, MLCSH; ref: 1, 9, 19, 65, 93, 95, 148, 700, 786
CAHILL, Martin; pvt; Stuart's Horse Arty, Breathed's Battery; ref: 1, 498
CAHILL, William Henry; pvt; 7th VA Cav, Co F; res: Emmitsburg, Frd Cty; MLCSH; ref: 1, 9, 19, 65, 92, 93, 95, 148, 627, 700, 735, 786
CAIN, A.; pvt; 1st SC Inf, Co G; res: Balt; ref: 1, 1613
CAIN, John; cpl; 2nd MD Inf, Co E; res: Balt; ref: 1, 2, 19, 21, 23
CALBRETH, John; pvt; 1st VA Cav, Co K; ref: 2, 19, 20
CALDWELL, Edward; pvt; 7th VA Cav, Co C; ref: 1, 3
CALDWELL, Harvey Cummings; ref: 12
CALDWELL, J. M.; pvt; 1st SC Inf, Co G; ref: 1
CALDWELL, William O.; pvt; Edelin's MD Heavy Arty; ref: 1, 1540
CALHOUN, John; pvt; MD American Rifles; ref: 1, 19
CALHOUN, William H.; pvt; 39th VA Inf; ref: 1, 735
CALHOUN, William H.; pvt; 2nd MD Inf, Co G; ref: 1, 2, 19, 21, 23
CALIS, Charles; pvt; 1st SC Inf, Co G; ref: 1
CALLAHAN, John E.; pvt; 1st VA Inf, Co E; ref: 1, 2, 21, 470, 735, 1523
CALLAM, John; pvt; 2nd MD Cav, Co F; ref: 1, 2, 19, 21
CALLAN, Christopher C.; Capt; 24th VA Cav, Scott's Partisan Rangers, Co A; res: Georgetown; ref: 1, 2, 316

CALLAN, James J.; Capt; TX Cav, Co I; ref: 1, 316, 730
CALLAN, John; pvt; 1st MD Inf, Co B; ref: 1, 2, 21, 316
CALLAN, Owen; pvt; 1st MD Cav, Co F; res: Balt; ref: 1, 2, 19, 21, 791
CALLEN, John; pvt; 2nd MD Cav, Co F; ref: 1
CALLIGAN, John T.; pvt; Purcell's Co, VA Lt Arty; ref: 1
CALLOWAY, W. A.; pvt; 3rd MD Lt Arty; ref: 1, 2, 19, 21, 160, 726
CALVERT, Charles Frederick; pvt; 43rd VA Cav (Mosby's), Co C; res: Balt; ref: 1, 8, 1540
CALVERT, E.S.; pvt; ref: 1690
CALVERT, Robert; pvt; Lucas' 15th SC Heavy Arty; ref: 1, 19
CALVERT, Seth; res: Tal Cty; ref: 19, 20, 645
CALVIN, John; res: Cumberland, All Cty; ref: 9, 19, 65, 95, 148
CAMALIER, Vincent; Capt; Signal Corps; res: St. M. Cty; MLCSH; ref: 1, 2, 14, 19, 700, 735, 786, 803, 1509, 1624, 1662, 1670
CAMBLE, Thomas; pvt; 2nd MD Inf, Co F; ref: 1, 2, 19, 21
CAMDEN, John Henry; pvt; Jacobs' Mounted Riflemen; res: Annapolis, AA Cty; ref: 1, 1539, 1628
CAMERON, Oliver; res: Har Cty; ref: 20
CAMERON, Stephen J. (Revd); Chaplain; 1st MD Inf; ref: 1, 2, 19, 21, 44, 746
CAMMACK, John; pvt; Conscript Mounted Guard; res: Georgetown; ref: 316
CAMP, George W.; pvt; 3rd MD Lt Arty; ref: 1, 2, 19, 21, 160, 726
CAMP, James R.; pvt; 3rd MD Lt Arty; ref: 1, 2, 160, 726
CAMPBELL, Alexander Mills (M.D. & D.D.S.); Asst Surg; Dental Corps, Nelson's MS Lt Arty; res: Bt Cty; ref: 1, 18, 1689
CAMPBELL, James; pvt; Davis's MD Cav, Co A; ref: 1, 735
CAMPBELL, John; pvt; 1st MD Lt Arty; ref: 1, 2, 19, 21
CAMPBELL, Joseph; pvt; MD Guerrilla Zouaves; ref: 1
CAMPBELL, R. A.; pvt; 1st VA Cav, Co K; ref: 1, 93
CAMPBELL, William; pvt; 2nd MD Lt Arty; ref: 1, 2, 19, 21, 1494
CAMPBELL, William H. H. (M.D.); sgt; Hospital Steward; 10th VA Inf; res: Owings Mills, Bt Cty; ref: 1, 18, 21, 70, 700, 1536
CAMPER, Napoleon; sgt; 1st MD Inf, Co E; ref: 1, 2, 19, 21, 23
CAN, Patrick; res: Balt; ref: 1540
CANBY, Benjamin D.; pvt; 1st MD; Cav, Co A; res: Rockville, Mont Cty; ref: 1, 2, 19, 21, 631, 1574
CANBY, William; pvt; 22nd NC Inf, Co F; res: Mont Cty; ref: 1, 20
CANDEN; Pat; pvt; Davis's MD Cav, Co C; ref: 1
CANE, James; pvt; 2nd MD Lt Arty; ref: 1
CANE, Ned; pvt; 3rd MD Lt Arty; ref: 1
CANE, Thomas H.; pvt; 4th MD Lt Arty; ref: 1
CANESI, Samuel P.; pvt; 1st VA Inf, Co E; ref: 1
CANFIELD, John H.; pvt; 4th MD Lt Arty; res: Dor Cty; ref: 1, 2, 19, 21
CANFIELD, Thomas; pvt; 4th MD Lt Arty; Dor Cty; ref: 1, 19, 112
CANNON, J. Faulk; pvt; 3rd MD Lt Arty; ref: 1, 2, 19, 21, 160, 461, 726
CANNON, John G.; pvt; 39th VA Cav, Co A; res: Bridgetown, Caro Cty; ref: 1, 19, 1543
CANNON, William Shipp; 4th MS Inf, Co F; ref: 70
CANTER, John; pvt; 7th VA Cav, Co G; res: Cha Cty; ref: 1, 3
CANTWELL, James; pvt; 2nd MD Inf, Co E; ref: 1, 2, 21, 1609
CANTWELL, John; pvt; 2nd MD Inf, Co E; Cornersville, Dor Cty; ref: 1, 2, 19, 21, 1547
CANTWELL, Michael; pvt; 35th VA Cav, Co B; res: Balt; ref: 1, 2, 19, 21, 1611, 1677
CAPERTON, George Henry (M.D.); Asst Surg; Montgomery Springs Hosptial South West Virginia; res:

Cumberland, All Cty; ref: 1, 18, 1534, 1596, 1610

CAPERTON, James Mosher; 13th VA Lt Arty, Co A; res: Georgetown; MLCSH; ref: 1, 2, 19, 21, 316, 627, 700, 786

CAPPS, Joseph B.; pvt; 9th VA Inf, Co B; ref: 1, 1576

CARBARY; pvt; Zarvona's MD Zouaves; ref: 735

CARBERRY, James L.; pvt; 6th VA Cav, Co K; res: Georgetown; ref: 1, 316

CARBERRY, Patrick; pvt; 3rd MD Lt Arty; ref: 1, 2, 19, 21, 160, 726

CARBERRY, Thomas A.; cpl; 4th MD Lt Arty; res: Balt; ref: 1, 2, 19, 21, 34, 64

CARDER, Joseph F.; pvt; 2nd MD Cav, Co E; ref: 1, 19, 1609

CARE, W. W.; pvt; 2nd MD Cav, Co D; ref: 1, 19, 1609

CAREY, Alexander G.; pvt; 43rd VA Cav (Mosby's), Co E; res: Balt; ref: 1, 2, 8, 21, 70, 601, 700, 1571, 1578, 1579, 1613, 1654

CAREY, James; Capt; Signal Corps; res: Balt; ref: 1, 2, 14, 19, 431, 735,791, 803

CAREY, James E.; pvt; 2nd MD Inf, Co A; ref: 1, 2, 21, 681

CAREY, Michael; gun, Navy; ref: 1, 2, 19, 21

CAREY, Thomas W.; sgt; 2nd MD Cav, Co D; res: Balt; ref: 1, 19, 21, 469, 700, 1609

CAREY, Timothy; pvt; 1st MD Inf, Co A; res: Frederick, Frd Cty; ref: 1, 2, 19, 21, 90

CARLIN, Laurence; pvt; 2nd MD Inf, Co H; ref: 1, 2, 21

CARLISLE, Charles; pvt; 33rd VA Inf, Co A; res: Merryland Tract, Frd Cty; ref: 1, 3, 90, 1573

CARLISLE, D. Grafton; pvt; 43rd VA Cav (Mosby's), Co A; res: Bt Cty; ref: 1, 8, 70, 86, 735, 1523, 1579, 1613

CARLISLE, David G.; pvt; 35th VA Cav, Co B; res: Barnesville, Mtg Cty; ref: 1, 3, 21, 1611, 1677

CARLISLE, George; pvt; 2nd MD Cav, Co F; res: Bt Cty; ref: 1, 2, 19, 21

CARLISLE, John A.; sgt; 7th VA Cav, Co C; ref: 1, 1148

CARLISLE, William; pvt; 35th VA Cav, Co B; res: Adamstown, Frd Cty; ref: 1, 3, 1611, 1677

CARMAN, Robert; pvt; 1st MD Cav, Co A; res: Balt; ref: 1, 19

CARNEAL, G. T.; pvt; 9th VA Cav, Co F; res: Balt; ref: 1, 700

CARNES, John; pvt; 1st SC Inf, Co G; ref: 1

CARNEY, Michael Luke; pvt; 9th VA Inf, Co B; res: Balt; ref: 1, 735, 1540, 1576

CARNIE, Jacob; pvt; Ashby's Cav; ref: 3

CARPENTER, George Henry; pvt; 1st VA Cav, Co I; ref: 1, 1536

CARPENTER, Lee; sgt; 2nd MD Cav, Co D; ref: 1, 19

CARPER, Philip W.; pvt; 35th VA Cav, Co A; ref: 1, 3, 15

CARR, J. Randolph; pvt; Quartermaster Dept; res: Balt; MLCSH; ref: 93, 700

CARR, James; pvt; 2nd MD Cav, Co A; ref: 1

CARR, John C.; pvt; 2nd MD Lt Arty; ref: 1, 2, 21

CARR, Patrick; pvt; 3rd MD Lt Arty; ref: 1, 2, 19, 21, 160, 726

CARR, Thomas; pvt; 1st MD Inf, Co F; res: Balt; ref: 1, 2, 19, 21, 700

CARR, W. R.; pvt; 61st GA Inf, Co E; res: Balt; ref: 1, 1540

CARR, William; pvt; 2nd MD Cav, Co A; ref: 1, 19, 1609

CARR, Wilson Carry Nicholas; Capt; 21st VA Inf, Co B; res: Balt; ref: 1, 2, 18, 19, 35, 44, 312, 650, 690, 711, 735, 791, 1520

CARRICK, John; pvt; 1st MD Inf, Co A; ref: 1, 2, 19, 21

CARRINGTON, Eugene; Capt; Quartermaster Dept, Richmond VA; res: Balt; ref: 1, 21, 700, 791

CARROL, G. T.; pvt; 9th VA Cav, Co B; res: Balt; ref: 1, 21

CARROLL, Albert H.; Lt; Signal Officer, Gen R.S. Ewell's staff; res: Ellicott City, How Cty; ref: 1, 2, 10, 19, 21, 69, 86, 316, 511, 735, 748, 1550
CARROLL, Daniel; Midn, Navy; C.S.S Patrick Henry; res: Balt; ref: 1, 19, 58, 69, 97, 279, 316, 511, 1564
CARROLL, Edmund; pvt; Holbrook's Independent MD Lt Arty; ref: 1
CARROLL, Edward; pvt; 2nd MD Inf, Co D; ref: 1
CARROLL, Hamilton; pvt; 31st VA Inf, Co B; ref: 20, 511
CARROLL, Harper; Lt; 1st VA Cav, Co K; res: Ellicott City, How Cty; ref: 1, 2, 19, 690, 700, 791, 1550
CARROLL, Henry; pvt; 28th LA INf, Co F; res: Annapolis, AA Cty; ref: 1, 1539
CARROLL, James P.; 2nd MD Inf, Co H; ref: 1, 2, 19, 21, 511
CARROLL, John; pvt; 3rd MD Lt Arty; ref: 1, 2, 19, 21, 160, 726
CARROLL, John C.; pvt; 1st MD Cav, Co F; res: Balt; ref: 1, 2, 19, 21, 51, 511, 1620
CARROLL, Lawrence; pvt; 2nd MD Inf, Co H; ref: 1, 2, 19, 21, 511
CARROLL, Muckell Philip; pvt; 21st VA inf, Co B; res: Great Mills, St. M. Cty; ref: 1, 2, 9, 19, 69, 70, 312, 316, 511, 592, 735, 1509, 1555, 1662
CARROLL, Philip Michael; pvt; 2nd VA inf, Co E; res: Balt; ref: 1, 70, 511
CARROLL, Robert G. Harper; Lt; Aid de Camp, Gen Ewell's staff; res: How Cty; ref: 1, 2, 10, 69, 316, 511, 748, 1577
CARROLL, T. Stapleton; pvt; 21st VA Inf, Co B; ref: 1, 2, 19, 511, 559, 681, 735
CARROLL, William Joseph; Midn, Navy; C.S.S. Tuscaloosa; ref: 1, 19, 58, 97, 279, 511, 1564
CARROLL, William L.; Lt; 9th VA Inf, Co B; res: Balt; ref: 1, 19, 1576
CARROLL, William Sterett; pvt; Norfolk Light Arty Blues; res: Bt Cty; ref: 1, 21, 70, 511, 700
CARRY, G. M.; pvt; 3rd MD Lt Arty; ref: 1, 2, 19, 21, 160, 461, 511, 726
CART, N.; pvt; Steuart's Horse Arty, Breathed's Battery; ref: 1
CARTER, Albert; pvt; 8th VA Inf, Co B; res: Mont Cty; ref: 1, 20, 1621
CARTER, Alexander; pvt; 3rd TX Cav, Co B; res: Bt Cty; ref: 1, 20
CARTER, George W.; Col; 21st TX Cav, Co F; res: Balt; MLCSH; ref: 1, 786, 791
CARTER, George W.; pvt; 21st VA Cav, Co D; ref: 1, 93, 700
CARTER, Grafton; pvt; 1st MD Cav, Co D; res: Libertytown, Frd Cty; ref: 1, 2, 19, 21, 90, 1601
CARTER, Henry Mayo; sgt; 44th VA Inf, Co E; res: Balt; ref: 1, 21, 56, 57, 70, 700
CARTER, James H.; pvt; 3rd NC Inf, Co K; res: Mont Cty; ref: 1, 20
CARTER, John P.; pvt; 51st VA Inf, Co D; ref: 1, 21, 700
CARTER, Philip W.; pvt; 35th VA Cav, Co A; res: Petersville, Frd Cty; ref: 1, 735, 1677
CARTER, Robert B.; pvt; 29th TN Inf, Co B; ref: 1, 700
CARTER, Robert W.; pvt; 1st MD Cav, Co A; res: Rockville, Mont Cty; ref: 1, 2, 19, 21, 879, 1552
CARTER, Thomas Henry (M.D.); Col; Chief of Arty, 2nd Corps; res: Balt; ref: 1, 18, 23, 105, 111, 126, 127, 129, 138, 347, 380, 403, 422, 478, 677, 791, 1600
CARTER, William; pvt; Lee's MD Cav; ref: 1, 19
CARTER, William Fitzhugh; Lt Commanding, Navy; C.S.S Louisa Anne Fanny; res: Balt; ref: 1, 21, 56, 57, 97, 700, 783, 1564
CARTER, William H.; pvt; 21st VA Inf, Co B; ref: St. M. Cty; ref: 1, 2, 6, 19, 312, 891, 1509

CARUSE, Samuel P.; pvt; 21st VA Inf, Co B; res: Balt; ref: 1, 2, 19, 312, 735
CARUTHERS, Illinois; sgt; 1st MD Cav, Co B; ref: 1, 2, 19, 21, 23
CARVELL, Robert W.; cpl; 1st MD Cav, Co B; res: Broad Creek, QA Cty; ref: 1, 2, 19, 21, 23, 785, 1554
CARVER, A.; pvt; 1st SC Inf, Co G; ref: 1
CARVER, J; pvt; 1st SC Inf, Co G; ref: 1
CARVER, J. Francis; pvt; 1st VA Inf, Co E; res: Cha Cty; ref: 1, 735
CARY, James; pvt; AR Inf, Co A; res: Balt; ref: 1, 757, 1540
CARY, John Boone; pvt; 1st MD Cav, Co A; res: Balt; ref: 1, 2, 11, 19, 21, 57, 70, 94, 511, 513, 690, 700, 724, 1634
CARY, Michael; gun, Navy; gunboat Bragg; res: Balt; ref: 1, 19, 1575
CARY, Timothy U.; sgt; 2nd MD Cav, Co C; ref: 1, 19
CARY, Wilson Miles; Maj; Quartermaster Dept, Montgomery, AL; res: Balt; ref: 1, 2, 19, 21, 22, 23, 53, 57, 70, 94, 511, 513, 689, 700, 735, 757, 791, 798, 1003, 1017, 1583
CASE, N. E. N.; pvt; res: Balt; ref: 20
CASEY, John; pvt, Marine Corps, Co A; res: Balt; ref: 1, 1540, 1594, 1598
CASEY, William; pvt; Lucas' 15th SC Heavy Arty; res: Balt; ref: 1, 1540
CASHEL, James; pvt; 1st MD Cav, Co A; ref: 1, 19
CASHMYER, ---; Gen C. S.Winder's staff; res: Balt; ref: 631
CASLOW, James; pvt; 1st MD Cav, Co F; ref: 1, 2, 19, 21
CASON, Benjamin F.; Lt; 9th VA Inf, Co B; ref: 1, 1576
CASPER, W.; pvt; 4th MD Lt Arty; ref: 1
CASS, Michael; pvt; MD Guerrilla Zouaves; ref: 1
CASSELL, Charles E.; Lt; Engr, Army of Northern Virginia; res: Balt; ref: 1, 56, 70, 791
CASSIN, William Deakins; pvt; 3rd VA Inf, Co F; res: Georgetown; ref: 1, 70, 1492
CASSON, John S.; pvt; 3rd MD Lt Arty; ref: 1, 1523
CASTELLO, Thomas; Lt; 2nd MD Inf, Co E; res: Balt; ref: 1
CASTH, J. S.; pvt; 1st MD Inf, Co B; ref: 1
CASTLE, James Luther; pvt; 2nd MD Inf, Co C; res: Frd Cty; MLCSH; ref: 1, 2, 19, 21, 72, 89, 90, 93, 627, 700, 786
CASTLEMAN, Charles W.; pvt; 2nd MD Cav, Co F; ref: 1, 2, 19, 21
CASTLEMAN, John R.; pvt; 43rd VA Cav (Mosby's), Co A; ref: 1, 8, 20
CASTLEMAN, Thomas; pvt; 2nd MD Cav, Co F; ref: 1, 2, 19, 21
CATHER, George Robert; cpl; 1st MD Cav, Co D; res: Kt Cty; ref: 1, 2, 19, 21, 23, 1540, 1591, 1601
CATOR, Benjamin; pvt; 1st MD Cav, Co E; res: PG Cty; ref: 1, 2, 19, 21, 730
CATOR, W. B.; pvt; 1st SC Lt Arty, Co A; ref: 1, 2, 19, 21, 23
CAULFIELD, James; pvt; 21st VA Inf, Co B; ref: 1, 2, 19, 312, 735
CAULK, William H.; pvt; 3rd MD Lt Arty; ref: 1, 2, 19, 21, 160, 726
CAUS, R. Brent; pvt; 1st MD Cav, Co A; ref: 1, 70
CAUTHORN, Andrew B.; Lt; 26th VA Inf; res: Balt; ref: 1, 70
CAUTHORN, L. Byran; pvt; 9th VA Cav, Co F; res: How Cty; ref: 1, 10, 19, 71
CAUTHORN, R. A.; pvt; 9th VA Cav, Co F; res: Balt; ref: 1, 21, 57, 700
CAVANAGH, Patrick; pvt; 2nd MD Cav, Co B; ref: 1, 1609
CAVANAUGH, Francis C.; pvt; 2nd MD Inf, Co H; ref: 1, 2, 19, 21
CAVANAUGH, John Moran; pvt; 3rd MS Inf, Co D; res: Balt; MLCSH; ref: 1, 93, 627, 786
CAVE, William W.; pvt; 2nd MD Cav, Co C; ref: 1

CAWOOD, Charles H.; Lt; Signal Corps; res: Cha Cty; ref: 1, 2, 14, 19, 20, 21, 133, 142, 251, 431, 735, 803, 1493, 1624, 1654, 1686
CAWOOD, E. Mathew; pvt; 1st MD Lt Arty; Homonky, Cha Cty; ref: 1, 2, 19, 21, 1546
CEANEY, Lloyd; pvt; Edelin's MD Heavy Arty; res: Frostburg, All Cty; ref: 1, 735
CECIL, Columbus C.; pvt; 35th VA Cav, Co B; res: Urbana, Frd Cty; ref: 1, 3, 90, 1611, 1677
CECIL, Frank; pvt; 16th VA Cav, Co F; res: AA Cty; ref: 1, 4, 5
CECIL, James; pvt; 4th MD Lt Arty; res: St. M. Cty; ref: 1, 2, 6, 19, 1509, 1627, 1662
CECIL, Randolphus; Lt; 1st VA Cav, Co K; res: Millersville, AA Cty; ref: 1, 2, 19, 23, 64, 445, 1523, 1539
CEISHING, Joseph E.; ref: 784
CESSELL, James T.; pvt; 1st MD Inf, Co I; res: St. M. Cty; ref: 1, 19
CESSLER, Henry; pvt; 4th MD Lt Arty; ref: 1, 2, 19
CHAFIN, S.; pvt; 3rd MD Lt Arty; ref: 1, 2, 19, 21, 160, 461, 726, 1460
CHALMERS, J. W.; pvt; 8th VA Inf, Co A; res: Balt; ref: 1, 21, 700
CHAMBERS, Charles; q.m. sgt; Chambers' Independent MD Lt Arty Bn; ref: 1, 55
CHAMBERS, John Edward; sgt; Rhett's 1st SC Heavy Arty; MLCSH; res: Balt; ref: 1, 2, 19, 21, 627, 700, 735, 786
CHAMBERS, John H.; sgt; Chambers' Independent MD Lt Arty Bn, Co A; ref: 1
CHAMBERS, Robert Marion, II; Lt Col; Chambers' Independent MD Lt Arty Bn; res: Balt; ref: 1, 19, 20, 21, 53, 79, 700, 735, 1540, 1598
CHAMBERS, Robert Marion, I; Capt; Chambers' Independent MD Lt Arty Bn, Co A; res: Balt; ref: 1, 2, 19, 20, 23, 93, 1540
CHANCELLOR, Charles William (M.D.); Surg; Medical Director Picket's Div; res: Balt; ref: 1, 18, 631, 700, 1533, 1534, 1536
CHANDLER, James; sgt; 16th GA Inf, Co A; ref: 1, 20
CHANDLER, William S. J.; pvt; 1st SC Inf, Co G; res: Balt; ref: 1, 2, 19, 21, 92, 93, 259, 650, 735
CHANEY, Alfred; pvt; 18th LA Cav, Co B; res: AA Cty; ref: 1, 20
CHANEY, George W.; res: St. Margarett, AA Cty; ref: 1539
CHANEY, Joshua; res: Millersville, AA Cty; ref: 20, 1539
CHANEY, Taylor; pvt; Jacobs' Mounted Riflemen; res: PG Cty; ref: 1
CHANEY, William; pvt; 1st MD Inf, Co B; ref: 1, 2, 19, 21
CHAPALIN, George; pvt; 1st MD Inf, Co I; ref: 1, 2, 19, 21
CHAPILOT, A.; pvt; MD Guerrilla Zouaves; ref: 1
CHAPIN, Charles; pvt; 1st MD Cav, Co F; ref: 1, 2, 19, 21
CHAPMAN, Isaac N.; pvt; 1st MD Cav, Co F; res: Balt; ref: 1, 2, 19, 21
CHAPMAN, John W.; pvt; 2nd VA Inf, Co G; res: Balt; ref: 1, 21, 469, 700
CHAPMAN, Nathaniel (M.D.); Lt; 1st MD Cav, Co E; res: Perrymansville, Cha Cty; ref: 1, 2, 18, 19, 20, 21, 23, 64, 68, 240, 498, 700, 730, 1536, 1546
CHAPMAN, Richard; sgt; 32nd VA Inf, Co K; res: Balt; ref: 1, 68, 1560
CHAPMAN, William; pvt; 2nd MD Cav, Co F; ref: 1, 2, 19, 21, 700
CHAPPELAIR, J.; res: Cha Cty; ref: 559, 1511
CHAPPELEAR, George W.; pvt; 6th VA Cav, Co A; res: St. M. Cty; ref: 1, 6, 1509
CHAPPELL, C. C.; pvt; 9th VA Inf, Co B; ref: 1, 1576
CHAPPELL, David; pvt; 12th SC Inf, Co F; ref: 1, 735
CHARLES, Jacob F.; pvt; MD Guerrilla Zouaves; res: E. New Market, Dor Cty; ref: 1, 1547

CHARLESWORTH, Joshua; sgt, Marine Corps; C.S.S. Virginia; res: Balt; ref: 1, 1594
CHARLOTTE, George W.; pvt; 2nd MD Lt Arty; ref: 1, 2, 19, 21
CHASLEY, T. O.; q.m. sgt; Holbrook's Independent MD Lt Arty; ref: 1
CHASTAIN, James B.; pvt; 53rd VA Inf, Co A; ref: 1, 57, 1001
CHASTEEN, R. L.; pvt; 1st SC Inf, Co G; ref: 1
CHATARD, Frederick; Commander, Navy; C.S.S. Patrick Henry; res: Balt; ref: 1, 19, 20, 21, 23, 58, 61, 64, 97, 279, 700, 735, 783, 789,791, 818, 1520, 1523, 1564, 1578
CHEASHAM, John W.; pvt; 3rd MD Lt Arty; ref: 1, 2, 19, 21, 160, 726
CHEEZAM, Richard Denny; 7th VA Cav, Co F; res: Cumberland, All Cty; ref: 1, 19, 20, 627
CHEEZUM, Daniel Richard; pvt; 14th TX Field Battery; res: Easton, Tal Cty; MLCSH; ref: 1, 645, 735, 786
CHERNE, J.; ref: 20
CHERRY, James; pvt; 2nd MD Cav, Co F; ref: 1, 2, 19, 21, 791
CHESELDINE, Columbus; res: St. M. Cty; ref: 6, 1509
CHESER, G. S.; pvt; 3rd MD Lt Arty; ref: 1, 2, 19, 21, 160, 726, 1460
CHESER, Richard; res: St. M. Cty; ref: 1670
CHESLER, Henry; pvt; 1st MD Cav, Co D; ref: 1, 2, 19, 21, 1601
CHESLEY, Daniel S.; pvt; 1st MD Cav, Co E; res: PG Cty; ref: 1, 2, 19, 21, 730, 1622
CHESTER, Harry; pvt; 4th MD Lt Arty; ref: 1, 19
CHESTNEY, Theodore O.; Maj; Asst A.G.,Gen A. Elzey's staff; ref: 1, 2, 19, 735, 789, 1365
CHEW, John A.; pvt; 43rd VA Cav (Mosby's), Co B; res: AA Cty; ref: 1, 8, 511
CHEW, Robert Bowie; sgt; 1st MD Lt Arty; res: Friendship, Cal Cty; MLCSH; ref: 1, 2, 8, 19, 20, 21, 34, 63, 64, 68, 92, 93, 215, 240, 311, 470, 511, 627, 700, 782, 786, 791, 1167, 1273, 1542, 1579
CHEW, Walter Scott; Capt; 4th MD Lt Arty; res: Georgetown; ref: 1, 2, 19, 21, 23, 35, 36, 64, 68, 94, 168, 316, 443, 450, 492, 733, 791, 1523
CHICHESTER, Arthur; res: Georgetown; ref: 12
CHILDERS, David; pvt; Davis's MD Cav, Co B; ref: 1
CHILDERS, Thadeus K.; pvt; Davis's MD Cav, Co B; ref: 1, 19
CHILDRES, J. Thomas, Jr; pvt; 1st SC Inf, Co G; ref: 1
CHILDRES, J. Thomas, Sr; pvt; 1st SC Inf, Co G; ref: 1
CHILDS, Nathan Soper; pvt; 1st MD Cav, Co A; res: Anne Cty; ref: 1, 2, 4, 5, 10, 19, 20, 21, 71
CHILDS, Owen; pvt; 2nd MD Inf, Co E; res: St. M. Cty; ref: 1
CHILDS, Walley; pvt; 1st VA Cav, Co K; res: Cha Cty; ref: 1, 2, 19
CHILDS, William H.; pvt; 1st MD Cav, Co A; res: Olney, Mont Cty; ref: 1, 19, 1552, 1574
CHILES, William L.; pvt; Hampton Leg Lt Arty, Co B; res: AA Cty; ref: 1, 2, 4, 5, 19, 20, 21, 70, 1628
CHILTON, William B.; pvt; 1st VA Inf, Co E; res: Blandensburg, PG Cty; rf: 1, 735
CHING, Jarrett; pvt; 2nd MD inf, Co B; res: St. M. Cty; ref: 1, 2, 19, 21
CHINOWETH, Joseph Hart; pvt; 1st MD Inf, Co B; ref: 1, 2, 19, 21
CHILCUTT, Joshua; pvt; 11th AL Inf, Co C; res: Carr Cty; ref: 1, 2, 19, 20, 21, 92, 93, 700
CHISHOLM, J. M.; Capt; 9th AL Cav, Co C; ref: 1, 735
CHISHOLM, Peter; cpl; 33rd VA Inf, Co F; Cumberland, All Cty; ref: 1, 9, 19, 65, 95, 148
CHISHOLM, Walter Wallace; pvt; McNeill's Rangers; res: Cumberland, All Cty; ref: 1, 9, 19, 65, 95, 148, 504, 519, 1610

CHISIDEINE, William C.; pvt; 1st MD Cav, Co C; res: Chaptico, St. M. Cty; ref: 1, 2, 21

CHISOLM, Julian J. (M.D.); Surg; Medical Purveyor Columbia, SC; res: Balt; ref: 1, 2, 18, 21, 700, 1527, 1532, 1533, 1534, 1536, 1674

CHISWELL, Edward Jones; Lt, 35th VA Cav, Co B; res: Dickerson, Frd Cty; ref: 1, 2, 3, 15, 19, 20, 23, 64,73, 86, 106, 371, 873, 1552, 1611, 1677

CHISWELL, George W.; Capt; 35th VA Cav, Co B; res: Poolesville, Mont Cty; ref: 1, 2, 3, 15, 23, 50, 64, 67, 72, 73, 106, 371, 518, 615, 791, 1078, 1560, 1611, 1670, 1677

CHISWELL, William T.; pvt; 35th VA Cav, Co B; res: Carrollton Manor, Frd Cty; ref: 1, 3, 72, 90, 643, 1552, 1611, 1677

CHITY, Caleb; pvt; 9th VA Inf, Co B; ref: 1, 1576

CHITY, John W.; pvt; 9th VA Inf, Co B; ref: 1, 1576

CHOWNING, William B.; pvt; Johnson's Co, VA Lt Arty; res: Balt; ref: 1, 21, 700

CHRISPIN, William L.; Capt; 55th VA Inf, Co K; res: Balt; ref: 1, 700

CHRISTIAN, John D.; pvt; 3rd VA Cav, Co F; ref: 1, 21, 700

CHRISTIAN, John H. (M.D); pvt; 24th VA Cav, Co G; res: Bt Cty; ref: 1, 8, 18, 21, 700, 1536

CHRISTIAN, William S.; pvt; 3rd VA Cav, Co B; res: Balt; ref: 1, 21, 700

CHRISTY, George W.; pvt; 2nd MD Lt Arty; res: St. M. Cty; ref: 1, 2, 6, 7, 21

CHRISTY, William; pvt; 2nd MD Inf, Co H; ref: 1, 2, 19, 21

CHUM, George A.; pvt; Richmond Howitzers; res: Mechanicsville, St. M. Cty; ref: 1, 7, 1662, 1670

CHUNN, John Henry; pvt; 2nd MD Inf, Co B; res: St. M. Cty; MLCSH; ref: 1, 2, 6, 19, 21, 93, 627, 700, 786, 1509, 1662

CHUNN, Severn B.; lmn, Navy; res: Mechanicsville, St. M. Cty; ref: 1, 1662, 1670

CHYZLER, Henry C.; pvt; 1st MD Inf, Co A; res: Bt Cty; ref: 1, 19, 1541

CISSELL, James T.; pvt; 1st MD Inf, Co I; ref: 1, 2, 19, 21

CITY, George Washington; Chief Engr, Navy; C.S.S. Arkansas; res: Balt; MLCHS; ref: 1, 627, 700, 786, 1564, 1598

CLABAUGH, Fenton Blackwell; Gen. J.H. Winder's Detectives; MLCSH; res: Cumberland, All Cty; ref: 1, 19, 21, 627, 700, 786

CLABBY, William; pvt; Zarvona's MD Zouaves; ref: 1, 735

CLAGETT, Charles; pvt; Edelin's MD Heavy Arty; res: AA Cty; ref: 1, 4

CLAGETT, David; pvt; 1st VA Cav, Co K; ref: 1, 735

CLAGETT, Edward L.; pvt; 2nd MD Inf, Co F; res: Buckeystown, Frd Cty; MLCSH; ref: 1, 2, 19, 20, 786, 1548, 1573, 1578, 1663

CLAGETT, George H.; pvt; 2nd MD Inf, Co F; res: Cha Cty; ref: 1, 2, 19, 21,23, 470, 700, 1523

CLAGETT, H. H.; pvt; 1st VA Cav, Co K; res: Frd Cty; ref: 1, 2, 19

CLAGETT, Jesse; VA Cav; ref: 1, 735

CLAGETT, John N.; pvt; 1st MD Cav, Co A; res: Mont Cty; ref: 1, 2, 19, 21, 1487, 1622

CLAGETT, John T. W.; pvt; 2nd MD Inf, Co F; res: Cha Cty; ref: 1, 2, 19, 21, 700

CLAGETT, John W.; pvt; 2nd MD Inf, Co F; ref: 1, 2, 19

CLAGETT, Johnson; pvt; 43rd VA Cav (Mosby's), Co B; ref: 1, 8

CLAGETT, Joseph Edward (M.D.); Chief Surg; Receiving & Forwarding Hopsital, Richmond; res: Rohrersville, Wash Cty; ref: 1, 18, 57, 65, 361, 631, 1534, 1536

CLAGETT, Morris; pvt; 1st VA Inf, Co H; ref: 1, 735

CLAGETT, Robert; pvt; 1st MD Cav, Co D; ref: 1601

CLAGETT, Thomas H., Jr; pvt; 17th VA Inf, Co C; res: Lime Kiln, Frd Cty; ref: 1, 19, 90, 142, 251
CLAGETT, William E. H.; sgt; 17th VA Inf, Co A; res: PG Cty; ref: 1, 12, 133, 142, 251
CLAGETT, William H.; pvt; 2nd MD Inf, Co C; res: AA Cty; ref: 1, 2, 19, 21, 79, 81, 470, 1523
CLAIBORNE, Charles Harrison; Lt; 1st SC Inf, Co G; res: Balt; ref: 1, 2, 19, 21, 23, 53, 70, 79, 488, 655, 700, 735, 848, 849, 866, 923
CLAIBORNE, Ferdinand O.; Capt; 3rd MD Lt Arty; ref: 1, 2, 19, 21, 23, 64,65, 160, 461, 479, 638, 726, 791, 1060, 1106, 1523
CLAIBORNE, J. F.; ordnance sgt; 3rd MD Lt Arty; ref: 1
CLAPHORN, William; res: AA Cty; ref: 4
CLAPP, Charles; pvt; 18th LA Inf, Co F; res: Wash Cty; ref: 1, 74
CLAREY, John; sgt; Lee's MD Cav; ref: 1, 19
CLARK, Alfred G.; pvt; Holbrook's Independent MD Lt Arty; ref: 1
CLARK, Basil Crawford; cpl; 1st MD Cav, Co A; res: Clarksville, Mont Cty; ref: 1, 2, 10, 19, 21, 71, 748
CLARK, C. S.; pvt; 1st MD Cav, Co E; res: Bt Cty; ref: 1, 19
CLARK, Charles; pvt; 3rd MD Lt Arty; res: Balt; ref: 1, 2, 19, 21, 160, 726
CLARK, Charles H.; pvt; 1st MD Cv, Co D; ref: 1, 19
CLARK, Charles H. "Monk"; pvt; Zarvona's MD Zouaves; ref: 1, 735
CLARK, Charles J.; pvt; 56th VA Inf, Co I; ref: 1, 19
CLARK, David J.; pvt; 2nd MD Cav, Co A; res: Clarksville, How Cty; ref: 1, 10, 19, 71, 748
CLARK, Duncan Chink; pvt; 2nd MD Cav, Co C; res: Balt; ref: 1, 19, 21, 70, 685, 700, 1636
CLARK, Edwin; res: Patuxent Forge, AA Cty; ref: 1539
CLARK, Frank Peyton; Capt; Paymaster, Gen W. E. Jones' staff; res: Balt; ref: 1, 20, 21, 23, 29, 44, 56, 57, 70, 700, 1636
CLARK, Franklin H.; pvt; 3rd MD Lt Arty; ref: 1, 2, 21, 160, 726
CLARK, F. T.; Acting Midn, Navy; ref: 19, 1564
CLARK, Ignatius; pvt; 1st VA Cav, Co K; res: St. M. Cty; ref: 1, 2, 6, 19, 1509
CLARK, J. G.; Rockbridge Lt Arty; ref: 1, 735
CLARK, James C.; pvt; 1st MD Cav, Co A; res: Ellicott City, How Cty; ref: 1, 10, 13, 19, 21, 71, 496, 748, 904, 1550
CLARK, James H.; pvt; 2nd MD inf, Co H; res: Mathews Store, How Cty; ref: 1, 2, 19, 21, 700, 1550
CLARK, James Louis; Capt; 2nd MD Cav, Co F; res: Balt; MLCSH; ref: 1, 2, 11, 19, 21, 39, 75, 93, 233, 445, 518, 601, 685, 690, 757, 786, 789, 791, 1562, 1565, 1577, 1578, 1579, 1609
CLARK, John; pvt; Lucas's 15th SC Heavy Arty; res: Balt; ref: 1
CLARK, John E.; pvt; 2nd MD Inf, Co B; res: Balt; ref: 1, 2, 19, 21
CLARK, John O.; pvt; 2nd MD Cav, Co C; res: Mathews Store, How Cty; ref: 1, 10, 748, 1550, 1574
CLARK, John R.; Lt; Aid de Camp, Gen L. Lomas's staff; res: Columbia, How Cty; ref: 1, 13, 19, 748
CLARK, Joseph; pvt; 1st Cav, Co D; ref: 1, 2, 19, 21, 1601
CLARK, Joseph B.; pvt; 43rd VA Cav (Mosby's), Co G; res: Bt Cty; MLCSH; ref: 1, 8, 92, 93, 700, 786
CLARK, M. H.; Capt; Chief Clerk Pres. Davis's office; res: Balt; ref: 592
CLARK, Matthew; 2nd Lt; 13th VA Inf, Co C; ref: 1, 21, 631, 700, 735
CLARK, Michael Richard; pvt; Purcell's Battery, Lt Arty; res: Balt; MLCSH; ref: 21, 627, 700, 735, 786, 1539
CLARK, Nicholas W.; 1st VA Cav, Co G; res: How Cty; ref: 10, 19, 502, 735, 748

CLARK, Robert; pvt; 9th VA Inf, Co B; res: St. M. Cty; ref: 1, 735, 1576, 1662, 1670
CLARK, Rody; pvt; 1st VA Cav, Co K; ref: 2
CLARK, T.; pvt; 1st MD Lt Arty; ref: 1, 19
CLARK, Thomas; pvt; 2nd MD Cav, Co A; ref: 1
CLARK, Thomas B.; pvt; 3rd MD Lt Arty; ref: 1, 2, 19, 21, 160, 726
CLARK, William J.; pvt; 1st MD Cav, Co A; res: Balt; ref: 1, 2, 21, 1487
CLARK, William Worthington; pvt; 2nd MD Inf, Co B; res: Ridge, St. M. Cty; ref: 1, 2, 6, 7, 19, 21, 70, 1509
CLARKE, Charles; pvt; 3rd MD Lt Arty; ref: 1
CLARKE, Charles A.; 19th VA Heavy Arty, Co C; ref: 1, 2, 19, 21, 23, 316, 1580
CLARKE, Charles H.; pvt; 1st MD Cav, Co D; ref: 1, 2, 21, 1601
CLARKE, David; pvt; 1st MD Cav, Co A; res: Balt; ref: 1, 2, 21, 1540
CLARKE, Duncan; pvt; 2nd MD Cav, Co C; ref: 1, 2, 21
CLARKE, J. Lyle; Lt Col; 30th VA Sharpshooters; res: Catonsville, Bt Cty; ref: 1, 2, 18, 19, 20, 21, 23, 34, 38, 44, 50, 53, 63, 64, 68, 70, 93, 110, 117, 124, 222, 240, 312, 456, 461, 518, 631, 638, 681, 686, 690, 700, 735, 781, 791, 893, 1485, 1520, 1523, 1584, 1585, 1586, 1600
CLARKE, James; pvt; 2nd MD Inf, Co H; ref: 1, 2, 19, 21
CLARKE, James A.; pvt; 9th VA Inf, Co B; ref: 1, 1576
CLARKE, John; pvt; 1st MD Cav, Co A; ref: 1, 2, 19, 21
CLARKE, John D.; pvt; 2nd MD Cav, Co F; ref: 1, 19
CLARKE, John T.; sgt; 1st VA Inf, Co E; ref: 1, 735
CLARKE, Joseph; pvt; 2nd MD Inf, Co E; Balt; ref: 1, 2, 19, 21, 69, 316
CLARKE, Powhatan (M.D.); Lt Col; Chief of Ordnance, Army of Western LA; res: Balt; ref: 1, 18, 21, 57, 700, 1533
CLARKE, Robert; pvt; 2nd SC Cav, Co H; res: St. M. Cty; ref: 1, 735, 1509, 1670
CLARKE, Thomas; pvt; 2nd MD Inf, Co A; ref: 1, 19
CLARKE, William E.; pvt; 9th VA Inf, Co B; res: St. M. Cty; ref: 1, 1576, 1598, 1662, 1670
CLARY, Lloyd L.; McNeill's Rangers; res: Cumberland, All Cty; ref: 1, 9,19, 65, 95, 148, 504, 519
CLARY, Richard L.; pvt; McNeill's Rangers; res: Cumberland, All Cty; ref: 1, 9, 19, 65, 95, 148, 504, 519
CLARY, Thaddeus W.; pvt; McNeill's Rangers; res: Cumberland, All Cty; ref: 1, 9, 19, 65, 95, 148, 504, 519, 735
CLASH, C. V.; cpl; 2nd MD Cav, Co D; ref: 1, 19, 1609
CLATTERBUCK; H.; pvt; Stuart's Horse Arty, Breathed's Battery; ref: 1, 498, 1677
CLATTERBUCK, Layton C.; pvt; 35th VA Cav, Co F; ref: 1, 1611
CLAUDE, Hammond; pvt; 1st MD Cav, Co C; ref: 1, 2, 19, 21
CLAUS, Louis; commissary sgt; 2nd MD Lt Arty; ref: 1, 2, 19, 21, 64
CLAY, James W.; pvt; 18th VA Inf, Co G; res: Balt; ref: 1, 21, 700
CLAYES, Patterson; pvt; 35th VA Cav, Co B; ref: 1, 1611, 1677
CLAYLAND, James; pvt; 1st MD Cav, Co D; ref: 1, 19
CLAYTON, Charles McCeeney; cpl; 2nd MD Inf, Co C; res: Crownsville, AA Cty; ref: 1, 2, 19, 21, 70, 1539
CLAYTON, G. W.; pvt; 1st MD Lt Arty; ref: 1,2, 19, 21
CLAYVILLE, Moses; pvt; 2nd MD Inf, Co A; res: Wor Cty; ref: 1, 2, 19, 21, 650
CLEAL, Charles; pvt; 2nd MD Lt Arty; ref: 1, 2, 19, 21

CLEARY, J. H.; pvt; 2nd MD Lt Arty; ref: 1
CLEARY, James K.; Lt; 1st Foreign Bn, Co D; res: PG Cty; ref: 1, 316, 735, 1574
CLEARY, Paul W.; pvt; 1st MD Cav, Co E; ref: 1, 2, 19, 21, 730
CLEARY, Reuben; Capt; 7th VA Inf, Co H; res: PG Cty; ref: 1, 316
CLEARY, Robert E.; pvt; 1st MD Lt Arty; ref: 1, 2, 19, 21, 470
CLEARY, Vachel T.; pvt; 1st MD Cav, Co D; ref: 1, 2, 19, 21, 1601
CLEM, John A.; 2nd MD Cav; ref: 1590
CLEM, W. B.; pvt; Stuart's Horse Arty, Breathed's Battery; ref: 1
CLEMENS, Ridgley; pvt; 7th VA Cav, Co G; ref: 1, 3
CLEMENTS, Francis J.; pvt; 2nd MD Inf, Co F; res: Allens Fresh, Cha Cty; ref: 1, 2, 19, 21, 316, 1546
CLEMENTS, Frank; pvt; 1st VA Cav, Co K; ref: 1,2, 19
CLEMENTS, Lawrence; pvt, Marine Corps; Norfolk Navy Yard; ref: 1, 1594
CLEMENTS, Peter; pvt; Zarvona's MD Zouaves; ref: 1, 735
CLEMENTS, Ridgley; 7th VA Cav; ref: 1098
CLEMENTS, William; pvt; 1st MD Cav, Co C; res: Port Tobacco, Cha Cty; ref: 1,2, 19, 21, 1546
CLEMSON, John Calhoun; Lt; Nitre & Mining Bureau; Bladensburg, PG Cty; ref: 1, 1579, 1582, 1622
CLENDENIN, Alexander F. (M.D.); Surg; 5th VA Cav; ref: 1, 18
CLENDINEN, Thomas Rufus; pvt; Cadet, V.M.I.; res: Balt; ref: 1, 20, 21, 23, 107, 700, 1687
CLEWELL, Augustus A.; pvt; 21st NC Inf, Co E; res: Balt; ref: 1, 18,720, 1536
CLIFFORD, Harry A.; smn, Navy; res: Balt; ref: 1
CLIFTON, Louis R.; pvt; 1st MD Inf, Co E; ref: 1,2,19, 21
CLINGAN, G. Frank; pvt; Jacobs' Mounted Riflemen; ref: 1, 643
CLINGAN, John W.; pvt; 10th MS Cav, Co A; res: Frd Cty; ref: 1, 72
CLINTON, Henry De Witt; pvt; 1st VA Cav, Co K; res: Balt; MLCSH; ref: 1,2, 19, 21, 627, 700, 786
CLINTON, Lewis R.; pvt; 1st MD Inf, Co E; ref: 1, 2,21
CLIPP, Hiram O.; res: Sharpsburg, Wash Cty; ref: 361
CLOSE, James; pvt; 21st VA Inf, Co B; res: Balt; ref: 1, 2, 19, 21, 312, 559, 700, 735
CLOTWORTHY, George W.; pvt; 2nd MD Lt Arty; res: Balt; ref: 1, 2, 19, 21, 23, 700
CLOTWORTHY, S.; ref: 53
CLOUD, Mountjoy; pvt; 2nd MD Cav, Co C; ref: 1, 11, 19, 194
CLOUGH, C. E.; pvt; Davis's MD Cav, Co B; ref: 1, 19
CLOUGH, Robert H.; pvt; 2nd MD Inf, Co C; res: Royal Oak, Tal Cty; ref: 1, 2, 19, 21, 595, 645, 1557
CLOWE, John H.; sgt; 2nd NC Inf, Co C; res: Balt; ref: 1, 21, 700
CLUM, John; res: St. M. Cty; ref: 94
COAKSLEY, Philip H., Jr; pvt; 1st MD Inf, Co H; res: Balt; ref: 1, 2, 19, 21, 559, 650, 711, 735, 1511
COAKLEY, John; pvt; 2nd MD Cav, Co E; ref: 1, 19, 1609
COALE, William Augustus; pvt; 1st MD Lt Arty; res: AA Cty; MLCSH; ref: 1, 2, 19, 21, 627, 700, 786, 1628
COBERTH, David; pvt; 35th VA Cav, Co B; res: Darnestown, Mtg Cty; ref: 1, 3, 1611, 1622, 1677
COBOURN, James M.; Lt; 2nd MD Cav, Co A; ref: 1, 17, 1609
COBURN, Chauncey; pvt; 19th VA Heavy Arty, Co C; ref: 1, 1580
COBURN, John; pvt; Davis's MD Cav, Co B; ref: 1, 2, 21, 735
COCHRAN, Henry King (M.D.); Asst Surg; Old Seabrook Hospital; res: Peterville, Frd Cty; ref: 1, 18, 19, 124, 1534
COCHRAN, James; pvt; 35th VA Cav, Co A; ref: 1, 7, 1611, 1677
COCKERVILLE, Samuel Johnson (D.D.S.); Lt; Dental Corps; ref: 1, 18, 1677
COCKEY, Charles R.; sgt; 1st MD Cav, Co A; res: Balt; ref: 1, 2, 19,

21, 23, 781, 824, 1562, 1609, 1634
COCKEY, John Powell; pvt; 1st MD Cav, Co E; res: Worthington Valley, Bt Cty; ref: 1, 2, 19, 21, 94, 730, 825, 1562
COCKEY, Sabastian Sprigg; pvt; 1st MD Cav, Co; res: Urbana,Frd Cty; ref: 1, 2, 19, 21, 90, 643, 700, 1548, 1573
COCKRELL, James Daniel; pvt; 1st MD Cav, Co D; res: Doubs, Frd Cty; ref: 88, 90
CODD, W. M.; pvt; 1st MD Inf, Co C; ref: 1, 2, 19, 21, 789
CODD, William H.; Chief Engr, Navy; C.S.S. Shenandoah; ref: 1, 2, 19, 21, 58, 64, 70, 97, 107, 283, 700, 735, 783, 964, 1564, 1673, 1676
COE, Aurelius; pvt; 35th VA Cav, Co A; ref: 1, 3, 1611, 1677
COE, Charles Hanson Pitts; 2nd MD Cav, Co D; res: Balt; ref: 70
COFFEE, M. J.; pvt; 2nd MD Lt Arty; ref: 1, 2, 19, 21
COFFEY, Matthew; pvt; Martin's TX Cav, Co F; res: Cumberland, All Cty; ref: 1, 9, 19, 65, 95, 148
COFFSOTH, George R.; res: Balt; ref: 1540
COLE, Charles N.; pvt; 1st MD Cav, Co D; res: Balt; ref: 1, 2, 19, 21, 1601
COLE, James; pvt; MD Line, Co D; res: Bristol, AA Cty; ref: 1, 1539
COLE, Thomas of Joseph; pvt; 27th LA Inf, Co A; res: Elk Ridge Landing, AA Cty; ref: 1, 1539
COLE, W.; pvt; 1st SC Inf, Co G; ref: 1, 1599
COLE, William H.; (M.D.); Acting Asst Surg; Howard Grove Hospital Richmond; res: Balt; ref: 1, 2, 18, 19, 21, 631, 700, 735, 1533
COLEMAN, Charles; cpl; MD Guerrilla Zouaves; ref: 1, 19
COLEMAN, Henry Eaton; Col; 12th NC Inf; ref: 1, 21, 105, 134, 700, 791, 1600
COLEMAN, James; pvt; MD Guerrilla Zouaves; ref: 1
COLEMAN, John A.; pvt; Letcher's Lt Arty Battery; MLCSH: res: Balt; ref: 1, 2, 19, 21, 93, 700, 735, 786
COLEMAN, Lewis; pvt; 1st MD Inf, Co C; 1, 19
COLL, Charles; pvt; 1st MD Cav, Co D; ref: 740
COLLIER, E. J.; pvt; Stuart's Horse Arty, Breathed's Battery; ref: 1
COLLIER, James L.; pvt; 12thVA Cav, Co F; res: Carr Cty; ref: 1, 7
COLLINS, Charles; sgt; 2nd MD Inf, Co H; ref: 1, 2, 21
COLLINS, H. E.; pvt; Barry's MD Vols; ref: 1, 19
COLLINS, John; pvt, Marine Corps; C.S.S. Raleigh; MLCSH; ref: 1, 19, 20, 21, 700, 783, 1594
COLLINS, John W.; pvt; 7th NC Independent Inf, Co D; res: Balt; MLCSH; ref: 1, 2, 19, 21, 23, 700, 786
COLLINS, Martin; sgt; 34th GA Inf, Co A; res: Annapolis, AA Cty; ref: 1, 1539
COLLINS, Peter; pvt; 2nd MD Inf, Co H; ref: 1, 1628
COLLINS, Richard; pvt; 2nd MD Inf, Co H; ref: 1, 2, 21
COLLINS, Thomas; pvt; 1st VA Inf, Co E; ref: 1
COLLINS, Walter; pvt; Rhett's 1st SC Heavy Arty; ref: 1, 735
COLLINS, William G.; pvt; 1st VA Inf, Co E; res: East New Market, Dor Cty; ref: 1, 1547
COLSTON, Frederick Morgan; Capt; Ordnance Dept, Asst to Chief; res: Balt; ref: 1, 2, 19, 20, 21, 53, 69, 111, 150, 272, 316, 469, 507, 510, 511, 601, 684, 700, 727, 758, 777, 858, 866, 869, 877, 906, 976, 1058, 1187, 1293, 1577, 1599
COLSTON, William E.; pvt; 43rd VA Cav (Mosby's), Co B; res: Balt; ref: 1, 2, 8, 19, 35, 44, 92, 93, 257, 258, 259, 511, 559, 650, 711, 1511, 1519, 1520, 1579

COLSTON, William G.; pvt; 32nd NC Inf, Co F; ref: 1, 735
COLTON, Lodge; Mast. M., Navy; C.S.S. Shenandoah; ref: 19, 58, 93, 107, 283, 716, 964, 1564, 1620, 1673, 1676
COLTON, Walter; pvt; 47th VA Inf, Co B; res: PG Cty; ref: 1, 82, 83
COLUMBINE, Lungi; pvt; 2nd MD Cav, Co C; res: 1
COLYER, William; pvt; 13th VA Inf, Co G; res: 1
COMBS, Benjamin; pvt; Lee's MD Cav; MD Cav; ref: 1
COMBS, Edgar; pvt; 2nd MD Inf, Co B; res: St. M. Cty; ref: 1, 2, 19, 21, 1509, 1662
COMBS, Edward John; res: St. M. Cty; ref: 6, 1662
COMPTON, J. C.; pvt; 43rd VA Cav (Mosby's), Co C; ref: 1, 8, 20
COMPTON, William Penn; sgt; 1st MD Lt Arty; res: Port Tobacco, Cha Cty; MLCSH; ref: 1, 2, 19, 21, 23, 26, 34, 63, 64, 68, 93, 215, 700, 782, 786, 791, 1020, 1273, 1523, 1546
CONAWAY, Joel; pvt; Jacobs' Mounted Riflemen; res: Elk Ridge Landin, AA Cty; ref: 1, 1539
CONCANNIN, Martin; res: Millersville, AA Cty; ref: 1539
CONDELL, Samuel C.; pvt; 2nd MD Cav, Co C; res: Balt; ref: 1, 2, 19, 21
CONKLING, Charles; res: Millersville, AA Cty; ref: 1539
CONDEY, Edgar Thomas; pvt; MD Guerrilla Zouaves; ref: 1, 2, 20, 21, 86
CONLEY, Martin V.; pvt; 1st MD Cav, Co E; ref: 1, 2, 19, 21, 730
CONLEY, Michael E.; pvt; Epps' Lt Arty Co; ref: 1, 2, 19, 21, 470, 700
CONLEY, William; pvt; 9th VA Inf, Co B; res: Balt; MLCSH; ref: 1, 21, 92, 93, 627, 786, 1540, 1576
CONLEY, William P.; pvt; 2nd MD Cav, Co C; res: Balt; ref: 1, 19, 1540, 1609
CONN, William D.; pvt; 1st MD Inf, Co D; res: Balt; ref: 1, 2, 19, 21
CONNELL, A.; pvt; MD Guerrilla Zouaves; ref: 1
CONNELL, Thomas; pvt; Davis's MD Cav, Co C; res: Balt; ref: 1, 1540
CONNELLY, Edward T.; pvt; 1st MD Inf, Co D; ref: 1, 2, 19, 21
CONNELLY, Nicholas; pvt; 1st SC Inf, Co G; ref: 1
CONNELLY, Patrick; pvt; Davis's MD Cav, Co C; ref: 1
CONNER, William; pvt; 1st MD Lt Arty; res: Frd Cty; ref: 1, 2, 21
CONNERARY, John; pvt; Jacobs' Mounted Riflemen; res: Balt; ref: 1, 1540
CONNOLLEY, Edward; pvt; MD American Rifles; res: Balt; ref: 1, 2, 21
CONNOLLY, Patrick; sgt; 1st SC Inf, Co E; res: Bt Cty; MLCSH; ref: 1, 21, 627, 700, 735, 786
CONNOLLY, William; pvt; 1st MD Inf, Co F; ref: 1, 2, 21
CONNOR, Alexander; pvt; 3rd MD Lt Arty; ref: 1, 2, 19, 21, 160, 726
CONOR, Andrew; pvt; Stuart's Horse Arty, Breathed's Battery; ref: 1, 498
CONNOR, James; pvt; 1st VA Inf, Co E; ref: 1, 2, 21, 160, 726, 735
CONNOR, Jonathan; artificer; Stuart's Horse Arty, Breathed's Battery; ref: 1, 498
CONNOR, William; pvt; Staurt's Horse Arty, Breathed's Battery; ref: 1
CONNORS, Michael; pvt; 19th VA Heavy Arty, Co C; res: Balt; ref: 1, 1580, 1613
CONOWAY, William Henry; pvt; 1st SC Inf, Co G; res: Balt; MLCSH; ref: 1, 21, 93, 627,. 700, 735, 786
CONRAD, Ephraim; pvt; 1st VA Cav, Co K; ref: 1, 2, 19
CONRAD, George W.; pvt; 43rd VA Cav (Mosby's), Co C; ref: 1, 2, 8, 19, 21
CONRAD, James M. Monroe; pvt; 12th VA Cav, Co B; res: Balt; ref: 1, 21, 255,700, 761

CONRAD, John Summerfield (M.D.); Asst Surg; Engineers Corps, Army of Northern Virginia; res: Balt; ref: 1, 18, 631, 1533, 1536
CONRAD, M. O.; pvt; 43rd VA Cav (Mosby's), Co C; ref: 1, 8, 20
CONRAD, Peter M.; pvt; 10th VA inf, Co F; Reisterstown, Bt Cty; ref: 1, 21, 124, 700
CONRAD, Thomas Nelson; Chaplain; 3rd VA Cav; res: Georgetown; ref: 1, 973, 1492, 1493, 1523
CONRAD, Townsend N.; vpt; Dixie VA Lt Battery; res: Balt; ref: 1, 1008
CONRADT, C. S.; res: Balt; ref: 20
CONRADT, Christian J.; pvt; 1st VA Cav, co K; res: Balt; ref: 1, 2, 19, 21, 56, 70, 700, 899
CONROY, Dennis; pvt; Stuart's Horse Arty, Breathed's Battery; ref: 1, 498
CONROY, John J.; smn; Privateer Schooner Beauregard; res: Balt; ref: 1, 1332
CONSTANTINE, Daniel; cpl; 4th Bn VA Inf, Co A; res: Balt; ref: 1, 1540
CONTEE, Charles Snowden; Lt; 1st MD Lt Arty; res: Pleasant Prospect Plantation, PG Cty; ref: 1, 2, 4, 5, 19, 35, 63, 64, 68, 70, 215, 443, 458, 627, 782, 791, 1273, 1523, 1553
CONTEE, John; Pleasant Prospect, PG Cty; ref: 12
CONTEE, Philip Ashton Lee, Jr; cpl; 1st MD Lt Arty; res: Charlotte Hall, Cha Cty; ref: 1, 2, 12, 19, 20, 21, 26, 1546
CONTEE, Richard S.; Maj; Adj & I.G. Gen A. Elzey's staff; res: Pleasant Prospect Plantation, PG Cty; MLCSH; ref: 1, 2, 4, 19, 34, 70, 627, 685, 687, 735, 786, 789, 1579
CONTTRELL, Edward C.; pvt; 4th MD Lt Arty; ref: 1, 2, 21
CONTWELL, Joseph; pvt; 7th VA Cav, Co G; ref: 1, 3
COODE, Demetrius A. G., "Mett"; cpl; Stuart's Horse Arty, Breathed's Battery; Skipping Point, St. M. Cty; ref: 1, 2, 6, 19, 21, 498, 650, 700, 822, 1509, 1555
COOK, Adolphus; Lt; 1st MD Cav, Co B; PG Cty; ref: 1, 2, 19, 21, 23, 45, 62, 68, 69, 316, 486, 700, 785, 791, 816, 1523, 1553, 1622
COOK, Charles; pvt; 3rd MD Lt Arty; ref: 1, 2, 19, 21, 160, 726
COOK, Frederick; pvt; 8th KY Cav, Co I; res: Balt; ref: 1, 21, 70, 700
COOK, George Anderson; pvt; Lee's MD Cav; ref: 1, 686, 1577
COOK, George R.; pvt; 1st MD Cav, Co C; res: Chaptico, St. M. Cty; ref: 1, 2, 6, 19, 21, 650, 1509, 1555, 1627
COOK, George Wythe (M.D.); pvt; 7th VA Cav, Co E; res: Balt; ref: 1, 23, 677
COOK, Jacob F.; pvt; 4th MD Lt Arty; res: Balt; ref: 1, 2, 19, 21, 700, 1523
COOK, John H.; pvt; 12th VA Cav, Co F; ref: 1, 70, 677
COOK, Rudolphus; pvt; 1st VA Cav, Co K; res: 1, 2, 19
COOK, Stephen L.; pvt; 1st VA Inf, Co E; ref: 1
COOK, Steve J.; sgt; 2nd MD Cav, Co A; ref: 1, 19, 693, 735
COOK, Thomas W.; pvt; Lee's MD Cav; res: Balt; ref: 1, 19
COOK, W. J.; pvt; Lucas's 15th Heavy SC Arty; ref: 1, 7
COOK, William; pvt; 1st MD Inf, Co A; ref: 1, 2, 19, 21
COOK, William S.; pvt; 5th VA Cav, Co E; ref: 1, 21, 93, 700
COOKE, Benjamin Dorsey; Lt; Edelin's MD Heavy Arty; res: Cookesville, How Cty; ref: 1, 13, 19, 748
COOKE, George A.; pvt; Hampton Leg Lt Arty; ref: 1, 2, 19, 21, 70
COOKE, Giles Buckner (Revd); Maj; Asst Adj & I.G., Gen R. E. Lee's staf; res: Cec Cty; ref: 1, 30, 111, 114, 122, 127, 791, 825, 1004, 1022, 1180, 1274, 1300, 1437, 1438, 1449

COOKE, James Philip (M.D.) Contract Surg; res: Chaptico, St. M. Cty; ref: 1, 6, 18, 1509, 1670
COOKE, Robert Corbin; cpl; 24th NC, Co G; res: Balt; MLCSH; ref: 1, 93, 786
COOKE, Robert E.; pvt; MD Cav; ref: 20
COOKE, William; pvt; 21st VA Inf, Co B; res: How Cty; ref: 1, 2, 20, 312, 735
COOKE, William P.; pvt; Weston's Inf, Co B; res: Balt; ref: 1, 69, 70, 316
COOKSEY, Benjamin; res: Davidsonville, AA Cty; ref: 1539
COOKSEY, Theodore C.; pvt; 2nd MD Inf, Co C; res: Crownsville, AA Cty; ref: 1, 2, 4, 5, 19, 21, 70, 79, 86, 469, 700, 1539
COOLEY, Ambrose; pvt; 2nd MD Cav, Co F; res: Har Cty; ref: 1, 2, 19, 20, 21
COOLEY, William L.; pvt; 2nd MD Cav, Co D; res: Har Cty; ref: 1, 20
COOMBS,George Griswold (D.D.S.); pvt; Hampton Leg Lt Arty, Co B; res: Balt; MLCSH; ref: 1, 2, 19, 21, 93, 627, 786
COOMBS, Charles; pvt; 1st MD, Co G; res: Southern MD; ref: 1, 2, 19, 21, 69, 316
COONAN, James; pvt; 13th VA Inf, Co G; ref: 1
COOPER, Charles E.; pvt; 1st MD Inf, Co E; ref: 1
COOPER, J. B.; Navy; C.S.S. Albermarle; res: St. M. Cty; ref: 1, 1627
COOPER, James; sgt; 1st Regt Engineers, Co C; res: Balt; ref: 1, 2, 19, 21, 690, 700
COOPER, James; pvt; Lucas' 15th SC Heavy Arty; ref: 1, 20
COOPER, John M.; 2nd Lt; Davis's MD Cav, Co C; res: Junction, AA Cty; ref: 1, 19, 1539, 1609
COOPER, Samuel; pvt; 2nd MD Cav, Co C; res: St. M. Cty; ref: 1, 1627
COOPER, W.; pvt; 4th MD Lt Arty; ref: 1
COOPER, William; pvt; 2nd MD Cav, Co D; res: Annapolis, AA Cty; ref: 1, 19, 1539
COOPER, William T.; pvt; 1st MD Cav, Co B; res: Som Cty; ref: 1, 2, 19, 21, 785
COPE, J.; pvt; 1st MD Lt Arty; ref: 1
COPELAND, John; carpenter; Richard Naval Station; res: Carrollton Manor, Frd Cty; ref: 1, 643
COPELAND, Phillip D.; pvt; 12th VA Cav, Co B; res: Balt; ref: 1, 21, 255, 700
CORBIN, John W.; sgt; 43rd VA Cav (Mosby's), Co A; res: Balt; ref: 1, 8, 70, 1579, 1598
CORBIN, W. F.; pvt; 1st SC Inf, Co G; ref: 1
CORCORAN, James W.; pvt; ref: 1690
CORCORAN, Thomas W.; pvt; 1st MD Cav, Co D; res: Carroll Cty; ref: 1, 2, 19, 21, 1601
CORDELL, Eugene Fauntleroy (M.D.); Capt; Adj, 51st VA Inf; res: Balt; ref: 1, 18, 23, 1533, 1536
CORKLEY, J.; pvt; 2nd MD Cav, Co A; ref: 1, 19
CORLIDGE, Theodore; pvt; 2nd MD Cav, Co B; ref: 1, 19
CORMICK, Robert; pvt; 1st MD, Cav, co E; ref: 1, 2, 19, 21, 730
CORNWELL, Charles C.; pvt; Davis's MD Cav, Co B; ref: 1, 2, 19, 21
CORNWELL, George; pvt; 43rd VA Cav (Mosby's), Co H; ref: 1, 8, 20
CORNWELL, James A.; pvt; 22nd SC Inf, Co K; res: Mont Cty; ref: 1, 20
CORNWELL, James L.; pvt; 43rd VA Cav (Mosby's), Co H; ref: 1, 8, 20
CORNWELL, R. H.; pvt; 43rd VA Cav (Mosby's), Co H; ref: 1, 8, 20
CORRELL, John William (M.D.); Asst Surg, Army of Northern Virginia; ref: 1, 18, 1536
CORRY, Henry; pvt; 4th MD Lt Arty; res: Cha Cty; ref: 1, 2, 19, 21
CORRY, James B.; pvt; 2nd MD Inf, Co B; ref: 1, 2, 19, 21
CORUTHERS, Illinois; Cpl; 13th VA Inf, Co G; ref: 1, 735

COSGRIFF, James O.; pvt; 2nd MD Lt Arty; ref: 1, 2, 19, 21

COSGROVE, James William; Lt; Stuart's Horse Arty, Breathed's Battery; res: Park Mills, Frd Cty; ref: 1, 90, 498, 700

COSSON, John S.; pvt; 3rd MD Lt Arty; ref: 1, 2, 19, 21, 160, 461, 726, 1460

COSTELLO, Thomas; Lt; 1st MD Inf, Co B; ref: 1, 2, 19, 21, 23, 64, 456, 791, 1609

COSTEN, Isaac Thomas (M.D.); Contract Surg; res: Pocomoke City, Wor Cty; ref: 1, 18

COSTIGAN, C. of Silvester; pvt; Edelin's MD Heavy Arty; res: Oakville, St. M. Cty; ref: 1, 6, 1555, 1627

COSTIGAN, Dorsey, T.; pvt; 1st MD Inf, Co H; res: St. M. Cty; ref: 1, 2, 6, 19, 21, 259, 650, 1509, 1520

COTCHETT, George M.; sgt; ref: 700

COTTER, J. J.; pvt; 3rd MD Lt Arty; ref: 1, 2, 19, 160, 461, 726, 1460

COTTINGHAM, James Thomas; Lt; 5th GA Reserves, Co A; res: Princeland, AA Cty; MLCSH; ref: 1, 21, 93, 627, 700, 735, 786, 1539

COTTMAN, Herman Stuart; pvt; 43rd VA Cav (Mosby's), Co A; ref: 1, 70

COTTON, M. Augustus; Lt; 17th NC Inf, Co E; res: Balt; ref: 1, 70

COTTRELL, Edward C.; pvt; 4th MD Lt Arty; res: Balt; ref: 1, 2, 19, 21, 470, 700

COULDER, Harry; res: Annapolis, AA Cty; ref: 1539

COULTER, William M.; pvt; Jacobs' Mounted Riflemen; res: Rohrersville, Wash Cty; ref: 1, 361

COURT, Michael; pvt; 2nd MD Inf, Co H; ref: 1

COURTNEY, Patrick; pvt; 2nd MD Inf, Co E; ref: 1, 19

COUSINS, J. H.; pvt; 3rd MD Lt Arty; ref: 1, 2, 19, 21, 160, 726

COUSINS, Thomas J.; pvt; 1st MD Cav, Co; ref: 1

COVEY, Edward Napoleon; (M.D.) Surg, Medical Director of General Hospital of NC; res: St. Michaels, Tal Cty; ref: 1, 18, 19, 645, 1152, 1370, 1579

COVINGTON, Allen J.; pvt; 4th MD Lt Arty; res: QA Cty; ref: 1, 2, 19, 21, 470, 1612

COVINGTON, George W.; pvt; Stuart's Horse Arty, Breathed's Battery; ref: 1, 498

COVINGTON, Jesse H.; pvt; 1st MD Lt Arty; res: How Cty; ref: 1, 2, 19, 21

COVINGTON, T. B.; pvt; 36th NC Inf, Co F; res: Balt; ref: 1, 70

COWARDIN, W. R. (Revd); sgt; 3rd VA Ragulars, Co B; res: Balt; ref: 1, 21, 700, 866, 906, 1053

COWLING, John; Q.M.; MD Line; ref: 1

COX, Abraham C.; cpl; 3rd MD Lt Arty; ref: 1,2, 19, 21, 23, 160, 461, 726, 1460

COX, C. M.; pvt; 2nd MD Cav, Co E; res: Balt; ref: 1, 1609

COX, Fleet W.; Capt; 40th VA Inf, Co K; res: Southern MD; ref: 1, 818

COX, George; pvt; 2nd MD Lt Arty; ref: 1, 2, 19, 21, 55, 1523

COX, George Thomas; Lt; 1st VA Inf, Co F; ref: 1, 685

COX, George W.; pvt; 23rd GA Inf, Co E; res: Balt; ref: 1, 784

COX, James; pvt; 3rd MD Lt Arty; ref: 1, 2, 19, 21, 160, 726

COX, James B.; pvt; 1st MD Cav, Co E; ref: 1, 2, 19, 21, 730

COX, Richard Smith; Maj; Asst Q.M.; VA Reserves; res: Georgetown; ref: 1, 1492

COX, Thomas G.; Lt; 1st VA Inf, Co F; res: Bristol, AA Cty; rf: 1, 685, 735, 1539

COX, William H. H.; pvt; 2nd MD Lt Arty; ref: 1, 2, 19, 21

COYLE, James; pvt; Davis's MD Cav, Co C; ref: 1

COYLE, John Henry (D.D.S.); 5th VA Cav, Co C; res: Balt; ref: 1689

COYLE, Patrick Henry; pvt; 1st MD Inf, Co D; res: Balt; MLCHS; ref: 1, 2, 19,21, 627, 700, 786

COYLE, Wilbur F.; pvt; 1st MD Inf, Co D; ref: 1, 19, 1279
COYNER, Samuel F. (M.D.); pvt; 7th VA Cav, Co D; res: Balt; ref: 1, 18, 631
COYNER, William Renic; pvt; 1st KY Inf, Co E; Res: Balt; MLCSH; ref: 1, 627, 700, 786
COZZENS, Henry B.; pvt; 28th MS Inf, Co K; ref: 1, 70
CRABB, Richard; pvt; 34th AL Inf, Co D; ref: 1, 20
CRABB, Robert; pvt; Stuart's Horse Arty, Breathed's Battery; ref: 1
CRABTREE, Albert P.; pvt; Freeman's NC Bn, Co C; res: Balt; ref: 1, 21, 700
CRAFT, Henry B.; gun, Navy; Gunboat Fredericksburgh; res: Balt; ref: 1
CRAFT, John B.; pvt; Davis's MD Cav, Co C; res: Frd Cty; ref: 1, 1611, 1677
CRAIG, Alexander; pvt; Zarvona's MD Zouaves; ref: 1, 735
CRAIG, Edward; pvt; 3rd MD Lt Arty; ref: 1, 2, 19, 21, 160, 726
CRAIG, George W.; pvt; 35th VA Cav, Co A; ref: 1, 15
CRAIG, William R.; pvt; Davis's MD Cav, Co A; ref: 1, 735
CRAIGVILLE, A. W.; pvt; 1st MD Cav, Co D; ref: 1, 19
CRALLE, Richard K.; pvt; 46th VA Inf, Co B; res: Balt; ref: 1, 21, 700
CRAMPTON, Benjamin Philpott; Capt; 7th Cav, Co G; res: Merryland Tract, Frd Cty; ref: 1, 3, 64, 90, 517, 518, 791, 1154, 1278
CRANDALL, Joseph N.; VA Inf; res: AA Cty; ref: 20
CRANDELL, Charles P.; Lt; 19th VA Heavy Arty; ref: 1, 735, 1580
CRANDELL, Robert C.; pvt; 6th NC Inf, Co G; res: Friendship, AA Cty; ref: 1, 1539
CRANE, Charles T.; sgt; Richmond Howitzers, 2nd Co; res: Balt; ref: 1, 20, 21, 23, 70, 700, 906, 1058
CRANE, Henry Ryland; pvt; Richmond Howitzers, 2nd Co; res: Balt; ref: 1, 20, 21, 23, 56, 57, 700, 720
CRANE, James Parran; Maj; 2nd MD Inf; res: St.M. Cty; ref: 1, 2, 6, 19, 21, 23, 63, 64, 68, 86, 94, 105, 107,240, 443, 462, 511, 791, 1509, 1520, 1523, 1578, 1600, 1624, 1627, 1634
CRANE, Robert Brent; pvt; 1st MD Cav, Co A; res: Towson, Bt Cty; ref: 1, 2, 6, 19, 20, 21, 23, 92, 1509
CRANE, William; pvt; 1st MD Cav, Co C; res: St. M. Cty; ref: 1, 2, 6, 19, 21, 511
CRANGLE, Robert; pvt; 3rd MD Lt Arty; ref: 1, 2, 19, 21, 160, 726
CRAPSTER, Thaddeus; ref: 20
CRASK, Selden F.; pvt; 9th VA Cav, Co C; res: St. M. Cty; MLCSH; ref: 1, 21, 93, 700, 786
CRATE, Frederick Thomas; cpl; Lucas's 15th SC Heavy Arty; res: Fort Washington, PG Cty; ref: 1, 20, 70, 1541
CRAVEN,, B. L.; pvt; 1st MD Lt Arty; ref: 1, 2, 19, 21
CRAVER, Moses M.; pvt; 1st VA Lt Arty, Co A; res: Balt; ref: 1, 21, 23, 57, 700
CRAWFORD, George R.; pvt; 1st MD Cav, Co E; res: PG Cty; MLCSH; ref: 1, 2, 19, 21, 730, 786
CRAWFORD, George William; pvt; 2nd Cav, Co D; ref: 1, 8, 70, 700
CRAWFORD, Henry H.; pvt; 2nd MD Inf, Co C; res: PG Cty; ref: 1, 2, 19, 21
CRAWFORD, Henry Van Bibber; pvt; 1st MD Cav, Co B; res: Middletown, Cec Cty; ref: 1, 2, 19, 20, 21, 122, 785
CRAWFORD, James W.; pvt; McNeill's Rangers; Cumberland, AA Cty; ref: 1, 1010
CRAWFORD, John T.; pvt; 1st MD Cav, Co A; res: How Cty; ref: 1, 10, 19

CRAWFORD, Richard; cpl; 16th TN Cav, Co D; res: Crownsville, AA Cty; ref: 1, 1539
CRAWFORD, Thomas; pvt; 1st MD Cav, Co A; res: How Cty; ref: 1, 2, 19, 21
CRAWLEY, Barney; pvt; 43rd VA Cav (Mosby's), Co A; ref: 1, 8, 20
CRAWLEY,George Fitzhugh; pvt; 6thVA Inf, Co C; ref: Rockville, Mont Cty; ref: 1, 86
CRAYON, Porte; ref: 456
CREAGER, Frank A. W.; Lt; 35th TX Cav, Co I; ref: 1, 2, 19, 735
CREAMER, Jacob J.; pvt; 1st MD Inf, Co D; ref: 1, 2, 19, 21
CREEL, Barnett; pvt; 2nd MD Cav, Co A; ref: 1
CREMMIN, S.; LA; res: Balt; ref: 816
CRENSHAW, A. W.; pvt; 1st SC Inf, Co G; ref: 1
CRENSHAW, S. P.; pvt; 1st SC Inf, Co G; ref: 1
CRESAP, Van; pvt; McNeill's Rangers; ref: 1, 504
CRETIN, Andrew L.; pvt; 2nd MD Inf; res: Emimitsburg, Frd Cty; ref: 1, 2, 19, 21, 90
CRETIN, Henry; pvt; 2nd MD Inf, Co F; res: St. M. Cty; ref: 1, 2, 19, 21
CRETIN, Hillary; pvt; 2nd MD Inf, Co F; res: Emmitsburg, Frd Cty; ref: 1, 2, 19, 21, 90
CRETIN, John H.; pvt; 1st MD Cav, Co C; res: Wash Cty; ref: 1, 19
CRETIN, John T.; pvt; 2nd MD Inf, Co G; res: Emmitsburg, Frd Cty; ref: 1, 2, 19, 21, 90, 735
CRIDER, J. M.; pvt; 3rd MD Lt Arty; ref: 1, 2, 19, 160, 726
CRIDER, W. R.; pvt; 3rd MD Lt Arty; ref: 1, 2, 19, 21, 160, 726
CRIDLIN, Jacob H.; Lt; 30th VA Inf, Co A; res: Balt; ref: 1, 21, 700
CRIDLIN, Thomas L.; sgt; 30th VA Inf, Co F; res: Balt; Ref: 1, 21, 700
CRIMMONS, Daniel; pvt; 1st MD Inf, Co F; res: Balt; ref: 1
CRIPPS, Frederick; pvt; 9th VA Inf, Co B; ref: 1, 1576
CRISALL, George W.; pvt; Lucas' 15th SC Heavy Arty; ref: 1
CRISALL, J; pvt; 2nd MD Arty; ref: 1
CRISE, George W.; pvt; 21st VA Inf, Co B; res: Balt; ref: 1, 2, 312, 735, 781, 1540
CRISE, John L.; CSA medicine purchasing; res: Balt; ref: 1, 781, 1540
CRIST, Ephraim; pvt; 2nd VA Inf, Co A; res: Frd Cty; ref: 1, 90
CRISTY, George; res: Leonardtown, St. M. Cty; ref: 1509, 1555
CRISWELL, John O.; pvt; 1st MD Cav, Co D; ref: 1, 2, 19, 21, 1601
CRITTENDEN, Churchill; pvt; 1st MD Cav, Co C; ref: 1, 2, 21
CROAKER, Rufus K.; pvt; 19th VA Heavy Arty, Co C; ref: 1, 1580
CROFTON, James L.; pvt; 24th VA Cav, Co C; ref: 1, 21, 700
CROGAN, William W.; pvt; 9th VA Inf, Co B; ref: 1, 1576
CROMWELL, Benjamin Mellicamp (M.D.) Asst Surg; 3rd LA Bn; res: Eckhart Mines, All Cty; ref: 1, 18, 148, 1190, 1532
CROMWELL, Charles; pvt; Davis's MD Cav, Co B; ref: 1
CROMWELL, Joshua; pvt; Jacobs' Mounted Riflemen; res: AA Cty; ref: 1, 1539, 1628
CROMWELL, Oliver; pvt; 17th VA Inf, Co K; ref: 1, 142, 251
CROMWELL, Stephen A.; pvt; 1st VA Inf, Co E; res: Mont Cty; ref: 1, 735
CROMWELL, William; pvt; 43rd VA Cav (Mosby's), Co A; ref: 1, 8, 1539
CRONE, Gittings; pvt; Jacobs' Mounted Riflemen; res: Balt; ref: 1, 735
CRONE, Michael; pvt; 1st VA Inf, Co C; res: Balt; ref: 1, 21, 700, 735
CRONE, Robert; pvt; 1st VA Inf, Co A; res: Balt; ref: 1, 735
CROP, Charles Lewis; pvt; Davis's MD Cav, Co A; res: Govenstown, Bt Cty; ref: 1, 735, 1541

CROPPER, Thomas E.; pvt; 1st MD Cav, Co B; res: Cec Cty; ref: 1, 2, 19, 21, 785
CROSBY, R. H.; pvt; 1st SC Inf, Co G; ref: 1
CROSBY, Samuel; pvt; 20th MS Inf, Co I; res: West River, AA Cty; ref: 1, 1539
CROSHAW, William; pvt; 1st MD Inf, Co B; ref: 1, 2, 19, 21
CROSS, Alexander; Lt; 1st MD Inf, Co G; res: Balt; ref: 1, 2, 19, 21, 23, 64, 456, 1510
CROSS, Charles F.; pvt; 9th VA Inf, Co B; ref: 1, 1576
CROSS, Charles Louis; sgt; 7th VA Cav, Co G; res: Balt; ref: 1, 3, 21, 23, 700
CROSS, George W.; pvt; 2nd MD Cav, Co A; res: Balt; ref: 1, 19, 1609
CROSS, James W.; pvt; 1st TN Inf, Co B; res: Hagerstown, Wash Cty; MLCSH; ref: 1, 93, 700,786, 855, 905
CROSS, Lewis; sgt; Davis's MD Cav, Co A; res: Balt Cty; ref: 1, 1371
CROUCH, Bernard Spotswood; pvt; 24th VA Cav, Co B; ref: 1, 70
CROUCH, Frederick William Nicholls (Prof.); pvt; Richmond Howitzers, 1st Co; res: Balt; ref: 1, 21, 23, 56, 93, 700
CROUGHAN, Michael; pvt; 2nd MD Cav, Co F; ref: 1, 2, 21
CROUSE, W. Frank; Lt; Secret Service, Gen J.H. Winder's staff; res: Frederick, Frd Cty; ref: 1, 89, 90
CROUSE, William J.; Navy; res: Balt; ref: 1
CROW, ---; sgt; 1st VA; res: Balt; rf: 30, 55, 117
CROW, S. W.; pvt; 1st VA Inf, Co E; ref: 1
CROWDER, Jesse J.; Co F; ref: 70
CROWLEY, James; pvt; 1st MD Lt Arty; res: PG Cty; ref: 1, 2, 19, 21
CROWLEY, Michael; pvt; 3rd MD Lt Arty; ref: 1, 2, 19, 21, 160, 726
CROWLEY, Robert A.; sgt; 4th MD Lt Arty; res: Balt; ref: 1, 2, 19, 21, 23, 64, 1613
CROWLING, Michael; pvt; 2nd MD Cav, Co C; ref: 1, 19, 1609
CROWN, Frank H.; pvt; 35th VA Cav, Co B; ref: 1677
CROWN, Frederick N.; pvt; 35th VA Cav, Co B; res: Adamstown, Frd Cty; ref: 1, 3, 19, 90, 643, 1611, 1677
CROWN, John R.; pvt; 7th VA Cav, Co G; res: Adamstown, Frd Cty; ref: 1, 3, 15, 19, 64, 69, 643, 1560, 1611, 1677
CROWN, Joshua R.; Lt; 35th VA Cav, Co B; res: Adamstown, Frd cty; ref: 1, 2, 3, 15, 19, 62, 64, 70, 73, 90, 316, 371, 643, 733, 791, 816, 1611, 1677
CROGAN, Edward A.; pvt; 21st VA Inf, Co B; res: Balt; ref: 1, 2, 19, 312, 735
CROZART, J. A.; pvt; 3rd MD Lt Arty; ref: 1, 2, 19, 21, 160, 726
CRUDUP, John; Lt; ref: 1690
CRUDUP, Josiah; pvt; ref: 1690
CRUGHAN, Michael; pvt; 2nd MD Cav, Co F; ref: 1, 2, 21
CRUM, Louis; pvt; 2nd MD Inf, Co D; res: Annapolis, AA Cty; ref: 1, 70
CRUMMER, Armstrong; pvt; 2nd MD Inf, Co D; res: Balt; ref: 1, 2, 19, 21, 70
CRUMP, W. G.; pvt; Lee's MD Cav; ref: 1
CRUTHERS, Illinois; sgt; 1st MD Cav, Co C; res: Balt; ref: 1, 19
CRYER, Joseph Francis; pvt; 40th VA Inf, Co F; res: St. M. Cty; MLCSH; ref: 1, 21, 627, 700, 786, 1509, 1670
CRYER, Thomas E.; pvt; 2nd TN Inf, Co H; res: Tal Cty; ref: 1, 19, 20, 645
CUIPACK, F.; pvt; 4th MD Lt Arty; ref: 1, 34
CULBERSON, G. W.; pvt; 1st SC Inf, Co G; ref: 1
CULBRETH, John; pvt; Steuart's Horse Arty, Breathed's Battery; res: Balt; MLCSH; ref: 1, 2, 8, 19, 20, 21, 93, 498, 786

CULLINGSWORTH, Robert; pvt; 17th VA Inf, Co H; ref: 1, 21, 700
CULVER, E. K.; pvt; 4th MD Lt Arty; ref: 1, 2, 19, 21
CULVER, William; pvt; 4th MD Lt Arty; ref: 1, 2, 19
CUMMINS, Edward H.; Lt; 1st VA Inf, Co F; res: Georgetown; ref: 1, 316, 735, 1492
CUMMINS, Daniel; pvt; 1st MD Inf, Co F; ref: 1, 2, 19, 21
CUMMINGS, James; pvt; 25th MS Inf, Co B; res: Balt; ref: 1, 1540
CUMMINGS, Robert; res: Balt; ref: 1540
CUNNANE, Edward J.; pvt; Zarvona's MD Zouaves; ref: 1, 735
CUNNANE, Henry S.; pvt; Zarvona's MD Zouaves; ref: 1, 735
CUNNINGHAM, Albert; pvt; 5th TX Cav; res: Balt; ref: 1, 20
CUNNINGHAM, Albert B.; pvt; 18th LA Inf,, Co C; res: Balt; ref: 23
CUNNINGHAM, George W.; pvt; 43rd VA Cav (Mosby's), Co C; res: Old-town, All Cty; ref: 1, 2, 8, 19, 21, 1010
CUNNINGHAM, Jacob V.; res: Frd Cty; ref: 643
CUNNINGHAM, James; pvt; 10th LA Inf, Co D; res: Friendship, AA Cty; ref: 1, 1539
CUNNINGHAM, Robert H.; pvt; 1st VA Cav, Co K; res: Balt; ref: 1, 2, 19, 21, 700
CUNNINGHAM, T. E.; pvt; 35th VA Cav, Co B; ref: 1, 1611
CUNNINGHAM, William N.; Capt; ref: 1690
CURLETT, Edward W.; 1st MD Lt Arty, Co K; res: Balt; ref: 1, 1540
CURRAN, John; pvt; 3rd MD Lt Arty; ref: 1, 2, 19, 21, 160, 726
CURRY, Benjamin; res: St. M. Cty; ref: 1670
CURRY, Jabez Lamar Monroe; Lt Col; 5th AL Cav; res: Balt; ref: 1, 20, 23, 108, 110, 447, 523, 791
CURRY, William; pvt; Edelin's MD Heavy Arty; res: Annapolis, AA Cty; ref: 1, 1539, 1628
CURTIS, Charles J. (Revd); pvt; 2nd VA Inf, Co E; res: Lappans, Wash Cty; ref: 1, 361
CURTIS, J. B.; Navy; res: Balt; ref: 1
CUSHING, John, Jr; Lt; 1st MD Inf, Co E; res: Balt; ref: 1, 2, 19, 21, 23, 64, 70, 456
CUSHING, Joseph H.; 1st MD Co C; res: Balt; ref: 141
CUSHING, Robert H.; sgt; 1st MD Inf, Co E; res: Balt; ref: 1,2, 19, 21, 23, 141, 1510, 1540, 1598
CUSICK, Frederick; pvt; 4th MD Lt Arty; ref: 1, 2, 19
CUSTARD, George; pvt; 33rd VA Inf, Co I; res: Frederick, Frd Cty; ref: 1, 89
CUSTIS, William P.; Lt Col; 2nd VA Militia Inf; res: Balt; ref: 1, 70, 105
CWYN, John Tomkies; Lt; 26th VA Inf, Co B; ref: 1, 70

D'ANTIGNAC, A.; Capt; ref: 1690
DABNEY, Frederick Y.; Lt; 1st MD Lt Arty; ref: 1, 2, 19, 21, 23, 34, 64, 1523
DACHARIAS, Granville; ref: 735
DACHARIAS, John; ref: 735
DADE, Lee M.; pvt; 35th VA Cav, Co B; res: Buck Lodge, Dor Cty; ref: 1, 3, 1611, 1677
DADE, Oscar; cpl; Davis's MD Cav, Co A; ref: 1, 735
DADE, Robert L.; cpl; 35th VA Cav, Co B; res: Buck Lodge, Dor Cty; ref: 1, 3, 15, 1552, 1611, 1677
DADE, William F.; pvt; 1st MD Cav; res: Old Medley's, Mont Cty; ref: 1, 2, 19, 21, 73, 86, 106, 1601
DAFFIN, Benjamin; pvt; Zarvona's MD Zouaves; ref: 1, 735
DAFFIN, Francis D.; sgt; Zarvona's MD Zouaves; res: Balt; ref: 1, 2, 19, 21, 735, 1540
DAFFIN, Joseph; pvt; Jacobs' Mounted Riflemen; res: Balt; ref: 1, 1540, 1599
DAGNON, Michael; pvt; 33rd VA Inf, Co A; ref: 1, 145, 735

DAILEY, Benjamin; pvt; Courier for Gen T. L. Rosser; res: Cumberland, All Cty; ref: 1, 18, 1610
DAILEY, Charles James; pvt; McNeill's Rangers; res: Oakland, Gar Cty; ref: 1, 9, 19, 65, 95, 125, 145, 148, 372, 431, 519, 1010, 1560, 1636
DAILEY, James; pvt; Stuart's Horse Arty, Breathed's Battery; res: Cumberland, All Cty; ref: 1, 18
DAILEY, John; sgt; 2nd NC Inf, Co H; ref: 1, 735
DAILEY, Robert Wood (M.D); Surgeon-in-Charge, Gen Hospital, Lexington, VA; res: Cumberland, All Cty; ref: 1, 18, 1635
DAILEY, Thomas J.; pvt; 35th VA Cav, Co C; res: Point of Rocks, Frd Cty; ref: 1, 1611
DAILEY, William H.; pvt; 3rd MD Lt Arty; ref: 1, 2, 19, 21, 160, 726
DAILEY, John; pvt; 2nd MD Cav, Co D; ref: 1
DALEY, John; pvt; Zarvona's MD Zouaves; ref: 1, 19, 58, 92, 93, 97
DALL, Horatio McPherson; pvt; 21st VA Inf, Co B; res: Frederick, Frd Cty; ref: 1,2, 19, 21, 23, 312, 700, 735
DALL, Rash M.; pvt; 1st VA Cav, Co K; res: Williamsport, Wash Cty; ref: 1, 2, 19, 827, 1558
DALLAM, Charles Francis; pvt; 4th MD Lt Arty; res: Balt; MLCSH; ref: 1, 2, 19, 21, 627, 700, 786
DALLAM, Henry Clay; pvt; 3rd VA Inf, Co F; res: Balt; ref: 1, 19, 21, 44, 700, 724
DALLAM, William; pvt; 1st MD Lt Arty; ref: 1, 2, 21, 782, 791, 1273
DALLAM, William W.; Lt; 1st Engineers Corps. Co A; res: Trevanion, Carr Cty; ref: 1, 19, 21, 34, 40, 700, 791, 806
DAMAR, John Stralford; pvt; 1st MD Lt Arty; res: Frd Cty; MLCSH; ref: 1, 2, 19, 21, 82, 93, 700, 786
DAME, William Meade (Revd); pvt; Richmond Howitzers, 1st Co; res: Balt; ref: 1, 20, 21, 23, 53, 56, 70, 86, 101, 118, 493, 700, 866, 906, 936, 944, 1058, 1295, 1333, 1343, 1579
DAMERON, Thomas LeRoy; pvt; 40th VA Inf, Co C; res: St. M. Cty; ref: 1, 7, 1670
DAMMER, Joseph F.; pvt; 1st MD Inf, Co B; ref: 1, 2, 19, 21, 272
DANCE, E. Scott; pvt; 1st MD Cav, Co C; res: Bt Cty; ref: 1, 2, 19, 20, 21
DANDRIDGE, Phillip P.; Lt; 9th CA Cav, Co F; ref: 1, 21, 700
DANIEL, John S. (M.D.); Acting Asst Surg, Farmsville Hospital; ref: 1, 18, 1690
DANIEL, John W.; Lt, Navy; Richmond Naval Office; ref: 1, 1621
DANIEL, William H.; pvt; Castle Pinkney, SC Heavy Arty; ref: 1, 735
DANIELS, Joseph D.; lmn, Navy; ref: 1, 20
DANIELS, R. M.; pvt; 30th NC Inf, Co G; ref: 1, 92
DANIELS, William C.; pvt; 2nd MD Cav, Co C; ref: 1, 2, 19, 21
DANN, John; pvt; 43rd VA Cav (Mosby's), Co A; res: St. M. Cty; ref: 1,6, 1627
D'ARCY, J. H. B.; Capt; Quartermaster Dept; res: Carr Cty; MLCSH; ref: 700, 786
DARDEN, Francis W.; pvt; 43rd VA Cav (Mosby's), Co A; ref: 1, 8, 21, 700
DARDEN, George Freeman; Lt; 31st NC Inf, Co K; res: Balt; MLCSH; ref: 1, 21, 56, 57, 627, 700
DARDEN, Robert R.; pvt; 9th VA Inf, Co B; ref: 1, 1576
DARMADY, John; pvt; 7th VA Cav, Co G; res: Cumberland, All Cty; ref: 1, 3
DARNE, William; pvt; 35th VA Cav, Co B; res: Darnestown, Mont Cty; ref: 1, 1611, 1677
DARNELL, J. L.; pvt; 2nd MD Cav, Co B; ref: 1, 19, 1609

DARR, James W.; pvt; 35th VA Cav, Co A; ref: 1, 3, 7, 15, 1677
DASHIELD, Benjamin; pvt; Hampton Leg Lt Arty, Co B; ref: 1, 19
DASHIELD, Francis S.; pvt; 17th VA Inf, Co H; res: Princess Anne, Som Cty; ref: 1, 20, 1556
DASHIELD, George H.; pvt; 1st MD Inf, Co D; res: Balt; ref: 1, 2, 19, 21
DASHIELD, J. M.; pvt; 13th VA Inf, Co H; ref: 1, 20
DASHIELL, George; Maj; Chief Paymaster, Gen N. B. Forrest's staff; res: Elk Ridge, Bt Cty; ref: 1, 556, 735, 791
DASHIELL, Jeremiah Yellott; Col; Asst Adj Gen; Austin, TX; res: Balt; ref: 1, 18, 19, 127, 205, 546, 791
DAVENPORT, Jack; pvt; 4th AL Cav, Co B; ref: 1, 735
DAVENPORT, William H.; sgt, 11th GA Inf, Co E; res: Balt; ref: 1, 700
DAVIAGE, J. B. F.; pvt; 1st VA Inf, Co E; ref: 1, 735
DAVID, S. B.; Lt; 14th GA Inf, Co E; res: Balt; ref: 1, 70
DAVIDGE, J. D.; pvt; 1st VA Inf, Co E; res: Balt; ref: 1
DAVIDSON, E.; pvt; 3rd MD Lt Arty; ref: 1, 2, 19, 21, 160, 726
DAVIDSON, Hunter; Commander, Navy; Torpedo Boat; res: Stevensville, QA Cty; ref: 1, 61, 97, 543, 550, 1578
DAVIDSON, J. E.; pvt; 24th Cav, Co K; res: Balt; ref: 1, 21, 93, 700
DAVIDSON, Joseph H.; pvt; 1st MD Inf, Co F; res: Balt; ref: 1, 19
DAVIDSON, Robert; pvt; 1st MD Cav, Co E; res: Balt; ref: 1, 2, 19, 21, 730
DAVIDSON, Rufus C.; pvt; Davis's MD Cav, Co A; res: PG Cty; ref: 1, 735
DAVIDSON, Thomas H.; cpl; 1st MD Inf, Co E; ref: 1, 2, 19, 21, 23
DAVIDSON, Wallace C.; pvt; 30th VA Inf, Co F; ref: 1, 70
DAVIDSON, William H.; pvt; 2nd MD Cav, Co G; res: Balt; ref: 1, 19, 1609, 1611
DAVIES, A. B.; pvt; 34th VA Inf, Co A; res: Balt; MLCSH; ref: 1, 19, 786
DAVIES, Howard; pvt; 2nd MD Inf, Co G; ref: 1
DAVIES, John Franklin; Lt; 14th GA, Co I; res: Balt; ref: 1,70, 791
DAVIES, William; pvt; 2nd VA Cav, Co E; ref: 1, 2, 19
DAVIES, William H.; pvt; 1st MD Inf, Co H; res: AA Cty; MLCSH; ref: 1, 2, 19, 21, 93, 650, 700, 786
DAVIES, William T.; Lt; 3rd AR Inf, Co D; res: Balt; ref: 1, 21, 700
DAVIS, A.; Lt; Davis's MD Cav, Co F; res: Carrollton Manor, Frd Cty; ref 1, 643
DAVIS, A. David; pvt; 19th VA Heavy Arty, Co C; ref: 1, 1580
DAVIS, A. J.; sgt; 3rd MD Lt Arty; ref: 1, 2, 19, 21, 23, 160, 461, 511, 726
DAVIS, Daniel M.; pvt; 30th VA Inf, Co C; ref: 1, 720
DAVIS, Edward D.; smn, Navy; C.S.S. Georgia; ref: 1, 19, 58, 97, 1564
DAVIS, Evan; pvt; 1st MD Cav, Co D; res: Libertytown, Frd Cty; ref: 1, 2, 19, 21, 90, 511, 735, 1601
DAVIS, Frank R.; pvt; MD Guerrilla Zouaves; ref: 1
DAVIS, George; pvt; 43rd VA Cav (Mosby's), Co H; ref: 1, 8, 19, 74
DAVIS, George Howard; pvt; 1st MD Inf, Co E; ref: 1, 2, 19, 21, 511
DAVIS, George W.; pvt; 2nd MD Inf, Co A; res: AA Cty; ref: 1, 2, 4, 5, 19, 21, 511, 650
DAVIS, Henry B.; pvt; 1st VA Cav, Co K; res: Wor Cty; ref: 1, 2, 19, 21, 700
DAVIS, Henry Campbell; Capt; 12th SC Inf, Co C; res: Frd Cty; ref: 1, 72
DAVIS, Henry H.; pvt; 35th VA Cav, Co B; res: Darnestown, Mont Cty; ref: 1, 1552, 1677

DAVIS, Howard; pvt; 40th TN Inf, Co B; res: Balt; ref: 1, 1540
DAVIS, J. A.; Lt; Davis's MD Cav, Co B; ref: 1, 20, 511
DAVIS, Jacob N.; 2nd MD Inf, Co A; res: Clearsprings, Wash Cty; ref: 1, 2, 19, 21, 93, 259, 511, 650, 1558
DAVIS, James A.; Lt 2nd MD Inf, Co G; res: Dor Cty; ref: 1, 2, 19, 21, 23, 64, 68, 511, 650, 700, 1523
DAVIS, James Calvin; pvt; 1st TX Cav, Co I; res: Balt; ref: 1, 70
DAVIS, James W.; sgt; 35th VA Cav, Co B; res: Darnestown, Mont Cty; ref: 1, 3, 1552, 1677
DAVIS, James W.; pvt; 2nd MD Cav, Co G; res: Cambridge, Dor Cty; ref: 1, 1578, 1609
DAVIS, John A.; pvt; 7th VA Cav, Co G; res: St. M. Cty; ref: 1, 1670
DAVIS, John B.; Lt; 2nd VA Inf, Co K; ref: 1, 735
DAVIS, John Colbert; smn, Navy; C.S.S. Jamestown; res: Balt; MLCSH; ref: 1, 627, 700, 786
DAVIS, John G.; pvt; 2nd MD Inf, Co G; res: Port Tobacco, Cha Cty; ref: 1, 2, 19, 21, 511, 1546
DAVIS, John Ignatius (M.D.); Asst Surg; 6th NC Inf; res: Lime Kiln, Frd Cty; ref: 1, 2, 18, 19, 90, 700, 735
DAVIS, John J.; pvt; 12th VA Inf, Co C; res: Buckeystown, Frd Cty; ref: 1, 93, 1543
DAVIS, John Robinson; Captain's clerk, Navy, C.S. Florida; res: Balt; MLCSH; ref: 1, 21, 93, 627, 700, 783, 786, 1673
DAVIS, John S.; pvt; 19th VA Heavy Arty; ref: 1, 2, 19, 21, 511, 1580
DAVIS, John T.; pvt; 1st MD Lt Arty; ref: 1, 2, 19, 21, 70, 511
DAVIS, Joseph G.; pvt; 9th VA Inf, Co B; res: Balt; ref: 1, 1576
DAVIS, Joshua, Jr; bugler; 2nd MD Lt Arty; res: Princess Anne, Som Cty; ref: 1, 2, 19, 21, 511, 1556
DAVIS, Leslie H. (Revd); 7th VA Cav, Co F; res: Frederick, Frd Cty; ref: 1, 1129, 1137
DAVIS, M. H. Mc; pvt; 1st SC Inf, Co G; ref: 1
DAVIS, Mark N.; pvt; 13th VA Cav, Co D; res: Balt; ref: 1, 21, 700
DAVIS, Michael; pvt; 2nd MD Inf, Co C; ref: 1, 2, 19, 21, 23, 511
DAVIS, Moscow; pvt; 2nd MD Cav, Co C; ref: 1, 2, 19, 21, 511
DAVIS, Peter A.; cpl; 43rd VA Cav (Mosby's), Co C; ref: 1,2, 8, 21, 511
DAVIS, Phineas J.; sgt; 1st MD Cav, Co D; res: Libertytown, Frd Cty; ref: 1, 2, 19, 21, 23, 90, 511, 735, 1601
DAVIS, Richard; res: St. M. Cty; ref: 1670
DAVIS, Robert; pvt; 1st MD Cav, Co E; res: Balt; ref: 1, 2, 20, 92, 93, 730, 1540
DAVIS, Robert T.; pvt; 1st SC Inf, Co G; ref: 1
DAVIS, Samuel T; pvt; 14th MS Inf, Co A; ref: 1, 693
DAVIS, Samuel Boyer; Lt; Aid de Camp, I.R. Trimble's staff; res: Princess Anne, Som Cty; ref: 1, 678, 1124, 1489, 1556
DAVIS, Stephen; pvt; 1st SC Inf, Co G; ref: 1
DAVIS, T. Sturgis; Lt Col; Davis's MD Cav; res: Towson, Bt Cty; ref: 1, 2, 3, 11, 18, 19, 44, 50, 64, 70, 72, 81, 88, 91, 107, 127, 168, 256,457, 499, 518, 735, 778, 789, 791, 824, 1177, 1371, 1485, 1486, 1560
DAVIS, Thomas K.; pvt; 1st VA Inf, Co E; res: Princess Anne, Som Cty; ref: 1, 735, 1556
DAVIS, Thomas Sappington; pvt; 1st MD Cav, Co D; res: Libertytown, Frd Cty; ref: 1, 2, 19, 21, 72, 90, 511, 1579, 1601
DAVIS, Travers; pvt; 9th VA Cav, Co A; res: Taylor's Island, Dor Cty; ref: 1, 19, 112

DAVIS, Tyler Edward; pvt; 40th VA Cav, Co G; res: Frederick, Frd cty; ref: 1, 89
DAVIS, W. A.; pvt; 2nd MD Lt Arty; res: Mont Cty; ref: 1, 2, 19, 21, 511
DAVIS, W. E.; pvt; 3rd MD Lt Arty; ref: 1, 2, 19, 21, 160, 461, 511, 726
DAVIS, W. J.; pvt; 3rd MD Lt Arty; ref: 1, 2, 19, 21, 160, 511, 726
DAVIS, William; pvt; 1st AL Lt Arty, Co A; res: Johnson's Store, AA Cty; ref: 1, 2, 21, 511, 1534
DAVIS, William B.; res: Salisbury, Wic Cty; ref: 1666
DAVIS, William F.; cpl; 43rd VA Cav (Mosby's), Co E; ref: 1, 2, 8, 19, 21
DAVIS, William Henry; pvt; 35th VA Cav, Co C; ref: 1, 2, 3, 19, 20, 21, 511, 650, 1677
DAVIS, William L.; Capt; 2nd MS Inf, Co F; res: Cumberland, All Cty; ref: 1, 735
DAVIS, William M.; pvt; 2nd MD Cav, Co C; ref: 1, 1609
DAVIS, Z. O.; pvt; 4th VA Inf, Co D; res: Balt; MLCSH; ref: 1, 21, 700, 786
DAVISON, George; sgt; Davis's MD Cav, Co A; ref: 1, 735
DAVISON, J.; Letchers Battery, VA Lt Arty; ref: 735
DAVISON, John H.; pvt; 35th VA Cav, Co B; res: Balt; ref: 1, 3, 1677
DAVISON, Joseph G.; pvt; Davis's MD Cav, Co A; res: Georgetown; ref: 1, 735
DAVISON, Marcelus; pvt; Davis's MD Cav, Co A; ref: 1, 735
DAVISON, Thomas H.; pvt; 35th VA Cav, Co B; ref: 1, 2, 21, 23, 70, 80, 700, 1677
DAVISSON, John E.; pvt; 1st MD Cav, Co D; ref: 1, 19
DAVY, John; pvt; 2nd MD Cav, Co B; ref: 1, 2, 21, 1609
DAWEES, John; pvt; 2nd MD Inf, Co D; ref: 1, 19
DAWES, Samuel S.; pvt; 9th VA Inf, Co B; ref: 1, 1576
DAWSON, Charles; Lt; 8th VA Inf, Co H; res: Balt; ref: 1, 70
DAWSON, George; pvt; MD American Rifles; ref: 1
DAWSON, J.E.; pvt; 1st SC Inf, Co G; ref: 1
DAWSON, J. L.; pvt; 1st SC Inf, Co G; ref: 1
DAWSON, John W.; pvt; Letcher's Battery; res: West River, AA Cty; ref: 1, 2, 21, 735, 1539
DAWSON, Joseph R.; pvt; 1st VA Inf, Co E; ref: 1, 735
DAWSON, Lambden T.; pvt; 4th MD Lt Arty; res: St. Michaels, Tal Cty; ref: 1, 2, 19, 21, 1557
DAWSON, Levin G.; pvt; 2nd MD Inf, Co E; res: Trappe, Tal Cty; ref: 1, 2, 19, 21, 645, 1162, 1557
DAWSON, Nathan; pvt; 17th TX Inf, Co C; res: Hancock, Wash Cty; ref: 1, 361
DAWSON, Robert Alexander; pvt; 2nd MD Inf, Co E; res: Trappe, Tal Cty; ref: 1, 2, 19, 21, 93, 645, 1557
DAWSON, Robert L.; pvt; 1st VA Inf, Co E; res: Upper Marlboro, PG Cty; ref: 1
DAWSON, Robert Morris (M.D.); pvt; 2nd MD Inf,Co C; res: Royal Oak, Tal Cty; ref: 1, 2, 18, 19,21, 595, 645, 1536, 1557, 1612
DAWSON, Theodore; pvt; 15th TX Cav, Co B; res: Cumberland, All Cty; ref: 1, 9, 19, 65, 95, 148
DAWSON, Thomas W.; sgt; 1st SC Inf, Co G; res: Hancock, Wash Cty; ref: 1, 361, 1610
DAWSON, William A.; Lt; 27th VA Inf, Co D; res: Balt; ref: 1, 1540
DAY, Edward N.; pvt; 42nd NC Inf, Co K; res: Balt; ref: 1, 1540
DAY, M. V.; sgt; 1st SC Inf, Co G; ref: 1
DAY, William A.; pvt; 4th LA Inf, Co G; res: Millersville, AA Cty; ref: 1, 1539
DEAKINS, James R. H.; cpl; 1st MD Cav, Co B; res: Bladensburg, PG Cty; ref: 1, 2, 19, 21, 23, 785, 1553, 1622

DEALE, E. W.; pvt; 2nd MD Inf, Co A; ref: 1, 7, 19
DEALE, Theophilus Norman; pvt; 2nd MD Inf, Co A; res: West River, AA Cty; ref: 1, 2, 7, 19, 21, 70, 259, 650, 1628
DEAN, James E.; pvt; 4th MD Lt Arty; Lakesville, Dor Cty; ref: 1, 2, 19, 21, 1547
DEAN, Thomas; pvt; 4th MD Lt Arty; ref: 1, 2, 19, 21
DEAN, William H.; pvt; 1st MD Lt Arty; ref: 1, 2, 19, 21
DEANE, Frank; pvt; 4th VA Cav, Co I; res: East New Market, Dor Cty; ref: 1, 70, 1547
DEANE, T. M.; Capt; Orleans Light Guards, Co B; ref: 70
DEARBECK, Charles; pvt; 14th SC Inf, Co C; res: Balt; ref: 1, 93, 1677
DEAVER, John R.; pvt; 1st MD Cav, Co F; res: Balt; ref: 1, 2, 19
DEBRIL, Charles; pvt; 2nd MD Cav, Co C; ref: 1, 2, 11, 19, 21, 349
DEBROW, John; pvt; 11th Bn, TN Cav, Co E; res: How Cty; ref: 1, 10, 19
DECATUR, L. M.; pvt; Holbrooks' MD Lt Arty; ref: 1, 19
DECHAINE, Augustus; pvt; 2nd MD Cav, Co D; ref: 1, 19
DECKER, Lee W.; pvt; 1st MD Cav, Co A; res: Frd Cty; ref: 1, 19
DEERBACH, Charles; pvt; 1st SC Inf,Co G; res: Balt; ref: 1, 735, 1599
DEES, Daniel B.; pvt; 1st SC Inf, Co G; ref: 1
DEFEE, James; pvt; 1st SC Inf, Co G; ref: 1
DE FORD, Diogener N.; pvt; Norfolk Lt Arty Blues; res: Balt; MLCSH; ref: 1, 786
DEGAN, Casper; pvt; 3rd MD Lt Arty; ref: 1, 2, 14, 21, 160, 726
DE GOURNAY, Paul FranciEs; Lt Col; De Gournay LA Arty Bn; res: Balt; ref: 1, 2, 19, 21, 57, 92, 93, 700, 962, 969, 1424
DE GREY, Louis F.; pvt; 2nd MD Inf, Co H; ref: 1, 2, 19, 21
DELANEY, Francis; pvt; 3rd MD Lt Arty; ref: 1, 2, 19, 21, 160, 726
DELANEY, Jeremiah: pvt; Lucas' 15th SC Heavy Arty; ref: 1, 20
DE LASHMUTT, John M.; sgt; 6th TX Cav, Co L; res: Frd Cty; ref: 1, 70, 72, 90, 735, 1573
DE LASHMUTT, William; pvt; 1st MD Cav, Co D; res: Frederick, Frd Cty; ref: 1, 2, 19, 21, 90, 91, 1151, 1301, 1601
DELCHER, Edward; Mississippi; res: Balt; ref: 118
DELCHER, Harley; Mississippi; res: Balt; ref: 118
DELCON, M. J.; pvt; 56th NC Inf, Co H; ref: 1, 735
DELEVIE, Jacob; pvt; 1st MD Inf, Co C; ref: 1, 2, 19
DELISLE, William; pvt; 2nd MD Cav, Co A; res: Carr Cty; ref: 1, 19
DELLINGER, James N.; pvt; Edelin's MD Heavy Arty; res: Balt; ref: 1, 70, 1599
DELOZIER, George E.; pvt; 2nd MD Inf, Co B; Pisgah, Cha Cty; ref: 1,2, 19, 21, 700, 1546
DELOZIER, John M.; pvt; 2nd MD Inf, Co B; res: Pisgah, Cha Cty; ref: 1, 2, 19, 21, 1546
DELOZIER, Thomas J.; pvt; 2nd MD Inf, Co B; res: Pisgah, Cha Cty; ref: 1, 2, 19, 21, 1546
DEMENT, Benjamin Frank; sgt maj; 2nd MD Inf, Co F; res: Pisgah,Cha Cty; ref: 1, 2, 19, 21, 511, 700, 1523, 1546
DEMENT, John L.; pvt 2nd MD Inf, Co F; res: Pisgah, Cha Cty; ref: 1, 19, 1546
DEMENT, William Fendlay; Capt; 1st MD Lt Arty; res: Duffield, Cha Cty; ref: 1, 2, 19, 21, 23, 26, 34, 35, 50, 63, 64, 68, 88, 94, 104, 105, 126, 129, 215, 240, 443, 459, 470, 492, 511, 631, 700, 782, 791, 794, 823, 838, 1273, 1520, 1523, 1546, 1634, 1652
DEMENT, William Francis; pvt; 25th VA Inf, Co B; res: Oxon Hill, PG Cty; ref: 1, 2, 21, 316

DEMETTER, Alexander; 13th VA Cav, Co F; ref: 735
DEMING, A. J.; pvt; 2nd FL, Co A; res: Frd Cty; ref: 1, 677
DEMPSEY, Austin Nelson; pvt; Lecher's Battery, VA Lt Arty; res: Balt; MLCSH; ref: 1, 92, 93, 627, 700, 735, 786
DEMPSEY, Joseph; pvt; 4th MD Lt Arty; ref: 1, 2, 19, 21, 55, 700
DENEGRE, John; V.M.I. Cadet; res: Balt; ref: 70, 1687
DENMEAD, Aquila; pvt; 2nd MD Cav, Co F; ref: 1, 2, 19, 21
DENNIS, C. H. pvt; 43rd VA Cav (Mosby's), Co E; ref: 1, 8, 20
DENNIS, James; pvt; 1st MD Inf, Co E; res: Balt; ref: 1, 2, 19, 21
DENNIS, W. F.; pvt; 43rd VA Cav (Mosby's), Co E; ref: 1, 8, 20
DENNISON, George W.; pvt; 2nd MD Cav, Co C; res: Balt; ref: 1
DENNISON, George W.; pvt; 13th VA Inf, Co G; ref: 1, 735
DENNISON, John E.; pvt; Davis's MD Cav, Co B; ref: 1, 19
DENNY, James W.; pvt; 39th VA Cav, Co A; res: Balt; ref: 1,2, 21, 23, 56, 57, 511, 513, 700, 891, 916, 976, 994, 1001
DENT, Ferguson; pvt; 1st MO Inf, Co C; res: Cha Cty; ref: 1, 185
DENT, George H., Jr; pvt; 43rd VA Cav (Mosby's), Co C; res: Cha Cty; ref: 1, 2, 8, 19, 21, 735, 1609
DENT, Henry Clay; pvt; 2nd MD Inf, Co B; res: Allens Fresh, Cha Cty; ref: 1, 2, 7, 19, 21, 700, 1546
DENT, John Marshall; pvt; 1st MD Cav, Co B; res: Chaptico, St. M. Cty; ref: 1, 2, 19, 21, 785, 1509, 1555
DENT, Joseph H.; pvt; 12th GA Bn; res: St. M. Cty; ref: 1662, 1670
DENT, S. H.; Capt; Dent's Lt Arty Battery; res: Cha Cty; ref: 1, 19, 1188
DENT, Simon Magrauder, Capt; 5th VA Cav, Co B; res: Pomonkey, Cha Cty; ref: 1, 185
DENTON, George; cpl; 2nd MD Inf, Co A; res: Cal Cty; ref: 1, 2, 19, 21, 259, 650, 1520
DENTON, William; pvt; 1st MS Cav, Co F; ref: 1, 735
DEPPISH, Edward C; Lt; 1st MD Inf, Co G; res: Balt; res: 1, 2, 19, 21, 23
DEPPISH, Edward Christian; Lt; 1st MD Inf, Co G; res: Balt; MLCSH; ref: 1, 21, 64, 456, 502, 627, 700, 735, 786
DEPPISH, Frank; pvt; 1st MD Inf, Co G; ref: 1, 2, 19, 21
DERING, George M.; Capt; Asst Q.M.; 19th VA Cav; res: Germantown, Mont Cty; MLCSH; ref: 1, 21, 700, 786, 1621
DERMODY, John; pvt; 3rd Bn, SC Lt Arty, Co B; res: Cumberland, All Cty; ref: 1, 19, 65, 95, 148
DEROUGES, Alphonse; pvt; Jacobs' Mounted Riflemen; res: Junction, AA Cty; ref: 1, 1539
DERR, Thomas S.; pvt; 60th TN Mounted Inf, Co A; res: Frederick, Frd Cty; ref: 1, 89
DERRICK, Clarence; Lt Col; 23rd VA Inf; ref: 1, 735, 787, 791, 1019, 1485, 1600
DERRIERS, John; pvt; 2nd MD Cav, Co F; ref: 1
DERROW, Marlin; pvt; 19th VA Heavy Arty, Co C; res: Carr Cty; ref: 1, 1580
DERRY, Samuel; pvt, 2nd MD Cav, Co A; ref: 1
DESHAM, Augustus Wesley; pvt; 2nd MD Cav, Co D; ref: 1, 1540
DESNEY, John; pvt; 2nd MD Cav, Co D; res: AA Cty; ref: 1, 1628
DE SPAIN H. B.; pvt; Davis's MD Cav, Co B; res: Wor Cty; ref: 1, 19
DEUBLER, Constantine; pvt; 3rd SC Cav, Co C; res: Balt; ref: 1, 70
DEVECMON, Peter; McNeill's Rangers; res: Cumberland, All Cty; ref: 19, 95, 148, 504, 519, 735
DEVERIES, Octavius; pvt; 1st MD Cav, Co E; res: Balt; ref: 1, 19

DEVIEN, Thomas Jefferson; pvt; 13th VA Inf, Co G; res: Balt; MLCSH; ref: 1, 627, 786
DEVINNEY, Benjamin F; Lt; 2nd MD Inf, Co H; ref: 1, 19
DEVITT, Edward J.; pvt; 1st MD Inf, Co D; res: Frederick, Frd Cty; ref: 1, 2, 19, 21, 89, 90
DEVRIES, William; pvt; 2nd MD Cav,Co C; ref: 1, 2, 21
DEWEES, Jonathan; pvt; 2nd MD Inf, Co A; ref: 1
DIBBLE, ---; Gen J.H. Winder's Detectives; res: Balt; ref: 30
DIBRELL, C. L.; pvt; 2nd MD Cav, Co C; ref: 1, 1609
DICE, William T.; pvt; 27th VA Inf, Co D; ref: 1, 700
DICKEL, Harry L.; pvt; 8th KY Cav, Co I; ref: 1, 700
DICKERSON, William H.; pvt; 35th VA Cav, Co F; res: Old Medley's, Mont Cty; ref: 1, 106, 1611, 1677
DICKINSON, Elveno; pvt; 2nd Fl Cav, Co I; res: Tal Cty; ref: 1, 592, 645, 1612
DICKINSON, George C.; Capt; Engineers Corps, Co E; ref: 1, 21, 700, 800
DICKINSON, Lairie T.; pvt; 1st MD Cav, Co A; ref: 1, 2, 19, 21, 700, 841, 881
DICKSON, John Hamilton (D.D.S.); Lt; Dental Corps; res: Balt; ref: 1, 8, 18, 20, 1529, 1579, 1690
DIDLAKE, William F.; cpl; 26th VA Inf, Co B; res: Balt; ref: 1,21, 700
DIGGES, John T. (M.D.); pvt; 1st MD Lt Arty; res: Laplata, Cha Cty; ref: 1, 2, 19, 21, 26, 69
DIGGS, ---; pvt; Davis's MD Cav, Co A; ref: 735
DIGGS, Eugene; Capt; 2nd MD Cav, Co B; res: Port Tobacco, Cha Cty; ref: 1, 2, 11, 19, 21, 23, 64, 70, 316, 456, 693, 794, 901, 1609
DIGGS, William J.; pvt; 61st VA Inf, Co C; res: Georgetown; ref: 1, 316
DILLER, Anthony; pvt; Stuart's Horse Arty, Breathed's Battery; ref: 1, 498
DILLON, E. G.; pvt; 7th VA Cav, Co G; ref: 1
DIMITRY, Alexander; pvt; Castle Pinkney, SC Heavy Arty; ref: 1, 735
DIMMOCK, William; sgt; 1stEngineer Corps, Co E; res: Balt; ref: 1, 21, 700
DINEY, William; pvt; 2nd MD Cav, Co D; res: Balt; ref: 1, 2, 19, 21
DINKLE, J. H.; pvt; 7th VA Cav, Co G; ref: 1
DISENBERGER, George; pvt; 1st MD Inf, Co C; ref: 1, 19
DISHAROON, John W.; pvt; 1st MD Cav, Co E; res: Som Cty; ref: 1, 2, 21, 730
DISNEY, Andrew Jackson; pvt; MD Guerrilla Zouaves; res: Balt; ref: 1, 1540
DISNEY, Andrew J.; pvt; 9th VA Inf, Co B; res: Patuxent Forge, AA Cty; ref: 1, 1539, 1576
DISNEY, John William; sgt; 9th VA Inf, Co B; res: Patuxent Forge, AA Cty; ref: 1, 735, 1539, 1576
DISNEY, Nicholas; res: Princeland, AA Cty; ref: 1539
DISNEY, William J. of Julia; res: Elk Ridge Landing, AA Cty; ref: 1539
DISNEY, Wilson E.; pvt; 2nd MD Cav; res: Princeland, AA Cty; ref: 1539, 1609
DITMORE, J. C.; pvt; Davis's MD Cav, Co C; ref: 1
DITTERS, John Frederick; pvt; 1st MD Cav, Co C; res: Balt; MLCSH; ref: 1, 2, 19, 21, 93, 627, 700, 786
DITTY, Cyrus Irving; Lt; 1st MD Cav, Co F; res: West River, AA Cty; ref: 1, 2, 13, 19, 21, 23, 64, 70, 509, 631, 700, 827
DIVINE, James W.; pvt; 9th VA Inf, Co B; res: Balt; ref: 1, 1540, 1576, 1613
DIVINE, Thomas; pvt; 13th VA Inf, Co G; ref: 1, 735

DIX, William T.; pvt; 1st MD Cav, Co B; res: St. M. Cty; ref: 1, 2, 19, 21, 785, 1509
DIXON, Bradley S.; pvt; 2nd SC Inf, Co F; res: Balt; ref: 1, 1540
DIXON, J. J.; pvt; 2nd MD Cav, Co B; ref: 1
DIXON, James H.; cpl; 2nd MD Inf, Co F; ref: 1, 2, 19, 21, 23
DIXON, James W.; pvt; Griffin's Co, VA Lt Arty; res: Frd Cty; ref: 1, 19, 72, 90
DOBBIN, Robert; Nitre & Mining Bureau; res: St. Dennis, Howard Cty; ref: 735, 757, 1550
DOBBIN, Thomas M.; Nitre & Mining Bureau; ref: 735, 757
DOBBS, Thomas E.; pvt; 2nd MD Cav, Co A; res: Balt; ref: 1, 2, 11, 19, 21, 70, 1609
DOBSON, William H.; pvt; 2nd MD Cav, Co G; ref: 1
DODE, Samuel; pvt; 2nd MD Inf, Co D; ref: 1, 2, 19, 21
DODSON, John E.; pvt; 30th GA Inf, Co E; res: Crownsville, AA Cty; ref: 1, 1539
DODSON, Joseph; Crownsville, AA Cty; ref: 1539
DODSON, R. Town, sgt maj; Stuart's Horse Arty, Breathed's Battery; ref: 1, 498
DOFFLEMYER, George Washington; pvt; 7th VA Cav, Co D; res: Laurel, PG Cty; MLCSH; ref: 1, 92, 93, 627, 700, 786
DOHERTY, Charles; sgt; 30th VA Sharpshooters, Co E; ref: 1, 21, 700
DOLAN, Patrick H.; sgt; 1st MD Cav, Co C; ref: 1, 19, 21, 700
DOLL, George; 15th Mo Cav, Co E; res: Frederick, Frd Cty; ref: 1, 89
DOLLAR, A.; pvt; 3rd MD Lt Arty; ref: 1, 2, 461
DONAHUE, Charles R.; pvt; 1st VA Inf, Co E; ref: 1, 735
DONOHUE, Joseph P. O.; pvt; 1st MD Inf, Co E; res: Balt; ref: 1, 2, 19, 21
DONAHUE, Michael; pvt; 2nd MD Cav, Co C; ref: 1, 735
DONOAHUE, Thomas; pvt; 1st MD Inf, Co E; ref: 1, 2, 19, 21
DONALD, J. W.; pvt; 2nd MD Cav, Co A; ref: 1, 19, 1609
DONALDSON, John; pvt; 2nd MD Cav, Co D; ref: 1
DONALDSON, Owen; res: McPherson Pack, AA Cty; ref: 1539
DONCASTER, James W.; Lt; 3rd MD Lt Arty; ref: 1, 2, 19, 21, 23, 160, 461, 726, 791, 1060, 1523
DONGLADS, William; West River, AA Cty; ref: 1539
DONIPHAN, John W. (D.D.S.); pvt; ref: 1690
DONLAN, J. R.; pvt; 9th VA Inf, Co B; ref: 1, 1576
DONLAN, Thomas; pvt; Davis's MD Cav, Co C; ref: 1, 19
DONLEY, Charles A.; pvt; 2nd MD Cav, Co C; ref: 1
DONNELLY, Charles Aloysious; pvt; Lucas' 15th SC Heavy Arty; res: Emmitsburg, Frd Cty; MLCSH; ref: 1, 627
DONNELSON, Samuel; pvt; 2nd SC Rifles, Co A; res: Patuxent Forge, AA Cty; ref: 1, 1539
DONOHOE, Le Grand; pvt; 35th VA Cav, Co A; ref: 1, 3, 1677
DONOHUE, Edward; pvt; 3rd MD Lt Arty; ref: 1, 2, 21, 160, 726
DONOHUE, John; pvt; 2nd MD Inf, Co H; ref: 1, 2, 19, 21
DONOHUE, John C.; pvt; res: Balt; ref: 700, 1110
DONOHUE, William; pvt; 27th NC, Co A; res: Balt; MLCSH; ref: 1, 21, 93, 700, 735, 786
DONOVAN, Cornelius; pvt; 2nd MD Inf, Co C; ref: 1
DONOVAN, Thomas J.; pvt; 32nd TN Inf, Co A; ref: 1, 93
DOOLEY, Bernard; pvt; 2nd MD Inf, Co F; ref: 1, 2, 19, 21
DOOLEY, E. G.; Lt; 1st MD Cav, Co A; res: Mont Cty; ref: 1, 19
DOOLEY, Francis; pvt; 3rd MD Lt Arty; ref: 1, 2, 19, 21, 160, 726

DOOLEY, Robert; pvt; 1st MD Inf, Co I; ref: 1, 2, 19, 21
DOOLEY, Theodore W.; pvt; 2nd MD Cav, Co D; ref: 1, 19, 1609
DOOLEY, Thomas; pvt; 1st MD Cav, Co F; ref: 1, 2, 19, 21
DORAN, William; pvt; 2nd MD Cav, Co C; ref: 1, 2, 11, 21
DORE, Samuel B.; pvt; 2nd MD Inf, Co D; ref: 470
DORMANDY, John; pvt; 7th VA Cav, Co G; res: Cumberland, All Cty; ref: 1, 2, 19, 21, 1601
DORNIN, Franklin B.; Midn, Navy; C.S. Roanoke; res: Annapolis, AA Cty; ref: 1, 58, 59, 97, 1523, 1539, 1564
DORNIN, Thomas Lardner; Lt, Navy; C.S.S. Gaines; ref: 1, 21, 97, 279, 700, 783, 1564, 1677
DORSETT, J. Hawkins; pvt; 1st MD Lt Arty; res: PG Cty; ref: 1, 2, 19, 21, 26, 57, 70, 700
DORSETT, James A.; pvt; 1st MD Inf, Co I; res: Aquasco, PG Cty; ref: 1, 2, 19, 21, 1553, 1665
DORSETT, Walter C.; pvt; 6th VA Inf, Co K; res: AA Cty; ref: 1, 1539, 1628
DORSEY, Albert A.; pvt; 2nd MD Cav, Co F; ref: 1, 2, 21, 1609
DORSEY, Andrew I.; pvt; 1st MD Cav, Co A; res: Randallstown, Bt Cty; ref: 1, 2, 19, 21, 93, 233, 700, 720, 1295, 1539, 1565
DORSEY, B. Harrison; res: How Cty; ref: 10, 19, 748
DORSEY, C.; sgt; 7th VA Cav, Co G; res: How Cty; ref: 1, 71, 748
DORSEY, C. H.; pvt; 1st VA Cav, Co K; ref: 1, 2, 19, 21
DORSEY, Caleb; Col; Missouri; ref: 1, 2, 19, 735, 791
DORSEY, Charles R.; pvt; 1st VA Cav, Co K; res: How Cty; ref: 1, 2, 10, 19, 748
DORSEY, Charles Worthington; pvt; 43rd VA Cav (Mosby's), Co D; res: How Cty; MLCSH; ref: 1, 2, 3, 8, 10, 19, 21, 70, 92, 93, 627, 700, 735, 748, 786, 1523
DORSEY, Daniel B.; pvt; Hampton Leg Lt Arty, Co B; ref: 1, 2, 19, 21
DORSEY, Edward R.; Lt Col; 1st MD Inf; res: How Cty; ref: 1, 2, 19, 21, 23, 34, 38, 44, 64, 68, 240, 456, 493, 559, 583, 638, 684, 711, 715, 748, 789, 1313, 1491, 1511, 1523, 1600
DORSEY, Edward W.; pvt; 2nd VA Inf, Co A; res: Williamsport, Wash Cty; ref: 1, 361
DORSEY, Evan L.; pvt; 1st MD Lt Arty; res: Frd Cty; ref: 1, 2, 19, 21, 88, 559
DORSEY, Ezekiel S.; sgt; 2nd MD Inf, Co A; res: Balt; ref: 1, 2, 19, 21, 23, 650, 700, 1511
DORSEY, Frank; pvt; 1st SC Inf, Co G; res: Balt; ref: 1, 735, 947, 1025, 1026
DORSEY, George; pvt; 1st SC Inf, Co G; res: Balt; ref: 1, 735
DORSEY, Gustavus W.; Lt Col; 1st MD Cav; res: Brookeville, Mont Cty; ref: 1, 2, 10, 11, 13, 19, 21, 23, 35, 45, 46, 50, 118, 222, 443, 445, 462, 497, 505, 509, 511, 518, 560, 602, 638, 668, 684, 693, 722, 748, 791, 825, 827, 853, 947, 952, 981, 1025, 1027, 1068, 1071, 1108, 1338, 1387, 1519, 1523, 1550, 1574, 1584, 1600, 1634
DORSEY, Hammond; cpl; 1st VA Cav, Co K; res: Ellicott City, How Cty; ref: 1, 2, 10, 19, 21, 71, 240, 511, 735, 748, 881, 1550
DORSEY, Harry C.; pvt; 43rd VA Cav (Mosby's), Co D; res: How Cty; ref: 1, 2, 8, 10, 21, 511, 735, 740, 748
DORSEY, Harry Woodward, Jr (M.D.); Asst Surg; 1st MD Cav; res: Urbana, Frd Cty; ref: 1, 18, 19, 89, 90, 735, 1548, 1596
DORSEY, Ignatious Walter; Capt; Q.M., 1st MD Cav, Co A; res: New Market, Frd Cty; ref: 1, 2, 13, 18, 19, 21, 23, 63, 64, 67, 90, 740, 1523, 1634
DORSEY, J. Pembroke; pvt; 1st MD Cav, Co A; ref: 1, 19, 1634

DORSEY, James E., Jr; pvt; 2nd MD Inf, Co C; ref: 1, 2, 19, 21, 595
DORSEY, John; pvt; 1st SC Inf, Co G; ref: 1
DORSEY, John; pvt; Stuart's Horse Arty, Breathed's Battery; ref: 1, 498
DORSEY, John Cummings; pvt; 1st MD Cav, Co A; res: How Cty; MLCSH; ref: 1, 2, 10, 19, 21, 71, 511, 628, 700, 748, 786
DORSEY, John T. B.; Capt; Asst Q.M., Gen S. Garland, Jr's staff; res: Clarksville, How Cty; ref: 1, 10, 19, 93, 511, 735, 748, 791, 1550, 1583
DORSEY, John W.; Asst Engr, Navy; C.S.S. Missouri; res: How Cty; ref: 1, 2, 10, 19, 68, 511, 735, 740, 748, 1564
DORSEY, Lloyd E.; pvt; 1st VA Cav, Co A; res: Junction, AA Cty; ref: 1, 2, 19, 21, 687, 1539
DORSEY, Nicholas Worthington (M.D.); Lt; 35th VA Cav, Co B; res: Urbana, Frd Cty; ref: 1, 2, 3, 15, 18, 64, 73, 88, 90, 371, 643, 1548, 1560, 1611, 1677
DORSEY, Oscar; pvt; 5th VA Cav, Co C; res: Carr Cty; ref: 1, 19, 40, 1544
DORSEY, Pulaski; pvt; 43rd VA Cav (Mosby's), Co D; res: Simpsonville, How Cty; ref: 1, 2, 8, 10, 19, 21, 71, 511, 735, 748, 1550
DORSEY, Reuben Meriwether; pvt; 43rd VA Cav (Mosby's), Co D; ref: 1, 8, 19, 1523
DORSEY, Richard Brook, Jr; 21st VA Inf, Co B; res: Bt Cty; ref: 1, 2, 19, 23, 312, 650, 690, 735, 1539, 1575
DORSEY, Samuel of B.; pvt; 5th AR Inf, Co H; res: How Cty; ref: 1, 10, 19, 511, 748
DORSEY, Samuel Worthington; Lt; 1st VA Cav, Co K; res: How Cty; ref: 1, 2, 10, 11, 19, 21, 511, 687, 700, 748, 1523
DORSEY, Thomas B.; Missouri; ref: 2, 19, 735
DORSEY, Upton L.; sgt; 1st MD Cav, Co D; res: Carr Cty; ref: 1, 2, 19, 21
DORSEY, Upton W.; pvt; 1st MD Cav, Co A; res: Clarksville, How Cty; ref: 1, 2, 10, 21, 40, 71, 73, 90, 748, 1550, 1601
DORSEY, William; Lt; 2nd MD Cav, Co F; res: Mathews Store, How Cty; ref: 1, 2, 10, 11, 21, 23, 511, 748, 1550, 1631
DORSEY, William; pvt; 1st VA Cav, Co K; ref: 2, 21
DORSEY, William F.; sgt; 1st MD Cav, Co C; ref: 1, 2, 21, 23
DORSEY, William H. B.; Lt; 1st MD Cav, Co D; res: Mt Airy, Frd Cty; ref: 1, 2, 13, 19, 21, 23, 64, 66, 67, 68, 72, 79, 80, 90, 91, 614, 643, 693, 700, 789, 791, 827, 1301, 1523, 1544, 1577, 1578, 1579, 1601, 1609, 1634
DOSENBERRY, H. B.; pvt; 2nd MD Lt Arty; res: Balt; ref: 1, 2, 19, 21
DOSIER, Charles; pvt; 2nd MD Cav, Co D; ref: 1, 19, 1609
DOUGHERTY, Cornelius; pvt; 1st MD Inf, Co F; res: Balt; ref: 1, 2, 19, 21
DOUGHERTY, Daniel; cpl; 4th MD Lt Arty; ref: 1, 2, 19, 21, 34, 64
DOUGHERTY, George A.; pvt; 1st MD Lt Arty; ref: 1, 2, 19, 21
DOUGHERTY, Joseph; pvt; 9th VA Inf, Co B; ref: 1, 2, 19, 21, 93, 1576
DOUGHERTY, Henry C.; pvt; 19th VA Heavy Arty, Co C; res: Balt; ref: 1, 21, 700, 1580
DOUGHERTY, William E.; cpl; 19th VA Lt Arty, Co C; res: Balt; ref: 1, 21, 700, 1580
DOUGLAS, Bernard; pvt; 21st VA Inf, Co B; ref: 1, 2, 19, 312
DOUGLAS, Henry Kyd; Lt Col; Asst I.G., Gen T.J. Jackson's staff; res: Hagerstown, Wash Cty; ref: 1, 2, 11, 19, 21, 22, 23, 32, 35, 42, 44, 46, 48, 49, 64, 65, 66, 68, 72, 88, 91, 117, 118, 121, 125, 126, 127, 129, 145, 165, 289, 340, 347, 352, 361, 362,

469, 475, 517, 580, 601, 603, 612, 685, 686, 700, 735, 782, 789, 791, 816, 821, 873, 954, 1079, 1114, 1304, 1331, 1337, 1374, 1398, 1486, 1520, 1523, 1560, 1569, 1577, 1578, 1579, 1588, 1592, 1633, 1642, 1647, 1648, 1650, 1674

DOUGLAS, Henry Thompson; Lt Col; Engineerss Corps, Trans-Mississippi Dept; res: Balt; ref: 1, 21, 23, 56, 57, 62,127, 175, 700, 791

DOUGLAS, Hugh Thomas; Capt; 1st Regt Engineers, Co F; ref: 1, 21, 700, 791

DOUGLAS, Jackson; sgt; 1st MD Inf, Co H; refr: 1, 2, 21, 650

DOUGLAS, James Ross; pvt, 35th VA Cav, Co A; res: Frd Co; ref: 1, 3, 15, 735, 1677

DOUGLAS, John; pvt; 35th VA Cav, Co A; res: Frd Cty; ref: 1, 3, 735, 1677

DOUGLAS, Thomas T.; pvt; 1st VA Inf, Co E; ref: 1

DOUZIE, Lucien; pvt; LA Washington Lt Arty; ref: 1

DOVE, John, Jr; sgt; 35th VA Cav, Co A; res: Friendship, AA Cty; ref: 1, 3, 15, 371, 1539, 1677

DOVE, Joseph; pvt; 35th VA Cav, Co B; ref: 1, 3, 1677

DOVE, Robert; pvt; 1st VA Inf, Co E; ref: 1, 735

DOVE, Samuel B.; pvt; 2nd MD Inf, Co D; res: Bristol, AA Cty; ref: 1, 2, 21, 23, 70, 1523, 1539

DOVE, W. S.; pvt; 3rd MD Lt Arty; ref: 1, 2, 19, 21, 160, 726

DOWELL, Conard F.; pvt; 1st VA Cav, Co H; res: Balt; ref: 1, 70

DOWNEY, Jesse Wright (M.D.); pvt; 1st MD Cav, Co D; res: New Market, Frd Cty; ref: 1, 19, 64, 67, 72, 90, 1601

DOWNEY, John; sgt; MD American Rifles; ref: 1, 19

DOWNING, John Z.; cpl; 2nd MD Inf, Co B; res: Cha Cty; ref: 1, 2, 19, 21, 23, 1509

DOWNING, Samuel; Capt; 55th VA Inf, Co L; ref: 1, 21, 700

DOWNING, T. Jerome; pvt; 9th VA Cav, Co D; res: Balt; ref: 1, 21, 57, 700

DOWNS, Cicero; pvt; 35th VA Cav, Co F; res: Hyattstown, Mont Cty; ref: 1, 1611, 1677

DOWNS, Henry; pvt; 35th VA Cav, Co F; resd: Hyattstown, Mont Cty; ref: 1, 1611, 1677

DOWNS, James S.; pvt; 3rd MD Lt Arty; res: St. M. Cty; ref: 1, 2, 19, 21, 160, 726, 775

DOWNS, John H.; pvt; 2nd MD Cav, Co E; ref: 1, 19, 596, 693, 1609

DOWNS, Pierson; pvt; 35th VA Cav, Co F; res: Hyattstown, Mont Cty; ref: 1, 1611, 1677

DOYLE, Edwin T.; sgt; 13th TN Inf, Co E; ref: 1, 456

DOYLE, John; pvt; 19th VA Heavy Arty, Co C; ref: 1, 2, 19, 21, 1580

DOYLE, Joseph T.; sgt; 1st MD Inf, Co E; ref: 1, 2, 19, 21, 23

DOYLE, Philip; pvt; 2nd MD Inf, Co F; McPherson Pack, AA Cty; ref: 1, 2, 19, 21, 1539

DOYLE, T. Harry; Norfolk Lt Arty Blues; res: Balt; ref: 70

DOYLE, Walter J.; Capt; 41st VA Inf, Co F; res: Balt; ref: 1, 70

DRAKE, David W.; pvt; 5th VA Inf, Co L; res: Ft Washington, PG Cty; ref: 1, 70

DRAKE, Lloyd W.; pvt; 9th VA Inf, Co B; ref: 1, 1576

DRAWBRIDGE, George Manning; sgt; 2nd MD Inf, Co G; res: Dor Cty; ref: 1, 112

DRERS, ---; pvt; Co H; ref: 456

DRESSER, Lemuel B.; Acting Mast.M., Navy; C.S. Launch No. 5, New Orleans; ref: 1, 1564

DREW John W.; Capt; 23rd VA Cav, Co H; ref: 1, 2, 19, 735

DREWRY, Emmett A.; Lt; 9th VA Inf, Co B; ref: 1, 1576

DRISCALL, James; pvt; 3rd MD Lt Arty; ref: 1, 2, 19, 21, 160, 726

DRISKELL, James; pvt; 2nd MD Inf, Co H; ref: 1, 2, 19, 21
DROPMAN, Charles; pvt; 1st MD Inf, Co B; ref: 1, 2, 19, 21
DRURY, Charles T.; musician; 2nd MD Inf, Co B; res: Leonardtown, St. M. Cty; ref: 1, 2, 19, 21, 23, 64, 470, 1509, 1523, 1555
DRURY, Samuel; pvt; 14th LA Inf, Co F; res: Bristol, AA Cty; ref: 1, 1539
DRURY, Walter; pvt; Rhett's 1st SC Heavy Arty; res: Balt; ref: 1, 735
DRURY, William C.; pvt; 2nd MD Inf, Co B; res: Leonardtown, St. M. Cty; ref: 1, 2, 19, 21, 1509, 1555
DRYDEN, Robert H. (M.D.); Asst Sur; Baird's TX Cav; res: Balt; ref: 1, 18, 1533
DRYDEN, Robert J.; pvt; 1st MD Lt Arty; res: Som Cty; ref: 1, 2, 19, 21, 470
DU BARRY, W. D.; pvt; 27th SC Inf, Co A; ref: 1, 21, 700, 1598
DUBELL, Frederick; pvt; 24th VA Cav, Co F; ref: 1, 735, 976
DUCK, Henry R. S.; pvt; 1st MD Inf, Co C; res: Balt; ref: 1, 2, 19, 21
DUDLEY, Hamilton M.; pvt; 40th VA Inf, Co B; res: Balt; ref: 1, 21, 93, 700
DUDLEY, Thomas; pvt; Stuart's Horse Arty, Breathed's Battery; ref: 1
DUDLEY, Thomas W.; Maj; Asst Commissary of Subsistence, Gen R. E.Colston's staff; ref: 1, 700
DUERSON, W. H.; pvt; 1st MD Cav, Co K; res: Caro Cty; ref: 1, 19
DUEY, David E.; pvt; MD Guerrilla Zouaves; ref: 1
DUFF, Jason L.; res: Balt; ref: 1540
DUFF, Jonathan R.; pvt; 33rd MS Inf, Co K; res: Balt; ref: 1, 1540
DUFFAN, Henry; pvt; 3rd MD Lt Arty; ref: 1, 2, 19, 21, 160, 726
DUFFER, John; pvt; 44th VA Inf, Co C; res: McPherson Pack, AA Cty; ref: 1, 1539
DUFFEY Jefferson Waite (M.D.); pvt; McNeill's Rangers; ref: 1, 70, 148, 372, 431, 519, 1357, 1415, 1426, 1459
DUFFIN, Francis; sgt; Zarvona's MD Zouaves; ref: 19, 58, 61, 97, 703
DUFFY, James G.; pvt; 2nd MD Cav, Co C; ref: 1
DUFFY, Michae; pvt; Davis's MD Cav, Co C; ref: 1
DUFRIEND, James; pvt; Davis's MD Cav, Co A; ref: 1
DUGAN, Hammond; pvt; 21st VA Inf, Co B; res: Balt; ref: 2, 19, 312
DUGAN, Pierre C.; pvt; 21st VA Inf, Co B; res: Balt; ref: 1, 2, 19, 312, 592
DUGGAN, Patrick; pvt; 1st VA Inf, Co B; res: Balt; MLCSH; ref: 1, 21, 627, 700, 786
DUKE, Daniel J.; pvt; 2nd MD Inf, Co G; ref: 1
DUKE, George W.; pvt; 17th VA Inf, Co B; ref: 1, 142, 251
DUKE, James Basil VII; Lt; Aid de Camp, Gen B.Bragg's staff; res: Brook Place Manor, Cal Cty; ref: 19, 760, 1663
DUKE, John Edgar; Lt; 30th GA inf, Co F; res: Cumberland, All Cty; ref: 1, 148
DUKE, John Francis; pvt; 2nd MD Inf, Co B; res: Leonardtown,St. M. Cty; ref: 1, 2, 7, 19, 21, 70, 1509, 1555, 1627, 1663
DUKE, John Thomas; 5th AL Inf, Co F; res: Cal Cty; ref: 1663
DUKEHART, John M.; bsn, Navy; C.S.S. Stonewall; ref: 1564
DULANEY, Jeremiah; pvt; 2nd MD Inf, Co C; ref: 1, 2, 19, 21
DULANEY, Josiah L.; Kt Cty; ref: 1584
DULANY, Daniel F.; pvt; 43rd VA Cav (Mosby's), Co A; ref: 8
DULEY, E. C.; res: Mont Cty; ref: 901
DUMINGAN, Edward; res: Balt; ref: 1540
DUMNE, James; pvt; Stuart's Horse Arty, Breathed's Battery; ref: 1, 498

DUNCAN, Frank W.; pvt; 1st MD Cav, Co D; res: Balt; ref: 1, 19
DUNCAN, James A.; pvt; 2nd MD Lt Arty; res: Balt; ref: 1, 2, 19, 21, 70
DUNCAN, John J.; 2nd TX Inf, Co D; res: Balt; ref: 1, 21, 700, 735
DUNCAN, Lawrence W.; pvt; MD Guerrilla Zouaves; res: Wash Cty; ref: 1
DUNCAN, Thomas (Revd); Chaplain; MD Line; res: Easton, Tal Cty; ref: 2, 23, 240, 825, 1523
DUNCAN, William C.; gun, Navy; C.S. Virginia; MLCSH; ref: 1, 21, 684, 700, 786
DUNDAS, William O.; Lt; Asst Paymaster, Gen K. Smith's staff; ref: 1, 700
DUNEGAN, Philip; pvt; 2nd MD Cav, Co F; ref: 1, 2, 19, 21
DUNLAP Donald M.; pvt; 12th VA Inf, Co C; res: Balt; ref: 1, 21, 70, 700
DUNLOP Henry J.; pvt; 17th TN Cav, Co A; res: Merryland Tract, Frd Cty; ref: 1, 90
DUNLOP, John; pvt; 7th VA Cav, Co G; res: Frd Cty; ref: 1, 3, 1278
DUNLOP, Joseph L.; pvt; 1st MD Cav, Co A; ref: 1, 2, 19, 21
DUNLOP, S. O.; pvt; Hampton Leg Lt Arty, Co B; ref: 1, 2, 21
DUNN, Benjamin F.; pvt; 1st MD Cav, Co E; res: Wash Cty; ref: 1, 19
DUNN, James; pvt; Davis's MD Cav, Co C; ref: 1, 735
DUNN, John W. H.; pvt; 1st SC Inf, Co G; ref: 1, 2, 19, 21, 735
DUNN, R. J.; 1st VA Inf; ref: 70
DUNN, W. W.; pvt; 15th AL Inf, Co B; ref: 1, 70
DUNN, William C.; Capt; 37th VA Cav, Co E; res: Balt; ref: 1, 2, 19, 21, 23, 124, 700, 1540
DUNNING, John; pvt; 43rd VA Cav (Mosby's), Co D; res: Greensborough, Caro Cty; MLCSH; ref: 1, 8, 627, 700, 786, 1613
DUNNING, Thomas B.; res: Annapolis, AA Cty; ref: 1539
DUNNINGTON, Charles Allen; pvt; 4th VA Cav, Co A; ref: 1, 8, 21, 677, 700
DUNNINGTON, J. Lemuel; 2nd MD Inf, Co F; ref: 1, 2, 19, 21
DUNNINGTON Virginius G.; pvt; 2nd VA Cav, Co B; ref: 1, 21, 700
DURBOROW, John C.; pvt; 1st MD Cav, Co A; ref: 1, 2, 19, 21, 628
DURFEY, James W.; pvt; 9th VA Inf, Co B; res: Balt; ref: 1, 1576
DURHAM, James E.; pvt; 35th VA Cav, Co B; res: Balt; ref: 1, 3, 1540, 1611, 1677
DURHAM, James S.; sgt; 28th NC Inf, Co G; MLCSH; ref: 1, 2, 19, 21, 93, 786
DURKIN, John Henry; pvt; 1 VA Cav, Co K; res: Balt; MLCSH; ref: 1, 2, 19, 627, 700, 786, 1598, 1613
DURNER, John F.; pvt; 2nd MD Inf, Co A; res: Patuxent, AA Cty; ref: 1, 2, 19, 21, 650, 1539
DURST, John F.; pvt; 1st MD Inf, Co F; ref: 1, 2, 19, 21
DUSENBERRY, B.; pvt; 1st VA Cav, Co K; ref: 1, 2, 19
DUSENBERRY, H. Bowie; pvt; Stuart's Horse Arty, Breathed's Battery; res: Annapolis, AA Cty; ref: 1, 2, 19, 312, 498, 735
DUTTON, Benjamin Z.; pvt; Lucas' 15th SC Heavy Arty; ref: 1, 20
DUTTON, Edward V.; pvt; 1st SC Inf, Co G; ref: 1
DUTTON, James L.; pvt; 1st SC Inf, Co G; ref: 1
DUTTON, John T.; pvt; 1st MD Cav, Co B; res: Cha Cty; ref: 1, 2, 19, 21, 93, 700, 785
DUTTON, S. S.; pvt; 1st MD Cav, Co B; ref: 2, 19, 21
DUTTON, Thomas W.; sgt; 15th KY Cav, Co C; res: Balt; MLCSH; ref: 93, 700, 735, 786
DUTTON, W. J.; pvt; 1st MD Cav, Co B; res: Balt; ref: 1, 2, 21
DUVAL, Frank M.; pvt; 17th VA inf, Co F; res: Balt; ref: 1, 19, 21, 53, 70, 93, 133, 142, 251, 700

DUVAL, Henry Rieman; pvt; McNeill's Rangers; res: Balt; ref: 19, 70, 504, 511, 685
DUVAL, Louis; Lt; 8th TX Cav, Co C; res: Balt; MLCSH; ref: 1, 19, 21, 119, 700, 786
DUVALL, Andrew; 17th VA Inf, Co F; ref: 735
DUVALL, Beal; res: Millersville, AA Cty; ref: 1539
DUVALL, Charles; pvt; 3rd MD Lt Arty; ref: 1, 2, 19, 21, 160, 316, 511, 726
DUVALL, Daniel; pvt; 2nd MD Inf, Co C; res: Crownsville, AA Cty; ref: 1, 2, 19, 21, 34, 81, 511, 595, 700, 1539, 1664
DUVALL, Edward Mitchell; pvt; Signal Corps; res: Balt; ref: 1, 735, 959
DUVALL, Eli; Lt; Signal Corps; ref: 1, 2, 14, 19, 735, 791, 1335, 1523
DUVALL, Evans; pvt; 2nd MD Inf, Co C; res: Crownsville, AA Cty; ref: 1, 2, 19, 21, 23, 81, 470, 511, 595, 700, 1523, 1539, 1664
DUVALL, Ferdinand C.; Capt; 2nd MD Inf, Co C; res: Millersville, AA Cty; ref: 1, 2, 19, 21, 23, 64, 68, 81, 127, 240, 511, 595, 674, 700, 1520, 1523, 1664, 1666
DUVALL, G.; ref: 1664
DUVALL, Franklin; pvt; 2nd MD Inf, Co C; res: Beltsville, PG Cty; ref: 1, 2, 19, 21, 23, 470, 511, 595, 1664
DUVALL, Henry Claggett; sgt; Williams' Co, MS Cav; res: Petersville, Frd Cty; ref: 1, 65
DUVALL, James E.; pvt; 17th VA Inf, Co E; res: PG Cty; ref: 1, 2, 19, 21, 133, 142, 251, 677, 1622
DUVALL, John H.; pvt; 2nd MD Inf, Co G; ref: 1, 2, 19, 21
DUVALL, Joseph W.; pvt; 2nd MD Inf, Co C; ref: AA Cty; ref: 1, 19, 1539, 1664
DUVALL, Leonidas; pvt; 21st VA Inf, Co B; res: Balt; ref: 1, 2, 19, 312
DUVALL, Philip Barton (M.D.); pvt; 1st MD Lt Arty; res: Crownsville, AA Cty; ref: 1,2, 18, 19, 21, 34, 63, 64, 68, 93, 511, 1539
DUVALL, Ridgeley; pvt; 1st MD Inf, Co D; res: Balt; ref: 1, 2, 19, 21, 511, 700, 1540, 1664
DUVALL, S. E.; pvt; 1st MD Lt Arty; ref: 1, 19, 470, 511
DUVALL, Samuel Coleman; pvt; 2nd MD Inf, Co C; res: Millersville, AA Cty; ref: 1, 2, 19, 21, 23, 595, 784, 1539
DUVALL, Samuel Fulton (M.D.); pvt; Hampton Leg Lt Arty, Co B; res: AA Cty; ref: 1, 2, 18, 19, 21, 720, 1664
DUVALL, Thomas Mitchell; pvt; 1st La Cav, Co B; res: Forest Home, AA Cty; ref: 1, 1539
DUVALL, Tobias; pvt; 2nd MD Inf, Co C; res: PG Cty; ref: 1, 2, 19, 21, 70, 511, 595, 700, 1664
DUVALL, William G.; pvt; 2nd MD Lt Arty; res: Johnsons Store, AA Cty; ref: 1, 2, 19, 21, 511, 1539
DWYER, Martin; pvt; 3rd MD Lt Arty; ref: 1, 2, 19, 21, 160, 726
DWYER Thomas J. R.; sgt; 1st VA Inf, Co E; ref: 1, 735
DWYRA, James; pvt; Davis's MD Cav, Co C; ref: 1
DYER, Algernon Miles; pvt; 1st MD Cav, Co B; res: Frederick, Frd Cty; ref: 1, 2, 19, 21, 89, 785
DYER, Stephen; pvt; Zarvona's MD Zouaves; res: Leonardtown, St. M. Cty; ref: 1, 19, 735, 1509, 1555, 1627
DYSER, Luke J.; pvt; 41st VA Inf, Co F; res: Balt Cty; ref: 1, 2, 21, 92, 93, 700, 1099, 1158
DYTYMYER, Henry; res: AA Cty; ref: 1539

EADER, Charles Williams; pvt; 35th VA Cav, Co B; res: Park Mills, Frd Cty; ref: 1, 3, 90, 1548, 1611, 1677
EADER, Lewis A.; pvt; 35th VA Cav, Co B; res; Park Mills, Frd Cty; ref: 1,3, 90, 1548, 1611, 1677

EAGAN, Daniel; pvt; 13th VA Inf, Co G; ref: 1
EAGAN, Henry; pvt; 13th VA Inf, Co G; ref: 1
EAGAN, Peter; pvt; 2nd MD Inf, Co G; ref: 1, 2, 19, 21
EAGAN, Thomas T.; pvt; 2nd MD Inf, Co H; res: Annapolis, AA Cty; ref: 2, 19, 21, 1539
EAGGER, Henry; pvt; 1st MD Inf, Co G; ref: 1, 2, 19, 21
EANS, John; sgt; 9th VA Inf, Co B; ref: 1, 1576
EARICKSON, Frederick G.; pvt; 1st MD Cav, Co B; res: QA Cty; ref: 1, 2, 19, 21, 785
EARLE, James T.; pvt; 1st MD Cav, Co B; res: Centreville, QA Cty; ref: 1, 2, 19, 21, 785, 1554
EARLE, John; pvt; 1st VA Inf, Co E; ref: 735
EARLY, Thomas; pvt; 3rd MD Lt Arty; ref: 2, 19, 21, 160, 461, 726
EARNEST, Thomas J.; pvt; 2nd MD Lt Arty; ref: 1, 2, 19, 21
EATON, J. H.; pvt; 3rd MD Lt Arty; ref: 1, 2, 19, 21, 160, 726, 1460
EATON, Joseph; pvt; Lucas' 15th SC Heavy Arty; res: Balt; ref: 1
EASTON, R. S.; Stuart's Horse Arty, Breathed's Battery; res: New Windsor, Carr Cty; ref: 1
EASTRIDGE, S.; pvt; 1st SC Inf, Co G; ref: 1
ELBERT, Charles; pvt; 1st MD Cav, Co D; ref: 2, 21, 1601
ELBERT, Charles S.; pvt; 1st MD Inf, Co A; res: Frederick; ref: 19, 90
EBERT, Charles; pvt; 1st MD Cav, Co B; res: QA Cty; ref: 1, 2, 19, 21, 785
EBERT, Valerins J.; pvt; 8th LA Inf, Co I; res: Frederick, Frd Cty; ref: 1, 89
ECKER, William; courier, Gen R. E. Lee; ref: 735
ECKHART, Augustus; pvt; 1st MD Inf, Co B; ref: 1, 2, 19, 21
ECKHART, Charles H.; 1st MD Cav, Co B; res: Tal Cty; ref: 1, 2, 19, 21, 645, 785
ECKMAN, John G.; cpl; 12th GA Inf, Co H; res: Balt; MLCSH; ref: 1, 93, 700, 786
EDDINS, Richard Winslow; color bearer; 13th VA Inf, Co D; res: Balt; ref: 70, 700
EDELEN, Alexander W.; pvt; 1st MD Inf, Co E; ref: 1, 2, 19, 21
EDELIN, Boyd; Lt; 1st VA Inf, Co F; ref: 1, 735
EDELIN, Charles Columbus; Capt; Edelin's MD Heavy Arty; res: Balt; ref: 1, 2, 19, 21, 23, 64, 68, 456, 462, 789, 923, 1511, 1520, 1523
EDELIN, Francis D.; pvt; 2nd MD Inf, Co G; ref: 1, 2, 19, 21
EDELIN, Jesse R.; pvt; 1st MD Cav, Co E; ref: 1, 2, 19, 21, 94, 730
EDELIN, John D.; pvt; 2nd MD Inf, Co G; ref: 1, 2, 19, 21
EDELIN, Jospeh B.; pvt; 7th VA Inf, Co H; res: PG Cty; ref: 1, 316, 1622
EDELIN, Philip F.; pvt; 1st MD Lt Arty; res: Leonardtown, St. M. Cty; ref: 1, 2, 7, 19, 21, 1509, 1555
EDELIN, Thomas Boyd; Lt Col; 16th NC Cav; ref: 19, 211, 735, 791, 1600
EDELIN, William, "Tip"; pvt; 1st VA Inf, Co F; ref: 1, 456, 735
EDELIN, William H. H.; Lt; Barry's Co, MD vols; ref: 1, 19, 21, 23, 316
EDELIN, William Marshal; 2nd VA Cav, Co; res: Leonardtown, St. M. Cty; ref: 1, 2, 7, 19, 21, 735, 1555
EDELIN, William Samuel; pvt; 2nd MD Inf, Co A; res: Leonardtown, St. M. Cty; ref: 1, 2, 19, 21, 23, 470, 650, 1509, 1520, 1523, 1555, 1670
EDELL, Henry J.; pvt; 2nd MD Lt Arty; res: Balt; ref: 1, 2, 19, 21, 700
EDGAR, Joseph; cpl; 3rd MD Lt Arty; ref: 1, 2, 19, 21, 23, 160, 461, 726
EDGAR, Thomas J.; pvt; 2nd MD Inf, Co C; res: St. Michaels, Tal Cty;

ref: 1, 2, 19, 21, 595, 645, 1557, 1612
EDGE, Joseph G.; pvt; Rhett's 1st SC Heavy Arty; ref: 1, 2, 21, 470
EDGELEY, William; pvt; MD Guerrila Zouaves; ref: 1
EDMONDS, John J.; pvt; 47th NC Inf, Co C; res: Balt; MLCSH; ref: 21, 93, 700, 786
EDMUNDS, George; pvt; 4th VA Cav, Co I; ref: 1, 19
EDMUNDS, Nicholas E.; 1st Lt; Davis's MD Cav, Co C; ref: 1
EDWARD, Eli H.; pvt; 2nd MD Cav, Co E; res: Bt Cty; ref: 1, 1609
EDWARD, J. C.; pvt; 13th VA Inf, Co G; ref: 1, 735
EDWARDS, Alexander G. (M.D.); pvt; 1st VA Cav, Co K; res: Brownsville, Wash Cty; ref: 1, 2, 18, 19, 21, 69, 316, 1558
EDWARD, Frank K.; pvt; 30th GA Inf, Co D; ref: 1, 2, 19, 21, 160, 726
EDWARDS, George T.; pvt; 1st VA Inf, Co E; ref: 1, 735
EDWARDS, J. H. (M.D.); Asst Surg; Eastern District of FLorida; res: Frd Cty; ref: 1, 18
EDWARDS, John R.; pvt; 12th GA Lt Arty; res: Balt; ref: 1, 70
EDWARDS, Newit J.; pvt; 9th VA Inf, Co B; ref: 1, 1576, 1598
EDWARDS, William T.; pvt; 9th VA Inf, Co B; res: Balt; ref: 1, 1540, 1576
EDWARDS, William H.; pvt; 7th Cav, Co G; res: Balt; ref: 1, 2, 3, 8, 19, 21, 72
EFF, John; pvt; Lucas' 15th SC Heavy Arty; ref: 1, 19
EGAN, Andrew H.; pvt; 4th MD Lt Arty; res: Balt; ref: 1, 2, 21
EGEN, Daniel; pvt; 9th MS Inf, Co B; res: Balt; ref: 1, 1540
EGEN, Eugene; res: Balt; ref: 1540
EGEN, Thomas G.; pvt; 2nd MD Inf, Co H; ref: 1, 2, 21
EICHELBERGER, Daniel G.; pvt; 35th VA Cav, Co B; res: Point of Rocks, Frd Cty; ref: 1, 19
EICKELBERGER, George F.; pvt; 2nd VA Inf, Co G; MLCSH; ref: 786, 866
EIGER, John H.; pvt; 1st MD Cav, Co F; ref: 1, 2, 21
EISBERGER, C.; pvt; 1st MD Inf, Co C; ref: 1
EISENBERG, George; pvt; 1st MD Inf, Co F; res: Balt; ref: 1, 2, 19, 21, 700
EISENBISE, Thaddeus B.; Lt; 19th VA Heavy Arty, Co C; ref: 1, 1580
ELAM, Thomas H. E.; pvt; Stuart's Horse Arty, Breathed's Battery; ref: 1, 498
ELAM, W. A.; pvt; Stuart's Horse Arty, Breathed's Battery; ref: 1
ELDER, George Howard, Jr; pvt; 1st MD Cav, Co C; res: Garrison, Bt Cty; ref: 1, 2, 19, 21, 70, 233, 511, 700, 1565
ELDER, Henry; pvt; 3rd MD Lt Arty; ref: 1, 2, 19, 21, 160, 511, 726
ELDER, Phillip Laurence; pvt; 21st VA Inf, Co B; res: Balt; ref: 1, 2, 19, 312, 511, 735
ELGIN, John Ogilvie; pvt; 35th VA Cav, Co B; res: Poolesville, Mont Cty; ref: 1, 3, 73, 1358, 1552, 1611, 1677
ELGIN, Thomas G.; pvt; 35th VA Cav, Co C; ref: 1, 3, 15, 1611, 1677
ELIASON, Henry A.; pvt; 1st VA Lt Arty, Co C; ref: 1, 735
ELLERY, Albert; Capt; 3rd VA local Defence Inf, Co D; ref: 1, 1620
ELLICOTT, Charles J.; pvt; 9th VA Inf, Co B; res: Frd Cty; ref: 1, 19, 1576
ELLICOTT, Charles J. F.; pvt; 3rd MD Lt Arty; res: Balt; ref: 1, 2, 19, 21, 160, 726, 1540
ELLICOTT, David E. B.; pvt; 4th VA Cav, Co F; res: Balt; ref: 1, 1540
ELLICOTT, J. T.; cpl; 3rd AL Cav, Co H; res: Balt; ref:1, 690
ELLICOTT, John; Maj; Nitre & Mining Bureau; res: Balt; ref: 1, 2, 19, 34, 157, 735, 753, 791
ELLIGETT, Michael; pvt; 19th VA Heavy Arty, Co C; ref: 1, 2, 21, 1580

ELLIOTT, G. M.; pvt; 1st MD Cav, Co B; res: Eastern Shore; MLCSH; ref: 1, 2, 19, 21, 786
ELLIOTT, John B.; pvt; 2nd MD Inf, Co D; res: Woodberry Factory, Bt Cty; ref: 1, 1541
ELLIOTT, J. Wesley; Lt; 32nd VA Inf, Co A; res: Balt; ref: 1, 21, 53, 700
ELLIOTT, James T.; pvt; 1st MD Cav, Co B; ref: 1, 2, 19, 21
ELLIOTT, Joseph W.; pvt; 1st MD Inf, Co E; ref: 1, 2, 19, 21
ELLIS, B. F.; pvt; 1st MD Cav, Co A; ref: 1, 19
ELLIS, Edward; pvt; Lucas' 15th SC Heavy Arty; res: Balt; ref: 1
ELLIS, Henry; pvt; 2nd MD Cav, Co E; res: AA Cty; ref: 1, 1628
ELLIS, John; pvt; 28th MS Cav, Co D; res: Cracthers Ferry, Dor Cty; ref: 1, 19, 21, 92, 93, 700, 1547
ELLIS, John Thomas; pvt; 1st VA Cav, Co K; ref: 1, 2, 19, 21
ELLIS, William H. C.; pvt; 9th VA Inf, Co B; res: Cratchers Ferry, Dor Cty; ref: 1, 1547, 1576
ELLMORE, John D.; pvt; 35th VA Cav, Co A; ref: 1, 3, 1611, 1677
ELSESSER, Henry; pvt; 1st SC Inf, Co G; ref: 1, 735
ELSESSER, Peter; sgt; 1st SC Inf, Co G; res: Balt; MLCSH; ref: 1, 21, 700, 735, 786
ELTA, F. T.; 2nd MD; ref: 93
ELZEY, Arnold; Maj Gen; Department of Richmond & Army of Tennessee; res: Som Cty; ref: 1, 2, 11, 13, 15, 18, 19, 21, 22, 23, 24, 30, 32, 34, 35, 37, 38, 39, 43, 44, 45, 47, 48, 50, 53, 63, 68, 70, 88, 97, 100, 105, 110, 111, 120, 123, 125, 126, 127, 129, 130, 137, 138, 145, 152, 154, 155, 159, 161, 165, 209, 211, 215, 222, 240, 266, 320, 347, 385, 397, 404, 422, 426, 431, 443, 456, 462, 501, 503, 511, 559, 583, 601, 631, 638, 674, 684, 686, 693, 724, 735, 748, 757, 769, 778, 789, 791, 794, 825, 838, 857, 873, 893, 895, 900, 990, 1006, 1053, 1158, 1279, 1282, 1365, 1367, 1486, 1491, 1511, 1519, 1520, 1523, 1561, 1568, 1569, 1577, 1578, 1579, 1583, 1588, 1623, 1624, 1633, 1638, 1642, 1644, 1672, 1674
ELZEY, Robert; pvt; 43rd VA Cav (Mosby's), Co C; ref: 8, 20
ELZEY, William; pvt; 43rd VA Cav (Mosby'), Co A; ref: 1, 8, 20
EMACK, George W.; Capt; 1st MD Cav, Co B; res: PG Cty; ref: 1, 2, 11, 12, 19, 21, 23, 44, 45, 46, 63, 64, 68, 70, 113, 122, 240, 443, 462, 511, 638, 693, 785, 791, 825, 941, 1260, 1383, 1466, 1520, 1523, 1582, 1634
EMACK, James W.; Lt; 7th NC Inf, Co F; ref: 1, 2, 19, 511, 735
EMANUEL, B. F.; pvt; Barry's Co, MD vols; res: St. M. Cty; ref: 1, 19, 1627
EMBERT, John; pvt; 4th MD Lt Arty; res: Balt; ref: 2, 19, 1540
EMBERT, John R. H.; pvt; 1st MD Cav, Co B; res: Queenstown, QA Cty; ref: 1, 2, 19, 21, 70, 785, 1612
EMMERICH, George H.; pvt; 2nd MD Cav, Co C; res: Balt; ref: 1, 2, 19, 21, 70, 86, 1609
EMMERICH, George W.; pvt; Lee's MD Cav; res: Balt; ref: 1, 19, 70, 72, 700
EMMERICH, John W.; cpl; 2nd MD Cav, Co C; res: Balt; ref: 2, 19, 21, 23, 70, 72, 75, 79, 86, 494
EMMERSON, Henry; pvt; 7th VA Cav, Co G; res: Patuxent; ref: 1539
EMMITT, ---; pvt; 3rd MD Lt Arty; ref: 461
EMORY, Albert T.; q.m sgt; 3rd MD Lt Arty; res: QA Cty; ref: 1, 2, 19, 21, 23, 64, 160, 461, 726, 735
EMORY, Daniel Grant; pvt; 1st MD Cav, Co C; res: Balt; ref: 1, 2, 19, 21, 690, 700
EMORY, Frederick; Capt; Asst Q.M., Gen T. Pegram's staff; ref: 1, 592
EMORY, George; pvt; 2nd MD Cav, Co A; res: Balt; ref: 1, 19, 1609

EMORY, J. H.; pvt; 2nd MD Cav, Co E; res: Balt; ref: 1, 352
EMORY, Richard (M.D.); Asst Surg; Gen Hospital, No. 13 Richmond Phoenix; res: Bt Cty; ref: 1, 2, 18, 19, 21, 700, 720, 1534, 1536, 1578, 1579
EMORY, Thomas Hall, Sr (M.D.); Asst Surg, Navy; C.S. Florida; res: QA Cty; ref: 1, 18, 19, 58, 97, 279, 1536, 1564
EMORY, William W.; pvt; 57th NC, Co A; res: Balt; MLCSH; ref: 1, 93, 700, 786, 1599
ENGELFIELD, Giles; pvt; 2nd MD Cav, Co E; ref: 1
ENGLAND, Joseph R.; pvt; 14th VA Cav, Co D; res: Frd Cty; ref: 1, 90, 1573
ENGLEHARDT, Edward C.; pvt; 1st MD Inf, Co F; res: Balt; ref: 19, 21, 700
ENGLISH, B.; pvt; 7th AR Cav, Co E; ref: 1, 93
ENNIS, Joseph H.; 4th MD Lt Arty; res: Wor Cty; ref: 1
ENNIS, Philip J.; sgt; 1st VA Inf, Co E; ref: 1, 735
ENNIS, Thomas H.; pvt; 4th MD Lt Arty; res: Wor Cty; ref: 1, 2, 19, 21
ENO, Charles E.; pvt; 1st MD Inf, Co D; res: Bt Cty; ref: 1, 2, 19, 21, 700
ENO, Charles Edward; pvt; 3rd VA Inf, Arsenal Bn; res: Balt; ref: 1, 1540, 1613
ENSEBIO, Giacomo; pvt; 9th VA Inf, Co B; ref: 1, 1576
ENSOR, Zadock; pvt; 1st MD Cav, Co D; ref: 1, 2, 19, 21, 1601
EPPERLY, Addison; pvt; Stuart's Horse Arty, Breathed's Battery; ref: 1, 498
EPPERLY, William H.; pvt; Stuart's Horse Arty, Breathed's Battery; ref: 1, 498
ERICKSON, G. M. F. G.; pvt; 1st MD Cav, Co B; ref: 1
ERNULL, A. W.; pvt; 21st VA Inf, Co B; ref: 1, 2, 19, 312, 735
ERWIN, A. D.; Capt; Davis's MD Cav, Co F; ref: 1
ERWIN, Holmes; Lt; 3rd MD Lt Arty; ref: 1, 2, 19, 21, 23, 64, 160, 461, 726, 1460, 1523
ERWIN, William H.; cpl; 3rd MD Lt Arty; ref: 1, 2, 19, 21, 23, 160, 726
ESPEY, James; pvt; 1st VA Inf, Co E; ref: 1, 735
ESSENDER, William F.; pvt; 1st MD Inf, Co E; res: Balt; ref: 1, 2, 19, 21, 1540
ESSEX, George W.; sgt; Clutter's Co, VA Lt Arty; ref: 1, 21, 119, 700
ESTES, Carter C.; pvt; 3rd KY Inf, Co B; ref: 1, 70
ESTES, David N.; Lt; 9th Bn, TN Cav, Co A; res: Carollton, PG Cty; ref: 1, 23
ESTES, William; pvt; MD Guerrilla Zouaves; ref: 1
ETCHISON, William L.; pvt; 2nd MD Inf, Co G; res: Cha Cty; ref: 1, 2, 19, 21
ETHERIDGE, Roscoe; pvt; 1st NC Lt Arty, Co K; ref: AA Cty; MLCSH; ref: 1, 627, 700, 786
EVANS, Benjamin; pvt; 1st VA Cav, Co K; ref: 1, 2, 19
EVANS, C. Benton; pvt; Stuart's Horse Arty, Breathed's Battery; ref: 1, 40, 498, 806
EVANS, Charles A.; sgt maj; Stuart's Horse Arty, Pelham's Battery; ref: 1, 19, 21, 498, 700
EVANS, Charles S.; pvt; 2nd MD Lt Arty; ref: 1, 2, 21, 1509
EVANS, Dallas J.; pvt; 2nd MD Co B; res: St. M. Cty; ref: 1, 2, 19, 21, 1509
EVANS, Dudley; Lt Col; 20th VA Cav; ref: 1, 21, 700, 791, 1600
EVANS, George; pvt; 38th Bn, VA Lt Arty; res: Annapolis, AA Cty; ref: 1, 1539
EVANS, John; Acting Mast. M., Navy; C.S.S. Launch No. 6, New Orleans; ref: 1, 1564
EVANS, W. B.; pvt; DAvis's MD Cav, Co C; ref: 1

EVANS, William; pvt; 9th VA Inf, Co B; ref: 1, 1576
EVANS, William Oliver; pvt; Davis's MD Cav, Co A; ref: 1, 735
EVATT, W. H.; pvt; 1st SC Inf, Co G; ref: 1
EVELINE, John; pvt; 1st MD Inf, Co F; ref: 1, 2, 19, 21
EVERETT, William B. (M.D., Revd); Acting Asst Surg; Marquis's VA Battery; res: Kt Cty; ref: 1, 18, 19, 315, 358, 1363, 1584
EVERGAN, Thomas J.; pvt; 4th MD Lt Arty; ref: 1, 2, 19, 21
EVERAM, William H.; pvt; Lees' MD Cav; ref: 1, 19, 1622
EWELL, George Shelton Ross; sgt; 4th MD Lt Arty; ref: 1
EWEN, William T.; pvt; 1st MD Cav, Co E; res: Tal Cty; ref: 1, 2, 19, 21, 730
EWING, Harvey S.; pvt; 1st MD Cav, Co D; res: Cec Cty; ref: 1, 2, 19, 21, 1601
EWING, William J.; pvt; 1st MD Cav, Co D; ref: 1, 2, 19, 21, 1601
EWING, William Thomas; pvt; Davis's MD Cav, Co A; res: Tal Cty; ref: 1, 19, 645, 1612
EXALL, Turner P.; pvt; 3rd VA Cav, Co G; res: Balt; ref: 1, 21, 700
EYSTER, George Hupp (M.D.); Maj; Asst A.G., Gen J. A. Early's staff; res: Balt; ref: 1, 18, 631, 1536
EZELL, Malachai; pvt; 13th MS Inf, Co C; res: How Cty; MLCSH; ref: 1, 21, 93, 700, 735, 786

FAGAN, William Thomas; pvt; 9th VA Inf, Co B; res: Balt; ref: 1, 57, 1576
FAHERTY, William James; Lt; 23rd VA Cav, Co F; res: Balt; MLCSH; ref: 1, 93, 627, 700, 986
FAHEY, Alexander A.; pvt; Courier for Gen R. E. Lee; res How Cty; ref: 10, 19, 21, 700
FAIR, John W.; pvt; Davis's MD Cav, Co C; ref: 1
FAIRBANKS, Francis M.; cpl; 4th MD Lt Arty; res: Tal Cty; ref: 1, 2, 19, 21, 645, 1612
FAIRFAX, Carlyle; res: Balt; ref: 38
FAIRFAX, Charles Snowden; res: PG Cty; ref: 34
FAIRFAX, John Contee; res: PG Cty; ref: 34
FALCONER, Edward W.; pvt; MD American Rifles; res: Balt; ref: 1, 2, 19, 21, 1540
FALL, Martin Y.; sgt; 1st MD Inf, Co A; ref: 92
FALLIN, John H.; Capt; Asst Commissary of Supply, Gen A. Thomas' staff; ref: 1, 70
FALLIN, Joseph H.; cpl; 92nd VA Militia, ref: 1, 70
FALLIS, Edwarard; pvt; 2nd MD Inf, Co E; ref: 1, 2, 19, 21
FALLIS, William R.; pvt; 1st MD Cav, Co A; res: Balt; ref: 1, 19, 1540
FALLON, James; pvt; 2nd MD Inf, Co E; ref: 1, 2, 19, 21
FALLS, Jeremiah; pvt; 25th VA Inf, Co D; res: Frederick, Frd Cty; ref: 1, 72
FARINHOLT, Benjamin Lines; Col; 1st Farinholts' VA Reserves Inf; res: Balt; ref: 1, 875, 876, 1600
FARINHOLT, William H.; pvt; 24th VA Cav, Co C; res: Balt; ref: 1, 57, 974
FARING, James; pvt; 1st SC Inf, Co G; ref: 1
FARLAND, Robert; res: Balt; ref: 1540
FARLEY, Hugh; cpl; Lucas' 15th SC Heavy Arty; res: Balt; ref: 1, 1540
FARLEY, Lawrence; pvt; 1st SC Inf, Co G; ref: 1
FARLEY, Richard G.; pvt; 3rd VA Cav, Co F; res: Balt; MLCSH; ref: 1, 21, 700, 786
FARMER, James; pvt; 2nd MD Lt Arty; ref: 1, 2, 19, 21
FARMER, Thomas; pvt; 3rd MD Lt Arty; res: Cha Cty; ref: 1, 2, 19, 21, 160, 726
FARR, Francis; pvt; 2nd MD Lt Arty; res: Havre de Grace, Har Cty;

ref: 1, 2, 19, 21, 456, 488, 700, 923, 1540
FARR, Joseph R.; pvt; 1st MD Inf, Co H; res: St. M. Cty; ref: 1, 2, 19, 21, 259, 559, 650, 1509, 1511
FARR, Peter; pvt; Lucas' 15th SC Heavy Arty; ref: 1
FARR, Resin S.; pvt; 43rd VA Cav (Mosby's), Co B; ref: 1, 8, 20
FARR, Richard R.; pvt; 43rd VA Cav (Mosby's), Co B; ref: 1, 8, 20
FARRALL, John H.; pvt; 1st MD Inf, Co I; ref: 1, 2, 19, 21
FARRELL, James; sgt; 1st MD Inf, Co G; res: Balt; ref: 1, 2, 19, 21, 23
FARRELL, John A.; pvt; 19th VA Heavy Arty, Co C; res: Cha Cty; ref: 1, 1580
FARRELL, William; pvt; 1st MD Inf, Co G; res: Balt; ref: 1, 2, 19, 21
FARROW, Thomas Stobo; Lt Col; 13th SC Inf; res: PG Cty; ref: 1, 23, 105, 791, 1600
FASSITT, William P.; pvt; 21st VA Inf, Co B; res: Eastern Shore; ref: 1, 2, 19, 312
FAUBLE, F. Marion; ref: 643
FAUCETT, James A.; pvt; 2nd MD Lt Arty; res: Balt; ref: 1, 2, 19, 21
FAUCETT, John R.; pvt; 55th VA Inf, Co C; res: Rock Hall, Kt Cty; ref: 1, 1584
FAULK, S.; pvt; 3rd MD Lt Arty; ref: 1, 2, 19, 21, 160, 726
FAULKNER, J. F.; pvt; 43rd VA Cav (Mosby's), Co E; res: Balt; ref: 1, 8, 20
FAULKNER, W. W.; pvt; 43rd VA Cav (Mosby's), Co E; res: Balt; ref: 1, 8, 20, 1613
FAULTZ, John H.; pvt; 1st MD Cav, Co A; res: Wash Cty; ref: 1
FAVOUR, Charles R.; sgt; 12th VA Inf, Co F; res: Sykesville, Carr Cty; ref: 1, 2, 21, 23, 1577
FAY, John; cpl; Stuart's Horse Arty, Breathed's Battery; ref: 1, 498
FAY, John B.; sgt; McNeill's Rangers; res: Cumberland, All Cty; ref: 1, 19, 23, 65, 88, 95, 145, 148, 372, 431, 473, 504, 519, 989, 1010, 1130, 1144, 1316, 1348, 1357, 1414, 1560, 1579, 1588, 1636
FAYER, Frederick; 1st MD Lt Arty; ref: 68
FEARKAKE, George; Lt; 20th TX Inf, Co H; res: Frederick; ref: 1, 90, 735
FEARLAKE, Adophus, Jr; pvt; 1st MD Cav, Co D; res: Braddock Heights, Frd Cty; ref: 1, 2, 19, 21, 67, 89, 90, 789, 1101, 1301, 1601
FEAST, Loudon; pvt; 2nd MD Cav, Co E; res: Balt; ref: 1, 2, 19, 21, 700, 1540
FEATHERSTONE, J. C.; Lt; 9th AL Inf, Co F; res: Balt; ref: 1, 11, 19
FEBREY, Moses A.; Lt; Stuarts' Horse Arty, Breathed's Battery; res: Balt; MLCSH; ref: 1, 21, 39, 93, 498, 700, 786
FEERKAKE, W.; pvt; 1st MD Cav, Co B; ref: 1, 19
FEIGE, Charles L.; pvt; 2nd MD Inf, Co A; res: Balt; ref: 1, 2, 19, 21, 650
FELIS, Carlis; pvt; 2nd MD Cav, Co F; ref: 1
FELLINS, J. W.; pvt; 1st MD Lt Arty; ref: 2, 19, 470
FELLON, R.; Zarvona's MD Zouaves; ref: 19, 58, 97
FENDALL, James R. Y.; Lt, Marine Corps; Asst Q.M., res: PG Cty; ref: 1, 792, 1349, 1495, 1564, 1593, 1594, 1622
FENETER, D. C.; pvt; 1st MD Cav, Co K; ref: 1, 19
FENNEY, L.; pvt; Stuart's Horse Arty, Breathed's Battery; ref: 1
FENTON, Daniel A.; sgt; 2nd MD Inf, Co G; res: Balt; ref: 1, 2, 19, 21, 23, 39, 150, 470, 493, 511, 700, 873, 1523
FENTON, Henry T.; sgt; 2nd MD Cav, Co B; ref: 1, 19, 1609
FENTON, John J.; sgt; Rhett's 1st SC Heavy Arty; res: Balt; ref: 1, 19, 21, 511, 700, 735, 1609

FENTRESS, Andrew B.; pvt; 9th VA Inf, Co B; ref: 1, 1576
FENWICK, Albert; cpl; 2nd MD Inf, Co B; res: Leonardtown, St. M. Cty; ref: 1, 2, 19, 21, 23, 1509, 1555, 1627
FERCOIT, Charles N.; cpl; 1st MD Inf, Co G; res: Balt; ref: 1, 2, 19, 21, 23, 456, 1540
FERGUSON, A. J.; pvt; 1st MD Cav, Co A; ref: 1, 2, 21
FERGUSON, James Duque; Maj; A.G., Gen F. Lee's staff; res: Balt; ref: 1, 44
FERGUSON, John; pvt; 1st MD Cav, Co E; res: Port Tobacco, Cha Cty; ref: 1, 2, 19, 21, 730, 1546
FERGUSON, W. J.; pvt; 40th VA Cav, Co B; res: Balt; ref: 1, 21, 700, 1598
FERRAL, Thomas, Jr; pvt; 1st MD Cav, Co B; res: Buena Vista, PG Cty; ref: 1, 2, 19, 21, 785, 1553, 1622
FERRELL, Benjamin; pvt; 2nd MD Cav, Co D; ref: 1, 19
FERRELL, John Thomas; pvt; 1st MD Cav, Co B; res: PG Cty; MLCSH; ref: 1, 2, 19, 21, 93, 627, 700, 786
FERRIOT, C. N. ref: 488
FERRIS, John; pvt; Davis's MD Cav, Co B; ref: 1, 19
FERRITER, Timothy C.; pvt; Davis's MD Cav, Co B; ref: 1, 19
FERRY, William S.; cpl; 2nd MD Lt Arty; res: Balt; ref: 1, 2, 19, 21
FEUTHSWAIT, J. R.; pvt; 2nd MD Inf, Co H; ref: 2, 19, 21
FIEGE, Charles E.; pvt; 1st MD Inf, Co E; ref: 1, 2, 19, 21
FIELD, Eugene William; ordnance sgt; 2nd MD Cav, Co C; ref: 1, 2, 11, 19, 21, 23, 93, 125, 349, 614, 1523, 1560, 1562, 1563, 1609, 1631
FIELD, George W.; sgt; 19th VA Heavy Arty, Co C; ref: 1, 2, 19, 21, 730, 1580
FIELD, Richard A.; pvt; 19th VA Heavy ArtY, Co C; res: Forktown, Som Cty; ref: 1, 1556, 1580
FIELDS, Edward W.; pvt; Hampton Leg Lt Arty, Co B; ref: 1, 2, 21
FIELDS, James; pvt; Zarvona's MD Zouaves; ref: 735
FIELDS, John; pvt; Holbrook's Independent MD Lt Arty; res: Balt; ref: 1, 1613
FIGG, John Q.; color sgt; 1st VA Inf, Co B; res: Balt; ref: 1, 21, 700
FILLER, F.; ref: 412
FILLINS, John W.; pvt; 1st MD Lt Arty; ref: 1, 2, 19, 21
FILLIS, Edward; pvt; 1st MD Inf, Co E; ref: 1, 2, 19, 21
FILMER, Frederick; pvt; 3rd MD Lt Arty; ref: 1, 2, 19, 21, 160, 726
FINK, Henry; pvt; 1st MD Inf, Co G; ref: 1, 2, 19, 21
FINNEGAN, James; Lt; 2nd MD Inf, Co H; ref: 1
FINNEGAN, Patrick; pvt; Stuart's Horse Arty, Breathed's Battery; res: Balt; MLCSH; ref: 700, 786
FINSTWAIT, J. P.; 2nd MD Inf, Co G; res: Federalsburg, Dor Cty; ref: 19, 112
FIPPS, John; pvt; 2nd MD Cav, Co F; ref: 1, 2, 21
FISHACK, George; pvt; 9th VA Inf, Co B; res: Balt; ref: 1, 735, 1576
FISHER, A. B.; Lt; 7th VA Cav, Co G; ref: 1
FISHER, Charles D.; pvt; 2nd MD Cav, Co F; res: Balt; ref: 1, 2, 19, 21
FISHER, Charles W.; pvt; Kevill's Co, VA Heavy Arty; ref: 1, 21, 700
FISHER, John W.; lmn, Navy; res: McPherson Pack, AA Cty; ref: 1, 1539
FISHER, W. C.; pvt; 1st SC Inf, Co G; ref: 1
FISHER, William J., Jr; pvt; 9th VA Inf, Co B; ref: 1, 1576
FISHER, William J., Sr; pvt; 9th VA Inf, Co B; ref: 1, 1576

FISHPACK, George; pvt; 13th VA Inf, Co G; ref: 1
FISHPAW, Eli; cpl; 1st MD Inf, Co G; ref: 1, 2, 19, 21, 23
FISKE, Henry; pvt; Barry's Co, MD Vols; ref: 1, 19
FITCH, William; sgt; 35th VA Cav, Co B; res: Barnesville, Mont Cty; ref: 1, 3, 1552, 1611, 1677
FITE, Lewis; res: Frederick, Frd Cty; ref: 89
FITTS, Tandy Walker; cpl; 20th VA Inf, Co K; res: Frd Cty; ref: 1, 71
FITZGERALD, John; cpl; 1st VA Inf, Co E; ref: 1
FITZGERALD, John E.; pvt; 2nd MD Cav, Co E; res: Balt; ref: 1, 2, 19, 21, 650, 735
FITZGERALD, R. E.; pvt; 20th VA Lt Arty, Co H; ref: 1, 2, 19, 21
FITZGERALD, Robert; pvt; Rhett's 1st SC Heavy Arty; ref: 735
FITZGERALD, Thomas; pvt; 1st MD Cav, Co D; res: Balt; ref: 1, 2, 19, 21, 93, 1601
FITZGERALD, W. H.; pvt; 12th VA inf, Co E; ref: 1, 735
FITZGERALD, William Bolton; pvt; Weston's Bn, Co A; res: Balt; ref: 1, 2, 19, 21, 69, 361, 700,
FITZGERALD, William H.; Mast. M, Navy; C.S.S. Indian Chief; res: Balt; ref: 1, 2, 21, 53, 58, 97, 700, 735, 783, 848, 1564
FITZHUGH, C. D.; pvt; 1st MD Cav, Co C; res: Hagerstown, Wash Cty; ref: 1, 19, 901
FITZHUGH, R. Allen; sgt; 26th VA Inf, Co B; ref: 1, 57
FITZPATRICK, Charles Howard; Lt; 9th VA Inf, Co B; res: Balt; MLCHS; ref: 627, 700, 786, 1576
FITZPATRICK, Daniel; pvt; 13th VA Inf, Co G; res: Balt; ref: 1, 2, 11, 19, 21, 735
FITZPATRICK, John D.; pvt; Zarvona's MD Zouaves; ref: 1, 2, 19, 21, 735
FITZSIMMONS, Michael; pvt; 35th VA Cav, Co B; ref: 1677
FITZSIMMONS, Nicholas C.; pvt; 35th VA Cav, Co B; res: Urbanna, Frd Cty; ref: 1, 3, 90, 1611, 1677
FLACK, Thomas J., Jr; pvt; 43rd VA Cav (Mosby's), Co D; res: Balt; ref: 1, 2, 8, 19, 21
FLAHERTY, James F.; pvt; 1st VA Inf, Co E; ref: 735
FLAHERTY, William J.; pvt; 1st VA Inf, Co F; ref: 735
FLANAGAN, Jefferson; pvt; 1st MD Inf, Co B; ref: 1, 2, 19, 21
FLANNAGAN, Patrick; pvt; 1st MD Cav, Co F; ref: 1, 2, 19, 21
FLANNAGAN, John; pvt; 1st MD Cav, Co C; res: Balt; ref: 1, 2, 19, 21
FLAXCOMB, Charles; res: Balt; ref: 1540
FLEINOR, Abraham; pvt; 3rd MD Lt Arty; ref: 1, 2, 19, 21, 160, 726, 1460
FLEINOR, Isaac; pvt; Holbrook's Independent MD Lt Arty; ref: 1
FLEINOR, Michael; res: Balt; ref: 1540
FLEMING, Charles C.; pvt; 1st SC Inf, Co G; ref: 1
FLEMING, William; sgt; 3rd MD Lt Arty; Funkstown, Wash Cty; ref: 1, 2, 19, 21, 23, 160, 726, 1558
FLETCHER, John W.; pvt; 35th VA Cav, Co A; ref: 1, 3, 15, 1611, 1677
FLETCHER, Joseph G., artificer; 3rd MD Lt Arty; ref: 1, 2, 19, 21, 23, 160, 726, 1460
FLETCHER, Madison, W.; cpl; 2nd MD Cav, Co D; ref: 1, 19, 86, 1609
FLETCHER, Solomon D.; pvt; 2nd MD Lt Arty; res: Carr Cty; ref: 1, 2, 19, 21, 645
FLINT, James U.; pvt; 1st MD Cav, Co D; ref: 1, 2, 21, 1601
FLIPPO, Major F.; pvt; 47th VA Inf, Co H; ref: 1, 1388
FLOOD, Peter; pvt; 2nd MD Inf, Co H; ref: 1, 2, 19, 21
FLORENCE, Lewis, Jr; pvt; 19th VA Heavy Arty; ref: 1, 1580
FLOWERS, John; pvt; 1st SC Inf, Co G; ref: 1
FLOWERS, John W.; pvt; 11th VA Inf, Co H; res: Balt; ref: 1, 21, 700

FLOWERS, W. Henry; pvt; 3rd MD Lt Arty; ref: 1, 2, 19, 21, 160, 726
FLOYD, ---; res: Rose Hill, Port Tobacco, Cha Cty; ref: 272
FLOYD, James Frederick; Lt; 39th VA Inf, Co E; res: Eastern Shore; ref: 1, 70, 684
FLOYD, John; pvt; 1st MD Cav, Co F; ref: 1, 19
FLOYD, Joseph Walker; pvt; 16th VA Inf, Co H; res: Frd Cty; ref: 1, 72
FLOYD, Robert Semmes; sgt; 1st VA Cav, Co K; res: Port Tobacco, Cha Cty; ref: 1, 2, 19, 21, 735, 1523, 1546
FLOYD, William Henry; chief musician; 14th VA Cav, Co C; res: Catonsville, Bt Cty; ref: 1, 71
FLOYD, William S.; pvt; 1st MD Cav, Co F; res: Eastern Shore; ref: 1, 2, 19, 21, 70
FLYHASTY, John; res: West River, AA Cty; ref: 1539
FOARD, Norvel E.; pvt; 3rd VA Inf, Co C; res: Balt; ref: 1, 986
FOLEY, Daniel; pvt; 3rd MD Lt Arty; ref: 1, 2, 19, 21, 160, 726
FOLEY, David R.; pvt; 13th VA Inf, Co G; res: Balt; MLCSH; ref: 1, 2, 19, 21, 93, 700, 735, 786
FOLEY, Fenton M.; pvt; 35th VA Cav, Co A; ref: 1, 3, 15, 1677
FOLEY, Frederick S.; pvt; 13th VA Inf, Co G; res: Balt; ref: 1, 735, 1540
FOLEY, John; pvt; 3rd MD Lt Arty; res: West River, AA Cty; ref: 1, 2, 19, 21, 160, 461, 726, 1539
FOLEY, Presley S.; res: Balt; ref: 1540
FOLEY, Richard Fleming; Master, Navy; C.S.S. Robert E. Lee; res: Balt; ref: 21, 97, 700, 735, 783, 1540, 1564
FOLLAS, Edward; res: Balt; ref: 1540
FOMAN, Charles; pvt; 2nd MD Cav, Co F; ref: 2, 11, 19, 21
FOMAN, Perry; pvt; 2nd MD Cav, Co F; ref: 2, 19, 21
FONERDEN, Clarence A.; cpl; Carpenter's Co, VA Lt Arty; ref: Balt; ref: 1, 44
FONTAIN, J.; sgt; 2nd MD Cav, Co A; ref: 1, 19, 456, 1609
FONTZ, Nicholas; res: Johnson's Store, AA Cty; ref: 1539
FOOKS, Josiah D.; pvt; 1st MD Inf, Co D; res: Berlin, Wor Cty; ref: 1, 19, 1559
FOOS, George W.; sgt; 1st MD Inf, Co F; res: Balt; ref: 1, 2, 19, 21, 23
FOOT, J. G.; 12th VA, Co K; ref: 92
FORBES, Henry Marshall; pvt; 1st MD Lt Arty; Aquaser, PG Cty; ref: 1. 2, 19, 21, 1520, 1553, 1665
FORBES, Joseph Harris; sgt; 1st MD Lt Arty; res: Aquaser, PG Cty; ref: 1, 2, 19, 21, 23, 690, 700, 1553, 1665
FORD, Benjamin E.; pvt; 1st MD Cav, Co B; ref: 1, 19
FORD, Edward Clement Samuel; pvt; 1st MD Inf, Co E; res: Pack Mills, Frd Cty; ref: 1, 2, 19, 21, 89, 90, 1548
FORD, Edwin; res: Princess Anne, Som Cty; ref: 1509, 1556
FORD, Flemming; pvt; 2nd MD Cav, Co C; ref: 1, 2, 11, 21
FORD, Henry; pvt; Zarvona's MD Zouaves; ref: 1, 19, 1599
FORD, Henry; pvt; 2nd MD Inf, Co B; res: St. M. Cty; ref: 1, 2, 19, 21, 23, 316, 470, 1509, 1523, 1579
FORD, James E.; pvt; 1st MD Lt Arty; ref: 1, 2, 19, 21
FORD, James W.; pvt; 3rd MD Lt Arty; res: Princess Anne, Som Cty; ref: 1, 2, 19, 21, 160, 726, 1556
FORD, John; pvt; 1st SC Inf, Co G; res: Balt; ref: 735
FORD, Louis; res: Tracey's Landing, AA Cty; ref: 1539
FORD, Patrick; pvt; 9th VA Inf, Co B; ref: 1, 1576
FORD, Stephen H.; mast. a., Navy; C.S.S. Indian Chief; res: Cec Cty; ref: 1, 70

FORD, Thomas; pvt; Holbrook''s Independent MD Lt Arty; res: Balt; ref: 1
FORD, Thomas F.; 13th VA Cav, Co F; ref: 735
FORD, William; Castle Pinkney's SC Heavy Arty; ref: 735
FOREMAN, Arthur L. (M.D.); Asst Surg; 25th LA Inf; res: Balt; ref: 1, 18
FOREMAN, P. G.; pvt; 43rd VA Cav (Mosby's), Co E; ref: 8, 20
FOREMAN, Valentine; pvt; 1st MD Inf, Co A; res: Frd Cty; ref: 1, 2, 19, 21, 90
FOREMAN, W. W.; pvt; S.L.S. Lt Arty; res: Balt; ref: 262
FORNANDIS, George G. (M.D.); Asst Surg; 2nd SC Inf; res: Balt; ref: 1, 18, 1532, 1536
FORNER, William; pvt; 2nd MD Lt Arty; res: Pikesville, Bt Cty; ref: 1, 2, 19, 21, 1541
FORNEY, George W.; Lt; 2nd MD Cav, Co C; ref: 1, 2, 19, 21, 23, 1609
FORREST, Andrew H.; pvt; 9th VA Inf, Co B; ref: 1, 1576
FORREST, David C.; Lt; 2nd MD Inf, Co F; ref: 1, 2, 19, 21, 23, 674
FORREST, Douglas F. (Revd), Paymaster, Navy; C.S.S. Arctic; res: Ellicott City, How Cty; ref: 1, 21, 58, 133, 142, 330, 601, 700, 783, 1127, 1523, 1564, 1578, 1579, 1673
FORREST, Dulany A.; Lt, Navy; C.S.S. Palmetto States; ref: 19, 58, 61, 97, 279, 1564
FORREST, French; Capt, Navy; Commanding the James River Squadron; ref: 1, 18, 19, 58, 61, 97, 279, 735, 791, 1118, 1126, 1499, 1523, 1554, 1564, 1568, 1579, 1616, 1620, 1632, 1673
FORREST, George W.; pvt; 9th VA Inf, Co B; res: Balt; ref: 1, 735, 1576
FORREST, J. J.; pvt; 43rd VA Cav (Mosby's), Co E; ref: 1, 8, 20
FORREST, J. M.; pvt; 29th Bn GA Cav, Co D; ref: 1, 93
FORREST, Joseph; Capt; 4th MD Lt Arty; res: Oakville, St. M. Cty; ref: 1, 2, 7, 19, 316, 1509, 1520, 1555
FORREST, Joseph; Lt; 2nd MD Inf, Co F; res: PG Cty; ref: 64, 68, 791
FORREST, Julius; Castle Pinkney SC Heavy Arty; ref: 735
FORREST, Pitt; pvt; 1st VA Cav, Co K; res: St. M. Cty; ref: 2, 19, 21, 1509
FORREST, W. S.; Acting Mast. M., Navy; C.S. Tennessee; ref: 1, 19, 1564
FORREST, Zachariah; pvt; 1st MD Inf, Co G; res: Balt; ref: 1, 2, 21
FORSYTH, A. M.; pvt; 21st VA Inf, Co B; ref: 1, 2
FORSYTHE, William Henry; pvt; 1st MD Cav, Co A; res: Sykesville, Carr Cty; ref: 1, 2, 10, 19, 21, 23, 70, 71, 72, 75, 86, 685, 700, 748, 1288, 1550
FORT, D.; pvt; MD Guerrilla Zouaves; ref: 1
FORT, W. E.; pvt; 12th NC Inf, Co G; ref: 1, 93, 735
FORWARD, R. (M.D.); pvt 5th LA Inf, Desota Rifles; res: Har Cty; ref: 1, 18, 86
FOSTER, James Harry; pvt; 5th GA Inf, Co A; ref: 1, 19
FOSTER, John Henry; pvt; 43rd Cav (Mosby's), Co A; res: Balt; MLCSH; ref: 1, 2, 8, 19, 21, 312, 627, 700, 735, 786, 1579
FOSTER, Michael; pvt; 1st MD Cav, Co A; ref: 1, 2, 19, 21
FOSTER, Peter; pvt; Lucas' 15th SC Heavy Arty; res: 1, 19
FOSTER, Robert E.; pvt; 21st VA Inf, Co B; ref: 1, 2, 19, 312
FOSTER, Samuel; pvt; 19th VA Heavy Arty, Co C; ref: 1, 1580
FOSTER, T. Gardiner; pvt; 18th GA Inf, Co C; ref: 1, 19
FOUCH, Amos; res: Annapolis, AA Cty; ref: 1539
FOUNTAIN, W. B.; pvt; 2nd MD Inf, Co G; ref: 2, 19, 21
FOUST, John; res: Friendship, AA Cty; ref: 1539

FOUT, John; Lt; res: Doubs, Frd Cty; ref: 19, 90, 615, 643
FOUTE, Augustus M.; Lt Col; Gen J. Pemberton's staff; res: Balt; MLCSH; ref: 1, 21, 93, 700, 786, 791, 846
FOWLER, A. J.; pvt; 3rd MD Lt Arty; ref: 1, 2, 19, 21, 160, 726
FOWLER, E. A.; pvt; 1st SC Inf, Co G; ref: 1
FOWLER, Elsburry, C.; pvt; 3rd MD Lt Arty; ref: 1, 2, 19, 21, 160, 726
FOWLER, Henry; pvt;39th VA Inf, Co B; res: Salisbury, Som Cty; ref: 1, 735, 1556
FOWLER, James H., Jr; pvt; 13th VA Inf, Co G; res: Balt; ref: 1, 735, 1540
FOWLER, John T., Navy; C.S.S. Atlanta; ref: 1, 93
FOWLER, Spencer D.; pvt; MD American Rifles; res: Horse Head, PG Cty; ref: 1, 1553, 1622
FOWLKES, Francis L.; pvt; 9th VA Inf, Co B; ref: 1, 1576
FOWLKES, Junius Woodson; pvt; Richmond Howitzers, 2nd Co; res: Balt; MLCSH; ref: 1, 627, 700, 786
FOX, ---; Capt; 5th VA Cav; ref: 735
FOX, A. G.; pvt; 43rd VA Cav (Mosby's), Co A; ref: 8, 10
FOX, C. A. (M.D.); pvt; 43rd VA Cav (Mosby's), Co A; res: Balt; ref: 1, 8, 20, 257
FOX, John; pvt; 2nd MD Cav, Co G; ref: 1
FOXWELL, Charles J.; pvt; 2nd MD Inf, Co B; res: Leonardtown, St. M. Cty; ref: 1, 2, 19, 21, 690, 700, 1509, 1555, 1670
FRAIL, C. M.; Lucas' 15th SC Heavy Arty; ref: 1, 470, 486
FRANCE, Robert Lee, Jr; ordnance sgt; Moore's Co, VA Lt Arty; res: Balt; ref: 1, 19, 69, 316
FRANCE, Spencer L.; Capt; King William VA Lt Arty; res: Tal Cty; ref: 1, 44, 69, 133, 316
FRANCIS, Thomas P.; petty officer, Navy; C.S.S. Virginia; res: Balt; ref: 1
FRANCIS, William M.; pvt; 9th VA Inf, Co B; ref: 1, 1576
FRANCK, W. Joseph; ref: 456
FRANKLIN, Benjamin E.; pvt; 3rd VA Inf, Co H; res: Balt; ref: 1, 21, 700
FRANKLIN, Joel W. (M.D.); Asst Surg; 56th GA Inf; ref: 1, 2, 18, 21, 23, 64, 160, 461, 1534
FRANKLIN, James Shaw; Lt; 2nd MD Inf, Co D; res: Annapolis, AA Cty; ref: 1, 2, 19, 21, 23, 35, 64, 68, 81, 674, 1519, 1523, 1539
FRANKLIN, John; pvt; 2nd MD Cav, Co A; ref: 1
FRANKLIN, Joseph; pvt; Hampton Leg Lt Arty, Co B; res: West River, AA Cty; ref: 1, 2, 21, 470, 700, 786, 1539, 1628
FRANTON, Joseph; res: Annapolis, AA Cty; ref: 1539
FRAYER, Frederick J.; pvt; 1st MD Lt Arty; res: Bt Cty; ref: 1, 2, 19, 21, 34, 63, 64, 470, 782, 791, 1273, 1575
FRAZIER, G. H.; pvt; Zarvona's MD Zouaves; res: Balt; ref: 1, 58, 97, 1520
FRAZIER, John; res: Annapolis, AA Cty; ref: 1539
FRAZIER, Louis H.; res: Annapolis, AA Cty; ref: 1539
FRAZIER, Lorenzo W.; sgt; 3rd MD Lt Arty; ref: 1, 2, 19, 21, 23, 160, 461, 726
FREAMER, George; Maj; Asst A.G., Gen F. Lee's staff; res: Hagerstown, Wash Cty; ref: 1, 19, 23, 65, 125, 361, 511, 693, 791
FREDERICK, Adolph; pvt; 2nd MD Lt Arty; res: Balt; ref: 1, 2, 21, 700
FREDERICK, W.; ref: 92
FREEBURGER, James H.; pvt; 2nd MD Cav, Co C; res: Balt; ref: 1, 11
FREEBURGER, William T.; pvt; 2nd MD Cav, Co C; res: Balt; ref: 2, 19, 21
FREELAND, Thomas E.; pvt; 2nd MD Inf, Co G; res: St. M. Cty; ref: 1, 2, 7, 19, 21, 822

FREEMAN, Bernard; pvt; 2nd MD Inf, Co A; res: Great Mills, St. M. Cty; ref: 1, 2, 19, 21, 23, 470, 650, 700, 1509, 1523, 1555
FREEMAN, E. T.; Gen S. G. French's staff; res: Som Cty; ref: 70
FREEMAN, James Marion; pvt; 2nd MD Inf, Co B; res: Cha Cty; ref: 1, 2, 19, 21
FREEMAN, Lewis; pvt; 21st VA Inf, Co B; res: Great Mills, St. M. Cty; ref: 2, 19, 233, 312, 1555
FREEMAN, Phillip; pvt; 1st MD Infj, Co I; ref: Cha Cty; ref: 1, 2, 19, 21
FREEMAN, R. M.; pvt; 21st VA Inf, Co B; res: Great Mills, St. M. Cty; ref: 1, 2, 21, 312, 592, 700, 735, 1509, 1555
FREEMAN, Robert J. (M.D.); Passed Asst Surg, Navy; Ram Atlanta; res: Som Cty; ref: 1, 18, 70, 97, 1534, 1564
FREEMAN, Thomas S.; pvt; Holbrook's Independent MD Lt Arty Battery; res: Cha Cty; ref: 1, 2, 19, 21
FREEMAN, Z. Francis; sgt; 2nd MD Inf, Co B; res: Cha Cty; ref: 1, 2, 19, 21, 23, 1509, 1565
FRENCH, William; res: Balt; ref: 1540
FREY, Gotlieb; Lucas' 15th SC Heavy Arty; res: Balt; ref: 1, 1540
FRICK, James; pvt; 1st MD Lt Arty; res: Balt; ref: 1, 470
FRICK, William, Jr; Acting Chief Engr, Navy; C.S.S. Gaines; ref: 19, 58, 61, 97, 279, 1564
FRIDHOFER, John G.; res: Patuxent Forge, AA Cty; ref: 1539
FRIESE, John; pvt; 1st SC Inf, Co G; ref: 735
FRIZZELL, Bull; res: Mont Cty; ref: 1493
FRONTAU, C. M.; 5th NC, Co B; ref: 92
FUGITT, Walter R.; pvt; 47th VA Inf, Co H; ref: 1
FULKERSON, J. K. P.; pvt; 3rd MD Lt Arty; ref: 1, 2, 21, 160, 726
FULLER, Richard; pvt; Zarvona's MD Zouaves; ref: 1, 19, 58, 97
FULMER, George W.; pvt; 19th VA Heavy Arty, Co C; ref: 1, 1580
FULTON, Alexander; pvt; 2nd MD Inf, Co A; res: AA Cty; ref: 1, 2, 19, 21, 259, 650, 1539
FUNCHEON, Martin; pvt; 19th VA Heavy Arty, Co C; ref: 1, 1580
FUNK, Charles Daniel; pvt; 5th VA Cav, Co C; res: Balt; MLCSH; ref: 1, 2, 19, 21, 93, 627, 700, 735, 786, 1601
FURRINGTON, John; pvt; Davis's MD Cav, Co; ref: 1

GADD, Alexander; res: Caro Cty; ref: 19, 523, 527
GADD, Frank; res: Caro Cty; ref: 19, 523, 527
GADD, William F.; pvt; 21st VA Inf, Co B; res: Balt; ref: 1, 2, 19, 312
GAGAN, Louis A.; pvt; 2nd MD Cav, Co G; ref: 1
GAILLARD, Edwin Samuel (M.D.); Surg; Surgical & Medical Inspector,Richmond; res: Balt; ref: 1, 2, 18, 19, 21, 64, 923, 1531, 1532, 1534
GAINER, John H.; pvt; 1st MD Lt Arty; res: Leonardtown, St. M. Cty; ref: 1
GAINES, John Mutiurs (M.D.); Asst Sur; 8th VA Inf, Boonsboro, Wash Cty; ref: 1, 18, 74, 78, 361, 486, 1534, 1536
GAINES, William W.; pvt; 1st MD Lt Arty; ref: 1
GAITHER, George Ridgely, Jr; Lt Co; 1st VA Cav; res: Ellicott City, How Cty; ref: 1, 2, 10, 18, 19, 21, 23, 34, 50, 53, 63, 64, 68, 79, 107, 117, 127, 222, 240, 445, 457, 488, 489, 518, 631, 638, 684, 700, 748, 789, 791, 848, 849, 866, 923, 981, 1519, 1523, 1550
GAITHER, George Washington; pvt; 1st VA Cav, Co K; res: Cooksville, How Cty; ref: 1, 2, 10, 13, 19, 21, 1550
GAITHER, William; res: Millersville, AA Cty; ref: 1539

GALE, Frank (M.D.); Asst Surg; Hampton Leg Lt Arty; ref: 1, 2, 18, 19, 21, 1690
GALE, George G.; pvt; Hampton Leg Lt Arty, Co B; ref: 1, 2, 19, 21, 685
GALE, John; Lt; 1st MD Lt Arty; Som Cty; ref: 1, 2, 19, 21, 23, 34, 64, 470, 782, 791, 1523
GALLAGHER, Charles H.; pvt; 2nd VA Inf, Co G; MLCSH; ref: 1, 3, 786, 1611, 1677
GALLAGHER, Charles K.; Capt; 4th NC Inf, Co E; ref: 1, 21, 700, 791
GALLAGHER, De Witt Clinton; pvt; 1st VA Cav, Co E; res: Balt; ref: 1, 70
GALLAGHER, Howard L.; pvt; 2nd MD Inf, Co A; res: Balt; ref: 1, 2, 19, 21, 650, 1520
GALLAGHER, Michael Patrick, gun, Navy; C.S.S. Atlanta; res: Frederick, Frd Cty; ref: 1, 89, 90, 735
GALLOWAY, William J.; pvt; 1st SC Inf, Co G; res: Crownsville, AA Cty; ref: 1, 1539
GALVIN, A.; pvt; MD Guerrilla Zouaves; ref: 1
GAMAGE, John O.; pvt; Norfolk Lt Arty Blues; res: Balt; ref: 1, 70
GAMBELL, A. A.; pvt; 1st MD Cav, Co A; ref: 1, 19
GAMBLE, Carey Breckinridge (M.D.); Chief Surg; District of Florida; res: Balt; ref: 1, 18, 21, 23, 53, 56, 700, 1533, 1536
GAMBRILL, James H.; res: Frd Cty; ref: 125, 361
GAMER, A. B.; pvt; 35th VA Cav, Co B; ref: 15
GANNON, William; drummer; 2nd MD Inf, Co A; ref: 1, 2, 19, 21, 64, 650
GARDEN, Alexander; pvt; 56th VA Inf, Co G;; res: Balt; MLCSH; ref: 1, 19, 93, 124, 627, 786
GARDENER, John B.; pvt; 1st MD Lt Arty; res: Silversburg, Wash Cty; ref: 1, 2, 19, 21, 1558
GARDENER, John H.; pvt; 4th MD Lt Arty; res: Princeland, AA Cty; ref: 1, 2, 19, 21, 1539
GARDENER, Richard A.; 45th VA Inf, Co F; res: Princeland, AA Cty; ref: 1, 687, 1539
GARDENER, Robert; res: West River, AA Cty; ref: 1539
GARDINER, Bernard; pvt; 18th VA Heavy Arty, Co A; res: St. M. Cty; ref: 1
GARDINER, F. A.; pvt; 1st MD Lt Arty; ref: 1, 2, 19, 21
GARDINER, James; pvt; 2nd MD Inf, Co F; res: Cha Cty; ref: 1, 2, 19, 21
GARDINER, John de Barth Walback; pvt; 1st MD Lt Arty; res: Cha Cty; ref: 1, 2, 19, 21, 1665
GARDINER, Joseph; cpl; 18th VA Heavy Arty, Co A; res: St. M. Cty; ref: 1
GARDINER, Louis de Barth; sgt; Robinson's VA Lt Arty; res: Cha Cty; ref: 21, 700, 1665
GARDINER, Lewis D.; 1st LA Cav; ref: 735
GARDINER, Thomas J.; pvt; 35th VA Cav, Co D; res: Balt; MLCSH; ref: 786, 1677
GARDINER, William F.; pvt; 1st MD Inf, Co H; res: Patuxent Forge, AA Cty; ref: 1, 2, 19, 21, 650, 1539
GARDNER, Benjamin; pvt; 2nd MD Inf, Co H; ref: 1, 2, 19, 21
GARDNER, Elijah; pvt; 2nd MD Lt Arty; ref: 1, 2, 19, 21
GARDNER, George Craftholder; Navy; C.S.S. Gaines; res: Balt; ref: 1, 1540
GARDNER, J. J.; pvt; 1st MD Cav, Co F; ref: 1, 2, 19, 21, 1523
GARDNER, John W.; pvt; Stuart's Horse Arty, Breathed's Battery; res: Balt; ref: 1, 2, 19, 498
GARDNER, Robert F.; pvt; Hospital Steward, Medical student; res: Annapolis, AA Cty; ref: 1, 1539
GARDNER, S. T.; pvt; Holbrook's Independent MD Lt Arty; res: Cha Cty; ref: 1, 68

GARDNER, Thomas J.; pvt; 35th VA Cav, Co D; res: Rockville, Mont Cty; ref: 1, 86, 92, 93, 1552
GARDNER, William F. (Revd); Chaplain; 19th VA Inf; res: How Cty; ref: 1, 21, 70, 650, 700, 735
GARIGAN, Michael; pvt; Stuart's Horse Arty, Breathed's Battery; ref: 1, 498
GARNER, Franklin Smith; Lt; 1st VA Lt Arty; res: Carr Cty; ref: 1, 70
GARNER, John; pvt; Zarvona's MD Zouaves; res: St. M. Cty; ref: 1, 735, 1509
GARNER, Robert; pvt; 1st MD Cav, Co B; res: Friendship, AA Cty; ref: 1, 19, 70, 1539
GARNETT, ---; pvt; 43rd VA Cav (Mosby's), Co G; ref: 8, 20
GARNETT, James Mercer (Prof); Capt; Ordnance Dept, Gen C. S. Winder's staff; res: Annapolis, AA Cty; ref: 1, 21, 44, 56, 70, 122, 150, 631, 700, 749, 791, 936, 1001, 1058, 1157, 1628
GARNETT, Reufus A.; sgt; 51st VA Inf, Co C; ref: 1, 21, 700
GARNETT, Robert Edward; 4th AL, Co C; res: Balt; ref: 70
GARRETSON, Frederick (M.D.); Passed asst Surg, Navy; C.S.S. Florida; ref: 1, 18, 1533, 1534, 1536, 1564
GARRETT, Charles D.; pvt; 4th MD Lt Arty; ref: 1, 19
GARRETT, E. W.; sgt; 1st SC Inf, Co G; ref: 1
GARRETT, Robert Edwdard; sgt; 4th AL Inf, Co C; res: Balt; ref: 996
GARRETT, W. A. K.; pvt; 46th Al, Co A; ref: 1, 2, 19, 21, 160, 726
GARRETTSON, William H.; pvt; Click's Ordnance Scouts & Guards; res: Balt; ref: 1, 1540
GARRIGUES, Henry H.; pvt; 14th TN Inf, Co A; ref: 1, 21, 70, 700
GARRISON, Henry; pvt; 9th VA Cav, Co A; ref: 1, 21, 700
GARRISON, Robert D.; pvt; 2nd MD Inf, Co C; res: Som Cty; ref: 1, 2, 19, 21
GARRISON, Samuel; res: Balt; ref: 1540
GARST, Benjamin; pvt; 3rd MD Lt Arty; ref: 1, 2, 19, 21, 160, 461, 726, 1460
GARST, Elias; pvt; 36th VA Inf, Co E; res: Frd Cty; ref: 72
GARTLAND, Frank P.; pvt; 1st VA Inf, Co E; res: PG Cty; ref: 1, 735
GASKINS, Benjamin; pvt; 1st SC Inf, Co G; ref: 1
GASKINS, D. M.; drummer; 1st SC Inf, Co G; res: Balt; ref: 1, 1613
GASKINS, Sebastian; pvt; 1st SC Inf, Co G; ref: 1
GASKINS, William H.; pvt; clerk to Gen Elzey, MD Line; res: Balt; ref: 1
GASSAWAY, Samuel; pvt; 1st MD Inf, Co C; res: Balt; ref: 1, 2, 19, 21, 685
GASSETT, C. W.; Maj; Q.M., Gen B. W. Duke's staff; ref: 1, 21, 700, 791
GASSMAN, Jacob; McNeill's Rangers; res: Cumberland, All Cty; ref: 19, 23, 65, 95, 148, 431, 519, 1560
GATCH, Joseph A. Ross; pvt; 1st KY Battery; res: Towson, Bt Cty; MLCSH; ref: 21, 93, 700, 735, 786
GATCH, Thomas Benton; Capt; Davis's MD Cav; res: Lauraville, Bt Cty; ref: 1, 2, 11, 19, 21, 23, 70, 86, 700, 735, 781, 824, 1371, 1375, 1485, 1541, 1562, 1575, 1609, 1675
GATCHELL, J. G.; pvt; 2nd MD Lt Arty; res: Balt; ref: 1, 2, 19 21
GATCHELL, Samuel H.; pvt; 2nd MD Cav, Co A; res: Balt; ref: 1, 19
GATELRY, John Thomas; smn, Navy; C.S.S. Gaines; res: Balt; ref: 1, 1540
GATES, Lewis R.; pvt; 3rd MD Lt Arty; ref: 1, 2, 19, 21, 160, 726
GATES, W.; pvt; 43rd GA Inf, Co E; ref: 1, 2, 19, 21, 160, 726

GATTON, Lloyd; res: St. M. Cty; ref: 1670
GATTON, William F.; pvt; 35th VA Cav, Co B; res: Point of Rocks, Frd Cty; ref: 1, 19, 90, 1611, 1677
GAULTY, Cyrus, Jr; pvt; 2nd MD Cav, Co F; ref: 1, 2, 19, 21, 757, 1609
GAUNA, ---; pvt Holbrook's Independent MD Lt Arty Battery; ref: 1, 19
GAVAN, William; sgt; 54th GA Inf, Co F; res: Balt; ref: 1, 21, 23, 57
GAVGING, Michael; pvt; 1st VA Cav, Co K; ref: 1, 2, 19
GAVIN, Michael F.; pvt; 12th VA Inf, Co K; ref: 21, 92, 93, 700
GAVIN, Thomas; pvt; 1st MD Inf, Co F; ref: 1, 2, 19, 21
GAVIN, William S.; pvt; 2nd MD Inf, Co E; res: Balt; ref: 1, 2, 19, 21, 470, 700, 1523
GAWTKIN, Charles; pvt; 7th VA Cav, Co G; ref: 1
GAYTHER, James W.; pvt; 2nd MD Lt Arty; ref: 2, 19, 21
GEASEY, Charles E.; pvt; 1st MD Cav, Co D; res: Libertytown, Frd Cty; ref: 1, 2, 19, 21, 90, 1601
GEASEY, James W.; pvt; 1st Md Cav, Co D; res: Libertytown, Frd Cty; ref: 1, 19, 90, 1601
GEDDING, Eli (M.D.); Surg; Gen Hospital Tallahassee, FL; res: Balt; ref: 1, 18, 1532, 1533, 1536
GEER, Edwin (Revd); Chaplain; Fort Fisher; res: Balt; ref: 1, 720, 1599
GEGAN, Louis A.; pvt; 2nd MD Cav, Co C; res: Balt; ref: 1, 19, 16C9
GEGAN, W.; pvt; 2nd MD Lt Arty; res: Balt; ref: 1, 2, 19, 21
GEIGER, George; Capt; Fire Bn LA Militia, Co C; res: New Windsor, Carr Cty; ref: 1, 19, 1620
GEIGER, Frederick; bugler; 3rd MD Lt Arty; ref: 1, 2, 19, 21, 23, 160, 726
GEIGER, John G. (M.D.); pvt; 1st MD Cav, Co D; res: Manchester, Carr Cty; ref: 1, 2, 19, 21, 1488, 1601
GEISE, Charles Richard; pvt; Rhett's 1st SC Heavy Arty; res: Balt; ref: 1, 735
GEMMILL, Thomas H.; sgt; 1st MD Cav, Co E; res: Kt Co; ref: 1, 2, 19, 21, 23, 107, 668, 730, 1584
GENTRY, Albert J.; pvt; Nelson Battery, Reserve Lt Arty; ref: 1, 93, 700
GEORGE, J. N.; cpl; 1st SC Inf, Co G; ref: 1
GEORGE, Thomas J.; pvt; 1st MD Cav, Co C; ref: 1, 2, 21
GEORGE, William T.; sgt; Zarvona's MD Zouaves; res: Rock Hall, Kt Cty; ref: 1584
GEPHART, Solomon Arthur; pvt; 1st MD Cav, Co A; Cumberland, All Cty; MLCSH; ref: 1, 2, 19, 21, 89, 90, 93, 627, 700, 786
GERDAN, William; pvt; 9th VA Inf, Co B; ref: 1, 1576
GERDING, S. G. W.; cpl; 3rd MD Lt Arty; ref: 1, 2, 19, 21, 23, 160, 726
GERMAN, John; pvt; Zarvona's MD Zouaves; ref: 735
GERMAN, Michael P.; pvt; Hampton Leg Lt Arty, Co B; res: Balt; ref: 1, 2, 19, 21, 1540
GERTRAM, G. L.; pvt; Zarvona's MD Zouaves; ref: 1
GERVIN, Peter M.; pvt; 2nd MD Inf, Co H; ref: 1, 2, 21
GETLING Fred; pvt; 2nd MD Cav, Co D; ref: 1, 19, 1609
GETZANDANNER, W. H.; Lt; 12th TX Cav, Co E; res: Frd Cty; ref: 1, 72
GIBBES, Robert R. (M.D.); Asst Surg, Navy, C.S.S. Savannah; res: Balt; ref: 1, 18, 1535
GIBBONS, Charles J.; MD American Rifles; res: How Cty; ref: 1, 10
GIBBONS, John S.; pvt; Zarvona's MD Zouaves; res: Beantown; ref: 1, 2, 21, 69, 316, 700, 735
GIBBONS, Simeon B.; Col; 10th VA Inf; res: St. M. Cty; ref: 1, 177, 250, 518, 530, 791

GIBBS, Thomas H.; pvt; 41st VA Inf, Co G; res: West River, AA Cty; ref: 1, 1539

GIBSON, Beverly William; Navy; prize, St. Minnes; ref: 1, 93

GIBSON, Charles Bell (M.D.); Surg; General Hospital No. 1, Richmond; res: Marrittsville; ref: 1, 18, 1534, 1536, 1550

GIBSON, Edward; pvt; 2nd MD Lt Arty; res: Tal Cty; ref: 1, 2, 19, 21, 645

GIBSON, Edward F.; pvt; Johnson's Battery LA Lt Arty; ref: 1, 2, 21, 1494

GIBSON, F.; pvt; Zarvona's MD Zouaves; ref: 19, 58, 97, 735

GIBSON, Fayette; cpl; Stuart's Horse Arty, Breathed's Battery; res: St. Michaels, Tal Cty; MLCSH; ref: 1, 19, 93, 498, 645, 786, 1557

GIBSON, George G.; Sgt; 21st VA Inf, Co B; ref: 1, 2, 19, 312, 681, 735, 1520

GIBSON, George T.; pvt; Holbrook's Independent MD Lt Arty Battery; res: AA Cty; ref: 1, 19

GIBSON, Henry Boteler; sgt; Castle Pinkney SC Heavy Arty; res: Bt Cty; MLCSH; ref: 1, 2, 19, 21, 70, 735, 786

GIBSON, Henry C.; pvt; 43rd VA Cav (Mosby's Cav), ref: 1, 8, 20, 123, 1601

GIBSON, James H.; pvt; 7th VA Cav, Co G; res: Horse Head, PG Cty; ref: 1, 800, 1553

GIBSON, Jonathan E.; pvt; 1st MD Cav, Co B; res: Bladensburg, PG Cty; ref: 1, 2, 19, 21, 1553

GIBSON, Mahlon; sgt; 1st VA Cav, Co H; ref: 1, 19, 21, 700

GIBSON, S.; pvt; 43rd VA Cav (Mosby's), Co E; ref: 1, 2, 8, 19, 21

GIBSON, Thomas P.; pvt; Marine Corps, Co H; res: Friendship, AA Cty; ref: 1, 1539, 1594

GIBSON, William C.; pvt; 2nd MD Inf, Co C; res: St. Michaels, Tal Cty; MLCSH; ref: 1, 2, 19, 21, 595, 645, 786, 1557

GIBSON, William E.; pvt; Lee's MD Cav; ref: 1, 19

GIDDINGS, Eugene J.; pvt; 35th VA Cav, Co B; res: Frd Cty; ref: 1, 1677

GIEGAN, William; 2nd MD Cav; ref: 680

GIESENDOFFER, Leonard; pvt; Davis's MD Cav, Co B; res: PG Cty; ref: 1, 19

GIFFEN, James Fortesue; sgt; Washington LA Arty, Co 5; res: Balt; ref: 1, 70

GIFFORD, James; pvt; MD Guerrilla Zouaves; ref: 1, 1621

GILBERT, James; 14th VA; res: Balt Cty; ref: 740

GILBERT, Stephen M.; pvt; 7th VA Cav, Co G; ref: 1, 3

GILBERT, William; pvt; Lee's MD Cav; ref: 1

GILDERSLEEVE, Basil L.; (Prof.); Capt; Asst Commissary of Supply, Gen J. B. Gordon's staff; res: Balt; ref: 30, 56, 57, 107, 108, 309, 753, 1143, 1174, 1261, 1327

GILES, Joseph; pvt; 9th VA Inf, Co B; res: AA Cty; ref: 1, 1576

GILES, Samuel N.; pvt; 7th VA Cav, Co G; ref: 1

GILES, Thomas D.; Lt; 3rd MD Lt Arty; ref: 1, 2, 19, 21, 23, 64, 160, 461, 726, 791, 1060, 1523

GILES, William Fell, Jr; pvt; 13th VA Inf, Co A; res: Balt; ref: 1, 2, 19, 21, 74, 559, 612, 700

GILL, George H.; pvt; 13th VA Inf, Co G; ref: 1, 1520

GILL, George Murray, Jr; pvt; 43rd VA Cav (Mosby's), Co D; res: Balt; ref: 1, 2, 8, 19, 21, 70, 107, 501, 511, 685, 757, 1519, 1579

GILL, H. C.; Lt; Zarvona's MD Zouaves

GILL, John; sgt; Signal Corps; res: Annapolis, AA Cty; ref: 1, 2, 8, 13, 14, 19, 21, 23, 44, 53, 56, 57, 70, 107, 503, 511, 650, 700, 715, 735, 781, 862, 869, 873,

881, 904, 994, 1519, 1539, 1628, 1635
GILL, Somerville Pinkney; cpl; 2nd MD Inf, Co A; res: Annapolis, AA Cty; ref: 1, 2, 19, 21, 107, 259, 511, 650, 1520, 1539
GILL, William H.; pvt; 1st MD Cav, Co C; res: Balt; ref: 1, 2, 19, 21, 486, 511, 690, 700
GILLAND, Charles; pvt; Barry's Co, MD Vols; res: Balt; ref: 1, 19, 628
GILLAND, S. R.; pvt; 32s. NC Inf, Co K; ref: 1, 735
GILLAND, Stephen; pvt; 2nd MD Cav, Co F; ref: 1, 2, 19, 21
GILMOR, Arthur; pvt; 2nd MD Cav, Co F; res: Balt; ref: 1, 2, 21, 233, 1565, 1583
GILMOR, C. Graham; pvt; 21st VA Inf, Co B; res: Balt; MLCSH; ref: 1, 2, 11, 19, 21, 312, 511, 681, 685, 693, 700, 735, 786, 1609
GILMOR, Harry W.; Lt Col; 2nd MD Cav; res: Towson, Bt Cty; ref: 1, 2, 3, 7, 11, 15, 17, 18, 19, 21, 23, 35, 36, 39, 40, 42, 44, 46, 47, 50, 62, 63, 64, 66, 67, 68, 70, 86, 88, 93, 94, 103, 105, 107, 113, 118, 125, 126, 127, 129, 145, 168, 171, 194, 222, 233, 240, 255, 256, 323, 331, 340, 349, 389, 408, 421, 443, 444, 455, 485, 489, 493, 496, 499, 501, 502, 507, 511, 517, 518, 559, 601, 602, 614, 631, 638, 680, 684, 685, 686, 693, 700, 740, 748, 753, 778, 781, 789, 791, 794, 824, 825, 829, 857, 860, 862, 873, 931, 1040, 1042, 1056, 1072, 1156, 1177, 1258, 1279, 1378, 1426, 1485, 1486, 1488, 1523, 1540, 1560, 1562, 1563, 1565, 1566, 1569, 1571, 1577, 1578, 1579, 1583, 1584, 1588, 1590, 1593, 1600, 1609, 1614, 1615, 1620, 1631, 1634, 1636, 1654, 1663, 1674, 1675
GILMOR, Hoffman; pvt; 2nd MD Cav, Co F; res: Balt; ref: 1, 2, 11, 19, 21, 88, 93, 145, 511, 614, 700, 1523, 1540, 1578, 1609
GILMOR, Howard; pvt; 7th VA Cav, Co G; res: Bt Cty; ref: 3
GILMOR, Meredith; Lt; 2nd MD Cav, Co A; res: Bt Cty; ref: 1, 2, 11, 19, 21, 23, 511, 700, 724, 1583
GILMOR, Richard Tilghman; Capt; 2nd MD Cav, Co C; res: Towson, Bt Cty; MLCSH; ref: 1, 2, 11, 19, 21, 23, 44, 64, 93, 456, 503, 511, 559, 650, 627, 631, 693, 700, 786, 1371, 1520, 1540, 1609
GILMOR, William of William; pvt; 2nd MD Cav, Co C; res: Balt; ref: 1, 2, 11, 19, 21, 56, 349, 511, 693, 724, 791, 1540, 1583, 1609
GILPIN, John; cpl; 1st MD Lt Arty; res: Elkton, Cec Cty; ref: 1, 2, 19, 21, 470, 700
GILROY, Thomas; pvt; 1st MD Cav, Co E; res: Cha Cty; ref: 1, 2, 19, 21, 730
GINDER, Fredrick; res: Balt; ref: 1540
GINNES, C. D.; pvt; Lee's MD Cav; res: St. M. Cty; ref: 1, 1627
GIPSEN, Thomas; pvt; MD American Rifles; ref: 1
GIRVIN, John; pvt; 1st MD Inf, Co F; ref: 1, 2, 19, 21
GISE, Andrew; res: Balt; ref: 1540
GISSIL, Henry; res: McPherson Pack, AA Cty; ref: 1539
GIST, Washington J.; pvt; 1st MD Inf, Co H; ref: 1, 2, 19, 21, 650
GITTINGER, Charles W.; pvt; 2nd VA Inf, Co D; ref: 1, 735
GITTINGS, Charles W.; 2nd VA Inf; ref: 735
GITTINGS, Edward L.; sgt; 7th VA Cav, Co G; res: Merryland Tract, Frd Cty; ref: 1, 3, 90
GITTINGS, Harry N.; pvt; 1st VA Cav, Co K; ref: 1, 2, 19, 21
GIVANS, G. W.; ref: 92
GIVINS, Charles; pvt; Davis's MD Cav, Co C; ref: 1
GIVINS, Marian; pvt; Davis's MD Cav, Co C; ref: 1
GLADDEN, George B.; smn, Navy; Allis Dixie; res: Frd Cty; ref: 1, 88

GLANDEL, John; drummer; Barry's Co, MD Vols; ref: 1, 19
GLASCOCK, Aquilla; pvt; 43rd VA Cav (Mosby's), Co A; ref: 1, 8, 20
GLASS, Alexander; cpl; 7th SC Reserves, Co B; ref: 1, 693
GLASS, Peter; pvt; 1st SC Inf, Co G; res: Balt; ref: 1, 19, 735
GLASS, Richard C.; pvt; 1st MD Lt Arty; ref: 1, 2, 19, 21, 34, 93
GLASSCOCK, John Edwin; sgt; 1st MD Lt Arty; ref: 1, 2, 19, 21, 34, 63, 64, 68, 104, 782, 791, 1523
GLASSCOCK, William Adams; Lt; 22nd VA Cav, Co G; ref: 1, 57, 513
GLASSETT, G. H.; pvt; 2nd MD Inf, Co F; ref: 1
GLAUDEL, John B.; pvt; 1st MD Inf, Co C; ref: 1, 2, 19, 21
GLEAVES, Samuel G. (M.D.); Asst Surg; 45th VA Inf; res: Chestertown, Kt Cty; ref: 1584
GLENN, Clement; pvt; 1st MD Cav, Co C; ref: 1, 2, 19, 21
GLENN, Elias; pvt; 1st MD Cav, Co C; ref: 1, 2, 19, 21, 1583
GLENN, Francis; pvt; 1st MD Cav, Co C; res: Har Cty; ref: 1, 2, 19, 21, 1634
GLENN, James S.; pvt; 1st MD Cav, Co E; res: Balt Cty; ref: 1, 2, 19, 21, 730, 1575
GLENN, James W.; Capt; 12th Cav, Co A; res: All Cty; ref: 1, 148, 791
GLENN, Joseph P.; pvt; Barry's Co, MD vols; ref: 1, 19
GLENN, N. C.; pvt; Stuart's Horse Arty, Breathed's Battery; ref: 1
GLENN, Samuel T.; pvt; 2nd MD Inf, Co A; res: Tal Cty; ref: 1, 2, 19, 21, 92, 93, 645
GLENN, Samuel Thomas; pvt; 39th Inf, Co B; res: QA Cty; MLCSH; ref: 1, 21, 627, 700, 786, 1612
GLENN, Walter; pvt; Davis's MD Cav, Co A; ref: 735
GLENN, William Y.; orderly; 2nd MD Lt Arty; res: Balt; ref: 1, 2, 19, 21, 23, 1540, 1598
GLANNAN, John; pvt; 1st MD Inf, Co B; ref: 1, 2, 19, 21
GLISAN, Rodney (M.D.); Physician; Medical Corps; ref: 1, 18
GLOCKER, Albert Campbell; pvt; 2nd MD Cav, Co A; res: Balt; ref: 1, 18, 19, 21, 23, 57, 513, 700
GLOCKER, Theodore W. (M.D.); Acting Surg; Staunton General Hospital; res: Balt; ref: 1, 2, 18, 19, 21, 1534, 1536
GLONDELL, John; pvt; 1st VA Cav, Co K; ref: 2, 19, 21
GLOSSNER, Hanus; pvt; 1st MD Inf, Co F; ref: 1, 2, 21
GLOVER, Thomas J.; pvt; 2nd MD Cav, Co B; ref: 1
GLOVER, W. H.; pvt; 3rd MD Lt Arty; ref: 1, 2, 19, 21, 160, 726
GLYNN, Patrick; pvt; 2nd MD Cav, Co D; ref: 1
GODDARD, George W.; pvt; Zarvona's MD Zouaves; res: St. Clements Bay, St. M. Cty; ref: 1, 735, 1509, 1555
GODFREY, A.; pvt; 1st SC Inf, Co G; ref: 1
GOING, Rozier; pvt; 2nd MD Cav, Co E; res: AA Cty; ref: 1, 1628
GOLDEN, H. F.; pvt; 3rd MD Lt Arty; ref: 2, 19, 21, 160, 726
GOLDEN, John; pvt; 1st MD Inf, Co F; ref: 1, 2, 19, 21
GOLDEN, W.; pvt; 3rd MD Lt Arty; ref: 2, 19, 21, 160, 726
GOLDER, Hamilton; pvt; 1st MD Inf, Co C; ref: 1, 2, 19, 21
GOLDING, Patrick; pvt; 19th VA Heavy Arty, Co C; ref: 1, 1580
GOLDSBERRY, Harrison; pvt; 1st MD CAv, Co E; ref: 1, 730
GOLDSBOROUGH, ---; pvt; 4th MD Lt Arty; ref: 2, 19, 511
GOLDSBOROUGH, Charles; pvt; 1st MD Lt Arty; ref: 1, 2, 19, 21, 470, 511
GOLDSBOROUGH, Charles; pvt; 43rd VA Cav (Mosby's), Co D; res: Balt; ref: 8, 23, 44, 56, 70, 511, 690, 1564
GOLDSBOROUGH, Edmund K. (M.D.); Asst Surg, Navy; C.S.S. Fredericksburg; res: Easton, Tal Cty; ref: 1, 18, 19, 23, 58, 59,

97, 511, 645, 677, 770, 1557, 1564, 1612

GOLDSBOROUGH, Eugene Yarbig; pvt; 2nd MD Cav, Co C; res: Carr Cty; ref: 1, 19

GOLDSBOROUGH, Harrison S.; pvt; Zarvona's Md Zouaves; res: Great Mills, St. M. Cty; ref: 1, 735, 1509, 1555

GOLDSBOROUGH, James; pvt; Zarvona's MD Zouaves; res: Great Mills, St. M. Cty; ref: 1, 735, 1509, 1555

GOLDSBOROUGH, McDowell Serpell; ref: 1589, 1590

GOLDSBOROUGH, N. Lee; pvt; 1st MD Inf, Co D; res: Frederick, Frd Cty; ref: 1, 2, 19, 21, 90, 493, 511, 700, 1523

GOLDSBOROUGH, Robert H.; Capt; Chamber's Independent MD Lt Arty, Co C; ref: 1, 19, 44, 511, 645, 685, 770, 1152, 1510, 1523, 1579

GOLDSBOROUGH, Thomas; Cumberland, All Cty; ref: 19, 65, 95, 148, 511

GOLDSBOROUGH, William Worthington; Maj; 2nd MD Inf; res: Balt; ref: 1, 2, 11, 19, 21, 23, 34, 35, 44, 50, 62, 63, 64, 68, 92, 93, 94, 105, 117, 126, 129, 222, 240, 431, 443, 444, 445, 456, 469, 476, 489, 493, 503, 511, 517, 559, 595, 601, 631, 638, 674, 700, 784, 789, 791, 825, 872, 901, 938, 1511, 1520, 1523, 1577, 1578, 1600, 1607, 1608, 1634, 1635

GOLDSCHNID, Solomon; res: Balt; ref: 1540

GOLDSMITH, George W.; pvt; Davis's Md Cav, Co A; res: Balt; ref: 1, 19, 735

GOLDSMITH, John; Master, Navy; res: St. M. Cty; ref: 1670

GOLDSMITH, John W.; pvt; 1st MD Inf, Co H; res: Miles Town, St. M. Cty; ref: 1, 2, 19, 21, 650, 1509, 1555

GOLDSMITH, William; sgt; 54th NC Inf, Co E; res: Balt Cty; MLCSH; ref: 21, 93, 700, 735, 786

GONDRIAN, Anthony; pvt; 3rd MD Lt Arty; ref: 1, 2, 19, 21, 160, 726

GONDRIAN, Stephen; pvt; 3rd MD Lt Arty; ref: 1, 2, 19, 21, 160, 726

GOODHAND, G. W.; pvt; 4th MD Lt Arty; res: Balt; ref: 1, 2, 19, 21

GOODLOE, William; pvt; 1st MD Cav, Co E; ref: 1, 2, 19, 21, 730

GOODMAN, B. W.; sgt; Stuart's Horse Arty, Breathed's Battery; ref: 1

GOODMAN, Hobson Charles; pvt; Stuart's Horse Arty, Shoemaker's Battery; res: Balt; MLCSH; ref: 1, 627, 700, 786

GOODMAN, Isaac; res: Balt; ref: 1540

GOODMAN, John W.; Lt; 2nd MD Lt Arty; res: Balt; ref: 1, 2, 19, 21, 23, 50, 64, 68, 740, 1540

GOODMAN, Julius B.; pvt; 1st MD Inf, Co E; ref: 1, 2, 19, 21

GOODMAN, Otho; pvt; 1st MD Cav, Co C; ref: 1, 2, 19, 21

GOODMAN, Zack; pvt; Davis's MD Cav, Co A; ref: 1, 735

GOODRICH, P. Washington; Gen J. H. Winder's Detectives; ref: 1533, 1563

GOODWIN, Claudius L., Sr; Maj; Paymaster, Gen W. Hempton's staff; ref: 1, 57

GOODWIN, Charles R.; pvt; Wheaton's GA Lt Arty; ref: 1, 685, 700

GOODWIN, Frank Greenwood; pvt; 8th GA Inf, Co B; ref: 1, 2

GOODWIN, J.; pvt; 2nd MD Cav, Co A; ref: 1, 19, 1609

GOODWIN, John; pvt; 2nd MD Inf, Co A; res: Balt; ref: 1, 2, 19, 21, 650

GOODWIN, Ridgely; Lt; Aid de Camp, Gen E. Alexander's staff; res: Balt; ref: 1, 2, 19, 21, 685

GOOLRICK, Peter (M.D.); Surg; Stark's Lt Arty Bn; res: Balt; ref: 1, 18, 21, 700, 1534

GORDON, Douglas Hamilton; Ambulance Corps; res: Bt Cty; ref: 70

GORDON, Henry; pvt; 3rd MD Lt Arty; res: Annapolis, AA Cty; ref: 1, 2, 19, 21, 160, 461, 726, 1267, 1539

GORDON, James; pvt; 2nd MD Inf, Co D; res: Balt; ref: 1, 23, 470
GORDON, John Henry; pvt; 35th VA Cav, Co B; res: AA Cty; MLCSH; ref: 1, 2, 3, 19, 21, 627, 786
GORDON, William A., Jr; Lt; 1st Engineers, Co G; res: Georgetown; ref: 1, 1492
GORDON, William J.; pvt; 2nd MD Lt Arty; ref: 1, 2, 19, 21
GORE, John W.; pvt; 4th MD Lt Arty; res: Tal Cty; ref: 1, 2, 21, 55
GOREY, John K.; pvt; Davis's MD Cav, Co C; res: Golden Hill, Dor Cty; ref: 1, 1547
GORINGS, Rozier; pvt; 2nd MD Cav, Co E; ref: 1
GORMAN, D.; pvt; 2nd MD Cav, Co A; ref: 1, 11, 1609
GORMAN, Patrick; pvt; 3rd MD Lt Arty; ref: 1, 2, 19, 21, 160, 726
GORMAN, William H.; pvt; 1st MD Lt Arty; res: Balt; ref: 1, 2, 19, 21, 34, 63, 64, 68, 700, 782, 791, 823, 1273
GORSUCH, Nathan; qm sgt; 2nd MD Cav; res: Bt Cty; ref: 1, 2, 11, 19, 21, 740, 791, 1609
GORSUCH, Theodore; pvt; 2nd MD Cav, Co B; res: Frd Cty; ref: 1, 1540
GOSDEN, Walter W.; pvt; 1st MD Inf, Co G; res: Balt; ref: 1, 2, 19, 21, 685
GOSSAGE, T.; pvt; 2nd MD Inf, Co A; ref: 1, 19, 650
GOSSAM, James H.; pvt; 19th VA Heavy Arty, Co C; ref: 1, 735, 1580
GOSSON, James H.; pvt; 17th VA Inf, Co D; res: Laurel, PG Cty; ref: 1, 2, 21, 142, 687, 735, 1553
GOTTIEIB, Friy; ref: 735
GOUGH, Benjamin (M.D.); pvt; 4th VA Cav, Co I; res: Leonardtown, St. M. Cty; MLCSH; ref: 1, 18, 19, 21, 93, 627, 700, 735, 786, 922, 1509
GOUGH, Charles E.; pvt; 1st MD Cav, Co C; res: Leonardtown, St. M. Cty; ref: 1, 2, 19, 21, 69, 316, 785, 1509
GOUGH, James; pvt; 3rd MD Lt Arty; ref: 1, 2, 19, 21, 160, 726
GOUGH, James H.; pvt; 1st MD Lt Arty; res: Cha Cty; ref: 1, 2, 19, 21, 86, 470
GOULD, Charles W.; pvt; 18th GA Inf, Co B; res: Balt; ref: 1, 1540
GOULDIN, Simon; pvt; 47th VA Inf, Co H; ref: 1
GOVER, Edwin P.; sgt; 2nd MD Inf, Co D; res: Friendship, AA Cty; MLCSH; ref: 1, 2, 19, 21, 23, 70, 786, 1539
GOVER, William E.; pvt; 7th VA Cav, Co G; ref: 3, 76
GOWDEY, James; pvt; 21st VA Inf, Co B; ref: 1, 2, 19, 312, 735
GOWL, George H.; pvt; 7th VA Cav, Co G; ref: 1
GOYN, John Lomkies; 26th VA Inf, Co D; res: Carr Cty; ref: 70
GRABILL, Abraham W., Jr; pvt; 1st MD Cav, Co D; res: Johnsville, Frd Cty; ref: 1, 2, 19, 21, 90, 1548, 1601
GRACE, William; pvt; 2nd MD Inf, Co C; res: Easton, Tal Cty; MLCSH; ref: 1, 2, 19, 21, 23, 470, 645, 700, 786, 1523
GRADY, Edward K.; pvt; 6th VA Cav, Co D; res: Balt; ref: 1, 21, 133, 700
GRADY, Frank T.; pvt; 17th VA Inf, Co A; res: Balt; ref: 1, 70, 133
GRADY, James O.; pvt; 1st VA Inf, Co E; ref: 1, 735
GRAFFIN, C. C.; 17th VA Inf, Co A; res: Balt; ref: 70, 133
GRAHAM, George H.; pvt; 4th MD Lt Arty; ref: 1, 2, 19, 64, 92
GRAHAM, Israel J.; pvt; 7th VA Cav, Co G; res: Burkittsville, Frd Cty; MLCSH; ref: 1, 2, 3, 19, 90, 92, 93, 627, 700, 786, 1278
GRAHAM, James M.; pvt; 35th VA Cav, Co C; res: McPherson Pack, AA Cty; ref:1, 3, 1539
GRAHAM, Jesse W.; pvt; 1st MD Cav, Co C; ref: 1, 2, 19, 21
GRAHAM, John T.; pvt; 2nd MD Cav, Co D; ref: 1, 1574
GRAHAM, Thomas; pvt; 17th VA CAv, Co A; ref: 1, 684

GRAHAM, Thomas; pvt; 2nd MD Inf, Co H; ref: 1, 2, 19, 21

GRAHAM, W.; pvt; 1st SC Inf, Co G; ref: 1

GRAHAM, Wellington; pvt; 2nd MD Lt Arty; ref: 1

GRAHAM, William Curran; pvt; 35th VA Cav, Co B; res: Bt Cty; ref: 1, 3, 1677

GRAHAM, William Francis; pvt; 3rd VA Inf, Co H; res: Balt; ref: 1, 1540

GRAMER, William G.; pvt; 3rd MD Lt Arty; ref: 1

GRAMMER, Frederick L.; pvt; 2nd MD Inf, Co A; res: Annapolis, AA Cty; ref: 1, 2, 19, 21, 650, 1539

GRANDCHAMPS, Emile; pvt; 26th LA Inf, Co G; res: Balt; ref: 1, 69, 316

GRANGER, Charles; pvt; 19th VA Heavy Arty, Co C; res: Balt; ref: 1, 1540, 1580

GRANGER, Nathan; res: McPherson Pack, AA Cty; ref: 1539

GRANT, D. J.; pvt; 1st SC Inf, Co G; res: Balt; ref: 1, 1598

GRANT, John; pvt; 2nd MD Inf, Co E; res: 1, 2, 19, 21

GRANT, Richard R.; Lt; 5th NC Inf, Co D; res: Balt; MLCSH; ref: 1, 21, 700, 786

GRASON, John; Lt; 4th MD Lt Arty; res: Queenstown, QA Cty; ref: 2, 19, 21, 23, 64, 1511, 1523, 1554, 1612

GRATIS, Joseph; Pvt; Lucas' 15th SC Heavy Arty; res: Bt Cty; ref: 1, 1541

GRAVES, Henry Montfort; Lt; Engineers, Richmond Defenses; res: Balt; ref: 1, 2, 19, 21, 70, 697, 700, 735, 866, 906, 1379

GRAVES, Richard; pvt; Davis's MD Cav, Co C; ref: 1

GRAVES, William B.; sgt; Utterbach's Co, VA Lt Arty; res: Pikesville, Bt Cty; ref: 1, 2, 19, 21, 70, 700

GRAY, J. Elijah; pvt; Marines, Co C, Wilmington Navy Station; res: Johnson's Store, AA Cty; ref: 1, 1529, 1594

GRAY, Francis; pvt; 2nd MD Inf, Co C; ref: 1

GRAY, Henry S.; pvt; 1st MD Cav, Co C; ref: 1, 2, 19, 21

GRAY, J. A.; pvt; 3rd MD Lt Arty; ref: 1, 2, 19, 21, 160, 726

GRAY, Joseph; pvt; 2nd MD Inf, Co F; ref: 1, 2, 19, 21, 23

GRAY, William R.; pvt; 1st MD Inf, Co D; ref: 1, 2, 19, 21, 1611, 1677

GRAYSON, George Mason; 8th VA, Co F; res: Frd Cty; ref: 72, 90

GRAYSON, James B.; pvt; 1st MD Inf, Co H; res: Queenstown, QA Cty; ref: 1, 2, 19, 21, 650, 1554

GRAYSON, Spence Monroe; pvt; 2nd MD Inf, Co A; res: Balt; ref: 1, 2, 19, 21, 23, 44, 56, 650, 685, 700, 1579

GREANOR, William; Maj; res: Balt; ref: 240

GREEN, Alexander; pvt; Davis's MD Cav, Co A; ref: , 1, 2, 19, 21, 735, 1609

GREEN, Charles; P.; sgt; 35th VA Cav, Co B; ref: 1, 2, 3, 15, 19, 21, 1611, 1677

GREEN, Daniel Smith (M.D.); Surg; Navy; C.S.S. Patrick Henry; res: Balt; ref: 1, 18, 1534, 1564

GREEN, Hugh T.; pvt; 1st MD Cav, Co F; res: Balt; ref: 1, 2, 19, 21

GREEN, James W.; 4th MD Lt Arty; ref: 93, 700

GREEN, John; sgt; 35th VA Cav, Co B; ref: 1611

GREEN, John; pvt; 7th VA Cav, Co G; res: Cha Cty; ref: 3

GREEN, John F.; pvt; 21st VA Inf, Co B; res: Balt; ref: 1, 2, 312, 735, 1540

GREEN, John F.; pvt; 4th MD Lt Arty; MLCSH; res: Dor Cty; MLCSH; ref: 1, 2, 19, 21, 112, 786

GREEN, John T.; pvt; Davis's MD Cav, Co A; ref: 1, 2, 19, 21, 735

GREEN, Joseph; Stonewall Brigade; res: Wash Cty; ref: 1359

GREEN, Louis; pvt; 2nd MD Inf, Co D; res: Annapolis, AA Cty; ref: 1, 2, 19, 21, 700, 852, 873
GREEN, Matthew; pvt; 43rd VA Cav (Mosby's), Lt Arty Co; res: Balt; MLCSH; ref: 1, 2, 8, 19, 21, 92, 93, 627, 700, 786, 1540
GREEN, Thomas J.; Lt; 61st AL Inf, Co B; res: Balt; MLCSH; ref: 1, 2, 19, 21, 23, 68, 496, 700, 786, 791, 1523, 1540, 1560, 1665
GREEN, Vincent; pvt; 4th MD Lt Arty; res: Bt Cty; MLCSH; ref: 1, 2, 19, 21, 92, 93, 627, 700, 786
GREEN, Wharton Jackson; Lt Col; 2nd NC Inf; ref: 1, 21, 110, 134, 700, 791, 1600
GREEN, William (M.D); Chief Surg; 2nd Corps of Arty; res: Balt; ref: 1, 18, 23, 56, 70, 1534, 1536, 1599
GREEN, William; pvt; 1st MD Cav, Co F; ref: 1, 2, 19, 21
GREEN, William; pvt; 3rd MD Lt Arty; res: Princess Anne, Som Cty; ref: 1, 1556
GREEN, William; pvt; Davis's MD Cav, Co A; ref: 1, 735
GREEN, William B.; pvt; 1st MD Cav, Co E; res: Balt; ref: 1, 2, 19, 21, 730
GREEN, William Oliver; pvt; 2nd VA Inf, Co B; res: Cec Cty; MLCSH; ref: 1, 2, 19, 21, 92, 93, 627, 785, 786
GREEN, Z. W.; pvt; Stuart's Horse Arty, Breathed's Battery; ref: 1
GREENFALL, William; pvt; 2nd VA Cav, Co E; res: Galena, Kt Cty; ref: 1, 1584
GREENFIELD, William; yeoman, Navy; C.S. Chicamauga; res: Balt; ref: 1, 2, 19, 21, 93, 700, 783
GREENTREE, Howard; res: Frederick; ref: 89
GREENWELL, Joseph A.; pvt; Stuart's Horse Arty, Breathed's Battery; res: Great Mills, St. M. Cty; ref: 1, 2, 19, 21, 312, 559, 681, 700, 735, 1509, 1555, 1662
GREENWELL, Thomas W. Herb; pvt; Sturat's Horse Arty, Breathed's Bn; res: Great Mills, St. M. Cty; ref: 1, 2, 19, 21, 44, 259, 498, 650, 1509, 1555, 1627, 1662
GREENWOOD, James W.; Navy; Receiving ship Meekanaw; ref: 1
GREGORY, Caleb H.; sgt; 9th VA Inf, Co B; ref: 1, 1576
GREGORY, James A.; pvt; 2nd MD Inf, Co A; ref: 1, 21, 23, 470, 650
GREGORY, Oliver F.; pvt; Hampton Leg SC Inf, Co H; res: Balt; ref: 1, 21, 700
GRESENDOFFER, William, Jr; res: Balt; ref: 1540
GRESENDOFFER, William, Sr; res: Balt; ref: 1540
GRESHAM, Thomas Baxter; pvt; 2nd GA Inf, Co B; res: Balt; ref: 1, 21, 56, 70, 272, 700
GREW, Thomas; Lt; ref: 64
GREY, Hugh; pvt; 1st VA Cav, Co K; res: Balt; ref: 2, 19, 1540
GREY, S. W.; pvt; 1st MD Cav, Co E; ref: 1
GRIDLIN, Jacob H.; Lt; 30th VA Sharpshooters, Co A; ref: 92, 93
GRIFFIN, Becy N.; pvt; 3rd MD Lt Arty; ref: 1
GRIFFIN, George C.; pvt; 43rd VA Cav (Mosby's), Co G; res: Har Cty; ref: 1, 2, 8, 19, 21, 511
GRIFFIN, Joseph; Lt; 1st MD Inf, Co B; ref: 1, 2, 8, 19, 21, 23, 64, 124, 511
GRIFFIN, Michael C.; pvt; Stuart's Horse Arty, Breathed's Battery; ref: 1, 498
GRIFFIN, Richard C.; pvt; Davis's MD Cav, Co B; res: How Cty; ref: 1, 10, 19, 511
GRIFFIN, W. B.; pvt; 3rd MD Lt Arty; ref: 2, 21, 160, 511, 726
GRIFFIN, William Hunter; Capt; 2nd MD Lt Arty; res: Balt; ref: 1, 2, 19, 21, 23, 45, 55, 64, 68, 94, 105, 240, 443, 462, 492, 496, 511, 685, 791, 872, 1523, 1577, 1579, 1613
GRIFFITH, Columbus B.; pvt; Lee's MD Cav; res: Millersville, AA Cty; ref: 1, 1539

GRIFFITH, David; pvt; 1st MD Cav, Co A; res: Redland, Mont Cty; ref: 1, 2, 19, 21, 86, 631, 1574
GRIFFITH, Edward; pvt; 1st MD Inf, Co F; ref: 1, 2, 19, 21
GRIFFITH, Festus Farmer; Capt; 8th VA Inf, Co H; res: Mont Cty; ref: 1, 19, 560, 631, 735
GRIFFITH, Frank; Lt; 1st MD Cav, Co A; res: Mont Cty; ref: 1, 2, 19, 21, 23, 631, 1634
GRIFFITH, George; pvt; 1st VA Cav, Co K; ref: 2
GRIFFITH, Greenberry; pvt; 1st MD Inf, Co G; ref: 1, 2, 19, 21
GRIFFITH, John A.; pvt; 6th SC Inf, Co K; res: Georgetown; ref: 1, 7
GRIFFITH, John B.; pvt; 43rd VA Cav (Mosby's), Co F; res: Millesvile, AA Cty; ref: 8, 20, 1539
GRIFFITH, John James; pvt; 1st MD Cav, Co E; ref: 1, 2, 19, 21, 730
GRIFFITH, Johnathan W.; pvt; 49th NC Inf, Co F; res: Millersville, AA Cty; ref: 1, 1539
GRIFFITH, Marion M.; pvt; Lucas' 15th SC Heavy Arty; ref: 1, 19
GRIFFITH, Lyde; pvt; 1st MD Cav, Co A; ref: 1, 19
GRIFFITH, Richard; pvt; 1st VA Cav, Co K; res: Laurel, How Cty; ref: 1, 2, 19, 687, 1550
GRIFFITH, Thomas; res: res: Princesland, AA Cty; ref: 1539
GRIFFITH, Thomas; Capt; 1st MD CAv, Co A; res: Olney, Mont Cty; ref: 1, 2, 19, 21, 23, 64, 68, 86, 240, 445, 560, 631, 881, 1037, 1096, 1108, 1519, 1523, 1574, 1620, 1634
GRIFFITH, Thomas W.; pvt; 22nd VA Cav, Co F; res: How Cty; ref: 1, 748
GRIFFITH, William Henry; Maj; 11th GA Inf; res: Laurel, How Cty; ref: 1, 748, 1550
GRIM, I.; pvt; 1st MD Lt Arty; ref: 34
GRIMES, Cornelius D.; pvt; 1st MD Cav, Co D; res: Balt; ref: 1, 2, 19, 21, 1601
GRIMES, Harry; pvt; 1st VA Cav, Co H; res: Carr Cty; ref: 1, 2, 19, 21, 1601
GRIMES, John Henry (M.D.); pvt; 1st VA Cav, Co A; res: New Windsor, Carr Cty; ref: 1, 18, 19, 21, 23, 57, 700, 720, 892, 916, 1533, 1536, 1540, 1544
GRIMES, Richard; pvt; Rhett's 1st SC Heavy Arty; ref: 1, 735
GRIMES, Robert; pvt; 4th MD Lt Arty; ref: 1, 2, 19, 21, 470
GRIMSBY, William; Navy; Charleston, Naval Station; ref: 1
GRISHAM, Thomas Baxter; 2nd GA, Co B; res: Balt; ref: 70
GRISWOLD, Elias; Maj; P.M. of Richmond; res: Cambridge, Dor Cty; ref: 1, 2, 19, 21, 30, 86, 112, 685, 735, 791, 1489, 1578, 1579, 1624
GROAES, Thomas T.; pvt; 700
GROGAN, Charles E.; Lt; 43rd VA Cav (Mosby's), Co D; res: Balt; ref: 1, 2, 8, 19, 21, 35, 38, 44, 64, 123, 393, 503, 511, 601, 650, 700, 710, 791, 875, 1058, 1571, 1578, 1579, 1613, 1620, 1654
GROGAN, George M.; sgt; Morris's Co, VA Lt Arty; res: Balt; ref: 1, 263, 511
GROGAN, James J.; pvt; 21st VA Inf, Co B; res: Balt; ref: 1, 2, 19, 21, 44, 312, 511, 690, 700, 1520
GROGAN, Kennedy O.; sgt; 35th VA Cav, Co F; res: Balt; ref: 1, 2, 15, 19, 21, 38, 44, 501, 511, 536, 791, 1037, 1611, 1677
GROGAN, Robert Reddle; pvt; 1st MD Cav, Co C; ref: 1, 2, 19, 21, 511, 700, 791
GROOM, William; Lt; ref: 1690
GROSHON, George; res: Frederick, Frd Cty; ref: 89
GROSHON, John F.; sgt; 1st MD Inf, Co A; res: Frd Cty; ref: 1, 2, 19, 21, 23, 89, 90
GROSS, John; Lt; 15th LA Inf, Co C; res: Balt; MLCSH; ref: 1, 21, 627, 700, 735, 786
GROVE, Benjamin F.; sgt; 43rd VA Cav (Mosby's), Co C; ref: 1, 8, 20

GROVE, Francis Thomas; pvt; 1st VA Cav, Co F; res: Sharpsburg, Wash Cty; MLCSH; ref: 1, 19, 627, 786, 1558, 1579
GROVE, John W.; pvt; 35th VA Cav, Co E; res: Frd Cty; ref: 1, 19, 89, 1611
GROVE, Lewis; pvt; 1st MD Inf, Co A; res: Frd Cty; ref: 1, 2, 19, 21, 89, 90
GROVE, Philip D. (M.D.) Asst Surg; 2nd MD Cav; ref: 1, 18
GROVE, Thomas H.; pvt; 1st MD Cav, Co C; ref: 1, 2, 19, 21, 827
GROVE, William H.; pvt; Stuart's Horse Arty, Breathed's Battery; res: Sharpsburg, Wash Cty; ref: 1, 1558
GROVER, Edwin Plummer; pvt; MD American Rifles; res: Friendship, AA Cty; ref: 1, 1135
GROVER, John H.; pvt; 2nd MD Cav, Co B; ref: 1,, 19
GROVES, Thomas Frederick; pvt; 2nd MD Inf, Co B; res: Nanjemoy, Cha Cty; ref: 1, 2, 19, 21, 1546
GRUBB, Amos B.; pvt; MD Guerrilla Zouaves; ref: 1
GRUBB, H. C.; pvt; 2nd MD Lt Arty; ref: 1, 2, 19, 21
GRUBBS, W. A.; pvt; Stuart's Horse Arty, Breathed's Battery; ref: 1, 800
GUAKLE, Albert; pvt; 1st MD Cav, Co K; ref: 1, 19
GUFFISS, John J.; pvt; 13th VA Inf, Co G; ref: 1, 735
GUGGENHEIMER, Isaac; Evans' Richmond Defense, Co A; res: Balt; ref: 70
GUGGENHEIMER, Maurice; ordnance sgt; 2nd VA Cav, Co C; res: Balt; ref: 1, 70
GUGGENHEIMER, Simon; pvt; 3rd MD Lt Arty; ref: 1, 2, 19, 21, 100, 726
GUILLETTE, Gilbert G.; Lt; 2nd MD Inf, Co G; res: Som Cty; ref: 1, 2, 19, 21, 23, 68
GUINN, Patrick; pvt; 2nd MD Cav, Co B; ref: 1, 19
GUIS, Andrew J.; pvt; 1st MD Inf, Co C; ref: 1, 2, 19, 21
GUNBY, Francis M.; pvt; 10th VA Inf, Co A; res: Salisbury, Wic Cty; ref: 1, 1523, 1626, 1666
GUNBY, J.; pvt; Davis's MD Cav, Co B; ref: 1
GUNBY, John W.; pvt; Hampton Leg Lt Arty, Co B; res: Salisbury, Wic Cty; ref: 1, 2, 19, 21, 1523, 1626, 1666
GUNDERMAN, Louis, drummer; Rhett's 1st SC Heavy Arty; res: Balt; MLCSH; ref: 1, 21, 700, 735, 786
GUNDLASH, Charles; sgt; 1st SC Inf, Co G; res: Balt; ref: 1, 1598
GUNDLASH, Conrad; pvt; 1st SC Inf, Co G; ref: 1
GUNNING, John; res: Annapolis, AA Cty; ref: 1539
GUNTAN, G.A.; pvt; 1st SC Inf, Co G; ref: 1
GUTHRIE, John G. T.; pvt; 9th VA Inf, Co B; ref: 1, 1576
GUTHRIE, John Julius, Jr; Acting Mast. M., Navy; C.S. Gen Polk; res: Balt; ref; 1, 21, 97, 700, 783, 1564
GUY, George Henry; pvt; 41st VA Cav, Co F; res: How Cty; ref: 1, 71
GUY, George W.; pvt; 2nd MD Inf, Co F; res: St. M. Cty; ref: 1, 2, 19, 21, 23, 470, 1523, 1662
GUYTHER, Jack W.; pvt; 2nd MD Lt Arty; res: St. M. Cty; ref: 1, 1509
GUYTHER, W. H. W.; sgt; 1st MD Cav, Co B; res: Great Mills, St. M. Cty; ref: 1, 2, 19, 21, 23, 650, 785, 1509, 1555
GUYTHER, William H.; pvt; 21st VA Inf, Co B; res: great Mills, St. M. Cty; ref: 1, 2, 19, 312, 1555
GWATHMEY, Robert W.; pvt; 3rd VA Inf, Co F; ref: 1, 21, 700
GWYN, John Tomkins; Lt; 26th VA Inf, Co B; res: Middle River, Bt Cty; ref: 1, 21, 70, 700
GWYNN, Andrew Jackson; Capt; 2nd MD Inf, Co F; res: Pleasant Springs, PG Cty; ref: 1, 2, 12, 19, 21, 23, 64, 68, 70, 83, 791, 1523

GWYNN, Charles L. (M.D.) Acting Asst Surg; 26th VA Inf; ref: 1, 18, 1534, 1690
GWYNN, George A.; pvt; MD Line; res: Piscataway, PG Cty; ref: 3216
GWYNN, George E.; pvt; 17th VA Inf, Co A; ref: 1, 2, 133, 142
GWYNN, Henry; Capt; 9th VA Inf, Co F; ref: 1, 19, 57, 462, 513
GWYNN, James E.; pvt; 47th VA Cav, Co C; res: PG Cty; ref: 1, 69, 316
GWYNN, James J.; pvt; 1st MD Inf, Co A; ref: 2, 19, 21
GWYNN, John M.S.; 1st MD Cav, Co E; ref: 92
GWYNN, Thomas N.; Lt; 29th VA Inf, Co E; res: Piscataway, PG Cty; ref: 1, 69, 316
GWYNN, William H.; pvt; 2nd MD Inf, Co E; res: Piscataway, PG Cty; ref: 2, 69, 316
GWYNN, Wizzie; pvt; 4th MD Lt Arty; ref: 2, 19

HAAS, Isaac C.; pvt; 10th VA Inf, Co F; res: Balt; ref: 1, 2, 19, 21, 700, 1199, 1523
HAASE, Thomas H. B.; pvt 21st VA Inf, Co B; res: Westminister, Carr Cty; ref: 1, 2, 19, 312, 735, 1523
HACK, A. C.; pvt; McNeill's Rangers; ref: 1, 504
HACK, H. R.; pvt; 2nd MD Cav, Co A; ref: 1, 19, 1523, 1609
HACK, Henry Clay; sgt; 16th VA Inf, Co H; res: Balt; ref: 1, 21, 700
HACK, John W.; pvt; 9th VA Inf, Co F; ref: 1, 93
HACKET, John; pvt; 2nd MD Cav, Co D; res: Balt; ref: 1, 19, 1523, 1609
HACKETT, F. C.; pvt; Dor Cty; ref: 1523
HACKETT, Luke T.; pvt; Commissary Dept; res: Dor Cty; ref: 1, 19, 112, 1523
HACKMON, B. F.; pvt; 1st VA Inf, Co D; ref: 1, 677
HACKNEY, Benjamin S.; pvt; 34th VA Inf, Co A; res: Balt; MLCHS; ref: 1, 21, 53, 93, 700, 786
HADIN, J. F.; pvt; 12th MS Cav, Co F; res: Balt; ref; 1, 1540
HADLEY, John; Cumberland, All Cty; ref: 19, 65, 95, 148, 1523
HAFFEY, John; smn, Navy; C.S.S. Palmetto State; res: Balt; ref : 1, 2, 19, 21, 1523
HAFFEY, William; cpl; 1st MD Inf, Co B; ref: 1, 2, 19, 21, 23, 1523
HAGAN, Frank T.; pvt; 1st VA Cav, Co A; ref: 1, 735
HAGAN, Henry; pvt; cpl; 1st VA Cav, Co F; ref: 1, 2, 735
HAGAN, John; pvt; 1st MD Inf, Co F; res Wash Cty; ref: 1, 2, 19, 21, 92, 1523
HAGAN, Michael; Gen J. E. B. Stuart's staff; res: Braddock Heights, Frd Cty; ref: 45, 46, 90, 113
HAGAN, R.; pvt; 2nd MD Cav, Co F; ref: 1, 2, 19, 21, 1523
HAGAN, Thomas; Lt; LA Crescent Heavy Arty; ref: 1, 1523
HAGER, John H.; pvt; 1st MD Cav, Co; res: Wash Cty; ref: 1, 2, 19, 21, 700, 827, 1523
HAGLEY, Alphonsus; pvt; Zarvona's MD Zouaves; res: Balt; ref: 1, 2, 19, 21, 1523
HAHN, Reuben H.; sgt; 2nd MD Cav, Co F; res: Frd Cty; ref: 1, 2, 19, 21, 89, 1523, 1609
HAIGHLEY, Frank; pvt; Zarvona's MD Zouaves; ref: 735
HAIL, Francis; pvt; 3rd MD Lt Arty; ref: 1, 2, 19, 21, 160, 726, 1523
HAILEY, C. Parker; ref: 735
HAILY, James; res: Oakland, Ga Cty; ref: 735
HAINES, George; ref: 55
HAINES, John J.; Lt; 2nd VA Inf, Co E; res: Balt; ref: 1, 21, 56, 57, 700
HALBIG, John Stephen pvt; 47th VA Inf, Co H; res: Balt; MLCSH; ref: 19, 21, 93, 627, 700, 786, 1523
HALBROOK, William G.; Lt; Senior TN Inf, Co I; res: Balt; ref: 1, 461, 1540
HALEY, John; pvt; Zarvona's MD Zouaves; ref: 1, 735

HALL, Alfred; res: St. M. Cty; ref: 1670
HALL, Edward Howard; pvt; 1st MD Cav, Co A; res: Har Cty; ref: 1, 2, 19, 21, 70, 601, 685, 1523, 1579
HALL, Francis M.; Lt; Engineers Corps; res: PG Cty; ref: 1, 86
HALL, Frank; pvt; 19th VA Heavy Arty, Co C; ref: 1, 1580
HALL, Ira; pvt; 47th VA Inf, Co H; ref: 1
HALL, James; pvt; 12th VA Inf, Co C; ref: 1, 70
HALL, James R.; sgt; 40th VA Inf, Co A; res: Balt; ref: 1, 21, 700
HALL, John Thomas; pvt; 2nd MD Inf, Co F; res: Aquaser, PG Cty; ref: 1, 21, 141, 1523, 1553
HALL, Joseph H.; pvt; 40th VA Inf, Co F; res: Balt; ref: 1, 21, 700, 862
HALL, Martin Y.; sgt; 31st VA Inf, Co A; res: Balt; MLCSH; ref: 1, 21, 93, 700, 786
HALL, Richard B.; pvt; 2nd MD Inf, Co F; res: Aquaser, PG Cty; ref: 1, 1553
HALL, Theodore F.; pvt; 2nd MD Cav, Co C; ref: 1
HALL, Thomas John; cpl; MD Guerrilla Zouaves; ref: 1, 19, 1523
HALL, Thomas W.; sm, Navy; Shrevesport Naval Station; Millersville, AA Cty; ref: 1, 1539
HALL, Thomas William, Jr; Maj; Asst Inspector General, Dept of Alabama, Mississippi & East Louisiana; res: Balt; ref: 1, 2, 19, 21, 23, 50, 53, 56, 57, 63, 68, 70, 88, 110, 256, 494, 558, 559, 611, 685, 700, 791, 826, 1523, 1539, 1560, 1578, 1620, 1654
HALL, W. Carvel; Maj; Asst A.G., Valley District; res: Balt; ref: 1, 2, 19, 21, 34, 38, 44, 240, 681, 690, 700, 753, 791, 1523
HALL, Wilburn Briggs; Lt, Navy; C.S.S. Huntress; res: Balt; ref: 1, 21, 97, 700, 783, 1564
HALL, William D.; pvt; Edelin's MD Bn; res: Aquaser, PG Cty; ref: 1, 42, 1553
HALL, William H.; Asst Engr, Navy; C.S.S. Virginia; ref: 1, 19, 58, 97, 1523, 1564
HALL, William S.; pvt; 55th VA Inf, Co E; res: Locust Grove, Kt Cty; ref: 1, 1584
HALLAY, James; pvt; 2nd MD Inf, Co A; ref: 1
HALLER, Charles P.C.; cpl; 4th LA Inf, Co B; res: Balt; ref: 1, 1540
HALLER, John E. of Jacob; pvt; 2nd MD Inf, Co C; res: Frd Cty; ref: 1, 2, 19, 21, 89, 90, 1523
HALLER, Uriah H.; pvt; Stuart's Horse Arty, Breathed's Battery; ref: 1, 498
HALLMAN, Martin; pvt; 13th SC Inf, Co K; res: Balt; ref: 1, 21, 93
HALPIN, Thomas P.; pvt; 2nd MD Cav, Co F; res: Balt; ref: 1, 2, 19, 21, 1523, 1540, 1609
HALSEY, William; pvt; 2nd MD Cav, Co D; ref: 1
HALSTEAD, Charles; pvt; 1st MD Lt Arty; ref: 1, 2, 19, 21, 1523
HALTON, R. H. S.; 1st MD Lt Arty; ref: 93
HALTZMAN, Andrew J.; pvt; 13th Inf Co G; ref: 1
HAM, H. U.; Engr, Navy; C.S. Gen Clinch; res: Balt; MLCSH; ref: 700, 786
HAM, James; pvt; 3rd MD Lt Arty; ref: 1, 2, 21, 160, 726, 1523
HAMBLETON, James P. (M.D.); sgt; 35th GA Inf; res: Easton, Tal Cty; ref: ref: 1, 2, 19, 21, 511, 645, 677, 785, 1523, 1557
HAMBLETON, Thomas Edward; pvt; 1st MD Cav, Co E; ref: 1, 2, 19, 21, 511, 730, 994, 1523
HAMBLETON, Varland Edward; pvt; 19th VA Inf, Co G; res: Bt Cty; ref: 1, 70, 511, 1580
HAMBLETON, William H.; pvt; 9th VA Inf, Co K; res: Tal Cty; ref: 1, 19, 645, 1523

HAMES, Zealous; pvt; 15th SC Inf, Co H; ref: 1, 92
HAMILL, Charles Webb; res: Balt; ref: 631
HAMILL, Henry Jackson; pvt; 1st NC Inf, Co D; res: Balt; MLCSH; ref: 1, 93, 700, 735, 786
HAMILL, R. S.; 1st VA Inf, Co H; ref: 735
HAMILTON, Alexander C.; pvt; 43rd VA Cav (Mosby's), Co B; res: Cha Cty; ref: 1, 69, 258, 316
HAMILTON, Beale D.; pvt; 2nd MD Inf, Co F; res: West River, AA Cty; ref: 1, 2, 19, 21, 1523, 1539
HAMILTON, Edward R.; pvt; 1st MD Inf, Co A; 1, 2, 19, 21
HAMILTON, Jacob; pvt; MD American Rifles; 1, 2, 21, 1523, 1622
HAMILTON, John of Woodward; res: Frederick, Frd Cty; ref: 89
HAMILTON, Samuel H.; pvt; 2nd MD Inf, Co C; ref:" 1, 2, 19, 21, 1523
HAMILTON, Theodore; pvt; Edelin's MD Bn; res: Balt; ref: 1, 1599
HAMILTON, Thomas; sgt; 1st SC Inf, Co G; ref: 1, 735
HAMILTON, W. W.; pvt; 1st SC Inf, Co G; ref: 1
HAMILTON, William Campbell; pvt; 2nd MD Cav, Co F; res: Cha Cty; ref: 1, 2, 19, 21, 69, 70, 316, 1523
HAMMEL, Edward; pvt; 1st MD Inf, Co A; ref: 1, 2, 19, 21, 1523
HAMMEL, Peter; pvt; Lee's MD Cav; res: Balt; ref: 1, 1540
HAMMER, F. H.; pvt; 2nd MD Lt Arty; ref: 1, 2, 19, 21, 1523
HAMMETT, Charles M. (M.D.); res: St. M. Cty; ref: 1670
HAMMETT, Daniel; pvt; 2nd MD Lt Arty; res: St. Gregors, St. M. Cty; ref: 1, 2, 19, 21, 1509, 1523, 1555, 1563
HAMMETT, David; pvt; 2nd MD Inf, Co D; res: St. M. Cty; ref: 1, 2, 19, 21, 1509, 1523, 1665
HAMMETT, John H.; pvt; 1st MD Cav, Co F; res: St. M. Cty; ref: 1, 2, 19, 21, 1509, 1523
HAMMETT, John M.; pvt; 1st MD Inf, Co A; res: St. Gregers, St. M. Cty; ref: 1, 2, 19, 21, 1523, 1555
HAMMETT, John Thomas; pvt; 2nd MD Inf, Co A; ref: 1, 2, 19, 21, 92, 93, 259, 1509, 1520, 1523
HAMMETT, Whittingham (D.D.S.); sgt; 2nd MD Inf, res: St. M. Cty; ref; 1, 2, 19, 21, 23, 677, 1509, 1523, 1627
HAMMOND, Alexander L.; Acting Asst Surg; Howard Grove Hospital, Richmond; res: AA Cty; ref: 1, 18
HAMMOND, Arthur; res: Millersville, AA Cty; ref: 1539
HAMMOND, Charles H.; pvt; 2nd MD Inf, Co C, res: Annadale; MLCSH; ref: 1, 2, 10, 19, 21, 700, 748, 786, 1523, 1540
HAMMOND, Charles M.; pvt; 1st MD Cav, Co A; res: Millersville, AA Cty; ref: 1, 2, 21, 71, 1487, 1523, 1539
HAMMOND, Claude; pvt; 1st Md Cav, Co C; res: How Cty; ref: 1, 19, 1523
HAMMOND, Denton; pvt; 1st MD Cav, Co D; res: New Market, Frd Cty; ref; 1, 2, 19, 21, 64, 67, 89, 90, 1523, 1548, 1601
HAMMOND, George B. (M.D.); Surg; 18th VA, Heavy Arty; res: Millersville, AA Cty; ref: 1, 18, 735, 883, 1539
HAMMOND, Harry (M.D.); Maj; Gen M. Grigg's staff; res: AA Cty; ref: 1, 12, 18
HAMMOND, Henry R.; sgt; 7th MS Inf, Co D; res: Millersville, AA Cty; ref: 1, 1539, 1628
HAMMOND, John S.; sgt; SC Hampton Leg Inf, Co E; ref: 1, 21, 70, 684, 868, 700, 1613
HAMMOND, Oliver B.; pvt; 1st MD Cav, Co D; res: New Market, Frd Cty; ref: 1, 2, 19, 21, 90, 1523, 1601
HAMMOND, W. H.; pvt; 3rd MD Lt Arty; ref: 2, 19, 21, 160, 726, 782, 1523
HAMMOND, William Edgar; pvt; 53rd VA Inf, Co H; res: Millersville, AA

Cty; ref: 1, 2, 21, 70, 93, 1523, 1539, 1628
HAMPTON, Thomas; pvt; 1st MD Cav, Co F; ref: 1, 2, 19, 21, 1523
HANCE, James J.; pvt; 1st MD Cav, Co C; res: Cal Cty; ref: 1, 2, 19, 21, 650, 1523
HANCE, William H. C.; pvt; 2nd MD Inf, Co A; res: PG Cty; ref: 1, 2, 19, 21, 92, 650, 1523, 1622
HANCOCK, Beverley O.; Dancers Div; ref: 72
HANCOCK, George W.; cpl; 3rd MD Lt Arty; ref: 1, 2, 19, 21, 23, 160, 726, 1523
HANCOCK, Hartwell P.; cpl; 14th VA Inf, Co D; res: Balt; MLCSH; ref: 1, 19, 21, 93, 700, 786
HANCOCK, James W.; pvt; 35th VA Cav, Co A; ref: 1, 3, 1677
HANCOCK, Johnathan H.; pvt; 2nd MD Cav, Co C; ref: 1, 2, 21, 791, 1523
HANDS, Alfred; res: Junction, AA Cty; ref: 1539
HANDS, Washington; pvt; 2nd MD Lt Arty; ref: Balt; ref: 1, 2, 21, 23, 700, 890, 893, 900, 1523
HANDY, Frederick George A.; cpl; 1st Co, Independent Signal Corps; res: Balt; ref: 1, 14
HANDY, John C.; pvt Hampton Leg Lt Arty, Co B; ref: 1, 2, 19, 21, 1523
HANDY, John Huston; pvt; 2nd VA Reserves, Co E; res: Som Cty; ref: 1, 631
HANDY, John T.; sgt; LA Washington Lt Arty, 3rd Battery; res: Balt; MLCSH; ref: 1, 92, 93, 786
HANDY, Luther; res: Melitota, Kt Cty; ref: 1584
HANDY, Moses Purnell; Maj; Asst I.G., Gen W. Stephen's staff; res: Berlin; Wor Cty; ref: 1, 96, 735, 791
HANDY, Thomas; Lt; LA Cresent Heavy Arty, Co A; ref: 1, 2, 19, 735
HANEY, James; pvt; 22nd VA Inf; res: Balt; ref: 70
HANK, John; sgt; 20th SC Inf, Co E; ref: 1, 735
HANK, Thomas; pvt; 20th SC Inf, Co E; res: Balt; ref: 1, 735
HANLEY, James; pvt; 13th VA Inf, Co G; MLCSH; ref: 1, 2, 19, 21, 735, 786, 1523
HANLEY, Thomas J.; pvt; 1st MD Inf, Co G; ref: 1, 2, 19, 21, 700
HANDY, Richard; pvt; MD Guerrilla Zouaves; ref: 1, 1523
HANNA, Alexander B.; pvt; 1st MD Cav, Co C; res: Balt; ref: 1, 19
HANNA, George; pvt; 1st MD Inf, Co E; ref: 1, 2, 19, 21, 1523
HANNA, James L.; pvt; 47th VA Inf, Co H; res: Balt; ref: 1
HANNA, John; pvt; 1st MD Inf, Co F; ref: 1, 2, 21, 1523
HANNICK, George; pvt; MD Guerrilla Zouaves; ref: 1
HANNIGAN, William; pvt; 1st MD Cav, Co F; ref: 1, 2, 19, 21, 1523
HANNON, Lemuel M.; pvt; 1st MD Lt Arty; res: Homonky, Cha Cty; ref: 1, 2, 19, 21, 1546
HANNON, Sherrod B.; pvt; 1st MD Lt Arty; res: Homonky, Cha Cty; ref: 1, 2, 19, 21, 1546
HANNON, Thomas L.; cpl; 1st MD Inf, Homonky, Cha Cty; ref: 1, 2, 19, 21, 23, 1546
HANPT, John; res: Frederick, Frd Cty; ref: 89
HANS, H.; sgt; 2nd MD Cav, Co C; ref: 1, 19, 1523
HANSDAFFER, John; pvt; 2nd MD Cav, Co E; ref: Bt Cty; ref: 1, 19, 1523, 1609
HANSEN, Warren; pvt; Edelin's MD Bn; ref: 1
HANSON, Edward; pvt; Gillward's Co, sappers and miners; res: Frederick, Frd Cty; ref: 1, 89
HANSON, John D.; sgt; 25th VA Inf, Co B; res: Port Tobacco, Cha Cty; MLCSH; ref: 1, 2, 19, 21, 627, 700, 786, 1523, 1546
HANSON, Notley; pvt; 2nd MD Inf, Co A; ref: 1, 2, 19, 21, 650, 1523
HANWAY, William; pvt; 1st MD Cav, Co A; res: Har Cty; ref: 1, 2, 19, 21, 1523

HARBAUGH, George H.; pvt; Staurt's Horse Arty, Breathed's Battery; res: Balt; MLCSH; ref: 1, 786
HARBAUGH, Ignatious; Maj; Gen J. E. B. Stuart's staff; res: Silverburg, Wash Cty; ref: 735, 1559
HARBIN, Thomas H.; pvt; 1st MD Cav, Co B; res: PG Cty; ref: 1, 19, 1523
HARDCASTLE, Aaron Bascom; Col; 33rd MS; res: Denton, Caro Cty; ref: 1, 2, 19, 21, 70, 127, 645, 700, 791, 1134, 1152, 1523
HARDCASTLE, Jerome Humphrey; Asst Surg, Richmond Defense; ref: 1, 18, 1536
HARDCASTLE, William R.; pvt; 2nd MD Inf, Co C; res: Tal Cty; ref: 1, 2, 19, 21, 595, 645, 1523
HARDESTY, James Richard; pvt; 4th MD Lt Arty; res: Annapolis, AA Cty; ref: 1, 2, 19, 93, 1523, 1539
HARDESTY, John W.; sgt; MD American Rifles; res: St. Leonards, Cal Cty; ref: 1, 2, 19, 21, 259, 650, 1523, 1542
HARDESTY, William; pvt; Zarvona's MD Zouaves; res: Balt; ref: 1540, 1613
HARDING, Albert; 35th VA Cav, Co A; res: Adamstown, Frd Cty; ref: 1, 3, 15, 86, 1611, 1677
HARDING, Babe; pvt; 2nd MD Cav, Co C; res: How Cty; ref: 2, 21, 71, 791, 1523
HARDING, Charles A. (M.D.); pvt; 2nd MD Cav, Co C; ref: 1, 18, 457
HARDING, Charles R.; Maj; Q.M., MD Line; ref: 1, 2, 19, 68, 110
HARDING, Columbus; res: Frd Cty; ref: 90
HARDING, Hiram W. (M.D.) Acting Asst Surg; Breckinridge's Hospital, Marion VA; ref: 1, 18, 1690
HARDING, John E.; pvt; 7th VA Cav, Co G; res: How Cty; ref: 1, 2, 10, 19, 21, 23, 70, 1523
HARDING, John W.; pvt; 2nd MD Cav, Co F; ref: 1, 2, 19, 21, 1523
HARDING, Joseph F.; pvt; 35th VA Cav, Co A; ref: 1, 1677
HARDING, Nicholas; pvt; 2nd MD Cav, Co C; res: Carr Cty; ref: 1, 19, 1523, 1609
HARDING, W. M. B.; pvt; 5th VA Inf, Co A; ref: 1, 70, 93
HARDWOOD, Thomas; pvt; 35th VA Cav, Co B; res: Carrollton Manor; Frd Cty; ref: 3, 90, 1523, 1611, 1677
HARDWOOD, William; pvt; 35th VA Cav, Co B; ref: 1677
HARDY, A. J.; pvt; Davis's MD Cav, Co B; ref: 1, 19, 1523
HARDY, Samuel B.; pvt; 2nd MD Lt Arty; res: Balt; ref: 1, 2, 19, 21, 1523
HARE, Silas; Maj; Q.M., Gen B. E. Bee's staff; ref: 1, 23, 791
HARGAVE, E. P. pvt; Davis's MD Cav, Co C; ref: 1, 19
HARGEY, William; pvt; 2nd MD Inf, Co H; ref: 1, 2, 19, 21, 1523
HARKINS, James L.; pvt; 1st MD Cav, Co E; ref: 1, 2, 19, 21, 72, 730, 1523
HARLEY, Albert G.; Lt; 22nd VA Inf, Co A; res: QA Cty; ref: 1, 75
HARLEY, Job; pvt; 2nd MD Inf, Co D; ref: 2, 19, 21, 1523
HARMAN, Andrew of James; pvt; MD American Rifles; res: Patxuent, AA Cty; ref: 1, 1539
HARMAN, Henry W.; pvt; 7th VA Cav, Co G; res: Cha Cty; ref: 1, 3
HARMAN, John T.; pvt; 13th VA Inf, Co G; res: Balt; ref: 1, 70
HARMAN, Victor; pvt; 3rd MD Lt Arty; ref: 1, 2, 19, 21, 160, 726, 1523
HARMISON, Malcolm G.; pvt; 7th VA Cav, Co F; res: Cumberland, All Cty; ref: 1, 19, 95, 1523
HARNEY, Daniel; pvt; 2nd MD Inf, Co D; ref: 1, 2, 7, 19, 21, 1523
HARNEY, Lawrence; pvt; MD Guerrilla Zouaves; ref: 1
HARNEY, Thomas F.; pvt; 43rd VA Cav (Mosby's), Co H; ref: 8
HARPER, James; Lt; Adj, 1st AR Mounted Rifles; res: Upper Marlborough, PG Cty; ref: 1, 83, 735
HARPER, James Kenper; pvt; 4th MD Lt Arty; res: Easton, Tal Cty; ref:

1, 2, 19, 21, 69, 70, 316, 645, 1523, 1557, 1612
HARPER, John; pvt; 2nd MD Lt Arty; ref: 1
HARPER, John R.; pvt; 4th MD Lt Arty; ref: 1
HARPER, Lloyd; pvt; 1st MD Inf, Co E; ref: 1, 2, 19, 21, 1523
HARPER, Robert W.; Col; 3rd Brigade, Army of Tennessee; Upper Marlborough, PG Cty; ref: 2, 12, 19, 81, 735, 791, 1523, 1547
HARPER, William H.; pvt; 1st MD Lt Arty; Upper Marlborough, PG Cty; ref: 1, 19, 21, 83, 700, 1523
HARRELL, Edward R.; pvt; 9th VA, Co I; ref: 1, 700
HARRINGTON, C. M.; pvt 2nd MD Cav, Co A; ref: 1, 19, 1523, 1609
HARRINGTON, Daniel; pvt; 17th VA Inf, Co F; ref: 1, 133, 142, 251
HARRIS, Albert G.; pvt; 19th VA Heavy Arty, Co C; ref: 1, 1580
HARRIS, Alexander; pvt; Stuart's Horse Arty, Breathed's Battery; ref: 1
HARRIS, Baldwin G.; pvt; 5th VA Inf, Co H; ref: 1, 700
HARRIS, Charles H.; pvt; 1st MD Lt Arty; ref: 1, 2, 21, 34, 782, 791, 1273, 1523
HARRIS, E. L.; pvt; 1st MD Cav, Co C; ref: 1
HARRIS, Edwin H.; Maj; Q.M., 3rd Brigade, 3rd Div, at Montgomery Alabama; ref: 1, 21, 93, 700, 791
HARRIS, Fabian L.; cpl; 9th VA Inf, Co B; res: Rockville, Mont Cty; ref: 1, 1552, 1576, 1621
HARRIS, G. M.; pvt; 3rd MD Lt Arty; ref: 2, 19, 21, 160, 726, 1523
HARRIS, James Howard (M.D.); Asst Surg; Dental Corps, Harrisonburg General Hospital; res: Balt; ref: 1, 18, 70, 1536, 1689
HARRIS, John F.; pvt; 1st MD Lt Arty; ref: 1, 2, 19, 21, 1523
HARRIS, John G.; sgt; 1st MD Lt Arty; res: Cha Cty; ref: 1, 2, 19, 21, 23, 34, 63, 64, 68, 215, 782, 791, 1273, 1523
HARRIS, John T.; pvt; 9th VA Inf, Co B; ref: 1, 1576, 1621
HARRIS, Joseph; pvt; 1st MD Lt Arty; res: Cha Cty; ref: 1, 2, 19, 21, 1523
HARRIS, Joseph H.; pvt; 9th VA Inf, Co B; ref: 1, 1523, 1576
HARRIS, Madison William; 17th MS Inf, res: Catonsville, Bt Cty; ref: 71
HARRIS, Marcellus W.; pvt; Andersons' Co, VA Lt Arty; res: Balt; MLCSH; ref: 1, 93, 786
HARRIS, Morgan; pvt; LA Washington Lt Arty, 1st Co; ref: 1, 203
HARRIS, N. Frank; gun, Navy; Floating Battery; ref: 1, 718, 1520
HARRIS, W. H.; smn, Navy; C.S.S. Albemarle; ref: 1
HARRIS, William; pvt; 19th VA Heavy Arty, Co C; res: East New Market, Dor Cty; ref: 1, 1547, 1580, 1666
HARRIS, William E.; pvt; 35th VA Cav, Co D; res: Balt; ref: 1, 2, 19, 21, 259, 559, 650, 711, 791, 1511, 1523, 1677
HARRISON, ---; pvt; Davis's MD Cav, Co A; ref: 735
HARRISON, C. J.; pvt; 2nd MD Cav, Co A; ref: 1
HARRISON, Charles H., Jr; pvt; 6th VA Inf, Co E; ref: 1, 2, 19, 21, 1523
HARRISON, Edwin J.; pvt; 1st MD Cav, Co A; res: Balt; ref: 1, 19, 1523
HARRISON, George E.; Lt; Signal Corps; res: PG Cty; ref: 1, 2, 14, 735, 791
HARRISON, James E.; pvt; Davis's MD Cav, Co C; res: Cambridge, Dor Cty; ref: 1, 1547
HARRISON, J. W.; pvt; 21st VA Inf, Co B; ref: Carr Cty; ref: 1, 2, 21, 312
HARRISON, John Spencer; Lt; 2nd MD Cav, Co B; res: Church Hill, QA Cty; ref: 1, 2, 19, 21, 23, 791, 1523, 1609
HARRISON, John W.; pvt; 21st MD Inf, Co B; ref: 1, 2, 21, 735, 1523

HARRISON, Joseph; pvt; 1st SC Inf, Co G; ref: 1, 1576
HARRISON, Malcom G.; pvt; 14th NC Inf, Co K; res: Cumberland, All Cty; ref: 1, 65, 148, 735
HARRISON, Philip Littig; pvt; 4th MD Lt Arty; res: Queens Town, QA Cty; ref: 1, 2, 19, 21, 70, 1523, 1554
HARRISON, Theodore Perry; pvt; 5th VA Cav, Co D; ref: 1, 19, 1523
HARRISON, Thomas; pvt; 1st MD Cav, Co D; ref: 1, 19, 1523
HARRISON, Thomas D.; pvt; 2nd MD Inf, Co A; res: Balt; ref: 1, 2, 19, 21, 493, 650, 700, 1523
HARRISON, W. W.; pvt; Stuart's Horse Arty, Breathed's Battery; ref: 1
HARRISON, William; pvt; Davis's MD Cav, Co C; ref: 1
HARRISON, William H.; pvt; 1st MD Cav, Co D; ref: 1, 2, 19, 21, 1523, 1601
HARRISON, William H.; pvt; 2nd MD Inf, Co A; res: Balt; ref: 1, 2, 19, 21, 23, 650, 684, 700, 1523
HARRISON, William L.; pvt; 3rd MD Lt Arty; ref: 1
HARROLL, Thompson; pvt; 1st SC Inf, Co G; ref: 1
HARRY, Albert; pvt; 39th MS Inf, Co E; ref: 1, 2, 19, 21, 1523
HARRY, George; pvt; 1st MD Cav, Co C; res: Hagerstown, Wash Cty; ref: 1, 19, 1523
HARRY, James T.; pvt; 1st MD Cav, Co A; ref: 1, 2, 19, 21, 1523
HARRY, John; pvt; 30th NC Inf, Co K; ref: 1, 2, 19, 21, 1523
HART, C. C.; Arty Battery; ref: 1082
HART, Frank; pvt; Stuart's Horse Arty, Breathed's Battery; ref: 1, 498
HART, William A.; cpl; 13th Bn, VA Lt Arty, Battery A; res: Balt; ref: 1, 21, 70, 93, 700, 1599
HART, William E.; pvt; 2nd MD Lt Arty; res: Kt Cty; MLCSH; ref: 1, 2, 19, 21, 786, 1523, 1584
HARTIGAN, John J.; pvt; 1st MD Cav, Co C; ref: 1, 2, 19, 21, 1523
HARTIGAN, John J.; pvt; 13th VA Inf, Co G; ref: 1, 735
HARTLEY, William B.; pvt; 1st MD Inf, Co G; ref: 1, 2, 19, 21, 1523
HARTLEY, William D.; pvt; 35th VA Cav, Co B; res: Balt; ref: 1
HARTMAN, Michael H.; pvt; 1st Bn VA Inf, Co B; res: Johnson's Store, AA Cty; ref: 1, 1539
HARTMEYER, Richard J.; pvt; 1st VA Cav, Co K; res: Balt; ref: 1, 2, 19, 21, 1523, 1540
HARTZ, David; pvt; 1st MD Inf, Co F; res: Balt; ref: 1, 2, 19, 21, 1523
HARTZELL, John C.; sgt; Davis's MD Cav, Co A; ref: 1, 735
HARVERSON, Elisha; pvt; 1st SC Inf, Co G; ref: 1
HARVEY, James E. S.; Holbrook's Independent MD Lt Arty; res: Governor's Bridge, AA Cty; ref: 1, 1529
HARVEY, James C.; pvt; 3rd MD Lt Arty; ref: 1, 2, 19, 21, 160, 725, 1523
HARVEY, John L.; pvt; McNeill's Rangers; res: Gorman; ref: 1010
HARVEY, Martin L.; orderly sgt; 19th VA Heavy Arty, Co C; ref: 1, 2, 19, 21, 64, 1523, 1580
HARVEY, W.; pvt; 3rd MD Lt Arty; ref: 1, 2, 19, 21, 160, 726, 1523
HARWOOD, Francis N.; pvt; 9th VA Inf, Co A; ref: 1, 700
HARWOOD, James Kemp; Paymaster, Navy; Richmond Naval Station; res: Balt; ref: 1, 19, 21, 53, 58, 59, 61, 97, 700, 783, 1523, 1564, 1578, 1674
HARWOOD, Richard L.; pvt; 1st MD Cav, Co E; ref: 1, 2, 19, 21, 730, 1523
HARWOOD, William Thomas; pvt; 35th VA Cav, Co B; res: Adamstown, Frd Cty; ref: 1, 19, 72, 643, 1523, 1573
HASKELL, Alexander M.; Maj; Asst A.G., Gen E. Van Dorn's staff; ref: 1, 2, 19, 735, 791, 1523

HASKELL, William T.; cpl; 1st SC Inf, Co A; res: Balt; ref: 1, 38
HASLETT, Robert E.; Capt; Wise Leg, McLean's LA Inf; res: Balt; ref: 1, 2, 19, 93, 97, 735, 791
HASSKINS, Cor R.; 4th MD Lt Arty; ref: 34
HASSON, John; Lt; 2nd MD Cav, Co A; res: Cec Cty; ref: 1
HASTINGS, Hugh; pvt; 1st MD Inf, Co A; ref: 1, 2, 19, 21, 1523
HATTAWAY, W., Jr; pvt; 3rd MD Lt Arty; ref: 1, 2, 19, 21, 160, 726, 1523
HATTAWAY, W., Sr; pvt; 3rd MD Lt Arty; ref: 1, 2, 19, 21, 160, 726, 1523
HATTON, J. W. F. (M.D.); pvt; 1st MD Lt Arty; ref: 1, 2, 18, 19, 21, 1523
HATTON, Joseph; pvt; 1st MD Lt Arty; ref: 1, 2, 19, 21, 1523
HATTON, R. H. S.; pvt; 1st MD Lt Arty; ref: 1, 2, 21
HAUGHTON, Thomas H.; Lt; McRae's Bn, NC Cav, Co C; res: Balt; ref: 1, 1147
HAUPT, Edward; pvt; 13th VA Inf, Co G; ref: 1
HAUPTMAN, Gerhardt; pvt; 13th VA Inf, Co G; ref: 1, 735
HAUSE, La Fayette; cpl; 1st MD Cav, Co C; res: Bt Cty; ref: 1, 2, 19, 21, 23, 690, 1523, 1575
HAVENER, Charles W.; pvt; 1st VA Inf, Co E; ref: 1, 735
HAWELL, E. R.; pvt; 23rd NC Inf; res: Balt; ref: 70
HAWKEN, James E.; sgt; res: Williamsport, Wash Cty; ref: 361
HAWKINS, A. W.; Maj; 12th MS; ref: 2, 19, 735, 791, 1523
HAWKINS, C. M.; pvt; 2nd MD Cav, Co C; ref: 1, 19, 1523, 1609
HAWKINS, Joseph J.; pvt; 7th NC Inf, Co H; res: Balt; MLCSH; ref: 21, 92, 93, 700, 786
HAWKINS, Joseph S.; pvt; Rhett's 1st SC Heavy Arty, Co A; ref: 1, 2, 19, 21, 470, 1523
HAWKINS, Wallace W.; cpl; 5th VA Cav, Co B; res: Balt; ref: 1, 70, 86
HAWKS, A. W.; courier; res: Ruxton, Bt Cty; ref: 1376, 1613
HAWKS, Wells J.; Maj; Chief Commissary, Gen T. Jackson's staff; res: Ruxton, Bt Cty; ref: 1, 42, 70, 127, 570, 602, 684, 693, 791, 1063, 1376, 1391, 1569, 1642
HAWLEY, George W.; pvt; 3rd MD Lt Arty; ref: 1, 2, 19, 21, 160, 726, 1523
HAWN, David; pvt; 1st MD Inf, Co F; ref: 1, 19, 1523
HAWTHORN, George W.; pvt; MD Guerrilla Zouaves; ref: 1
HAWTHORNE, Robert; pvt; 2nd MD Lt Arty; ref: 1
HAYDEN, A.; pvt; 1st VA Cav, Co K; ref: 1, 2, 19, 21, 1523
HAYDEN, Charles Greenwell; pvt; 1st MD Inf, Co I; res: St. M. Cty; ref: 1, 2, 19, 21, 1509, 1523
HAYDEN, Edwin A.; pvt; 2nd MD Inf, Co B; ref: 1
HAYDEN, George; pvt; 2nd MD Inf, Co B; res: Chaptico, St. M. Cty; ref: 1, 2, 19, 21, 86, 1509, 1523, 1555, 1627
HAYDEN, Horace Edwin (Revd); pvt; 3rd VA Cav, Co A; res: How Cty; ref: 1, 2, 13, 19, 21, 56, 445, 457, 602, 700, 1155, 1198, 1523, 1579
HAYDEN, John Alexander; pvt; 2nd MD Inf, Co B; res: St. M. Cty; ref: 1, 2, 19, 21, 70, 1509, 1523, 1577, 1578, 1662
HAYDEN, John F.; sgt; 2dn MD Lt Arty; res: Balt; ref: 1, 2, 18, 19, 21, 23, 70, 488, 686, 700, 848, 849, 866, 906, 923, 976, 1058, 1523
HAYDEN, Richard A.; pvt; 1st MD Inf, Co C; res: St. M. Cty; ref: 1, 2, 19, 21, 1523, 1627
HAYDEN, William; pvt; 1st VA Cav, Co K; ref: 2, 19, 21, 1523
HAYES, Hayden; pvt; Stuart's Horse Arty, Breathed's Battery; ref: 1

HAYES, John F.; pvt; Davis's MD Cav, Co C; ref; 1
HAYES, Thomas; sgt; 17th VA Inf, Co G; ref: 1, 133, 142, 251
HAYES, Thomas Gordon; sgt; Maj; 10th VA Cav; res: Balt; ref: 21, 41, 70, 107, 700, 1687
HAYNES, J. L.; cpl; 1st SC Inf, Co G; ref: 1
HAYNES, James A.; Capt; 55th VA Inf, Co K; ref: 1, 21, 700
HAYNES, Mitchell; pvt; Davis's MD Cav, Co A; ref: 735
HAYNES, Thomas R.; sgt; 55th VA Inf, Co K; ref: 1, 21, 700
HAYNES, Virgil S.; pvt; Stuart's Horse Arty, Breathed's Battery; ref: 1
HAYNES, William H.; Lt; 55th VA Inf, Co K; res: Balt; ref: 1, 21, 700
HAYNIE, Edward Theodore; Acting Mast. M., Navy; Yazoo City MS Dept; ref: 1, 1529, 1564
HAYS, Samuel Brook; pvt; 35th VA Cav, Co A; res: Barnesville, Mont Cty; ref: 3, 19, 371, 1523, 1611, 1677
HAYS, J. G.; pvt; 2nd MD Inf, Co H; ref: 1, 2, 19, 21, 1523
HAYS, John; pvt; 2nd MD Inf, Co D; ref: 1, 2, 19, 21, 1523
HAYS, Richard Poole; pvt; 35th VA Cav, Co B; res: Old Medley's, Mont Cty; ref: 1, 3, 72, 73, 86, 106, 718, 1078, 1108, 1574, 1611, 1677
HAYWARD, Charles Eccleston; Lt; 1st FL Inf, Co A; res: Cambridge, Dor Cty; ref: 1, 19, 312, 631, 681, 685, 1520, 1523, 1547, 1579
HAYWARD, James C.; pvt; 40th VA Cav, Co D; ref: 1, 685
HAYWOOD, Henry Peabody; pvt; 1st MD Cav, Co C; res: Balt; ref; 1, 2, 19, 21, 70, 685, 1523, 1579
HAYWOOD, Thomas B.; pvt; Davis's MD Cav, Co B; Libertytown, Frd Cty; ref: 1, 19, 1523
HAZEL, Patrick; pvt; 2nd MD Cav, Co B; res: St. M. Cty; ref: 1, 2, 19, 21, 1509, 1523
HEAD, William Edward; pvt; 60th TN Mounted Inf, Co A; res: Balt; MLCSH; ref: 1, 92, 627, 786
HEADLY, P. D.; Capt; 6th NC Sharpshooters, Co B; ref: 1, 735
HEALEY, Frederick; Forrest's Cav; res: Cumberland, All Cty; ref: 631
HEALEY, Maurice Aloysius; pvt; 7th VA Cav, Co F; res: Cumberland, All Cty; ref: 1, 65, 95, 148, 631, 1610
HEALEY, Thomas A. (M.D.); Surg; Mariett's Academy Hospital, South Carolina; res: Cumberland, All Cty; ref: 1, 2, 18, 19, 65, 95, 148, 735, 1523, 1536, 1610
HEALEY, Thomas M.; Capt; Engineer Officer, Gen J. E. Johnson's staff; res: Cumberland, All Cty; ref: 1, 65, 92, 95, 148, 631
HEALL, William Carvil; Gen I. R. Trimble's staff; ref: 70, 735
HEAPHY, John; Navy; ref: 1, 735
HEAPHY, William; sgt; 2nd MD Inf, Co E; ref: 1, 2, 19, 21, 23, 1523, 1609
HEARD, John L.; pvt; 1st MD Cav, Co F; res: Balt; ref: 1, 2, 19 21, 700, 1523
HEARD, John William; Capt; 2nd MD Inf, Co A; res: Frederick, Frd Cty; ref: 1, 2, 19, 21, 23, 64, 72, 88, 89, 91, 650, 1523, 1670
HERLAHY, Cornelius; pvt Lucas' 15th SC Heavy Arty; ref: 1
HEARNE, Benjamin G.; pvt; 1st MD Cav, Co B; res: Som Cty; ref: 1, 2, 19, 21, 785, 1523
HEARNE, Samuel B.; pvt; 1st MD Cav, Co B; ref: 1, 2, 19, 21, 200, 1523
HEARNE, William H.; pvt; 2nd MD Inf, Co F; res: Som Cty; ref: 1, 2, 19, 21, 1523
HEATH, Edward A.; d.h., Navy; Memphis Naval Station; res: Johnson's Store, AA Cty; ref: 1, 1539
HEATH, George R.; sgt; 1st VA Inf, Co B; res: Balt; ref: 1, 21, 700

HEATH, Horace M. (M.D.); Asst Surg; Young's VA Battery; ref: 1, 18, 1534, 1690
HEATH, William H.; pvt; MD American Rifles; res: Johnson's Store, AA Cty; ref: 1, 1539
HEBB, Henry James; pvt; 1st MD Inf, Co H; res: Great Mills, St. M. Cty; ref: 1, 2, 18, 19, 21, 650, 1509, 1523, 1555
HEBB, John W.; Acting Master, Navy; Richmond Station; res: St. M. Cty; ref: 1, 1509, 1564
HEBB, John Wise (M.D.); Asst Surg; 7th LA Inf; How Cty; MLCSH; ref: 1, 18, 21, 700, 720, 735, 786, 1670, 1690
HEBB, Thomas Alexander; pvt; 1st MD Inf, Co H; res: St. M. Cty; ref: 1, 2, 18, 19, 21, 44, 93, 259, 650, 690, 1509, 1523
HECHT, Robert H.; pvt; 1st MD Inf, Co A; res: Frederick, Frd Cty; ref: 1, 2, 19, 21, 89
HECK, Jacob; pvt; 2nd MD Inf, Co G; res: Boonsboro, Wash Cty; ref: 1, 2, 19, 21, 1523, 1558
HECK, Robert A.; pvt; 19th VA Heavy Arty, Co C; res: Boonsboro,. Wash Cty; ref: 1, 2, 19, 21, 1523, 1558, 1580
HECKETT, F. C.; pvt; res: Dor Cty; ref: 112
HEDEN, Thomas; pvt Davis's MD Cav, Co C; ref: 1
HEDGES, Enoch George; pvt; 11th VA Cav, Co A; res: Balt; MLCSH; ref: 1, 93, 627, 700, 786, 1598
HEENAN, N.; pvt; 2nd MD Inf, Co A; ref: 2, 19, 21, 1523
HEFFNER, Daniel Stephen; pvt; 35th VA Cav, Co B; res: Poolesville, Mont Cty; ref: 1, 3, 73, 1552, 1611, 1677
HEFFNER, John; pvt; Lee's MD Cav; res: Annapolis, AA Cty; ref: 1, 1539, 1628
HEFLEBORNER, John N.; pvt; 43rd VA Cav (Mosby's), Co C; res: Balt; ref: 8, 70
HEIFER, John Wallace; Navy; Annapolis, AA Cty; ref: 1, 1539
HEIGHE, John M.; pvt; 2nd VA Cav, Co A; res: Balt; ref: 1, 2, 19, 21, 70, 71, 700, 881, 1419, 1523
HEIGHTS, Thomas B.; pvt; 2nd VA Inf, Co B; ref: 1, 735
HEIMILLER, Herman; pvt; 1st MD Cav, Co C; res: Balt; ref: 1, 2, 19, 21, 700, 827, 1058, 1523
HEIMILLER, William; pvt; 2nd MD Cav, Co A; res: Balt; ref: 1, 2, 19, 21, 412, 700, 866, 1058, 1523
HEINEMAN, Herman; pvt; 3rd MD Lt Arty; ref: 1, 2, 19, 21, 160, 726, 1523
HEINER, Charles M.; pvt; 21st VA Inf, Co B; res: Balt; ref: 1, 2, 312, 735
HEINZ, Ferdenand; musician; 2nd VA Reserves, Co L; res: Balt; MLCSH; ref: 1, 21, 700, 786
HEISKELL, Henry Lee; Capt 20th VA Inf, Co I; res: Balt; MLCSH; ref: 1, 19, 21, 700, 786
HEISKELL, James Monroe; pvt; 43rd VA Cav (Mosby's), Co D; ref: 1, 2, 8, 19, 21, 119, 601, 700, 735, 791, 1571, 1578, 1579, 1654
HEISTER, Frederick; pvt; 2nd MD Inf, Co A; res: Balt; ref: 1, 2, 19, 21, 650, 1523
HEITZELBARGER, S. V.; pvt; Richmond Howitzers, 2nd Co; ref: 1
HELBIG, John Stephen; pvt Zarvona's MD Zouaves; res: Balt; ref: 1, 2, 19, 21, 92, 735, 1523
HELDT, John; pvt; 1st MD Cav, Co D; ref: 1, 19, 1523
HELFRICK, John A.; pvt; Davis's MD Cav, Co B; ref: 1, 19, 1523
HELM, John; pvt; 2nd MD Cav, Co G; ref: 1
HELMLING, Charles A.; sgt; Zarvona's MD Zouaves; ref: 1, 61, 703, 735
HELMLING, James E.; pvt; Zarvona's MD Zouaves; ref: 1, 735
HELMUTH, M.; pvt; MD American Rifles; ref: 1
HELWIG, Lewis; pvt; 3rd MD Lt Arty; ref: 1, 2, 21, 160, 726, 1523
HEMICK, Dudge; res: Balt; ref: 1540

HEMMELL, John C.; pvt; 9th VA Inf, Co B; res: Balt; ref: 1, 1576, 1598
HEMMELL, Robert F.; pvt; 9th VA Inf, Co B; ref: 1, 1576
HEMMINS, Andrew; pvt; 13th VA Inf, Co G; ref: 735
HEMPSTON, Alexander Tounder; pvt; 1st MD Inf, Co C; ref: 1, 2, 19, 21, 1523
HEMPSTONE, Robert T.; pvt; 8th VA Inf, Co H; res: Mont Cty; ref: 1, 1102
HEMSLEY, William; pvt; 1st SC Inf, Co G; res: Balt; ref: 1, 735
HENDERSON, Charles; pvt; 35th VA Cav, Co C; ref: 1, 1523, 1611
HENDERSON, Gaither; pvt; 1st MD Cav, Co A; res: How Cty; ref: 1, 2, 19, 19, 21, 1523
HENDERSON, George; sgt; 35th VA Cav, Co B; ref: 1, 2, 3, 19, 21, 1523, 1677
HENDERSON, H. F.; pvt; 1st MD Cav, Co B; ref: 1, 19, 1523
HENDERSON, Henry; pvt; Stuart's Horse Arty, Breathed's Battery; ref: 1, 498
HENDERSON, John; sgt; 35th VA Cav, Co B; ref: 1161
HENDERSON, Ladson M., fifer; 25th NC Inf, Co H; res: Balt; MLCSH; ref: 1, 21, 93, 700, 786
HENDERSON, Larkin T.; pvt; Stuart's Horse Arty, Breathed's Battery; ref: 1, 735
HENDERSON, Peter; pvt; 19th VA Heavy Arty, Co C; ref: 1, 2, 19, 21, 1523, 1580
HENDERSON, William; Capt; ref: 1690
HENDERSON, William H.; pvt; 14th NC Inf, Co B; res: Balt; MLCSH; ref: 700, 786
HENDERSON, William W.; pvt; 2nd MD Inf, Co G; res: Wor Cty; ref: 1, 2, 19, 21, 1523
HENDON, Thomas; pvt; 1st MD Cav, Co A; res: Har Cty; ref: 1, 2, 19, 21, 1487, 1523
HENDORF, Frederick; pvt; 1st MD Inf, Co A; ref: 1, 2, 19, 21, 412, 1523
HENDRY, W.; pvt; 3rd MD Lt Arty; ref: 2, 19, 21, 160, 726, 1523
HENLEY, George A.; pvt; Signal Corps; res: Balt; ref: 1578
HENNESSY, John William; pvt; Lucas' 15th SC Heavy Arty; ref: 1
HENNICK, Marion; pvt; 2nd MD Lt Arty; ref: 1, 2, 21, 1523
HENNING, Charles M.; pvt; 1st VA Inf, Co E; ref: 1, 735
HENRY, Algernon; sgt; 2nd MD Inf, Co G; res: East New Market, Dor Cty; ref: 1, 2, 19, 21, 23, 1523, 1547
HENRY, John Campbell; pvt; 2nd MD Inf, Co A; res: Cambridge, Dor Cty; ref: 1, 2, 19, 21, 112, 650, 685, 700, 902, 1523, 1547, 1578, 2579
HENRY, John W.; pvt; 2nd MD Cav, Co A; ref: 1
HENRY, L. H.; pvt; 1st VA Inf, Co E; ref: 1, 735
HENSHAW, George; pvt; 47th VA Inf, Co H; ref: 1
HENSHAW, Howard; cpl; Davis's MD Cav, Co A; ref: 1, 735
HERBERT, Charles; pvt; 2nd MD Cav, Co D; ref: 1, 1609
HERBERT, Charles Frederick; pvt; 2nd MD Inf, Co C; res: Balt; ref: 1, 2, 19, 21, 70, 1523
HERBERT, James R.; pvt; 2nd MD Inf, Co B; res: Newberg, Chas Cty; ref; 1, 2, 19, 21, 1546
HERBERT, James R.; Lt Col; 2nd MD Inf; res: Woodstock, How Cty; ref: 1, 2, 10, 11, 13, 15, 18, 19, 21, 23, 34, 35, 38, 42, 50, 62, 63, 64, 68, 70, 88, 94, 105, 107, 122, 129, 222, 240, 443, 444, 456, 462, 469, 488, 493, 501, 503, 517, 559, 595, 631, 638, 674, 685, 689, 690, 700, 711, 748, 757, 784, 789, 790, 791, 816, 825, 856, 857, 860, 862, 873, 881, 893, 923, 1042, 1081, 1361, 1511, 1520, 1523, 1563, 1578, 1579, 1585, 1586, 1600, 1620, 1624, 1634
HERBERT, John C.; pvt; 35th VA Cav, Co B; res: How Cty; ref: 1, 86, 1677

HERBERT, John P.; pvt; 1st MD Inf, Co I; ref: 1, 2, 19, 21, 1523
HERBERT, Lawrence M.; pvt; 2nd MD Cav, Co D; ref: 1
HERBERT, William; pvt; 2nd MD Inf, Co B; ref: 1, 2, 19, 21, 1523
HERBERT, William E.; pvt; 3rd Inf, Co B; res: Balt; ref: 1, 21, 700
HERBERT, William H.; pvt; 12th VA Cav, Co C; res: Hagerstown, Wash Cty; ref: 1, 3, 15, 19, 735, 987, 1677
HERGESHEIMER, David J.; pvt; 1st MD Cav, Co D; res: Frd Cty; MLCSH; ref: 1, 2, 19, 21, 90, 93, 700, 786, 1601
HERING, Francis L.; pvt; 1st MD Cav, Co D; res: Finksburg, Carr Cty; ref: 1, 2, 19, 21, 323, 1523, 1601, 1620
HERMAN, Solomon; pvt; 3rd MD Lt Arty; ref: 1, 2, 19, 21, 160, 726, 1523
HERMANDIES, John; pvt; 1st SC Inf, Co G; ref: 1
HERMANTROUT, W. F.; pvt; 4th MD Lt Arty; ref: 1, 2, 19, 21, 1523
HERNANDEX, Richard; sgt; 13th VA Inf, Co G; ref: 735
HERDON, E. M.; pvt; 3rd MD Lt Arty; ref: 2, 19, 21, 461, 1523
HERON, A.; pvt; 2nd MD Lt Arty; ref: 1, 2, 19, 21, 1523
HERR, E. G. W.; pvt; 12th VA Cav, Co D; res: Williamsport, Wash Cty; ref: 1, 735
HERRON, B.C.; pvt; 3rd MD Lt Arty; ref: 1, 2, 19, 21, 160, 726, 1523
HERRON, D. A.; pvt; MD Guerrilla Zouaves; ref: 1
HERRON, George S.; pvt; 2nd MD Cav, Co C; res: Har Cty; ref: 1, 2, 19, 21, 1523, 1609
HERRON, Virgie P.; cpl; 3rd MD Lt Arty; ref: 1, 2, 19, 21, 23, 160, 726, 1523
HERSON, Cornelius; pvt; 2nd MD Inf, Co C; ref: 1
HERSTER, Frederick; pvt; 1st MD Inf, Co E; ref: 1, 2, 19, 21, 1523
HERZOG, J. Lewis; sgt; Moorehead's VA Rangers; ref: 1, 21, 700, 1580
HESS, Casper; pvt; Holbrook's Independent MD Lt Arty; ref: 1
HESSE, Edward; pvt; 48th VA Inf, Co K; res: Balt; ref: 1, 21, 700
HESSEY, David S.; pvt; 13th VA Inf, Co G; ref: 1
HEWES, James; pvt; 1st MD Inf, Co A; res: Balt; ref: 1, 2, 19, 21, 56, 511, 700, 1145, 1523
HEWES, Michael Warner; pvt; 1st VA Cav, Co K; res: Balt; ref; 1, 2, 19, 21, 57, 75, 84, 511, 777, 878, 891, 904, 916, 994, 1523
HEWITT, David M.; pvt; 21st AL Inf, Co E; res: How Cty; ref: 1, 107
HEWITT, H. N.; ref: 800
HEWITT, Henry Clay; Lt; 1st VA Inf, Co C; res: Balt; ref: 1, 23, 1687
HEWITT, Razin Davis; pvt; 12th VA Cav, Co B; res: Sykesville, Carr Cty; ref: 1, 10, 36, 1550
HICHCOCK, J.; pvt; 2nd MD Cav, Co D; ref: 1
HICKEY, Edmund P.; pvt; 1st MD Cav, Co B; res: Hyattsville, PG Cty; ref: 1, 2, 19, 21, 316, 785, 1523
HICKEY, John Francis; pvt; 1st MD Cav, Co B; res: Hyattsville, PG Cty; ref: 1, 2, 19, 21, 76, 150, 316, 785, 941, 976, 1523
HICKEY, John M.; Capt; 38th MO Inf, Co F; res: How Cty; ref: 1, 23, 677, 735, 791, 859, 997, 1356, 1406, 1407
HICKEY, John P.; commissary sgt; 4th MD Lt Arty; res: Carr Cty; ref: 1, 2, 19, 21, 23, 64, 1523
HICKEY, Patrick; pvt; Davis's MD Cav, Co B; ref: 1, 19, 1523
HICKEY, W.; pvt; 35th VA Cav, Co B; ref: 1, 1677
HICKMAN, Joshua; pvt; 2nd MD Lt Arty; ref: 1, 2, 19, 21, 1523
HICKS, Crowder; pvt; Davis's MD Cav, Co A; ref: 1, 735
HICKS, George L.; pvt; 17th VA Inf, Co H; ref: 1, 133, 142, 251
HICKS, W. Granville; pvt; Stuart's Horse Arty, Breathed's Battery; ref: 1
HICKSON, George; pvt; 14th VA Inf, Co I; ref: 1, 735

HICKSON, William A.; pvt; 15th LA Inf, Co D; ref: 1, 735
HIGDON, Francis Leonard; ordnance sgt; 2nd MD Inf; res: Pisgah, Cha Cty; MLCSH; ref: 1, 2, 19, 21, 23, 92, 93, 470, 700, 786, 1523, 1546, 1665
HIGGINS, Eugene; pvt; 21st VA Inf, Co B; res: Balt; ref: 1, 2, 69, 316, 631, 735, 1540
HIGGINS, Henry A.; pvt; Davis's MD Cav, Co A; Little Orleans, All Cty; ref: 1, 19, 65, 95, 148, 735, 1538
HIGGINS, James F.; lmn, Navy; C.S Virginia; res: Balt; ref: 1
HIGGINS, James L.; pvt; Stuart's Horse Arty, Breathed's Battery; ref: 1, 498, 1575
HIGGINS, James R.; pvt; Davis's MD Cav, Co A; res: Little Orleans, All Cty; ref: 1, 3, 65, 95, 148, 735
HIGGINS, John P.; pvt; 21st VA Inf, Co A; ref: 1, 2, 19, 735, 1523
HIGGINS, Owen F.; pvt; 12th VA Cav, Co D; res: Balt; MLCSH; ref: 1, 786
HIGGINS, William George; pvt; 1st MD Lt Arty; res: Millersville, AA Cty; ref: 1, 2, 19, 21, 34, 70, 700, 1523, 1539
HIGGONS, ---; Gen J. H. Winder's Detectives; ref: 30
HIGGONS, Eugene; pvt; 21st VA Inf, Co B; res: Balt; ref: 1, 2, 312, 592
HIGGONS, John P.; cpl; 21st VA Inf, Co B; ref: 1, 2, 312
HIGHFIELD, Thomas N.; smn, Navy; C.S. Albermarle; res: La Plata, Cha Cty; MLCSH; ref: 1, 19, 21, 58, 700, 783, 786, 1523, 1662
HIGHLEY, Burton S. (Revd); Chaplain; 51st VA Inf; res: 1, 19
HILBERT, George; pvt; Lucas' 15th SC Heavy Arty; res: Balt; ref: 1, 255, 700
HILDT, John; pvt; 1st MD Inf, Co A; res: Frd Cty; ref: 1, 2, 19, 21, 1523
HILIARD, R. E.; pvt; 1st MD Cav, Co D; ref: 1, 1523
HILL, Amos; pvt; 2nd MD Cav, Co G; ref: 1
HILL, Augustus; pvt; 1st MD Lt Arty; ref: 1, 34
HILL, Charles D.; Capt; 13th NC Inf, Co C; res: Balt; ref: 1, 21, 700, 791
HILL, Charles S.; Lt; 1st VA Inf, Co F; res: Nottingham, PG Cty; ref: 1, 2, 19, 735, 1523, 1553
HILL, Clayton; 13th VA Inf; ref: 50, 64
HILL, Edgar; Lt; Stuart's Horse Arty, Breathed's Battery; ref: 1, 498
HILL, Edward; pvt; Davis's MD Cav, Co C; ref: 1
HILL, Elias; pvt; 1st SC Inf, Co G; ref: 1
HILL, Eugene Francis; Lt; Aid de Camp, Gen F. A. Shoup's staff; ref: 1, 34, 69, 316
HILL, Frank T.; Capt; 13th VA Inf, Co G; ref: 1, 518, 735, 791
HILL, Frederick R.; cpl; 25th VA Inf, Co G; res: Millersville, AA Cty; ref: 1, 1539
HILL, John; pvt; 4th MD Lt Arty; res: Cambridge, Dor Cty; ref: 1, 2, 10, 19, 21, 1523
HILL, John A.; pvt; 1st MD Inf, Co A; res: Carr Cty; ref: 1, 2, 19, 21, 1523
HILL, John Beall; pvt; 1st MD Cav, Co B; res: PG Cty; ref: 1, 2, 19, 21, 785, 1523, 1540, 1622
HILL, John L.; Lt; 14th VA Cav, Co I; res: How Cty; MLCSH; res: 1, 470, 700, 786
HILL, John O.; pvt; 2nd MD Inf, Co F; Cornersville, Dor Cty; ref: 1, 2, 21, 470, 1523, 1547
HILL, Nichols Snowden; Maj; Chief Commissary, District of AK; res: PG Cty; ref: 1, 2, 13, 19, 21, 23, 34, 57, 69, 316, 791, 916, 994, 1523
HILL, Thomas R.; Lt; Poague's Co, VA Lt Arty; ref: 57, 513

HILL, William; pvt; 1st MD Cav, Co D; res: Balt; ref: 1, 2, 19, 1523
HILL, William I.; Lt; 1st MD Lt Arty; res: Bladensburg, PG Cty; ref: 1, 2, 19, 21, 23, 63, 64, 68, 81, 791, 1523
HILL, William M.; pvt; 1st MD Inf, Co D; res: PG Cty; ref: 1, 19, 69, 316, 1523
HILLARY, W. M. (M.D.); pvt; 1st MD Lt Arty; ref: 19, 93, 1523
HILLEARY, Clarence Worthington; 7th VA Cav, Co G; res: Petersville, Frd Cty; ref: 1, 3, 67, 90, 1278
HILLEARY, George H.; cpl; Hampton Leg Lt Arty, Co B; ref: 1, 2, 21, 23, 1523
HILLEARY, Thomas; pvt; 7th VA Cav, Co G; res: Petersville, Frd Cty; ref: 1, 2, 3, 19, 21, 90, 1154, 1278, 1601
HILLEARY, Washington M. (M.D.); pvt; Hampton Leg Lt Arty, Co B; ref: 1, 2, 18, 21, 1523
HILLERY, J.; 1st MD, Co C; ref: 93
HILLEY, M.; pvt; 1st SC Inf, Co G; ref: 1
HILTON, Joseph B.; sgt; 1st SC Inf, Co G; ref: 1
HILTON, Sebastian; pvt; 1st SC Inf, Co G; ref: 1
HINDES, George; pvt; 1st MD Inf, Co D; ref: 1
HINES, J. W.; pvt; Epps Lt Arty; ref: 1, 2, 21, 470, 1523
HINES, Michael; pvt; 19th VA Heavy Arty; ref: 1, 2, 19, 21, 1523, 1580
HINES, Thomas J.; pvt; 2nd MD Inf, Co D; ref: 1, 2, 19, 21, 1523
HINKEY, John; pvt; Davis''s MD Cav, res: Annapolis, AA Cty; ref: 1, 1539
HINNICK, Marion; pvt; 2nd MD Lt Arty; ref: 2, 19, 21, 1523
HINNICKS, T. E. C.; pvt; 1st MD Lt Arty; res: PG Cty; ref: 1
HINTON, Nicholas J.; pvt; 3rd MD Lt Arty; ref: 1, 2, 19, 21, 160, 726, 1523
HINTON, William; res: Birdsville, AA Cty; ref: 1539
HIPKINS, John; pvt; 43rd VA Cav (Mosby's), Co H; res: Balt; MLCSH; ref: 8, 93, 627, 700, 786
HIPKINS, Richard; pvt; 6th VA Inf, Co G; ref: 21, 700
HIPSLEY, Thomas; pvt; 10th VA Cav, Co D; res: Balt; ref: 1, 19, 21, 700, 1523
HIRST, James P.; pvt; 1st MD Inf, Co E; ref: 1
HISSEY, John H.; pvt; Holbrook's Independent MD Lt Arty; res: Balt; ref: 1, 2, 19, 21, 1523, 1540
HITCHCOCK, Robert Fielding; pvt; 1st VA Inf, Co B; res: Balt; MLCSH; ref: 1, 21, 92, 93, 627, 700, 786, 1609
HITZILBERGER, Charles F.; pvt; 1st MD Inf, Co D; res: Libertytown, Frd Cty; ref: 1, 2, 19, 21, 90, 559, 1511, 1523
HITZILBERGER, Stephen V.; pvt; Richmond Howitzers, 2nd Co; ref: 1, 686
HOAX, Robert; pvt; 7th VA Cav, Co G;ref: 3
HOBBS, Charles; res: Frederick, Frd Cty; ref: 89
HOBBS, J.; pvt; 2nd MD Cav, Co F; ref: 1, 2, 19, 21, 1523
HOBBS, Jarrett; pvt; 1st VA, Co K; res: How Cty; ref: 1, 2, 10, 19, 21, 93, 748, 1523
HOBBS, John; pvt; Zarvona's MD Zouaves; ref: 1, 735, 888
HOBBS, Nathan Chew; Capt; 1st VA Cav, Co K; res: Cooksville, How Cty; ref: 1, 2, 10, 19, 21, 23, 64, 70, 240, 445, 700, 748, 791, 1523, 1577, 1578
HOBBS, Townsend R.; pvt; 1st VA Cav, Co K; res: How Cty; ref: 1, 2, 10, 19, 21, 1523
HOBBS, William H.; drummer; Lucas's 15th SC Heavy Arty; res: Balt; MLCSH; ref: 1, 2, 19, 21, 627, 700, 786, 1523

HOBLITZELL, Fetter S.; pvt; 1st MD Inf, Co H; res: Cumberland, All Cty; ref: 1, 2, 19, 21, 57, 65, 95, 95, 148, 650, 700, 1523, 1610, 1635
HOBSON, Dean; pvt; Stuart's Horse Arty, Breathed's Battery; ref: 1, 498
HODGE, William; pvt; 2nd MD Cav, Co D; ref: 1, 1609
HODGES, Benjamin; pvt; 2nd MD Inf, Co F; res: Port Tobacco, Cha Cty; ref: 1, 2, 19, 21, 1523, 1546
HODGES, Charles W.; Lt; 2nd MD Inf, Co C; ref: 1, 2, 19, 21, 23, 64, 68, 511, 595, 693, 1523
HODGES, Henry; cpl; Lee's Balt Lt Arty, Alexander's Bn; res: Governor's Bridge, AA Cty; ref: 1, 1539
HODGES, J. N.; pvt; 7th VA Cav, Co G; ref: 1
HODGES, J. W.; Lt; Farinholt's VA Reserves, Co B; res: St. M. Cty; ref: 1, 7
HODGES, Robert T.; sgt; 2nd MD Inf, Co C; ref: 1, 2, 19, 21, 23, 511, 690, 1523
HODGES, Thomas O.; sgt; 2nd MD Inf, Co F; res: Port Tobacco, Cha Cty; ref: 1, 2, 19, 21, 23, 1523, 1546
HODGES, William Ringgold (M.D.); Asst Surg; General Hospital Grenada Mississippi; res: Ellicott City, How Cty; ref: 1, 18, 1584, 1690
HODGKIN, J. B.; pvt; 3rd VA Inf, Co E; ref: 1689
HODGKINS, James B.; pvt; 3rd VA Inf, Co E; ref: 1, 1529
HODSON, Emmory Payton; pvt; 21st VA Inf, Co B; ref: 1, 2, 19, 141, 1523
HOERSTER, Frederick; pvt; 2nd MD Inf, Co A; res: Balt; MLCSH; ref: 19, 21, 700, 786, 1523, 1540
HOFF, George W.; pvt; Chew's Lt Arty; ref: 93, 700
HOFFAR, Daniel; pvt; 1st MD Cav, Co B; ref: 1, 19, 1523
HOFFMAN, Alfred; Maj; Asst I.G., Gen I. R. Trimble's staff; res: Balt; ref: 1, 501
HOFFMAN, C. S.; pvt; Jackson's Co, GA Inf; ref: 1, 93
HOFFMAN, George William; pvt; 1st MD Inf, Co F; res: Balt; MLCSH; ref: 1, 2, 19, 21, 92, 93, 627, 700, 786, 1523
HOFFMAN, Henry; pvt; 2nd MD Cav, Co E; ref: 1, 791
HOFFMAN, Howard S.; Lt; 10th VA Inf, Co L; ref: 1, 693
HOFFMAN, John; pvt; Davis's MD Cav, Co A; ref: 1, 735
HOFFMAN, John; pvt; 43rd VA Cav (Mosby's); ref: 21, 700
HOFFMAN, John H.; pvt; 3rd MD Lt Arty; ref: 1, 2, 19, 21, 160, 461, 726, 1523
HOFFMAN, Richard Curzon; Capt; 30th VA Inf, Co E; res: Balt; ref: 1, 2, 19, 21, 23, 44, 53, 56, 57, 64, 70, 592, 681, 684, 685, 700, 735, 798, 1520, 1523, 1540, 1579
HOFFMAN, William H.; pvt; 2nd MD Inf, Co A; res: Catonsville, Bt Cty; ref: 1, 2, 19, 21, 650, 1523
HOGAN, James; pvt; 3rd MD Lt Arty; ref: 1, 2, 19, 21, 160, 726, 1523
HOGAN, Thomas J.; pvt; 1st MD Inf, Co E; ref: 1, 2, 19, 21, 88, 1523
HOGARTHY, William; pvt; 2nd MD Inf, Co D; res: AA Cty; MLCSH; ref: 1, 2, 19, 21, 700, 786, 1523
HOGE, Charles A.; pvt; 2nd MD Inf, Co F; ref: 1, 2, 19, 21, 70, 888, 1523
HOGG, Thomas Francis; Mast, Navy; ref: 70, 1564
HOLBAND, John W.; pvt; LA Washington Lt Arty; res: Dickerson, Frd Cty; ref: 86
HOLBROOK, A.; pvt; 3rd MD Lt Arty; ref: 1, 2, 19, 21, 160, 726, 1523
HOLBROOK, G. J.; pvt; 3rd MD Lt Arty; ref: 1, 2, 19, 21, 160, 726, 1523
HOLBROOK, John F.; pvt; 1st MD Cav, Co C; ref: 1, 2, 19, 21, 1523

HOLBROOK, Patrick M.; pvt; 35th VA Cav, Co D; res: Balt; ref: 1, 1611, 1677
HOLBROOK, Thomas H.; Capt; Holbrook's Independent MD Lt Arty; ref: 1, 2, 17, 19, 64, 68, 456, 1523
HOLDEN, Robert Randolph (M.D.); Asst Surg, Jackson Hospital Richmond; ref: 1, 2, 18, 19, 21, 1523
HOLDER, John; pvt; 3rd MD Lt Arty; ref: 1, 2, 19, 21, 160, 726, 1523
HOLIDAY, Clement W.; pvt; 1st MD Cav, Co B; res: Nottingham, PG Cty; ref: 1, 19, 1523, 1553
HOLLAHAN, M.; pvt; 1st SC Inf, Co G; res: Balt; ref: 735
HOLLAND, Albert; pvt; Purcell battery, VA Lt Arty; ref: 1, 2, 19, 21, 677, 735, 1523
HOLLAND, J. J. J.; pvt; 1st VA Cav, Co K; ref: 1, 2, 19, 21, 1523
HOLLAND, John R.; pvt; 1st VA Cav, Co K; res: AA Cty; ref: 1, 2, 19, 21, 687, 700, 1523
HOLLAND, John W.; Capt; Q.M., Libby Prison; res: Old Medley's, Mont Cty; ref: 86, 106, 557, 718, 1574
HOLLAND, Josiah; 39th VA Inf, Co B; ref: 735
HOLLAND, Michael; pvt; 6th VA Inf, Co I; res: Bt Cty; MLCSH; ref: 1, 2, 19, 21, 92, 93, 700, 735, 786, 1523
HOLLAND, P. R.; pvt; 1st VA Cav, Co K; ref: 1, 2, 19, 21, 1523
HOLLAND, Peter; 39th VA Inf, Co B; ref: 735
HOLLAND, Thomas R.; pvt; 1st MD Inf, Co E; res: Balt; ref: 1, 2, 19, 21, 1523
HOLLAND, W. W.; 6th NC, Co J; ref: 92
HOLLAND, William J.; pvt; 17th VA Inf, Co A; Balt; ref: 1, 735
HOLLAND, William J.; pvt; 19th VA Heavy Arty, Co C; ref: 1, 1580
HOLLAND, William James Canady; pvt; 1st VA Cav, Co K; res: Wor Cty; MLCSH; ref: 2, 93, 133, 142, 627, 786
HOLLINGFIELD, Jacob; pvt; 1st SC Inf, Co G; ref: 1
HOLLINGSWORTH, Thomas J.; pvt; 17th VA Inf, Co C; res: Balt; ref: 142, 251, 1331
HOLLINGSWORTH, William T.; pvt; 1st MD Cav, Co E; ref: 1, 2, 19, 21, 730, 1523
HOLLINS, Frederick H.; sgt; Zarvona's MD Zouaves; ref: 1, 14, 19, 58, 97, 608, 757, 1523
HOLLINS, George Nicholas, Jr; Asst Engineer, Navy; C.S.S. Ivy; ref: 19, 58, 97, 279, 608, 1523, 1564
HOLLINS, George Nicholas, Sr; Commodore, Navy; Richmond Naval Station; res: Balt; ref: 1, 17, 19, 21, 23, 24, 25, 43, 44, 50, 58, 59, 61, 63, 64, 68, 70, 97, 125, 127, 130, 166, 271, 274, 275, 276, 277, 279, 372, 480, 501, 511, 593, 602, 608, 674, 700, 703, 735, 757, 781, 783, 791, 818, 838, 857, 1165, 1297, 1520, 1523, 1560, 1564, 1568, 1569, 1577, 1578, 1579, 1583, 1588, 1620, 1623, 1632, 1676
HOLLINS, J. W.; pvt; 21st VA Inf, Co H; ref: 1
HOLLIS, Isaac; pvt; 7th VA Cav, Co G; ref: 1
HOLLOWAY, Michael; pvt; 2nd MD Inf, Co H; ref: 1, 2, 19, 21, 1523
HOLLOWAY, O. A.; pvt; 1st SC Inf, Co G; ref: 1
HOLLYDAY, Clement W.; pvt; 1st MD Cav, Co B; res: PG Cty; ref: 1, 785
HOLLYDAY, Floyd S.; pvt; 2nd MD Cav; ref: 70
HOLLYDAY, George T. of G.; sgt; 1st MD Cav, Co E; res: Balt; ref: 1, 2, 19, 21, 23, 57, 70, 469, 700, 1520, 1523
HOLLYDAY, George Tilghman of W.; pvt; 35th VA Cav, Co B; res: Kt Cty; ref: 1, 2, 19, 21, 70, 700, 1584, 1677
HOLLYDAY, Henry Sr.; pvt; 2nd MD Inf, Co A; res: QA Cty; ref: 1, 2, 17, 19, 21, 23, 81, 470, 650,

700, 1001, 1162, 1176, 1275, 1285, 1520, 1523

HOLLYDAY, John Geiger (M.D.); pvt; 1st MD Cav, Co C; res: Pt. Comfort; ref: 1, 2, 19, 21, 23, 70, 700, 1523

HOLLYDAY, Lamar; pvt; 2nd MD Inf, Co A; res: Balt; MLCSH; ref: 1, 2, 19, 21, 39, 70, 71, 79, 107, 441, 443, 445, 493, 650, 686, 693, 700, 784, 976, 1058, 1297, 1523

HOLLYDAY, William H.; pvt; 2nd MD Inf, Co A; res: Hagerstown, Wash Cty; ref: 1, 2, 19, 21, 70, 92, 93, 259, 650, 888, 1523

HOLMEAD, Charles H.; pvt; 1st VA Inf, Co F; ref: 1, 2, 19, 21, 735, 1523

HOLMES, James Gadson; Capt; Asst Q.M., Gen E. Law's staff; res: Balt; ref: 1, 21, 700

HOLMES, John W.; pvt; 2nd MD Cav, Co A; ref: 1, 7, 19, 1523

HOLMES, Julius Charles; sgt; 2nd MD Cav, Co A; res: Balt; ref: 1, 21, 23, 700

HOLOHAN, Michael C .; sgt; 19th VA Heavy Arty, Co C; ref: 1, 2, 19, 21, 23, 1523, 1580

HOLSTON, George; pvt; 19th VA Heavy Arty, Co C; ref: 1, 1580

HOLT, Jonathan T.; Mast. A., Navy; C.S. Tennessee; res: Balt; ref: 1, 1540

HOLT, Thomas; pvt; MD Guerrilla Zouaves; ref: 1

HOLTZ, Randolph; pvt; 2nd MD Cav, Co A; ref: 1, 19, 1523, 1609

HOLTZEL, F. S.; pvt; Barry's Co, MD Vols; ref: 1, 19, 1523

HOLTZMAN, William H. F.; pvt; 5th VA Cav, Co C; res: Balt; ref: 1, 2, 19, 21, 700, 735, 1523

HONEA, F.; pvt; 1st SC Inf, Co G; ref: 1

HOOD, George L.; pvt; 1st MD Inf, Co G; ref: 1, 2, 19, 21, 819, 1523

HOOD, John D.; pvt; 2nd MD Cav, Co D; ref: 1

HOOD, John Miffin; Lt; 2nd Regt, Eng'r Corps, Co B; res: Sykesville, Carr Cty; ref: 1, 2, 13, 19, 21, 23, 56, 57, 65, 361, 748, 994, 995, 1523, 1578

HOOD, Joseph J.; pvt; 13th VA Inf, Co G; ref: 1

HOOD, William; pvt; Lee's Balt Lt Arty, Alexander's Bn; res: Millersville, AA Cty; ref: 1, 1539

HOOFF, John J.; pvt; 4th MD Lt Arty; MLCSH; ref: 1, 2, 19, 21, 133, 786, 1523

HOOK, John; res: Balt; ref: 1540

HOOK, Robert Bruce; pvt; 2nd MD Cav, Co F; res: Reisterstown, Bt Cty; ref: 1, 2, 19, 21, 70, 1523

HOONEY, D. I.; 2nd MD Inf, Co D; ref: 1, 7, 19, 1523

HOOPER, James; Adj; 1st AR Rifles; ref: 2, 19, 1523

HOOPER, John Pitt; sgt; 3rd MD Lt Arty; res: Hoopersville, Dor Cty; ref: 1, 2, 19, 21, 23, 64, 70, 160, 461, 726, 1523, 1547

HOOPER, Richard H.; Acting Mast., Navy; C.S.S. Curlew; res: Carr Cty; ref; 1, 21, 700, 783

HOOVER, George; Junction, AA Cty; ref: 1539

HOOVEY, John; pvt; 2nd MD Cav, Co B; ref: 1, 1609

HOPE, Samuel; pvt; MD Guerrilla Zouaves; ref: 1

HOPKINS, Alexander Rigby; cpl; 4th MD Lt Arty; res: Tal Cty; ref: 1, 2, 19, 93, 1523

HOPKINS, Andrew Jackson; pvt; 15th VA Inf, Co H; res: Balt; MLCSH; ref: 1, 93, 627, 786

HOPKINS, Ben; cpl; 4th MD Lt Arty; ref: 64

HOPKINS, Frank; pvt; 32nd VA Inf, Co I; res: Davidsonville, AA Cty; ref: 1, 1539

HOPKINS, H.; pvt; 1st VA Cav, Co K; ref:1, 2, 19, 21, 46, 1523

HOPKINS, Henry; pvt; 1st MD Lt Arty; ref: 1, 2, 21, 1523

HOPKINS, Henry Hal; cpl; Stuart's Horse Arty, Breathed's Battery; ref: 1, 2, 19, 21, 498

HOPKINS, John; pvt; Davis's MD Cav; res: Annapolis, AA Cty; ref: 1, 1539
HOPKINS, Luther W.; pvt; 6th VA Cav, Co H; res: Bt Cty; ref: 1, 7, 37, 513, 1028, 1130, 1143, 1523
HOPKINS, Montgomery; pvt; Zarvona's MD Zouaves; res: Millersville, AA Cty; ref: 1, 1539
HOPKINS, Samuel Isaac; pvt; 2nd MD Inf, Co A; res: PG Cty; ref: 1, 2, 19, 21, 1523, 1589
HOPKINS, Thomas J.; res: Queen Anne, AA Cty; ref: 1539
HOPKINS, William Fayette; pvt; Stuart's Horse Arty, Breathed's Battery; ref: 1, 498
HOPKINS, William Rigby; pvt; 1st MD Cav, Co K; res: Tal Cty; ref: 1, 19, 645, 1612
HOPPELL, George W.; pvt; 1st MD Inf, Co A; ref: 1, 2, 19, 21, 1523
HOPPER, Hanson W.; pvt; 17th VA Inf, Co B; ref: 1, 142, 251
HORBACK, James P.; Maj; Q.M.; Dept of Tennessee; res: PG Cty; ref: 1, 23, 677, 791
HORN, H. C.; pvt; 2nd MD Cav, Co F; ref: 1, 2, 19, 21, 1523, 1609
HORN, William C.; pvt; Lee's MD Cav; ref: 1, 735
HORNER, David H.; pvt; 6th VA Cav, Co F; res: Rockville, Mont Cty; ref: 1, 718, 1574
HORNER, Frank B.; pvt; 1st MD Cav, Co A; res: Rockville, Mont Cty; ref: 1, 2, 19, 21, 86, 1523, 1574
HORNER, Robert C.; pvt; 43rd VA Cav (Mosby's), Lt Arty Co; ref: 8
HORNING, George; res: Frederick, Frd Cty; ref: 89
HORSEMAN, William H.; pvt; 35th VA Cav, Co A; res: Urbana, Frd Cty; ref: 1, 3, 1611, 1677
HORTON, B. F.; pvt; 1st SC Inf, Co G; ref: 1
HORTON, William R.; cpl; 63rd VA Inf, Co G; ref: 1, 1563
HORUSLY, Reuben Andrew Jackson; Navy; C.S.S. Virginia; res: Williamsport, Wash Cty; ref: 1359
HOSHBERGER, S. D.; pvt; 2nd MD Cav, Co D; ref: 1, 19, 1523, 1609
HOSKINS, James H.; pvt; 35th VA Cav, Co B; ref: 1
HOTTINGER, Moses; pvt; 2nd MD Lt Arty; ref: 1, 2, 19, 21, 1523
HOUGH, Gresham; pvt; 43rd VA Cav (Mosby's), Co D; res: Balt; ref: 1, 2, 8, 17, 19, 21, 70, 93, 469, 511, 601, 650, 685, 700, 735, 1519, 1520, 1523, 1571, 1578, 1579, 1602, 1654
HOUGH, Harry; pvt; 17th VA Inf, Co H; ref: 1, 70, 133, 142
HOUGH, Oscar R.; Lt; 1st VA Inf, Co H; ref: 1, 735
HOUGH, Robert; Gen A. S. Johnston's staff; res: Balt; ref: 1013, 1018
HOUGH, Samuel J.; pvt; 1st MD Cav, Co A; res: Balt; ref: 1, 2, 19, 21, 36, 70, 511, 685, 690, 700, 976, 1523, 1579, 1634
HOUGH, William Dickinson; Midn, Navy; C.S. Florida; res: Balt; ref: 1, 2, 19, 21, 70, 650, 724, 791, 1523, 1564, 1578, 1579, 1602
HOUPE, Edward; res: Balt; ref: 1540
HOUSE, Christian; sgt; 32nd AL Inf, Co K; res: Balt; ref: 1, 1540
HOUSE, Robert; Lt; 22nd GA Inf, Co I; res: West River, AA Cty; ref: 1539
HOUSER, John E.; pvt; 35th VA Cav, Co C; res: West River, AA Cty; ref: 1, 1539, 1677
HOUSTON, James P. S.; res: Bt Cty; ref: 70
HOWARD, Benjamin; pvt; Rhett's 1st SC Heavy Arty; res: Balt; ref: 735
HOWARD, Carvil C.; pvt; 1st MD Cav, Co C; res: Balt; MLCSH; ref: 1, 2, 19, 21, 92, 93, 511, 753, 786, 1523
HOWARD, Charles; pvt; 4th MD Lt Arty; ref: 1
HOWARD, Charles, Jr; Maj; Chief Commissaray, Gen A. Elzey's staff; res: Balt; ref: 1, 2, 18, 19, 21, 44, 54, 86, 256, 511, 722, 791, 826, 1523, 1541, 1579, 1583, 1634

HOWARD, David Ridgely; pvt; 2nd MD Inf, Co A; res: Balt; ref: 1, 2, 19, 21, 34, 441, 469, 493, 511, 650, 700, 753, 866, 906, 976, 1058, 1523, 1540, 1577, 1578

HOWARD, Edward Lloyd (M.D.) Asst Surg; Courtney Lt Arty; res: Balt; ref: 1, 2, 18, 21, 38, 44, 70, 511, 690, 700, 753, 1491, 1523, 1533, 1534, 1536, 1541, 1583

HOWARD, George; Castle Pinkney's SC Heavy Lt Arty; ref: 735

HOWARD, George T.; Lt; 22nd VA Inf; ref: 21, 86, 677, 700

HOWARD, George W.; Capt; 1st MD Cav, Co C; res: How Cty; ref: 1, 2, 10, 19, 21, 23, 64, 68, 445, 511, 686, 748, 901, 1523, 1583

HOWARD, James; Lt Col; 18th & 20th VA Bn Heavy Arty; res: Balt; ref: 1, 19, 21, 23, 44, 56, 500, 511, 684, 700, 735, 753, 791, 1107, 1254, 1255, 1523, 1578, 1593, 1600

HOWARD, James McHenry (M.D.); Capt; Engineer Corps; res: Balt; ref: 1, 2, 18, 19, 21, 22, 23, 34, 35, 38, 44, 94, 154, 511, 583, 650, 685, 700, 735, 753, 791, 1523, 1533, 1541, 1577, 1578, 1579

HOWARD, John Eager of Charles; Capt; Asst Commissary of Supply, 2nd MD Inf; res: Balt; ref: 1, 2, 17, 18, 19, 21, 38, 44, 63, 64, 68, 511, 559, 638, 700, 753, 789, 1520, 1523, 1540, 1541, 1583

HOWARD, John Eager of James; pvt; 1st MD Cav, Co C; ref: 1, 2, 19, 21, 44, 735, 1523

HOWARD, McHenry; Capt; Asst I.G., staff of Gen G. H. Steuart, Jr.; res: Balt; ref: 1, 2, 17, 18, 19, 21, 23, 35, 38, 44, 53, 63, 65, 66, 70, 117, 126, 240, 469, 493, 500, 501, 503, 511, 602, 643, 650, 690, 700, 735, 753, 754, 791, 798, 828, 829, 906, 931, 944, 1058, 1255, 1519, 1523, 1541, 1577, 1579, 1638, 1647

HOWARD, Richard; 1st VA Cav, Co L; res: Har Cty; ref: 233, 976

HOWARD, Richard McG; pvt; 1st MD Cav, Co C; res: Monkton, Balt Cty; ref: 1, 2, 19, 21, 700, 1523, 1541

HOWARD, Robert; pvt; 1st MD Inf, Co I; ref: 1, 2, 21, 1523

HOWARD, Washington; pvt; Hampton Leg Lt Arty, Co B; res: Cha Cty; ref: 1, 2, 19, 21, 1523

HOWARD, William; pvt; 2nd MD Lt Arty; ref; 1, 2, 19, 21, 1523

HOWARD, William Key; Lt; 1st MD Inf, Co D; res: Balt; ref: 1, 2, 19, 21, 23, 44, 64, 240, 272, 456, 511, 559; 690, 693, 753, 1523, 1577

HOWELL, Charles L.; Lmn, Navy; C.S. Savannah; res: Balt; ref: 1, 19, 21, 58, 97, 700, 783, 1523

HOWELL, Gustvus; pvt; Hampton Leg Lt Arty, Co B; ref: 1, 2, 19, 21, 1523

HOWELL, Rodney C.; Lt; 35th VA Cav, Co B; res: Frd Cty; ref: 1, 3, 64, 1371

HOWELL, Thomas; pvt; Barry's Co, MD Vols; ref: 1, 19, 1523

HOXTON, Lywellyn Griffith; Lt Col; Chief of Arty, Gen W. J. Hardee's staff; res: Georgetown; ref: 1, 127, 791

HOXTON, William; Lt; Stewart's Horse Arty, Breathed's Battery; res: Annapolis, AA Cty; ref: 1, 70, 498, 791

HOY, F. J.; pvt; Davis's MD Cav, Co C; ref: 1

HOYE, James; pvt; MD Guerrilla Zouaves; res: St. Margarett, AA Cty; ref: ref: 1, 1539

HOYE, Samuel H.; pvt; 24th VA Inf, Co B; res: Cumberland, All Cty; ref: 1, 19, 65, 95, 148, 1523

HOYE, William D.; pvt; McNeill's Rangers; res: Deer Park, Ga Cty; ref: 1, 19, 65, 95, 148, 1010, 1523, 1310

HOYLE, George W.; pvt; 43rd VA Cav (Mosby's), Co D; res: Derwood, Mont Cty; ref; 1, 8, 70, 71, 86, 557, 735, 1574

HOYLE, Nathan L. S.; pvt; 1st MD Cav, Co D; res: Poolesville, Mont Cty; ref: 1, 2, 19, 21, 70, 71, 1523, 1552, 1601

HUBBALL, Bernary; pvt; Rhett's 1st SC Heavy Arty; res: Balt; ref: 1, 2, 19, 21, 735, 1523, 1575

HUBBARD, Alexander J.; Chief Musician; 1st MD Inf, Co A; res; Frd Cty; ref: 1, 2, 19, 21, 57, 89, 90, 92, 93, 513, 686, 700, 1523

HUBBARD, John A.; pvt; ref: 700

HUBBARD, John L.; pvt; 2nd MD Inf, Co F; res: Hagerstown, Wash Cty; ref: 1, 2, 19, 21, 1523

HUBBARD, William H.; pvt; 35th VA Cav, Co B; ref: 1, 1677

HUBBARD, William L.; pvt; 2nd MD Inf, Co A; res: Balt; ref: 1, 2, 19, 21, 259, 650, 1523

HUBER, Paul; pvt; 4th MD Lt Arty; ref: 1, 2, 19, 21, 1523

HUCHT, Albert; pvt; MD American Rifles; ref: 1, 2, 19, 21

HUCORN, John F.; pvt; 1st MD Cav, Co B; res: Broad Creek, QA Cty; ref; 1, 2, 19, 21, 785, 1523, 1554

HUDDLE, John; pvt; Davis's MD Cav, Co A; ref: 1, 735

HUDGINS, Charles H.; Lt; 24th VA Cav, Co E; res: Balt; MLCSH; ref: 1, 21, 57, 700, 730, 735, 786, 1523

HUDGINS, Ezekiel L.; pvt; Navy; Local Defense Naval Bn; ref: 1, 70

HUDSON, Isham; pvt; 1st SC Inf, Co G; ref: 1

HUDSON, John D.; pvt; 7th VA Cav, Co G; ref: 1

HUDSON, John J.; pvt; 19th VA Heavy Arty, Co C; res: Balt; ref; 1, 1580, 1599

HUDSON, Louis; pvt; MD Guerrilla Zouaves; ref: 1

HUDSON, Samuel Sylvester; pvt; 2nd VA Inf, Co B; res: Mont Cty; MLCSH; ref: 1, 627, 700, 786

HUDSON, T. J.; pvt; 1st SC Inf, Co G; ref: 1

HUFFINGTON, John; pvt; 2nd MD Inf, Co F; res: Barren Creek Springs, Som Cty; ref: 1, 2, 19, 21, 1523, 1556

HUGER, Eustis; Lt; Aid de Camp, Gen B. Huger's staff; res: Balt; ref: 1, 631

HUGHBUCK, J. T.; pvt; 47th VA Inf, Co H; ref: 1

HUGHES, Alexander; pvt; 2nd MD Inf, Co A; ref: 1, 2, 19, 21, 650, 1523

HUGHES, Alfred (M.D.); Physician, Medical Corps; res: Balt; ref: 1, 18, 685

HUGHES, Evan R.; pvt; 7th VA Cav, Co G; res: Ellicott City, How Cty; ref: 1, 3, 10, 19, 1550

HUGHES, G. N.; pvt; 17th VA Regulars, Co K; res: Balt; ref: 21, 700

HUGHES, James Fritz (M.D); Asst Surg; General Hospital No. 24, Richmond; ref: 1, 18, 1534, 1690

HUGHES, James O.; pvt; 43rd GA Inf, Co F; ref: 1, 2, 19, 21, 160, 726, 1523

HUGHES, Jonathan; pvt; 14th VA Inf, Co K; res: Balt; ref: 1, 1540

HUGHES, Maxey; pvt; Davis's MD Cav, Co B; res: West River; ref: 1, 19, 1523, 1539

HUGHES, Patrick; pvt; 1st MD Inf, Co G; ref: 1, 2, 19, 21, 1523

HUGHES, William Jasper Skaife; pvt; 5th VA Cav, Co A; res: Cratchers Ferry, Dor Cty; ref: 1, 70, 1547

HULL, George; 9th VA Cav,; ref: 1563

HULL, John; pvt; 21st VA Inf, Co B; res: Balt; ref: 1, 2, 19, 312, 592, 681, 1523

HULL, Napoleon B., Sr.; pvt; 14th VA Cav, Co H; res: Clearspring; ref: 1, 361

HULL, William; Capt; res: Balt; ref: 19

HULL, William Janney; pvt; 5th VA Cav; res: Balt; ref: 21, 107, 700

HUME, ---; 1st VA Cav, Co G; ref: 502, 735

HUME, Charles; pvt; Davis's MD Cav; ref: 1

HUME, Frank; pvt; 1st MD Cav, Co B; ref: 2, 19, 21, 1523
HUME, J. R. F.; pvt; 1st MD Cav, Co C; ref: 1, 2, 19, 21, 1523
HUMMER, Braden E.; pvt; 35th VA Cav, Co A; res: Darnestown, Mont Cty; ref: 1, 3, 1611, 1677
HUMMER, Joseph; pvt; 1st MD Cav, Co F; res: Balt; MLCSH; ref: 1, 2, 19, 21, 93, 700, 786, 1523
HUMPHREY, John T.; pvt; 1st MD Cav, Co E; ref: 1, 19, 730, 1523
HUMPHREY, T. G.; pvt; 1st SC Inf, Co G; ref: 1
HUMPHREYS, J. H.; pvt; Stuart's Horse Arty, Breathed's Battery; ref: 1
HUMPHREYS, Milton Wylie; sgt; King's Lt Arty; ref: 72
HUMPHREYS, Nelson; pvt; Davis's MD Cav; res: Balt; ref: 1, 1540
HUMPHREYS, Richard W.; pvt; Lucas' 15th SC Heavy Arty; ref: 1
HUMPSTONE, Robert G.; res: Mont Cty; ref; 86
HUNDLEY, William T.; pvt; 9th VA Inf, Co B; res: Balt; ref: 1, 1576
HUNGERFORD, Thomas W.; pvt; 47th VA Inf, Co C; PG Cty; ref: 1, 23, 677, 1622
HUNLEY, W. R. B.; Lt; Starkis's VA Lt Arty; ref: 1, 57, 70
HUNT, Austace; pvt; 19th VA Heavy Arty, Co C; ref: 1, 1580
HUNT, Charles William; pvt; 1st MD Cav, Co E; res: Friendship, AA Cty; ref: 1, 2, 19, 21, 1523, 1539
HUNTER, Alexander; Maj; Black Horse Cav; res: Silver Spring, Mont Cty; ref: 1105
HUNTER, Andrew; pvt; Stuart's Horse Arty, Breathed's Battery; ref: 1
HUNTER, Charles; Mast. M., Navy; C.S. Chicora; res: PG Cty; ref: 1, 19, 58, 97, 1523, 1564
HUNTER, Frederick (M.D.); Asst Surg; Pettigrew's Lt Arty; ref: 1, 2, 18, 21, 34, 700, 1523
HUNTER, Harry Warring; pvt; 19th VA Heavy Arty, Co C; ref: 1, 69, 316, 1580
HUNTER, Jacob; pvt; Lucas's 15th SC Heavy Arty, Co B; ref: 1, 7
HUNTER, James P.; pvt; 3rd MD Lt Arty; ref: 1, 2, 19, 21, 160, 726, 1523
HUNTER, John J.; pvt; 2nd MD Inf, Co A; res: Balt; ref; 1, 2, 19, 21, 23, 470, 650, 700, 1523
HUNTER, Joseph; Lmn, Navy; res: Balt; ref: 1
HUNTER, Robert; pvt; 2nd MD Lt Arty; ref: 1, 2, 19, 21, 1494, 1523
HUNTER, Robert W.; Maj; Asst A.G., Gen J. Gordon's staff; ref: 1, 23, 111, 677, 791
HUNTER, Thomas; sgt; 2nd VA Cav, Co A; res: Long Green, Bt Cty; MLCSH; ref: 1, 2, 19, 21, 627, 700, 786, 1523
HUNTER, Thomas T., Jr; passed Mast. M., Navy; C.S.S. Curlew; res: Rockville, Mont Cty; ref: 1, 19, 58, 61, 97, 1523, 1564
HUNTER, W.; pvt; 3rd MD Lt Arty; ref: 2, 21, 160, 726
HUNTER, William; Midn, Navy; C.S.S. Curlew; ref: 1, 19, 58, 61, 97, 279, 1523, 1564
HUNTINGTON, S.; pvt; 2nd MD Cav, Co C; ref: 1
HUPPMAN, Henry; pvt; 20th VA Cav, Co C; ref: 1, 735
HURD, Joseph; musician; 1st AL Inf, Co K; res: Wash Cty; ref; 1, 361
HURLEY, Abel; pvt; 2nd MD Inf, Co F; res: Drawbridge, Dor Cty; ref; 1, 2, 19, 21, 1523, 1547
HURLEY, Charles; pvt; 3rd MD Lt Arty; ref: 1, 2, 19, 21, 160, 726, 1263, 1523
HURLEY, Jobe; pvt; 2nd MD Inf, Co D; res: Drawbridge, Dor Cty; ref: 1, 2, 19, 21, 1523, 1547, 1666
HURLEY, Otho J.; pvt; 1st VA Cav, Co K; res: Hagerstown, Wash Cty; ref: 1, 2, 19, 21, 74, 1523, 1558
HURRY, John C.; pvt; 1st MD Lt Arty; ref: 1

HURST, E.; Lt; 2nd MD Cav, Co F; ref: 2, 11, 19, 21, 23, 194, 1523
HURST, Edward S; pvt; 43rd VA Cav (Mosby's), Co A; ref: 1, 8
HURST, Thomas F.; pvt; 2nd MD Cav, Co F; ref: 1
HURST, William; pvt; 2nd MD Lt Arty; res: Balt; ref: 1, 2, 19, 21, 1523
HURTT, Cornelius; ref: 93
HURTT, Henry N.; pvt; Zarvona's MD Zouaves; res: Balt; ref: 1, 21, 735, 1598
HUTCHINS, Joseph; pvt; 19th VA Heavy Arty, Co C; ref: 1, 2, 19, 21, 1523, 1580
HUTCHINSON, John T.; pvt; 2nd MD Inf, Co G; res: PG Cty; ref; 1, 2, 19, 21, 1523
HUTCHINSON, Joseph; pvt; Barry's Co, MD, Vols; ref: 1, 2, 19, 21, 1523
HUTCHINSON, Philip A.; pvt; 35th VA Cav, Co A; ref: 1, 1611, 1677
HUTCHINSON, Thomas; pvt; 1st MD Inf, Co F; ref: 1, 2, 19, 21, 1523
HUTCHISON, George C.; pvt; 35th VA Cav, Co A; ref: 1, 3, 1611, 1677
HUTTON, Charles C.; pvt; 1st MD Cav, Co A; res: Mont Cty; ref: 1, 2, 19, 21, 1523, 1574, 1621
HUTTON, S.; pvt; 3rd MD Lt Arty; ref: 2, 19, 21, 160, 726, 823, 1523
HYATT, Robert U.; pvt; 7th VA Cav, Co G; ref: 1, 316
HYDE, Jacob W.; pvt; Cav; died of wounds, Savannah GA; res: West River, AA Cty; ref: 19, 1523, 1539
HYDE, John Poisal (Revd); Chaplain; 2nd VA Inf; res: Annapolis, AA Cty; ref: 749, 1539
HYLAND, John G.; Lt; 2nd MD Inf, Co F; res: Som Cty; ref: 1, 2, 19, 21, 23, 64, 68, 685, 1523
HYLAND, Matthew; pvt; 1st SC Inf, Co G; res: Balt; ref: 1, 735
HYLTON, Solomon; cpl; 3rd MD Lt Arty; ref: 1, 2, 21, 23, 160, 461, 726, 1460, 1523
HYNES, Edward; pvt; 2nd MD Lt Arty; ref; 1, 2, 21, 1523
HYNSON, Medford; pvt; 2nd Palmetto Sharp Shooters, Co H; res: Still Pond, Kt Cty; ref: 1584
HYNSON, Nathaniel; ref: 86

IGLEHART, James I., Jr; pvt; 2nd MD Inf, Co A; res: Annapolis, AA Cty; ref: 2, 19, 21, 35, 259, 715, 1520, 1523, 1539
IGLEHART, William T.; Lt; 30th VA Sharpshooters, Co E; ref: 1, 2, 19, 21, 64, 70, 312, 681, 1523
IJAMS, Jacob W.; pvt; 1st NC Inf, Co B; res: Patuxent Forge, AA Cty; ref: 1, 1539
ILER, J. J.; pvt; 1st SC Inf, Co G; ref: 1
INGLEHART, Edward; pvt; 1st MD Inf, Co F; ref: 1, 2, 19, 21
INGLEHART, Osborn S. (M.D.); Passed Asst Surg, Navy; C.S.S. Gaines; res: Annapolis, AA Cty; ref: 1, 18, 58, 61, 279, 1539, 1564
INGLIS, John Henry; Midn, Navy; C.S.S. Palmetto States; res: Balt; ref: 70, 1564, 1598
IGNLIS, Lawrence Charles; cpl; 2nd SC Lt Arty, Co D; res: Balt; ref: 1, 70
INGRAHAM, Charles H.; pvt; 40th VA Inf, Co A; res: Balt; ref: 21, 700
INGRAHAM, Duncan N.; Capt, Navy; Commandant Charleston Station; ref: 1, 21, 97, 700, 1564
INGRAHAM, Pretiss; Col; Regimental Hdqtrs, Mississippi Dept; res: Easton, Tal Cty; ref: 1, 23, 677, 965
INGRAHAM, William H.; pvt; 20th AL Inf, Co I; res: Balt; ref: 1, 21, 700
INLOES, Alfred J.; pvt; 1st MD Inf, Co C; ref: 1, 2, 19, 21, 1523
INLOES, Charles E.; pvt; 1st MD Cav, Co C; res: Balt; ref: 1, 2, 7, 19, 21, 650, 1523
INLOES, William H.; pvt; 2nd MD Inf, Co B; res: Balt; ref: 1
IRVIN, David S.; pvt; 1st SC Inf, Co G;r ef: 1

IRVIN, John; pvt; 4th MD Lt Arty; ref: 1, 2, 19, 21, 1523
IRVIN, Michael; pvt; 2nd MD Lt Arty; ref: 1, 2, 19, 21, 1523
IRVINE, George W.; ymn, Navy; res: Balt; ref: 1
IRVINE, Jesse B.; pvt; VA Horse Arty, McGreggor's Battery; res: Balt; ref: 1, 21, 700
IRVING, James; pvt; Holbrook's Independent MD Lt Arty; res: Balt; ref: 93, 1523, 1540, 1613
IRVING, Joseph K.; 3rd VA Cav, Co G; ref: 1, 35
ISAACS, Joseph; pvt; 1st VA Cav, Co K; res: How Cty; ref: 1, 23
ISAACS, Thomas; pvt; Stuart's Horse Arty, Breathed's Battery; ref: 1
ISAACS, William E.; pvt; 1st MD Inf, Co G;r ef: 1, 2, 19, 21, 1523
ISHAM, J. H.; pvt; 3rd MD Lt Arty; ref: 2, 19, 21, 160, 461, 726, 1523
ISRAEL, G. P.; pvt; Lee's MD Lt Arty, Alexander's Bn; ref: 1, 2, 19, 21, 1523
IVES, Leoanrd W.; pvt; 2nd MD Inf, Co A; ref: 2, 19, 21, 259, 1523
IVEY, John P.; cpl; 9th VA Inf, Co B; ref: 1, 1576

JACKINS, William H.; pvt; 1st VA Cav, Co K; res: Balt; ref: 1, 2, 19, 21, 1523, 1540
JACKSON, Andrew J.; pvt; 1st MD Cav, Co A; ref: 1, 2, 19, 21, 1523
JACKSON, Charles Murry; Lt; Hood's Bn, Co C; res: Balt; ref: 21, 57, 513, 700, 791
JACKSON, Elijah; pvt; Davis's MD Cav; res: Millersville, AA Cty; ref: 1, 1539
JACKSON, E. J.; Capt; 22nd VA Inf, Co E; res: Balt; ref: 1, 21, 70, 700
JACKSON, Henry Inloes; pvt; 2nd MD Lt Arty; ref: 1, 2, 19, 21, 890, 1523
JACKSON, J. C.; pvt; 3rd MD Lt Arty; ref: 2, 19, 21, 160, 726, 1523
JACKSON, John W.; pvt; Prucell Battery; res: Laurel, PG Cty; ref: 21, 700
JACKSON, L. M.; pvt; 2nd MD Cav, Co B; ref: 1, 19, 1523, 1609
JACKSON, O.; pvt; 3rd MD Lt Arty; ref: 1, 2, 19, 21, 160, 726, 1523
JACKSON, Thomas Alphonse; Chief Engr, Navy; C.S. Florida; res: Rockville, Mont Cty; ref: 1, 1523, 1564
JACKSON, Thomas G.; pvt; 4th MD Lt Arty; ref: 1, 2, 19, 21, 1523
JACKSON, William; cpl; 43rd VA Cav (Mosby's), Co C; ref: 1, 8
JACOBS, Benjamin L.; Lt; Q.M. Dept; Army of Northern Virginia; ref: 1, 735
JACOBS, John H., Jr; pvt; 11th TX Inf, Co A; res: Millersville, AA Cty; ref: 1, 1539
JACOBS, Juliua E.; pvt; 6th VA Inf, Co H; res: Balt; ref: 1, 21, 700
JACOBS, Michael; pvt; Stuart's Horse Arty, Breathed's Battery; ref: 1, 1621
JACOBS, Richard J.; res: Patuxent Forge, AA Cty; ref: 1539
JACOBS, William H.; Capt Jacob's Mounted Riflemen; res: QA Cty; ref: 1, 789
JACGEN, Henry; res: Balt; ref: 1540
JAMES, Alfred Randolph; Lt; 28th VA Inf, Co E; res: Balt; ref: 1, 21, 93, 700, 1540
JAMES, Daniel; pvt; Lee's MD Cav; res: Annapolis, AA Cty; ref: 1, 1539
JAMES, Edwin; q.m. sgt; 1st VA Inf, Co H; res: Wash Cty; MLCSH; ref: 1, 2, 19, 21, 23, 64, 470, 627, 700, 786, 1523
JAMES, George W. B. E. S.; pvt; Davis's MD Cav, Co A; res: Balt; ref: 1, 11, 19, 735, 1523, 1609
JAMES, J. W.; pvt; MD American Rifles; ref: 1
JAMES, James P.; pvt; 1st VA Cav, Co K; ref: 1, 2, 19, 21, 1523
JAMES, John Claiborne; pvt; 4th VA Cav, Co F; res: Balt; ref: 1, 70

JAMES, Neal; bsn, Navy; C.S. Charleston; res: Bt Cty; ref: 1, 1541
JAMES, R.; pvt; 1st MD Inf, Co A; ref: 1, 1523
JAMES, Thomas; pvt; Lee's MD Cav; res: Annapolis, AA Cty; ref: 1, 1539
JAMES, Titus R.; pvt; 1st SC Inf, Co G; ref: 1
JAMES, Walter; pvt; 2nd MD Cav, Co A; ref: 1
JAMES, William H. H.; pvt; Lucas' 15th SC Heavy Arty; ref: 1
JAMESTON, S.; ref: 141
JAMISON, Frank A.; pvt; 1st VA Cav, Co K; ref: 1, 2, 19, 21, 1523
JANNEY, John W.; pvt; 54th VA Inf, Co H; res: East River Landing, AA Cty; ref: 1, 1539
JANNOK, J. H.; 13th GA, Co D; ref: 92
JARBOE, Charles; G. T.; pvt; 9th VA Inf, Co B; res: Old Fields, PG Cty; ref: 1, 735, 1553, 1576
JARBOE, George Benedict; 1st VA Inf, Co E; ref: Carr Cty; ref: 1, 19, 21, 23, 700, 735, 1523
JARBOE, Samuel; pvt; 35th VA Cav, Co B; res: Poolesville, Mont Cty; ref: 1611, 1677
JARBOE, Thomas W.; pvt; 9th VA Inf, Co B; ref: 1, 643, 1576
JARBOE, William Alfred; pvt; 43rd VA Cav (Mosby's), Co D; res: Carr Cty; MLCSH; ref: 1, 8, 627, 700, 786
JARBOE, William S.; pvt; 1st MD Cav, Co E; res: PG Cty; ref: 1, 2, 19, 21, 730, 1523
JARNER, John; pvt; Zarvona's MD Zouaves; ref: 735
JARRETT, Martin L.; Acting Asst Surg; 1st MD Cav; res: Jarrettsville, Har Cty; ref: 1, 18, 511, 720
JARVIS, Thomas W.; pvt; 19th Heavy Arty, Co E; ref: 1, 70, 677, 1580
JARVIS, William S.; pvt; Armistead's VA Lt Arty; ref: 1, 700
JEFFERS, Thomas Anderson; Lt; 2nd SC Cav, Co B; res: Balt; MLCSH; ref: 1, 627, 700, 786
JEFFERS, William H.; pvt; 1st MD Cav, Co B; res: Kent Island, QA Cty; ref: 1, 2, 19, 21, 700, 785, 1523, 1554
JEFFERSON, Thomas H.; pvt; Edelin's MD Bn; res: Annapolis, AA Cty; ref: 1, 1539
JEFFERSON, Warren; pvt; 2nd MD Cav, Co A; ref: 1
JENIFER, Walter Hanson; Col; 8th VA Cav; res: St. M. Cty; ref: 1, 19, 23, 29, 34, 70, 110, 137, 154, 289, 361, 371, 518, 791, 1002, 1520, 1523, 1600
JENKINS, A. Poland; pvt; 1st MD CAv, Co C; res: Balt; ref: 1, 2, 19, 21, 23, 511, 1523, 1578
JENKINS, Asa; pvt; 2nd VA Inf, Co E; res: Balt; ref: 1, 70, 511
JENKINS, David W.; pvt; 2nd MD Cav, Co D; ref: 1
JENKINS, E. D.; pvt; 1st VA Cav, Co K; ref: 1, 2, 19, 21, 1523
JENKINS, Edward Courtney, Jr; Flag Officer's Secretary, Navy; Jackson Naval Station; res: Balt; ref: 1, 2, 19, 69, 312, 316, 511, 592, 685, 690, 735, 1523, 1564
JENKINS, George Carroll; Capt; Q.M., Gen L. L. Lomax's Staff; res: Balt; ref: 1, 2, 21, 23, 53, 56, 69, 91, 316, 469, 511, 700, 798, 1461, 1520, 1523, 1579, 1599
JENKINS, George Taylor, Jr; pvt; Holbrook's Independent MD Lt Arty; res: Balt; ref: 1, 1540
JENKINS, Henry; Lt; Wood's MO Bn Cav, Co C; res: Sykesville, Carr Cty; ref: 1, 2, 19, 21, 511, 677, 700, 735, 1523
JENKINS, James E.; pvt; 2nd MD Inf, Co B; ref: 1, 2, 19, 21, 1523
JENKINS, James Wilcox, Jr; pvt; 1st MD Cav, Co E; res: Balt; ref: 1, 2, 19, 21, 69, 316, 511, 685, 700, 730, 976, 1523, 1540, 1577

JENKINS, John Carroll; pvt; 21st VA Inf, Co B; res: Balt; ref: 2, 23, 93, 312, 511, 592, 690, 1540
JENKINS, John E.; pvt; 1st MD Inf, Co I; ref: 1, 2, 19, 21, 1523
JENKINS, John W.; sgt; 9th VA Inf, Co B; ref: 1, 1576
JENKINS, John Z.; pvt; 1st MD Lt Arty; res: PG Cty; ref: 1, 2, 19, 21, 70, 470, 511, 1523
JENKINS, Lewis B.; sgt; 9th VA Inf, Co B; res: PG Cty; ref: 1, 1553, 1576, 1622
JENKINS, Louis William; pvt; 1st MD Lt Arty; res: Balt; ref: 1, 2, 19, 21, 34, 69, 316, 511, 687, 1523
JENKINS, Oliver L.; Acting Mast. M., Navy; C. S. Raleigh; res: Balt; ref: 1, 19, 58, 97, 511, 1523, 1564
JENKINS, Samuel; pvt; 35th VA Cav, Co A; res: Frd Cty; ref: 3, 15, 90, 511, 735, 1611, 1677
JENKINS, Samuel; pvt; Davis's MD Cav; res: Annapolis, AA Cty; ref: 1, 1539
JENKINS, Simeon Tazwell; Lt; 47th GA Inf, Co B; res: Balt; ref: 1, 21, 511, 700
JENKINS, Theodore Robert, Jr; cpl; 21st VA Inf, Co B; res: Laurel, PG Cty; ref: 1, 2, 19, 21, 34, 69, 74, 312, 316, 511, 687, 735, 823, 1523, 1553
JENKINS, Thomas; pvt; Stuart's Horse Arty, Breathed's Battery; ref: 1, 498
JENKINS, W. W.; pvt; 2nd MD Cav, Co C; res: Bt Cty; ref: 1, 1541
JENKINS, William; sgt; 1st MD Inf, Co D; res: Har Cty; MLCSH; ref: 1, 2, 19, 21, 23, 69, 316, 511, 786, 1523
JENKINS William Kennedy; pvt; 1st MD Lt Arty; res: Balt; ref: 1, 2, 19, 21, 69, 316, 511, 700, 823, 1523, 1540
JENNINGS, Benjamin Rush (D.D.S.); pvt; Lt; Dental Corps; res: Balt; MLCSH; ref: 1, 2, 19, 21, 93, 627, 650, 700, 746, 786, 1053, 1523
JENNINGS, Henry T.; Lt; 5th GA Inf, Co K; ref: 1, 70
JENNINGS, Jacob Mead; Caplain; 3rd AL Inf; res: Balt; ref: 1, 1185
JENNINGS, Matthew; pvt; 43rd VA Cav (Mosby's), Co F; ref: 1, 8
JENNINGS, Samuel; 8th GA Inf, ref: 735
JESSUP, William; res: Balt; ref: 1540
JESTER, William; 2nd MD Cav, Co D; res: Church Creek, Dor Cty; ref; 93, 1547
JETER, Reuben T.; pvt; 47th VA Inf, Co H; ref: 1
JETT, John; ref: 93
JIMISON, John W.; pvt; Stuart's Horse Arty, Breathed's Battery; ref: 1
JNELL, Joseph; res: Annapolis, AA Cty; ref; 1539
JOBE, Richard M.; pvt; 5th VA Inf, Co A; res: Balt; ref: 21, 23, 700
JOHNEES, Benjamin; pvt; Zarvona's MD Zouaves; res: Bristol, AA Cty; ref: 1, 1539
JOHANNES, Martin J.; pvt; 17th VA Inf, Co C; res: Balt; ref: 1, 2, 19, 21, 142, 1523
JOHNS, Edward W.; Asst Surg; ref: 1, 19
JOHNS, John; Lt; Aid de Camp, Gen B. Huger's staff; res: Balt; ref: 1, 70
JOHNSON, Alfred C.; cpl; 1st VA Inf, Co E; ref: 1
JOHNSON, Andrew; smn, Navy; C.S. Palmetto State; res: Balt; ref: 1
JOHNSON, Anthony; pvt; 2nd MD Cav, Co B; ref: 1
JOHNSON, B. C.; pvt; 1st VA Inf, Co E; ref: 735
JOHNSON, Bartlett Shipp; Midn, Navy; C.S.S. Virginia; ref: 1, 21, 22, 44, 58, 70, 97, 700, 727, 783, 869, 873, 915, 918, 1564
JOHNSON, Benjamin F.; pvt; 2nd MD Cav, Co B; ref: 1
JOHNSON, Bradley Tyler; Brig Gen, Army of Northern Virginia; res:

Frederick, Frd Cty; ref: 1, 2, 7, 11, 13, 15, 17, 18, 19, 21, 23, 24, 25, 29, 34, 35, 38, 39, 40, 42, 44, 45, 46, 47, 48, 50, 53, 54, 62, 63, 64, 66, 68, 70, 82, 88, 89, 90, 91, 93, 94, 96, 102, 103, 105, 107, 110, 113, 117, 125, 126, 127, 129, 130, 131, 140, 150, 159, 165, 169, 171, 173, 194, 209, 211, 215, 222, 233, 240, 272, 290, 320, 330, 347, 349, 361, 371, 380, 385, 386, 389, 403, 408, 409, 422, 431, 443, 448, 455, 456, 457, 459, 462, 463, 464, 465, 466, 467, 469, 481, 485, 488, 492, 493, 494, 496, 501, 502, 503, 507, 509, 511, 512, 515, 517, 530, 541, 559, 560, 583, 595, 601, 602, 603, 614, 631, 638, 643, 674, 684, 686, 689, 700, 738, 746, 748, 753, 757, 778, 787, 789, 790, 791, 794, 806, 821, 822, 825, 827, 829, 838, 839, 840, 841, 843, 849, 857, 866, 881, 882, 893, 896, 906, 914, 923, 928, 931, 941, 950, 990, 1006, 1053, 1072, 1095, 1110, 1178, 1258, 1282, 1303, 1323, 1339, 1347, 1374, 1378, 1398, 1436, 1447, 1470, 1483, 1486, 1487, 1494, 1511, 1519, 1520, 1523, 1560, 1562, 1563, 1565, 1572, 1577, 1578, 1579, 1582, 1584, 1588, 1605, 1607, 1608, 1609, 1616, 1619, 1620, 1623, 1624, 1627, 1631, 1634, 1636, 1642, 1644

JOHNSON, Charles W.; pvt; 2nd MD Lt Arty; ref: 1

JOHNSON, D. W.; pvt; 3rd MD Lt Arty; ref: 1, 2, 19, 21, 160, 511, 726

JOHNSON, Edward; pvt; 9th VA Inf, Co B; res: Annapolis, AA Cty; ref: 1, 1539, 1576

JOHNSON, Edward C.; q.m. sgt; 1st MD Cav; res: Balt; ref: 1, 2, 8, 19, 21, 23, 44, 68, 69, 94, 240, 316, 511, 650, 740, 1037, 1523, 1540

JOHNSON, F. N.; pvt; Stuart's Horse Arty, Breathed's Battery; ref: 1, 498

JOHNSON, G. M.; pvt; 2nd MD Lt Arty; ref; 1

JOHNSON, George; pvt; 1st MD Cav, Co F; ref; 1, 2, 19, 21, 827, 1523

JOHNSON, George W.; pvt; 3rd MD Lt Arty; ref: 1, 2, 19, 21, 160, 511, 726, 1523

JOHNSON, Henry B.; pvt; 1st SC Inf, Co G; ref: 1, 2, 19, 21, 1523

JOHNSON, J. Newman; pvt; 1st MD Cav, Co A; res: Urbana, Frd Cty; ref: 1, 2, 19, 21, 90, 643, 1487, 1523

JOHNSON, J. W.; pvt; 3rd MD Lt Arty; ref: 1, 2, 19, 21, 160, 511, 700, 726, 1523

JOHNSON, James; pvt; 43rd VA Cav (Mosby's), Co G; ref: 1, 8, 735

JOHNSON, James K.; lmn, Navy; prize steamer Hope; res: Balt; ref: 1

JOHNSON, James Thomas, Jr (M.D.); Asst Surg, Medical Purveyor, Charlotte NC; res: Urbana, Frd Cty; ref: 1, 18, 90, 1534, 1536

JOHNSON, John; pvt; 1st MD Cav, Co F; ref: 1, 2, 19, 21

JOHNSON, John; pvt; 2nd MD Inf, Co D; ref: Annapolis, AA Cty; ref: 1, 2, 19, 21, 1523, 1539

JOHNSON, John J.; pvt; 1st MD Cav, Co F; ref: 1, 2, 19, 21

JOHNSON, John N.; pvt; 1st MD Cav, Co A; res: Balt; ref: 1, 2, 18, 19, 21, 1523, 1540

JOHNSON, John Q. A.; pvt; 1st VA Cav, Co K; ref: 2, 19, 21, 1523

JOHNSON, John R.; pvt; 9th VA Inf, Co B; ref: 1, 1576

JOHNSON, John W.; pvt; Norfolk Lt Arty Blues; res: Balt; ref: 1, 21, 55

JOHNSON, John W.; pvt; 1st MD Inf, Co C; ref: 2, 21, 1523

JOHNSON, Joshua; pvt; 9th VA Inf, Co B; res: Balt; ref: 1, 1576, 1598

JOHNSON, Meredith B. (M.D.); Surg; ref: 1, 2, 1494

JOHNSON, O. M.; pvt; 2nd MD Lt Arty; ref: 2, 19, 21, 511, 1494, 1523

JOHNSON, Oliver Perry; Capt; 32nd VA Inf, Co F; res: Lakesville, Dor Cty; ref: 1, 21, 700, 1547

JOHNSON, Osborn; pvt; Zarvona's MD Zouaves; res: Patuxent, AA Cty; ref: 1, 1539
JOHNSON, Otis; Lt; 1st MD Cav, Co A; res: Urbana, Frd Cty; ref: 1, 2, 18, 19, 21, 23, 90, 511, 643, 1523, 1634
JOHNSON, Philip Preston; Maj; Stuart's Horse Arty; ref: 1, 11, 19, 24, 45, 46, 113, 498, 791, 890, 1523, 1600
JOHNSON, R.; res: Johnsons Store, AA Cty; ref: 1539
JOHNSON, Richard Potts (M.D.); Surg; MD Line; res: Frederick, Frd Cty; ref: 1, 2, 18, 21, 38, 44, 72, 90, 240, 456, 511, 643, 923, 1520, 1634
JOHNSON, Rizin; pvt; 31st NC Inf, Co D; res: Millersville, AA Cty; ref: 1, 1539
JOHNSON, Robert; pvt; 1st SC Inf, Co G; ref: 1
JOHNSON, S.; pvt; 3rd MD Lt Arty; ref: 2, 19, 21, 160, 511, 726, 1523
JOHNSON, Stephen; pvt; 3rd MD Lt Arty; res: Annapolis, AA Cty; ref: 1, 2, 19, 21, 160, 511, 726, 1539, 1628
JOHNSON, Thomas C.; pvt; 9th VA Inf, Co B; res: Balt; ref: 1, 1576, 1613
JOHNSON, Thomas Somerville; pvt; 2nd MD Lt Arty; res: Balt; MLCSH; ref: 1, 2, 19, 21, 50, 93, 511, 627, 700, 786, 1523
JOHNSON, W. E.; pvt; Davis's MD Cav, Co A; ref: 1, 19, 1523
JOHNSON, William; cpl; 1st SC Inf, Co G; res: Chaptico, St. M. Cty; ref: 1, 1555
JOHNSON, William; Lt; 33rd VA Inf, Co A; res: All Cty; ref: 1, 145
JOHNSON, William H.; pvt; 19th VA Heavy Arty, Co C; ref: 1, 19, 1580
JOHNSON, William H.; pvt; 1st GA Inf, Co H; res: Balt; ref: 21, 57, 72, 469, 700
JOHNSON, William Hilleary (M.D.); Asst Surg; Missouri State Guards; res: Adamstown, Frd Cty; ref: 1, 18, 67, 90, 735, 891, 930
JOHNSON, William N.; pvt; MD Guerrilla Zouaves; res: Johnsons Store, AA Cty; ref: 1, 1539
JOHNSON, William P.; pvt; 1st MD Cav, Co E; res: East New Market, Dor Cty; ref: 1, 2, 19, 21, 730, 1523, 1547
JOHNSON, Zachariah T.; pvt; 9th VA Inf, Co B; res: Johnson Store, AA Cty; ref: 1, 1539, 1576
JOHNSTON, Charles W.; pvt; Goods Co, TX Lt Arty Battery; res: Hagerstown, Wash Cty; MLCSH; ref: 700, 735, 786
JOHNSTON, Elliott; Maj; Asst A.G., Gen R. Ewell's staff; res: Balt; ref: 1, 42, 63, 68, 70, 685, 735, 791, 1540, 1578
JOHNSTON, Henry E.; res: Balt; ref: 70
JOHNSTON, John J.; gun, Navy; Richmond Naval Station; res: Balt; MLCSH; ref: 1, 2, 19, 21, 93, 627, 786
JOHNSTON, John R.; pvt; 1st MD Inf, Co E; ref: 1, 2, 19, 21
JOHNSTON, Malcolm H.; cpl; 27th GA Inf, Co A; res: Balt; ref: 1, 70
JOHNSTON, Philip; pvt; 1st MD Inf, Co C; ref: 1, 2, 19, 21, 1523
JOHNSTON, Richard Malcolm; Col; GA Militia; res: Balt; ref: 70, 126, 791
JOHNSTON, Robert W.; sgt; Davis's MD Cav, Co C; res: Frederick, Frd Cty; ref: 1, 89
JONE, Roby C.; res: Tal Cty; ref: 645
JONE, William G.; pvt; 1st MD Cav, Co C; ref: 1, 2, 19, 21
JONES, A. H.; pvt; 43rd VA Cav (Mosby's), Co F; ref: 8, 19
JONES, Albert; Lt; Aid de Camp, Gen B. T. Johnson's staff; res: Mt. Airy, Carr Cty; ref: 1, 2, 19, 21, 23, 40, 70, 90, 511, 700, 1523, 1601
JONES, Albert J.; pvt; 47th VA Inf, Co H; ref: 1

JONES, Benjamin John; pvt; 35th VA Cav, Co B; res: Barnesville, Mont Cty; ref: 1, 3, 72, 73, 74, 86, 106, 1552, 1611, 1677
JONES, Burkley; pvt; Zarvona's MD Zouaves; res: Annapolis, AA Cty; ref: 1, 1539
JONES, Courtney A.; pvt; Jacobs Mounted Riflemen; res: Balt; ref; 1, 2, 19, 21, 160, 511, 726, 1523, 1540
JONES, Charles Tiberghein; pvt; 3rd VA Richmond Defense; res: Balt; MLCSH; ref: 93, 627, 700, 786
JONES, Custis; pvt; Richmond Departmental Inf Bn; res: Balt; ref: 30
JONES, Edward L.; pvt; 1st MD Cav, Co D; res: Libertytown, Frd Cty; ref: MLCSH; ref: 1, 2, 19, 21, 90, 511, 700, 786, 1301, 1523, 1601
JONES, Edwin J.; res: Patuxent Forge, AA Cty; ref: 1539
JONES, Edwin P.; pvt; 23rd VA Cav, Co F; res: PG Cty; ref: 23, 677
JONES, F. J.; pvt; 43rd VA Cav (Mosby's), Co E; ref: 8
JONES, Francis Buckner; Maj; 2nd VA Inf; res: Frd Cty; ref: 1, 44, 791, 1519
JONES, Frank H.; Col; 2nd AL Inf; res: Dor Cty; ref: 19, 112, 1523
JONES, George; pvt; 3rd MD Lt Arty; ref: 1, 21, 160, 511, 1523
JONES, George W.; pvt; 18th VA Cav, Co H; res: Friendship, AA Cty; MLCSH; ref: 1, 2, 19, 21, 70, 93, 700, 727, 786, 1523, 1539, 1620
JONES, Griffith; smn, Navy; res: Balt; ref: 1
JONES, Henry M. (M.D.); Asst Surg; Trans Mississippi Dept; ref: 1, 18, 1690
JONES, Henry W.; pvt; Davis's MD Cav, Co B; res: Tobaccostick, Dor Cty; ref: 1, 19, 1523, 1547
JONES, J. W.; pvt; Edelin's MD Heavy Arty; ref: 1
JONES, James E.; sgt; Parker's VA Lt Arty Battery; res: Balt; ref: 1, 1595
JONES, John; lmn, Navy; Richmond Naval Station; res: Frederick, Frd Cty; ref: 1, 72
JONES, John; pvt; Berry's Co MD Vols; res: West River, AA Cty; ref: 1, 1539
JONES, John; pvt; 1st MD Cav, Co A; ref: 1, 2, 19, 21, 1523, 1634
JONES, John; pvt; 1st MD Cav, Co B; res: PG Cty; ref: 1, 2, 21, 785
JONES, John H. C.; pvt; 3rd MD Lt Arty; res: Church Creek, Dor Cty; ref: 1, 1547
JONES, John T.; sgt; 2nd MD Cav, Co C; ref: 1, 2, 19, 21
JONES, John W.; pvt; MD Line; ref: 1
JONES, Joseph A.; Texas Rangers, Co F; ref: 685
JONES, M. M.; 13th MS, Co E; ref: 92
JONES, Pembroke B.; cpl; 1st MD Cav, Co B; res: Beltsville, PG Cty; ref: 1, 2, 19, 21, 23, 785, 1523, 1553, 1622
JONES, R. Emmett; Lt; 10th FL Inf, Co A; ref: 1, 631
JONES, Richard T.; pvt; Davis's MD Cav; res: Annapolis, AA Cty; ref: 1, 1539
JONES, Robert; pvt; MD American Rifles; res: Mont Cty; ref: 1, 735
JONES, Robert; pvt; 4th MD Lt Arty; res: Tal Cty; ref: 2, 19, 511, 1523
JONES, Robert Chew; 2nd MD Inf, Co B; res: QA Cty; ref: 70, 148, 511, 631, 1523
JONES, Robert H.; pvt; 1st MD Cav, Co E; res: Som Cty; ref: 1, 2, 21, 730, 1523
JONES, Samuel; pvt; Barry's Co, MD Vols; ref: 1
JONES, Samuel; pvt; 3rd MD Lt Arty; res: Annapolis, AA Cty; ref: 1, 2, 19, 21, 160, 511, 726, 1539
JONES, Spencer Cone; pvt; 1st MD Cav, Co D; res: Frederick, Frd Cty; ref: 1, 2, 19, 21, 23, 73, 86, 88, 90, 222, 469, 511, 700, 718, 789, 825, 885, 1001, 1520, 1523, 1574, 1601

JONES, Thomas; pvt; 2nd MD Cav, Co C; res: Frd Cty; ref: 1, 233
JONES, Thomas; pvt; Richmond Departmental Inf Bn; res: Balt; ref: 30
JONES, Thomas A., Chief Agent, Secret Service in Maryland; res: La Plata, Cha Cty; MLCSH; ref: 2, 19, 21, 92, 125, 132, 431, 700, 786, 1482, 1523, 1560, 1608, 1654, 1662
JONES, Thomas A.; pvt; Davis's MD Cav, Co C; ref: 1, 735
JONES, Thomas H.; cpl; 3rd MD Lt Arty; ref: 1, 2, 19, 21, 23, 160, 461, 511, 726, 1523
JONES, W.; pvt; Davis's MD Cav, Co A; ref: 1
JONES, W. J. W.; pvt; 3rd MD Lt Arty; res: Tobaccostick, Dor Cty; ref: 1, 2, 19, 21, 160, 511, 726, 1523, 1547
JONES, William; pvt; Lee's MD Cav; res: Patuxent Forge, CA Cty; ref: 1, 1539
JONES, William; pvt; 2nd MD Lt Arty; ref: 1, 2, 19, 21, 511, 1523
JONES, William; pvt; 23rd MD Lt Arty; res: Balt; ref: 1, 2, 19, 21, 160, 511, 690, 726, 1523
JONES, William F.; Asst Engr, Navy; C.S.S. Patrick Henry; ref: 21, 97, 700, 1564
JONES, William G.; pvt; 1st MD Cav, Co C; ref: 1, 2, 19, 21
JORDAN, George; pvt; Jacob's Mounted Rifles; res: Balt; ref: 1, 735, 1599, 1613
JORDON, B.; pvt; 3rd MD Lt Arty; ref: 2, 19, 21, 160, 726, 1523
JORDON, John R.; Chief Engr, Navy; C.S. Huntsville; ref: 21, 97, 700, 783, 1564
JORDON, S. B.; sgt Maj; 27th NC Inf; ref: 735
JOY, James E.; pvt; 2nd MD Inf, Co B; res: Great Mills, St. M. Cty; ref: 1, 2, 19, 21, 141, 1509, 1523, 1555, 1627, 1662
JOYNER, Jeremiah E.; pvt; 9th VA Inf, Co B; ref: 1, 1576
JOYNES, Levin Smith (M.D.); Asst Surg; Virginia State Troops; rs: Balt; ref: 1, 18, 1534, 1536
JUDGE, Edward S.; pvt; 2nd MD Inf, Co C; res: Balt; ref: 1, 2, 19, 21, 64, 700, 1001, 1523
JUDGE, John M.; pvt; 1st VA Inf, Co E; res: Cha Cty; ref: 1, 735
JUMP, Charles M.; pvt; 1st MD Cav, Co E; res: QA Cty; ref: 1, 2, 19, 21, 730, 1523
JUNGER, John H.; pvt; 2nd MD Inf, Co B; ref: 2, 19, 21, 1523

KAELCHER, John; pvt; 1st VA Inf; ref: 21, 700
KAGLEMAN, H.; pvt; 1st SC Inf, Co G; res: Balt; ref: 735
KAHLER, Adam; pvt; 7th VA Cav, Co G; res: 1
KAHLER, Charles Porterfield; pvt; 2nd MD Cav, Co E; res: Bt Cty; ref: 1, 2, 19, 21, 1523, 1609
KAMLEL, William; res: Balt; ref; 1540
KANE, Bernard; pvt; 2nd MD Inf, Co D; res: Balt; ref; 1, 2, 19, 21, 1523
KANE, George Proctor; Col; MD Line, Inspector, Gen B.T. Johnson's staff; res: Balt; ref: 2, 17, 18, 23, 25, 88, 96, 110, 125, 132, 349, 350, 386, 431, 438, 490, 494, 515, 558, 559, 606, 614, 616, 631, 655, 658, 678, 685, 689, 693, 776, 781, 791, 826, 1446, 1494, 1523, 1560, 1562, 1638, 1654
KANE, James C.; pvt; 43rd VA Cav (Mosby's), Co D; res: Balt; ref: 1, 2, 8, 19, 21, 257, 258, 498, 1523, 1578, 1579
KANE, Jeremiah; pvt; Davis's MD Cav; ref: 1
KANE, John C.; pvt; 43rd VA Cav (Mosby's), Co D; ref: 8, 257, 498, 1578, 1579
KANE, Thomas; pvt; Rhett's 1st SC Heavy Arty; res: Balt; ref: 1, 735

KANOUFE, George W.; 1st MD Cav, Co D; res: Licksville, Frd Cty; ref: 90

KARL, Charles; pvt; 1st SC Inf, Co G; res: Balt; ref: 735

KARNES, Benjamin; sgt Maj; Carpenter's Co, VA Lt Arty; ref: 1, 34

KARNES, Peter; res: Annapolis; ref: 1539

KARNEY, Michael S.; cpl; 9th VA Inf, Co B; ref: 1, 1576

KASTEN, Charles A.; sgt; Zarvona's MD Zaouaves; ref: 1, 735

KATING, George P.; pvt; Davis's MD Cav, Co B; ref: 1

KAUFFMAN, Carl; pvt; 39th VA Cav, Co B; res: Frd Cty; ref; 1, 2, 19, 21, 94, 1523

KAUFFMAN, Jacob; pvt; 1st SC Inf, Co G; ref: 1

KAULIMBUC, James; Letcher's Battery, VA Lt Arty; ref: 735

KAVALIDGE, John A.; pvt; 1st MD Inf, Co B; ref: 1, 2, 21

KEARNEY, ---; Lt; 2nd MD Cav, Co B; ref: 11

KEARNS, John; Navy; New Orleans, Naval Station; res: South River, AA Cty; ref: 1, 1539

KEATING, Edward; pvt; 1st MD Cav, Co E; ref: 1, 2, 19, 21, 730, 1523

KEATING, George P.; pvt; MD Guerrilla Zouaves; ref: 1, 693, 1523

KEATING, James E.; pvt; LA Washington Lt Arty; res: Balt; ref: 21, 700

KEATS, John Thomas (M.D.); Acting Asst Surg; 1st MD Cav; res: QA Cty; MLCSH; ref: 1, 2, 18, 21, 93, 627, 700, 785, 786, 1523

KEBAUGH, William; pvt; 1st VA Cav, Co K; ref: 2, 21, 1523

KECHBERGER, Albert; pvt; 1st MD Cav, Co C; ref: 1, 19, 1523

KEDGELY, John; pvt; 1st MD Inf, Co D; ref: 1, 2, 19, 21, 1523

KEECH, Chilton A.; pvt; 3rd VA Cav, Co J; ref: St. M. Cty; MLCSH; ref: 1, 21, 93, 700, 735, 786, 1627

KEECH, James F.; pvt; 2nd MD Inf, Co B; res: Charlotte Hall, St. M. Cty; ref: 1, 2, 19, 21, 1509, 1523, 1555

KEECH, Shelton A.; pvt; 21st VA Inf, Co B; res: Cha Cty; ref: 2, 312, 1523, 1670

KEELAN, John, Jr; pvt; Barry's Co MD Vols; res: Balt; ref: 1, 1540

KEELING, E. D.; pvt; 3rd MD Lt Arty; ref: 1

KEELING, Edward; pvt; 13th VA Inf, Co G; res: Balt; ref: 1, 735

KEELING, John L.; pvt; Norfolk Lt Arty Blues; res: Balt; ref: 1, 21, 93, 700

KEEMAN, Henry; pvt; 13th VA Inf, Co G; res: Balt; ref: 735, 1540

KEENAN, Patrick; cpl; 2nd MD Inf, Co H; ref: 1, 2, 19, 21, 23, 1523

KEENE, Robert Goldsborough; pvt; 1st VA Cav, Co K; res: Balt; ref: 1, 2, 19, 21, 23, 56, 700, 881, 1519, 1523

KEENE, W. H.; pvt; 1st MD Inf, Co A; ref: 1, 1523

KEEPERS, Alexius V.; pvt; 2nd MD Inf, Co G; res: Emmitsburg, Frd Cty; ref: 1, 2, 19, 21, 23, 90, 470, 1523

KEEPERS, Louis; Capt; MD Guerrilla Zouaves; ref: 1, 19

KEER, John; sgt; 7th Bn VA Reserves, Co D; ref: 1, 1533

KEESLER, D. Windsor; sgt; 1st MD Inf, Co A; ref: 2, 19, 21, 1523

KEESLLER, J. M.; pvt; 20th NC Inf, Co B; res: Balt; ref: 21, 56, 700

KEESTER, W. A.; pvt; 1st MD Lt Arty; ref: 2, 19, 21, 63, 1523

KEGLER, Francis; pvt; Davis's MD Cav, Co A; ref: 1, 735

KEHNS, Charles A.; pvt; TX Cav; res: Frederick, Frd Cty; ref: 90

KEIDEL, Herman F.; Lt; Adj, 2nd MD Cav; res: Balt; ref: 1, 2, 11, 19, 21, 23, 70, 412, 690, 791, 1523, 1609

KEIFER, Frederick; 12th VA Cav, Co C; ref: 735

KEILHOLTY, William; pvt; Holbrook's Independent MD Lt Arty; res: Balt; ref: 1, 1540
KEIN, Charles W.; Asst Paymaster, Navy; C.S.S. Macon; ref: 21, 97, 700, 783, 1564
KEINNINGHAM, S. E.; pvt; 2nd MD Cav, Co B; ref: 1
KEIRL, Mathew; res: Balt; ref: 1540
KELB, Philip; cpl; 30th VA Inf, Co F; res: Balt; MLCSH; ref: 1, 786
KELCHER, P. H.; pvt; Stuart's Horse Arty, Breathed's Battery; ref: 1
KELLAM, J. Leroy; pvt; 6th VA Inf, Co C; res: Balt; ref: 1, 1540
KELLAM, Stewart; pvt; 1st TX Lt Arty, Co H; res: Balt; ref: 21, 700
KELLBAUGH, George M.; pvt; 1st VA Cav, Co K; res: Balt; ref: 1, 2, 1540
KELLBAUGH, Henderson; sgt; Lucas's 15th Bn, SC Heavy Arty; res: Balt; ref: 1, 1540
KELLBAUGH, Jonathan; res: Balt; ref: 1540
KELLER, Ab; pvt; 7th VA Cav, Co G; res: all Cty; ref: 1, 3
KELLER, Daniel T.; Lt; 13th VA Inf, Co I; res: Barton; ref: 1, 65
KELLER, James H.; sgt; 1st VA Inf, Co F; ref: 1, 70, 316, 1622
KELLEY, E. F.; pvt; MD American Rifles; res: Balt; ref: 1
KELLEY, G.; pvt; 1st SC Inf, Co G; ref: 1
KELLEY, James; pvt; 2nd MD Inf, Co H; ref: 1, 2, 21
KELLEY, John C.; pvt; 43rd VA Cav (Mosby's), Co F; ref: 1, 2, 8, 21
KELLEY, M.; pvt; 1st SC Inf, Co G; ref: 1
KELLEY, Stewart; pvt; 1st MD Inf, Co B;r ef: 1, 2, 19, 21, 1523
KELLEY, Thomas S.; pvt; Marine Corps; res: Annapolis; ref: 1, 1539, 1594
KELLO, James R.; sgt; 9th VA Inf, Co B; ref: 1, 1576
KELLO, John G.; pvt; 9th VA Inf, Co B; ref: 1, 1576
KELLROY, ---; pvt; 1st MD Cav, Co C; ref: 1, 19
KELLUM, Peter W.; pvt; 19th VA Heavy Arty, Co C; ref: 1, 1580
KELLY, Charles; pvt; 2nd MD Cav, Co C; ref: 1, 19, 1523
KELLY, Daniel B.; pvt; 1st MD Cav, Co F; ref: 1, 2, 19, 21, 1523
KELLY, Edward F.; pvt; Lucas' 15th SC Heavy Arty; res: Bt Cty; ref: 1, 19, 1523, 1541, 1575, 1609
KELLY, Francis Patrick; pvt; 12th VA Inf, Co B; res: Balt; MLCSH; ref: 21, 93, 627, 786
KELLY, Frank; pvt; 35th VA Cav, Co B; ref: 1, 1611, 1677
KELLY, James S.; pvt; 1st MD Inf, Co D; res: Balt; ref: 1, 2, 19, 21, 1540
KELLY, John; pvt; 1st SC Lt Arty, Co G; res: Balt; ref: 1, 735
KELLY, John; sgt; 13th VA Inf, Co G; ref: 1, 2, 19, 21, 735
KELLY, John F.; pvt; 3rd MD Lt Arty; res: Princess Anne, Som Cty; ref: 1, 2, 19, 21, 160, 726, 1523, 1556
KELLY, John L.; pvt; 2nd MD Inf, Co H; ref: 1, 2, 19, 21
KELLY, L.; pvt; Stephen's GA Lt Arty; ref: 1, 2, 19, 21, 160, 726, 1523
KELLY, Lewis H.; pvt; Davis's MD Cav; res: Frd Cty; ref: 1
KELLY, Michael; pvt; Lucas' 15th SC Heavy Arty; ref: 1
KELLY, Patrick; Navy, Gun boat crew, Vicksburg Naval Station; MLCSH; ref: 1, 700
KELLY, Peter; pvt; 3rd MD Lt Arty; ref: 1, 2, 19, 21, 160, 726, 1523
KELLY, Richard; pvt; 1st MD Cav, Co F; ref: 1, 2, 19, 21, 1523
KELLY, Samuel L.; pvt; 38th NC Inf, Co B; res: Kt Cty; ref: 1, 668, 1584, 1612
KELLY, William; pvt; 2nd MD Lt Arty; res: Princess Anne, Som Cty; ref: 1, 2, 21, 1523, 1556
KELLY, William D.; cpl; 19th VA Heavy Arty, Co C; ref: 1, 1580

KELTON, Carlton B.; pvt; 2nd MD Cav, Co E; res: Cal Cty; ref: 1, 2, 19, 21, 700, 1301, 1523
KELTON, John C.; pvt; 1st MD Inf, Co D; res: Balt; ref: 1, 2, 19, 21, 1523, 1589
KEMER, James A.; ref: 457
KEMP, Charles; pvt; 1st MD Cav, Co D; ref: 1, 2, 19, 21, 1523, 1601
KEMP, Fred; pvt; Davis's MD Cav, Co B; ref: 1, 19, 1523
KEMP, O. Wesley; res: Frederick, Frd Cty; ref: 89
KEMP, Theodore; pvt; 1st MD Cav, Co D; res: Balt; ref: 1, 1523, 1601
KEMP, Thomas F.; cpl; 5th VA Cav, Co E; ref: 1, 21, 93, 700
KEMP, William H.; Lt; 2nd MD Cav, Co C; res: Bt Cty; ref: 1, 2, 3, 11, 19, 21, 23, 70, 82, 349, 791, 1523, 1560, 1609, 1631
KENDAL, George E.; cpl; 38th VA Lt Arty, Co D; res: Balt; ref: 1, 21, 700
KENDALL, Henry La Fayette; gun, Navy; C.S. Hampton; res: Balt; ref: 70, 79, 1673
KENDRICK, William H.; cpl; 2nd MD Lt Arty; ref: 1, 2, 19, 21, 23, 1523
KENLEY, John Reese; pvt; 1st MD Cav, Co A; res: How Cty; ref: 1, 2, 10, 19, 21, 904, 1414
KENLEY, Oliver G.; pvt; 1st VA Cav, Co K; res: Balt; MLCSH; ref: 1, 21, 700, 786
KENLEY, Richard; pvt; Lee's MD Cav; ref: 2, 19, 21, 1523
KENN, Edward; pvt; 3rd MD Lt Arty; ref: 1, 2, 19, 21, 160, 461, 726, 1523
KENNARD, James Alfred; pvt; 8th VA Inf, Co C; res: Still Pond, Kt Cty; ref: 1, 69, 70, 107, 316, 668, 1557, 1584
KENNARD, John H., Jr; Fenner's Battery, LA Lt Arty; res: Kt Cty; ref: 1, 1584
KENNEDY, Arthur T.; pvt; 1st MD Inf, Co A; res: Cal Cty; ref: 1, 2, 19, 21, 259, 1523
KENNEDY, D. Stile; 8th NC; ref: 735
KENNEDY, J. M.; pvt; 1st SC Inf, Co G; ref: 1
KENNEDY, McPherson; Lt; Davis's MD Cav, Co B; res: Frd Cty; ref: 1, 2, 19, 21, 90, 1523
KENNEDY, Price; pvt; 1st MD Cav, Co A; res: Hagerstown, Wash Cty; ref: 1, 19, 1523
KENNEDY, Samuel A.; sgt; 1st MD Inf, Co F; res: Balt; ref: 1, 2, 19, 21, 23, 1523
KENNEDY, Thomas; pvt; 1st SC Inf, Co G; ref: 1
KENNEDY, William H.; pvt; 43rd VA Cav (Mosby's), Co G; res: 1, 2, 8, 19, 21
KENNEDY, William R.; pvt; 2nd MD Inf, Co F; res: Har Cty; ref: 1, 2, 19, 21, 1523
KENNEY, Bernard; pvt; 2nd MD Inf, Co C; ref: 1, 2, 19, 21, 1523
KENNEY, Charles; pvt; Barry's Co, MD Vols; ref: 1, 19, 1523
KENNEY, John; pvt; Lucas' 15th SC Heavy Arty; ref: 1
KENNEY, Patrick; pvt; 1st MD Inf, Co F; ref: 1, 2, 19, 21, 1523
KENNINGHAM, Gideon E.; cpl; Woolfolk's Co, VA Lt Arty; ref: 1, 693, 1523, 1609
KENNON, Beverly; Lt Commanding, Navy; C.S. Governor Moore; res: Georgetown; ref: 1, 21, 97, 700, 783; 1564
KENT, Daniel M.; ordnance sgt; 39th VA Cav, Co B; res: Davidsonville, AA Cty; ref: 1, 1539
KENT, H. Bland; Maj; 39th VA Cav; ref: 735
KENT, Joseph, Jr (M.D.); Surg; 1st AR Inf; res: Davidsonville, AA Cty; ref: 1, 18, 70, 1511
KENT, Joseph B.; pvt; 9th VA Cav, Co C; res: St. Margarett; ref: 1, 730, 1539, 1628
KEPHART, Charles; res: Licksville, Frd Cty; ref: 19, 90, 643, 1523
KEPHART, George A.; res: Licksville, Frd Cty; ref: 19, 90, 643, 1523
KEPHART, J. W.; pvt; 35th VA Cav, Co B; ref: 1, 15, 1677

KEPHART, Jasper C.; pvt; 35th VA Cav, Co A; res: Point of Rocks; ref: 1, 3, 1677
KEPHART, William F.; Lt; 2nd LA Cav, Co B; res: Frederick, Frd Cty; ref: 1, 69, 316, 791
KEPLER, John Hanson; cpl; 1st VA Inf, Co D; res: Balt; MLCSH; ref: 1, 627, 700, 786
KER, John (M.D.) Contract Surg; Chinborago Hospital Richmond; res: Balt; ref: 1, 18, 70
KERBY, Joseph A.; pvt; 3rd MD Lt Arty; ref: 1, 2, 19, 21, 160, 726, 1523
KERNAN, James L.; pvt; 2nd MD Lt Arty; res: Balt; ref: 1, 2, 19, 21, 70, 700, 1001, 1523
KERNS, Cornelius; pvt; 2nd MD Inf, Co D; ref: 2, 19, 21, 1523
KERNS, G. A.; pvt; 3rd MD Lt Arty; ref: 1, 2, 19, 21, 160, 726, 1523
KERREGAN, John; pvt; 2nd MD Cav, Co G; ref: 1
KERRUS, John H.; Commissaary Dept; res: Balt; ref; 70, 1540
KERSAY, John; pvt; 9th VA Inf, Co B; res: How Cty; ref: 1, 1576
KERSEY, Edward; pvt; 19th VA Heavy Arty, Co C; ref: 1, 1580
KERSHAW, Edwin; pvt; Stuart's Horse Arty, Graham's Battery; res: Balt; ref: 21, 57, 513, 700, 916
KESLER, William Henry Harrison; pvt; 35th VA Cav, Co B; res: Buckeystown, Frd Cty; ref: 1, 1548, 1611, 1677
KESSLER, Windsor G.; sgt; 1st MD Inf, Co A; res: Urbana, Frd Cty; ref: 1, 2, 19, 21, 23, 90, 1523
KESTER, John S.; pvt; Rice's Co VA Lt Arty; ref: 1, 46, 68
KESTERSON, W. A.; Navy; Prize, St. Nicholas; res: Balt; MLCSH; ref: 786
KETTLEWELL, Charles; sgt; 1st MD Cav, Co C; res: AA Cty; ref: 1, 2, 19, 21, 23, 687, 700, 848, 1523
KETTLEWELL, Edward R.; pvt; 1st MD Cav, Co A; ref: 1, 2, 19, 21, 1523
KETTLEWELL, Samuel H.; pvt; 13th VA inf, Co G; ref: 1, 21, 700, 735
KEY, Clarence; pvt; 26th TN Inf, Co E; res: Balt; MLCSH; ref: 1, 93, 511, 786, 1038, 1046, 1061, 1069, 1093
KEY, Daniel Murry; pvt; 35th VA Cav, Co B; res: AA Cty; MLCSH; ref: 1, 2, , 15, 19, 21, 44, 92, 93, 511, 627, 700, 786, 1093, 1523, 1611, 1677
KEY, Henry J. (M.D.); Asst Surg; Courtney's Battery, Army of Tennessee; res: Balt; ref: 1, 18, 56, 511
KEY, John Francis; pvt; Stuart's Horse Arty, Breathed's Battery; res: Annapolis, AA Cty; MLCSH; ref: 1, 52, 92, 93, 498, 511, 559, 627, 700, 786, 1093
KEY, John Ross; pvt; 1st MD Inf, Co D; ref: 1, 2, 19, 21, 44, 70, 511, 559, 1511, 1523
KEY, Philip; pvt; 1st MD Cav, Co C; res: St. M. Cty; ref: 1, 19, 68, 511, 1509, 1523
KEY, Richard Hammond; pvt; 1st Md Cav, Co B; res: Cal Cty; ref: 1, 2, 19, 21, 45, 93, 146, 511, 785, 1523
KEYS, William Wilfred; pvt; 1st MD Cav, Co C; ref: 1, 19, 1523
KEYSER, Herman; pvt; 1st MD Inf, Co G; ref: 1, 2, 19, 21, 1523
KEYWORTH, Robert W.; Maj; Chief of Subsistence Dept, Trans Mississippi Dept; ref: 1, 2, 19, 735, 791, 1523
KIBLER, Charles P.; sgt; Davis's MD Cav, Co B; ref: 1, 19, 1523
KICKSON, John; pvt; 17th VA Inf, Co D; ref: 735
KIDD, T. O. G.; cpl; 2nd MD Cav, Co F; ref: 1, 2, 11, 19, 21, 1523, 1609
KILGORE, Francis Stribling; pvt; 35th VA Cav, Co C; res: Potomac, Mont Cty; ref: 1, 3, 86, 557, 718, 1552, 1560, 1574, 1677
KILGORE, John Mortimer; Capt; Q.M., 35th VA Cav; res: Rockville, Mont

Cty; ref: 2, 3, 15, 19, 72, 88, 371, 1011, 1523, 1611, 1677

KILGOUR, J. Michael; pvt; 35th VA Cav, Co A; ref: 1, 64

KILLMAN, Richard G.; pvt; 2nd MD Inf, Co D; res: Annapolis, AA Cty; ref: 1, 2, 19, 21, 70, 93, 700, 1494, 1523

KIMBALL, Henry C.; pvt; Davis's MD Cav, Co B; res: Balt; ref: 1, 19, 1523

KIMBALL, S. H.; pvt; 1st MD Cav, Co C; res: Balt; ref: 1, 2, 19, 21, 1523

KIMBLE, Louis F.; pvt; 1st MD Cav, Co F; ref: 1, 2, 7, 19, 21, 1523

KIMBLE, William H.; pvt; 3rd MD Lt Arty; ref: 1, 2, 19, 21, 160, 726, 1523

KIMERY, James R.; pvt; 1st SC Inf, Co G; ref: 1

KINCANNON, John; res: Governor Bridge, AA Cty; ref: 1539

KING, A. H.; sgt; Davis's MD Cav, Co D; res: Point of Rocks, Frd Cty; ref: 1, 19, 1523

KING, Albert; pvt; Holbrook's Independent MD Lt Arty; res: Princess Anne, ref: 1, 7335

KING, Christian; Ashby's Cav; res: Frd Cty; ref: 89, 90

KING, E. C.; ordnance sgt; 17th VA Inf; res: Balt; ref: 21, 700

KING, Edward S.; pvt; Stuart's Horse Arty, Breathed's Battery; res: Balt; MLCSH; ref: 1, 2, 19, 21, 23, 92, 498, 627, 786, 1523

KING, Elmer; pvt; Holbrook's Independent MD Lt Arty; ref: 1

KING, George W.; pvt; Herding Dept; res: Balt; ref: 21, 700

KING, Henry; pvt; 9th VA Inf, Co B; ref: 1, 735, 1576

KING, James A.; pvt; 2nd MD Lt Arty; res: Balt; ref: 1, 2, 19, 21, 1523

KING, James B.; pvt; Barry's Co, MD Vols; rf: 1, 19, 1523

KING, James E.; pvt; 13th VA Inf, Co g; ref: 1, 735

KING, John; sgt; 13th VA Inf, Co G; ref: 1, 735

KING, John A.; pvt; 9th VA Inf, Co B; res: Balt; ref: 1, 893, 1576

KING, John C.; pvt; 15th VA Inf, Co B; res: Balt; ref: 1, 21, 700, 1540

KING, John F.; pvt; Marine Corps; C.S.S. Savannah; res: St. M. Cty; ref: 1, 7, 822, 1509, 1594, 1670

KING, John William; pvt; 1st MD Inf, Co G; res: Delight, Bt Cty; ref: 1, 2, 19, 21, 708, 1523

KING, Mitchell; Capt; Adj, 1st SC Regulars; res: Balt; ref: 1, 1169

KING, R. K.; pvt; Lee's MD Cav, ref: 1, 2, 68

KING, R. S.; Lt; 2nd MD Cav, Co C; ref: 1, 19, 1523, 1609

KING, Robert; pvt; 19th VA Heavy Arty, Co C; ref: 1, 1580

KING, Thomas; pvt; 19th VA Heavy Arty, Co C; ref: 1, 1580

KING, Thomas; pvt; 6th GA Inf, Co G; MLCSH; ref: 1, 700

KING, Thomas S.; pvt; 55th VA Inf, Co E; res: Bowie, PG Cty; ref: 1, 21, 700

KING, Thomson; pvt; 7th VA Cav, Co G; res: AA Cty; ref: 1, 3, 21, 62, 700

KING, Walter; pvt; 1st MD Inf, Co D; ref: 1, 2, 19, 21, 1523

KING, William John; pvt; 1st MD Inf, Co G; res: Reisterstown, Bt Cty; ref: 19, 21, 700, 1523

KING, William K.; pvt; 3rd MD Lt Arty; res: Crownsville, AA Cty; ref; 2, 19, 21, 160, 1523, 1539

KINGSBURG, Charles F.; 2nd NC Inf, Co B; res: Balt; MLCSH; ref: 1, 93, 786

KINLOCK, William; pvt; Lee's Balt Lt Arty, Alexander's Bn; res: Balt; ref: 1, 21, 700

KINNIAN, Frank; pvt; Zarvona's MD Zouaves; ref: 735

KINSEY, Howard H.; sgt; 1st MD Cav, Co F; res: Mont Cty; ref: 1, 2, 19, 21, 23, 1523, 1574

KIRBY, Benjamin F.; sgt; 61st VA Inf, Co C; res: Cambridge, Dor Cty; ref: 1, 735, 1547

KIRBY, Francis M.; pvt; 4th MD Lt Arty; ref: 1, 2, 19, 21, 1523
KIRBY, James R.; pvt; Lucas's 15th SC Heavy Arty; ref: 1, 8, 19, 93, 1523, 1609
KIRBY, Patrick; cpl; 2nd MD Lt Arty; res: Balt; ref: 1, 2, 19, 21, 23, 1523
KIRCHNER, William; res: West River, AA Cty; ref: 1539
KIRK, James A.; res: St. M. Cty; ref: 1670
KIRK, Charles R.; sgt; 9th VA Cav, Co D; ref: 1, 57
KIRK, Samuel; sgt; 2nd MD Inf, Co E; res: Balt; ref: 1, 2, 19, 21, 23, 1523
KIRKLAND, Edward P.; Engr, Navy; Prize Steamer Borton; res: How Cty; MLCSH; ref: 1, 21, 93, 700, 735, 783, 786
KIRKLAND, J. T.; pvt; 3rd MD Lt Arty; ref: 2, 19, 21, 160, 726, 1523
KIRKLAND, William C. (M.D.); Asst Surg, Navy; res: Balt; ref: 1, 18, 58, 97
KIRLL, George W.; res: Balt; ref: 1540
KITCHEN, Collin E.; pvt; 9th VA Inf, Co B; ref: 1, 1576
KITCHEN, Francis; pvt; 9th VA Inf, Co b; ref: 1, 1576
KITCHEN, James; pvt; 9th VA Inf, Co B; ref: 1, 1576
KITCHEN, John G.; pvt; 9th VA Inf, Co B; res: Balt; ref: 1, 1576, 1598
KITZMILLER, C.; pvt; 2nd MD Cav, Co D; ref: 1, 19
KITZMILLER, Henry; pvt; 3rd MD Lt Arty; ref: 1, 2, 19, 21, 160, 461, 726, 1523
KIVERT, Alexander L.; pvt; 9th VA Inf, Co B; ref: 1, 1576
KLEINSCHMIDT, Karl A. H. (M.D.); Asst Surg; 3rd AR Inf; res: Georgetown; ref: 1, 18, 316
KLEMKWITZ, Benjamin; pvt; 1st MD Inf, Co I; ref: 1, 2, 19, 21, 1523
KLIMKIEWIEZ, Thaddius A.; pvt 2nd MD Inf, Co A; ref: 1, 2, 19, 21, 650, 1523
KLINE, Ferdinand; bugler; 2nd MD Cav; ref: 1
KLINE, John D.; Capt; Chief of Ordnance, Gen E. F. Paxton's staff; res: Balt; ref: 1, 19, 733, 1523, 1579
KLINN, Charles; pvt; 1st S C Inf, Co G; ref: 735
KLISER, Augustus; pvt; 1st MD Inf, Co B; ref: 1, 2, 19, 21, 1523
KLOMAN, E. F.; pvt; 43rd VA Cav (Mosby's), Co B; ref: 1, 21, 700
KLOMAN, William C. (M.D.) Asst Surg; 6th VA Inf; res: Balt; ref: 1, 2, 18, 21, 23, 412, 700, 1523, 1533, 1534, 1536
KNAFF, August; res: McPherson's Pack, AA Cty; ref: 1539
KNAPP, Henry; pvt; 1st MD Inf, Co F; ref: 1, 2, 19, 21, 1523
KNAUFF, George W.; pvt; 1st MD Cav, Co D; res: Balt; ref: 1, 2, 19, 21, 93, 700, 1523, 1601, 1613
KNELLER, Jacob S.; pvt; 6th VA Cav, Co D; res: Balt; ref; 1, 2, 19, 21, 57, 412, 700, 1523
KNIGHT, Benjamin F.; pvt; 9th VA Inf, Co B; ref: 1, 1576
KNIGHT, Dennis; pvt; Jacobs' Mounted Riflemen; res: Millersville, AA Cty; ref: 1, 1539
KNIGHT, J. E.; pvt; 1st SC Inf, Co G; ref: 1
KNIGHT, J. M.; pvt; 1st MD Cav, Co A; ref: 1, 19, 1523
KNIGHT, John; pvt; 2nd MD Lt Arty; res: Darlington, Har Cty; ref: 1, 2, 19, 21, 1523, 1549
KNIGHT, John J.; sgt; 5th VA Cav, Co F; res: Balt; ref: 1, 21, 700
KNIGHT, Louis W. (M.D.); pvt; 2nd MD Cav, Co D; res: Balt; ref: 1, 2, 18, 19, 21, 23, 57, 513, 700, 891, 1523, 1533, 1575
KNIGHT, M. R.; pvt; 1st SC Inf, Co G; ref: 1
KNIGHT, Reuben; pvt; MD Guerrilla Zouaves; res: Frd Cty; ref: 1

KNOPP, Peter; pvt; 6th TX Inf, Co A; res: West River, AA Cty; ref: 1, 1539
KNOTT, Francis Rodney; cpl; 7th VA Cav, Co G; res: Merryland Tract, Frd Cty; ref: 1, 3, 90, 1278
KNOTT, James F.; pvt; Barry's Co, MD Vols; ref: 1, 19, 1523
KNOTT, Loyisis L.; pvt; Lee's Balt Lt Arty, Alexander's Bn; res: Balt; ref: 1, 1540
KNOTT, M. T.; pvt; 2nd MD Inf, Co F; ref: 2, 19, 21, 1523
KNOTT, Minion F.; pvt; 2nd MD Inf, Co F; ref: 1, 2, 19, 21, 1523
KNOWLES, Raymond; sgt; 62nd AL Inf, Co B; ref: 1, 21, 700
KNOX, James; pvt; 1st MD Inf, Co D; ref: 1, 2, 19, 21, 1523
KNOX, Richard T.; color sgt; 1st MD Cav, Co C; res: Balt; ref: 1, 2, 19, 21, 23, 56, 57, 493, 511, 513, 700, 891, 916, 1523
KNOX, William Francis; pvt; 2nd MD Lt Arty; res: Balt; MLCSH; ref: 1, 2, 19, 21, 93, 511, 627, 700, 786, 1523
KOBRIDGE, Theodore; pvt; 2MD MD Cav, Co B; ref: 1
KOBURG, Charles; pvt; 3rd MD Lt Arty; ref: 1, 2, 19, 21, 160, 726, 1523
KOESTER, Lewis H.; pvt; 1st MD Lt Arty; res: Johnsville, Frd Cty; ref: 1, 2, 19, 21, 34, 72, 89, 90, 470, 782, 1523
KOESTER, William A.; pvt; 1st MD Lt Arty; res: Johnsville, Frd Cty; ref: 1, 2, 19, 21, 90, 215, 791, 1273, 1523
KOFELMAN, J.; SC; ref: 693
KOFFMAN, George; pvt; 2nd MD Cav, Co E; ref: 1, 19, 1523, 1609
KOHLHEPP, John; pvt; 1st MD Inf, Co B; ref: 1, 2, 19, 21, 1523
KOINER, Simeon; pvt; 5th VA Inf, Co H; res: Carr Cty; ref: 1, 773
KONIG, Henry S.; pvt; 1st MD Cav, Co F; res: Balt; ref: 1, 2, 19, 21, 92, 93, 1523
KONNE, Charles; Gen D. H. Hill's staff; ref: 2, 19, 1523
KOONS, Abraham; pvt; Hampton Leg Lt Arty, Co B; res: Westminster, Carr Cty; MLCSH; ref: 1, 2, 19, 21, 93, 700, 786, 1523
KOONTZ, Edgar; res: St. M. Cty; ref: 1670
KOPPLEMAN, John; pvt; 2nd MD Inf, Co E; res: Balt; ref: 1, 2, 19, 21, 1523
KRAFT, John; pvt; LA Washington Arty; ref: 1, 735
KRAFT, John; pvt; 35th VA Cav, Co B; res: Frederick, Frd Cty; ref; 1, 89, 1677
KRAGER, Joseph H.; Lt; 9th VA Inf, Co B; res: Balt; ref: 1, 76, 735, 1576
KRAUS, Charles Agustus; pvt; 7th VA Cav, Co A; res: Balt; MLCSH; ref: 1, 2, 19, 21, 92, 93, 627, 700, 730, 786, 1523
KREBS, Charles; pvt; 21st VA Inf, Co B; res: Balt; ref; 1, 2, 19, 21, 312, 735, 1523
KREIS, George; pvt; 1st MD Inf, Co B; res: Balt; ref: 1, 2, 19, 21, 1523, 1549
KREMER, Frederick M.; pvt; 13th VA Inf, Co G; res: Balt; MLCSH; ref: 1, 19, 21, 700, 735, 786, 1523, 1540
KREPPTS, M. J.; pvt; 2nd MD Cav, Co D; ref: 1, 19, 1523, 1609
KRETZER, Hiram; pvt; 1st MD Inf, Co A; res: Funkstown, Wash Cty; ref: 1, 2, 19, 21, 1523, 1558
KRISCHMAN, James R.; pvt; Stuart's Horse Arty, Breathed's Battery; ref: 1
KUBLE, Adolphus; pvt; 2nd MD Lt Arty; ref: 1, 2, 19, 21, 1523
KUHN, John A.; pvt; 2nd MD Cav, Co A; ref: 1, 2, 19, 21, 352, 1523, 1609
KULLE, Louis; res: Annapolis, AA Cty; reff: 1539
KUNKEL, John; pvt; Zarvona's MD Zouaves; ref: 1, 735
KYLE, George H.; Maj; Chief Commissary of Supply, Gen G. H. Steuart's staff; res: Balt; ref:

1, 2, 44, 55, 68, 559, 690, 791, 1634

LACEY, James; pvt; 1st MD Inf, Co I; res: Cha Cty; ref: 1, 2, 19, 21, 1523

LACEY, Robert S.; pvt; 1st MD Inf, Co I; res: Cha Cty; ref: 1, 2, 19, 21, 1523

LACKEY, Joseph W.; sgt; 3rd MD Lt Arty; ref: 1, 2, 21, 23, 160, 726, 1523

LACKLAND, William L.; sgt; 6th LA Inf, Co E; res: Balt; MLCSH; ref: 1, 21, 93, 700, 786

LADD, N. E.; pvt; 2nd MD Lt Arty; ref: 1, 2, 19, 21

LAENY, Jules; pvt; 2nd MD Cav, Co G; ref: 1, 19, 1523, 1609

LAGARDE, Ernest; pvt; 2nd LA Inf, Co A; res: Emmitsburg, Frd Cty; ref: 1, 90

LAHMAN, R.; pvt; 2nd MD Cav, Co F; ref: 1, 19, 1523, 1609

LAIN, John; pvt; Lucas' 15th SC Heavy Arty; ref: 1

LAIRD, Edward; pvt; Davis's MD Cav; ref: 1

LAIRD, J. Winder; Lt; Adj; 2nd MD Inf; res: Cambridge, Dor Cty; ref: 1, 2, 19, 21, 23, 44, 64, 112, 259, 511, 674, 685, 746, 1520, 1523, 1547, 1578, 1579

LAIRD, Severn; pvt; Davis's MD Cav; res: South River, AA Cty; ref: 1, 1539

LAIRD, William H.; pvt; 2nd MD Inf, Co A; res: Cambridge, Dor Cty; ref; 1, 2, 19, 21, 23, 44, 470, 511, 650, 700, 1520, 1523, 1547

LAKE, Albert Crawford; pvt; Stanford's Co, MS Lt Arty; res: Dor Cty; ref: 1, 112, 970

LAKE, Alexander Fridge; pvt; 54th TN Inf, Co B; res: Dor Cty; ref; 1, 112

LAKE, Augustus Washington; pvt; 15th MS; res: Dor Cty; ref: 1, 112

LAKE, Charles Henry; bugler; Stanford's Co, MS Lt Arty; res: Dor Cty; ref: 1, 112

LAKE, Craig; pvt; 2nd MD Inf, Co A; res: Cambridge, Dor Cty; ref: 2, 19, 21, 112, 259, 1523, 1578, 1579

LAKE, Edwin B.; pvt; 77th VA Militia, Co C; res: Dor Cty; ref: 1, 112

LAKE, Gabriel Perry; Capt; 3rd MS Inf, Co B; res: Dor Cty; ref: 1, 19, 86, 112

LAKE, George of Wm.; pvt; Stanford's Co, MS Lt Arty; res: Dor Cty; ref: 112

LAKE, George W.; pvt; 2nd MS Reserves Cav, Co B; res: Dor Cty; ref: 1, 112

LAKE, George W., Jr; pvt; Stanford's Co, MS Lt Arty; res: Dor Cty; ref: 112

LAKE, James Bushrod, Jr; Capt; Asst Commissary of Supply, Gen B. T. Johnson's staff; res: Dor Cty; ref: 1, 112, 791

LAKE, John Craig; pvt; 2nd MD Inf, Co E; res: Dor Cty; ref: 1, 2, 19, 21, 112, 486, 685, 1523

LAKE, John Jemison; sgt; 1st AL Inf, Co K; res: Dor Cty; ref: 1, 112

LAKE, Levin, Jr; Lt; Aid de Camp, Gen J. Early's staff; res: Dor Cty; ref: 1, 112, 129, 1547

LAKE, Levin, Sr; Capt; Q.M. Dept, Mississippi; res: Dor Cty; ref: 1, 53, 791, 970, 1064

LAKE, Richard Pinkney; Lt; 4th MS Cav; res: Dor Cty; ref: 1, 112

LAKE, Walter Scott; ordnance sgt; 17th TN Inf; res: Dor Cty; ref: 112

LAKEMAN, Richard; pvt; 1st VA Inf, Co E; ref: 1, 1609

LAKINS, Charles; pvt; 2nd MD Cav, Co F; ref: 1, 2, 19, 21, 1523, 1609

LAKINS, Edward; Lt; 19th VA Heavy Arty, Co C; ref: 1, 1580

LAMAN, Martin; pvt; Holbrook's Independent MD Lt Arty; res: Annapolis, AA Cty; ref: 1, 1539

LAMAN, Randolph; pvt; Holbrook's Independent MD Lt Arty; res: Annapolis, AA Cty; ref: 1, 1539

LAMAN, Robert; pvt; 2nd MD Cav, Co F; res: Balt; MLCSH; ref: 1, 2, 19, 21, 786, 1523
LAMAR, Abb; 35th VA Cav, Co B; res: Adamstown, Frd cty; ref: 643
LAMAR, Baker H.; res: Frederick, Frd Cty; ref: 89
LAMAR, George Albert; pvt; 35th VA Cav, Co B; res: Carrollton Manor; Frd Cty; ref: 1, 3, 19, 90, 643, 1290, 1573, 1611, 1677
LAMAR, John T.; pvt; 7th VA Cav, Co G; ref: 1
LAMAR, Robert; pvt; 2nd MD Cav, Co F; ref: 2, 21
LAMAR, William; pvt; Lee's MD Cav; res: Cumberland, All Cty; ref: 1, 19, 65, 95, 1523, 1610
LAMATES, James; sgt; 1st MD Inf, Co B; res: Balt; MLCSH; ref: 1, 2, 19, 21, 23, 627, 700, 786, 1523
LAMB, John H. of Andrew; pvt; 2nd MD Inf, Co D; res: Annapolis, AA Cty; ref; 1, 2, 19, 21, 1523, 1539, 1628
LAMBDIN, George T.; Lt; 17th VA Inf, Co C; ref: 1, 142, 251, 791, 1523
LAMBERT, Maurice William; pvt; 43rd VA Cav (Mosby's), Co D; res: PG Cty; ref: 1, 2, 8, 19, 21, 677, 1523
LAMBSON, James B.; pvt; 2nd MD Inf, Co B; ref: 1, 19, 1523
LAMDEN, Charles; pvt; 1st MD Cav, Co D; res: Frd Cty; ref: 1, 2, 19, 21, 791, 1601
LAMKIN, Samuel L.; pvt; 40th VA Inf, Co B; ref: 1, 1119
LAMSDON, Charles; pvt; Davis's MD Cav, Co A; ref: 1
LANAHAN, Daniel; pvt; 2nd MD Inf, Co Co; ref: ref: 1, 2, 19, 21, 23, 1523
LANCASTER, Andrew; pvt; Stuart's Horse Arty, Breathed's Battery; ref: 1
LANCASTER, Samuel G.; pvt; 1st MD Cav, Co E; ref: 1, 2, 21, 730, 1523
LANDEE, Isaac; pvt; 2nd MD Cav, Co C; ref: 1, 19, 1523, 1609
LANDIN, Daniel; res: Balt; ref: 1540
LANDRETH, R. P.; pvt; 1st SC Inf, Co G; ref: 1
LANDSTREET, Aristides, C.; pvt; 6th VA Cav, Co F; res: Green Spring Valley, Bt Cty; ref: 1, 94
LANDSTREET, Edward; pvt; 1st VA Cav, Co A; res: Geen Spring Valley, Bt Cty; ref; 1, 21, 94, 556, 700
LANDSTREET, John (Revd); Chaplain; 1st VA Cav; ref: 1, 559
LANE, Benjamin A.; pvt; 30th VA Inf, Co; res: Balt; MLCSH; ref: 1, 21, 93, 700, 786
LANE, Francis; pvt; 43rd VA Cav (Mosby's), Co A; ref: 1, 8
LANE, George M.; Steward, Navy; Richmond Navy Station; res: Cec Cty; ref: 1
LANE, John; pvt; 2nd MD Cav, Co E; ref: 1, 19, 1523, 1574, 1609
LANE, John A.; pvt; 4th MD Lt Arty; res: Royal Oak, Tal Cty; ref; 1, 2, 19, 21, 470, 1523, 1557, 1612
LANE, John N.; pvt; 10th VA Lt Arty, Co D; res: Tal Cty; ref: 1, 645
LANE, Richard; cpl; 8th NC Inf, Co F; ref: 1, 735
LANE, William Benjamin; pvt 2nd MD Inf, Co C; res: Royal Oak, Tal Cty; ref: 1, 2, 8, 19, 21, 92, 93, 595, 645, 1523, 1557, 1612
LANERA, Frank C.; pvt; Zarvona's MD Zouaves; ref: 735
LANG, Henry; pvt; Lucas' 15th SC Heavy Arty; ref: 1
LANGFORD, George W.; pvt; 2nd MD Inf, Co G; res: Galestown, Dor Cty; ref: 1, 2, 19, 21, 1523, 1547
LANGFORD, Wiley; pvt; 9th VA Inf, Co B; ref: 1, 1576
LANGLEY, Edward H.; sgt; 3rd MD Lt Arty; ref: 1, 2, 19, 21, 23, 64, 160, 440, 461, 726, 791, 813, 1523
LANGLEY, Richard E.; pvt; 4th MD Lt Arty; res: St. Gregors, St. M. Cty; ref: 1, 2, 19, 21, 34, 1523, 1555
LANGLY, Thomas; pvt; 1st MD Cav, Co A; res: St. M. Cty; ref; 1, 2, 19, 21, 1509, 1523

LANGSDALE, Henry J.; sgt; 1st MD Lt Arty; res: Quantico, Som Cty; ref: 1, 2, 19, 21, 34, 70, 215, 470, 782, 791, 1273, 1523, 1556
LANGSTON, Elias; pvt; 1st SC Inf, Co G; ref: 1
LANHAM, Benjamin L.; pvt; 2nd MD Inf, Co C; ref: 2, 19, 21, 1523
LANIER, James B.; pvt; 2nd MD Lt Arty; ref: 1, 2, 19, 21
LANIER, John; pvt; Davis's MD Cav, Co B; ref: 1, 19, 781, 1523
LANIER, M.; pvt; 1st SC Inf, Co G; ref: 1
LANIER, Sidney; pvt; 2nd GA Inf, Co B; ref: 1, 1247, 1276, 1315, 1350, 1429, 1484
LANKFORD, George W.; pvt; 49th TN Inf, Co D; res: Linwood, Dor Cty; ref: 1, 19, 112, 1523, 1547
LANNAHAN, Thomas; pvt; 4th MD Lt Arty; ref: 2, 19, 1523
LANNERS, John H.; pvt; 2nd MD Cav, Co A; res: Balt; ref: 1, 19, 1609
LANTZ, Noah; pvt; 19th VA Heavy Arty, Co C; ref: 1, 1580
LAPOLE, Andrew T.; sgt; 12th VA Cav, Co D; res: Sharpsburg, Wash Cty; ref: 1, 19, 88, 352, 1523, 1560
LARABEE, George S.; pvt; 1st MD Inf, Co D; ref: 1, 2, 19, 21, 1523
LARINION, Richard; res: Birdsville, AA Cty; ref: 1539
LARKER, T.; pvt; 2nd MD Cav, Co A; ref: 1, 19, 1609
LARKINSON, N.; pvt; 1st MD Cav, Co E; ref: 1, 2, 19, 21, 1523
LARMOUR, Robert B.; Lt, Navy; C.S.S. Missouri; res: Balt; ref: 1, 19, 58, 97, 279, 1523, 1564
LARRABEE, H. Clay; pvt; 21st VA Inf, Co B; res: Balt; ref: 1, 2, 19, 312, 735
LASHOW, William; pvt; 2nd VA Inf, Co D; ref: 1, 700
LASSELL, James T.; (Revd); Lt; 7th NC Inf, Co E; res: Chestertown, Kt Cty; ref: 1, 1584
LASSELL, William H. (M.D.); res: Chestertown, Kt Cty; ref: 1584
LATHAM, James; pvt; Stuart's Horse Arty, Breathed's Battery; ref: 1
LATHAM, Joseph W.; cpl; 1st MD Cav, Co F; res: Frederick, Frd Cty; ref: 1, 2, 19, 21, 23, 92, 93, 1523
LATHAM, Thomas R.; pvt; 43rd VA Cav (Mosby's), Co E; res: Balt; ref: 1, 8, 19, 1613
LATIMER, George S.; pvt; Stuart's Horse Arty, Breathed's Battery; res: Har Cty; ref; 1, 2, 19, 21, 38, 498, 1523
LATIMER, James B.; pvt; 2nd MD Inf, Co C; res: Cha Cty; ref: 1, 141
LATIMER, Thomas Sargent (M.D.); Asst Surg; 1st MD Inf; res: Balt; ref: 1, 2, 18, 19, 21, 38, 68, 240, 456, 700, 1491, 1523, 1533, 1534, 1536
LATON, J. N.; pvt; 3rd MD Lt Arty; ref: 2, 19, 21, 160, 726, 1523
LATROBE, Henry B.; Capt; 3rd MD Lt Arty; res: Balt; ref: 1, 2, 19, 21, 23, 42,50, 64, 65, 68, 160, 222, 443, 461, 462, 479, 492, 511, 638, 726, 791, 838, 1060, 1106, 1523
LATROBE, Osmun; Lt Col; Asst A.G., Gen J. Longstreet; res: Balt; ref: 1, 2, 19, 21, 22, 23, 56, 57, 100, 105, 111, 115, 127, 165, 324, 511, 700, 720, 735, 738, 739, 787, 791, 1523, 1577, 1578, 1579
LATROBE, R. Steuart; pvt; 1st MD Cav, Co C; res: Balt; ref: 1, 2, 19, 21, 56, 100, 700, 720, 738, 739, 771, 1523
LATTIMORE, C. W.; color sgt; 40th VA Inf; ref: 19, 21, 700, 1523
LAUGHLIN, James; pvt; Zarvona's MD Zouaves; ref: 1, 19, 58, 97, 1523
LAUGHTER, William H.; Lt; Adj; 18th VA Heavy Arty; rs: Balt; ref: 1, 21, 56, 57, 700
LAW, D. O.; Lt; Aid de Camp; MD Line; ref: 1, 1494
LAW, Edward; pvt; 1st MD Inf, Co E; ref: 2, 19, 21
LAW, Jacob G. Daires; pvt; 1st MD Inf, Co H; ref: 1, 2, 19, 21, 650
LAWLESS, W.; pvt; 3rd MD Lt Arty; ref; 2, 19, 21, 160, 726, 1523

LAWN, Edward; pvt; 2nd MD Inf, Co E; ref: 1, 2, 19, 21, 470, 1523
LAWRENCE, Frank; pvt; Barry's Co, MD Vols; res: Princeland, AA Cty; ref: 1, 1539
LAWRENCE, George Washington (M.D.); Surg; Medical Director, 3rd Corps, Army of Mississippi; res: Catonsville, Bt Cty; ref: 1, 18, 19, 1523, 1536, 1576
LAWRENCE, John H.; pvt; Lucas' 15th SC Heavy Arty; ref: 1
LAWRENCE, Stephen Demett; Lt; 1st MD Cav, Co D; res: Libertytown, Frd Cty; ref: 1, 2, 19, 21, 23, 64, 68, 90, 748, 1523, 1601
LAWSON, Campbell G.; Capt; 15th VA Inf, Co H; res: Clark Bay View; res: 1, 21, 93, 700
LAWSON, James A.; pvt; 2nd MD Inf, Co C; ref: 1, 2, 19, 21, 1523
LAWSON, S. A.; pvt; 3rd VA Local Defense Inf, Co K; ref: 1, 19, 690
LAWSON, William M.; Lt; 1st VA Inf, Co H; ref: 1, 21, 700
LAWTON, J. C.; pvt; ref: 1690
LAY, Henry C. (Revd); Chaplain; Edelin's MD Heavy Arty; res: Easton, Tal Cty; ref: 1, 70, 330
LAYDEN, Francis; pvt; 9th VA Inf, Co B; res: Bt Cty; ref: 1, 1576
LAYMAN, Charles; pvt; Zarvona's MD Zouaves; res: Balt; ref: 1, 1540
LAYTON, John H.; pvt; 2nd MD Cav, Co C; res: Drawbridge, Dor Cty; ref: 1, 19, 1523, 1547, 1609
LAYTON, R.; pvt; 1st SC Inf, Co G; ref: 1
LEACHE, Charles H.; Black Horse Cav; res: Balt; ref; 70
LEAGUE, John S.; pvt; 1st MD Inf, Co D; ref: 1, 2, 19, 21, 1523
LEAKFELT, Henry; pvt; 9th VA Inf, Co B; ref: 1, 1576
LEAR, Alpheus; pvt; 17th VA Inf, Co K; ref: 1, 21, 700
LEATSE, Charles; res: Balt; ref: 1540
LEAVING, Christopher; res: Annapolis, AA Cty; ref: 1539
LEAZEY, Joseph H.; pvt; 1st MD Cav, Co C; ref: 2, 19, 21, 1523
LECHLEIDER, George P.; pvt; 1st MD Inf, Co A; res: Frd Cty; ref: 1, 2, 19, 21, 89, 1523
LECHLEIDER, Thomas George; pvt; 2nd MD Inf, Co E; res: Frd Cty; MLCSH: ref: 1, 2,`19, 21, 88, 89, 93, 627, 700, 786, 1523
LE COMPT, Thomas P.; Lt; 4th MD Lt Arty; ref: 1, 2, 19, 21 64, 1523
LEDLIN, Norman; pvt; Davis's MD Cav; res: Annapolis, AA Cty; ref; 1, 1539
LEE, A.; pvt; 3rd MD Lt Arty; ref: 2, 19, 21, 160, 461, 726, 1523
LEE, Andrew; pvt; 9th VA Inf, Co B; ref: 1, 1576
LEE, Charles W.; pvt; 1st MD Inf; res: Aberdeen, Har Cty; ref: 19, 21, 700
LEE, Daniel Murray; Passed Midn, Navy; C.S.S. Chicanauge; res: Balt; ref: 1, 21, 97, 700, 783, 1564, 1598, 1674, 1687
LEE, Edgar A.; pvt; 35th VA Cav, Co A; ref: 1, 3, 15, 1611, 1677
LEE, Edmund J.; pvt; 7th VA Cav, Co G; ref: 1, 3
LEE, George W.; pvt; 7th VA Cav, Co I; ref: 1, 3, 15, 19, 1609, 1611, 1677
LEE, Humphrey W.; sgt; 32nd VA Inf, Co I; res: Balt; ref; 1, 21, 272, 700
LEE, J. Boykin; ordnance sgt; 7th SC Cav; res: Balt; ref: 1, 21, 53, 56, 700
LEE, J. C.; pvt; Hampton Leg Lt Arty, Co B; ref: 1, 2, 19, 21, 1523
LEE, J. T.; pvt; 1st SC Inf, Co G; ref: 1
LEE, J. Watkins; pvt; MD Guerrilla Zouaves; ref: 1, 70
LEE, James C.; pvt; 1st SC Inf, Co G; res: South River, AA Cty; ref: 1, 1539
LEE, Jeremiah; pvt; 1st SC Inf, Co G; ref: 1
LEE, John; pvt; Davis's MD Cav, Co A; ref: 1

LEE, John Frank; pvt; 35th VA Cav, Co A; ref: 1, 3, 15, 1611, 1677
LEE, John W.; pvt; 2nd MD Cav, Co E; res: Balt; ref: 1, 1609
LEE, John Mason; Maj; Asst I.G., Gen F. Lee's staff; ref: 1, 21, 154, 700, 791
LEE, M. L.; cpl; Lee's MD Cav; res: Woodberry; ref: 1
LEE, Otho Scott; sgt maj; Steuart''s Horse Arty; res: Bel Air, Har Cty; ref: 1, 2, 19, 21, 122, 700, 735, 1523, 1663
LEE, Philip Henry; Capt; Lee's MD Cav; ref: 1, 1628
LEE, R. J. D.; Lt; 1st MD Inf, Co C; ref: 1, 19, 1523
LEE, Richard Henry; pvt; Hampton Leg Lt Arty, Co B; res: Bt Cty; ref: 1, 2, 19, 21, 69, 316, 686, 1523
LEE, Robert; pvt; MD American Rifles; res: Tal Cty; ref: 1, 19, 645, 1523, 1612
LEE, Wezehiah C.; smn, Navy; Richmond Naval Station; res: St. Margarett, AA Cty; ref: 1, 1539
LEE, William; res: St. M. Cty; ref: 1509, 1670
LEE, William C.; pvt; 2nd MD Inf, Co E; res: Annapolis, AA Cty; ref: 1, 2, 19, 21, 69, 316, 1523, 1539
LEE, William W.; pvt; 35th VA Cav, Co A; ref: 1, 3, 15, 1611, 1677
LEE, Wills; pvt; Richmond Howitzers, 2nd Co; res: Balt; ref: 21, 56, 700
LEE, Z. Collins; 1st MD Lt Arty; res: Balt; ref: 70
LEEDS, John; res: Tal Cty; ref: 1152
LEEMAN, William M. (M.D.); Physician; Medical Corps; ref: 18, 735
LEFEVRE, Hamilton; pvt; 1st VA Cav, Co L; res: Har Cty; MLCSH; ref: 1, 2, 19, 21, 23, 233, 786, 1523, 1579
LEFEUVE, Jacob (Revd); res: Balt; ref: 1540
LEFFINGER, Isaac; pvt; 1st MD Cav, Co E; ref: 1, 2, 19, 21, 730, 1523
LEFTWICH, Alexander T.; pvt; Pemberton's Co, Signal Corps; res: Balt; ref: 1, 56, 57, 583, 1578
LEGG, E. A.; pvt; 2nd MD Lt Arty; ref: 1, 2, 19, 21, 1523
LEGG, Edgar K.; pvt; 13th VA Inf, Co H; res: Balt; ref: 1, 21, 23, 56, 700
LEGG, George Thomas; pvt; 23rd VA Cav, Co K; res: Bt Cty; MLDSH; ref; 1, 74, 786
LEGG, William E.; pvt; 1st MD Cav, Co K; res: Broad Creek, QA Cty; ref: 1, 19, 1523, 1554
LEGGETT, Andrew Jackson; pvt; 3rd NC Cav, Co K; ref: 1, 72
LEICH, Christopher C.; pvt; 2nd MD Inf, Co D; res: AA Cty; ref: 1, 2, 19, 21, 1523
LEIGH, Benjamin Watkins; Capt; Asst Q.M., Gen A. P. Hill's staff; ref: 1, 19, 1523
LEIGH, John H.; pvt; 5th VA Cav, Co A; res: Balt; ref: 1, 21, 93, 700
LEIGH, William G.; pvt; 1st MD Inf, Co I; res: Cha Cty; ref: 1, 2, 19, 21, 1523
LEISHEAR, George Washington; pvt; 1st MD Cav, Co A; res: Cooksville, How Cty; ref: 1, 2, 19, 21, 71, 1523, 1550
LEITCH, Collumbus; pvt; Barry's Co, MD Vols; res: Friendship, AA Cty; ref: 1, 1539
LEITCH, Marion; pvt; Barry's Co, MD Vols; res: Friendship, AA Cty; ref: 1, 1539
LEITER, Charles; pvt; 1st MD Cav, Co A; ref: 1, 2, 19, 21, 1523
LEMAR, William; res: Cumberland, All Cty; ref: 148
LEMATER, James; pvt; 2nd MD Inf, Co E; ref: 1, 2, 19, 21, 93, 1523
LEMMON, David H.; pvt; 7th VA Cav, Co G; ref: 1, 1621
LEMMON, George S.; Lt; Aid de Camp, Gen J. J. Archer's staff; res: Balt; MLCSH; ref: 1, 2, 19, 21, 30, 35, 38, 44, 503, 559, 627, 650, 681, 689, 700, 757, 782, 786, 1519, 1523, 1583

LEMMON, John S.; pvt; 1st MD Inf, Co H; ref: 1, 2, 19, 21, 650, 681, 757, 1520, 1523
LEMMON, Robert, Jr; Lt; Ordnance Officer, Gen J. J. Archer's staff; res: Balt; ref: 1, 2, 19, 70, 312, 592, 681, 689, 735, 1523, 1672
LEMMON, William Southgate; pvt; 1st MD Cav, Co C; res: Balt; ref: 1, 2, 19, 21, 53, 650, 681, 735, 1511, 1523
LEMOINE, John H.; pvt; 40th VA Inf, Co B; res: Balt; ref: 1, 70
LENHARD, John; pvt; 1st SC Inf, Co G; res: Balt; ref:735
LEON, Henry; pvt; 2nd MD Inf, Co C; ref: 1
LEONARD, Charles H.; pvt; 1st MD Inf, Co E; res: Balt; ref: 1, 2, 19, 21, 1523
LEONARD, Jacob Biddle; pvt; Lee's MD Cav; ref: 1, 735
LEONARD, John H.; pvt; 1st NC Inf, Co A; ref: 1, 735
LEONARD, Michael J.; pvt; 1st MD Inf, Co G; res: Balt; ref: 1, 2, 19, 21, 700, 1523
LEPINE, Charles; drummer; 1st SC Inf, Co G; ref: 1, 800
LEPPER, Charles V.; pvt; 1st VA Cav, Co K; res: Balt; ref: 1, 2, 19, 21, 700, 1523
LERESH, J.; pvt; MD Guerrilla Zouaves; ref: 1
LEROY, H. A.; pvt; 1st sC Inf, Co G; ref: 1
LESLIE, J. T.; pvt; 2nd MD Cav, Co A; ref: 1, 1609
LESLIE, John W.; pvt; 1st MD Cav, Co F; ref: 1, 19, 21, 1523
LESSEY, Samuel H.; pvt; Zarvona's MD Zouaves; ref: 1, 19, 1523
LESTER, William Wharton; Capt; Asst Q.M. Mississippi Dept; res: PG Cty; ref; 1, 71, 791
LEUTBECHER, Charles; pvt; 19th VA Inf, Co A; res: Balt; ref: 21, 124, 700
LEVERING, Thomas H.; pvt; Ward's Battery, AL Lt Arty; res: Balt; ref: 1, 2, 19, 21, 44, 312, 456, 592, 650, 689, 735, 1519, 1523
LEVINING, Joshua; pvt; 1st SC Inf, Co G; ref: 1, 800
LEVY, James C.; sgt; 2nd MD Cav, Co B; ref: 1, 2, 19, 21, 791, 1609
LEWIS, D. S. J.; Hospital Service; ref: 735
LEWIS, Edward T.; pvt; 19th VA Heavy Arty, Co C; ref: 1, 1580
LEWIS, Enock M.; pvt; 19th VA Heavy Arty, Co C; ref: 1, 1580
LEWIS, George C.; pvt; Griffin's Bn, TX Rangers, Co H; res: Kt Cty; ref: 1, 720
LEWIS, George S.; pvt; 4th VA Inf, Co H; ref: 1, 92
LEWIS, George T.; (M.D.); Physician; 47th VA Inf; ref: 1, 18, 19, 1523
LEWIS, George W.; sgt; 6th VA Inf, Co H; ref: 1, 21, 700
LEWIS, Henry H.; Lt, Navy; Steamer Spray; ref: 1, 53, 1564
LEWIS, Jason H.; Lmn, Navy; C.S. Florida; res: Balt; ref: 1, 1540
LEWIS, Joseph; res: Balt; ref: 1540
LEWIS, John William; color sgt; 8th VA Cav, Co H; res: Balt; ref: 1, 21, 23, 700
LEWIS, M.; pvt; 3rd MD Lt Arty; ref: 2, 19, 21, 160, 726, 1523
LEWIS, Robert; pvt; 9th VA Inf, Co B; ref: 1, 1576, 1613
LEWIS, Salathiel; pvt; 9th VA Inf, Co B; ref: 1, 1576
LEWIS, Samuel; pvt; Davis's MD Cav; ref: 1, 1563
LEWIS, Thomas; pvt; 9th VA Inf, Co B; ref: 1, 1576
LEWIS, W. J.; pvt; 3rd MD Lt Arty; ref: 461
LEWIS, Walter; pvt; Holbrook's Independent MD Lt Arty; ref: 1
LEWIS, William G.; pvt; Stuart's Horse Arty, Breathed's Battery; ref: 1, 498
LEYMAN, Robert; res: How Cty; ref: 10, 19
LIAMBAUGH, William C.; pvt; 1st MD Cav, Co C; res: Wash Cty; ref: 1, 2, 19, 21, 1523, 1634

LICHLENSTEIN, Reuben; Pickett's Div; res: Cumberland, All Cty; ref: 148

LICKER, W.; 1st MD Inf, Co G; ref: 93

LICKLE, John D. (M.D.); pvt; 1st MD Cav, Co D; res: New Market, Frd Cty; ref: 1, 2, 18, 19, 21, 90, 700, 1601

LIDIARD, Bernard H.; cpl; 1st MD Inf, Co E; ref: 1, 2, 19, 21, 1523

LIFFLER, George; res: Balt; ref: 1540

LIGHT, John; cpl; 3rd MD Lt Arty; ref: 1, 2, 19, 21, 23, 160, 726, 1460, 1523

LIGHTNER, Henry; pvt; 1st MD Cav, Co F; res: Balt; ref: 1, 19, 1523

LILES, Benjamin R.; pvt; 1st SC Inf, Co G; ref: 1

LILES, J. T.; pvt; 1st SC Inf, Co G; ref: 1

LILLISTON, Thomas P.; pvt; Edelin's MD Heavy Arty; ref: 1

LILLY, ---; cpl; res: Carr Cty; ref; 91

LINCOLN, J. Rush; pvt; 1st MD Cav, Co A; ref: 1, 2, 19, 21, 1523

LINDENBOURNE, John; pvt; Davis's MD Cav; res: Annapolis, AA Cty; ref: 1, 1539

LINDENBOURNE, Philip; pvt; 2nd MD Lt Arty; ref: 1, 2, 19, 21, 1523

LINDNER, Charles; pvt; Rhett's 1st SC Heavy Arty, Co H; ref: 1, 700

LINDSEY, Alexander (M.D.); Acting Asst Surg; Gen Hospital No. 4., Wilmington NC; res: Balt; ref: 1, 18, 70

LINDSEY, Elijah; pvt; Stuart's Horse Arty, Breathed's Battery; ref: 1, 498

LINDSEY, James; pvt; Stuart's Horse Arty, Breathed's Battery; ref: 1

LINDSEY, Richard; pvt; 34th AL Inf, Co D; res: Johnsons Store, aA Cty; ref: 1, 1539

LINDSEY, S. J.; pvt; 3rd MD Lt Arty; ref: 1, 2, 19, 21, 160, 726, 1523

LINSENMYER, George; res: McPherson Pack, AA Cty; ref: 1539

LINTHICUM, Abner; pvt; Jacobs Mounted Riflemen; res: AA Cty; ref: 1, 1539, 1628

LINTHICUM, Charles Frederick (Revd); Chaplain, 8th VA Inf; res: Frd Cty; ref: 1, 15, 23, 735, 791

LINTHICUM, Edwin; pvt; 1st MD Cav, Co A; res: How Cty; ref: 1, 2, 10, 19, 21, 700, 1523

LINTHICUM, Herman R.; Roadmaster; NC Railroad; res: Middletown, Frd cty; ref: 720

LINTHICUM, John; res: Annapolis, AA Cty; ref: 1539

LINTHICUM, John Warren; 43rd VA Cav (Mosby's); res: Clarksville, How Cty; ref: 1, 2, 10, 21, 23, 67, 687, 1523, 1548, 1550

LINTZ, Samuel; pvt; 1st VA Inf, Co E; ref: 1, 735

LINZEY, James H.; pvt; 1st MD Cav, Co C; res: Towson, Bt Cty; ref; 1, 19, 21, 1523, 1575

LIPSCOMB, Frank; pvt; 1st MD Cav, Co A; ref: 1, 2, 19, 21, 1523

LIPSCOMB, Philip; pvt; 2nd MD Inf, Co D; ref: 1, 2, 19, 21, 79, 1523

LIPSCOMB, Thomas; drummer; 2nd MD Inf, Co: 1

LISSTON, Thomas A.; pvt; 19th VA Heavy Arty, Co C; ref: 1, 1580

LITCHFIELD, C. W., Jr; pvt; 1st MD Lt Arty; ref: 1

LITTLE, Columbus M.; pvt; 19th VA Heavy Arty, Co C; ref: 1, 1580

LITTLE, Daniel C.; pvt; MD Guerrilla Zouaves; ref: 1

LITTLE, Lewis Henry; Brig Gen, Army of the West; res: Balt; ref: 1, 2, 18, 19, 23, 27, 39, 44, 50, 127, 130, 153, 158, 162, 164, 388, 431, 491, 511, 682, 674, 735, 791, 857, 864, 993, 1006, 1094, 1193, 1279, 12882, 1523, 1568, 1577, 1579, 1588, 1623, 1649

LITTLEFORD, John T.; pvt; Barry's Co, MD Vols; ref: 1, 2, 19, 21, 1523

LITTLEJOHN, Clifton W.; pvt; 2nd MD Cav, Co D; ref: 1, 19, 1523, 1609

LITTLEPAGE, James; pvt; Davis's MD Cav, ref: 1
LITTLEPAGE, Lewis Livingston; pvt; 53rd VA Inf, Co D; res: Balt; ref: 1, 70
LITTLESTON, T. P.; pvt; 21st VA Inf, Co B; ref: 1, 2, 19, 312, 1523
LITTLETON, R.; pvt; Davis's MD Cav, Co B; ref: 1, 19, 1523
LIUMAN, Gustan; pvt; 1st MD Cav, Co C; res: Catonsville, Bt Cty; ref: 70
LIVESAY, James A.; pvt; 3rd VA Inf, Co E; res: Balt; ref: 1, 21, 700
LIVESAY, T. T.; sgt; 3rd VA Inf, Co E; res: Balt; ref: 1, 21, 700
LLEWELLEN, John; pvt; Stuart's Horse Arty, Breathed's Battery; ref: 1
LLOYD, Charles Tilghman; pvt; 2nd MD Inf, Co A; res: Tal Cty; ref; 2, 19, 21, 107, 259, 645, 1520, 1523
LLOYD, Daniel, Jr; pvt; 1st MD Lt Arty; res: Cambridge, Dor Cty; ref: 1, 2, 19, 21, 112, 645, 1523, 1547
LLOYD, James A.; pvt; 1st VA Inf, Co E; res: Laurel Factory, AA Cty; ref: 1, 735, 1539
LLOYD, John A.; pvt; 1st MD Cav, Co F; ref: 1, 2, 19, 21, 1523
LOANE, William T. J.; pvt; 2nd MD Inf, Co A; ref: 1, 2, 21, 650
LOBBAN, John G.; Capt; 49th VA Inf, Co F; ref: 1, 57, 791
LOCKE, Leonard E.; Capt; 53rd AL Partisan Rangers, Co F; res: Balt; ref: 1, 18
LOCKERMAN, Theodore R.; pvt; 3rd VA Inf, Co D; res: Tal Cty; ref; 1, 645, 1612
LOCKETT, John B.; 4th NC Inf; ref: 93
LOCKINGTON, James A.; pvt; 1st MD Inf, Co E; ref: 1, 2, 19, 21, 1523
LOCKS, Leonard E. (M.D.); Surg; AL Cav; res: Balt; ref: 70
LODGE, John; pvt; 1st SC Inf, Co G; res: Balt; ref: 735
LOGAN, Alexander; pvt; 1st VA Cav, Co K; ref: 1, 2, 19, 21, 1523
LOGAN, James G.; pvt; 21st VA Inf, Co B; ref: 1
LOGAN, Robert; res: Annapolis, AA Cty; ref: 1539
LOGSDEN, John; pvt; 1st MD Inf, Co G; ref: 1, 2, 21
LOGSDEN, Nimrod; pvt; 2nd MD Cav, Co F; ref: 1, 2, 19, 21, 1523
LOGUE, John; pvt; 1st MD Inf, Co F; res: Balt; ref: 1, 2, 19, 21, 1523, 1598
LOGUE, Michael; pvt; 1st MD Inf, Co F; res: Balt; ref: 1, 2, 19, 21, 819, 1523
LOID, Robert; pvt; 1st MD Inf, Co E; ref: 1
LOID, William; pvt; 1st MD Inf, Co E; ref: 1
LOIECKY, Isadore; res: Balt; ref: 1540
LOKER, Edward T.; pvt; 1st MD Cav, Co A; res: St. M. Cty; ref: 1, 2, 19, 21, 1509, 1523
LOKER, James B.; res: St. M. Cty; ref: 1670
LOKER, William M.; pvt; 1st MD Cav, Co A; res: St. M. Cty; ref: 1, 2, 19, 21, 1509, 1523
LOMAX, Thomas Lunford; pvt; 3rd Bn, VA Inf Local Defense, Co D; res: Balt; MLCSH; ref: 1, 93, 627, 700, 786
LOMAX, William R.; pvt; 5th VA Cav, Co K; res: Balt; MLCSH; ref: 1, 21, 700, 786
LOMBARD, Henry C.; pvt; Zarvona's MD Zouave; ref: 1, 19, 735, 1523
LONDENSLAGER, Thomas; pvt; Stuart's Horse Arty, Breathed's Battery; res: Balt; ref: 1, 498
LONDON, W. L.; Capt; Asst A.G., Gen B. Grimes' staff; ref: 1, 862
LONG, Benjamin E.; pvt; 7th VA Cav, Co G; ref: 1, 1622
LONG, Edward S.; pvt; 2nd MD Lt Arty; res: Balt; ref: 1, 2, 19, 21, 1523, 1540
LONG, George E.; pvt; 2nd MD Lt Arty; res: Balt; ref; 1, 2, 19, 21, 700, 1523, 1540
LONG, John; pvt; Lucas' 15th SC Heavy Arty; ref: 1

LONG, Patrick; pvt; 60th VA Inf, Co A; res: Balt; ref: 1, 21, 700
LONG, Thomas Jefferson; pvt; 2nd MD Inf, Co B; res: Chaptico, St. M. Cty; ref; 1, 2, 19, 21 1509, 1555, 1670
LONG, William H.; pvt; Davis's MD Cav, Co A; ref: 1
LORD, William; cpl; 2nd MD Inf, Co G; res: QA Cty; ref: 1, 2, 19, 21, 1523, 1609
LORSCH, Henry; pvt; 19th VA Inf, Co A; res: Balt; MLCSH; ref; 21, 124, 700, 786
LOTT, James; pvt; Davis's MD Cav, Co C; ref: 1
LOTTS, Mackall; pvt; 1st SC Inf, Co G; res: Balt; ref: 1, 19, 735, 1523
LOUD, John J.; pvt; 4th MD Lt Arty; res: Dor Cty; ref: 1, 2, 19, 21, 1523
LOUGHBOROUGH, James Henry; pvt; 10th VA Cav, Co A; res: Bethesda, Mont Cty; ref: 1, 86, 316
LOUGHLIN, Michael; pvt; 17th VA Inf, Co C; ref: 1, 142, 251
LOUGHRAN, Henry; pvt; 2nd MD Inf, Co C; res: Balt; ref; 1, 2, 19, 21, 1523, 1613
LOUNES, Lloyd; ref: 23
LOUVIOT, Francis; cpl; Zarvona's MD Zouaves; ref: 1, 735
LOVE, Lucien; pvt; 43rd VA Cav (Mosby's), Arty Co; ref: 8, 19
LOVE, N. L.; pvt; 2nd MD Inf, Co A; ref: 2, 19
LOVE, Samuel; pvt; Dunn's Co, Mississippi Rangers; ref: 1, 70
LOVE, Thomas; Chaplain; ref: 70
LOVE, William; Chaplain; 3rd MD Lt Arty; ref: 1, 2, 19, 21, 70, 160, 726, 1523
LOVEDAY, Carl L.; pvt; 12th VA Cav, Co F; res: PG Cty; ref: MLCSH; ref: 1, 2, 19, 21, 700, 735, 786, 1609
LOVEDAY, William N.; pvt; 2nd MD Inf, Co C; res: Tal Cty; ref: 1, 19, 645
LOVELESS, Philip; pvt; 2nd MD Inf, Co G; ref: 1
LOVELL, Mansfield; Maj Gen; Department No. 1, New Orleans; res: Cec Cty; ref: 1, 18, 19, 23, 24, 30, 31, 64, 97, 109, 110, 126, 127, 130, 135, 137, 146, 153, 162, 164, 166, 206, 396, 397, 400, 401, 426, 431, 674, 735, 787, 789, 791, 1006, 1523, 1526, 1528, 1568, 1569, 1577, 1578, 1579, 1583, 1588, 1621, 1623, 1646
LOVELY, John Emanuel; pvt; 1st MD Inf, Co A; res: Frd Cty; ref: 1, 2, 19, 21, 89, 1523
LOWDES, James A.; pvt; 2nd MD Lt Arty; res: Balt; ref: 1, 2, 19, 21, 1523
LOWE, Daniel W.; pvt; 43rd VA Cav (Mosby's), Co F; ref: 1, 2, 8, 19, 21, 1523
LOWE, Henry C.; pvt; Lucas' 15th SC Heavy Arty; ref: 1
LOWE, James J.; pvt; 9th VA Inf, Co B; ref: 1, 1576
LOWE, William Edwin; pvt; 2nd MD Inf, Co A; res: Bayside, Tal Cty; ref; 1, 2, 19, 21, 23, 470, 645, 650, 700, 1162, 1281, 1523
LOWE, Wrightson L.; pvt; 2nd MD Inf, Co A; res: Tal Cty; ref: 1, 2, 19, 21, 23, 470, 645, 650, 700, 1281, 1523, 1612
LOWERY, James E.; pvt; 35th VA Cav, Co B; res: Balt; ref: 1, 3, 1523, 1611, 1677
LOWERY, Ross; pvt; 2nd MD Cav, Co B; ref: 1
LOWMAN, Lorenzo; pvt; Lee's Balt Lt Arty, Alexander's Bn; res: Millersville, AA Cty; ref: 1, 1539
LOWMAN, Martin; pvt; Lee's Balt Lt Arty, Alexander Bn; res: AA Cty; ref: 1, 1539
LOWMAN, Richard; pvt; Lee's Balt Lt Arty, Alexander's Bn; res: Millersville, AA Cty; ref: 1, 1539
LOWNDES, Charles; pvt; 4th VA Cav, Co E; res: How Cty; ref: 1, 70
LOWREY, F. M.; pvt; 3rd MD Lt Arty; ref: 1, 2, 19, 21, 160, 726, 1523

LOWREY, James E.; pvt; 1st MD Inf, Co G; ref: 1, 2, 19, 21, 1523
LOYSDEN, N.; pvt; 1st MD Cav, Co E; ref: 2, 19, 21, 1523
LOZZINS, Henry B.; pvt; 28th MS Inf, Co K; ref: 70
LUBER, David; pvt; Holbrook's Independent MD Lt Arty; ref: 1
LUCAS, Charles; pvt; 4th MD Lt Arty; ref: 2, 19, 1523
LUCAS, H. C.; pvt; 1st MD Cav, Co F; ref: 2, 19, 21, 1523
LUCAS, James Buchanan; pvt; 2nd MD Cav, Co B; res: Wash Cty; ref: 1, 19, 74, 1609
LUCAS, John A.; acting bsn, Navy; Drewey's Bluff, VA; res: Balt; ref: 1
LUCAS, William Henry; sgt; 1st SC Inf, Co C; res: Balt; MLCSH; ref: 92, 93, 627, 700, 786, 1540
LUCAS, William J.; pvt; 2nd MD Lt Arty; ref: 1, 2, 19, 21, 1523
LUCCHISE, David H.; pvt; 2nd MD Inf, Co A; res: Balt; ref: 1, 2, 19, 21, 650, 700, 1523
LUCKETT, Cooke D.; pvt; 6th VA Cav, Co A; res: Rockville, Mont Cty; ref: 1, 23, 557, 1574
LUCKETT, George T.; pvt; Stuart's Horse Arty, Breathed's Battery; ref: 1, 498, 1509
LUCKETT, S. T.; pvt; 43rd VA Cav (Mosby's), Co C; ref: 1, 8, 19
LUDEKSE, John; pvt; 1st SC Inf, Co G; res: Balt; ref: 735
LUDWIG, Romanus Philip; pvt; 35th VA Cav, Co D; res: Balt; MLCSH; ref: 627, 700, 786, 1599, 1677
LUITZ, Cornelius; res: St. M. Cty; ref: 1509
LUIZAY, James H.; res: Towson, Bt Cty; ref: 700
LUKE, Williamson; pvt; McNeill's Rangers; ref: 1, 504
LUKEMAN, R.; pvt; 1st VA Inf, Co E; ref: 735
LUM, Benjamin F.; pvt; 1st MD CAv, Co E; ref: 1, 2, 19, 21, 730, 1523
LUMAN, G. W.; res: Balt; ref: 700
LUMAN, H. E.; pvt; 1st MD CAv, Co F; ref: 1, 19
LUMKIN, E. T.; pvt; 1st SC Inf, Co G; ref: 1
LUMKIN, Gilmor A.; pvt; 19th VA Heavy Arty, Co C; ref: 1, 1580
LUMKIN, James T.; pvt; 1st MD Cav, Co C; res: Balt; ref: 1, 2, 19, 21, 1523
LUMSDEN, Drury Lacy; pvt; 2nd SC Cav, Co H; res: How Cty; MLCSH; ref: 1, 21, 93, 627, 700, 786
LUPTON, Thomas N.; pvt; 51st VA Militia, Co F; ref: 1, 70
LURMAN Gustav W.; pvt; 1st MD Cav, Co C; res: Balt; ref: 1, 2, 19, 21, 53, 56, 57, 513, 1519, 1523
LURTZ, Connel J.; pvt; 2nd MD Inf, Co B; ref: 1
LUSBY, James; pvt; Stuart's Horse Arty, Breathed's Battery; res: Balt; MLCSH; ref: 1, 2, 19, 21, 93, 498, 627, 786, 1027, 1523
LUSHER, Robert M.; pvt; 3rd Bn, VA Local Defense Inf, Co D; res: Georgetown; ref: 1;
LUTTS, John J.; pvt; 1st MD Inf, Co E; ref: 1, 2, 19, 21, 23, 64, 456, 599, 700, 791, 1523, 1593
LUTTZ, Conrad; pvt; 1st MD Inf, Co B; ref: 1, 2, 19, 21, 1523
LUTZ, John; Gen J. H. Winder's Detectives; res: Frederick, Frd Cty; ref; 89, 700, 1563
LUTZ, Nicholas T.; pvt; 1st MD Inf, Co A; ref: 1, 2, 19, 21, 1523
LYELL, George J.; pvt; 1st VA Lt Arty, Co D; res: Georgetown; ref: 1, 316
LYELL, Henry; pvt; 9th VA Cav, Co K; res: Balt; ref: 1, 21, 700
LYELL, John W.; Lt Col; 47th VA Inf, res: PG Cty; ref: 1, 23, 105, 124, 316, 791, 1574
LYLE, Duncan C.; Lt; 4th VA Reserves; res: Bt Cty; ref: 21, 700
LYLES, William; Lucas's 15th SC Heavy Arty; ref: 7
LYMAN, William R.; pvt; Stuart's Horse Arty, Breathed's Battery; ref: 1, 70

LYNCH, ---; pvt; 13th VA Inf, Co G; ref: 735

LYNCH, Christopher G.; pvt; 4th MD Lt Arty; res: QA Cty; ref: 1, 2, 19, 21, 1523

LYNCH, Daniel; pvt; 3rd MD Lt Arty; res: Balt; ref: 1, 2, 19, 21, 160, 461, 726, 1523, 1540

LYNCH, Daniel; pvt; Lucas' 15th SC Heavy Arty; ref: 1

LYNCH, George; Capt; 6th AL Inf, Co C; res: St. M. Cty; ref; 1, 70, 631, 791

LYNCH, James Ireton; Capt, Navy; Coast of NC Defences; res: Balt; ref: 1, 61, 97, 127, 269, 274, 279, 282, 284, 431, 543, 628, 654, 682, 700, 721, 774, 1495, 1499, 1515, 1632, 1671

LYNCH, John; pvt; 2nd MD Inf, Co D; ref: 1, 2, 19, 21, 1523

LYNCH, John P.; pvt; 2nd MD Lt Arty; res: Balt; ref: 1, 2, 19, 21, 1523

LYNCH, John Stevens (M.D.); Lt; 6th AL Inf, Co C; res: St. M. Cty; ref: 1, 18, 70, 631

LYNCH, Junius J.; Asst Paymaster, Navy; C.S. Florida; ref: 19, 58, 97, 279, 1523, 1564

LYNCH, William B.; Capt; 17th VA Inf, Co C; res: Frd Cty; ref: 1, 1032

LYNE, John; Capt; res: Sharpsburg, Wash Cty; ref: 361

LYNE, Thomas; Commissary Dept; Sharpsburg, Wash Cty; ref: 361

LYNN, David; Capt; 19th VA Cav, Co F; res: Cumberland, All Cty; ref: 1, 19, 65, 95, 148, 735, 1330, 1523

LYNN, John F.; pvt; 43rd VA Cav (Mosby's), Co H; ref: 1, 1428

LYNN, John Hallaway, Jr; pvt; McNiell's Rangers; res: Cumberland, All Cty; MLCSH; ref: 19, 65, 95, 148, 431, 504, 519, 627, 700, 786, 989, 1523, 1588

LYNN, Sprigg S.; pvt; McNiell's Rangers; res: Cumberland, All Cty; ref: 1, 19, 64, 95, 145, 148, 473, 504, 519, 735, 1010, 1523, 1560, 1579, 1610, 1636

LYON, James Thomas; sgt; MD Guerrilla Zouaves; res: Cha Cty; ref: 1, 2, 19, 21, 650, 1523, 1677

LYON, James William; Maj; Commissary of Supply, Gen I. R. Trimble's staff; res: Bt Cty; ref; 1, 2, 8, 19, 21, 44, 57, 70, 449, 503, 650, 700, 724, 791, 1523, 1578, 1674

LYON, Samuel H.; pvt; 1st MD Cav, Co C; res: Bt Cty; ref: 1, 2, 19, 21, 56, 233, 690, 777, 1523, 1565

LYONS, Burton; pvt; 1st MD Cav, Co B; res: Bt Cty; ref: 1, 2, 19, 21, 785, 1523

LYONS, Thomas; pvt; 13th VA Inf, Co G; ref: 1

LYONS, William H.; pvt; 2nd MD Inf, Co E; res: South River, AA Cty; ref: 1, 2, 19, 21, 645, 1523, 1539, 1557

LYTLE, William A.; pvt; 19th VA Heavy Arty, Co C; ref: 1, 1580

McALEER, Joseph L.; Capt; 2nd MD Inf, Co D; res: Emmitsburg, Frd Cty; ref: 1, 2, 19, 21, 23, 64, 66, 68, 90, 462, 700. 791, 1520, 1523

McALEESE, Francis L.; pvt; 35th VA Cav, Co F; res: Leonardtown, St. M. Cty; ref: 1, 1509, 1555, 1662, 1677

McALEESE, James; Lt; 12th VA Cav, Co F; ref: 1, 2, 11, 21, 23, 194,

McALEVEE, George W.; cpl; 2nd MD Lt Arty; MLCSH; ref: 1, 2, 19, 21, 700, 786, 1494

McARDLE, Henry A.; pvt; 21st VA Inf, Co B; ref: 1, 2, 19, 312

McATEE, George W.; cpl; 2nd MD Inf, Co D; res: Har Cty; ref: 1, 2, 19, 21, 23

McATEE, Henry; pvt; 2nd MD Inf, Co D; res: Har Cty; ref: 1, 2, 19, 21

McATEE, J. M.; pvt; 2nd MD Cav, Co A; ref: 1, 19

McATEE, Samuel E.; pvt; 1st MD Cav, Co C; res: Har Cty; ref: 1, 2, 19, 21
McAVOY, John F.; Lt; McNally's AR Battery; ref: 735
McAVOY, Joseph Y.; pvt; 22nd MS Inf, Co D; res: Balt; MLCSH; ref: 1, 21, 93, 700, 735, 786
McAVOY, Peter; pvt; MD Guerrilla Zouaves; ref: 1
McAVOY, William F.; pvt; 2nd MD Lt Arty; res: Balt; ref: 1, 2, 19, 21
McBLAIR, Charles R.; pvt; 43rd VA Cav (Mosby's), Co D; ref: 1, 8
McBLAIR, Charles Henry; Commander, Navy; C.S. Huntsville; res: Cumberland, All Cty; ref: 1, 19, 21, 58, 61, 64, 65, 70, 95, 97, 148, 279, 700, 735, 783, 791, 1515, 1523, 1564
McBLAIR, Charles R.; Acting Mast. M., Navy; C.S.S. Tennessee; ref: 1, 735, 1564
McBLAIR, Duncan; Mast. M., Navy; C.S.S. Isondiga; ref: 1, 19, 65, 95, 148, 1564
McBLAIR, William, Jr; Acting Mast. M., Navy; C.S.S. Atlanta; ref: 1, 1564
McBLAIR, William, Sr; Commander, Navy; C.S.S. Atlanta; ref: 1, 2, 19, 21, 58, 61, 70, 97, 279, 700, 735, 783, 791, 1564
McBRIDE, E. Thomas; pvt; 1st MD Cav, Co C; res: Emmitsburg, Frd Cty; ref: 1, 2, 19, 21, 90
McCABE, George; pvt; 2nd MD CAv, Co G; res: Balt; ref: 1, 2, 19, 21, 1540
McCabe, George W. E.; pvt; Stuart's Horse Arty, Breathed's Battery, res: Balt; ref: 1, 2, 19, 21, 498
McCABE, Luke; pvt; 1st MD inf, Co E; ref: 1, 2, 19, 21
McCADE, William; Castle Pinkney's SC Heavy Arty; ref; 735
McCAFFERTY, James F.; pvt; 41st AL Inf, Co C; res: Annapolis, AA Cty; ref: 1, 1539, 1628
McCAFFERTY, John; pvt; 50th AL Inf, Co B; res: Cumberland, All Cty; ref: 1, 65, 95, 148
McCAFFRAY, George; res: Balt; ref; 631
McCAHAN, Hugh; pvt; 13th VA inf, Co G; ref: 1
McCAHAN, J. H.; smn, Navy; C.S.S. Albemarle; ref: 1
McCALEB, James H.; pvt; 12th TX Inf, Co C; ref: 1, 2, 19, 312, 592, 1519
McCALL, Alexander; pvt; 1st MD Inf, Co B; ref: 1, 2, 19, 21
McCALL, R.; pvt; 1st MD Cav, Co B; ref:1, 2, 19, 21
McCALOP, James J.; sgt; ref: 1690
McCAMPBELL, Andrew W.; pvt; 1st MD Cav, Co A; ref: 1, 19
McCANN, Charles; Lt; 3rd VA Inf, Co E; res: Balt; ref: 1, 21, 700
McCANN, James K.; pvt, Marine Corps; C.S.S. Gaines; res: Balt; ref: 1, 1540, 1594
McCANN, Patrick; Artificer; 3rd MD Lt Arty; ref: 1, 2, 19, 21, 23, 160, 726
McCANN, William V.; pvt; 2nd MD Inf, Co C; res: Balt; MLCSH; ref: 1, 2, 19, 21, 700, 786
McCARDELL, Thomas F.; Lt; 64th VA Inf, Co C; res: All Cty; ref; 1, 21, 700, 1610
McCARROLL, William J.; Lt; 2nd MD Cav, Co D; ref: 1, 19, 1609
McCARTHY, Daniel; pvt; 1st MD inf, Co F; ref: 1, 2, 19, 21
McCARTHY, James; pvt; 3rd MD Lt Arty; ref: 1, 2, 19, 21, 160, 726
McCARTHY, John T.; pvt; Lucas' 15th SC Heavy Arty; ref: 1
McCARTHY, Martin; pvt; MD Guerrilla Zouaves; ref: 1
McCARTHY, Timothy J.; pvt; Lucas' 15th SC Heavy Arty; ref: 1
McCARTY, John; pvt; 19th VA Heavy Arty, Co C; ref: 1, 19, 1580
McCARTY, Neil; mach, Navy; C.S. Gen M. Jeff Thompson; ref: 1, 1564, 1580

McCASKER, Luke; pvt; Rhett's 1st SC Heavy Arty, Co A; res: Balt; ref: 1, 735
McCAUL, ---; 2nd MD Cav; ref: 11
McCAULEY, Daniel; pvt; Paris's Co, VA Lt Arty; res: Balt; MLCSH; ref: 1, 627, 786
McCAULEY, John; pvt; Edelin's MD Heavy Arty; res: St. Margarett, AA Cty; ref; 1, 1539
McCAULIFF, Daniel; pvt; 19th VA Heavy Arty, Co C; ref: 1, 1580
McCAULL, John A.; sgt; Lucas' 15th SC Heavy Arty; ref: 1, 2, 19, 240
McCAULY, Angles; pvt; 1st SC Inf, Co G; ref: 1
McCAWLEY, William N.; Lt; 9th VA Cav, Co K; res: Balt; ref: 21, 23, 700
McCEENY, Rufus; sgt; 3rd MD Lt Arty; ref: 1, 2, 19, 21, 23, 160, 726
McCEVITT, Arthur; pvt; 2nd MD Inf, Co A; res: Balt; ref; 1, 2, 19, 21, 650
McCHUE, David; cpl; Lucas' 15th SC Heavy Arty; res: Balt; ref: 1
McCLANE, Asbury; pvt; Lee's MD Cav; res: McPherson Pack, AA Cty; ref: 1 1539
McCLANE, Hector; smn, Navy; res: Balt; ref; 1
McCLAFFERTY, John; pvt; 7th VA Cav, Co G; ref: 1
McCLEARY, Douglas; Capt; 7th VA; ref: 70
McCLEARY, John W.; sgt; 12th VA Cav, Co D; res: Balt; ref: 1, 1419
McCLEERY, Peter Henry; pvt; 1st MD Cav, Co C; res: All Cty; MLCSH; ref: 1, 19, 21, 93, 627, 700, 786
McCLELLAN, S.; pvt; Holbrook's Independent MD Lt Arty; ref: 1, 19
McCLEMMY, George T.; pvt; 1st MD Cav, Co E; ref: 1, 2, 19, 21, 730
McCLENAHAN, W.; pvt; 1st MD Inf, Co A; ref: 1, 19
McCLENNY, James M.; pvt; 9th VA Inf, Co B; ref: 1, 1576
McCLERNAN, James; pvt; 1st MD Inf, Co C; res: Balt; ref: 1, 2, 19, 21, 1540
McCLERNAN, John H.; pvt; 2MD Cav, Co B; res: Balt; ref: 1, 1540
McCLERNAN, Samuel T.; pvt; 2nd MD Lt Arty; res: Balt; ref: 1, 2, 19, 21, 1540, 1609
McCLINTOCK, Richard; pvt; Davis's MD Cav; res: Balt; ref: 1
McCLINTOCK, Samuel; pvt; 1st MD Lt Arty; ref: 1, 2, 21
McCLUNG, David G.; pvt; Barry's Co MD Vols; ref: 1
McCLURE, George Douglas; pvt; 4th MD Lt Arty; res: Balt Cty; MLCSH; ref: 1, 2, 19, 21, 70, 93, 627, 700, 786
McCLURE, James N.; sgt; 6th VA Cav, Co D; res: Balt; MLCSH; ref: 1, 21, 786
McCLURE, Thomas; pvt; 4th MD Lt Arty; ref: 1, 2, 19, 21
McCLUSTER, John; pvt; Davis's MD Cav, Co B; ref: 1
McCLUTCHY, John F.; pvt; 1st MD Inf, Co F; ref: 1, 2, 19, 21
McCOBB, Joseph; pvt; 43rd VA Cav (Mosby's), Co D; res: Balt; ref; 8, 823
McCOFFREY, Thomas; pvt; 9th AL Inf, Co K; res: Balt; ref: 1, 1540
McCOLD, James; Castle Pinkney's SC Heavy Arty; ref: 735
McCOOL, Dennis; pvt; 2nd MD Cav, Co A; ref: 1, 19, 1609
McCORMICK, Henry Alexander; pvt; 2nd MD Inf, Co A; ref: 1, 2, 19, 21, 259, 650
McCORMICK, James W.; pvt; 35th VA Cav, Co B; res: Mont Cty; ref: 1, 3, 15, 1611, 1677
McCORMICK, John Edward; pvt; 1st MD Inf, Co F; res: Balt; ref; 1, 2, 21, 700, 1523
McCORMICK, Lewis D.; pvt; 2nd MD Inf, Co A; ref: 1, 2, 19, 21, 650
McCORMICK, Van H.; pvt; 1st VA Cav, Co A; res: PG Cty; ref: 1, 2, 19, 21, 470, 735, 785
McCOULEY, Daniel; pvt; Staunton Hill Lt Arty; MLCSH; ref: 21, 93, 700
McCOURT, C. A.; pvt; 43rd VA Cav (Mosby's), Co E; ref: 1, 8

McCOURT, James R.; pvt; 1st MD Cav, Co C; ref: 1, 2, 19, 21
McCOURT, Michael; pvt; 2nd MD Inf, Co A; res: Balt; ref: 1, 2, 19, 21, 23, 650
McCOY, Henry; Capt; Asst Q.M., Gen J. H. Winder's staff; res: Kt Cty; ref: 1, 2, 19, 64, 68, 70, 456, 668, 781, 791, 1523, 1584
McCOY, James; cpl; 13th VA Inf, Co G; res: Balt; ref: 1, 735, 1540
McCOY, Robert H.; pvt; 7th VA Cav, Co E; res: Kt Cty; ref: 1, 1584
McCREADY, John; cpl; 2nd MD Inf, Co D; res: Dor Cty; ref: 1, 2, 19, 21, 112
McCREADY, Thomas B.; pvt; 2nd MD Inf, Co D; res: Dor Cty; ref: 1, 2, 19, 21, 112
McCREERY, J. N. L.; sgt; Richmond Howitzers, 1st Co; ref: 19, 21, 101, 700, 1523
McCUBBIN, Clarence, H.; pvt; 1st VA Cav, Co K; ref: 1, 92, 93
McCUBBIN, Edward; pvt; 1st VA Cav, Co K; ref: 1, 2, 19, 21
McCUBBIN, George B.; q.m. sgt; 4th MD Lt Arty; res: Queens Town, QA Cty; ref: 1, 2, 19, 21, 64, 1554
McCUBBIN, Robert W., Jr; pvt; 2nd MD Lt Arty; res: Balt; ref: 1, 2, 19, 21
McCULLARS, James O.; Stuart's Horse Arty, Breathed's Battery; ref: 1
McCULLEY, William; pvt; 3rd MD Lt Arty; ref: 1, 2, 19, 21, 160, 726
McCULLOUGH, J.; pvt; Davis's MD Cav; ref: 1, 19
McCULLOUGH, Samuel Thomas; Lt; 2nd MD Inf, Co D; res: Annapolis, AA Cty; ref: 1, 2, 13, 19, 21, 23, 64, 68, 674, 700, 1628
McCULLOUGH, William R.; sgt maj; 2nd MD Inf; res: Cec Cty; ref: 1, 2, 19, 21, 23, 1523
McCURDIE, J. W.; pvt; 2nd MD Cav, Co D; ref: 1, 19, 1609
McCURE, Thomas; pvt; 4th MD Lt Arty; ref: 1, 2, 19, 21
McCURRY, L.; pvt; 3rd MD Lt Arty; ref: 461
McCUSKER, Lewis C.; pvt; 3rd SC Cav, Co H; res: Balt; ref: 1, 70
McDANIEL, James; res: Frederick, Frd Cty; ref; 89
McDANIEL, John T.; pvt; 1st MD Cav, Co D; res: Frederick, Frd Cty; ref; 1, 2, 19, 21, 90, 1601
McDANIEL, John W.; hospital steward; 2nd MD Inf, Co A; res: Tal Cty; ref; 1, 2, 19, 21, 23, 64, 470, 645, 1523
McDANIEL, Martin; pvt; 1st SC Inf, Co G; ref: 1
McDERMOTT, James; pvt; 1st MD Inf, Co F; ref: 1, 2, 19, 21
McDERMOTT, John; pvt; 2nd MD Cav, Co B; ref: 1, 19
McDONALD, Daniel M.; Lt; 56th NC Inf, Frd Cty; ref: 1, 19, 1579, 1620
McDONALD, Edward Hitchcock; Maj; 11th VA Cav; res: Balt; ref: 1, 18, 23, 371, 490, 791, 1600
McDONALD, John; pvt; 2nd MD Cav, Co A; ref: 1, 1609
McDONALD, John W.; pvt; 4th VA Cav, Co D; ref: 1, 57
McDONALD, John W.; pvt; 13th VA Inf, Co C; res: Balt; ref: 1, 56
McDONALD, Patrick; pvt; 2nd MD Inf, Co A; res: Balt; MLCSH; ref: 1, 2, 19, 21, 650, 700, 786
McDONALD, Stephen; pvt; 10th VA Bn Heavy Arty, Co A; res: Balt; MLCSH; ref: 1, 93, 627, 700, 786
McDONALD, Thomas; pvt; 3rd MD Lt Arty; ref: 1, 2, 19, 21, 160, 726
McDONALD, Thomas Alexander; Maj; Asst Adj & I.G., Gen D. H. Maury's staff; res: Frederick, Frd Cty; ref: 1, 72, 129, 789
McDONOUGH, William W.; pvt; 35th VA Cav, Co A; res: Hyattstown, Mont Cty; ref; 1, 3, 15, 1611, 1677
McDOWELL, Charles; pvt; 1st MD Cav, Co A; ref: 1, 2, 19, 21, 769
McDOWELL, James; pvt; Teal's TX Lt Arty; res: Balt; MLCSH; ref: 93, 627, 700, 786
McDOWELL, Perry; cpl; 1st MD Inf, Co A; res: Frd Cty; ref; 1, 2, 19, 21, 23, 90

McELWEE, Andrew J.; pvt; 4th MD Lt Arty; ref: 1, 2, 19, 21
McELWEE, George W.; cpl; 2nd MD Lt Arty; ref; 1, 2, 11, 19, 240, 1258, 1523, 1560
McELWEE, Jack; 3rd VA Inf, Co H; ref: 735
McENTEE, James J.; pvt; 1st SC Inf, Co G; res: Balt; ref: 1, 21, 693, 700
McEVANEY, Charles; pvt; 2nd MD Lt Arty; ref; 1, 2, 19, 21
McFALL, J. C.; pvt; 1st SC Inf, Co G; ref; 1
McGARRITY, James H.; pvt; 9th VA Inf, Co B; res: Bt Cty; ref: 1, 1576
McGARY, Charles P.; Lt Commanding, Navy; C.S.S. Tuscaloosa; ref: 19, 58, 61, 97, 279, 791, 1564
McGEARY, J.; pvt; 2nd MD Cav, Co B; ref: 1, 19
McGEE, Daniel; pvt; 1st MD Inf, Co B; ref: 1, 2, 19, 21
McGEE, George R.; pvt; 21st VA Inf, Co B; res: Balt; ref: 1, 2, 21, 312, 700, 735, 1540
McGEE, John; pvt; 1st MD Inf, Co B; ref: 1, 2, 19, 21
McGEEGAN, Patrick; res: Balt; ref: 1540
McGILL, Thomas H.; pvt; 4th VA Cav, Co C; res: Georgetown; ref: 1, 72, 316
McGILL, Thomas J. (M.D.); Acting Asst Surg, Richmond; ref: 1, 18
McGINN, John; pvt; 2nd MD Inf, Co C; ref: 1, 2, 19, 21
McGINNIS, Frank; pvt; 1st VA Cav, Co K; ref: 1, 2, 19, 21, 1523
McGINNIS, James R.; pvt; 1st MD Inf, Co E; ref: 1, 2, 19, 21
McGINNIS, John B.; pvt; Davis's MD Cav, Co C; res: Bt Cty; ref: 1, 93, 1575
McGINNIS, Patrick; pvt; 1st SC Inf, Co G; ref: 1
McGLONE, Bernard, F.; pvt; Zarvona's MD Zouaves; res: Timonium, Bt Cty; ref: 1, 2, 19, 21, 700, 735, 823, 1540, 1677
McGOLRICK, Thomas; cpl; 1st SC Inf, Co G; ref: 1
McGOVERN, John; pvt; 3rd MD Lt Arty; res: Balt; ref; 1, 2, 21, 160, 726, 1540
McGRAW, Joseph; Maj; Commissary of Supply, Gen J. Pegram's staff; res: Sharpsburg, Wash Cty; ref: 1, 2, 19, 735, 1600
McGRAW, Stephen; pvt; 2nd MD Cav, Co F; ref: 1, 19
McGREGOR, James; pvt; Lucas' 15th SC Heavy Arty; res: Balt; ref: 1
McGREGOR, John J.; pvt; 8th AL Inf, Co G; res: Balt; ref: 1, 511, 700
McGUGGIN, Bernard; pvt; 1st MD Inf, Co E; res: Bt Cty; ref: 1
McGUIRE, Charles E.; sgt; 2nd MD Inf, Co A;re f: 21, 700, 1523
McGUIRE, Dennis; pvt; 9th KY Cav, Co E; res: Balt; ref: 1, 1540
McGUIRE, George Lavender; pvt; 8th GA Inf, Co A; res: Balt; MLCSH; ref: 1, 93, 627, 786
McGUIRE, Henry A. W.; pvt; 1st VA Cav, 2nd Co K; res: Balt; ref: 1, 1540
McGUIRE, James W.; pvt; 1st MD Inf, Co C; res: Balt; ref: 1, 2, 19, 1540
McGUIRE, John; pvt; Barry's Co, MD Vols; ref: 1
McGUIRE, Joseph; pvt; 3rd MD Lt Arty; ref: 1, 2, 19, 21, 160, 726
McGUIRT, J.; pvt; 1st SC Inf, Co G; ref: 1
McGUIRT, Thomas; pvt; 1st SC Inf, Co G; ref: 1
McHEIR, John; 2nd VA Inf, Co B; ref: 735
McHENRY, ---; McNiell's Rangers; ref: 735
McHENRY, Hugh; mast. m., Navy; Richmond Naval Battery; res: Balt; ref: 1, 1564
McINTIRE, James; pvt; MD American Rifles; ref: 1, 70, 559
McINTIRE, Malcolm; pvt; MD American Rifles; ref: 1, 70
McINTOSH, David Gregg; Col; McIntosh Lt Arty Bn; res: Towson, Bt Cty; ref; 1, 18, 21, 22, 29, 30, 32,

53, 104, 105, 107, 126, 127, 169, 209, 290, 385, 431, 460, 684, 700, 720, 791, 860, 862, 873, 976, 1058, 1065, 1070, 1074, 1179, 1183, 1342, 1362, 1486, 1575, 1600
McINTYRE, George W.; pvt; 2nd MD Inf, Co A; res: Balt; ref: 19, 259
McINTYRE, Joseph; pvt; 1st MD Inf, Co D; ref: 1, 2, 19, 21
McINTYRE, Robert; pvt; 1st MD Inf, Co D; ref: 1, 2, 19, 21
McINTYRE, Thomas Joseph; pvt; 13th VA Inf, Co G; ref: 1, 735
McINTYRE, William H.; pvt; 1st MD Cav, Co B; ref: 1
McKAIG, John V. L.; McNeill's Rangers; res: Cumberland, All Cty; ref: 1, 19, 65, 95, 148, 504, 519, 1610, 1636
McKAIG, Thomas I., Jr; res: all Cty; ref: 19, 65, 95, 148, 1523, 1538, 1636
McKAIG, William W., Jr; Lt; 2nd MD Cav; res: Cumberland, All Cty; ref: 1, 2, 11, 19, 21, 23, 65, 95, 148, 735, 791, 1538, 1609, 1610, 1636
McKEAN, J.; pvt; Barry's Co, MD Vols; ref: 1, 19
McKEE, Charles W.; cpl; Lucas' 15th SC Heavy Arty; res: Balt; ref: 1, 19, 1609
McKEE, James; pvt; 1st MD Cav, Co C; res: Bt Cty; MLCSH; ref: 1, 2, 19, 21, 53, 93, 786
McKEEN, W. R.; pvt; Davis's MD Cav, Co B; ref: 1, 19
McKEHAN, W.; pvt; 3rd MD Lt Arty; ref: 2, 19, 21, 160, 726
McKELVEY, Charles M.; sgt; 36th VA Cav, Co D; res: Balt; ref; 1, 21, 700
McKENNA, Patrick J.; commissary sgt; 1st VA Inf; res: Balt; ref: 21, 57, 513, 700, 1613
McKENNA, Peter; pvt; Stewart's Horse Arty, Co E; res: Balt; MLCSH; ref: 1, 2, 19, 21, 700, 735, 786
McKENNY, James M.; pvt; 2nd MD Cav, Co D; ref: 1, 2, 1601
McKENZIE, E. H.; pvt; 2nd MD Lt Arty; ref: 1, 2, 21
McKEVITT, Arthur; pvt; 1st MD Inf, Co F; res: Balt; ref: 19, 21, 700
McKEY, Charles W.; pvt; Edelin's MD Heavy Arty; ref: 1
McKEY, J. B. L.; pvt; Davis's MD Cav, Co B; ref: 1, 19
McKIEMER, F. M.; pvt; 2nd MD cav, Co A; ref: 1, 19, 1609
McKIM, Allan; pvt; 43rd VA Cav (Mosby's), Co C; ref: 8, 511, 764
McKIM, B. A.; pvt; 43rd VA Cav (Mosby's), Co B; ref: 1, 8, 511
McKIM, James H.; pvt; Lucas' 15th SC Heavy Arty; ref: 1
McKIM, Randolph Harrison (Revd); Lt; Aid de Camp, Gen G. H. Steuart's staff; res: Balt; ref: 1, 2, 19, 21, 23, 34, 35, 44, 63, 64, 70, 107, 111, 118, 126, 144, 168, 209, 259, 331, 385, 443, 444, 469, 503, 511, 668, 677, 685, 700, 715, 782, 787, 791, 972, 1034, 1054, 1062, 1077, 1109, 1273, 1283, 1296, 1520, 1523, 1579, 1652
McKIM, Robert Buckinridge; pvt; Graham's Co, VA Lt Arty; res: Balt; ref: 1, 2, 35, 70, 107, 272, 501, 511, 559, 681, 685, 735, 1511
McKIM, Simeon; ref: 685
McKIM, William Duncan; Maj; Asst A.G., Gen I. R. Trimble's chief of staff; res: Balt; ref: 1, 2, 19, 35, 44, 68, 259, 501, 511, 650, 681, 724, 753, 764, 791, 1520, 1523
McKIMZIE, Michael; pvt; 19th VA Heavy Arty, Co C; ref: 1, 1580
McKINTEE, J.; pvt; 2nd MD Cav, Co C; ref: 1, 19, 1609
McKISSICK, H. L.; pvt; 3rd MD Lt Arty; ref: 1, 2, 19, 21, 160, 461, 726
McKLA, John; pvt; 2nd MD Inf, Co H; ref: 1, 2, 21
McKNEW, Mason E.; Lt; 1st MD Cav, Co B; res: Beltsville, PG Cty ref: 1, 2, 11, 19, 21, 23, 62, 68, 785, 816, 1553, 1582, 1634

McKNEW, Wilberforce Richmond (M.D.); Surg; 1st MD Cav; res: Beltsville, PG Cty; ref: 1, 2, 18, 19, 21, 23, 57, 63, 64, 68, 94, 700, 916, 1523, 1533, 1536, 1553, 1634
McKNIGHT, Robert; pvt; res: Point of Rocks; ref: 90
McLANAHAN, William H.; pvt; 1st MD Cav, Co D; res: Frederick, Frd Cty; ref; 1, 2, 19, 21, 72, 89, 90, 700, 1601
McLAUGHLIN, Augustus; Lt, Navy; C.S.R.S. United States; ref: 19, 58, 61, 97, 279, 791, 1564
McLAUGHLIN, Ephraim K.; Acting Mast. M., Navy; S.S.S. Virginia; ref: 1, 2, 19, 21, 1564
McLAUGHLIN, Frank A.; pvt 13th VA Inf, Co G; MLCSH; ref: 1, 21, 93, 316, 700, 735, 786
McLAUGHLIN, Hugh; pvt; 1st VA Inf, Co E; ref: 1
McLAUGHLIN, Martin; pvt; 1st MD Inf, Co B; ref: 1, 2, 19, 21
McLAUGHLIN, Thomas; pvt; Lucas' 15th SC Heavy Arty; res: Balt; ref: 1
McLAUGHLIN, Thomas G.; pvt; 2nd MD Cav, Co B; ref: 1, 2, 19, 21, 1609
McLAUGHLIN, William; pvt; 9th VA Inf, Co B; res: Balt; ref: 1, 1576, 1613
McLAURIN, George W.; pvt; 4th VA Cav, Co E; res: Hoods Mill, Carr Cty; ref: 21, 700, 1544
McLEAN, Eugene Eckel; Maj; Chief Q.M., J. E. Johnson's staff; ref: 1, 19, 735, 787, 791
McLEAN, Francis; pvt; Lucas' 15th sC Heavy Arty; ref: 1
McLEESSE, Frank L.; pvt; 2nd MD Cav, Co D; res: Balt; ref: 1, 19, 1609
McLEOD, Harry C.; pvt; 2nd MD Inf, Co B; ref: 1, 2, 19, 21
McLEOD, James M.; pvt; 9th TX Inf, Co C; res: Georgetown; ref: 316
McLEOD, Wilford M. (M.D.); 1st MD Cav, Co B; res: Georgetown; ref: 1, 2, 18, 19, 21, 316, 785, 1574
McLOCKLIN, H.; pvt; 1st VA Inf, Co E; r ef: 735
McLOID, Matthew; pvt; 2nd MD Lt Arty; ref: 1, 2, 19, 21
McLURE, James W.; pvt; 17th MS Inf, Co B; ref: 1, 700
McMAHAN, Wrightson E.; pvt; Zarvona's MD Zouaves; res: Tal Cty; ref; 1, 645, 735
McMAHON, Andrew; pvt; 2nd MD Cav, Co A; ref: 1, 19
McMAHON, Charles; pvt; 3rd MD Lt Arty; ref: 1, 2, 19, 21, 160, 726
McMAHON, E. W.; 1st VA Cav, Co G; ref: 735
McMAHON, Francis T.; d.h., Navy; C.S.S. Palmetto State; res: Bt Cty; ref: 1, 2, 19, 21
McMAHON, Hugh; pvt; 3rd MD Lt Arty; ref: 1, 2, 21, 160, 726
McMAHON, James T.; pvt; 1st MD Inf, Co F; ref: 1, 2, 19, 21
McMAHON, John Charles; pvt; 3rd MD Lt Arty; ref: 1, 2, 19, 21, 160, 726, 1523
McMAHON, Michael; pvt; Woolfolk Co, VA Lt Inf; ref: 1, 735
McMANN, Thomas; pvt; 9th VA Inf, Co B; res: Balt; ref: 1, 1576, 1598
McMANUS; James; pvt; 1st MD Inf, Co F; res: Balt; ref: 1, 2, 19, 21
McMEE, George; Castle Pinkney's SC Heavy Arty; ref: 735
McMILLAN, William; pvt; 3rd MD Lt Arty; ref: 1, 2, 19, 21, 160, 726
McMINN, Peter; pvt; 2nd MD Cav, Co E; ref: 1, 19, 1609
McMULLEN, Charles; pvt; Stuart's Horse Arty, Breathed's Battery; res: Frd Cty; ref: 1, 2, 19, 21, 89, 90
McMULLEN, L.; sgt; 2nd MD Cav, Co F; ref: 1, 2, 19, 21, 23, 1609
McMURRAY, ---; Maj; ref: 92, 93
McNABB, A.; pvt; 3rd MD Lt Arty; ref: 2, 19, 21, 160, 726
McNALLY, Felix; pvt; 1st MD Inf, Co F; ref: 1, 2, 19, 21
McNALLY, Peter; pvt; MD American Rifles; res: Bladensburg; ref: 1, 1523, 1622
McNAMARA, Lake Chaplain; Army of Northern Virginia; res: Dor Cty; ref: 112

McNAMARA, William Henry; pvt; Mississippi Cav; res: Dor Cty; ref: 112
McNAMEE, James F.; sgt; 1st VA Inf, Co E; res: Balt; ref: 1, 2, 19, 21, 735
McNAMEE, Thomas; pvt; 1st VA Inf, Co E; ref: 1, 735
McNEAL, Charles L.; pvt; Hampton Leg Lt Arty, Co B; ref: 1, 2, 19, 21, 34
McNEAL, William; pvt; Stuart's Horse Arty, Breathed's Battery; res: Annapolis, AA Cty; ref: 1
McNEALY, David; pvt; 1st SC Inf, Co G; ref: 1
McNEIGH, Richard; 43rd VA Cav (Mosby's); ref: 735
McNEIL, Henry; pvt; 35th VA Cav, Co B; ref: 1, 1611, 1677
McNELIS, James; pvt; Stuart's Horse Arty, Breathed's Battery; ref: 1, 498
McNULTY, James; pvt; 1st VA Cav, Co K; res: Balt; MLCSH; ref: 1, 2, 19, 21, 511, 627, 700, 786
McNULTY, John R.; Lt; 2nd MD Lt Arty; res: PG Cty; ref: 1, 2, 11, 19, 21, 23, 50, 55, 62, 64, 68, 88, 94, 240, 511, 512, 687, 700, 791, 816, 829, 931, 1258, 1523, 1553
McNULTY, Stephen; res: How Cty; ref; 10, 19
McNULTY, Thomas; ref: 511
McPHERSON, George; Castle Pinkney's SC Heavy Arty; ref: 735
McPHERSON, Henry S.; 1st VA Inf, Co E; ref: 1, 1622
McPHERSON, Lewis; pvt; Jacobs Mounted Riflemen; res: Princeland, AA Cty; ref: 1, 735, 1539
McQUEEN, Andrew M.; pvt; 25th NC Inf, Co G; res: Balt; ref: 21, 700
McREARY, J. N. L.; sgt; Richmond Howitzers, 1st Co; ref: 1, 265, 267
McSHERRY, Edward Coale (M.D.); 1st MD Cav, Co D; res: Frederick, Frd Cty; ref: 1, 2, 18, 19, 21, 72, 90, 1529, 1601
McSHERRY, James W. (M.D.); Surg; McCausland's Kanawha Inf; res: Balt; ref: 1, 18, 23, 791
McSHERRY, Richard M.; pvt; Signal Corps; res: Frd Cty; ref: 1, 2, 19, 21, 69, 316, 785
McVEIGH, Richard Newton; pvt; 43rd VA Cav (Mosby's), Co B; res: Balt; MLCSH; ref: 1, 8, 627, 700, 786, 1579
McWHORTER, J. D.; pvt; 3rd MD Lt Arty; ref: 2, 19, 21, 160, 726
McWILLIAMS, Daniel; Engr, Navy; C.S.S Florida; ref: 1, 19, 1564
McWILLIAMS, Frank; pvt; 1st MD Lt Arty; Allens Fresh, Cha Cty; ref: 19, 21, 700, 1546, 1563
McWILLIAMS, Hugh; pvt; 1st MD Cav, Co C; res: Balt; ref: 1, 2, 19, 21, 23, 70, 79, 700, 866, 1598
McWILLIAMS, J. Francis; pvt; Hampton Leg Lt Arty, Co B; ref: 1, 2, 19, 21
McWILLIAMS, James; pvt; 2nd MD Inf, Co F; res: Balt; ref: 1, 2, 19, 21
McWILLIAMS, James; sgt maj; 13th VA Inf, Co G; res: Balt; MLCSH; ref: 1, 2, 19, 735, 786
McWILLIAMS, John; pvt; 2nd MD Cav, Co C; ref: 1, 19, 1609
McWILLIAMS, John Ignatius; sgt Maj; 19th VA Inf; res: Balt; MLCSH; ref: 1, 19, 21, 56, 316, 672, 631, 700

MABIER, Henry T.; res: Frederick, Frd Cty; ref: 89
MACATEE, Henry; pvt; 1st MD Cav, Co C; ref: 1, 2, 19, 21, 1523, 1578, 1579
MACATEE, Ignatius; pvt; 1st MD Cav, Co C; res: Har Cty; MLCSH; ref: 1, 2, 19, 21, 700, 786, 1523
MACCUBBIN, ---; Chief of Richmond Police, Gen J. H. Winder's Detectives; ref: 30
MACCUBBIN, Clarence H.; pvt; res: Balt; ref: 700

MACCUBBIN, F. M.; pvt; 4th MD Lt Arty; ref: 1, 2, 21, 1523
MACCUBBIN, George B.; pvt; Holbrook's Independent MD Lt Arty; res: QA Cty; ref: 1, 1613
MACCUBBIN, R. W., Jr; pvt; 1st MD Inf, Co F; res: Balt; ref: 1, 70, 700, 1523
MACCUMMINS, F.; pvt; 4th MD Lt Arty; ref: 1, 2, 19, 21
MACGILL, Charles (M.D.); Surg; Lynchburg Hospital; res: Hagerstown, Wash Cty; ref: 1, 18, 361, 559, 611, 685, 720, 744, 791, 826, 1024, 1360, 1523, 1533, 1536, 1577, 1578, 1579
MACGILL, Charles G. W. (M.D.); Regimental Surg, Stonewall Brigade; res: Hagerstown, Wash Cty; ref: 1, 2, 18, 21, 23, 54, 56, 63, 65, 68, 70, 88, 259, 361, 559, 611, 685, 700, 720, 1511, 1533, 1536
MACGILL, Davidge; pvt; 1st MD Cav, Co C; res: Hagerstown, Wash Cty; ref: 1, 2, 19, 21, 23, 70, 361, 511, 1523
MACGILL, James; pvt; 1st MD Cav, Co C; res: Hagerstown, Wash Cty; ref: 23, 70, 361, 511, 685
MACGILL, William D.; 1st MD Cav, Co C; res: Hagerstown, Wash Cty; ref: 1, 2, 19, 21, 23, 70, 361, 511, 1523
MACIVOR, Henry Ronald Hislop; Lt; Aid de Camp, Gen T. Jackson's staff; res: Balt; MLCSH; ref: 1, 786
MACK, Thomas; pvt; 3rd MD Lt Arty; ref: 1, 2, 19, 21, 160, 726, 1523
MACKALL, Lenard Covington; Acting Master, Navy Richmond Station; ref: 1, 2, 19, 21, 70, 511, 700, 1523, 1564
MACKALL, Richard Covington; cpl; 1st MD Inf, Co H; ref: 1, 2, 19, 21, 23, 44, 259, 511, 650, 1520
MACKALL, Richard L.; Asst Paymaster, Navy; C.S.S. Morgan; res: Georgetown; ref: 1, 19, 58, 279, 316, 1523, 1564
MACKALL, Robert L.; pvt; Stuart's Horse Arty, Breathed's Battery; ref: 1, 498
MACKALL, Robert M.; pvt; 43rd VA Cav (Mosby's), Co D; res: PG Cty; ref: 1, 2, 8, 21, 677, 1613
MACKALL, Thomas B.; Lt; Aide de Camp, Gen W. W. Mackall's staff; res: Cal Cty; ref: 1, 2, 19, 21, 23, 53, 57, 503, 650, 700, 735, 891, 916, 1523, 1672
MACKALL, William Whann; Brig Gen; District of The Gulf & Army of Tennessee; res: Cec Cty; ref: 1, 2, 18, 19, 23, 29, 39, 44, 50, 64, 70, 97, 100, 125, 127, 153, 158, 163, 175, 266, 313, 388, 431, 511, 628, 674, 735, 789, 791, 1006, 1279, 1523, 1579, 1588, 1623, 1672
MACKEBEE, Richard T.; pvt; 2nd MD Inf, Co C; res: AA Cty; ref; 1, 2, 19, 21, 1523
MACKEBEE, William S.; pvt; 2nd MD Inf, Co C; res: AA Cty; ref: 1, 2, 19, 21, 1523
MACKEN, T. H.; pvt; 5th VA Cav, Co F; res: Balt; ref: 21
MACKEN, Thomas H.; pvt; 5th VA Cav, Co E; res: Balt; MLCSH; ref: 627, 700, 786
MACKENHEIMER, C. Page; pvt; 1st MD Lt Arty; ref: 1, 2, 19, 21, 1523
MACKEY, M.; pvt; 3rd MD Lt Arty; ref: 2, 19, 21, 160, 726, 1523
MACKHAM, J.; pvt; 3rd MD Lt Arty; ref: 2, 19, 21, 160, 726, 1523
MACKLIN, James; pvt; 3rd MD Lt Arty; ref: 1, 2, 19, 21, 160, 726, 1523
MACKLIN, Patrick; pvt; 2nd VA Inf, Co D; ref: 1, 19, 735, 1523, 1609
MACKUBIN, Clarence Nelson; pvt; 1st VA Cav, Co K; res: Balt; MLCSH; ref: 19, 21, 627, 786, 1523
MACILEER, Joseph; ref: 1135
MADDOX, Martin H. C.; pvt; 43rd VA Cav (Mosby's), Co A; ref: 1, 8, 19, 21, 700
MADDOX, Thomas Clay (M.D.); Surg; Barnesville, GA, Hospital; res: Hagerstown, Wash Cty; ref: 1, 18, 631, 1533, 1536

MADDOX, William J.; Capt; MD American Rifles; ref: 1
MADIGAN, Dennis T.; pvt; Richmond Howitzers; res: Balt; MLCSH; ref: 627, 700, 786
MAGAHA, Joseph; pvt; Lee's MD Cav; ref: 1, 3, 1611, 1677
MAGERSUPP, William; pvt; Barry's Co, MD Vols; ref: 1
MAGILL, Thomas T.; pvt; 2nd MD Inf, Co B; res: Great Mills, St. M. Cty; ref; 1, 2, 19, 21, 23, 470, 1509, 1523, 1555
MAGNESS, William; pvt; 1st MD Inf, Co F; res: Balt; ref: 1, 2, 19, 21, 1523
MAGRAW, Stephen C.; cpl; 2nd MD Cav, Co F; res: Bt Cty; ref: 1, 2, 19, 21, 23, 1523
MAGRUDER, Edward W.; bugler; 1st MD Cav, Co E; res: Upper Marlboro, PG Cty; ref: 1, 2, 19, 21, 69, 316, 700, 730, 1523
MAGRUDER, John R.; pvt; 2nd KY Cav, Co C; res: Annapolis, AA Cty; ref: 1, 1539
MAGRUDER, Richard H.; pvt; Edelin's MD Heavy Arty; Governor's Bridge, AA Cty; ref: 1, 1539
MAGRUDER, William Thomas; Capt; Asst A.G., Davis's Brigade, Heth's Div; res: Upper Marlboro, PG Cty; ref: 1, 19, 735, 787, 791, 1523
MAGRUDER, Zachariah; pvt; 1st MD Cav, Co A; res: Goshen Hills, Mont Cty; ref: 1, 2, 19, 21, 1523, 1552, 1574
MAGUIRE, Charles E.; pvt; 21st VA Inf, Co B; res: Balt; ref: 1, 2, 19, 312, 511, 650, 735, 1523, 1540
MAGUIRE, George C.; MLCSH; ref: 700
MAGUIRE, George W.; pvt; 1st MD Inf, Co A; ref: 1, 2, 19, 21, 511, 700, 1523
MAGUIRE, H. A. W.; pvt; 1st VA Cav, Co K; res: Balt; ref: 1, 2, 19, 21, 1523, 1540
MAGUIRE, James Louis; Navy; Franklin Buchanan Guards; res: Balt; MLCSH; ref: 627, 700, 786, 1540
MAGUIRE, John; pvt; Davis's MD Cav, Co C; ref: 1
MAGUIRE, Joseph E.; pvt; 1st MD Cav, Co D; res: Balt; ref: 1, 2, 21, 1523, 1601
MAGWOOD Edwin; pvt; 15th SC Heavy Arty; ref: 1
MAHARD, William; pvt; Holbrook's Independent MD Lt Arty; ref: 1
MAHOFFEY, William A.; pvt; Stuart's Horse Arty, Breathed's Battery; ref: 1
MAHOMER, Mathias; pvt; 1st MD Cav, Co C; ref: 1, 2, 19, 21, 1523
MAHOMY, James W.; pvt; Purcell's Lt Arty, Pegran's Bn; res: Balt; MLCSH; ref: 1, 2, 19, 21, 93, 511, 627, 700, 786, 1523
MAHONEY, John; pvt; Rhett's 1st SC Heavy Arty; res: Har Cty; MLCSH; ref: 1, 21, 93, 627, 700, 735, 786
MAHOOL, Thomas; Capt; 3rd GA Inf; ref: 21, 700
MAIRVY, Thomas F. (M.D.); Surg; 1st VA Inf; ref: 735
MAJORS, G. W.; pvt; 2nd MD Cav, Co G; ref: 1, 19, 1523, 1609
MALARD, M.; pvt; 2nd MD Lt Arty; ref; 2, 19, 1523
MALLER, Henry B.; pvt; 1st MD Inf, Co A; ref: 1, 2, 19, 21, 700, 1523
MALLORY, Charles A.; pvt; 1st VA Inf, Co E; ref: 1, 735
MALLORY, Mat; cpl; Steuart's Horse Arty, Breathed's Battery; ref: 1
MALLONEY, Brice M.; pvt; Barry's Co, MD Vols; res: Patuxent Forge, AA Cty; ref: 1, 1539
MALONE, Daniel; pvt; 2nd MD Lt Arty; ref: 1, 2, 19, 21, 1523
MALONEY, James A. (M.D.); pvt; 4th MD Lt Arty; ref: 1, 2, 19, 21, 677, 1523
MALONEY, William H.; pvt; McNiell's Rangers; res: All Cty; ref: 1, 2, 19, 21, 148, 519, 1425, 1523, 1610
MALOY, William C. (Revd); Chaplain; 44th MS Inf; res: Tal Cty; ref:

1, 21, 57, 70, 513, 700, 735, 891, 916, 1058, 1612

MALTBIE, J. R.; pvt; 4th TN Inf, Co C; res: Balt; ref: 1, 21, 700

MANEY, Thomas F. (M.D.); Acting Asst Surg; 1st VA Inf; ref: 2, 18

MANGUM, E. J.; pvt; Stuart's Horse Arty, Breathed's Battery; ref: 1, 498

MANGUM, W. W.; pvt; Stuart's Horse Arty, Breathed's Battery; ref: 1, 498

MANLEY, Nelios; pvt; 2nd MD Cav, Co B; res: Cha Cty; ref: 1

MANLEY, Nicholas P.; pvt; 9th VA Inf, Co B; res: Cec Cty; ref: 1, 1576

MANLY, Gaston; sgt maj; Manly's Lt Arty; res: Ellicott' City, How Cty; ref: 21, 700

MANLY, Joseph; pvt; 9th VA Inf, Co B; ref: 1, 2, 19, 21, 23, 470, 1523, 1576

MANN, Charles S.; pvt; 1st MD Lt Arty; ref: 1, 2, 19, 21, 1523

MANN, James; pvt; Davis's MD Cav, Co C; ref: 1, 19, 1523

MANN, John; Asst Engr, Navy; C.S.S. McRae; res: Frd Cty; ref: 1, 735, 1573, 1564

MANN, Samuel; pvt; 3rd MD Lt Arty; ref: 1, 2, 19, 21, 160, 726, 1523

MANNAN, Bartley; pvt; 1st MD Inf, Co B; ref: 1, 2, 19, 21, 1523

MANNERY, Thomas; pvt; Davis's MD Cav, Co B; ref: 1, 1523

MANNING, Edward; fmn, Navy; res: Balt; ref: 1

MANNING, E. S.; pvt; 7th VA Cav, Co G; ref: 1

MANNING, George W.; sgt; 2nd MD Inf, Co G; res: Drawbridge, Dor Cty; ref: 1, 2, 21, 23, 1523

MANNING, John A.; pvt; Rhett's 1st SC Heavy Arty, Co G; res: Balt; ref: 1, 735

MANNING, Richard I.; Maj; Q.M., Gen J. E. Johnston's staff; ref: 1, 21, 53, 700, 724

MANNING, Thomas S.; Acting Mast. M., Navy; C.S.S. Shenandoah; ref: 1, 19, 58, 97, 283, 1523, 1564

MANRY, Robert; pvt; 9th VA Inf, Co B; ref: 1, 1576

MANSFIELD, Wallace; res: Urieville, Kt Cty; ref: 1584

MANTZ, Ezra alias G. Wiskee WALTON; pvt; 4th KY Inf, Co B; ref: 1, 70

MARCERON, Albert; drummer; 1st MD Inf, Co I; ref: 1, 2, 19, 21 1523

MARCH, Elias; sgt; 5th VA Inf, Co K; res: Frd Cty; ref; 1, 72

MARCH, George; pvt; 5th VA Inf, Co K; res: Frd Cty; ref: 1, 72

MARCHANT, A. W.; pvt; 5th VA Cav, Co E; res: Balt; ref: 1, 21, 700

MARCK, Allen L.; pvt; Petersburg Defense; res: Balt; ref: 21, 700

MARCK, W. J.; Texas; ref: 735

MARCK, William B.; sgt; 30th VA Inf, Co B; res: Balt; ref: 1, 21, 700

MARCUS, James T.; pvt; 1st MD Inf, Co F; ref: 1, 2, 19, 21, 1523

MARDEN, George W.; pvt; 2nd MD Inf, Co A; ref: 1, 2, 19, 21, 650, 1523

MARINER, William H. C.; cpl; 60th TN Mounted Inf, Co B; res: Balt; ref: 1, 1540

MARKELL, Frederick; res: Frederick, Frd Cty; ref: 89

MARKOE, Francis, Jr; Lt; Signal Officer, Gen J. Gordon's staff; res: Balt; ref: 1, 2, 14, 19, 21, 38, 70, 469, 493, 503, 511, 650, 700, 735, 1335, 1519, 1520, 1523

MARKS, William B.; pvt; 55th VA Inf, Co K; ref: 1, 735

MARLEY, George; pvt; 2nd MD Cav, Co G; ref: 1

MARLOW, Richard C.; 2nd Lt; 35th VA Cav, Co A; res: Point of Rocks, Frd Cty; ref; 1, 3, 15, 371, 1677

MARLOW, Robert E.; pvt; 7th VA Cav, Co G; res: Knoxville, Frd Cty; ref: 1, 3, 89, 90, 1278

MARMADUKE, Henry Hungerford; Lt, Navy; C.S.S. Chicora; res: Annapolis, AA Cty; ref: 1, 23, 97, 281, 791, 1564, 1673

MARMILSTEIN, Adolphus F.; Q.M., Navy; C.S.S. Alabama; res: Balt; ref: 58, 59, 97, 278,. 281, 285, 1305, 1564, 1599, 1673

MARNEY, John; ordnance sgt; 1st MD Inf, Co F; res: Balt; MLCSH; ref: 1, 2, 19, 21, 627, 650, 700, 786, 1523
MARONEY, Z. T.; pvt; 3rd MD Lt Arty; ref: 2, 19, 21, 160, 726, 1523
MARRAN, John; pvt; Edelin's MD Heavy Arty; ref: 1, 735
MARRIOTT, Charles H.; pvt; 17th VA Inf, Co C; res: Fredeick, Frd Cty; ref: 1, 89, 727
MARRIOTT, George H.; pvt; Hampton Leg Lt Arty, Co B; res: Savage, How Cty; ref: 1, 2, 19, 21, 1523, 1550, 1553
MARRIOTT, Henry; Lt; 2nd MD Cav, Co E; ref; 1, 2, 19, 21, 93, 650, 791, 1523
MARRIOTT, John S.; pvt; MD American Rifles; res: Davidsonville, AA Cty; ref: 1, 1539
MARRIOTT, Joseph G. W.; Lt; 1st MD Inf, Co E; res: Frederick, Frd Cty; ref: 1, 2, 19, 21, 23, 64, 68, 88, 456, 488, 1511, 1523, 1666
MARROW, James E.; pvt; 1st VA Inf, Co E; ref; 1
MARSH, Walter W.; pvt; 9th VA Cav, Co K; res: Balt; MLCSH; ref: 1, 786
MARSHALL, Charles; Lt Col; Asst A.G., Gen R. E. Lee's staff; res: Balt; ref: 1, 2, 19, 21, 23, 30, 31, 34, 37, 38, 42, 44, 46, 53, 56, 57, 63, 64, 68, 100, 105, 110, 111, 113, 114, 115, 118, 123, 126, 127, 138, 139, 144, 145, 147, 148, 165, 169, 272, 289, 319, 431, 477, 495, 601, 603, 684, 685, 700, 787, 791, 815, 825, 840, 857, 1274, 1287, 1322, 1323, 1393, 1394, 1437, 1523, 1572, 1578, 1579, 1583, 1608, 1650
MARSHALL, George; pvt; 2nd MD Cav, Co G; res: Cambridge, Dor Cty; ref: 1, 1547
MARSHALL, Humphrey; pvt; 7th VA cav, Co G; ref: 1, 3
MARSHALL, Jackson; Lt; Gen J. H. Winder's staff, Andersonville; res: Balt; ref: 1489
MARSHALL, James; Lt; 12th VA Cav, Co F; ref: 1, 11, 194
MARSHALL, John P.; Lt; Barry's Co, MD Vols; res: Old Field, PG Cty; ref: 1, 69, 316, 456, 724, 1553
MARSHALL, Peter B.; pvt; 2nd MD Lt Arty; ref: 1, 2, 21, 1523
MARSTON, Frederick A.; pvt; Zarvona's MD Zouaves; ref: 1, 2, 19, 21, 700, 735, 1523
MARSTON, Harry A.; sgt; 2nd MD Lt Arty; ref: 1, 2, 19, 21, 64, 700, 1523
MARTIN, Benjamin; pvt; 19th VA Heavy Arty, Co C; ref: 1, 1580
MARTIN, Charles; pvt; Davis's MD Cav; res: Annapolis, AA Cty; ref: 1, 1539
MARTIN, George; pvt; 2nd MD Lt Arty; ref: 2, 19, 21, 1523
MARTIN, George; pvt; 2nd MD Cav, Co F; res: Bt Cty; ref: 1, 2, 19, 21, 233, 1523, 1565
MARTIN, Henry; pvt; 15th NC Inf, Co K; ref: 1, 735
MARTIN, Hugh (M.D.); pvt; 2nd MD Cav, Co C; res: Balt; ref: 1, 2, 18, 19, 21, 690, 791, 1523, 1609
MARTIN, J. G.; pvt; 3rd MD Lt Arty; ref: 2, 19, 21, 160, 461, 726, 1523
MARTIN, James; pvt; 5th VA Cav, Co C; res: Balt; ref: 1, 21, 700, 735
MARTIN, James, Jr; pvt; Lee's MD Cav; res: Millersville, AA Cty; ref: 1, 1539
MARTIN, James E.; Capt; 2nd MS Inf, Co I; res: Hagerstown, Wash Cty; ref: 1, 291
MARTIN, John; pvt; 2nd MD inf, Co H; res: Elk Ridge Landing, AA Cty; ref: 1, 2, 19, 21, 1523, 1539
MARTIN, John A.; pvt; ref: 700
MARTIN, John N. S.; pvt; 2nd MD Inf, Co E; res: Har Cty; MLCSH; ref: 1, 2, 19, 21, 70, 93, 645, 786, 1523

MARTIN, Joseph T.; pvt; 2nd MD Inf, Co F; res: Frd Cty; ref: 1, 2, 19, 21, 1523
MARTIN, Patrick H.; pvt; 21st VA Inf, Co B; res: Balt; MLCSH; ref: 1, 2, 19, 93, 312, 735, 786, 1523
MARTIN, Robert; pvt; 1st SC Inf, Co G; ref: 1, 1575
MARTIN, Samuel; 13th VA Inf, Co F; ref: 735
MARTIN, Thomas; pvt; 13th VA Inf, Co F; res: 1, 735, 1576
MARTIN, Thomas Brumley; pvt; 24th VA Cav, Co F; res: Balt; MLCSH; ref: 1, 21, 627, 700, 786
MARTIN, Thomas Henry; pvt; MD American Rifles; ref: 1
MARTIN, Washington; cpl; 2nd MD Inf, Co F; res: Som Cty; ref: 1, 2, 19, 21, 23, 1523
MARTIN, William D.; Lt; Lucas's 15th SC Heavy Arty; ref: 1, 21, 700, 791
MARTIN, William Pinkney; Lt; 43rd VA Cav (Mosby's), Co E; res: Frd Cty; ref: 1, 2, 3, 8, 15, 19, 21, 72, 393, 710, 1523, 1611, 1677
MARTINDALE, Henry H.; sgt; 14th NC Inf, Co K; res: Balt; ref: 1, 21, 23, 57, 513, 700
MARTY, Gabriel; pvt; Lucas' 15th SC Heavy Arty; ref: 1
MARYE, J. L., Jr; sgt; Pollock's Co, VA Lt Arty; res: Balt; ref: 1, 21, 700
MASLIN, James M.; pvt; 7th VA Cav, Co F; res: Balt; ref; 1, 21, 700
MASLIN, William H.; pvt; 7th VA Cav, Co F; ref: 1, 70
MASON, Augustine Smith (M.D.); Chief Surg; Medical Director, Dept of Richmond; res: Hagerstown, Wash Cty; ref: 1, 18, 21, 23, 72, 361, 700, 1534, 1536
MASON, Charles James; McNeill's Rangers; res: Cumberland, All Cty; ref: 148
MASON, Daniel Murray; pvt; 43rd VA Cav (Mosby's); ref: 8, 601, 1523, 1571, 1578, 1579, 1654
MASON, Frank J. (M.D.); Capt; 7th VA Cav, Co G; ref: 1, 2, 3, 11, 15, 18, 88, 222, 255, 256, 371, 517, 518, 1154, 1371, 1486, 1609
MASON, George F.; cpl; 5th VA Cav, Co F; res: Balt; ref: 1, 21, 700
MASON, Henry C.; pvt; 49th VA Inf, Co E; res: Old Medley's, Mont Cty; ref: 1, 106
MASON, James A.; pvt; 1st VA Cav, Co B; res: Oakland, Gar Cty; ref: 1, 19, 65, 72, 95, 148, 519, 685, 1010, 1610
MASON, James Edward; lmn, Navy; Ram Tennessee; res: West River, AA Cty; ref: 1, 1539
MASON, John Stevens; Acting Master, Navy; C.S.S. Patrick Henry; ref: 2, 14, 735, 936, 1564
MASON, John T. of R.; Passed Midn, Navy; C.S.S. Shenandoah; res: Balt; ref; 1, 19, 21, 316, 700, 783, 1520, 1571, 1564
MASON, John Thompson O. (M.D.); Asst Surg, Navy; C.S. Huntsville; res: Balt; ref: 1, 2, 18, 21, 23, 56, 70, 97, 469, 601, 684, 700, 716, 783, 791, 964, 1515, 1523, 1564, 1578, 1579, 1620
MASON, Murray; Commander, Navy; Richmond Naval Station; res: Georgetown; ref: 1, 44, 482, 1564
MASON, R. R.; pvt; 1st MD Cav, Co A; ref: 1, 2, 19, 21, 1523
MASON, Thomas P.; pvt; 26th VA Inf, Co B; res: Balt; ref; 1, 21, 700
MASON, William; pvt; Stuart's Horse Arty, Breathed's Battery; ref: 1, 498
MASON, William H.; pvt; 4th MD Lt Arty; ref: 1, 2, 19, 21, 1523
MASON, William Pinckney; Lt, Navy; C.S.S. Beaufort; res: Rockville, Mont Cty; ref: 1, 19, 1314, 1564, 1673
MAS...IEU, John B.; pvt; Norfolk Lt Arty Blues; MLCSH; ref: 786
MASSENBERG, R. C.; Adj; Findlay's Bn; res: Towson; ref: 21, 700
MASSEY, Oliver; pvt; Lucas 15th SC Heavy Arty; res: Balt; ref: 1

MATHER, Joseph; cptr, Navy; C.S.S. Stonewall; ref: 1, 1564
MATLOCK, Samuel A.; cpl; 35th VA Cav, Co D; res: Rockville, Mont Cty; ref: 1, 1552, 1611, 1677
MATTBIE, James R.; pvt; 4th TN Inf; ref: 93
MATTHEWS, Albert E.; Capt; 8th VA Inf, Co H; res: Balt; ref: 1, 21, 700, 735, 1492
MATTHEWS, C. J.; pvt; Edelin's MD Heavy Arty; res: Balt; ref: 1, 1574
MATTHEWS, Charles W.; pvt; 35th VA Cav, Co B; res: Poolesville, Mont Cty; ref: 1, 316, 1552, 1611, 1677
MATTHEWS, H. John; sgt; 1st SC Inf, Co G; res: Balt; ref; 1, 1540, 1598, 1613
MATTHEWS, Henry Haw; pvt; Stuart's Horse Arty, Breathed's Battery; res: Georgetown; MLCSH; ref; 1, 2, 19, 21, 46, 103, 498, 627, 700, 786, 905, 981, 1016, 1091, 1492, 1523, 1601
MATTHEWS, James Monroe; pvt; 35th VA Cav, Co B; res: Poolesville, Mont Cty; ref: 1, 1552, 1611, 1677
MATTHEWS, James W.; pvt 19th VA Inf, Co D; ref: 1, 93, 700
MATTHEWS, William G.; pvt; 2nd MD Inf, Co B; res: Cha Cty; ref: 1, 2, 19, 21, 23, 470, 1523
MATTHEWS, William H., Jr; 2nd MD Cav, Co B; res: Poolesville, Mont Cty; ref: 1, 1523, 1552, 1609
MATTISON, Samuel J.; ordnance sgt; 2nd MD Lt Arty; res: Tobaccostick, Dor Cty; ref: 1, 2, 19, 21, 700, 1523, 1547
MAUGHAN, Patrick; pvt; 15th VA Inf, Co F; ref: 1, 700, 1621
MAUPHIN, Chapman; Lt; 1st Regt Enginners, Co I; res: Ellicott City, How Cty; ref: 1, 21, 56, 700, 873
MAUPHIN, Robert W.; Passed Midn, Navy; C.S.S. Patrick Henry; ref: 1, 21, 58, 700, 783, 873, 1564
MAURY, John Soffrien; Lt Commanding, Navy; C.S.S. Hampton; ref: 1, 21, 53, 97, 469, 685, 700, 783, 1520, 1564
MAURY, Richard B. (M.D.); Surgeon-in-Charge, Greenville Alabama Hospital; res: Georgetown; ref: 1, 18, 556
MAURY, Robert H., Jr; Master, Navy; res: Mont Cty; ref: 1
MAXEY, P. B.; pvt; Davis's MD Cav, Co C; ref: 1
MAXWELL, James A.; Capt; Maxwell's GA Lt Arty; ref: 1, 21, 105, 700
MAXWELL, John Thomas (Revd); pvt; 35th VA Cav, Co B; res: Park Mills, Frd Cty; ref: 2, 3, 19, 21, 86, 90, 1523, 1611, 1677
MAXWELL, William B.; Lt; 1st VA Inf, Co E; res: Easton, Tal Cty; ref: 1, 735, 1557
MAY, Harvey; pvt; 13th VA Inf, Co G; ref: 1
MAY, William H.; cpl; 1st MD Lt Arty; ref: 1, 2, 19, 21, 23, 34, 68, 782, 791, 1273, 1523
MAY, Yancy; pvt; 146th VA Militia, Co A; res: Lewistown, Frd Cty; ref: 1, 1573, 1663
MAYBERRY, James Polk; pvt; 1st MD Inf, Co A; res: Frd Cty; ref; 1, 2, 19, 21, 89, 90, 1523
MAYER, Charles F.; ref: 412
MAYNADIER, John H.; pvt; 1st VA Cav, Co K; res: Har Cty; ref: 1, 2, 19, 21, 57, 122, 700, 1523
MAYNADIER, John M.; pvt; 1st VA Cav, Co K; res: Har Cty; ref: 1, 2, 19, 21, 122, 1523
MAYNARD, Albert; pvt; 1st MD Cav, Co D; res: Libertytown, Frd Cty; ref: 1, 2, 19, 21, 90, 1523, 1601
MAYNARD, John; Lt; ref: 1690
MAYNARD, Thomas B.; pvt; 1st MD Cav, Co D; res: Libertytown, Frd Cty; ref: 1, 2, 19, 21, 90, 1405, 1523
MAYS, Stephen; pvt; Stuart's Horse Arty, Breathed's Battery; ref: 1
MEACHORN, Horace B.; pvt; 21st VA Inf, Co G; res: Balt; MLCSH; ref: 700, 786
MEAD, Charles; pvt; 1st VA Inf, Co E; ref: 1, 735

MEAGHER, James; pvt; 1st MD CAv, Co F; ref: 1, 2, 19, 21, 1523
MEALY, Patrick; pvt; 2nd MD Cav, Co A; res: Balt; ref; 1, 19, 1523, 1609
MEARS, A. DeR (Revd); ref: 53
MEDARY, Samuel; pvt; 2nd MD Cav, Co A; ref: 1
MEDINGER, Edward G.; pvt; MD Guerrilla Zouaves; res: Balt; ref: 1, 1540
MEEHAN, Cornelius J.; sgt; 8th LA Inf, Co H; res: Elysville, MLCSH; ref: 1, 21, 700, 786
MEEKINS, Joseph; res: Bristol, AA Cty; ref: 1539
MEELY, John; pvt; 20th SC Inf, Co D; ref: 1
MEINCOMB, George; res: Balt; ref: 1540
MEIRE, Julius Ernest (M.D.); Capt, Marine Corps, Mobile Statoin; res: Tal Cty; ref: 1, 18, 19, 735, 792, 1349, 1495, 1515, 1523, 1564, 1593, 1594
MEISTER, Charles; pvt; 10th GA Inf, Co B; ref: 1, 2, 19, 21, 1523
MELTON, James M.; pvt; 43rd VA Cav (Mosby's), Co F; ref: 1, 8, 19
MELTON, Samuel; pvt; 3rd MD Lt Arty; ref: 1, 2, 19, 21, 160, 726, 1523
MELTON, William; pvt; Barry's Co, MD Vols; ref: 1
MELVIN, George F.; pvt; 1st MD Inf, Co E; res: Balt; ref; 1, 2, 19, 21, 700, 1523
MENDEZ, Samuel P.; pvt; Mahone's Command; res: Balt; ref: 1366
MENG, John William; ref: 1529
MENSHAW, Frank; Davis's MD Cav; res: East River Landing, AA Cty; ref: 1, 1539
MENTZER, Samuel; pvt; Stuart's Horse Arty, Breathed's Battery; ref: 1, 2, 19, 21, 498, 1474, 1523
MENZIES, Thomas A.; Asst Engr, Navy; C.S.S. Bienville; ref: 1, 19, 58, 97, 279, 282, 1523, 1564
MENZZO, Joseph; pvt; 2nd MD Cav, Co D; ref: 1, 19, 1523, 1609
MERCER, Elihu Washington; pvt; 1st VA Cav, Co K; res: Point of Rocks, Frd Cty; ref: 1, 2, 19, 21, 72, 90, 1523
MERCER, George Douglas; Maj; Quartermaster Corps; res: West River, AA Cty; ref; 1, 2, 19, 44, 312, 791, 1388, 1539, 1665
MERCER, George W.; Capt; 29th VA Inf, Co B; res: How Cty; ref: 1, 10, 19
MERCER, R.; pvt; MD Line, Co B; ref: 1
MERCER, Samuel B.; pvt; 1st MD Cav, Co D; res: Unionville, Frd Cty; ref: 1, 2, 19, 21, 72, 1523, 1601
MERCER, Wilson Carey; Lt; 37th VA Cav, Co A; res: West River, AA Cty; ref: 1, 1539, 1665
MERCIER, George C.; res: Point of Rocks, Frd Cty; ref: 643
MERCIER, William F.; 12th VA Cav, Co A; res: Mount Pleasant; ref: 67
MERRICK, Alfred Duhurst; pvt; Rockbridge Lt Arty; res: Wash Cty; MLCSH; ref: 1, 19, 700, 735, 786, 1523
MERRICK, George Clarence; Lt; Davis's MD Cav, Co A; res: Upper Marlborough, PG Cty; ref: 1, 2, 19, 21, 70, 81, 316, 730, 1371, 1523
MERRITT, James J.; pvt; 2nd MD Inf, Co D; ref: 1
MERRITT, Samuel; pvt; 1st VA Cav, Co K; ref: 1, 2, 19, 21, 1523
MERRIZE, Rocho; pvt; 2nd MD Cav, Co G; ref: 1
MERRYMAN, Joseph R.; pvt; 1st MD Cav, Co D; res: Bt Cty; ref: 1, 2, 19, 21, 1523, 1601
MERRYMAN, Richard S.; pvt; 7th VA Cav, Co G; res: Bt Cty; ref: 1, 3, 1010
MERRYMAN, Samuel; pvt; Stuart's Horse Arty, Breathed's Battery; ref: 498
MERSON, Basil; pvt; MD Guerrilla Zouaves; res: Laurel Factory, AA Cty; ref: 1, 1539, 1628
MERSON, George; pvt; MD Guerrilla Zouaves; res: Laurel Factory, AA Cty; ref: 1, 1539

MERSON, James; pvt; MD Guerrilla Zouaves; res: Laurel Factory, AA Cty; ref: 1, 1539
MESSICK, Hiram Ross; pvt; Davis's MD Cav, Co B; ref: 1, 2, 19, 21, 1523
MESSICK, James H.; ref: 93
METTAM, Henry Clay; pvt; 1st MD Cav, Co E; res: Pikesville, Bt Cty; ref: 1, 2, 19, 21, 70, 94, 730, 1523, 1560
METTEE, Charles H.; pvt; 4th MD Lt Arty; res: Balt; ref: 1, 2, 19, 21, 92, 93, 511, 700, 1523, 1575
MEWBORNE, Nathaniel J.; pvt; 1st MD Inf, Co A; ref: 1, 2, 19, 21, 1523
MEWSHAW, Ebenezer; pvt; 2nd MD Inf, Co F; res: McPherson Pack, AA Cty; ref; 1, 2, 19, 21, 1523, 1539
MEYERS, Henry; bugler; 1st SC Inf, Co G; res: Balt; ref: 1, 735
MEYERS, William H.; sgt; 55th VA Inf; res: Still Pond, Kt Cty; ref: 1584
MICHAEL, Hugh; pvt; Davis's MD Cav, Co A; ref: 1, 735
MICHAEL, John W.; pvt; 2nd MD Inf, Co C; res: Frederick, Frd Cty; MLCSH; ref: 1, 2, 19, 21, 700, 786, 1523
MICHAELS, Joseph; pvt; 1st MD Inf, Co B; ref: 2, 19, 21, 1523
MICHIE, Claudius Newton; pvt; Griffin's Bn, TX Inf, Co B; res: Balt; ref: 1, 70
MICOU, Thomas H.; pvt; 1st MD Inf, Co B; ref: 1, 2, 19, 21, 1523
MIDDLETON, Alexius L. (M.D.); Asst Surg; 2nd TX Inf, Upper Marlbor, PG Cty; ref: 1, 18, 1690
MIDDLETON, De Calb; pvt; Davis's MD Cav, Co A; ref: 1, 19, 735
MIDDLETON, Edward; pvt; Hampton Leg Lt Arty, Co B; ref: 1, 2, 19, 21, 1523
MIDDLETON, James E.; Quartermaster Dept, Lrings Brigade; res: Bladensburg, PG Cty; ref: 2
MIDDLETON, John I.; Capt; 28th MS Cav, Co K; res: Balt; ref: 1, 56, 105, 791
MIHON, Martin; pvt; 1st MD Inf, Co F; ref: 1, 2, 19, 21, 1523
MILES, Albano Rutledge; 9th VA Cav, Co H; res: Balt; MLCSH; ref: 1, 21, 70, 627, 700, 786
MILES, Francis Turguard (M.D.); Capt; 27th SC Inf, Co A; res: Balt; ref: 1, 18, 21, 56, 70, 272, 700, 791, 1523, 1533, 1536
MILES, George T.; pvt; 1st MD Cav, Co D; res: Frd Cty; ref; 1, 2, 19, 21, 90, 1523, 1601
MILES, John C.; pvt; 2nd MD Inf, Co B; ref: 470
MILES, Nicholas J.; sgt; 2nd MD inf, Co F; res: Cha Cty; ref: 1, 2, 21, 23
MILES, W.; pvt; 1st MD Cav, Co C; ref: 1, 19, 1523
MILLAN, George S.; pvt; 17th VA Inf, Co D; res: Balt; MLCSH; ref: 1, 21, 700, 786
MILLER, ---; Lt; 12th VA Cav, Co F; ref: 11, 735
MILLER, Aaron W.; pvt; 1st VA Inf, Co E; ref: 1
MILLER, Adam; pvt; Zarvona's MD Zouaves; res: McPherson Pack, AA Cty; ref: 1, 1539
MILLER, Andrew T.; pvt; Rhett's 1st SC Heavy Arty; res: Balt; ref: 1, 2, 7, 19, 21, 70, 650, 690, 735, 1523
MILLER, B. F.; pvt; Stuart's Horse Arty, Breathed's Battery; ref: 1
MILLER, Charles; pvt; 3rd MD Lt Arty; ref: 1, 2, 19, 21, 160, 726, 1523
MILLER, Charles; pvt; 2nd MD Inf, Co F; ref: 1
MILLER, Charles; pvt; Davis's MD Cav, Co A; ref: 1
MILLER, Charles M.; pvt; Richmond's Howitzers, 2nd Co; res: Scranton, Gar Cty; ref: 1, 1421
MILLER, Collins; pvt; 4th LA Inf, Co C; ref: 1, 352

MILLER, Edward B.; pvt; 18th VA Inf, Co F; res: Hamden, Bt Cty; MLCSH; ref: 786
MILLER, Frank C.; pvt; 2nd MD Cav, Co B; ref: 1
MILLER, George; pvt; 47th NC Inf, Co F; ref: 1, 735
MILLER, George; 3rd TX Inf; ref: 735
MILLER, George; pvt; 3rd MD Lt Arty; ref; 1, 2, 19, 21, 160, 726, 1523
MILLER, George R.; pvt; Davis's MD Cav, Co A; ref: 1, 316, 735
MILLER, H. D.; pvt; 1st MD Lt Arty; res: Elkton, Cec Cty; ref: 1, 2, 19, 21, 470, 1523
MILLER, Henry; pvt; Edelin's MD Heavy Arty; res: McPherson Pack, AA Cty; ref: 1, 1539, 1628
MILLER, Henry; pvt; 2nd MD Cav, Co C; res: Frd Cty; ref; 2, 19, 21, 291, 352, 1523
MILLER, Howard; pvt; 40th VA Inf, Co B; ref: 1, 21, 700, 735
MILLER, J. Parkins; pvt; 7th VA Cav, Co C; res: Frederick, Frd Cty; ref: 1, 72
MILLER, Jacob; pvt; 2nd MD Inf, Co E; res: Balt; ref: 1, 2, 19, 21, 1523
MILLER, James C.; pvt; 2nd MD Cav, Co D; ref: 1, 19, 1523, 1609
MILLER, Joel; Col; Gen Price's Missouri Army; ref: 21, 700
MILLER, John C.; pvt; 2nd MD Inf, Co C; ref: 1, 2, 19, 21, 1523
MILLER, John H.; pvt; 40th VA Inf, Co B; ref: 21, 700
MILLER, Joseph; smn, Navy; C.S.S. Gaines; ref: 1
MILLER, Lafayette; pvt; 9th VA Inf, Co B; res: Balt; ref: 1, 1576
MILLER, Lineaus Franklin; pvt; 5th VA Cav, Co A; MLCSH; ref: 93, 786
MILLER, Otto; pvt; Lee's MD Cav; res: Balt; ref: 1, 1540
MILLER, Peter; pvt; Barry's Co, MD Vols; res: McPherson Pack, AA Cty; ref; 1, 1539
MILLER, Shepard G.; Lt; 26th VA Inf, ref: 70
MILLER, Thadeus; pvt; 3rd MD Lt Arty; ref: 1, 2, 19, 21, 160, 726, 1523
MILLER, Thomas; pvt; 3rd MD Lt Arty; ref: 1, 2, 19, 21, 160, 726, 1523
MILLER, W. A.; pvt; Navy; Semmes Naval Brigade; res: Balt; ref: 1
MILLER, William; Capt; res: Balt; ref: 517
MILLER, William; pvt; MD Guerrilla Zouaves; ref: 1
MILLER, William; pvt; 2nd MD Cav, Co D; res: Carr Cty; ref: 1, 2, 3, 19, 21, 1523, 1609
MILLER, William H.; pvt; 1st MD Cav, Co A; res: Clarksville, How Cty; ref; 1, 2, 10, 19, 21, 71, 1523
MILLER, William S.; pvt; 9th VA Inf, Co B; ref: 1, 1576
MILLS, John C.; pvt; 17th VA Inf, Co A; res: Leonardtown, St. M. Cty; ref; 1, 2, 19, 21, 23, 133, 142, 1509, 1523, 1555, 1670
MILLS, Robert M.; pvt; 1st MD Cav, Co B; ref: 1, 19, 1523
MILLS, William B. P.; Farrier; 3rd MD Lt Arty; res: Tobaccostick, Dor Cty; ref: 1, 2, 19, 21, 23, 160, 726, 1523, 1547
MILLS, William P.; pvt; 1st MD Inf, Co F; res: Balt; ref; 1, 2, 21, 735
MILLSTEAD, Joseph H.; pvt; 2nd MD Inf, Co B; ref: 2, 21, 1523
MILNE, John S.; pvt; 1st MD Cav, Co F; ref: 1, 19, 1523
MILTON, John; pvt; 43rd VA Cav (Mosby's), Co E; ref: 1, 2, 8, 19, 21, 160, 726, 1523
MINN, James P.; Lt; 2nd MD Inf, Co H; ref: 1, 19
MINNAHAM, John; pvt; 1st MD Inf, Co A; ref: 1, 2, 19, 21, 1523
MINNIGERODE, Charles; Lt; Steuart's Horse Arty, Breathed's Battery, ref: 1, 498
MINNIHAN, Thomas; pvt; 1st MD Cav, Co F; ref: 1, 2, 19, 21, 1523
MINOR, Fairfax Catlett; pvt; 7th VA Cav, Co G; ref: 3, 316, 1677

MINOR, George C.; sgt; 55th VA Co D; res: Balt; ref: 1, 21, 57, 513, 700, 891, 916
MINOR, Robert; pvt; Zarvona's MD Zouaves; ref: 1, 480
MINOR, William B.; pvt; 20th VA Heavy Arty; res: Cec Cty; ref: 1, 1412
MINTER, William; pvt; 3rd MD Lt Arty; ref: 2, 19, 21, 160, 726, 1523
MINTY, J. M.; pvt; 2nd MD Cav, Co E; ref: 1
MISTER, Henry; pvt; MD American Rifles; res: McPherson Pack, AA Cty; ref: 1, 1539
MISTER, James F.; Lt; 2nd Partisan Rangers, MS Cav; res: Dor Cty; ref: 1, 112
MISTER, John J.; pvt; 1st SC Inf, Co G; ref: Balt; ref: 1, 735
MISTER, Matthew Keene; Capt; 12th MS Cav, Co E; res: Dor Cty; ref: 1, 112
MISTER, Wilbur Fisk (Revd); Chaplain; 15th MS Inf; res: Dor Cty; ref: 1, 112
MITCHEL, Joseph; pvt; 1st MD Cav, Co D; ref: 1, 19
MITCHELL, Andrew; res: St. M. Cty; ref: 1509
MITCHELL, George; pvt; 3rd MD Lt Arty; ref: 1, 2, 19, 21, 160, 726, 1523
MITCHELL, Hugh; Lt; 1st MD Inf, Co I; res: Port Tobacco, Cha Cty; ref: 1, 2, 19, 21, 23, 64, 456, 791, 1520, 1523, 1546
MITCHELL, James; pvt; 12th VA Cav, Co F; res: Balt; MLCSH; ref: 1, 2, 19, 21, 93, 786, 1523, 1609
MITCHELL, James Jackson; pvt; 43rd VA Cav (Mosby's), Co G; res: QA Cty; MLCSH; ref: 8, 627, 700, 786, 1509, 1579
MITCHELL, John; Navy; res: Balt; ref: 1
MITCHELL, John; pvt; 1st MD Lt Arty; res: Som Cty; ref: 1, 2, 19, 21, 470, 1523
MITCHELL, John D.; cpl; Zarvona's MD Zouaves; res: Som Cty; ref: 1, 61, 97, 703, 735, 1611, 1677
MITCHELL, Joseph H.; pvt; 24th VA Cav, Co B; res: Glyndon, Bt Cty; ref: 1, 69, 316, 1523
MITCHELL, Joshua; pvt; Barry's Co MD Vols; res: Balt; ref: 1, 1540
MITCHELL, Levin; pvt; 1st MD Cav, Co C; ref: 1, 2, 19, 21, 1523
MITCHELL, Oliver; pvt; 1st MD Cav, Co C; res: Dor Cty; ref: 1, 19, 1523
MITCHELL, Robert S.; sgt; Davis's MD Cav, Co A; ref: 1, 2, 19, 21, 730, 1523
MITCHELL, Thomas Holcombe; pvt; 11th VA Inf, Co A; res: Towson, Bt Cty; ref; 1, 21, 700, 1575
MITCHELL, Thomas L.; pvt; 2nd MD Inf, Co C; res: PG Cty; ref: 1, 2, 19, 21, 23, 470, 1523, 1553, 1622
MITCHELL, William D. A.; pvt; 24th VA Inf, Co C; res: Glyndon, Bt Cty; ref: 1, 69, 316
MITCHELL, William J.; pvt, Marine; Mobiel Marine Barracks; res: Annapolis, AA Cty; ref: 1, 1539, 1594
MITTAN, Henry C.; pvt; 1st MD Cav, Co E; res: Balt; ref; 1, 700, 825, 1523
MOBBERLY, Bradley (M.D.); pvt; 1st VA Cav; res: Frd Cty; ref: 18, 19, 72, 90, 1523
MOBERLY, John W.; pvt; 35th VA Cav, Co A; res: Mont Cty; ref; 1, 3, 15, 735, 1677
MOCKABEE, Joseph; pvt; Hampton Leg Lt Arty, Co B; ref: 1, 2, 19, 21, 34, 68, 141, 782, 1273, 1523
MODLIN, W. W.; sgt; 2nd MD Cav, Co D; ref: 1, 19, 1609
MOELLER, George H.; pvt; 10th VA Cav, Co H; res: Balt; ref: 21, 700
MOFFITT, William; pvt; Lucas' 15th SC Heavy Arty; res: Cec Cty; ref: 1

MOISE, A. W.; pvt; GA Sharpshooters, 2nd Co; ref: 1, 2, 19, 21, 730, 1523
MOISE, John; pvt; 3rd VA Reserves, Co D; res: Annapolis, AA Cty; ref: 1, 1539
MOLDEN, Elias; pvt; 1st MD Inf, Co G; ref; 1, 2, 19, 21, 73, 1523
MONAHAN, James J.; sgt; Davis's MD Cav, Co A; res: Carr Cty; MLCSH; ref: 1, 2, 19, 21, 627, 735, 786
MONCARE, Charles H.; pvt; 1st MD Lt Arty; ref: 1, 2, 19, 21, 784, 1523
MONCURE, E. C.; cpl; 1st MD Lt Arty; ref: 1, 2, 19, 21, 23, 1523
MONDAY, Albert; pvt; 7th VA Cav, Co G; ref: 1
MONEHAN, James; pvt; 8th LA Inf, Co C; ref: 1, 2, 19, 21, 1523
MONIER, John; pvt; 35th VA Cav, Co B; ref: 1, 1677
MONK, Christopher; pvt; 1st MD Cav, Co E; ref: 21, 700
MONMONIER, John N. K. (M.D.) Surg; Inspector of Hospital, Army of Northern Virginia; res: Balt; ref: 1, 2, 18, 21, 650, 700, 1523, 1533, 1536
MONNEY, Ephraim S.; pvt; 7th VA Cav, Co G; ref: 1, 3, 735
MONROE, Robert; pvt; 1st MD Cav, Co C; ref: 1, 19, 1523
MONTAGUE, Thomas; pvt; Lucas' 15th SC Heavy Arty; ref: 1
MONTAGUE, W. Powhattan; pvt; 21st VA Inf, Co B; res: Balt; ref: 1, 2, 19, 312, 735, 833, 1523
MONTEITH, George W.; pvt; 3rd MD Lt Arty; ref: 1, 2, 19, 21, 160, 726, 1460, 1523
MONTEITH, Mark; pvt; 3rd MD Lt Arty; ref: 1, 2, 19, 21, 160, 726, 1460, 1523
MONTEREY, Andrew; pvt; 1st MD Cav, Co F; ref: 1, 2, 19, 21, 1523
MONTGOMERY, J. Norris; Capt; 19th VA Heavy Arty, Co C; res: Balt; ref: 1, 17, 518, 791, 1580
MONTGOMERY, John; pvt; Jacob's Mounted Riflemen; res: Balt; ref: 1, 735
MONTGOMERY, John Craig; pvt; 4th MD Lt Arty; res: Balt; MLCSH; ref: 1, 2, 19, 627, 689, 700, 786, 1523
MONTGOMERY, William T. (M.D.); Surg; 10th AL Inf; res: Har Cty; ref: 1, 2, 18, 21, 70, 735, 1523, 1536
MONTIGNEY, Henry; pvt; 1st MD Cav, Co F; ref: 1
MONTJOY, William; pvt; Lucas' 15th SC Heavy Arty; ref: 1
MONTROSE, Charles; pvt; 2nd MD Cav, Co B; res: Balt; ref: 1
MOOG, George W.; sgt; 1st MD Inf, Co B; ref: 1, 2, 19, 21, 23, 1523
MOOG, Jacob J.; pvt; 2nd MD Cav, Co F; res: Har Cty; ref: 1, 2, 19, 21, 1523, 1609
MOOG, James R.; pvt; 1st MD Inf, Co B; res: Balt; ref: 1, 2, 19, 21, 23, 470, 700, 1523
MOONEY, Francis; pvt; 1st VA Inf, Co E; ref: 1, 1622
MOONEY, John B.; pvt; 1st MD Cav, Co A; res: Balt; ref: 1, 2, 19, 21, 1523, 1666
MOONEY, Thomas; pvt; Barry's Co, MD Vols; ref: 1
MOONEY, William; pvt; 7th VA Cav, Co G; ref: 3
MOORE, Augustus M.; pvt; 2nd MD Inf, Co E; res: Som Cty; ref: 1, 2, 19, 21, 645, 1523, 1556
MOORE, C. A.; pvt; Young's Co, VA Lt Arty; res: Balt; ref: 1, 1540
MOORE, Cole; color sgt; 2nd MD Inf; res: Tal Cty; ref: 64
MOORE, Daniel; pvt; 17th VA Inf, Co K; ref: 142, 251
MOORE, E. P.; pvt; 1st MD Inf, Co A; ref: 1, 19, 1523
MOORE, Edward A.; pvt; Graham's Co, VA Lt Arty; res: Salisbury, Wic Cty; ref: 1, 1170
MOORE, George; pvt; Holbrook's Independent MD Lt Arty; res: Annapolis, AA Cty; ref: 1, 1539
MOORE, George T.; smn, Navy; C.S.S. Atlanta; res: St. M. Cty; ref: 1, 7
MOORE, Henry; pvt; 2nd MD Cav, Co C; ref: 1

MOORE, Isadore; res: St. M. Cty; ref: 1670
MOORE, J. D.; Capt; Huger's Lt Arty; ref: 21, 88, 700
MOORE, James T.; pvt; 4th MD Lt Arty; res: Mont Cty; ref: 1, 2, 19, 21, 1523, 1574
MOORE, James W.; pvt; 2nd MD Cav, Co E; res: Balt; ref: 1, 1609
MOORE, John N.; pvt; Stuart's Horse Arty, Breathed's Battery; ref: 1, 498, 1523
MOORE, John S.; pvt; ref: 1690
MOORE, Percolus M.; cpl; Zarvona's MD Zouaves; res: Tal Cty; ref: 1, 2, 19, 21, 645, 735, 1523, 1540
MOORE, Philip L.; pvt; 1st MD Inf, Co A; ref: 1, 2, 19, 21, 700, 1523
MOORE, R. T.; pvt; MD American Rifles; ref: 1, 718, 1523
MOORE, Robert; pvt; 1st MD Inf, Co B; ref: 1, 2, 19, 21, 1523
MOORE, S. O.; pvt; 1st SC Inf, Co G; ref: 1
MOORE, Thomas; pvt; 1st MD Lt Arty; ref: 2, 19, 34, 63, 64, 68, 782, 791, 1273, 1523
MOORE, Thomas; pvt; 2nd MD Cav, Co B; ref: 1, 19, 1523, 1609
MOORE, W. C.; pvt; Davis's MD Cav, Co C; ref: 1
MOORE, W. D.; pvt; 2nd MD Cav, Co E; ref: 1
MOORE, Warren F.; 2nd MD Inf, Co B; res: Leonardtown, St. M. Cty; ref: 1, 2, 19, 21, 141, 1509, 1523, 1555, 1627
MOORE, William; drummer; 9th VA Inf, Co B; ref: 1, 1576
MOORE, William Martin Van Buren; 3rd VA Inf, Co G; res: Balt; MLCSH; ref: 71, 93, 786, 1484
MOORE, William P.; pvt; 9th VA Inf, Co B; res: Som Cty; ref: 556, 1576
MOORE, William S.; pvt; 2nd MD Cav, Co D; ref: 1, 19, 1523, 1609
MOORE, William Watts; musician; 1st NC Inf, Co H; res: Balt; MLCSH; ref: 1, 627, 700, 786
MORAN, Edward; pvt; Davis's MD Cav, Co C; ref: 1, 93
MORAN, John; pvt; MLCSH; ref: 700
MORAN, Michael G.; pvt; 2nd MD Lt Arty; ref: 1, 2, 19, 21, 1523
MORAN, Patrick Thomas; c. hr., Navy; C.S.S. Greyhound; res: Balt; ref: 1, 70, 1574
MORAN, Rinaldo, J.; pvt; 2nd MD Inf, Co B; ref: 1, 2, 19, 21, 1523
MORAN, Thomas F.; pvt; Berry's Co, MD Vols; res: Cha Cty; ref: 1
MORAN, William; pvt; Davis's MD Cav, Co C; ref: 1
MORAN, William P.; pvt; 2nd MD Inf, Co E; res: Balt; ref: 1, 2, 19, 21, 1523
MORDECAI, J. Randolph; Capt; 3rd SC Lt Arty, Co E; res: Luthersville, Bt Cty; ref: 1, 21, 70, 105, 700, 791
MORFIT, Charles; McL. (M.D.); Passed Asst Surg; Navy; C.S. Raleigh; res: Balt; ref: 1, 2, 18, 58, 70, 97, 279, 511, 700, 735, 1533, 1534, 1564
MORFIT, Clarence; Capt; Quarter Master Dept; res: Balt; ref: 1, 18, 79, 700, 791
MORFIT, Mason; Maj; Quarter Master Dept; res: Balt; ref: 1, 2, 18, 19, 21, 56, 70, 378, 511, 700, 735, 791, 1306, 1523, 1577
MORGAN, Benjamin H.; Lt; 1st VA Cav, Co K; res: Chaptico, St. M. Cty; ref: 1, 2, 19, 21, 69, 700, 720, 1523, 1555
MORGAN, Charles H.; pvt; Davis's MD Cav, Co C; ref: 1
MORGAN, Charles S.; pvt; 2nd MD Cav, Co B; res: Balt; ref: 1, 70
MORGAN, Francis; pvt; Barry's Co MD Vols; ref: 1, 2, 19, 21, 160, 726, 1523
MORGAN, James Morris; Passed Midn, Navy; C.S. Georgia; res: Mont Cty; ref: 1, 97, 1413, 1564, 1616, 1619, 1620
MORGAN, John A.; Lt; 1st MD Lt Arty; ref: 34

MORGAN, John A.; Lt; 1st NC Inf; res: Leonardtown, St. M. Cty; ref: 69, 316, 1670
MORGAN, Hayden; res: St. M. Cty; ref: 1509
MORGAN, Patrick; pvt; Steuart's Horse Arty, Breathed's Battery; ref: 1
MORGAN, R. Reese; res: Salisbury, Wic Cty; ref: 98
MORGAN, Thomas G.; pvt; 1st MD Lt Arty; res: Leonardtown, St. M. Cty; ref: 1, 2, 19, 21, 69, 316, 1509, 1523, 1555, 1627, 1662
MORGAN, William; pvt; 19th VA Heavy Arty, Co C; ref: 1, 2, 19, 21, 1523, 1580
MORGAN, William L. (M.D.); sgt; 31st VA Inf, Co A; res: Balt; ref: 1, 18, 21, 57, 513, 700, 891
MORGAN, William Thomas; cpl; Armistead's Co, VA Lt Arty; res: Balt; MLCSH; ref: 1, 21, 56, 93, 627, 700, 786
MORICE, Isidore; cpl; 1st VA Inf, Co E; ref: 1, 735
MORMEBECK, Henry; pvt; Lee's MD Cav; res: Crownsville, AA Cty; ref: 1, 1539
MORRIS, Alfred L.; pvt; 9th VA Inf, Co B; ref: 1, 1576
MORRIS, Charles Manigult; Lt Commanding, Navy; C.S. Florida; res: Balt; ref: 21, 53, 97, 469, 700, 783, 1520, 1564
MORRIS, Edwin; pvt; 1st MD Cav, Co E; ref: 1, 2, 7, 19, 21, 730, 1523
MORRIS, George; pvt; 35th VA Cav, Co B; res:Balt; ref: 1, 2, 3, 19, 21, 1523, 1611, 1677
MORRIS, Harry; pvt; 1st MD Inf, Co G; ref; 1, 2, 19, 21, 1523
MORRIS, John; pvt; 35th VA Cav, Co B; ref: 1, 3, 1611, 1677
MORRIS, John J.; sgt; 1st MD Inf, Co F; res: Balt; ref; 1, 2, 19, 21, 23, 1523
MORRIS, John M.; pvt; 2nd MD Cav, Co B; ref: 1
MORRIS, John R.; pvt; 9th VA Inf, Co B; res: Cambridge, Dor Cty; ref; 1, 1547, 1576
MORRIS, Lewis; pvt; O'Ferrall's Bn, VA Cav, Co; ref: 1, 2, 19, 21
MORRIS, R.; pvt; Lee's Balt Lt Arty, Alexander's Bn; ref: 1
MORRIS, William T.; pvt; 2nd MD Cav, Co E; ref: 1, 7, 1523
MORRISON, D. B.; pvt; 7th VA Cav, Co G; ref: 1
MORRISON, George W.; pvt; 2nd MD Cav, Co C; ref: 1, 19, 1523, 1609
MORRISON, James S.; sgt; 2nd MD Lt Arty; ref: 1, 2, 19, 21, 64, 1523
MORRISON, John C.; McNiell's Rangers; res: Merryland Tract, Frd Cty; ref; 70, 90, 148, 519
MORRISON, Joseph; fmn, Navy; prize steamer Stagy; res: Balt; ref: 1
MORRISON, Wilbur; pvt; 2nd MD Inf, Co A; res: Balt; ref: 2, 19, 21, 70, 259, 650, 1520, 1523
MORROW, James G.; pvt; 2nd MD Lt Arty; ref: 1
MORROW, John; pvt; MD Line, Co B; ref: 1
MORTIMER, Edwin J.; sgt; 13th VA Inf, Co G; ref: 1, 735
MORTON, Clement R.; pvt; Stuart's Horse Arty, Breathed's Battery; res: Balt; ref: 1, 70, 498
MORTON, Nicholas Samuel Merryman; pvt; Stuart's Horse Arty, Breathed's Battery; ref: 1, 498
MORTON, Richard; Col; Nitre & Mining Bureau; res: Balt; ref; 1, 21, 23, 56, 791
MORTON, Robert S.; pvt; 2nd NC Inf; res: Chesterville, Kt Cty; ref: 1584
MORTON, Thomas; pvt; 1st VA Cav, Co K; res: Aquaser, PG Cty; ref: 1, 2, 21, 1523, 1553
MORTON, William C.; pvt; 7th MD Cav, Co M; res: Balt; ref: 1, 1540
MOSES, J.; pvt; 3rd MD Lt Arty; ref: 1, 2, 19, 21, 160, 726, 1523
MOSES, William; pvt; 2nd MD Inf, Co H; ref: 1
MOTH, E.; pvt; 2nd MD Lt Arty; ref: 1, 2, 19, 21, 1523

MOTHERSHEAD, Samuel D.; pvt; 40th VA Inf, Co B; res: Balt; MLCSH; ref: 1, 93, 700, 786
MOTTER, Edward S.; Capt; res: Middletown VAlley; ref: 88
MOTTER, Jacob; pvt; 7th VA Cav, Co G; ref: Emmitsburg, Frd cty; ref: 3, 90
MOTTER, John Carlton; cpl; 1st MD Inf, Co E; ref: 1, 2, 19, 21, 72, 1523
MOUAHAN, James J.; sgt; MLCSH; ref: 700
MORIGHAN, Patrick; pvt; 15th VA Inf, Co F; res: Balt; ref: 1, 21
MOULDEN, Eli; pvt; 7th VA Inf, Co H; res: Mtg Cty; ref: 1, 735
MOULDEN, W. Elias; pvt; 35th VA Cav, Co B; res: Old Medley's Mont Cty; ref: 106, 1611
MOULTON, William; pvt; 2nd MD Cav, Co F; ref: 1, 2, 19, 21, 1523
MOUNTDZ, John D.; McNeill's Rangers; res: Cumberland, All Cty; ref: 19, 65, 95, 148, 504, 519, 1523
MOUNTZ, Joseph; pvt; 18th VA Cav, Co F; res: Georgetown; ref: 1, 316
MOURING, William C.; pvt; 5th VA Cav, Co A; ref: 1, 57
MOWBRAY, John; pvt; 4th MD Lt Arty; res: Cornersville, Dor Cty; ref: 1, 2, 19, 21, 112, 470, 1523, 1547
MOYLAN, William; pvt; 32nd VA Inf, Co C; res: Balt; ref: 1, 19, 21, 1523
MUCER, G. D.; 21st VA Inf, Co B; ref: 70
MUDD, Edward M.; pvt; 1st MD Lt Arty; Nottingham, PG Cty; ref: 1, 2, 19, 21, 470, 1523
MUDD, Edwin C.; pvt; 1st MD Lt Arty; res: Cha Cty; ref: 1, 2, 19, 21, 1523
MUDD, John F.; pvt; 2nd MD Lt Arty; ref: 1, 2, 19, 21, 1494, 1523
MUDD, Joseph A.; A.A. Surg; res: Hyattsville, PG Cty; ref: 1, 1139
MUHLY, Charles W.; pvt; 6th SC Cav; res: Balt; ref: 21, 700
MUIRHEAD, Philip T.; sgt; 2nd MD Inf, Co F; ref: 1, 2, 19, 21, 23, 1523
MULEARY, Stephen; pvt; 2nd MD Inf, Co E; ref: 1
MULHARE, Bernard; pvt; 1st MD Inf, Co E; ref: 1, 2, 19, 21, 1523
MULHEARN, James; pvt; 1st MD Inf, Co F;ref: 1, 19, 1523
MULL, James M.; musician; Lucas's 15th SC Heavy Arty; res: Frederick, Frd Cty; ref; 1, 1111
MULLAN, James; Lt; 1st MD Inf, Co B; ref: 1, 2, 21, 23, 1523
MULLANEY, Patrick; pvt; Lucas' 15th SC Heavy Arty; ref: 1, 1609
MULLANS, Patrick; pvt; 1st VA Inf, Co E; res: Mont Cty; ref: 1
MULLEN, Ambrose F.; pvt; 9th VA Inf, Co B; ref: 1, 735, 1576
MULLEN, Charles; Sharpshooters, Co E; ref: 1, 700
MULLEN, Charles X.; pvt; 1st SC Inf, Co G; MLCSH; ref: 1, 2, 19, 21
MULLEN, James; Lt; 1st MD Inf, Co B; ref: 1, 64, 456, 791
MULLEN, John; pvt; 35th VA Cav, Co B; res: Balt; ref; 1, 1611, 1677
MULLEN, Joseph, Jr; cpl; 27th NC Inf, Co F; res: Balt; ref: 1, 21, 56, 70, 93, 700
MULLEN, Patrick; pvt; Jacob's Mounted Riflemen; res: Balt; ref; 1, 1540
MULLEN, William H. (M.D.); pvt; 1st VA Inf, Co B; MLCSH; ref: 1, 18, 786
MULLER, A.; pvt; 4th SC State Troops, Co A; res: Balt; ref: 1, 735
MULLEY, Timothy; pvt; Zarvona's MD Zouaves; ref: 1, 735
MULLIKIN, Archibald; pvt; 35th VA Cav, Co B; res: Mont Cty; ref: 1, 1677
MULLIKIN, Beale Duvall; cpl; 2nd MD Inf, Co C; res: PG Cty; ref: 1, 2, 19, 21, 23, 70, 470, 700, 1523
MULLIKIN, Frank; pvt; Zarvona's MD Zouaves; ref: 735

MULLIKIN, H. Clay; pvt; Lee's MD Cav; res: Patuxent, AA Cty; ref: 1, 1539, 1628
MULLIKIN, Walter; pvt; 2nd MD Inf, Co C; ref: 1, 2, 19, 21, 1523
MULLIN, Charles H.; pvt 1st SC Inf, Co G; res: Balt; MLCSH; ref: 735, 786
MULLIN, Cornelius Saxton; pvt; 1st MD Cav, Co E; res: How Cty; ref: MLCSH; ref: 1, 2, 19, 21, 71, 79, 92, 93, 627, 730, 786, 1523
MUMFORD, Henry A.; cpl; 2nd MD Inf, Co G; res: Wor Cty; ref: 1, 2, 21, 23, 700
MUMFORD, William R.; pvt; 2nd MD Inf, Co G; ref: 1, 2, 19, 21, 1523
MUMMEY, Thomas Worthington; cpl; 4th MD Lt Arty; ref: 1, 2, 19, 21, 23, 1523
MUNDER, John B.; res: Old Medley's Mont Cty; ref: 106
MUNFORD, William; Lt Col; 17th VA Inf; res: Fairlee, Kt Cty; ref: 1, 19, 21, 30, 127, 133, 700, 791, 1584, 1600
MUNFORD, William Robert; pvt; 2nd MD Inf, Co G; ref: 2, 19, 21, 470, 1523
MURDOCH, Augustus; pvt; 1st MD Cav, Co A; res: Urbana, Frd Cty; ref: 1, 2, 19, 21, 90, 1523, 1549
MURDOCH, Fred; pvt; Lee's Balt Lt Arty, Alexander's Bn; res: Balt; ref: 1, 1540
MURDOCH, George W.; pvt; 39th NC Inf, Co M; res: Annapolis, AA Cty; ref: 1, 1539
MURDOCH, James Campbell; Lt; Marine Corps; C.S.S. Richmond; res: Balt; ref: 1, 2, 19, 21, 58, 70, 97, 279, 674, 685, 792, 1349, 1523, 1564, 1579, 1593, 1594, 1620
MURDOCH, John; 25th LA Inf; ref: 70
MURDOCH, William B.; 25th LA Inf; ref: 70
MURDOCK, Russell (M.D.); Surg; 1st Regt Engineer Corps; res: Balt; ref: 1, 18, 82, 995, 1533, 1534, 1536
MURDOCK, William; pvt; 2nd MD Cav, Co C; ref: 1, 70, 1609
MURGOTTEN, Charles; pvt; Lucas' 15th SC Heavy Arty; ref: 1
MURKLAND, W. J. (Revd); sgt maj; 3rd VA Inf, Local Defense, Co A; res: Balt; ref: 1, 21, 70, 107, 700, 866
MURPHY, Daniel E.; pvt; 2nd MD Cav, Co C; res: Cratchers Ferry, Dor Cty; ref: 1, 1511, 1547
MURPHY, Dennis; pvt; 1st MD Inf, Co G; res: Balt; ref: 1, 2, 19, 21, 1523
MURPHY, Edward; pvt; 1st MD Inf, Co D; ref: 1, 2, 19, 21, 1523
MURPHY, Frank; pvt; 2nd MD Cav, Co C; ref: 2, 21, 1523
MURPHY, George; pvt; 2nd MD Cav, Co C; res: Carr Cty; ref: 2, 19, 21, 1523, 1609
MURPHY, James F.; ordnance sgt; 1st SC Inf, Co C; res: Balt; ref: 1, 21, 700
MURPHY, John; cpl; 2nd MD Inf, Co H; ref: 1, 2, 19, 21, 1523
MURPHY, John; pvt; 1st SC Inf, Co G; ref: 1
MURPHY, John; pvt; Stuart's Horse Arty, Breathed's Battery; ref: 1, 2, 19, 21
MURPHY, John; pvt; Lucas' 15th SC Heavy Arty; ref: 1
MURPHY, M.; pvt; 2nd MD Cav, Co D; ref: 1, 1609
MURPHY, Michael; pvt; 9th VA Inf, Co B; res: Balt; ref: 1, 1523, 1576, 1598
MURPHY, Nicholas; pvt; 15th LA Inf, Co C; res: Frederick, Frd Cty; ref: 1, 89, 559
MURPHY, Patrick; pvt; Stuart's Horse Arty, Breathed's Battery; ref: 1, 1580
MURPHY, Richard Davis; sgt; 1st VA Cav, Co B; res: Balt; ref: 1, 601, 735, 934
MURPHY, Samuel W. (M.D.) Asst Surg; Page's TN Lt Arty; MLCSH; ref: 1, 18, 786
MURPHY, Thomas; pvt; 19th VA Heavy Arty, Co C; ref: 1, 1580

MURRAY, Alexander; pvt; 2nd MD Inf, Co A; res: West River, AA Cty; ref: 1, 2, 19, 21, 23, 259, 470, 645, 650, 685, 700, 715, 1355, 1523, 1539, 1577

MURRAY, Clapham; Lt; 2nd MD Inf, Co A; res: West River, AA Cty; ref: 1, 2, 19, 21, 23, 44, 64, 68, 70, 75, 259, 493, 503, 511, 650, 674, 685, 690, 700, 715, 753, 1353, 1355, 1520, 1523, 1579

MURRAY, David; 27th GA Inf, Co C; ref: 70

MURRAY, Edward; Lt Col; 49th VA Inf, res: How Cty; ref: 1, 13, 19, 735, 787, 791, 985, 1523, 1577, 1600

MURRAY, Edward C.; pvt; 19th VA Heavy Arty, Co C; res: Balt; ref: 1, 2, 21, 700, 730, 1540, 1580, 1578

MURRAY, George; pvt; 2nd MD Cav, Co F; res: Carr Cty; ref: 1, 2, 19, 21, 1523

MURRAY, J. A.; pvt; Davis's MD Cav; res: Tal Cty; ref: 2, 784

MURRAY, James; sgt; 6th LA Inf, Co F; res: Balt; ref: 1, 21, 53, 700, 1540

MURRAY, James S.; cpl; 13th VA Inf, Co G; ref: 1, 735

MURRAY, John H.; pvt; 2nd MD Inf, Co E; ref: 1, 2, 19, 21, 1523

MURRAY, Michael; pvt; 13th VA Inf, Co G; res: Balt; ref: 1, 735, 1540

MURRAY, Peter; pvt; 13th VA Inf, Co G; ref: 1, 735

MURRAY, Sterling; sgt; Stuart's Horse Arty, Breathed's Battery; ref: 1, 2, 19, 21, 44, 498, 700, 735, 1523

MURRAY, Thomas; pvt; 1st MD Inf, Co B; res: Balt; ref: 1, 2, 19, 21, 1523, 1540

MURRAY, William; pvt; 2nd MD Inf, Co A; ref: 1, 2, 19, 21, 1523

MURRAY, William H.; Asst Surg; Stuart's Horse Arty; res: Balt; ref: 1, 18, 19, 498, 1475, 1523, 1534

MURRAY, William H.; Capt; 2nd MD Inf, Co A; res: West River, AA Cty; ref: 1, 2, 19, 21, 23, 34, 35, 38, 44, 63, 64, 68, 75, 80, 92, 93, 107, 240, 259, 347, 444, 456, 462, 469, 493, 501, 503, 511, 517, 559, 595, 602, 631, 638, 650, 674, 681, 685, 686, 690, 715, 746, 753, 757, 789, 791, 825, 857, 877, 990, 1275, 1279, 1281, 1285, 1353, 1355, 1511, 1519, 1520, 1523, 1577, 1578, 1579, 1635, 1674

MURREL, Jesse F.; cpl; 9th VA Inf, Co B; ref: 1, 1576

MURRY, Robert W.; Lt; 9th VA Inf, Co B; ref: 1, 1576

MURRY, W. A.; pvt; 1st MD Cav, Co B;r f: 1, 2, 19, 21, 1523

MURTAY, J.; pvt; 2nd MD Cav, Co E; ref: 1

MURTHE, Christopher; pvt; Zarvona's MD Zouaves; ref: 1, 735

MURTY, Patrick; pvt; MD Guerrilla Zouaves; ref: 1

MUSE, Samuel W.; orderly sgt; 5th VA Cav, Co E; res: Balt; ref: 1, 21, 57, 700

MUSGROVE, Thomas H.; pvt; 1st MD Lt Arty; ref: 1, 2, 19, 21, 1523

MUSSER, William H.; pvt; 43rd VA Cav (Mosby's), Co G; res: Middlebrook, Mtg Cty; ref: 1, 8

MUTH, Alfred; pvt; 1st MD Inf, Co D; ref: 1, 2, 19, 21, 1523

MYERS, Abraham; pvt; 17th VA Inf, Co E; ref: 1, 133, 142, 735

MYERS, Andrew; drummer; 1st MD Inf, Co G; res: Balt; ref: 1, 2, 19, 21, 1523

MYERS, Calvin; pvt; 2nd TX Cav, Co D; ref: 1, 456, 488, 923

MYERS, Charles; pvt; Rhett's 1st SC Heavy Arty; res: Balt; MLCSH; ref: 1, 93, 627, 708, 786

MYERS, Charles F.; pvt; 1st VA Inf, Co E; ref: 1, 1622

MYERS, Charles Thomas; pvt; 2nd MD Cav, Co C; res: Frd Cty; ref: 1, 1301

MYERS, Christopher P.; pvt; 1st MD Inf, Co A; res: Frd Cty; ref: 1, 2, 19, 21, 89, 90, 1523
MYERS, Clinton; pvt; 1st MD Cav, Co C; ref: 2, 19, 21, 1523
MYERS, Daniel; pvt; Holbrook's Independent MD Lt Arty; res: Balt; ref: 1, 1540
MYERS, David; pvt; Jacob's Mounted Riflemen; res: Annapolis, AA Cty; ref: 1, 1539
MYERS, Henry; pvt; 1st SC Inf, Co G; ref: 1
MYERS, Henry; pvt; 3rd MD Lt Arty; ref: 1, 2, 19, 21, 160, 726, 1523
MYERS, Herman; 24th VA Cav, Co F; ref: 735
MYERS, J. H.; pvt; Stuart''s Horse Arty, Breathed's Battery; ref: 1, 498
MYERS, John; pvt; 4th MD Lt Arty; ref: 1, 2, 19, 21, 1523
MYERS, John A.; pvt; Lucas' 15th SC Heavy Arty; ref: 1
MYERS, Joseph; res: Frederick, Frd Cty; ref: 88, 89
MYERS, Joseph D.; Lt; 67th NC Inf, Co B; res: Millersville, AA Cty; ref: 1, 1539
MYERS, Mahlon L.; pvt; 6th VA Cav, Co K; res: Doubs, Frd Cty; ref: 1, 19, 90, 643, 1523, 1548, 1611
MYERS, Thomas S.; pvt; 1st MD Cav, Co D; res: Frd Cty; ref: 1, 2, 19, 21, 90, 1523, 1601
MYLAN, William; pvt; 32nd VA Inf, Co C; res: Balt; ref: 21
MYNCH, Christopher L.; pvt; 2nd MD Inf, Co E; res: Balt; ref: 1, 2, 19, 21, 1523
MYRES, P.; pvt; Lee's MD Cav; ref: 1
MYRICK, John D.; Capt; 9th VA Inf, Co B; res: Balt; ref: 1, 18, 518, 735, 791, 1576
MYRICK, John T.; pvt; 34th VA Inf, Co K; res: Balt; MLCSH; ref: 1, 21, 700, 786

NAILOR, N. J.; pvt; Lee's MD Cav; ref: 1, 1622
NAPOLEON, Louis; pvt; 3rd MD Lt Arty; ref: 1, 2, 19, 21, 160, 726
NASH, James; pvt; 2nd MD Inf, Co C; ref: 1, 2, 19, 21, 784
NASH, Wadsworth; pvt; Norfolk Lt Arty Blues, Co C; res: Balt; ref: 1, 21, 57, 700
NASH, William F.; sgt; Parker's VA Lt Arty Battery; ref: 1, 1595
NAVY, Samuel; res: Patuxent Forge, AA Cty; ref: 1539
NAYLOR, J. M.; pvt; 1st MD Cav, Co D; ref: 2, 19, 21
NAYLOR, Magill L.; pvt; 3rd TX Cav Co H; res: Patuxent Forge, AA Cty; ref: 1, 1539
NAYLOR, Thomas K.; pvt; 1st MD Cav, Co B; res: Westwood, PG Cty; ref: 1, 2, 19, 21, 785, 1466, 1553, 1622
NAYLOR, William E.; pvt; 2nd MD Lt Arty; res: Frd Cty; ref: 1, 2, 19, 21, 520
NEAL, D.; pvt; 43rd VA Cav (Mosby's), Co D; ref: 8
NEAL, Francis W.; pvt; 1st MD Cav, Co D; res: Westminster, Carr Cty; ref: 1, 2, 19, 21, 40, 70, 323, 498, 806, 1601
NEAL, George C.; pvt; 1st VA Inf , Co E; ref: 1, 735
NEAL, Harry S.; pvt; 1st MD Cav, Co D; res: Westminster, Carr Cty; ref: 1, 2, 19, 21, 40, 70, 323, 498, 806
NEAL, Henry; pvt; 2nd MD Lt Arty; ref: 2, 19, 21, 685
NEALE, Augustus Wills; pvt; 2nd MD Inf, Co B; res: Port Tobacco, Cha Cty; ref: 1, 2, 19, 21, 23, 69, 316, 700, 1523, 1546, 1665
NEALE, Charles A.; pvt; Hampton Leg Lt Arty, Co B; ref: 1, 2, 19, 21, 69, 316
NEALE, Edmund Clarence; pvt; 21st VA Inf, Co B; res: Balt; ref: 1, 2, 19, 21, 69, 312, 316, 1523
NEALE, Eustace C.; pvt; 3rd Bn, VA Inf Local Defense, Co D; ref: 1
NEALE, Francis; pvt; 2nd MD Lt Arty; res: Port Tobacco, Cha Cty; ref: 69, 316
NEALE, Hamilton S.; Lt; 39th V AInf, Co B; ref: 1, 70

NEALE, Walter; sgt maj; 39th VA Inf, Co B; ref: 1, 70
NEALE, Wilford; pvt; 1st MD Cav, Co C; res: Balt; ref: 1, 2, 19, 21, 69, 316, 1598
NEEDHAM, George; pvt; 2nd MD Inf, Co H; ref: 1, 2, 19, 21
NEER, N. Frank; pvt; 35th VA Cav, Co C; res: Balt; ref: 1,3 , 57, 513, 1677
NEIDHAMMER, Louis; pvt; 35th VA Cav, Co B; res: Balt; ref: 1, 2, 3, 15, 19, 21, 23, 1540, 1611, 1677
NEIL, Howard; pvt; Stuart's Horse Arty, Breathed's Battery; ref: 1
NELSON, Andrew J.; pvt; 12th SC Inf, Co I; res: Balt; ref: 1, 1540
NELSON, Caleb W.; pvt; 1st MD Lt Arty; ref: 1, 2, 19, 21, 470
NELSON, Francis Fletcher; pvt; 1st MD Lt Arty; res: Snow Hill, Wor Cty; MLCSH; ref: 1, 2, 19, 21, 627, 700, 786
NELSON, Hugh (M.D.); pvt; 2nd VA Cav, Co K; res: Balt; ref: 1, 18, 631
NELSON, John L.; cpl; 19th VA Heavy Arty, Co C; res: Balt; ref: 1, 1580, 1613
NELSON, Nathan, Jr; pvt; 2nd MD Cav, Co E; res: New Market, Frd Cty; ref: 67, 72
NELSON, Rawling W.; pvt; 1st MD Cav, Co A; ref: 1, 2, 19, 21
NELSON, Robert; pvt; Davis's MD Cav, Co B; ref: 1
NELSON, Robert; pvt; Rhett's 1st SC Heavy Arty; res: Balt; ref: 693, 735
NESBIT, James; pvt; Stuart's Horse Arty, Breathed's Battery; ref: 1
NETHKIN, Charles O.; pvt; Holbrook's Independent MD Lt Arty; res: All Cty; ref: 1
NEVETT, James Buchanan; Lt; MD American Rifles; ref: 1, 19, 1494
NEVITT, John J.; ref: 70
NEVITT, Philip; res: St. M. Cty; ref: 1670
NEWBERRY, D. M.; pvt; ref: 700
NEWBREY, John W.; pvt; 17th NC, Co H; res: Silversburg, Wash Cty; ref: 1, 93, 1558
NEWELL, William Henry (M.D.); Asst Surg; General Hostpial, Richmond; res: Frederick, Frd Cty; ref: 1, 18, 90, 1534, 1579
NEWKERKE, J. V.; pvt; 2nd MD Cav, Co F; res: Frd Cty; ref: 1, 2, 19, 21, 1609
NEWKIRK, Josiah; pvt; 1st MD Cav, Co E; res: Balt; ref; 1, 2, 19, 21, 730
NEWMAN, George; pvt; 1st MD Cav, Co C; res: Balt; ref: 1, 19
NEWMAN, John W.; cpl; 23rd VA Cav, Co G; res: Frederick, Frd Cty; ref: 1, 72
NEWPORT, Clarence; res: Frederick, Frd Cty; ref; 89
NEWTON, Charles Augustine; pvt; 6th VA Inf, Co G; res: Balt; MLCSH; ref: 1, 627, 700, 786
NEWTON, F. M.; pvt; 3rd MD Lt Arty; ref: 1, 2, 19, 21, 160, 461, 726, 1460
NEWTON, James W.; sgt; Davis's MD Cav, Co C; ref: 1, 2, 19, 21, 160, 726
NEWTON, John L.; smn, Navy; C.S.S. Albion; res: Wash Cty; ref; 1, 291
NEWTON, Samuel M.; pvt; 3rd MD Lt Arty; ref: 1, 2, 19, 21, 160, 726
NICHOLAS, Herman; pvt; 2nd MD Inf, Co A; ref: 2, 19, 21
NICHOLAS, Robert Carter; Capt; 59th VA Inf, Co F; MLCSH; ref: 1, 627, 700
NICHOLAS, Thomas; smn, Navy; C.S.S. Albemarle; ref: 1
NICHOLAS, William C.; Capt; Davis's MD Cav, Bn, Co E; ref: 1, 21, 923
NICHOLAS, Wilson Carey; Capt; 1st MD Inf, Co G; res: Owings Mills, Bt Cty; ref: 1, 2, 19, 21, 23, 34, 38, 39, 50, 57, 64, 68, 70, 86, 94, 240, 456, 462, 488, 493, 496, 511, 559, 580, 685, 700, 757, 791, 824, 1523, 1541, 1560, 1634

NICHOLS, Charles; pvt; McNeill's Rangers; res: Oakland, Gar Cty; ref: 1, 19, 65, 95, 148, 1010, 1538, 1610
NICHOLS, Christopher B.; pvt; 29th NC Inf, Co A; res: Annapolis, AA Cty; ref: 1, 1539
NICHOLS, J. P.; pvt; 3rd MD Lt Arty; ref: 2, 19, 21, 160, 461, 726
NICHOLS, John; pvt; 2nd MD Inf, Co H; res: Annapolis, AA Cty; ref: 1, 2, 19, 21, 1539
NICHOLS, Robert Carter; cpl; 53rd VA Inf, Co E; res: Balt; MLCSH; ref: 93, 786
NICHOLS, William L.; pvt; 2nd MD Inf, Co C; ref: 1, 2, 19, 21
NICKERON, Charles E. V.; Contract Surg; Walker Hospital, Columbia; ref: 1, 18
NICHOLSON, A. S.; pvt; Davis's MD Cav, Co C; ref: 1
NICHOLSON, Thomas Franklin; pvt; 1st MD Inf, Co I; ref: 1, 2, 19, 21
NICHOLSON, William; pvt; 18th VA Heavy Arty, Co E; ref: 1, 316, 735
NICOLAI, Herman; pvt; 2nd MD Inf, Co A; res: Balt; ref: 19, 259
NIGHTHART, Charles; res: Annapolis, AA Cty; ref: 1539
NIGHTINGALE, John A.; drummer; 13th VA Inf, Co G; ref: 1, 21, 700
NOBLE, Josiah; res: Tal Cty; ref: 645
NOBLE, William F.; pvt; 13th SC Inf, Co G; ref: 1, 72
NOCK, George S.; pvt; 46th VA Inf, Co F; res: Balt; ref: 1, 21, 700
NOEL, C. E.; pvt; 1st MD Cav, Co B; ref: 1, 2, 21, 785
NOEL, Henry Reginald; Surg; 60th VA Inf; ref: 1, 18, 1533, 1534, 1536
NOLAN, G.; pvt; 1st SC Inf, Co G; res: Balt; ref: 735
NOLAN, James; pvt; 1st MD Inf, Co F; res: Balt; ref: 1, 2, 19, 21, 791
NOLAND, George W.; pvt; 2nd VA Inf, Co A; res: Balt; ref: 1, 21, 93, 700
NOLL, Charles; pvt; 2nd SC Inf, Co K; res: Balt; MLCSH; ref: 1, 627, 700, 786
NOLLEY, M. J.; sgt; 31st NC Inf, Co G; res: Balt; ref: 1, 21, 57, 700, 891
NOMEY, H.; North Carolina; ref: 92
NOONAN, Michael; pvt; 2nd MD Inf, Co E; ref: 1, 2, 19, 21
NOONAN, Robert E.; Capt; Asst Q.M., Gen J. Johnston's staff; res: Libertytown, Frd Cty; ref: 1, 72, 90, 559, 643, 681, 735, 791
NORCUM, William Augustus Blount; Asst Surg; No. 2 North Carolina Hospital, Peteresburg, Virginia; res: Balt; ref: 1, 18, 1534, 1596
NORFOLK, George S.; pvt; 21st VA Inf, Co B; res: How Cty; ref: 1, 2, 8, 19, 312, 735, 1540
NORFOLK, William Hinton; pvt; 1st MD Inf, Co C; ref: 1, 2, 19, 21, 93
NORRIS, Alexander, Jr; pvt; 1st VA Cav, Co L; res: Har Cty; ref: 1, 2, 19, 21, 233
NORRIS, Daniel; sgt; 13th VA Inf, Co G; ref: 1, 735
NORRIS, George; pvt; 35th VA Cav, Co B; ref: 1611
NORRIS, George Smith; sgt; Signal Corps; res: Bel Air, Har Cty; ref: 1, 2, 14, 19, 21, 23, 1084, 1351, 1540, 1579
NORRIS, Lewis F.; pvt; 1st MD Cav, Co E; res: Balt; ref: 1, 2, 19, 21, 57, 730, 827
NORRIS, Oliver Philip; pvt; Zarvona's MD Zouaves; res: St. M. Cty; ref: 1, 735, 873, 1509, 1670
NORRIS, R. James; 7th VA Cav, Co G; res: Bt Cty; ref: 1, 3
NORRIS, Richard H.; cpl; 1st MD Cav, Co D; res: Libertytown; ref: 1, 2, 19, 21, 90, 1601
NORRIS, T. R.; pvt; 1st SC Inf, Co G; ref: 1
NORRIS, W. Epa; Lt; 46th VA Inf, Co D; res: Balt; ref: 1, 2, 19, 124, 312, 681, 735
NORRIS, William; Col; Chief-Signal Corps and Chief-Secret Service Bureau; res: Reisterestown, Bt

Cty; ref; 1, 2, 14, 19, 21, 63, 110, 431, 654, 700, 724, 735, 791, 803, 911, 1335, 1480, 1482, 1511, 1523, 1577, 1578, 1579, 1581, 1583, 1624, 1654, 1664
NORRIS, Williamson; pvt; 9th VA Cav, Co D; ref: 1, 8, 1583
NORTHROP, Charles; pvt; Holbrook's Independent MD Lt Arty; ref: 1
NORTHROP, Lucius Bellinger (M.D.); Col; commissary General; res: Bt Cty; MLCSH; ref: 1, 18, 21, 124, 133, 700, 722, 791, 1583, 1617, 1623
NORTON, James; sgt; MD Guerrilla Zouaves; ref: 1
NORTON, John J.; pvt; 1st MD Inf, Co D; ref: 1, 2, 19, 21
NORWOOD, James; res: Annapolis, AA Cty; ref: 1539
NORWOOD, Jeremiah; res: Hyattstown, Mont Cty; ref: 19
NORWOOD, Lewis; pvt; 2nd MD Cav, Co A; ref: 2, 21, 1523
NORWOOD, Richard R.; Md American Rifles; res: Annapolis, AA Cty; ref: 1, 1539
NORWOOD, Rufus F.; pvt; 5th NC Cav, Co F; res: Balt; ref: 1, 1540
NORWOOD, William (Revd); pvt; 2nd MD Cav, Co A; ref: 1, 2, 11, 19, 21, 700
NOSS, William; pvt; Barry's Co, MD Vols; ref: 1
NOTT, Josiah Clark; Surg; Medical Director, District of the Gulf; res: Balt; ref: 1, 18, 1532
NOTTINGHAM, John J.; pvt; 43rd VA Cav (Mosby's), Co D; ref: 1, 8
NOTTINGHAM, Lloyd H.; pvt; 2nd KY Cav, Co D; res: Balt; MLCSH; ref: 1, 700, 786
NOTTINGHAM, Trobe; pvt; 43rd VA Cav (Mosby's), Co D; ref: 8
NOUSE, Charles H., Jr (M.D.); 35th VA Cav, Co B; res: Darnestown, Mont Cty; ref; 1, 18, 316, 557, 735, 1002, 1574, 1677
NOWELL, Edward; Lt; 13th Bn, VA Lt Arty, Co A; ref: 1, 21, 700
NOWELL, John M.; sgt; 44th VA Inf, Co C; ref: 1, 684
NOWELL, Ottway; Lt; 26th VA Inf; ref: 735
NUGENT, Reginald; pvt; 1st SC Cav, Co M; res: Fairlee, Kt Cty; ref: 1, 1584
NUSE, Frederick; res: Frederick, Frd Cty; ref: 89
NUTT, James M.; pvt; 40th VA Inf, res: Balt; ref: 21, 700

OAKES, Charles C.; pvt; 9th VA Inf, Co B; ref: 1, 19, 70, 1576
OAKES, Patrick H.; pvt; Edelin's MD Heavy Arty; ref: 1
OAKES, Patrick Henry; pvt; Davis's MD Cav, Co A; ref: 1, 735
OATES, Charles T.; pvt; 2nd MD Cav, Co C; res: Frederick, Frd Cty; ref: 1, 2, 19, 21, 90, 240, 643, 1609
OATES, James F.; pvt; 1st MD Cav, Co C; ref: 1, 2, 19, 21
OBENDERFER, Augustus A.; pvt; 2nd MD Inf, Co F; res: Frederick, Frd Cty; ref: 19, 21, 67, 90, 643, 700, 873
OBENDERFER, Frederick W.; res: Frederick, Frd Cty; ref; 67
OBENDERFER, John Leonard; pvt; 1st MD Cav, Co D; res: Frederick, Frd Cty; MLCSH; ref: 1, 2, 19, 21, 67, 90, 786, 1301, 1601
OBENDOFFER, Augustus; pvt; 2nd MD Inf, Co F; ref: 1, 2, 21
OBENDORF, A., Jr; pvt; 10th AL Inf; res: Balt; ref: 21, 700, 735
O'BERG, Henry; pvt; Lee's MD Cav; res: Annapolis, AA Cty; ref: 1, 1539, 1628
O'BOYLE, Charles M.; pvt; 35th VA Cav, Co B; res: Poin of Rocks, Frd Cty; ref: 1, 3, 90, 1611, 1677
O'BOYLE, James A.; pvt; 35th VA Cav, Co B; res: Carrollton Manor, Frd Cty; ref: 1, 3, 90, 1611, 1677
O'BRIAN, Dennis; pvt; 2nd MD Cav, Co B; res: Balt; ref: 1, 2, 19, 21, 23
O'BRIAN, James; pvt; 2nd MD inf, Co D; res: Balt; ref: 1, 2, 19, 21, 1540, 1613

O'BRIAN, James; pvt; 3rd MD Lt Arty; ref: 1, 2, 21, 160, 461, 726, 1523
O'BRIEN, Edmund W.; Lt; 1st MD Inf, Co E; ref: 1, 2, 19, 21, 23, 64, 456, 559, 1511
O'BRIEN, Edward; pvt; 21st VA Inf, Co B; res: Carr Cty; ref: 2, 19, 312, 323
O'BRIEN, Edward H.; pvt; Stuart's Horse Arty, Breathed's Battery; ref: 1, 498
O'BRIEN, Edward H.; pvt; 43rd VA Cav (Mosby's), Co D; res: Carr Cty; ref: 1, 2, 8, 19, 21, 1511
O'BRIEN, John N.; pvt; 43rd VA Cav (Mosby's), Co G; res: How Cty; ref: 1, 2, 8, 19, 19, 21, 687
O'BRIEN, Michael J.; d.h., Navy; Gun boat Price; ref: 1, 735
O'BRIEN, Nicholas; pvt; 1st VA Inf, Co E; res: Bladensburg, PG Cty; ref: 1, 735
O'BRIEN, Patrick H.; pvt; 1st GA Inf, Co B; ref: 1, 72
O'BRIEN, Thomas; sgt; 2nd MD Inf, Co H; res: Balt; ref: 1, 2, 19, 21, 23, 650, 700
O'BYRNE, William E.; sgt; 7th VA Cav, Co G; ref: 1, 1156
O'CONNEL, Charles; pvt; 2nd MD Cav, Co D; ref: 1, 19, 1609
O'CONNELL, David Joseph; pvt; Lucas's 15th SC Heavy Arty; res: Balt; ref: 1
O'CONNELL, Edward; pvt; 2nd MD Cav, Co D; ref: 1
O'CONNELL, Michael H.; cpl; 3rd MD Lt Arty; ref: 1, 2, 19, 21, 23, 160, 461, 726
O'CONNELL, Patrick; pvt; 1st MD Inf, Co A; res: Frd Cty; ref: 1, 2, 19, 21, 23, 90
ODEN, Archibald; pvt; 43rd VA Cav (Mosby's), Co A; res: Frd Cty; ref: 1, 49
ODEN, William Samuel; pvt; 35th VA Cav, Co B; res: Frd Cty; ref: 1, 3, 15, 90, 1611, 1677
ODER, Joseph Benson (Hon.); pvt; 10th VA Inf, Co B; res: Frostburg, All Cty; ref: 1, 148, 631
ODONDERLOW, John R.; pvt; 9th VA Inf, Co B; ref: 1, 70, 1576
O'DONNELL, John E.; Lt; 9th VA Inf, Co B; res: Balt; ref: 1, 2, 19, 735, 1576
O'DONNELL, Patrick; pvt; 9th VA Inf, Co B; res: Balt; ref: 1, 735, 1576
O'DONOVAN, Edward; pvt; 2nd MD Inf, Co A; res: Bt Cty; ref: 1, 2, 19, 21, 23, 470, 650, 700, 1523
O'FARRAR, James; pvt; Davis's MD Cav, Co B; ref: 1, 19
OFFATT, George W.; Lt; 1st VA Inf, Co E; ref: 1, 2, 19, 735
OFFATT, John R.; pvt; 1st VA Inf, Co E; ref: 1, 2, 735, 1523
OFFATT, William; pvt; 1st VA Cav, Co K; ref: 2, 19, 21
OFFATT, Zac A., gun, Navy; C.S.S. Gaines; ref: 1, 2, 19, 735, 1564
OFFUTT, Thomas Zadac; Surg; 4th VA Inf, Towson, Bt Cty; ref; 1, 18, 720, 1596, 1613
O'GRADY, James; cpl; 2nd MD Lt Arty; res: Carr Cty; ref: 1, 2, 19, 21, 23, 786
O'HALLAN, Martin; pvt; 2nd MD Inf, Co E; ref: 1, 2, 19, 21
O'HANLON, John; pvt; 3rd MD Lt Arty; ref: 1, 2, 19, 21, 160, 726
O'HARA, Dennis P. H.; smn, Navy; ref: 1, 735
OHENHEIMER, Falk; pvt; Holbrook's Independent MD Lt Arty; res: Balt; ref: 1, 1540
OHILDRESS, ---; pvt; Davis's MD Cav, Co A; ref: 735
OHILDRESS, David; pvt; Davis's MD Cav, Co A; ref: 735
OHLGART, G. Philip, Jr; pvt; 2nd MD Inf, Co D; res: Balt; ref: 1, 19, 21, 70, 700
O'KEEFE, Matthew (Revd); Chaplain; Manhone's Brigade; res: Balt; ref: 1, 720
O'KEEFE, William; pvt; Zarvona's MD Zouaves; ref: 1, 19, 58, 97

OLAUGHLIN, John; cpl; 1st MD Inf, Co C; res: Balt; ref: 1, 2, 19, 21, 23

OLDNER, Philip E.; pvt; 4th MD Lt Arty; res: QA Cty; ref: 1, 2, 19, 34, 93, 1523

OLDSON, W. H. C.; pvt; 4th MD Lt Arty; res: QA Cty; ref: 1, 2, 19, 21

OLDSON, William O.; pvt; 4th MD Lt Arty; res: QA Cty; ref: 1, 2, 19, 21

O'LEARY, Jerome; pvt; 1st MD Cav, Co D; ref: Frederick, Frd Cty; ref; 1, 2, 19, 21, 89, 90, 700, 1548, 1601

OLGAND, Philip; res: Balt; ref: 1540

OLIVER, J. P.; pvt; 3rd MD Lt Arty; ref: 2, 19, 21, 160, 726

OLIVER, James R.; pvt; 1st VA Cav, Co K; ref: 1, 2, 19, 21, 46, 952

OLIVER, T. Harry; pvt; MD American Rifles; res: Tal Cty; ref: 1, 35, 44, 645, 1612

OLIVER, William H.; sgt; 5th VA Cav, Co F; res: Balt; ref: 1, 21, 700

OLNDOFF, John; pvt; 2nd MD Cav, Co D; ref: 1, 19, 1609

O'LOUGHLIN, Michael; pvt; 1st MD Inf, Co D; res: Balt; ref: 1, 2, 19, 21, 1540, 1578, 1607, 1608

O'NEAL, James; pvt; 2nd MD Cav, Co D; res: Havre de Grace, Har Cty; ref: 1, 350

O'NEAL, Thomas H.; pvt; MD Guerrilla Zouaves; res: Frederick, Frd Cty; ref: 1, 89

O'NEIL, Andrew; pvt; 1st MD Inf, Co B; res: Balt; ref: 1, 2, 19, 21

O'NEIL, John H.; pvt; 43rd VA Cav (Mosby's), Co G; ref: 1, 2, 8, 19, 21, 88

O'NEIL, Daniel P.; pvt; 3rd MD Lt Arty; ref: 1, 2, 19, 21, 160, 726

O'NEILL, G. W.; pvt; 3rd MD Lt Arty; ref: 2, 19, 21, 160, 726

O'NIEL, Patrick; pvt; 1st MD Inf, Co B; ref: 1, 2, 19, 21

ONION, Richard T.; pvt; 2nd MD Inf, Co C; res: Bladensburg, PG Cty; ref: 1, 2, 19, 21, 1553

ONLEY, John; pvt; 9th VA Inf, Co B; res: Balt; ref: 1, 1576

OPEL, John; pvt; 1st MD Inf, Co B; ref: 1, 2, 19, 21

OPIE, Thomas (M.D.); Asst Surg; 25th VA Inf; res: Balt; ref: 1, 18, 19, 21, 23, 56, 70, 631, 700, 791, 1533, 1534, 1536

OPPER, Conrad; pvt; 2nd MD Inf, Co F; res: Som Cty; ref: 1, 2, 19, 21

ORDAMAN, Charles (M.D.); Asst Surg; 21st TN Inf; res: Park Mills, Frd Cty; ref: 1, 18, 19, 72, 90

ORDAMAN, John Harman; pvt; 35th VA Cav, Co B; res: Park Mills, Frd Cty; ref: 1, 19, 72, 90, 643, 1548, 1677

ORENDORFF, John; pvt; Carpenter's Co, Virginia, Lt Arty; res: Frederick, Frd Cty; ref: 1, 89

ORFRAY, James L.; pvt; Barry''s Co, MD Vols; ref: 1

ORIN, Walter; pvt; 2nd MD Cav, Co B; res: Balt; ref: 1, 19

ORISON, T.; cpl; 7th VA Cav, Co G; ref: 1, 11

ORME, Henry C.; pvt; 35th VA Cav, Co D; res: Barnesville, Mont Cty; ref: 1, 3, 15, 1611, 1677

ORME, Lindley, H.; pvt; 35th VA Cav, Co D; res: Barnesville, Mont Cty; ref: 1, 3, 1611, 1677

ORMES, Nathan; pvt; 1st MD Cav, Co F; ref: 1, 2, 19, 21

ORNDORFF, James; pvt; 7th VA Cav, Co G; ref: 1, 3

ORNDORFF, John; pvt; 2nd MD Cav, Co D; ref; 1, 19

ORR, Peter; pvt; 2nd MD Inf, Co C; res: Carr Cty; ref: 1, 2, 19, 21, 23, 470

ORRICK, John C.; pvt; 43rd VA Cav (Mosby's), Co C; ref: 1, 8, 70

ORRICK, Johnson; Capt; 12th VA Cav, Co I; ref: 1, 798

ORRISON, George; pvt; 35th VA Cav, Co C; res: Frd Cty; ref: 1, 19, 1611, 1677

ORRISON, John W.; pvt; 35th VA Cav, Co A; res: Frd Cty; ref: 1, 90, 1611, 1677

ORRISON, Townsend; pvt; 7th VA Cav, Co G; ref: 1, 3
OSBORN, Harry; pvt; 48th NC Inf, Co E; res: Cumberland, All Cty; ref: 1, 19, 65, 95, 148
OSBORN, Joseph C.; pvt; 7th VA Cav, Co G; ref: 1, 3
OSBORN, Robert L.; pvt; 30th VA Bn Sharpshooteres, Co E; ref: 1, 70
OSBORN, William F.; pvt; 13th VA Inf, Co G; res: Balt; ref: 1, 735
OSBOURN, James E.; pvt; 1st MD Inf, Co C; ref: 1, 2, 19, 21
O'SHIELDS, J. P.; pvt; 3rd MD Lt Arty; ref: 1, 2, 19, 21, 160, 726
O'SULLIVAN, John; pvt; MD Guerrilla Zouaves; ref: 1
OTEY, Kirkwood; Col; 11th VA Inf; ref: 1, 21, 700, 791, 1600
OTT, George Michael; pvt; 1st MD Cav, Co D; res: Frederick, Frd Cty; ref: 1, 19, 21, 66, 72, 90, 700
OTT, George W.; pvt; 1st MD Cav, Co D; ref: 1, 2, 21, 1601
OTT, Theophilus; pvt; 7th VA Cav, Co G; ref: 1
OUTLAW, T.; pvt; 1st SC Inf, Co G; ref: 1
OUTTEN, William T.; sgt; 2nd MD Inf, Co C; ref: 1, 2, 19, 21, 23
OVERSISKY, Joseph; pvt; Edelin's MD Heavy Arty; res: Balt; ref: 1, 1540
OWENGS, Welsh; pvt; 1st MD Lt Arty; ref: 2, 19, 21, 215
OWENS, Addison; pvt; Lee's MD Cav; res: Bristol, AA Cty; ref: 1, 1539
OWENS, Beale; pvt; MD Guerrilla Zouaves; res: Friendship, AA Cty; ref: 1, 1539
OWENS, Benjamin Welch; pvt; 1st MD Lt Arty; res: AA Cty; MLCSH; ref: 1, 19, 21, 34, 63, 64, 68, 92, 93, 511, 627, 700, 786
OWENS, Charles E.; sgt; Baker's Co, GA Lt Arty; res: West River, AA Cty; ref: 1, 3, 1539
OWENS, David; pvt; Stuart's Horse Arty, Breathed's Battery; ref: 1
OWENS, Dawson; pvt; Lee's Balt Lt Arty, Alexander's Bn; res: Balt; ref: 1, 1540
OWENS, George W.; smn, Navy; C.S.S. Torpedo; res: West River, AA Cty; ref: 55, 97, 511, 1539
OWENS, Henry C.; pvt; 1st SC Inf, Co G; res: West River, AA Cty; ref: 1,80, 1539
OWENS, Henry C.; pvt; 2nd MD Inf, Co A; res: AA Cty; ref: 1, 2, 19, 21, 70, 259, 511, 650, 715
OWENS, J. F.; pvt; 2nd MD Lt Arty; res: Friendship, AA Cty; ref: 1, 2, 19, 21, 511, 1539
OWENS, James III; pvt; Barry's Co, MD Vols; res: Bristol, AA Cty; ref: 1, 1539
OWENS, James F.; cpl; 2nd MD Lt Arty; res: Balt; ref: 1, 2, 19, 21, 64, 93, 511
OWENS, James S. of Joseph; pvt; Stuart's Horse Art, Breathed's Battery; res: West River, AA Cty; ref: 93, 511, 498, 1539
OWENS, James William; cpl; 1st MD Lt Arty; res: Bristol, AA Cty; MLCSH; ref: 1, 2, 19, 21, 23, 34, 68, 150, 458, 470, 511, 700, 782, 786, 791, 852, 873, 1104, 1273, 1539
OWENS, John; gun, Navy; Gosport Navy Yard; ref: 1, 19, 58, 61, 97, 279, 511, 1564
OWENS, John G.; pvt; 9th VA Cav, Co I; res: West River, AA Cty; ref: 1, 1539
OWENS, Joshua; cpl; 2nd MD Inf, Co D; res: Friendship, AA Cty; ref: 1, 2, 19, 21, 70, 160, 726, 1539, 1574
OWENS, Mich B.; pvt; 43rd VA Cav (Mosby's), Co H; ref: 8, 735, 1519
OWENS, Summers, of Joseph; pvt; Barry's Co, MD Vols; res: West River, AA Cty; ref: 1, 1539
OWENS, T. P.; pvt; 1st SC Inf, Co G; ref: 1
OWENS, Thomas; pvt; Stuart's Horse Arty, Breathed's Battery; ref: 498

OWENS, W. E. H.; pvt; 1st SC Inf, Co G; ref: 1

OWENS, Wallace; pvt; 4th NC Cav, Co G; res: Friendship, AA Cty; ref: 1, 1539

OWENS, Wyatt H.; pvt; 3rd TX Cav, Co E; res: Balt; ref: 1, 21, 511, 700

OWENSBY, G.; pvt; 3rd MD Lt Arty; ref: 1, 2, 19, 21, 160, 726

OWINGS, John Hammond; Lt; Ordnance Officer, Gen F. Lee's staff; res: Elliott City, How Cty; ref: 1, 2, 10, 19, 21, 71

OWINGS, L. I. Gillis; res: Clarksville, How Cty; ref: 10, 1550

OWINGS, Nicholas W.; Capt; Q.M.; 2nd MD Cav; res: Owings Mills, Bt Cty; ref; ref: 1, 2, 11, 19, 21, 23, 66, 233, 643, 693, 740, 791, 1541, 1560, 1562, 1565, 1609, 1631

OWINGS, Samuel A.; Lt; Davis's MD Cav, Co F; res: Bt Cty; ref: 1, 2, 19, 21

OWINGS, W. Bealle; pvt; 2nd MD inf, Co D; res: All Cty; MLCSH; ref: 1, 2, 19, 21, 70, 786

OWINGS, William Henry; pvt; Lucas's 15th SC Heavy Arty; res: Balt; MLCSH; ref: 1, 700, 786, 1540

PACA, Edward Tilghman; pvt; 1st MD Cav, Co E; res: QA Cty; ref: 1, 2, 19, 21, 661, 700, 730, , 1523, 1583, 1690

PACE, H. B.; sgt; 2nd MD Cav, Co A; ref: 1, 19, 1609

PACE, John Trimble; pvt; 7th TX Inf, Co C; res: Cha Cty; ref: 1, 185

PACK, John Anderson; Capt; 60th VA Inf, Co H; ref: 1, 72

PACKARD, Joseph, Jr; Lt; Ordnance Dept, Army of Northern Virginia; res: Balt; ref: 1, 21, 23, 44, 53, 56, 70, 700, 906, 1058, 1295

PACKER, T.; pvt; 4th MD Lt Arty; ref: 34

PAGE, C. R. (Revd); 4th VA Inf; ref: 1293

PAGE, Charles Craig; sgt; 2nd MD Ind, Co B; ref: 1, 2, 19, 21, 1609

PAGE, G. F.; pvt; 19th VA Inf, Co I; res: Balt; ref: 1, 1540

PAGE, Isham R. (M.D.); Surg; Asst Medical Purveyor, Richmond; res: Balt; ref: 1, 18, 21, 23, 1534, 1536

PAGE, John P.; Lt; 43rd VA Cav (Mosby's), Arty Co; res: Balt; ref: 8, 393, 710, 1613

PAGE, John Randolph (M.D.); Surgeon-in-Charge, General Hosptial No. 2, Lynchburg; res: Carr Cty; ref: 1, 18, 124, 700, 791, 1533, 1534, 1536, 1579

PAGE, Mortimer M.; pvt; 43rd VA Cav (Mosby's), Co A; ref: 1, 8

PAGE, Walker Y.; pvt; Meads Cav, Co K; res: Frederick, Frd Cty; ref: 1, 89

PAGE, Washington; pvt; 2nd MD Inf, Co B; ref: 1, 2, 19, 21

PAGE, William; pvt; 2nd MD Cav, Co B; res: Cha Cty; MLCSH; ref: 1, 2, 19, 21, 786, 1609

PAGE, William; pvt; 2nd MD Inf, Co B; res: Cha Cty; ref: 1, 21, 700

PAGOCED, Joseph Stuart; pvt; Jefferson Mounted Guards; res: Balt; ref: 21, 631, 700, 1613

PAINE, William; pvt; Castle Pinkney SC Heavy Arty; ref: 1, 2, 18, 21, 735

PALMER, Andrew J.; pvt; 55th VA Inf, Co C; res: Balt; ref: 1, 2, 19, 21, 57, 700

PALMER, Charles H.; pvt; 19th VA Heavy Arty Co C; res: Cambridge, Dor Cty; ref: 1, 1580

PALMER, Francis LeRoy; 1st TX Inf, Co L; ref: 70

PALMER, J. B.; pvt; 1st SC Inf, Co G; ref: 1

PALMER, John; pvt, Marine Corps; C.S.S. Tennessee; res: Cumberland, All Cty; ref: 1, 19, 65, 95, 148, 735, 1523, 1594

PALMER, John A.; Lt; 3rd VA Cav, Co C; res: Emmitsburg, Frd Cty; ref: 1, 72

PALMER, John Williamson (M.D.); Capt; Aid de Camp, Gen R. C. Tyler's staff; res: Balt; ref: 1, 18, 1230, 1533, 1686
PANCOST, Page; pvt; MD Guerrilla Zouaves; ref: 1
PANGBURN, James; pvt; Barry's Co, MD Vols; ref: 1
PANGLE, Watson; pvt; 2nd MD Cav, Co G; ref: 1, 19, 1609
PANNEL, T. A.; pvt; 3rd MD Lt Arty; ref: 1
PARAGOY, John; pvt; Barry's Co MD Vols; ref: 1
PARE, David P.; pvt; 2nd MD Inf, Co A; ref: 2, 19, 21, 650
PARIS, Samuel A.; pvt; 1st VA Inf, Co E; ref: 1, 735
PARISH, John W.; pvt; Jacobs Mounted Riflemen; res: Annapolis, AA Cty; ref: 1, 1539
PARKER, George S.; pvt; 1st MD Cav, Co B; res: Fishing Creek, Dor Cty; ref: 1, 2, 19, 21, 68, 700, 785, 1547
PARKER, J. B.; pvt; 3rd MD Lt Arty; ref: 1, 2, 19, 21, 160, 726
PARKER, John ; pvt; 2nd MD Inf, Co H; res: Church Creek, Dor Cty; ref: 1, 2, 19, 21, 23, 470, 1547
PARKER, John R.; Capt; 9th VA Inf, Co B; ref: 1, 19, 518, 791, 1523, 1596
PARKER, John Thomas (M.D.); Asst Surg; 19th VA Bn, res: Snow Hill, Wor Cty; ref: 1, 18, 1580
PARKER, Joseph; pvt; Stuart's Horse Arty, Breathed's Battery; ref: 498
PARKER, Peter Henry; pvt; 4th MD Lt Arty; ref: 1, 2, 19, 21
PARKER, Thaddeus M.; pvt; 4th MD Lt Arty; ref: 1, 2, 19, 1523
PARKER, William; pvt; 3rd MD Lt Arty; ref: 1, 2, 19, 21, 160, 726
PARKER, William Harwar; Capt, Navy; Commandant, Naval Academy; ref: 18, 955, 1138, 1385, 1464, 1564, 1581, 1632
PARKHILL, Charles; pvt; Richmond Howitzers, 3rd Co; res: Balt; ref: 1, 57, 700, 916
PARKINSON, James S.; pvt; 3rd MD Lt Arty; ref: 1, 2, 19, 21, 160, 726
PARKINSON, Richard A.; pvt; Holbrook's Independent MD Lt Arty; res: Annapolis, AA Cty; ref; 1, 1539
PARKINSON, Richard B.; pvt; Holbrook's Independent MD Lt Arty; res: Annapolis, AA Cty; ref: 1, 1539
PARKINSON, Thomas A.; pvt; Lee's MD Cav; res: Annapolis, AA Cty; ref: 1, 1539
PARKINSON, Thomas Richard; pvt; Davis's MD Cav; res: Annapolis, AA Cty; ref; 1, 1539
PARNILL, T. A.; pvt; 3rd MD Lt Arty; ref: 2, 19, 21, 160, 726
PARR, David Preston, Jr; pvt; 2nd MD Inf, Co A; res: Balt; MLCSH; ref: 1, 2, 14, 19, 21, 70, 650, 700, 786
PARR, William Joseph C.; pvt; Parker's VA Lt Arty Battery; res: Chevy Chase, Mont Cty; ref: 1, 1595
PARRATT, Joseph; pvt; 9th AR Inf, Co D; res: Balt; ref: 1, 1540
PARSETT, Benjamin; pvt; MD American Rifles; ref: 1
PARSONS, Frank M., Jr; Lt; Zarvona's MD Zouaves; ref: 1, 61, 64, 735
PARSONS, James Thomas; pvt; 2nd MD Cav, Co B; res: Chaptico, St. M. Cty; ref: 1, 2, 7, 19, 21, 69, 70, 316, 1509, 1555
PARSONS, John H.; res: St. M. Cty; ref: 1670
PARSONS, Joseph F.; pvt; 2nd MD Cav, Co F; ref: 1, 19
PATRICK, Charles R.; pvt; 1st MD Cav, Co A; res: Balt; MLCSH; ref: 1, 2, 19, 21, 786
PATRICK, James Thomas; pvt; 12th VA Cav, Co G; res: Balt; MLCSH; ref: 1, 2, 21, 93, 700, 735, 786, 1598
PATRICK, John; pvt; 1st MD Cav, Co A; ref: 1, 2, 19, 21
PATRICK, John H.; pvt; 17th VA Inf, Co H; ref: 1, 2, 19, 133, 142
PATTEN, James W.; pvt; 1st MD Cav, Co F; ref: 1, 2, 19, 21

PATTEN, William Thompson; Lt; 3rd MD Lt Arty; res: Port Deposit, Cec Cty; ref: 1, 2, 19, 21, 23, 64, 65, 160, 440, 461, 726, 791, 1106, 1523
PATTERSON, E.; pvt; 2nd MD Cav, Co C; ref: 1, 19, 1609
PATTERSON, Francis W. (M.D.); Surg; 25th GA Inf; res: Catonsville, Bt Cty; ref: 1, 18, 21, 700, 1536
PATTERSON, George; sgt; ref: 1690
PATTERSON, James; pvt; Barry's Co, MD Vols; ref: 1, 93
PATTERSON, Reynolds S.; pvt; 35th VA Cav, Co D; res: Gaithersburg, Mont Cty; ref: 1677
PATTERSON, Thomas Leiper; pvt; 8th Bn, NC Junior Reserves, Co A; res: Cumberland, All Cty; ref: 1, 980
PATTERSON, William W.; pvt; 1st MD Lt Arty; ref: 1, 2, 19, 21
PATTIE, H. W.; pvt; 43rd VA Cav (Mosby's), Co D; res: St. M. Cty; ref: 8, 1627
PATTON, James W.; 1st MD Cav, Co F; ref: 1, 19, 355
PATTON, William; cpl; 1st MD Inf, Co b; ref: 1, 2, 19, 21
PAUGLE, Watson; pvt; Davis's MD Cav, Co A; ref: 1
PAUL, William James; pvt; 7th VA Cav, Co G; res: Buck Town, Dor Cty; ref: 1, 2, 3, 19, 21, 1547
PAXSON, Charles; 43rd VA Cav (Mosby's); res: Balt; ref: 8
PAXSON, Thompson M. C.; pvt; 39th VA Cav, Co A; ref: 1, 481
PAYNE, Benjamin; sgt; Lee's MD Cav; res: Bt Cty; ref: 1, 2, 19, 21, 86
PAYNE, George W.; pvt; 43rd VA Cav (Mosby's); res: Balt; ref: 56
PAYNE, James R.; pvt; 9th VA Inf, Co B; ref: 1, 1576, 1662
PAYNE, Joseph T.; pvt; 38th VA Inf, Co C; ref: 1, 92, 93, 1098
PAYNE, Josiah Thomas (M.D.); Asst Surg; 4th VA Reserves; res: Black Horse, Har Cty; ref: 1
PEAK, Charles Davis; pvt; 2nd MD Lt Arty; res: AA Cty; ref: 1, 2, 19, 21, 1539
PEARCE, Alfred; cpl; 1st MD Inf, Co E; ref: 1, 2, 19, 21, 23, 1523
PEARCE, Isaac; Edelin's MD Heavy Arty; res: Elk Ridge Landing, AA Cty; ref: 1, 1539
PEARCE, John F.; Lt; Engineers; res: Georgetown; ref: 1, 2, 19, 21, 1492
PEARCE, Walter; pvt; 1st AL Inf, Co D; res: Georgetown; ref: 1, 1492
PEARMAN, W. C.; pvt; 15th GA Inf, Co H; res: Balt; MLCSH; res: 1, 21, 700, 786
PEARRE, Aubrey; Lt; Ordnance Officer, Gen P. R. Cleburne's staff; res: Unionville, Frd Cty; ref: 1, 57, 90, 511, 791
PEARRE, Charles Morgan; Lt Col; 8th TX Rangers; res: Unionville, Frd Cty; ref: 1, 984
PEARRE, James A. (Hon.); cpl; 1st MS Cav, Co F; res: Chestertown, Kt Cty; ref: 1, 1100
PEARRE, James W.; res: Frederick, Frd Cty; ref: 89
PEARRE, Oliver H.; cpl; 1st Co Independent Signal Corps; res: Unionville, Frd Cty; ref: 1, 90, 511
PEARSON, Charles; pvt; 21st VA Inf, Co B; res: Balt; ref; 1, 2, 19, 312, 735
PEARSON, James F.; sgt; 2nd MD Inf, Co A; res: Balt; ref: 1, 2, 19, 21, 23, 650, 681, 700, 1520, 1523
PEARSON, Walter H.; pvt; 1st MD Lt Arty; ref: 1, 2, 19, 21
PEASE, Charles C.; pvt; Hampton Leg Lt Arty, Co B; res: Balt; ref: 1, 2, 19, 21, 34, 63, 64, 68, 215, 700, 782, 791, 823, 1273, 1540, 1599
PEASE, George W.; sgt; 22nd VA Inf, Swann's Co; res: Balt; ref: 1, 1540
PEAY, Augustus; pvt; Davis's MD Cav, Co A; ref: 1
PEAY, B. C.; pvt; 2nd MD Cav, Co A; ref: 1, 19, 1609

PEAY, Benjamin; pvt; Davis's MD Cav, Co A; ref: 1, 735
PEAY, Rossen; pvt; Davis's MD Cav, Co A; ref; 1, 735
PEDDICORD, Bascom E.; pvt; 1st MD Cav, Co A; res: How Cty; ref: 1, 10, 19, 748
PEDDICORD, C. A. L.; pursers steward, Navy; Drewry's Bluff; res: How Cty; ref; 1, 19, 21, 700
PEDDICORD, George Thomas Randall; pvt; 9th VA Lt Arty, Co A; res: How Cty; ref: 1, 71, 86, 1125
PEDDICORD, S.; pvt; 1st MD Cav, Co A; ref; 2, 19, 21
PEDCRICK, John; Lee's Balt Lt Arty, Alexander's Bn; res: Balt; ref: 1, 1540
PEDRICK, Charles; pvt; Zarvona's MD Zouaves; res: Balt; ref: 1, 735, 1540
PEELER, Mallard T.; pvt; 1st MD Cav, Co E; ref: 1, 2, 19, 21, 730
PEERCE, John T.; pvt; 7th VA Cav, Co F; ref: 1, 21, 700
PEGRAM, William M.; pvt; 4th VA Cav, Co H; res: Balt; ref: 1, 56, 976, 1096, 1120, 1160, 1257, 1540
PELTYN, Samuel; sgt; 1st SC Inf, Co G; ref: 1
PEMEND, B. E.; pvt; Davis's MD Cav, Co B; res: Balt; ref: 1
PENBROKE, George W.; pvt; 2nd MD Lt Arty; res: Great Mills,St. M. Cty; ref: 1, 2, 19, 21, 1509, 1555
PENDALL, Philip; pvt; Barry's Co, MD Vols; ref: 1
PENDELTON, Charles A.; smn, Navy; Norfolk Navy Yard; res: Balt; ref: 1
PENDERGRASS, Charles; drummer; Wheat's Special Bn, LA Inf; res: Balt; MLCSH; ref: 1, 21, 627, 700, 786
PENDLETON, C. Mason; pvt; 43rd VA Cav (Mosby's), Co E; ref: 8
PENDLETON, David E.; pvt; 7th VA Cav, Co A; res: Balt; ref: 1, 2, 21, 70, 700
PENDLETON, Frank; pvt; 2nd MD Cav, Co A; ref: 2, 19, 21
PENDLETON, Laurence B.; sgt; 30th VA Inf, Co D; res: Washington Grove; ref: 1, 961, 966
PENDLETON, Samuel H.; Lt; Carter's Bn, VA Lt Arty; res: Balt; ref: 1, 907
PENDLEY, John C.; cpl; 3rd MD Lt Arty; ref: 1, 2, 19, 21, 23, 160, 461, 726, 1460
PENICK, Charles C.; q.m. sgt; 38th VA Inf, res: Balt; ref: 1, 56, 70
PENN, John F.; pvt; 2nd MD Inf, Co B; res: Cha Cty; ref: 1, 2, 19, 21
PENNIE, G. V.; pvt; Hospital Steward; ref: 1
PENNINGTON, Harry C.; pvt; 1st MD Lt Arty; res: Balt; ref: 1, 2, 19, 21, 44, 500
PENNINGTON, Joseph, Jr; pvt; 35th TN Inf, Co A; res: Cumberland, All Cty; ref: 1, 19, 65, 95, 148
PERARLL, George W.; Lt; 2nd MD Cav, Co B; ref: 1, 2, 19, 21, 23
PERCIVAL, C. Dabney; pvt; 11th VA Inf, Co G; res: Balt; ref: 1, 21, 700
PERDUE, John; pvt; 1st MD Cav, Co A; res: Monkton, Bt Cty; ref: 21, 700
PEREGOY, Charles E.; pvt; 2nd MD Lt Arty; ref: 1, 2, 19, 21
PEREGOY, H.; pvt; 2nd MD Cav, Co F; ref: 1, 2, 19, 21, 1609
PEREGOY, James A.; pvt; 2nd MD Inf, Co A; res: Balt; ref: 1, 2, 19, 21, 650, 1523, 1613
PEREGOY, John T.; pvt; 1st MD Inf, Co C; res: Balt; ref; 1, 2, 19, 21
PEREGOY, Lewis A.; sgt; Davis's MD Cav, Co A; ref: 1, 735
PERKINS, John W.; sgt; 41st VA Inf, Co E; ref: 21, 92, 93, 700
PERKINS, Levi Wroth; pvt; 1st MD Cav, Co B; res: Kt Cty; ref: 1, 2, 19, 21, 107, 785, 1584
PERKINS, Livius C.; pvt; 2nd NC Lt Arty, Kt Cty; ref; 1, 21, 668, 700
PERNEW, William; pvt; Davis's MD Cav, Co B; ref: 1, 19

PERRIE, Albert W.; pvt; Hampton Leg Lt Arty, Co B; res: Horse Head, PG Cty; ref: 1, 2, 19, 21, 1553
PERRIE, George W.; pvt; 1st MD Lt Arty; ref; 1, 2, 19, 21
PERRIE, I.; pvt; 1st MD Cav, Co B; ref: 2, 19, 21
PERRIE, Thomas H.; pvt; 1st MD Cav, Co B; res: PG Cty; ref: 1, 2, 19, 21, 700, 720, 785
PERRIN, John Taylor; Capt; 26th VA Inf, Co E; res: Balt; ref: 1, 21, 700 956
PERROW, Eber Rice; sgt; 15th VA Cav, Co B; ref: 1, 1529
PERRY, Gabriel; pvt; Barry's Co, MD Vols; res: St. M. Cty; ref: 1, 1509, 1555, 1627
PERRY, J. Taylor; pvt; 43rd VA Cav (Mosby's), Co C; ref: 8
PERRY, James; pvt; 4th MD Lt Arty; ref: 2, 19
PERRY, John, Jr; pvt; 15th VA Inf, Co E; res: Balt; ref: 21, 70, 700, 735
PERRY, John G.; pvt; 4th MD Lt Arty; ref: 1, 2, 19, 21
PERRY, Levi Lucas; pvt; 55th VA Inf, Co M; res: How Cty; ref: 1, 71
PERRY, Oliver Haggard; sgt; 1st MD Cav, Co B; res: PG Cty; MLCSH; ref: 1, 2, 19, 21, 23, 785, 786, 1383, 1474, 1484, 1522
PERRY, Samuel H.; pvt; 3rd MD Lt Arty; ref: 1, 2, 19, 21, 160, 726
PERRY, Thomas; res: Friendship, AA Cty; ref: 1539
PERRY, Van Lear; pvt; 2nd VA Inf, Co G; res: Cumberland, All Cty; ref: 1, 19, 65, 95, 148, 735
PERRY, W.; pvt; 3rd MD Lt Arty; ref: 1, 2, 19, 21, 160, 726
PERRY, William; sgt; 17th VA Inf, Co A; ref: 1, 133, 142, 251
PERRY, William F.; pvt; 3rd VA Inf, Co D; res: St. M. Cty; MLCSH; ref: 1, 2, 19, 21, 559, 650, 700, 711, 786, 1509, 1511, 1520, 1555
PERVIL, Leighton; pvt; 1st MD Cav, Co F; ref: 1, 2, 19, 21
PETER, Walter Gibson; Lt; Tobins Co, TN Lt Arty; res: Mont Cty; ref: 1, 1002, 1005, 1574
PETERKIN, George William (Revd); Aid de Camp, Lt Gen W. N. Pendleton's staff; res: Clear Spring, Wash Cty; ref: 1, 21, 23, 249, 700, 735, 791, 1192, 1374
PETERS, Andrew; pvt; 1st MD Inf, Co A; ref: 1, 2, 19, 21
PETERS, George; Col; Chief of Ambulance Corps, Army of Northern Virginia; res: Balt; ref: 18, 23, 70, 503, 511, 791, 990, 1540
PETERS, George Henry; pvt; 3rd VA Reserve Inf, Co G; ref: 1, 21, 511, 700, 735
PETERS, Gibson; pvt; Holbrook's Independent MD Lt Arty; ref: 1, 735
PETERS, John P. C.; pvt; Ambulance Corps; res: Darnestown, Mont Cty; ref: 1, 3, 15, 1552, 1574, 1611, 1677
PETERS, Joseph L.; pvt; 4th MD Lt Arty; ref: 1, 2, 19, 21, 511
PETERS, Thomas; pvt; 2nd MD Cav, Co D; res: Park Mills, Frd Cty; ref: 1, 19, 90, 261, 511, 1609
PETERS, Thomas; pvt; 2nd MD Inf, Co A; res: Balt; ref: 1, 2, 19, 21, 650
PETERS, William Thomas; pvt; 35th VA Cav, Co B; res: Frd Cty; ref: 1, 3, 1677
PETERS, Winfield; Lt; Ambulance Corps, Army of Northern Virginia; res: Balt; ref: 1, 2, 19, 21, 23, 53, 56, 57, 464, 489, 493, 503, 511, 512, 513, 650, 700, 873, 891, 916, 990, 994, 1001
PETERSON, Niles; pvt; 3rd MD Lt Arty; ref: 1, 2, 19, 21, 160, 726
PETIT, William; pvt; 19th VA Heavy Arty, Co C; ref: 1, 1580
PETROS, Thomas; ref: 700
PETTICORD, S.; pvt; 1st MD Cav, Co A; res: How Cty; ref: 1, 2, 19, 21
PETTINGALL, Daniel Carlton; cpl; 35th VA Cav, Co A; res: Lime

Kiln, Frd Cty; ref: 1, 3, 15, 90, 735, 1611, 1677
PETTIS, A.; pvt; 2nd MD Cav, Co F; ref: 1, 2, 19, 21
PETTIT, Henry; McEwen, Jr (M.D.); Asst Surg; Pettigrew Infirmary; res: Frederick, Frd Cty; ref: 1, 18, 72, 90
PETTITT, Allen O.; pvt; 2nd MD Cav, Co B; res: Balt; ref: 1, 21, 700
PEYTON, C. Henry; pvt; 7th VA Cav, Co G; ref: 1, 3
PFLASTERER, George; pvt; 1st SC Inf, Co G;r ef: 1
PFLOUNLACKY, Berry; res: Annapolis, AA Cty; ref: 1539
PHELPS, Caleb; pvt; Lee's MD Cav; res: AA Cty; ref: 1, 1539
PHELPS, Martin; pvt; 2nd MD Cav, Co A; ref: 1, 19
PHELPS, Richard; pvt; Edelins' MD Heavy Arty; res: Millersville, AA Cty; ref: 1, 1539
PHILIPS, George H.; pvt; 2nd MD Cav, Co E; ref: 1, 19
PHILIPS, James J.; pvt; 1st MD Inf, Co G; res: Balt; ref: 1, 2, 19, 21, 259
PHILIPS, John J.; pvt; 43rd VA Cav (Mosby's), Co C; res: Dor Cty; ref: 1, 2, 8, 19, 21, 112, 650
PHILIPS, Joshua A.; pvt; MD Guerrilla Zouaves; res: Patuxent Forge, AA Cty; ref: 1, 1539
PHILIPS, William; pvt; 2nd MD Cav, Co D; ref: 1, 19, 1609
PHILLIPS, Abraham A.; pvt; 2nd MD Inf, Co D; res: Balt; ref: 1, 2, 19, 21
PHILLIPS, B. J.; pvt; Davis's MD Cav, Co C; ref: 1
PHILLIPS, James Crome; bugler, 35th VA Cav, Co B; res: Hyattstown, Mont Cty; ref: 1, 2, 3, 15, 19, 21, 1548, 1574, 1611
PHILLIPS, George C.; pvt; 4th MD Lt Arty; ref: 1, 2, 19
PHILLIPS, J. P.; pvt; 1st SC Inf, Co G; ref: 1
PHILLIPS, John Crome; pvt; Stuart's Horse Arty, Brown's Battery; res: Hyattstown, Mont Cty; ref: 1, 86, 316, 498, 1574, 1677
PHILLIPS, John G.; Capt; Davis's MD Cav, Co C; res: Cambridge, Dor Cty; ref: 1, 518, 791, 1547
PHILLIPS, John M.; fmn, Navy; res: Annapolis, AA Cty; ref: 1, 1539
PHILLIPS, Samuel K.; 4th GA Inf, Co I; res: Vienna, Dor Cty; ref: 735, 1547
PHILLIPS, Samuel W.; pvt; 4th MD Lt Arty; res: Fishing Creek, Dor Cty; ref: 1, 2, 19, 21, 1547
PHILLIPS, William F., Sr; pvt; 1st VA Cav, Co E; ref: 1, 735
PHILPOT, Gowen Blanchard; Lt; 35th VA Cav, Co B; res: Merryland Tract, Frd Cty; ref: 1, 3, 11, 64, 90, 791, 1156, 1159, 1161, 1278, 1330, 1338
PHIPPS, James E.; pvt; Barry's Co MD Vols; res: Queen Ann, AA Cty; ref: 1, 1539
PHIPPS, Jefferson; pvt; MD American Rifles; St. Margarett, AA Cty; ref: 1, 1, 1539
PHIPPS, John; color bearer; 2nd MD Cav, Co F; res: AA Cty; ref: 1, 2, 11, 19, 21, 1609
PHIPPS, Nicholas; pvt; MD American Rifles; res: St. Margarett, AA Cty; ref: 1, 1539, 1628
PHIPPS, Richard; pvt; 2nd NC Lt Arty, Co A; res: West River, AA Cty; ref: 1, 1539
PHIPPS, William E.; bugler; 1st MD Lt Arty; res: Tracey Landing, AA Cty; ref: 1, 2, 19, 21, 1539
PHLEEGER, N. L.; pvt; Stuart's Horse Arty, Breatheds' Battery; ref: 1
PICKELL, John H.; pvt; Barry's Co, MD Vols; ref: 1
PICKELL, William; pvt; Barry's Co MD Vols; ref: 1, 2, 19, 21, 23, 470, 1523
PICKET, J.; pvt; 43rd VA Cav (Mosby's), Co E; ref: 1, 93
PICKET, Weston; ref: 689
PICKETT, Enoch F.; pvt; 35th VA Cav, Co A; ref: 1, 3

PICKETT, Joseph; pvt; Lee's Balt Lt Arty, Alexander's Bn, Annapolis, AA Cty; ref: 1, 1539
PICKLE, John; pvt; Davis's MD Cav, Co B; ref: 1, 2, 19, 21
PIELERT, George; amr., Navy; C.S.S. Torpedo; res: Catonsville, Bt Cty; MLCSH; ref: 1, 2, 19, 21, 55, 64, 700, 786, 1579, 1620
PIERCE, Alfred A.; pvt; 1st MD Cav, Co F; res: Balt; ref: 1, 2, 19, 21
PIERCE, John Abel; pvt; Lucas's 15th SC Heavy Arty; ref: 1
PIERCE, Richard; pvt; 1st MD Lt Arty; res: Balt; ref: 1
PIERCE, S. H.; Navy; res: Balt; ref: 1
PIERCE, William M.; pvt; Navy; Maury's Naval Bn, Co B; res: Balt; ref: 1, 21, 700, 783
PIERSON, L. D.; 38th GA Inf, Co G; ref: 1, 92
PIET, William E.; cpl; 21st VA Inf, Co F; ref: 1, 57, 117
PIGEON, Joseph; pvt; 1st MD Inf, Co G; ref: 1, 2, 19, 21
PIGGOT, Aaron Snowden (M.D.); Surgeon-in-Charge; Pharmaceutical Laboratory, Lincolnton, North Carolina; res: Balt; ref: 1, 18, 1533, 1534, 1536, 1583
PIKE, Henry; pvt; 4th MD Lt Arty; ref: 2, 19
PILKER, Michael; pvt; 1st MD Inf, Co G; res: Balt; ref: 1, 2, 19, 21, 93, 700
PILSON, Samuel F.; sgt; 23rd VA Cav, Co B; ref: 1, 687
PINDELL, Philip; pvt; 1st MD Inf, Co A; res: West River, AA Cty; ref: 1, 2, 19, 21, 259, 685, 1539
PINDELL, Robert Montgomery; pvt; Jacobs Mounted Riflemen; res: Bristol, AA Cty; ref: 1, 1539
PINDER, William; pvt; 4th MD Lt Arty; res: QA Cty; ref: 1, 2, 19, 21
PINKNEY, Campbell W.; pvt; 1st MD Inf, Co H; res: Balt; ref: 1, 2, 19, 21, 44, 650, 724, 1583
PINKNEY, Robert F.; Capt, Navy; C.S.S. Livingston; res: Balt; ref: 1, 19, 58, 61, 64, 97, 279, 282, 674, 735, 791, 1520, 1523, 1564
PINKNEY, Tominville, C.; Passed Midn, Navy; C.S.S. Nanesmond; ref: 1, 81, 1255, 1564
PINKNEY, William S.; pvt; 1st MD Inf, Co H; res: Balt; MLCSH; ref: 1, 2, 19, 21, 650, 700, 786, 1690
PIPPIN, Edward A.; sgt; 40th VA Cav, Co D; res: Balt; ref: 1, 21, 700
PIRKLE, William; cpl; 3rd MD Lt Arty; ref: 1, 2, 19, 21, 23, 160, 461, 726
PITTMAN, Alonzo Jenkins; 67th NC Inf, Co D; res: Balt; MLCSH; ref: 1, 21, 93, 627, 700, 786, 1575
PITTS, A. P.; pvt; 1st SC Inf, Co G; ref: 1, 81, 628
PITTS, Benjamin Franklin; cpl; 7th VA Inf, Co E; res: Eagles Nest, Caro Cty; MLCSH; ref: 1, 93, 511, 627, 700, 786
PITTS, Frederick L.; pvt; 1st VA Cav, Co K; res: Berlin, Wor Cty; ref: 1, 2, 19, 21, 46, 493, 503, 511, 650, 952, 1025, 1559
PITTS, Hosea; drum maj; 1st MD Inf; res: How Cty; ref: 1, 2, 19, 21, 23, 44, 511, 684, 686
PITTS, J. Emory; pvt; 43rd VA Cav (Mosby's), Co B; res: Pocomoke, Wor Cty; ref: 1, 2, 8, 19, 21, 511, 1559
PITTS, John William (M.D.); Asst Sur; General Hospital, Richmond; res: Berlin, Wor Cty; ref: 1, 2, 18, 19, 21, 1626
PITTS, William; pvt; Lucus's 15th SC Heavy Arty; ref: 1, 2, 19, 21
PLACIDE, Robert E.; pvt; 1st MD Cav, Co D; res: Balt; ref: 1, 2, 19, 21, 1601
PLANK, Augustus; pvt; 1st MD Inf, Co B; ref: 1, 2, 19, 21
PLANT, John J.; sgt; 1st MD Inf, Co G; res: Balt; ref: 1, 2, 19, 21, 23
PLANTZ, George W.; pvt; 15th VA Inf, Co K; res: Balt; ref: 1, 21, 700

PLATER, John E.; Lt; 4th MD Lt Arty; res: Nottingham, Bt Cty; ref: 1, 2, 19, 21, 23, 64, 69, 105, 316, 690, 791, 1523

PLATER, John Rousby; Capt; Asst I.G.,Gen A. Thomas's staff; res: Tal Cty; ref: 1, 19, 645

PLATTSMIEN, John T.; 21st LA Inf, Co E; ref: 1, 735, 791

PLAUTZ, George E.; 15th VA Inf, Co K; ref: 93

PLECKER, D.; pvt; 7th VA Cav, Co G; ref: 1

PLUMMER, John B.; pvt; 1st VA Cav, Co K; res: Elk Ridge Landing, AA Cty; ref: 1, 2, 19, 21, 1539

POACHAHUTAS, Oseola; pvt; Davis's MD Cav, Co C; ref: 1

POE, J. L.; pvt; 2nd MD Cav, Co C; ref: 1, 1609

POE, John A.; pvt; 20th VA Inf, Co E; res: Balt; ref: 1, 21, 272, 700

POE, Neilson, Jr; pvt; 3rd MS Inf, Co B; res: Balt; ref: 1, 2, 19, 21, 56, 700, 735, 757, 976

POEHLMANN, Christopher; pvt; 12th VA Cav, Co G; res: Bt Cty; ref: 1, 2, 19, 21, 55, 64

POINDEXTER, George W.; sgt; 2nd MD Lt Arty; ref: 1, 2, 19, 21, 23, 64

POINDEXTER, James Edward (Revd); Capt; 38th VA Inf, Co H; res: Port Tobacco, Cha; ref: 1, 21, 700

POINDEXTER, William M.; Steuart's Horse Arty, Breathed's Battery; ref: 677

POISEL, J. Henry; pvt; 4th MD Lt Arty; ref: 2, 19, 21

POLAND, John C.; pvt; 35th VA Cav, Co A; ref: 1, 1677

POLE, Henry S. (D.D.S.); res: Towson, Bt Cty; ref: 1590

POLK, James; sgt; 1st LA Inf, Co B; ref: 1, 70

POLK, John W.; Lt; 2nd MD Inf, Co F; res: Princess Anne, Som Cty; ref: 1, 2, 19, 21, 23, 64, 68

POLK, Josiah B.; cpl; 1st MD Inf, Co C; res: Balt; ref: 7, 70, 1540

POLK, Lucies Carey; Navy; res: Som Cty; ref: 70, 631, 689, 1540

POLK, Samuel; pvt; 1st MD Cav, Co A; res: Som Cty; ref; 1, 2, 19, 21, 734

POLK, Trusten; pvt; 12th VA Cav, Co K; res: Sykesville, Carr Cty; ref: 1, 2, 10, 19, 21, 23, 70, 71, 700, 937

POLK, William Stewart; Capt; Engineers Corps, Army of Northern Virginia; res: Balt; ref: 23, 56

POLLACK, James D.; pvt; 7th VA Cav, Co F; res: Cumberland, All Cty; ref: 1, 148

POLLARD, Charles R.; Lt; Adj, 30th VA Inf; res: Balt; MLCSH; ref: 1, 21, 57, 70, 700, 786, 926

POLLARD, James; pvt; 34th VA Inf, Co K; ref: 1, 57

POLLARD, Smith; pvt; 13th VA Inf, Co G; ref: 1, 735

POLLITT, Alexander; pvt; 1st MD Cav, Co E; res: Princess Anne, Som Cty; ref: 1, 2, 19, 21, 70, 730, 1666

POLLITTE, Nehemiah; pvt; 1st MD Lt Arty; res: Princess Anne, Som Cty; ref: 1, 2, 19, 21, 34, 70

POLLOCK, James Dickson; pvt; 7th VA Cav, Co F; res: Barton, Wash Cty; ref: 1, 65, 95, 1150, 1610

POLLOCK, William Winder; Lt, Navy; C.S. Roanoke; res: Balt; ref: 1, 19, 279, 1564

POMPHREY, G. W.; 1st MD Cav, Co E; ref: 352

PONTIER, Nathaniel; sgt; 43rd VA Cav (Mosby's), Art Co; res: Balt; ref: 1, 8

POOLE, ---; 12th MS; ref: 735

POOLE, Dennis H.; Maj; A.A.G., Gen W. J. Hardee's staff; res: Frederick, Frd Cty; ref: 1, 2, 19, 179, 735, 791

POOLE, Ephraim Howard; hospital std, Salisbury, North Carolina Hospital; res: Frd Cty; MLCSH; ref: 1, 18, 627, 700, 786

POOLE, Theodore W.; pvt; 1st MD Cav, Co C; res: Balt; ref: 1, 2, 19, 21

POOLE, William; Maj; Asst A.G., Gen W. Hardee's staff; res: Frd Cty; ref: 1, 2, 19, 735, 791
POOLE, William; pvt; 19th VA Heavy Arty, Co C; ref: 1, 800, 1580
POOLE, William C.; pvt; 1st MD Cav, Co C; ref: 1, 2, 19, 21
POOLE, William H.; pvt; 1st MD Cav, Co F; ref: 1, 2, 19, 21
POOR, Richard L.; Maj; Engineers Corps, Army of Northern Virginia; res: Balt; ref: 1, 21, 23, 56, 107, 700, 791
POPE, Jeremiah; pvt; 40th VA Inf, Co A; res: St. M. Cty; ref: 1670
POPE, Nathaniel; pvt; 41st VA Inf, Co M; res: Princeland, AA Cty; ref: 1, 1539
POPE, William Henry; cpl; 1st MD Inf, Co A; res: Frederick, Frd Cty; MLCSH; ref: 1, 2, 19, 21, 23, 39, 53, 70, 90, 469, 627, 684, 686, 700, 758, 830, 836, 838, 840, 848, 855, 866, 906, 932, 1520, 1601
POPE, William Thomas; pvt; Davis's MD Cav; res: Princeland, AA Cty; ref: 1, 1539
POPHAM, George; pvt; 2nd GA Inf, Co B; res: Annapolis, AA Cty; ref: 1, 1539
POPPLEIN, Nicholas; pvt; 4th NC Cav, Co E; res: Balt; ref: 1, 56
PORTER, Charles E.; gun, Navy; C.S.S. Neuse; ref: 1, 19, 58, 59, 61, 97, 279, 1564
PORTER, Gustavus; pvt; 4th MD Lt Arty; res: QA Cty; ref: 1, 2, 19, 21
PORTER, Hugh M.; pvt; 1st MD Inf, Co A; res: Balt; ref: 1, 2, 19, 21, 92, 93, 700
PORTER, John E.; pvt; Stuart's Horse Arty, Breathed's Battery; res: Drawbridge, Dor Cty; ref; 1, 498, 1547
PORTER, John J.; pvt; 43rd VA Cav (Mosby's), Co F; res: Rockville, Mont Cty; ref; 1, 2, 8, 19, 21, 1523
PORTER, John Mercer; pvt; 5th VA Cav, Co F; res: Balt; ref: 1, 70
PORTER, Mouina G.; pvt; Mast. M., Navy; C.S.S. Palmetto States; ref: 1, 316, 735, 1564
PORTER, Richard C.; pvt; 9th vA Inf, Co B; ref: 1, 1576
PORTER, Robert T.; pvt; Norfolk Lt Arty Blues; res: Balt; ref; 21, 700
PORTER, Wallace D.; pvt; Smith's Co, Richmond Howitzers; ref: 1, 21, 93
PORTER, William D.; Mast., Navy; C.S.S. Beaufort; ref: 19, 58, 97, 279, 700, 1564
PORTER, ---; Gen J. H. Winder's Detectives; ref: 30
PORTER, William J.; pvt; 2nd MD Inf, Co A; res: Tal Cty; ref: 1, 2, 19, 21, 645, 650, 1612
POSEY, John H.; pvt; res: Big Dick's Plantation, Cha Cty; ref: 700, 818
POST, Harry; ref: 233
POST, John Eager Howard; Lt; 1st MD Cav; Adj; res: Balt; ref: 1, 2, 19, 21, 68, 70, 233, 511, 601,650, 685, 686, 690, 711, 1520, 1565, 1577, 1579, 1634
POSTLEY, Charles T.; pvt; 1st Md Inf, Co C; ref; 1, 2, 19, 21
POTTER, Hugh; pvt; 13th VA Inf, Co G; ref: 1, 21, 700
POTTS, Arthur; Stuart's Cav; res: Frederick, Frd Cty; ref: 72, 89, 1548
POTTS, Hezekiah; pvt; 9th VA Cav, Co I; res: Frd Cty; ref: 1, 70
POTTS, Richard (M.D.); Surg; Medical Purveyor, Jackson Mississippi; res: Frederick, Frd Cty; ref: 1, 18
POULTON, Emory; res: Elk Ridge Landing, AA Cty; ref: 1539
POWELL, Alfred H. (M.D.); Surg; 16th VA Inf; res: Balt; ref: 1, 18, 21, 56, 70, 686, 700, 1533, 1534
POWELL, Edward B.; Capt; 6th VA Cav, Co F; res: Balt; ref: 1, 21, 700, 791
POWELL, George; pvt; 2nd MD Cav, Co C; ref: 2, 19, 21

POWELL, H. B.; pvt; 50th TN Inf, Co I; ref: 1, 2, 19, 21, 160, 726
POWELL, James J.; pvt; 3rd MD Lt Arty; ref: 1, 2, 19, 21, 160, 726
POWELL, Ransom; pvt; 1st MD Cav, Co A; ref; 1
POWELL, Robert; pvt; 17th GA Inf, Co A; res: Balt; MLCSH; ref: 93, 700, 786
POWELL, Robert Michael; Col; 5th TX Inf; ref: 1, 21, 119, 127, 700, 791, 1600
POWELL, W. B.; pvt; 3rd MD Lt Arty; ref: 2, 19, 21, 160, 726
POWERS, C. W.; pvt; Stuart's Horse Arty, Breathed's Battery; ref: 1
POWERS, John; sgt; 2nd MD Lt Arty; ref: 1, 2, 19, 21, 23
POWERS, John J.; pvt; 19th VA Heavy Arty, Co C; res: Balt; ref: 1, 70, 1580, 1599, 1613
POWERS, John J.; sgt; 2nd MD Inf, Co H; ref: 1, 2, 19, 21
POWERS, Nathaniel F.; pvt; 12th VA Inf, Co C; ref: 1, 93
POWERS, Michael F.; pvt, Marine Corps; C.S.S. Patrick Henry; res: Bt Cty; ref: 1, 1594
POWERS, Nicholas; Blacksmith; 3rd MD Lt Arty; ref: 1, 2, 19, 21, 23, 160, 726
POWERS, William; Zarvona's MD Zouaves; ref: 19, 58, 97
PRATT, James P.; pvt; 4th MD Lt Arty; res: QA Cty; ref: 1, 2, 19, 21, 470
PRATT, Thomas St. George; Lt, Marine Corps; C.S.S. Savannah; res: Annapolis, AA Cty; ref: 1, 2, 21, 650, 792, 1349, 1523, 1539, 1564, 1583, 1593, 1594, 1628
PRATT, William; pvt; 1st SC Inf, Co G; ref: 1
PREECE, Edward V.; vpt; 12th VA Inf, Co K; res: Kt Cty; ref: MLCSH; ref: 1, 21, 93, 700, 786
PRENTIS, William S.; pvt; 2nd MD Inf, Co A; res: Balt; ref: 1, 2, 19, 21, 259, 650
PRESSGRAVES, Philip W.; pvt; 35th VA Cav, Co A; ref; 1, 3, 15, 1611, 1677
PRESSON, James H.; sgt; 9th VA Inf, Co B; ref: 1, 1576
PRESSTMAN, F. F.; ref: 53
PRESSTMAN, George R.; pvt; 21st VA Inf, Co B; res: Bt Cty; ref: 1, 2, 19, 70, 312, 690, 1541
PRESTON, John J.; pvt; 3rd MD Lt Arty; ref: 1, 2, 21, 160, 726
PRETZMAN, David C.; pvt; 1st MD Cav, Co A; res: Wash Cty; ref: 1, 2, 19, 21
PRICE, Adrian D.; cpl; 21st VA Inf, Co B; res: Hagerstown, Wash Cty; ref: 1, 2, 19, 312, 735
PRICE, Alfred C.; Capt; 4th AL Inf, Co C; res: Tal Cty; ref: 1, 2, 19, 645, 735, 791
PRICE, C. D.; pvt; 43rd VA Cav (Mosby's), Co G; ref: 8
PRICE, Charles; pvt; 3rd MD Lt Arty; ref: 1, 2, 19, 21, 160, 726
PRICE, Charles Richard; pvt; 17th VA Inf, Co H; res: Balt; MLCSH; ref: 1, 92, 93, 133, 627, 700, 786
PRICE, David; pvt; 3rd MD Lt Arty; ref: 1, 2, 19, 21, 160, 726
PRICE, David; pvt; 19th VA Heavy Arty, Co C; ref: 1, 735, 1580
PRICE, Elias; pvt; 35th VA Cav, Co B; res: Old Medley's, Mont Cty; ref: 1, 3, 15, 73, 106, 1552, 1611, 1677
PRICE, Ferdinand B.; pvt; 3rd VA Cav, Co G; res: Kt Cty; ref: 1, 1584
PRICE, Frank S.; Capt; 1st MD Inf, Co C; res: Balt; ref: 1, 2, 19, 21, 23, 64, 68, 456, 781, 1523
PRICE, James Edward; pvt; 1st MD Cav, Co D; res: Bt Cty; ref: MLCSH; ref: 1, 2, 19, 21, 92, 93, 627, 786, 1601
PRICE, James H.; pvt; 1st MD Cav, Co B; res: Easton, Tal Cty; ref: 1, 2, 19, 21, 645, 700, 785, 1557, 1612
PRICE, James S.; pvt; 47th TN Inf, Co K; res: Kt Cty; ref: 1, 668, 1584
PRICE, John; pvt; 35th VA Cav, Co D; ref: 1, 1677

PRICE, John "Buck"; pvt; 2nd MD Cav, Co C; res: Balt Cty; ref: 1, 11, 1609
PRICE, Kennedy; pvt; 1st MD Cav, Co A; res: Wash Cty; ref: 1, 2, 19, 21, 827, 1558
PRICE, Luther F.; pvt; 1st MS Cav, Co I; res: Balt; ref: 1, 655
PRICE, Marcellus A.; pvt; 1st MD Cav, Co A; ref: 1, 2, 19, 21, 70, 628
PRICE, Orlando K.; pvt; 3rd VA Inf, Co E; res: Balt; ref: 21, 56, 57, 700
PRICE, Samuel; res: Smithsburg, Wash Cty; ref: 1636
PRICE, Thomas A.; Capt; 6th NC Inf, Co A; res: Balt; ref: 1, 731, 735
PRICE, William C.; cpl; 1st MD Cav, Co E; res: Kennedyville, Kt Cty; ref: 1, 2, 19, 21, 23, 94, 668, 730, 1523, 1584
PRICHARD, William; pvt; 2nd MD Inf, Co H; res: Cha Cty; ref: 1
PRINCE, Lawrence L.; pvt; Inglis Lt Battery; ref: 21, 700
PRINTZ, J. A.; pvt; 33rd VA Inf, Co M; res: Halethorpe, Bt Cty; ref: 1, 70
PROBEST, George E.; sgt; 2nd MD Inf, Co C; res: Balt; ref: 1, 2, 19, 21, 23, 700
PROUT, John William; sgt; 2nd MD Inf, Co D; res: Friendship, AA Cty; ref: 1, 2, 8, 19, 21, 23, 700, 1539, 1542
PRUITT, John; pvt; 1st MD Cav, Co E; ref: 1, 2, 19, 21, 730
PUE, Arthur; pvt; 1st MD Cav, Co C; res: Har Cty; MLCSH; ref: 1, 2, 19, 21, 627, 786
PUE, Edward H. D.; Lt; 1st VA Cav, Co K; res: Bel Air, Har Cty; ref: 1, 2, 19, 21, 23, 981
PUE, Ferdinand C.; pvt; 1st MD Cav, Co A; res: How Cty; ref: 1, 2, 10, 19, 21
PUE, H. D.; Capt; res: How Cty; ref: 122, 791
PUE, James A. Ventris; Lt; 1st MD Cav, Co A; res: How Cty; ref: 1, 2, 10, 19, 21, 23, 64, 68, 240, 445, 748, 881, 901, 1096, 1251, 1519, 1523, 1634
PUE, R. P.; pvt; 3rd MD Lt Arty; ref: 1, 2, 21, 160, 726
PUE, William H. (M.D.); Asst Surg; 50th GA Inf, ref: 1, 2, 18, 21, 1690
PUGH, Edward; pvt; 1st VA Cav, Co K; ref: 1, 2, 19, 21, 64
PUGH, Ferman G.; 18th VA Cav; res: Frostburg, All Cty; ref: 148
PUGH, P. W.; Lt; 62nd VA Inf, Co B; ref: 1, 145, 1574
PUGH, Thomas Cloman (M.D.); Asst Surg; 21st NC Inf; res: Balt; ref: 1, 18, 53, 1596
PULLEN, Henry; pvt; 1st Bn MS Inf, Co B; ref: 1, 2, 19, 21
PULLEN, John F.; sgt; 15th VA Cav, Co G; res: Balt; ref: 1, 21, 700
PUMPHREY, George W.; pvt; 1st MD Cav, Co E; res: PG Cty; ref: 1, 2, 19, 21, 730
PUMPHREY, Greenbury; pvt; MD Guerrilla Zouaves; Princeland, AA Cty; ref: 1, 1539
PUMPHREY, John T.; pvt; 1st MD Cav, Co E; res: Princeland, AA Cty; ref: 1, 2, 19, 21, 730, 1539
PUMPHREY, Lemuel; sgt; 6th VA Inf, Co C; res: Balt; ref: 1, 21, 700
PUMPHREY, Thomas W. of Charles; pvt; 5th VA Cav, Co B; res: Millersville, AA Cty; ref: 1, 1539
PUMPHREY, Walter James; pvt; Holbrook's Independent MD Lt Arty; res: Millersville, AA Cty; ref: 1, 1539
PUMPHREY, William; res: Millersville, AA Cty; ref: 1539
PURCELL, Franklin; pvt; 8th VA Inf, Co A; res: Frd Cty; ref: 1, 3, 67, 1677
PURCELL, Thomas H.; pvt; 56th VA Inf, Co G; ref: 1, 316
PURCELL, William H.; pvt; 37th VA Inf, Co E; res: St. M. Cty; ref: 1670
PURCELL, William T.; cpl; 17th VA Inf, Co A; res: 1, 57, 113, 142, 251, 700, 1025

PURDIE, John; pvt; 1st MD Cav, Co A; res: South River, AA Cty; ref: 1, 19, 1539

PURDIE, William E.; pvt; 3rd MD Lt Arty; res: South River, AA Cty; ref: 1, 2, 19, 21, 160, 726, 1539

PURNELL, George Washington; Lt; 2nd MD Cav, Co B; res: Snow Hill, Wor Cty; ref: 1, 2, 19, 21, 23, 631, 700, 733, 791, 1559, 1609, 1626

PURNELL, John J.; pvt; 2nd MD Inf, Co G; res: Berlin, Wor Cty; ref: 1, 2, 19, 21

PURNELL, William S.; pvt; 1st VA Cav, Co K; res: Wor Cty; ref: 1, 2, 19, 21, 650, 1523, 1626

PURT, Ely; pvt; Barry's Co, MD Vols; ref: 1, 93

PUSEY, Azariah C.; pvt; 1st MD Cav, Co E; res: Som Cty; ref: 1, 2, 19, 21, 730, 1666

PYE, Edward; chief musician; 22nd LA Inf, Cha Cty; ref: 1, 69, 316

PYE, James B.; pvt; 13th TX Cav, Co A; res: Cha Cty; ref: 1, 69, 316

PYE, William H.; pvt; 1st MD Cav, Co C; res: Port Tobacco, Cha Cty; ref: 1, 2, 19, 21, 69, 316

PYFER, Henry; pvt; 2nd MD Inf, Co A; res: Cal Cty; MLCSH; ref: 1, 2, 19, 21, 93, 627, 650, 700, 786

PYLER, W. C. W.; pvt; 1st SC Inf, Co G; ref: 1

PYLER, W. O.; pvt; 1st SC Inf, Co G; ref: 1

PYLES, Benjamin Franklin; pvt; 35th VA Cav, Co B; res: Old Medley's, Mont Cty; ref: 1, 3, 73, 86, 106, 1552, 1611, 1677

PYLES, James H.; pvt; 19th VA Heavy Arty, Co C; ref: 1, 70, 1580

PYLES, M. Thomas; pvt; 35th VA Cav, Co B; res: Old Medley's, Mont Cty; ref: 1, 3, 73, 106, 718, 1552, 1611, 1677

PYNE, A. C.; pvt; 2nd MD Cav, Co D; ref: 1, 19, 1609

PYNE, James F.; sgt; 1st VA Inf, Co B; res: Balt; ref: 1, 21, 700

QUAILES, J. C.; pvt; 2nd MD Lt Arty; ref: 1

QUEEN, T.; pvt; 1st SC Inf, Co G; ref: 1, 74

QUENSENBERRY, James G.; pvt; 22nd VA; res: Aberdeen, Har Cty; MLCSH; ref: 92, 93, 700, 786

QUICK, Noah; pvt; 1st SC Inf, Co G; ref: 1

QUIGLEY, G. M.; pvt; Davis's MD Cav, Co C; ref: 1

QUIGLEY, J. R.; pvt; Davis's MD Cav, Co C; ref: 1

QUIGLEY, R. S.; pvt; Davis's MD Cav, Co C; ref: 1

QUINLAN, Edward; pt; 3rd MD Lt Arty; ref: 1, 2, 19, 21, 160, 726

QUINN, John Henry; pvt; 1st MD Cav, Co E; res: Balt; MLCSH; ref: 1, 2, 19, 21, 93, 94, 700, 730, 786, 826

QUINN, John Skinner; pvt; 2nd MD Cav, Co C; res: Balt; ref: 1, 2, 19, 21, 72, 1562, 1609

QUINN, Joseph P.; sgt; Zarvona's MD Zouaves; res: Balt; ref: 1, 2, 19, 21, 23, 64, 68, 735

QUINN, Louis; pvt; Zarvona's MD Zouaves; ref: 1, 61, 703, 735

QUINN, Michael Aloysious; chief musician; 2nd MD Inf; res: Tal Cty; MLCSH; ref: 1, 2, 19, 21, 23, 64, 470, 627, 700, 786, 1523

QUINN, Patrick; pvt; Barry's Co, MD Vols; ref: 1

QUINN, Richard M.; chief engr, Navy; C.S.S. Virginia; ref: 21, 700, 1564

QUINN, Thomas; pvt; Lucas's 15th SC Heavy Arty; res: Balt; ref: 1

QUINN, William; ordnance sgt; 2nd MD Lt Arty; ref: 1, 2, 19, 21, 64, 684

RABERG (Raborg?), Samuel A. (M.D.); Asst Surg; Culpepper General Hospital; res: Emmitsburg, Fred Cty; ref: 1, 18, 69, 70, 316, 1520, 1690

RABORG, Christopher; pvt; 1st Md Cav, Co D; ref: 1, 2, 19, 21, 1601

RABORG, George G.; sgt; 1st MD Inf, Co E; res: Balt; ref: 1, 2, 19, 21, 23
RABORG, William R.; pvt; 1st MD Cav, Co D; ref: 1, 2, 19, 21, 1601
RADAY, Patrick; pvt; 12th VA Cav, Co F; ref: 1, 2, 19, 21
RADCLIFFE, Edward B.; pvt; 1st MD Cav, Co D; ref: 1, 2, 19, 21, 1601
RADDINGTON, G.; pvt; 1st SC Inf, Co G; res: Balt; ref: 735
RADECKE, Herman Henry; pvt; 4th SC Inf, Co E; res: Balt; ref: 1, 2, 19, 21, 23, 700, 768
RADY, Henry; cpl; 2nd MD Cav, Co E; ref: 1
RAGLAND, E. F.; pvt; 3rd MD Lt Arty; ref: 1
RAILING, George H.; pvt; 2nd MD Cav, Co C; res: Frd Cty; ref: 1, 19, 90, 1609
RAINS, K. P.; pvt; Davis's MD Cav, Co C; ref: 1
RAITT, Charles H.; pvt; 1st MD Cav, Co D; ref: 1, 19, 1601
RALEIGH, William H. H.; Lt; Engineer Corps, Carter's Bn; res: Dor Cty; ref: 1, 23, 56, 57, 70, 513, 685, 1341
RALEY, James S.; pvt; 2nd MD Inf, Co A; res: Chaptico, St. M. Cty; ref: 1, 2, 19, 21, 650, 1555, 1627
RALEY, Michael N.; pvt; 4th MD Lt Arty; res: St. M. Cty; ref: 1, 2, 19, 21
RALPH, George W.; pvt; 1st MD Cav, Co E; ref: 1, 700
RAMAN, J.; pvt; 1st SC Inf, Co G; ref: 1
RAMSBURG, Edward J.; pvt; 1st VA Inf, Co E; ref: 1, 735
RAMSAY, Henry Ashton; Chief Engr; Gosport Navy Yard; res: Balt; ref: 1, 19, 21, 56, 97, 127, 280, 429, 700, 735, 783, 791, 860, 862, 873, 1127, 1564, 1581
RAMSEY, Alfred; pvt; 13th VA Inf, Co G; ref: 1, 735
RAMSEY, William S.; Lt; 6th NC Inf, Co C; res: Balt; ref: 1, 21, 700
RAMSON, Ambrose R. H.; Maj; Ordnance Dept, Army of Northern Virginia; res: Balt; ref: 21, 700, 774, 1583
RANDALL, Walter J.; sgt; 2nd MD Inf, Co F; res: Cha Cty; ref; 1, 2, 19, 21, 23
RANDALL, J.; pvt; 4th MD Lt Arty; ref: 1, 2, 19, 21
RANDOLL, A.; 1st MD Inf, Co D; ref: 93
RANDOLPH, James Innis; Lt; Topographical Engr, Gen R. Ewell's staff; res: Cha Cty; ref: 11, 70, 559, 685, 791, 884, 1579
RANDOLPH, John; cpl; 1st VA Inf, Co E; ref: 1, 735, 1622
RANDOPH, Alfred Magill (Revd); Chaplain; Jackson's Corps; res: Balt; ref: 70, 631
RANDOPH, Tacker; ref: 681
RANIN, R. H.; pvt; 700
RANSLER, Andrew; pvt; 1st MD Inf, Co I; ref: 1, 2, 19, 21
RANSOM, B. B.; pvt; 43rd VA Cav (Mosby's), Co H; ref: 8
RANSON, John Frank; cpl; Hampton Leg Lt Arty, Co B; ref: 1, 2, 19, 21, 23, 782
RAPHEAL, Abraham; pvt; 9th VA Inf, Co B; ref: 1, 1576
RAPHEL, Eugene Fressenjat; pvt; 1st MD Cav, Co C; res: Bt Cty; ref: 1, 2, 19, 21, 720
RASIN, Macall Medford II; Lt; Moody's VA Lt Arty; res: Still Pond, Kt Cty; ref: 1, 2, 19, 21, 70, 511, 700, 1584
RASIN, William Independence; Capt; 1st MD Cav, Co E; res: Still Pond, Kt Cty; ref: 1, 2, 11, 19, 21, 23, 35, 56, 64, 68, 70, 94, 240, 316, 511, 559, 601, 638, 668, 684, 685, 700, 791, 823, 825, 1520, 1523, 1577, 1579, 1584, 1620, 1634
RATCLIFF, Edward B.; pvt; Davis's MD Cav, Co B; ref: 1, 2, 19, 21, 730
RATCLIFFE, George E.; Lt; 2nd MD Cav, Co E; res: Balt; ref; 1, 2, 19, 21, 23, 312, 1540

RATCLIFFE, John R.; pvt; 17th VA Inf, Co D; ref; 1, 142, 251
RATE, Charles; pvt; 7th VA Cav, Co G; res: Cha Cty; ref: 3
RATEGAN, John; pvt; MD Guerrilla Zouaves; ref: 1
RAY, Alexander B.; pvt; 1st MD Inf, Co D; res: Tal Cty; ref: 1, 2, 19, 21
RAY, Marion; pvt; 3rd MD Lt Arty; ref: 1, 2, 19, 21, 160, 726
RAY, William A.; pvt; Edelin's MD Heavy Arty; res: Princeland, AA Cty; ref: 1, 1539
RAYFIELD, W. C.; cpl; 1st MD Inf, Co F; ref: 1, 19
RAYFORD, Albert N.; pvt; 9th VA Inf, Co B; ref: 1, 70, 1576
RAYFORD, Edwin; pvt; 9th VA Inf, Co B; ref: 1, 70, 1576
RAYFORD, Everette; pvt; 9th VA Inf, Co B; ref: 1, 70, 1576
RAYMOND, C. C.; pvt; 2nd MD Lt Arty; res: Carr Cty; ref: 1, 2, 19, 21, 40, 806, 1523
RAYSOR, John Michael; sgt; 5th FL Inf, Co F; res: Frd Cty; ref: 1, 72
REA, George A.; pvt; 1st VA Inf, Co H; res: Balt; ref: 1, 21, 700
READ, N. M. (M.D.); Asst Surg, Navy; C.S.S. Pontachartrain; ref: 1, 18, 58, 97, 279, 791, 1534, 1564
READ, William H.; pvt; 32nd VA Inf, Co K; res: Balt; ref: 1, 68, 1560
REAGS, P. A.; pvt; 2nd MD Cav, Co A; ref: 1, 19, 1609
REAMER, John; pvt; 1st MD Cav, Co A; ref: 1, 19
REAMY, William A.; pvt; 6th VA Inf, Co K; res: Balt; ref; 1, 21, 700
REARDON, Henry; Capt; Nitre & Mining Bureau; ref: 1, 685, 735
REARDON, Louis M.; pvt; 43rd VA Cav (Mosby's), Co E; res: Balt; ref: 1, 8, 19, 21, 700, 1613
REARDON, Michael; pvt; 2nd MD Cav, Co D; ref: 1
REDDIE, James; cpl; 2nd MD Inf, Co E; res: Tal Cty; ref: 1, 2, 19, 21, 645
REDGELY, Charles H.; res: How Cty; ref: 10, 748
REDMETER, John W.; res: Patuxent, AA Cty; ref; 1539
REDMOND, George S.; pvt; 1st MD Inf, Co H; res: Tal Cty; ref: 1, 2, 19, 21, 35, 44, 259, 645, 1520, 1563
REDWOOD, Allen Christian; pvt; 1st MD Cav, Co C; ref: 1, 2, 19, 21, 70, 431, 684, 700, 1298, 1308, 1579, 1644
REDWOOD, Henry; pvt; 3rd VA Local Defense, Co B; res: Balt; ref: 1, 1328
REDWOOD, J. W.; pvt; 1st MD Cav, Co C; ref: 1, 2, 19, 21, 827
REECH, C. V. A.; pvt; 21st VA Inf, Co B; ref: 1
REED, J. W.; sgt; 1st MD Lt Arty; ref: 34
REED, James; pvt; 1st MD Cav, Co E; ref: 1, 19
REED, James F.; pvt; 35th VA Cav, Co B; res: Boyds, Mont Cty; ref: 1611
REED, James W.; smn, Navy; Drewry's Bluff; res: Old Medley's Mont Cty; ref: 1, 106, 1574
REED, Manuel; pvt; 1st MD Cav, Co B; ref: 1, 2, 19, 21
REED, Samuel E.; pvt; 1st MD Inf, Co G; res: Pikesville, Bt Cty; ref: 1, 2, 19, 21, 86
REED, William; pvt; 2nd MD Cav, Co F; ref: 1, 7, 11, 19, 272, 1258
REED, William; 1st Lt; Davis's MD Cav, Co D; res: Balt; ref; 1, 2, 19, 21, 1523, 1540
REED, William B.; smn, Navy; Norfolk Navy Yard; res: Balt; ref: 1, 1540
REED, William T.; pvt; 2nd MD Inf, Co G; ref: 1, 2, 19, 21
REEDER, Philip T.; sgt; 2nd MD Inf, Co B; res: Oakville, St. M. Cty; ref: 1, 2, 19, 21, 23, 470, 1509, 1523, 1555
REESE, Gideon Davis; pvt; 2nd MD Cav; ref: 70

REESE, John R. A.; sgt; 9th VA Inf, Co B; res: Carr Cty; ref: 1, 735, 1573, 1576
REEVES, Francis S.; pvt; 1st MD Inf, Co H; ref: 1
REGESTER, William Gray (M.D.); Roanoke College Lt Arty; res: Mont Cty; ref: 18, 19, 21, 70, 700, 1533, 1536
REH, William F.; pvt; Stuart's Horse Arty, Breathed's Battery; res: Church Creek, Dor Cty; ref: 1, 1547
REHWINKLE, Henry R.; pvt; 4th LA Inf, Co E; res: AA Cty; MLCSH; ref: 1, 93, 786
REICH, Isaac S.; pvt; 33rd NC Inf, Co H; ref: 1, 72
REID, Charles; pvt; 9th VA Inf, Co K; ref: 1, 70
REID, H. T.; pvt; 1st SC Inf, Co G; ref: 1
REID, James Henry; pvt; 18th LA Inf, Co C; res: Frd Cty; ref: 1, 90
REID, John; pvt; 19th VA Heavy Arty, Co C; ref: 1, 70, 1580
REID, John R.; pvt; 1st MD Cav, Co C; ref: 1, 19
REID, Joseph Thomas; pvt; 18th LA Inf, Co C; res: Frederick, Frd Cty; ref: 1, 19, 90
REIDER, John; pvt; 1st MO Inf, Co H; res: Elk Ridge Landing, AA Cty; ref: 1, 1539
REILLY, John; pvt; 2nd MD Cav, Co A; res: Balt; ref: 1, 19
REILEY, Frank J.; Lt; 13th VA Inf, Co G; ref: 1, 2, 21, 735, 1523
REILEY, John; pvt; 2nd MD Lt Arty; res: Balt; ref: 1, 2, 19, 21
REILEY, Patrick; sgt; 2nd MD Cav, Co C; ref: 1, 19, 1609
REILEY, Richard; cpl; MD Guerrilla Zouaves; ref: 1
REILLEY, John H. F.; pvt; 1st MD Cav, Co B; res: Balt; ref: 21, 700
REILLY, John T.; pvt; 1st MD Cav, Co C; res: Balt; ref: 21, 700
REILLY, Joseph C.; pvt; 1st VA Inf, Co E; ref: 1, 735
REILLY, Philip K.; pvt; 1st VA Cav, Co E; ref: 1, 735
REIMAN, W. H.; pvt; 2nd MD Lt Arty; ref: 1, 2, 19, 21
REINER, Henry; res: Balt; ref: 51
REINHARDT, J. M.; pvt; 1st SC Inf, Co G; ref: 1
REINICKER, ---; Capt; res: Balt; ref: 240
REISTER, Peter P.; pvt; 39th VA Inf, Co F; res: Balt; ref: 1, 21, 700
RELCHBERGER, A.; res: South Carolina; ref: 693
RELESTON, Charles; Castle Pinkney SC Heavy Arty; ref: 735
REME, Leon; pvt; 1st MD Cav, Co F; ref: 1, 2, 19, 21
RENCH, Charles; pvt; 7th VA Cav, Co G; res: Wash Cty; ref: 3
RENCH, John V.; pvt; 1st VA Cav, Co K; ref: 1, 2, 19, 21
RENCH, William; pvt; MD American Rifles; ref: 1
RENSHAW, William T.; pvt; 4th MD Lt Arty; ref: 1, 2, 19, 21
REYNOLDS, A. S.; pvt; Wise Leg VA Lt Arty; ref: 1
REYNOLDS, Charles W.; pvt; 2nd MD Cav, Co D; ref: 1, 1523
REYNOLDS, Daniel; pvt; 3rd MD Lt Arty; ref: 1, 2, 19, 21, 160, 726
REYNOLDS, John; pvt; 2nd MD Lt Arty; ref: 2, 19, 21, 700
REYNOLDS, John W.; mast. a., Navy; C.S. Albemarle; res: Balt; ref: 1
REYNOLDS, Patrick; pvt; 1st MD Inf, Co B; ref: 1, 2, 21, 1523
REYNOLDS, Richard Tyler; pvt; 40th VA Inf, Co C; res: Balt; MLCSH; ref: 1, 93, 627, 700, 786
REYNOLDS, W.; pvt; 3rd MD Lt Arty; ref: 1, 2, 19, 21, 160, 726
REYNOLDS, William L.; pvt; 2nd MD Cav, Co D; res: Balt; ref: 1, 19, 1540, 1609
REYNOLDS, William; pvt; ref: 1690
RHEA, George A.; 1st VA Inf; ref: 735
RHEAMS, Joseph Vinsen; cpl; Davis's MD Cav, Co A; ref: 1, 735

RHEIM, Henry; pvt; MD American Rifles; res: Annapolis, AA Cty; ref: 1, 1539
RHEIM, James J.; pvt; 17th VA Inf, Co C; ref: 1, 2, 19, 21, 735
RHEIM, William G.; pvt; 17th VA Inf, Co C; ref: 1, 2, 19, 21, 735
RHETT, Albert; cpl; Stuart's Horse Arty, Breathed's Battery; ref: 1, 70, 93, 789
RHETT, Charles H.; Lt; Asst Q.M., Gen W. W. Machell's staff; res: Balt; ref: 1, 92
RHETT, Roland; pvt; Rutledge's Co, Independent Cav; res: Bt Co; ref: 1, 92, 791
RHETT, Thomas Grimke; Maj; Art, Trans-Mississippi Dept; res: Bt Cty; ref: 1, 21, 34, 92, 97, 115, 127, 154, 517, 576, 578, 700, 787, 789, 791, 1579
RHETT, Thomas Smith; Col; Arty Corps, in charge of Richmond Defense; res: Bt Cty; ref: 1, 21, 97, 583, 594, 700, 787, 791 1273, 1579, 1600, 1620, 1638
RHOADS, George M.; pvt; 1st MD Inf, Co E; res: Balt; MLCSH; ref: 19, 93, 786
RHOADS, Philip; pvt; Lee's MD Cav; res: Laurel Factory, AA Cty; ref: 1, 1539, 1628
RHODES, B. F.; sgt; MD Guerrilla Zouaves; ref: 1
RHODES, Oliver L.; McNeill's Rangers; res: Balt; ref: 1, 21, 148, 504, 519, 700, 1010
RHODES, William Lee; Capt; 8th GA Cav, Co C; ref: 1, 2, 19, 21, 73, 700, 735
RIACH, John; pvt; 1st MD Cav, Co C; res: Balt; ref: 1
RICAMORE, George; pvt; 12th VA Cav, Co B; ref: 1, 19, 1609
RICE, Albert; pvt; 20th VA Cav, Co D; res: Cumberland, All Cty; ref: 1, 19, 65, 93, 95, 148
RICE, Charles; pvt; 2nd MD Cav, Co D; ref: 1
RICE, Francis W.; pvt; 22nd VA Inf, Co B; res: St. M. Cty; ref: 1, 92, 93, 259, 1509, 1520
RICE, George C.; pvt; 1st MD Cav, Co A; res: Darnestown, Mont Cty; ref: 1, 2, 19, 21, 1552
RICE, George R.; pvt; 4th FL Inf, Co F; res: Mont Cty; ref: 1, 23, 73, 86, 1574
RICE, George T.; pvt; 4th MD Lt Arty; res: Balt; ref: 1, 2, 19, 21, 1662
RICE, James R.; pvt; 9th VA Inf, Co B; res: Chaptico, St. M. Cty; ref: 1, 735, 1555, 1576, 1627, 1670
RICE, John; ref: 55
RICE, Michael; pvt; Zarvona's MD Zouaves; ref: 1, 735
RICE, William; res: St. M. Cty; ref: 1670
RICH, Edward Robins (Revd); cpl; 1st MD Cav, Co E; res: Reisterstown, Bt Cty; ref: 1, 2, 19, 21, 23, 70, 75, 94, 700, 730, 825, 1001, 1147, 1562, 1563, 1626
RICHARD, S. H.; Lt; 53rd VA Inf, Co B; res: Balt; ref: 21
RICHARDS, ---; sgt; 2nd MD Cav; ref: 431, 827
RICHARDS, George B.; pvt; 1st MD Inf, Co I; ref: 1, 2, 19, 21
RICHARDSON, Alexander; pvt; Lucas's 15th SC Heavy Arty; res: St. M. Cty; ref; 1, 1509
RICHARDSON, Benjamin; pvt; Davis's MD Cav, Co A; ref: 1
RICHARDSON, G. H.; pvt; 43rd VA Cav (Mosby's), Co H; res: 1, 8
RICHARDSON, G. W.; pvt; 2nd MD Lt Arty; res: Bt Cty; ref: 1, 2, 19, 21
RICHARDSON, George W.; pvt; Davis's MD Cav, Co A; res: Church Creek, Dor Cty; ref: 1, 735, 1547
RICHARDSON, H. G.; pvt; 2nd MD Lt Arty; ref: 1, 2, 19, 21, 93, 700
RICHARDSON, Howard; Beale; pvt; 1st MD Cav, Co A; res: Balt; ref; 1, 2, 19, 21
RICHARDSON, James; pvt; 19th VA Heavy Arty, Co C; ref: 1, 1580
RICHARDSON, John Duhamel; pvt; 4th MD Lt Arty; res: Gustsville, QA

Cty; MLCSH; 1, 2, 19, 21, 470, 627, 700, 786, 1612

RICHARDSON, John Summerfield (M.D.); Acting Asst Surg, 51st VA Inf; res: St. Margarett, AA Cty; ref: 1, 18, 141, 1539

RICHARDSON, M. L.; pvt; 43rd VA Cav (Mosby's), Co C; res: Balt; ref: 1, 19, 786

RICHARDSON, Nicholas T.; pvt; 4th MD Lt Arty; res: Royal Oak, Tal Cty; ref: 1, 2, 19, 21, 1557

RICHARDSON, Richard T.; pvt; 1st MD Lt Arty; res: West River, AA Cty; ref: 1, 2, 19, 21, 34, 70, 700, 782, 786, 791, 1273, 1539

RICHARDSON, S. H.; Capt; Asst Commissary of Supply, Gen R. C. Tyler's staff; ref: 1, 53, 700

RICHARDSON, Shepard D.; pvt; 26th VA Inf, Co D; res: Balt; ref: 1, 21, 700

RICHARDSON, T. J.; pvt; 2nd MD Lt Arty; ref: 1, 2, 19, 21

RICHARDSON, Wallace P.; pvt; 2nd MD Lt Arty; res: Whitemarsh, Bt Cty; ref: 1, 2, 19, 21, 700

RICHARDSON, William H.; Lt; 2nd MD Cav, Co F; res: Har Cty; ref: 1, 2, 11, 19, 21, 23, 1609

RICHARSON, Thomas; pvt; 2nd MD Cav, Co G; ref: 1

RICKETT, Daniel; pvt; 2nd MD Cav, Co A; ref: 1

RICHTER, Frederick; res: Westminster, Carr Cty; ref: 1, 19

RICHY, George; pvt; 2nd MD Cav, Co B; ref: 1, 19, 1609

RICHY, James P.; Lt; Davis's MD Cav, Co A; ref: 1, 735

RICO, George; pvt; 1st MD Cav, Co A; ref: 2, 19, 21, 628

RIDDER, Harry W.; pvt; McNeill's Rangers; res: Oakland, Gar Cty; ref: 1, 1144, 1610

RIDDICK, John Henry (M.D.); Contract Surg; Dept of North Carolina Hospital; res: Balt; ref: 1, 18, 1596

RIDDICK, Joseph; pvt; 56th NC Inf, Co B; res: Frd Cty; ref: 1

RIDDLE, Charles; pvt; 1st Md Lt Arty; res: Cha Cty; ref: 1, 2, 19, 21, 26

RIDDLE, Charles C.; pvt; 2nd MD Cav, Co C; ref: 1, 19

RIDDLE, John F.; pvt; Davis's MD Cav, Co A; ref: 1, 735

RIDDLEMOSER, Alfred; cpl; 2nd MD Inf, Co D; res: Emmitsburg, Frd Cty; ref: 1, 2, 19, 21, 23, 90, 412, 1573

RIDDLEMOSER, David; pvt; 2nd MD Inf, Co D; ref: 1, 2, 7, 19, 21

RIDDLEMOSER, Joseph (M.D.); pvt; 2nd MD Inf, Co H; res: Emmitsburg, Frd Cty; ref; 1, 18, 90, 1573

RIDDLEMOSER, S. D.; ref: 88

RIDER, George J.; pvt; 2nd MD Cav, Co C; res: Frd Cty; ref: 1, 2, 19, 21

RIDER, George W.; pvt; 2nd MD Inf, Co G; res: Som Cty; ref: 1

RIDER, Martin Luther S.; 2nd MD Inf, Co G; res: Frd Cty; ref: 1, 2, 19, 21, 89, 700

RIDER, William; pvt; 1st VA Cav, Co K; ref: 2, 19, 21

RIDGAWAY, Joseph A.; pvt; Martin's GA Lt Lt Arty; res: Tal Cty; ref: 1, 645

RIDGE, Emerson; pvt; 7th VA Cav, Co G; ref: 3

RIDGEL, Edward; pvt; 2nd MD Inf, Co E; ref: 470

RIDGEL, James; pvt; Zarvona''s MD Zouaves; res: Great Mills, St. M. Cty; ref: 1, 2, 19, 21, 23, 735, 1555

RIDGELEY, T. R.; pvt; 43rd VA Cav (Mosby's), Co F; ref: 8

RIDGELEY, Thomas A.; pvt; 1st MD Cav, Co A; res: How Cty; ref: 1, 10, 19, 748

RIDGELY, Charles L.; Capt; 3rd FL Inf, Co B; res: Towson, Bt Cty; ref: 1, 11, 19, 50, 63, 1523, 1575

RIDGELY, John T.; color sgt; 1st MD Cav; res: Cooksville, How Cty; ref: 1, 2, 19, 21, 70, 685, 700, 748, 827, 1550

RIDGELY, Randolph; Lt; Aide de Camp, Gen J. Early's staff; ref: 1, 19
RIDGLEY, Samuel; pvt; 1st VA Cav, Co K; res: How Cty; MLCSH; ref: 1, 2, 19, 21, 93, 700, 748, 786
RIDGWAY, Mordicai J.; pvt; 1st MD Lt Arty; ref: 1, 2, 19, 21, 730
RIDING, John; pvt; 1st MD Lt Arty; ref: 34
RIDEN, Joseph; pvt; 7th VA Inf; res: Southern Maryland; ref: 69
RIELY, Frank; pvt; 12th VA Cav, Co F; ref: 1, 141, 1609
RIELY, W.; pvt; 2nd MD Cav, Co A; ref: 1, 19
RIELY, W. Brent; pvt; Davis's MD Cav, Co A; ref: 1, 735
RIFE, J. H.; pvt; 2nd MD Cav, Co C; ref: 1
RIGDON, James; drummer; res: Frederick, Frd Cty; ref: 89
RIGGLE, Virgil M.; pvt; Holbrook's Independent MD Lt Arty; res: Millersvile, AA Cty; ref: 1, 1539
RIGGS, Joshua Warfield; pvt; 43rd VA Cav (Mosby's); res: Mont Cty; ref: 1, 2, 8, 19, 21, 23, 70, 80, 601, 735, 881, 1571, 1578, 1579, 1654
RIGGS, Reuben; pvt; 1st MD Cav, Co A; res: Goshen, Mont Cty; ref: 1, 2, 19, 21, 560, 1574
RIGGS, Samuel; sgt; Madison's Regt, TX Cav, Co A; ref: 1, 718
RILEY, Brent; pvt; Davis's MD Cav,Co A; ref: 1, 735
RILEY, Frank M.; pvt; 2nd MD Cav, Co F; ref: 11, 693
RILEY, James; pvt; Davis's MD Cav, Co C; ref: 1, 1371
RILEY, John; pvt; 5th LA Inf, Co G; res: Balt; MLCSH; ref: 1, 21, 93, 627, 700, 786
RILEY, John; sgt; Davis's MD Cav, Co C; ref: 1
RILEY, John P.; pvt; 1st MD Cav, Co C; res: Balt; ref: 1, 2, 19, 21, 1634
RILEY, Joseph C.; pvt; 2nd MD Inf, Co F; res: Balt; ref: 1
RILEY, Michael; res: Annapolis, AA Cty; ref: 1539
RILEY, Owen; fmn, Navy; C.S. Charleston; res: Balt; ref: 1
RILEY, Patrick; sgt; 2nd MD Cav, Co C; ref: 1, 19
RILEY, Thomas H.; pvt; Stuart's Horse Arty, Breathed's Battery; ref: 1, 498
RILEY, Thomas S.; pvt; 1st MD Cav, Co A; ref: 1, 2, 19, 21
RINEHART, William C.; pvt; 1st MD Inf, Co C; ref: 1, 2, 19, 21, 93
RINGGOLD, R. Samuel (M.D.); Asst Surg; Charpenter's AL Battery; res: Balt; ref: 1, 18, 742
RINKER, John A.; pvt; 35th VA Cav, Co A; ref: 1, 1611, 1677
RINSSELOT, C. A.; Lt; 2nd MD Cav, Co D; ref: 693
RIORDAN, John Daniel; pvt; Wise Lt Arty; res: Balt; MLCSH; ref: 21, 89, 627, 700, 786
RIORDAN, Michael; pvt; 2nd MD Cav, Co B; ref: 1, 19, 1609
RISON, William H.; sgt; 1st MD Inf, Co I; ref: 1, 2, 19, 21, 23
RITENOUR, W. H.; pvt; 7th VA Cav, Co G; ref: 1, 3
RITTER, David H.; pvt; 43rd VA Cav (Mosby's); ref: 1, 8, 511
RITTER, George; cpl; Jacobs Mounted Riflemen; res: Cumberland, All Cty; ref: 1, 19, 65, 95, 148, 511, 1610
RITTER, William; sgt; 2nd MD Inf, Co C; ref: 1, 2, 19, 21, 23
RITTER, William L.; Capt; 3rd MD Lt Arty; res: Carr Cty; ref; 1, 2, 19, 21, 23, 28, 50, 56, 57, 64, 65, 70, 72, 75, 90, 150, 160, 168, 412, 440, 443, 451, 454, 461, 479, 511, 638, 685, 686, 700, 726, 758, 791, 866, 873, 891, 906, 916, 935, 942, 945, 957, 976, 994, 1058, 1060, 1106, 1249, 1262, 1263, 1265, 1267, 1422, 1423, 1460, 1523, 1577, 1578, 1579
RIVERS, J. H.; pvt; 2nd MD Cav, Co C; ref: 1, 19, 1609
RIVES, Francis S.; pvt; 1st MD Inf, Co H; ref: 2, 19, 21, 650

ROACH, E. R.; pvt; 3rd MD Lt Arty; ref: 2, 19, 21, 461
ROACH, James Benjamin; drummer; 23rd VA Inf, MLCSH; ref: 786
ROACH, John; pvt; 1st SC Inf, Co B; res: Balt; ref: 1, 735, 1540
ROACH, K.; pvt; 1st SC Inf, Co B; res: Balt; ref: 1, 735, 1540
ROACH, Michael; pvt; 13th VA Inf, Co G; ref: 1
ROACH, Philip E.; pvt; 35th VA Cav, Co C; ref: 1, 316
ROACH, R. J.; pvt; Stuart's Horse Arty, Breathed's Battery; ref: 1
ROADES, John; pvt; 2nd MD Cav, Co G; ref: 1, 19
ROANE, James; pvt; 2nd MD Lt Arty; res: Balt; ref: 1, 2, 19, 21, 628
ROBBINS, William A.; pvt; 24th VA Cav, Co D; ref: 2, 19, 21, 684
ROBBINS, William H. (M.D.); Acting Asst Surg; 40th VA Inf; res: Balt; ref: 1, 18, 1690
ROBERTS, Benjamin J.; Lt; 4th MD Lt Arty; res: QA Cty; ref: 1, 2, 19, 21, 23, 34, 64, 93, 459, 1523, 1612
ROBERTS, Frank; pvt; 2nd MD Inf, Co B; ref: 1, 2, 19, 21
ROBERTS, George E.; sgt; Lee's MD Cav; ref: 1, 2, 19, 21, 740, 1621
ROBERTS, John A.; pvt; 1st MD Cav, Co K; ref: 1, 19
ROBERTS, John T.; pvt; Pollack's Co, VA Lt Arty; res: Balt; ref: 1, 21, 700
ROBERTS, Joseph K., Jr; Lt; 1st MD Cav, Co E; res: Bladensburg, PG Cty; ref: 1, 2, 19, 21, 23, 64, 68, 69, 316, 700, 730
ROBERTS, L. Edward; Lt; 1st MD Inf, Co A; res: Easton, Tal Cty; ref: 1, 2, 19, 21, 70, 645, 700
ROBERTS, N.; pvt; 1st SC Inf, Co H; ref: 1
ROBERTS, Richard; pvt; 1st MD Cav, Co E; res: Bladensburg, PG Cty; ref: 1, 2, 19, 21, 69, 316, 730, 1622
ROBERTS, T. J.; pvt; 2nd MD Cav, Co D; ref: 1, 19, 1609
ROBERTSON, A. J.; pvt; Stuart's Horse Arty, Breathed's Battery; ref: 1
ROBERTSON, Duncan, Jr; Lt; 6th VA Inf, Co G; res: Balt; ref: 1, 21, 511, 700
ROBERTSON, Fenwick (M.D.); Asst Surg; General Hospital, Richmond; res: Kingston, Som Cty; MLCSH; ref: 1, 2, 18, 19, 92, 93,627, 700, 786
ROBERTSON, George; pvt; 2nd MD Lt Arty; ref: 1, 2, 19, 21, 1511
ROBERTSON, George W.; pvt; Davis's MD Cav, Co C; res: Wash Cty; MLCSH; ref: 1,786, 1609
ROBERTSON, Henry G. of Jonathan; pvt; 2nd MD Inf, Co B; res: Port Tobacco, Cha Cty; ref: 1, 2, 19, 21, 93, 1546
ROBERTSON, Hugh Ligon; pvt; 25th VA Inf, Co B; res: How Cty; ref: 1, 71
ROBERTSON, Isaac W.; pvt; Stuart's Horse Arty, Breathed's Battery; ref: 1
ROBERTSON, J. A. G.; pvt; 3rd MD Lt Arty; ref: 2, 19, 21, 160, 511, 726
ROBERTSON, James F.; pvt; Davis's MD Cav, Co C; ref: 1
ROBERSTON, Jesse; pvt; Stuart's Horse Arty, Breathed's Battery; ref: 1
ROBERTSON, Michael Stone; Capt; 1st MD Inf, Co I; res: Allens Fresh, Cha Cty; ref: 1, 2, 19, 21, 23, 34, 64, 68, 88, 107, 240, 456, 462, 511, 711, 746, 789, 790, 791, 793, 1520, 1523, 1546
ROBERTSON, William George; pvt; 43rd VA Cav (Mosby's), Co D; res: Bt Cty; MLCSH; res: Bt Cty; ref: 8. 786
ROBEY, H. A.; pvt; 2nd MD Cav, Co B; res: Balt; ref: 1, 2, 19, 21.
ROBEY, Townley; sgt; 1st MD Cav, Co E; ref: 1, 2, 19, 21, 23, 700, 730
ROBEY, William; cpl; 19th VA Heavy Arty, Co C; ref: 1, 1580

ROBEY, William; pvt; 2nd MD Cav, Co G; ref: 1, 2, 19, 21, 1609

ROBEY, William S.; pvt; 17th VA Inf, Co E; ref: 1, 2, 19, 34, 133, 142

ROBEY, William T.; pvt; Hampton Leg Lt Arty; ref: 1, 2, 19, 21

ROBINS, Thomas; pvt; Edelin's MD Heavy Arty; res: Balt; ref: 1, 1540

ROBINSON, A.; Master, Navy; ref: 1564

ROBINSON, Algernon Sidney; pvt, Marine Corps, Richmond, Co C; ref: 1, 58, 97, 735, 1594

ROBINSON, Arthur; pvt; 1st SC Inf, Co G; ref: 1, 681, 800

ROBINSON, Claiborne; pvt; 43rd VA Cav (Mosby's), Co D; ref: 8, 601, 1571, 1578, 1579, 1654

ROBINSON, Charles; pvt; 3rd MD Lt Arty; ref: 2, 19, 21, 160, 726

ROBINSON, Edward W.; pvt; 1st MD Cav, Co C; ref: 1

ROBINSON, George H.; pvt; 2nd MD Lt Arty; res: Balt; ref: 1, 2, 19, 21, 51, 700

ROBINSON, George S.; pvt; 2nd MD Lt Arty; res: Balt; ref: 1, 1053, 1058

ROBINSON, George W.; pvt; 1st MD Lt Arty; res: Balt; ref: 1, 2, 19, 21, 1540

ROBINSON, Henry; Maj; Asst I.G., Gen J. Longstreet's staff; ref: 1, 21, 105, 700, 735

ROBINSON, Israel; Lt Col; 67th VA Inf; res: PG Cty; ref: 1, 71, 791

ROBINSON, J. E.; pvt; 1st SC Inf, Co G; ref: 1

ROBINSON, James B.; pvt; 7th VA Cav, Co G; res: Sharpsburg, Wash Cty; ref: 1, 1558

ROBINSON, John; smn, Navy; Privateer Tacony; res: Johnsons Store, AA Cty; ref: 1, 70, 1539

ROBINSON, John M.; pvt; 35th VA Cav, Co B; res: Balt; ref: 1, 1677

ROBINSON, John Moncure; Capt; Asst A.G., Gen J. Longstreet's staff; res: Cha Cty; ref: 21, 105, 559, 631, 700, 735, 1511

ROBINSON, Joseph; pvt; 2nd MD Inf, Co H; res: Balt; ref:1, 2, 19, 21

ROBINSON, Joseph B.; pvt; 47th VA Inf, Co H; ref: 1

ROBINSON, Logan; pvt; Home Guards; res: Balt; ref: 21, 700

ROBINSON, Monroe; pvt; 43rd VA Cav (Mosby's), Co C; res: Balt; ref: 8, 19, 21, 700, 1613

ROBINSON, T. L.; pvt; 2nd MD Inf, Co H; ref: 1

ROBINSON, Thomas J.; pvt; 2nd MD Cav, Co A; ref: 1

ROBINSON, William; pvt; 1st VA Inf, Co E; res: Bladensburg, PG Cty; ref: 1, 735

ROBINSON, William; pvt; Holbrooks' Independent MD Lt Arty; res: Balt; ref: 1, 1540

ROBINSON, William A.; pvt; 3rd MD Lt Arty; res: Som Cty; ref: 2, 19, 21, 160, 726, 1556

ROBINSON, William C.; 2nd Lt; 55th VA Inf, Co H; MLCSH; ref: 1, 21, 92, 93, 700, 786, 791

ROBINSON, William H.; pvt; 1st MD Cav, Co C; res: Bt Cty; ref: 1, 2, 19, 21, 1575

ROBINSON, William Wirt; sgt; 2nd MD Lt Arty; ref: 1, 2, 19, 21, 23, 34, 64, 685

ROBY, Henry Albert; sgt; 2nd MD Cav, Co B; res: Balt; ref: 1, 2, 19, 21, 70, 107, 685, 700, 1289, 1609

ROBY, William T. F.; pvt; 1st MD Lt Arty; res: Duffield, Cha Cty; ref: 1, 93, 823, 1546

ROCHE, John S.; pvt; Lee's Balt Lt Arty, Alexander's Bn; res: Balt; ref: 1, 1540

ROCHE, Michael Berry; pvt; 34th VA Inf, Co D; res: Balt; ref: 1, 1540

ROCHE, Thomas F.; pvt; 21st VA Inf, Co B; res: Balt; ref: 1, 2, 19, 312, 690, 735

RODDATZ, Charles F.; (Prof.); Lt; Ordnance Officer, Gen E. K. Kirby's staff; res: Balt; ref: 21, 23, 56, 700

RODERICK, Jacob; pvt; 2nd MD Cav, Co D; ref: 1609

RODEWALD, John; pvt; 2 AL Inf, Co C; res: Balt; ref: 1, 735
RODGERS, Ezekiel H.; pvt; 9th VA Inf, Co B; res: Balt; ref: 1, 1576, 1613
RODGERS, George; pvt; 1st MD Cav, Co C; ref: 1
RODGERS, James P.; 21st VA Inf, Co B; res: Balt; ref: 1, 2, 19, 312, 559, 726
RODGERS, John Monroe; pvt; 12th VA Inf, Co H; res: Balt; ref: 1, 21, 23, 70, 92, 93, 700, 1687
RODLEY, Edward Smith; pvt; Lucas' 15th SC Heavy Arty; res: Balt; ref: 1, 1663, 1664
RODNEY, Edward L.; pvt; 2nd MD Cav, Co D; res: Balt; ref: 1, 19, 1540, 1609
RODRIGUEZ, Francisco; pvt; 3rd MD Lt Arty; ref: 1, 2, 19, 21, 160, 726
ROE, David; pvt; Staurt's Horse Arty, Breathed's Battery; ref: 1, 498
ROE, Samuel; sgt; 1st MD Cav, Co E; res: Centreville, QA Cty; ref: 1, 2, 19, 21, 700, 730
ROGERS, Edward G.; pvt; 21st VA Inf, Co B; res: Balt; ref: 1, 2, 19, 312, 681, 735
ROGERS, Edward J.; pvt; 2nd MD Cav, Co A; ref: 1, 19, 1609
ROGERS, George W.; pvt; 13th VA Inf, Co G; ref: 1, 735
ROGERS, Henry Clay; pvt; 1st MD Inf, Co D; res: Balt; ref: 1, 2, 19, 21, 38, 690
ROGERS, James P.; pvt; 1st MD Cav, Co C; res: Brooklandville, Bt Cty; ref: 1, 2, 19, 21, 69, 90, 160, 316, 643, 735, 1541
ROGERS, James W.; smn, Navy; Prize St. Pevensey; res: West River,AA Cty; ref: 1, 1539
ROGERS, John C.; pvt; 1st MD Inf, Co C; res: AA Cty; ref: 1, 2, 19, 21
ROGERS, John G.; pvt; 7th VA Cav, Co G; res: West River, AA Cty; ref: 1
ROGERS, Philip; pvt; 1st MD Cav, Co C; res: Balt; ref: 1, 2, 19, 21, 877
ROGERS, Samuel B.; pvt; 1st MD Cav, Co C; res: Brooklandville, Bt Cty; ref: 1, 2, 11, 19, 21, 259, 559, 711, 757, 1511, 1541
ROGERS, Thomas H.; pvt; MD Guerrilla Zouaves; res: West River, AA Cty; ref: 1, 1539
ROGERS, Thomas J.; (M.D.); Asst Surg; 3rd MD Lt Arty; ref: 1, 2, 18, 19, 21, 23, 160, 461, 726, 1523
ROGERS, William; pvt; 3rd MD Lt Arty; ref: 1, 2, 19, 21, 160, 461, 726
ROGERS, William C.; pvt; 26th VA Inf, Co E; res: Balt; ref: 1, 2, 19, 21, 1523
ROGERS, William H.; sgt; 1st MD Inf, Co C; ref: 1, 2, 19, 21
ROHNER, John; pvt; 9th VA Inf, Co b; ref: 1, 1576
ROHR, Charles; pvt, Navy; purchasing agent, Wilmington, North Carolina; ref: 1, 21, 70, 700, 783
ROHR, Elias; 17th VA Inf, Co E; ref: 735
ROLING, T. J.; pvt; 1st SC Inf, Co G; ref: 1
ROLL, John; pvt; 19th MS Inf, Co C; MLCSH; ref: 1, 21, 700
ROLLEY, Thomas H.; pvt; 1st MD Cav, Co D; ref: 1, 2, 19, 21, 1601
ROLLINS, Stephen B.; Lt; 47th VA Inf, Co E; res: Carr Cty; ref: 1, 8, 70, 1194
ROLPH, George W.; pvt; 1st MD Cav, Co E; res: Kt Cty; ref: 1, 2, 19, 21, 56, 93, 730, 1584
ROLPH, Wilbert F.; cpl; 1st MD Cav, Co F; ref: 1, 2, 19, 21, 23
ROMMELL, J. W.; 24th VA Cav; ref: 735
RONAN, Martin; pvt; 2nd MD Cav, Co B; ref: 1, 19
RONEY, J. C.; pvt; 2nd MD Cav, Co A; ref: 1, 19, 1609
RONEY, John; cpl; 1st SC Inf, Co G; ref: 1
ROPER, James M.; ymn, Navy; C.S.S. Richmond; res: Balt; ref: 1, 21, 700, 783

ROPER, N. C.; pvt; 1st SC Inf, Co G; ref: 1
ROSAN, Charles W.; pvt; 1st MD Cav, Co D; res: Balt; ref: 1, 2, 19, 21, 1601
ROSAN, Sterling L.; pvt; 1st MD Cav, Co F; ref: 1, 2, 19, 21
ROSE, E. Porter; pvt; 1st MD Cav, Co C; ref: 1, 2, 19, 21
ROSE, Jesse; pvt; Stuart's Horse Arty, Breathed's Battery; ref: 1, 2, 19, 21
ROSE, L. J.; 1st MD Cav, Co E; ref: 352
ROSENSTEEL, James W.; pvt; 1st MD Inf, Co A; res: Emmitsburg, Frd Cty; ref: 1, 2, 19, 21
ROSIER, Charles; pvt; 1st MD Cav, Co A; ref: 1, 2, 19, 21
ROSS, Alexander; d.h., Navy; C.S. Palmetto State; ref: 1
ROSS, Anthony P.; pvt; 2nd Md Lt Arty; res: Tal Cty; erf: 1, 2, 19, 21, 645, 1612
ROSS, Charles C.; sgt; Lucas' 15th SC Heavy Arty; res: Balt; ref: 1
ROSS, David M.; Capt; 2nd MD Cav, Co C; res: Kt Cty; ref: 1, 2, 11, 19, 21, 23, 70, 233, 791, 1565, 1609
ROSS, Francis; pvt; 2nd MD Cav, Co C; ref: 1, 19, 1609
ROSS, George; Cadet Corps; ref: 1
ROSS, George L.; sgt; 2nd MD Inf, Co E; res: Balt; ref: 1, 2, 19, 21, 23, 92, 93, 700
ROSS, Missick; pvt; 1st MD Inf, Co G; ref: 1, 2, 19, 21
ROSS, P. J.; pvt; 1st MD Cav, Co F; ref: 1
ROSS, W. George; sgt; 1st MD Inf, Co G; ref: 1, 2, 19, 21, 23
ROTE, John T.; res: Annapolis, AA Cty; ref: 1539
ROUSS, Charles B.; 2nd VA Inf; ref: 735
ROUSSELOT, C. A.; Lt; 2nd MD Cav, Co D; ref: 1, 19, 1609
ROWAN, John B.; Capt; 3rd MD Lt Arty; res: Elkton, Cec Cty; ref: 1, 2, 19, 21, 23, 28, 64, 65, 70, 160, 168, 443, 461, 479, 511, 638, 686, 726, 791, 889, 1060, 1106, 1422, 1523
ROWE, Augustus H.; pvt; 1st Local GA Inf, Co A; res: Frederick, Frd Cty; ref: 1, 89, 1573
ROWE, James F.; pvt; 5th VA Cav, Co E; res: Balt; MLCSH; ref: 1, 21, 92, 93, 700, 786
ROWE, Vincent; pvt; Jacobs Mounted Riflemen; res: Frederick, Frd Cty; ref: 1, 89, 1573
ROWLAND, D. P.; pvt; 3rd MD Lt Arty; ref: 2, 19, 21, 160, 726
ROWLAND, H. R.; pvt; 2nd MD Cav, Co A; ref: 1, 19
ROWLAND, Thomas; Maj; Asst I.G., Gen S. Ramson's staff; ref: 1, 21, 70, 127, 684, 700, 722, 740, 791
ROWLEY, William; pvt; Davis's MD Cav; res: Johnsons Store, AA Cty; ref: 1, 1539, 1563
ROYSTER, William A.; pvt; 2nd MD Cav, Co B; ref: 1, 19
RUARK, Michael; pvt; 1st MD Inf, Co E; res: Balt; ref: 1, 2, 19, 21
RUCKER, William; pvt; 2nd MD Lt Arty; ref: 1, 2, 19, 21
RUDDEN, Thomas; pvt; Stuart's Horse Arty, Breathed's Battery, res: Balt; ref: 1, 2, 19, 21
RUFF, George Fredrick; sgt; 1st MD Inf, Co D; res: Balt; ref: 1, 2, 19, 21, 23, 700, 1540
RUFFIN, Emmett Forsyth; Acting Mate, Navy; Savannah Station; res: Balt; MLCSH; ref: 700, 786, 1564
RULEY, James M.; drummer; 1st MD Inf, Co D; ref: 1, 2, 19, 21
RUSH, Peter; pvt; 2nd MD Inf, Co E; res: Balt; ref: 1, 2, 19, 21
RUSH, S. G.; pvt; 1st SC Inf, Co G; ref: 1
RUSHING, John; pvt; 1st MD Cav, Co F; ref: 1, 2, 19, 21
RUSK, J.; pvt; 1st MD Cav, Co D; ref: 1, 19
RUSKELL, William; pvt; 46th VA Inf, Co A; ref: 1, 735
RUSSELL, B. F.; pvt; 1st SC Inf, Co G; ref: 1
RUSSELL, Charles F. (M.D.); pvt; 7th VA Cav, Co G; ref:1, 3, 18

RUSSELL, Elisha Torleton; sgt maj; Stuart's Horse Arty, Breathed's Battery; res: St. M. Cty; ref: 1, 2, 19, 21, 93, 259, 498, 650, 1509, 1520

RUSSELL, Frank; res: St. M. Cty; ref: 1670

RUSSELL, Henry; pvt; 4th MD Lt Arty; ref: 1, 2, 19, 21

RUSSELL, Jerry S.; pvt; 4th MD Lt Arty; res: Galestown, Dor Cty; ref: 1, 19, 1547

RUSSELL, John H.; cpl; Zarvona's MD Zouaves; ref: 61, 68, 97, 703, 735, 1509

RUSSELL, John T.; pvt, Marine Corps; Co D; Citronelle Alabama; res: Balt; ref: 1, 76, 1540, 1594

RUSSELL, Thomas Alfred; sgt; 43rd VA Cav (Mosby's), Co F; res: Easton, Tal Cty; ref: 1, 2, 8, 19, 21, 498, 650, 1509, 1612

RUST, Charles P.; pvt; 9th VA Cav, Co H; res: Eastern Shore of Maryland; ref: 1, 735, 1620

RUTHART, T. H.; res: Annapolis, AA Cty; ref: 1539

RUTHLEDGE, Charles A. (M.D.); Asst Surg; Warrenton General Hospital; res: Taylor, Har Cty; ref: 1, 18, 700, 735

RUTTER, Elisha; pvt; 2nd MD Inf, Co E; ref: 1, 2, 19, 21, 23, 470, 1523

RUTTER, H.; pvt; 43rd VA Cav (Mosby's), Co E; ref: 1, 8

RUTTER, John W.; pvt; 43rd VA Cav (Mosby's), Co A; ref: 8

RUTTER, Wilbur; sgt; 2nd MD Inf, Co E; ref: 1, 2, 19, 21, 23, 1523

RUTTER, William F.; pvt; Zarvona's MD Zouaves; ref: 1, 735

RYAN, Abram Joseph (Revd); Chaplain; 8th TN Inf; res: Hagerstown, Wash Cty; ref: 1, 1280, 1336, 1435, 1523, 1685

RYAN, Alfred T.; pvt; 35th VA Cav, Co A; ref: 1, 1611, 1677

RYAN, Henry Clay; pvt; 35th VA Cav, Co A; ref: 1, 3, 1611, 1677

RYAN, James; pvt; 19th VA Heavy Arty, Co C; res: Balt; ref: 1, 1540, 1580, 1613

RYAN, James Aloysius, Jr; pvt; Stuart's Horse Arty, Breathed's Battery; res: Frd Cty; MLCSH; ref: 1, 2, 19, 21, 92, 93, 498, 700, 786

RYAN, James Aloysius, Sr; pvt; Stuart's Horse Arty, Breathed's Battery; res: Frd Cty; ref: 1, 498

RYAN, James W.; pvt; 35th VA Cav, Co A; ref: 1, 3, 1611, 1677

RYAN, John; cpl; 1st MD Inf, Co F; ref: 1, 2, 19, 21

RYAN, John; pvt; MD Guerrilla Zouaves; ref: 1

RYAN, John Charles; pvt; Rhett's 1st SC Heavy Arty; res: Balt; MLCSH; ref: 1, 627, 700, 735, 786

RYAN, Joseph; pvt; 2nd MD Inf, Co E; res: Balt; ref: 1, 2, 19, 21

RYAN, Michael; pvt; 3rd MD Lt Arty; ref: 1, 2, 19, 21, 160, 726

RYAN, Patrick; pvt; 9th VA Inf, Co B; ref: 1, 2, 19, 21, 1576

RYAN, Robert S.; pvt; 1st MD Inf, Co D; res: Balt; ref: 1, 2, 19, 21, 700, 1540

RYAN, Samuel; pvt; 35th VA Cav, Co B; ref: 1, 1611, 1677

RYAN, William H.; pvt; 2nd MD Cav, Co C; res: Balt; ref: 1, 2, 19, 21, 44, 1523, 1577, 1579

RYAN, William R.; cpl; Zarvona's MD Zouaves; res: Balt; ref: 1, 61, 97, 703, 735, 1540, 1620

RYCE, Francis W.; pvt; 1st MD Inf, Co H; ref: 1, 2, 19, 21, 650

RYE, John M.; pvt; Hampton Leg Lt Arty, Co B; ref: 1, 2, 19, 21

RYE, John S.; pvt; 6th VA Inf, Co I; res: Balt; ref: 1, 21, 700

RYLAND, Samuel Peachy, Jr; pvt; 34th VA Inf, Co K: res: Balt; ref: 1, 21, 23, 56, 700

SADLER, David M.; pvt; 11th TX Cav, Co C; res: Balt; ref: 1, 21, 57, 700

SAFFIR, Benjamin F.; pvt; 35th VA Cav, Co A; ref: 1, 1611, 1677
SAHM, Joseph; pvt; 1st MD Inf, Co G; ref: 1, 2, 19, 21
SAILOR, M. D.; pvt; 3rd MD Lt Arty; ref: 1, 2, 19, 21, 160, 726
SAKERS, John T.; pvt; 1st VA, Co K; res: Laurel, PG Cty; ref: 1, 2, 19, 21, 687, 700
SAKERS, Samuel; pvt; 7th MD Cav, Co G; ref: 1, 3
SALANA, P. G.; sgt; ref: 700
SAMS, R. J.; pvt; 3rd MD Lt Arty; ref: 1, 2, 19, 21, 160, 726
SAMSON, Henry; pvt; 1st MS Cav, Buck's Co; res: AA Cty; ref: 1, 1539
SANCHEZ, Blas; cpl; 3rd MD Lt Arty; ref: 1, 2, 19, 21, 23, 160, 461, 726
SANDERS, D.; pvt; Davis's MD Cav, Co A; ref: 1, 735
SANDERS, Edward; pvt; Davis's MD Cav, Co A; ref: 1
SANDERS, James H.; pvt; 1st MD Inf, Co G; ref: 1, 2, 21
SANDERS, John Willis; cpl; Searcy's Sharpshooters, Co B; res: Bt Cty; ref: 1, 71
SANDERS, Joseph; pvt; Davis's MD Cav, Co A; ref: 1, 2, 19, 21, 735
SANDERS, T. Hillen; pvt; 1st VA Cav, Co L; ref: 1, 2, 19, 21, 700
SANDERS, W. B.; pvt; 1st SC Inf, Co G; ref: 1
SANDERS, William Harrison; pvt; 23rd VA Inf, Co E; res: Balt; ref: 1, 23
SANDERSON, Frank Henry; pvt; 2nd MD Inf, Co A; res: Balt; ref: 2, 21, 259, 650, 1540
SANDLER, William J.; pvt; 1st MD Inf, Co E; res: Balt; ref: 1, 2, 19, 21, 1540
SANDS, Joseph; pvt; Lynch's Co, TN Lt Arty; res: Annapolis, AA Cty; ref: 1, 1539
SANFORD, Edward; pvt; Hampton Leg Lt Arty, Co B; ref: 1, 2, 19, 21
SANFORD, Robert A.; pvt; 9th VA Cav, Co C; res: Balt; ref: 1, 21, 57, 700
SANGSTOCK, Charles; pvt; 1st VA Inf, Co E; ref: 735
SANNER, Alexander A.; pvt; Otey's Battery, VA Lt Arty; ref: 1, 2, 19, 21
SANNER, Joseph Carberry; orderly sgt; 16th VA Inf, Co C; res: St. M. Cty; MLCSH; ref: 1, 627, 700, 786, 1627
SANSBURG, James L.; Lt; 26th SC Inf, Co G; res: McPherson's Pack, AA Cty; ref: 1, 1539
SAPP, David; pvt; 21st VA Cav, Co C; res: Annapolis, AA Cty; ref: 1, 1539
SARGENT, Harry D. G. C.; pvt; 1st MD Lt Arty; res: Balt; MLCSH; ref: 1, 2, 19, 21, 92, 93, 690, 700, 786
SARGERS, Samuel; pvt; Davis's MD Cav, Co A; ref: 1
SARTIN, John; pvt; Davis's MD Cav, Co C; ref: 1
SAULS, James; pvt; 1st SC Inf, Co G; ref: 1, 93
SAUNDERS, Addison E.; cpl; 17th VA Inf, Co A; ref: 1, 133, 142, 251
SAUNDERS, John O.; pvt; Davis's MD Cav, Co C; ref: 1
SAUNDERS, John Selden; Lt Col; Ordnance Dept, Army of Northern Virginia; res: Balt; ref: 1, 21, 22, 23, 53, 56, 700, 735, 787, 791, 862, 873, 885, 1364, 1600
SAUNDERS, Richard; pvt; 47th VA Inf, Co H; ref: 1
SAVAGE, George; pvt; Otey's Battery, VA Lt Arty; res: Balt; ref: 1, 19, 21, 93, 700
SAVAGE, John H.; cpl; 19th VA Heavy Arty, Co C; ref: 1, 1580
SAVAGE, John H.; pvt; 17th VA Inf, Co A; ref: 1, 2, 19, 21, 23, 133, 142
SAVAGE, John N.; pvt; 13th VA Cav, Co B; ref: 1, 7, 19
SAVAGE, William H.; Acting Mast. M., Navy; C.S.S. Stonewall; res: Balt; ref: 19, 21, 58, 97, 279, 700, 735, 783, 1564
SAVELL, Thomas S.; pvt; 3rd MD Lt Arty; ref: 1, 2, 19, 21, 160, 726

SAYLOR, William J.; pvt; 20th SC Inf, Co E; res: East River Landing, AA Cty; ref: 1, 1539
SCAGGS, Edward O.; pvt; 1st MD Cav, Co B; res: PG Cty; ref: 1, 2, 19, 21, 785
SCAGGS, J.; pvt; 1st MD Cav, Co B; res: Mont Cty; ref: 1, 2, 19, 21, 1574
SCAGGS, Robert; pvt; 1st VA Cav, Co K; res: Clarksville, How Cty; ref: 1, 2, 10, 19, 21, 748, 1550
SCALES, J. S.; pvt; 38th GA Inf, Co H; ref: 1, 2, 19, 21, 160, 461, 726
SCALLY, Patrick; pvt; 1st LA Cav, Co F; Texas, Bt Cty; ref: 1, 1563
SCARBOROUGH, Miles; pvt; 9th VA Inf, Co B; ref: 1, 1576
SCHACKLEFORD, John L.; cpl; 43rd VA Cav (Mosby's), Co F; ref: 1, 8
SCHAEFER, John W.; pvt; 4th MD Lt Arty; ref: 1
SCHAEFER, William; pvt; 4th MD Lt Arty; ref: 1, 2, 19
SCHAEFFER, Benjamin; pvt; Davidson's Co, VA Lt Arty; ref: 1, 2, 19, 21, 735
SCHAEFFER, Francis B.; Capt; 1st VA Inf, Co F; ref: 1, 18, 19, 127, 951
SCHAEFFER, Luther M.; pvt; 4th VA Inf, Co L; res: Frd Cty; ref: 1, 19, 90
SCHAEFFER, P. W.; sgt; MD Line; ref: 1
SCHAFER, George William; pvt; 2nd MD Cav, Co E; res: Balt; erf: 1, 2, 19, 21, 700, 906, 1609
SCHAFFER, Adam F.; pvt; 2nd MD Lt Arty; ref: 1, 2, 19, 21
SCHAKLEY, H. B.; pvt; 1st MD Cav, Co E; ref: 2, 19, 21
SCHAKLEY, Warinus W.; pvt; 1st VA Inf, Co E; ref: 1, 1622
SCHARF, John Thomas; Midn, Navy; C.S.S. Patrick Henry; res: Balt; ref: 1, 2, 19, 21, 58, 61, 69, 97, 110, 244, 316, 443, 469, 527, 560, 604, 612, 631, 658, 700, 735, 783, 787, 817, 818, 823, 1136, 1138, 1310, 1464, 1520, 1564, 1632
SCHAUB, Henry; pvt; 2nd MD Cav, Co E; ref: 1, 19, 1609
SCHECKELL, William; pvt; 1st VA Inf, Co E; ref: 735
SCHEESLER, Henry; pvt; 4th MD Lt Arty; ref: 1, 2, 19, 1601
SCHELL, Joseph (M.D.); pvt; 1st VA Cav, Co G; res: Frederick, Frd cty; ref: 1, 18, 89, 502, 735
SCHELL, W. Horace; lmn, Navy; Naval Brigade, Co D; ref: 1, 91
SCHENBERGER, John F.; pvt; 2nd MD Lt Arty; res: Balt; ref: 1, 2, 19, 21
SCHILLING, George Barnhardt; cpl; 23rd VA Inf, Co K; res: Balt; MLCSH; ref: 627, 786
SCHINDEL, S. Milford; Cav; res: Wash Cty; ref: 361
SCHLEY, Lake R.; pvt; 1st MD Inf, Co H; res: Dor Cty; ref: 1, 2, 19, 21, 269, 559, 650, 690, 711, 791, 1511, 1520
SCHLEY, Tench; Capt; Q.M., Dept of Army of Northern Virginia; res: Frd Cty; ref: 1, 90, 643, 791
SCHLEY, William C.; Lt; Signal Corps; res: Balt; ref: 1, 2, 14, 19, 735, 803, 1335, 1523
SCHLIEPHAKE, Henry T.; pvt; 1st MD Inf, Co H; ref: 1, 2, 19, 21, 650
SCHLINE, Charles; pvt; 8th TX Inf, Co G; res: McPhersons Pack, AA Cty; ref: 1, 1539
SCHLUPHAKE, Henry F.; pvt; Barry's Co, MD Vols; ref: 1, 503
SCHMIDT, Peter; sgt; 3rd LA Inf, Co A; ref: 1, 735
SCHMITT, John; pvt; Keys Battery, AR Lt Arty; ref: 1, 735
SCHNEKBERGER, Adam; pvt; 1st SC Inf, Co G; ref: 1
SCHNIDER, George W.; sgt; 2nd MD Cav, Co D; res: Balt; ref: 1, 19, 1609
SCHOLL, Charles E.; sgt; 35th VA Cav, Co B; res: Monocacy, Mont Cty; ref: 1, 2, 3, 15, 19, 21, 1552, 1611, 1677

SCHOLL, Lewis Juliun; pvt; 5th LA Inf, Co A; res: McPhersons Pack, AA Cty; ref: 1, 1539

SCHOLL, John H.; sgt; 35th VA Cav, Co B; res: Monocacy, Mont Cty; ref: 1, 2, 3, 19, 21, 23, 1552, 1611, 1621, 1677

SCHOOLFIELD, L. H.; smn, Navy; C. S. Webb; res: Balt; ref: 1, 19, 21, 684, 700, 783, 1494, 1613

SCHOOLS, James I.; pvt; VA Inf, Co C; ref: 1, 93

SCHOPPERT, John H.; pvt; 2nd MD Cav, Co D; ref: 1, 19, 1334, 1609

SCHULBAK, William F.; sgt; MD American Rifles; ref: 1, 2, 19, 312, 1613

SCHULL, John; pvt; 1st VA Cav, Co K; ref: 2, 19, 21

SCHULTER, John; pvt; Lucas' 15th SC Heavy Arty; res: Balt; ref: 1

SCHULTZ, Henry; sgt; 1st SC Inf, Co D; res: Balt; MLCSH; ref: 1, 21, 93, 627, 700, 735, 786

SCHULTZ, Justus; pvt; Barry's Co MD Vols; ref: 1, 2, 19

SCHUMACHER, Lomall; pvt; Holbrook's Independent MD Lt Arty; res: Patuxent, AA Cty; ref: 1, 1539

SCHWAKE, Henry; res: Elk Ridge Landing, AA Cty; ref: 1539

SCHWAN, Francis; pvt; 3rd MD Lt Arty; ref: 1, 2, 19, 21, 160, 726

SCHWARAR, John (Revd); Chaplain; Army of Tennessee; res: Annapolis, AA Cty; ref: 70

SCHWARTZ, Augustus F.; Capt; 1st MD Cav, Co F; res: Balt; ref: 1, 2, 19, 21, 23, 64, 68, 240, 412, 462, 511, 611, 631, 638, 684, 758, 1027, 1523

SCHWARTZMAN, G. A.; Maj; Gen G. W. C. Lee's staff; erf: 21, 700, 791

SCKAM, Thomas; 1st KY; ref: 735

SCLEIGH, Lake; res: Dor Cty; ref: 112

SCOTT, Amos B.; pvt; 31st GA Inf, Co B; res: Frederick, Frd Cty; ref: 1, 89

SCOTT, Channing M.; sgt; 2nd MD Cav, Co B; ref: 1, 19, 21, 93, 462, 693, 700, 1609

SCOTT, Charles A.; pvt; 1st MD Inf, Co C; res: Balt; ref: 1, 2, 19, 21, 1540

SCOTT, Cooper B.; drummer; 1st SC Inf, Co G; ref: 1, 800

SCOTT, George; pvt; Rhett's 1st SC Heavy Arty; res: How Cty; ref: 1, 2, 10, 19, 21, 735

SCOTT, George F.; cpl; Hampton Leg Lt Arty, Co B; ref: 1, 2, 19, 21, 23

SCOTT, Henry C. (M.D.); Asst Surg; Jackson Hospital, Richmond; res: Balt; ref: 1, 2, 18, 19, 21, 685, 1523, 1534

SCOTT, John Emory; pvt; 12th VA Inf, Co E; res: Balt; ref: 1, 2, 19, 21, 1529, 1540, 1689

SCOTT, John White; sgt; 21st VA Inf, Co B; res: Balt; ref: 1, 2, 19, 21, 23, 57, 70, 92, 312, 592, 631, 681, 700, 735, 916, 1520, 1540

SCOTT, Robert M. K.; pvt; 2nd TX Inf, Co A; res: Mont Cty; MLCHS; ref: 1, 735, 786

SCOTT, Tarlton W.; pvt; 9th VA Inf, Co B; ref: 1, 1576

SCOTT, Thomas H.; pvt; 1st MD Lt Arty; res: Port Tobacco, Cha Cty; ref: 1, 2, 19, 21

SCOTT, W. H.; pvt; Jacobs Mounted Riflemen; ref: 1

SCROGGINS, Daniel; pvt; 19th VA Heavy Arty, Co C; ref: 1, 2, 19, 21, 1580

SCULLY, Patrick; pvt; 2nd MD Cav, Co F; res: Balt; ref: 1, 2, 19, 21, 1609

SEABET, August; pvt; Marine Corps; C.S.S. Fredericksburg; res: Balt; ref: 1, 1594

SEABRIGHT, Jonathan; Lt; 3rd Bn, VA Valley, Co A; res: Balt; ref: 1, 1540

SEACCOMB, Thomas; pvt; 1st KY Inf, Co D; res: Balt; MLCSH; ref: 700, 786

SEAMAN, William C.; pvt; 13th VA Inf, Co G; res: Balt; ref: 1, 92, 93, 735

SEARL, Samuel; pvt; 1st MD Inf, Co G; ref: 1, 2, 19, 21
SEARS, Charles E.; Col; North Carolina Troops; res: Tal Cty; ref: 19, 645, 1152
SEARS, De Witt Clinton; pvt; Richmond Howitzers, 1st Co; res: Balt; MLCSH; ref: 1, 627, 700, 786
SEAWRIGHT, William L.; pvt; 3rd MD Lt Arty; ref: 1, 2, 19, 21, 160, 726, 1460
SEDDEN, Frank; pvt; 2nd MD Cav, Co C; res: Caro Cty; ref: 1, 19
SEIGNOR, Thomas; pvt; 1st VA Cav, Co K; ref: 2, 19, 21
SEITHERN, Jacob; pvt; MD Guerrilla Zouaves; ref: 1
SELBY, James; cpl; 21st VA Inf, Co B; res: Annapolis, AA Cty; ref: 1, 2, 19, 312, 681, 690, 735, 1540, 1628
SELBY, John; pvt; 1st MD Inf, Co I; ref: 1, 2, 19, 21
SELBY, Joseph; Lt; 30th VA Sharpshooter Inf, Co E; res: Annapolis, AA Cty; ref: 1, 2, 19, 64, 312, 681, 1520, 1540, 1628
SELDEN, Robert T.; pvt; 3rd VA Cav, Co B; res: Balt; MLCSH; ref: 1, 21, 56, 700, 786, 873
SELDEN, W. A.; sgt; Marine Signal Corps; ref: 1, 14, 21, 700, 783, 1515, 1594
SELLERS, Charles; pvt; 13th VA Inf, Co G; ref: 1
SELLES, Henry; pvt; 13th VA Inf, Co G; ref: 1
SELLMAN, Alonzo; sgt; 35th VA Cav, Co B; res: Old Medley's, Mont Cty; ref: 3, 15, 70, 106, 1386, 1552, 1611, 1677
SELLMAN, Frank; res: Frd Cty; ref: 19, 90
SELLMAN, Henry Clay; pvt; 35th VA Cav; res: Mont Cty; ref: 1, 3, 15, 73, 1611, 1677
SELLMAN, James C., Jr; pvt; 1st MD Inf, Co C; res: Balt; ref: 1, 19, 1523, 1540, 1635
SELLMAN, John Poole; pvt; 1st VA Cav, Co K; res: Barnesville, Mont Cty; ref: 1, 2, 19, 21, 86, 106, 557, 685, 718, 1386, 1552, 1578, 1579
SELLMAN, Wallace; pvt; 35th VA Cav, Co B; res: Old Medley's, Mont Cty; ref: 19, 70, 106, 577, 1386, 1552, 1579, 1611
SELLMAN, William; pvt; 22nd MS Inf, Co B; ref: 1, 93
SELVAGE, Edwin; cpl; 1st MD Cav, Co D; res: Frd Cty; ref: 1, 2, 19, 21, 23, 38, 456, 488, 700, 923, 1301, 1540, 1601
SEMMES, Alexander Jenkins (M.D.); Senior Surg; Medical Examing Board, Jackson Hospital, Richmond; res: Carr Cty; ref: 1, 18, 316, 785
SEMMES, Charles W.; orderly sgt; Davidson's Co, VA Lt Arty; res: Bt Cty; MLCSH; ref: 1, 19, 21, 700, 735, 786
SEMMES, Floyd Robert; ref: 685
SEMMES, Francis X.; pvt; 2nd MD Inf, Co B; ref: 2, 19, 21, 470, 1523
SEMMES, H. F.; pvt; 2nd MD Inf, Co B; ref: 2, 19, 21
SEMMES, Lewis S.; pvt; 2nd MD Inf, Co B; ref: 1, 2, 19, 21
SEMMES, Oliver Joseph; Capt; 1st Battery, Confederate Lt Arty; ref: 1, 721, 791
SEMMES, P. Warfield; Capt; 2nd Regt, Engineers; res: Georgetown; ref: 1578
SEMMES, Raphael; Rear Admiral, Navy; res: Cha Cty; ref: 1, 2, 18, 19, 23, 24, 26, 30, 39, 50, 58, 59, 61, 64, 68, 97, 107, 109, 110, 127, 130, 135, 137, 148, 165, 166, 206, 209, 270, 271, 272, 274, 275, 276, 277, 278, 279, 280, 281, 285, 313, 340, 349, 372, 431, 510, 511, 516, 559, 601, 602, 616, 631, 674, 684, 686, 713, 716, 717, 721, 723, 735, 791, 792, 819, 822, 828, 857, 867, 917, 948, 1030, 1033, 1036, 1041, 1067, 1136, 1143, 1165, 1279, 1291, 1317, 1324, 1336, 1340, 1354, 1396, 1397, 1401, 1404, 1416, 1431, 1472,

1493, 1523, 1528, 1564, 1568, 1570, 1571, 1577, 1578, 1579, 1582, 1583, 1615, 1616, 1617, 1620, 1623, 1632, 1639, 1673, 1674, 1676, 1685

SEMMES, Raphael, Jr; Midn, Navy; C.S.S. Patrick Henry; res: Cha Cty; ref: 1, 279, 556, 717, 721, 1564

SEMMES, Robert; Stuart's Horse Cav; res: Cha Cty; ref: 26

SEMMES, Samuel Spencer; Capt; Q.M., 1st LA Inf; ref: 1, 556, 717, 721, 791, 1523

SENGSTOCK, Charles P.; Lt; Ordnance Dept; ref: 1

SEPTER, John H.; pvt; 2nd MD Inf, Co D; res: Emmitsburg, Frd Cty; ref: 1, 2, 19, 21, 90

SERPELL, G. M.; cpl; 1st MD Cav, Co B; res: PG Cty; ref: 1, 2, 19, 21, 23, 785

SERVIS, Thomas Browne; 2nd MD Cav; res: Balt; ref: 70

SETH, Joseph B.; res: Tal Cty; ref: 1152, 1162, 1370

SETTLE, Josiah T.; pvt; Kirkpatrick's VA Battery; MLCSH; ref: 93, 786

SEVERE, Francis M.; pvt; 12th AL Inf, Co I; res: Balt; MLCSH; ref: 1, 19, 21, 700, 783, 786, 1609, 1620

SEVERE, John O.; pvt; 59th VA Inf, Co I; res: Tal Cty; MLCSH; ref: 1, 21, 700, 735, 796

SEVERING, Lewis; LA Washington Lt Arty; ref: 735

SEWALL, James W.; pvt; 35th VA Cav, Co F; res: Cal Cty; ref: 1, 760, 1677

SEWARD, George H.; pvt; 2nd MD Cav, Co C; res: Balt; ref: 1, 19

SEWARD, George W.; pvt; Lucus' 15th SC Heavy Arty; res: Balt; MLCSH; ref: 1, 700, 786

SEWELL, Brice B.; Lt; 32nd TX Cav, Co K; res: Annapolis, AA Cty; ref: 1, 1539

SEWELL, George W.; Capt; 3rd Bn, Richmond Defense, Co H; MLCSH; ref: 1,786

SEWELL, Joseph; pvt; 31st NC Inf, Co G; res: South River, AA Cty; ref: 1, 1539

SEWELL, Samuel T.; pvt; Lee's MD Cav; res: South River, AA Cty; ref: 1, 1539

SEWELL, Thomas H.; cpl; 17th NC Inf, Co C; res: South River, AA Cty; ref: 1, 1539

SEXSMITH, Truman; pvt; 2nd MD Cav, Co C; ref: 1, 19

SEXTON, Charles; pvt; 1st SC Inf, Co G; ref: 1

SEYMOUR, Charles L.; sgt; Stuart's Horse Arty, Breathed's Battery; ref: 1, 498

SHACKELFORD, George; pvt; 21st VA Inf, Co B; ref: 1, 2, 19, 312, 735

SHACKLEFORD, Durand; pvt; 43rd VA Cav (Mosby's), Co E; ref: 1, 8, 1579

SHACKLEFORD, Elzey D.; pvt; 43rd VA Cav (Mosby's), Co E; ref: 8

SHACKLETT, Henry; prv; 7th VA Cav, Co G; ref: 1

SHAEFFER, George W.; pvt; 2nd MD Lt Arty; ref: 1, 2, 19, 21

SHAEFFER, Henry; pvt; 1st MD Inf, Co E; ref: 1, 2, 19, 21

SHAEFFER, William; pvt; 2nd MD Lt Arty; ref: 1, 2, 19

SHAFER, Cornelius L.; pvt; 1st MD Cav, Co D; res: Cooksville, How Cty; ref: 1, 2, 10, 19, 21, 1550, 1601

SHAFER, Henry; pvt; LA Zouave Bn, Co F; ref: 1, 2, 19

SHAFER, John S.; pvt; 4th MD Lt Arty; res: Har Cty; ref: 1, 19

SHAFER, Thomas H.; pvt; 1st MD Cav, Co D; ref: 1, 2, 19, 21, 1601

SHAFFER, Benjamin B.; pvt; 31st VA Inf, Co A; ref: 1, 735

SHAFFER, George W.; pvt; 2nd MD Cav, Co A; ref: 1, 19, 866

SHAFFER, John O.; pvt; Lucus' 15th SC Heavy Arty; res: Balt; ref: 1

SHAFFER, John W.; pvt; 24th VA Cav, Co F; ref: 1, 735

SHAKERS, John; res: How Cty; ref: 10

SHALL, J. C.; pvt; 1st MD Inf, Co A; ref: 1
SHALTON, R. H.; 2nd MD Lt Arty; ref: 93
SHANDLEY, Patrick; pvt; 20th GA Inf, Co I; res: Balt; MLCSH; ref: 1, 21, 700, 786
SHANKS, Daniel; Capt; Stuart's Horse Arty; res: Miles Twn, St. M. Cty; ref: 1, 2, 19, 21, 23, 64, 68, 443, 498, 511, 650, 791, 1509, 1555, 1627, 1666
SHANKS, James L.; cpl; 9th VA Inf, Co A; ref: 1, 456
SHANKS, Morris; pvt; Steuart's Horse Arty, Shanks Battery; res: Balt; ref: 1, 19, 21, 511, 700
SHANLEY, Thomas E.; pvt; 2nd MD Inf, Co A; res: Balt; ref: 1, 2, 19, 21, 70, 700
SHANLEY, Timothy; pvt; 1st MD Cav, Co B; ref: 1
SHANNACY, Patrick; Elk Ridge Landing, AA Cty; ref: 1539
SHANNAHAN, John H. K.; pvt; 4th MD Lt Arty; res: Tal Cty; ref: 1, 2, 19, 21, 645, 1162, 1163, 1612
SHANNON, Charles K.; Capt; 1st VA Inf, Co E; ref: 2, 19
SHANNON, Michael; pvt; 1st MD Inf, Co E; ref: 1, 2, 19, 21
SHANNON, Samuel D.; Capt; Asst I.G.; Gen R. H. Anderson's staff; MLCSH; ref: 93, 700, 786, 791
SHARKEY, S.; pvt; 2nd MD Lt Arty; ref: 1, 2, 19, 21
SHARKEY, William; pvt; 2nd MD Lt Arty; ref: 1
SHARP, Henry T. (Revd); pvt; Independent Signal Corps, Army of Northern Virginia; ref: 57, 513, 891, 916, 1001, 1058
SHARP, J.; pvt; 2nd MD Cav, Co D; ref: 1, 19, 1609
SHAVER, John; pvt; Stuart's Horse Arty, Breathed's Battery; ref: 1
SHAW, J. C.; pvt; 2nd MD Lt Arty; ref: 1, 2, 19, 21
SHAW, J. Emmett, Lt; 8th GA Inf, Co E; ref: 1, 735, 791
SHAW, James C.; sgt; Davis's MD Cav, Co B; ref: 1
SHAW, John; pvt; 2nd MD Cav, Co G; ref: 1, 19, 735, 1609
SHAW, Peter; pvt; 2nd MD Lt Arty; ref:1, 2, 19
SHEA, Thomas; pvt; 13th NC Inf, Co I; ref: 1, 735
SHEA, Timothy; pvt; 3rd MD Lt Arty; ref: 1, 2, 19, 21, 160, 726
SHEAN, Michael H.; pvt; 2nd MD Cav, Co B; ref: 1, 19, 1609
SHEANHAN, George H.; Midn, Navy; ref: 1
SHEARER, George M. E.; Capt; Davis's MD Cav, Co D; res: Frederick, Frd Cty; ref: 1, 2, 19, 21, 23, 64, 65, 68, 88, 89, 90, 456, 488, 700, 740, 791, 923, 1609
SHECKELL, Marinus; pvt; 1st VA Inf, Co E; res: Georgetown; ref: 1, 316
SHECKELLS, Richard H.; pvt; Lucas' 15th SC Heavy Arty; res: Balt; ref: 1
SHEEAN, James John; pvt; 2nd MD Cav, Co D; res: Millington, Kt Cty; ref: 1, 19, 1551, 1609
SHEEDY, Daniel; pvt; 2nd MD Inf, Co E; ref: 1, 2, 19, 21, 93
SHEEHAN, Edward; cpl; 1st MD Inf, Co F; res: Balt; MLCSH; ref: 1, 2, 19, 21, 23, 93, 786
SHEEHAN, William; pvt; 1st MD Inf, Co G; ref: 1, 2, 19, 21
SHEEKS, Edward A.; pvt; 2nd KY Cav, Co D; res: Balt; MLCSH; ref: 786
SHEELER, William; Artificer; Stuart's Horse Arty, Breathed's Battery; ref: 1, 498
SHEEON, Michael H.; pvt; Lucas' 15th SC Heavy Arty; ref: 1
SHEERWOOD, Isaac; pvt; 39th VA Inf, Co H; res: Balt; ref: 1, 1540
SHEETS, Edward Adolphus; pvt; 2nd KY Cav, Co D; res: Balt; MLCSH; ref: 93, 627, 700
SHEIL, Michael; pvt; 2nd MD Lt Arty; ref: 1, 2, 19
SHEKEL, Marenus W.; pvt; 2nd MD Cav, Co C; res: Georgetown; ref: 1, 19
SHELDON, David I.; pvt; Marine Corps, Co C; ref: 1, 73, 1529, 1594

SHELL, Horace E.; pvt; 1st MD Cav, Co D; res: Frederick, Frd Cty; ref: 1, 2, 19, 21, 90, 1601
SHELL, William; pvt; 2nd MD Cav, Co C; ref: 1, 19
SHELLMAN, George K.; Lt; 1st MD Inf, Co A; res: Frederick, Frd Cty; MLCSH; ref: 1, 2, 19, 21, 23, 64, 66, 67, 72, 89, 72, 89, 90, 92, 93, 456, 700, 786, 791
SHEMIRCANT, Peter; res: Sourth River, AA Cty; ref: 1539
SHENLY, Patrick; pvt; 2nd MD Inf, Co E; ref: 1
SHEPARD, Seth (Hon.); 5th TX Cav, Co F; res: Georgetown; ref: 1, 316
SHEPHERD, Henry E.; Capt; 43rd NC Inf; res: Balt; ref: 21, 57, 62, 70, 272, 700, 816, 936, 994, 1172, 1182, 1186, 1189, 1191, 1195, 1196, 1249, 1250, 1252, 1256, 1261, 1264, 1270, 1343, 1350, 1375, 1384, 1445
SHEPHERD, James T.; Lt; Stuart's Horse Arty, Breathed's Battery; ref: 1, 791
SHEPHERD, Richard H.; pvt; 2nd MD Inf, Co D; res: AA Cty; ref: 1, 2, 19, 21, 23, 470, 1523
SHEPHERD, Thomas R.; sgt; 8th VA Cav, Co I; res: Davidsonville, AA Cty; ref: 1, 93
SHEPPARD, Samuel R.; cpl; 3rd MD Lt Arty; ref: 1, 2, 19, 21, 23, 160, 726
SHEPPERD, Abe; pvt; Lee's MD Cav; ref: 1, 3
SHEPPERD, Thomas L.; pvt; 7th VA Cav, Co G; res: Bt Cty; ref: 1, 3
SHERBERT, Augustus H.; pvt; MD Guerrilla Zouaves; res: Bristol, AA Cty; ref: 1, 1539
SHERBERT, Leonard; res: St. Margarett, AA Cty; ref: 1539
SHERBURNE, William L.; pvt; 1st MD Lt Arty; ref: 1, 2, 19, 21, 34, 782, 791, 1273
SHERIFF, Benjamin R.; smn, Navy; C.S.S. Virginia; ref: 19, 58, 97, 735
SHERLER, H.; pvt; 1st MD Cav, Co D; ref: 1, 19
SHERLOCK, Thomas; pvt; 1st SC Cav, Co E; res: Annapolis, AA Cty; ref: 1, 1539
SHERMAN, Charles K.; Capt; 1st VA Inf, Co E; res: Bladensburg; ref: 1, 316, 735, 791
SHERMAN, Charles S.; pvt; 1st VA Inf, Co E; ref: 735
SHERMAN, Robert T.; pvt; 1st MD Inf, Co B; ref: 1, 2, 19, 21
SHERRINGTON, Henry W.; pvt; 1st MD Inf, Co E; ref: 1, 2, 19, 21
SHERRY, Charles; pvt; 1st MD Cav, Co F; ref: 1, 2, 19, 21
SHERRY, James; 1st SC Inf, Co G; ref: 1
SHERRY, Patrick; pvt; 13th VA Inf, Co G; res: Balt; ref: 1, 1540, 1613
SHERWIN, Thomas; pvt; 1st VA Cav, Co K; ref: 1, 2, 19, 21, 827, 1579
SHERWOOD, Isaac N.; sgt; 2nd MD Inf, Co D; res: Balt; ref: 1, 2, 19, 21, 23, 470, 1523
SHERWOOD, James; pvt; 17th VA Inf, Co F; ref: 1, 735
SHERWOOD, William W.; cpl; 17th VA Inf, Co F; ref: 1, 735
SHESHAN, William F.; pvt; 35th VA Cav, Co B; ref: 1, 3, 15, 371, 1677
SHESSLER, Henry; pvt; Holbrook's Independent Lt Arty; ref: 1, 2, 19, 21
SHETKINS, John; pvt; 2nd MD Inf, Co G; ref: 2, 19, 21
SHICKELS, Ezra R. W.; pvt; Davis''s MD Cav; res: Annapolis, AA Cty; ref: 1, 70, 1539
SHIELDS, James J.; sgt; 1st Md Inf, Co G; res: Balt; ref: 1, 2, 19, 21, 23
SHIELDS, Luke; pvt; Barry's Co, MD Vols; res: Princeland, AA Cty; ref: 1, 1539
SHIELDS, Michael; pvt; 4th MD Lt Arty; res: Balt; ref: 1, 2, 19
SHIELDS, Owen; pvt; 2nd MD Inf, Co E; ref: 1, 2, 19, 21
SHIERBORN, William; pvt; 1st MD Inf, Co I; ref: 1, 2, 19, 21

SHIERS, George E.; Capt; 2nd MD Cav, Co D; ref: 1, 19
SHILLING, George; cpl; 5th TX Inf, Co D; ref: 1, 700
SHINBURNE, W. L.; pvt; 1st MD Lt Arty; ref: 1, 2, 19, 21
SHIPLETT, P.; pvt; 1st MD Cav, Co C; ref: 1, 2, 19, 21
SHIPLEY, Albert E.; pvt; Davis's MD Cav, Co B; res: How Cty; ref: 1, 19
SHIPLEY, Charles M.; pvt; 2nd KY Mounted Inf, Co D; Bt Cty; ref: 1, 735
SHIPLEY, Columbus; pvt; 36th AR Inf, Co H; res: Princeland, AA Cty; ref: 1, 1539
SHIPLEY, E. George; pvt; Edelin's MD Heavy Arty; res: Princeland, AA Cty; ref: 1, 1539
SHIPLEY, Elmond; sgt; 17th VA Cav, Co F; res: How Cty; ref: 1, 10, 19, 748
SHIPLEY, George R.; pvt; 3rd MD Lt Arty; ref: 1, 2, 19, 21, 160, 461, 726
SHIPLEY, Joshua; pvt; 2nd MD Cav, Co A; res: Balt; ref: 1, 19
SHIPLEY, R. A.; res: Elk Ridge Landing, AA Cty; ref: 1539
SHIPLEY, Samuel T.; pvt; 59th TN Mounted Inf, Co F; res: Hoods Mill, How Cty; ref: 1, 10, 748, 1550
SHIPLEY, Samuel J.; pvt; 1st MD Cav, Co A; ref: 1, 2, 19, 21, 791
SHIPLEY, Thomas Benton; sgt; 43rd VA Cav (Mosby's), Co E; res: AA Cty; ref: 1, 8, 1539
SHIPLEY, Theodore; pvt; 61st TN Mouted Inf, Co E; res: Elk Ridge Landing, AA Cty; ref: 1, 1539
SHIPLEY, William H.; pvt; 2nd MD Inf, Co C; res: New Market, Frd Cty; ref: 1, 2, 19, 21, 67, 72, 73, 74, 89, 90, 784
SHMELZ, John; pvt; 1st SC Inf, Co G; res: Balt; ref: 735
SHOCK, W. G.; pvt; 2nd MD Lt Arty; res: Balt; ref: 1, 2, 19, 21
SHOCKLEY, H. B.; pvt; 1st MD Cav, Co E; res: Wor Cty; ref: 1, 730
SHOCKNEY, Samuel; pvt; 1st MD Inf, Co B; ref: 1, 2, 19, 21
SHAE, Thomas; Oliver; pvt; MD Guerrilla Zouaves; ref: 1
SHOE, William H.; cpl; 9th VA Inf, Co B; res: Balt; ref: 1, 735, 1576
SHOEMAKER, Newton; pvt; 50th GA Inf, Co I; ref: 1, 93
SHOEMAKER, William L.; pvt; 64th VA Cav , Co H; res: Georgetown; ref: 1, 316
SHOEMAKER, ---; 1690
SHOEMAKER, ---; 1690
SHOOKS, Justice; pvt; Barry's Co, MD Vols; res: McPherson's Pack, AA Cty; ref: 1, 1539
SHORB, Donald McM.; pvt; 1st MD Cav, Co C; res: Frd Cty; ref: 1, 2, 19, 21
SHORB, Joseph Casnac; cpl; Hardy's Heavy Arty, No. 4; res: Emmitsburg, Frd Cty; MLCSH; ref: 1, 2, 21, 23, 627, 735
SHORE, Eugene; pvt; 13th VA Inf, Co G; ref: 1
SHORT, James; pvt; 3rd MD Lt Arty; ref: 1, 2, 19, 21, 160, 726
SHORT, William; pvt; MD American Rifles; res: Millersville, AA Cty; ref: 1, 1539
SHORTER, Thomas O.; pvt; 1st MD Inf, Co I; ref: 1, 2, 19, 21
SHOW, Joseph; pvt; 1st VA Cav, Co K; ref: 1, 2, 19, 21
SHOWERS, George Theodore (M.D.); pvt; 1st MD Cav, Co D; res: Manchester, Carr Cty; ref: 1, 2, 18, 19, 21, 70, 720, 1318, 1488, 1601
SHREVE, Daniel T.; pvt; 6th VA Cav, Co K; res: Mont Cty; ref: 1, 73, 86, 1677
SHRIVER, Anthony; Lt; 77th VA Militia, Richmond Defense, Co C; res: Carr Cty; ref: 1, 19, 21, 40, 65, 70, 95, 148, 791
SHRIVER, B. Frank; pvt; Lee's MD Cav; res: Carr Cty; ref: 1, 40
SHRIVER, Charles Eltinge; pvt; 43rd VA Cav (Mosby's), Co B; res: Park

Mills, Frd Cty; ref: 8, 72, 258, 643, 735
SHRIVER, Christopher Columbus; sgt; 3rd VA Inf, Co I; res: Carr Cty; ref: 1, 19, 21, 40, 700
SHRIVER, Daniel; pvt; Lee's MD Cav; res: Carr Cty; ref: 1, 40
SHRIVER, J. Henry; res: Cumberland, All Cty; ref: 19, 65, 95, 148
SHRIVER, John H.; pvt; 1st LA Cav, Co F; res: Cumberland, All Cty; ref: 1, 19, 65, 95, 148
SHRIVER, Keiser; pvt; Barry's Co, MD Vols; res: Carr Cty; ref: 1, 19, 40, 70
SHRIVER, Mark O.; pvt; 1st VA Cav, Co K; res: Carr Cty; ref: 1, 2, 19, 21, 23, 40, 70, 488, 700, 848, 849, 866, 906, 923, 1058
SHRIVER, O. Columbus; pvt; Lee's Balt Lt Arty, Alexander's Bn; res: Carr Cty; ref: 1, 40
SHRIVER, Thomas Herbert; pvt; V.M.I. Cadet; res: Carr Cty; ref: 1, 19, 21, 40, 70, 735, 1687
SHROFF, Peter Franklin; pvt; 1st VA Cav, Co L; res: Fallston, Har Cty; ref: 1, 2, 19, 21, 87, 786
SHUCKS, J.; pvt; 1st MD Cav, Co C; ref: 1
SHUE, J. J.; pvt; 2nd MD Lt Arty; res: Balt; ref: 1, 2, 19, 21
SHULTZ, Justus; pvt; 2nd MD Inf, Co C; ref: 2, 19, 21
SHULTZ, William; pvt; 1st MD Cav, Co D; ref: 1, 2, 19, 21, 1601
SHUSTER, John M.; pvt; 1st MD Lt Arty; res: PG Cty; ref: 1, 2, 19, 21
SHUTT, Jonathan W.; pvt; Edelins' MD Heavy Arty; res: Balt; ref: 1, 1540
SIBET, J.; pvt; 2nd MD Cav, Co C; ref: 1, 19, 1609
SILAS, Daniel; pvt; 5th FL Inf, Co D; ref: 1, 2, 19, 21, 160, 726
SILAS, L.; pvt; 5th FL Inf, Co D; ref: 1, 2, 19, 160, 726
SILDELL, John; ref: 685
SILLY, P. S.; 12th VA Cav; res: Bt Cty; ref: 70
SILMON, Richard; pvt; 12th VA Cav, Co E; ref: 1
SILVER, S. M.; pvt; 3rd MD Lt Arty; ref: 2, 19, 21, 160, 726
SIMMES, Henry M.; pvt; 1st MD Inf, Co I; res: Doneotes, Cha Cty; ref: 1, 2, 19, 21, 1546
SIMMONS, Charles; pvt; MD Guerrilla Zouaves; res: Mont Cty; ref: 1, 1621
SIMMONS, Daniel S.; pvt; 4th NC, Co I; ref: 1, 21, 700
SIMMONS, J. Vernon; fmn, Navy; Drewy's Bluff; Park Mills, Frd Cty; ref: 1, 89, 90
SIMMONS, Jackson; cpl; 3rd MD Lt Arty; ref: 1, 2, 19, 21, 23, 160, 726, 1460
SIMMONS, W. E.; pvt; Wingfield's LA Cav, Co A; ref: 1, 93
SIMMS, Francis H.; pvt; 2nd MD Inf, Co B; res: Leonardtown, St. M. Cty; ref: 1, 2, 1509, 1555, 1627
SIMMS, John; pvt; 1st MD Inf, Co D; ref: 1, 2, 19, 21
SIMMS, Thomas Jamestown; cpl; 2nd MD Inf, Co B; res: Tompkinsville, Cha Cty; ref: 1, 2, 19, 21, 23, 69, 316, 1509
SIMMS, William H.; pvt; 2nd MD Inf, Co B; res: Leonardtown, St. M. Cty; ref: 1, 2, 7, 19, 21, 1555
SIMMS, Willis R.; pvt; 3rd MD Lt Arty; ref: 1, 2, 19, 21, 160, 726
SIMON, August; pvt; 1st MD Inf, Co D; res: Balt; ref: 1, 2, 19, 21, 23
SIMON, August G.; Maj; Commissary of Supply, Gen S. Price's staff; res: Balt; ref: 1, 2, 19, 488, 700, 735, 848, 866, 906, 923, 1058
SIMONDS, Albert; pvt; 1st MD Inf, Co E; res: Balt; ref: 1, 2, 19, 21
SIMONS, Albert; pvt; 1st MD Cav, Co D; res: Balt; ref: 1, 2, 19, 21, 1602
SIMPSON, Albert J.; pvt; 41st GA Inf, Co B; ref: 1, 700
SIMPSON, Edward B. (M.D); Asst Surg; Jackson Hospital, Richmond; res:

Libertytown, Frd Cty; ref: 1, 2, 18, 21, 90, 735, 1082, 1677
SIMPSON, George; pvt; 3rd MD Lt Arty; ref: 1, 2, 19, 21, 160, 726
SIMPSON, George L.; Medical Dept; ref: 75
SIMPSON, George R.; cpl; 1st MD Cav, Co D; res: Libertytown, Frd Cty; ref: 1, 2, 21, 19, 23, 90, 1601
SIMPSON, H. H.; pvt; 1st MD Inf, Co G; ref: 1, 2, 19, 21
SIMPSON, John A.; pvt; MD American Rifles; ref; 1, 92, 93, 559
SIMPSON, John French; pvt; 35th VA Cav, Co A; ref: 1, 3, 15, 19
SIMPSON, John T.; pvt; 1st MD Cav, Co E; res: PG Cty; ref; 1, 2, 19, 21, 730
SIMPSON, Joshua; pvt; 1st MD Inf, Co D; ref: 1, 2, 19, 21, 1511
SIMPSON, Nathaniel; pvt; 21st VA Inf, Co B; reff: 1, 2, 19, 312, 735
SIMPSON, William; res: Balt; ref: 7
SIMRALL, William S.; 8th KY Cav, Co B; ref; 70
SIMS, Charles E.; orderly sgt; Zarvona's MD Zouaves; ref: 1, 61, 703, 735
SIMS, John J.; pvt; 2nd MD Cav, Co B; res: Bt Cty; MLCSH; ref: 19, 21, 92, 93, 700, 735, 786
SIMS, Joseph; pvt; 1st MD Inf, Co B; ref: 2, 19, 21
SINCLAIR, John; pvt; 19th VA Heavy Arty, Co C; ref: 1, 19, 70, 1580
SINCLAIR, William Beverly (M.D.); Surg; New Orleans Naval Station; res: Balt; ref: 1, 2, 18, 19, 21, 700, 1534, 1564
SINCOE, A. A.; pvt; Barry's Co, MD Vols; ref: 1, 2, 19, 21
SINDALL, Henry S.; pvt; 1st MD Lt Arty; ref: 1, 2, 19, 21
SINDALL, Samuel W.; pvt; 1st MD Inf, Co H; res: Balt; ref: 1, 2, 19, 21, 249, 559, 650, 711, 1511, 1519
SINGER, G.; pvt; 3rd MD Lt Arty; ref: 2, 19, 21, 160, 726
SINGER, John G.; pvt; 31st GA Inf, Co E; ref: 1, 1149
SINGLETON, Thomas D.; pvt; 12th VA Cav, Co F; res: Mont Cty; ref: 1, 3, 735, 1574
SISSON, C.R.; pvt; Stuart's Horse Arty, Breathed's Battery; ref: 1, 498
SISSON, Christopher R.; pvt; 1st MD Cav, Co D; res: Bt Cty; ref: 1, 2, 19, 21, 1540, 1601
SISSON, Oscar B.; pvt; 1st VA Cav, Co K; res: Balt; ref: 1, 2, 19, 21, 1540
SKELTON, A. J.; pvt; Lucas' 15th SC Heavy Arty; ref: 1, 7
SKIDMORE, William S.; pvt; 9th VA Cav, Co A; res: Balt; ref: 1, 21, 53, 684, 700
SKINNER, Charles W.; Midn, Navy; C.S.S. Patrick Henry; ref: 1, 19, 21, 97, 700, 783
SKINNER, Frederick Gustavus; Col; 1st VA Inf; res: Annapolis, AA Cty; ref: 1, 21, 22, 100, 105, 116, 129, 146, 159, 289, 431, 518, 530, 601, 700, 735, 791, 842, 886, 1600, 1644
SKINNER, Levin D.; pvt; McClung's Battery, TN Lt Arty; ref: The Reserve, Cal Cty; ref: 1, 19, 760, 1523
SKINNER, William; pvt; 47th VA Inf, Co H; ref: 1
SKINNER, William Dorsey; pvt; 2nd MD Inf, Co C; res: Cal Cty; ref: 1, 2, 19, 21, 1523, 1579
SKAGGS, E. C.; pvt; 14th VA Cav, Co K; ref: 1, 21, 700
SLACK, T. A.; pvt; Stuart's Horse Arty, Breathed's Battery; ref: 1, 498
SLATER, George M., Jr; pvt; 43rd VA Cav (Mosby's), Co E; res: Balt; ref: 1, 2, 8, 19, 21, 735, 1313
SLATER, Henry B.; pvt; 43rd VA Cav (Mosby's), Co B; res: Balt; ref: 1, 8, 19, 69, 258, 261, 316, 601, 1571, 1578, 1579, 1654
SLATER, James F.; Lt; 4th MD Lt Arty; res: PG Cty; ref: 1, 1553
SLATER, John C.; pvt; 46th VA Inf, Co A; res: Balt; ref; 1, 21, 70, 700

SLATER, William J.; pvt; 1st MD Cav, Co c; ref: 1, 2, 19, 21
SLAUGHTER, Louis; pvt; Zarvona's MD Zouaves; res: Tal Cty; ref: 1, 19, 645, 735, 1612
SLAVEN, John W.; cpl; 1st MD Cav, Co E; ref: 1, 2, 19, 21, 23, 730
SLEEPACK, Henry Frederick; pvt; 3rd VA Inf, Co I; res: Bt Cty; MLCSH; ref: 1, 92, 93, 627, 700, 786
SLEEPER, Louis; pvt; 2nd MD Cav, Co C; ref: 1, 19, 1609
SLEIGHTON, Benjamin F.; pvt; Uttersback's Co, VA Lt Arty; ref: 1, 2, 19, 21
SLEMAKER, Janius S.; pvt; Hampton Leg Lt Arty, Co B; ref: 1, 2, 19, 21
SLEMBER, Benjamin; pvt; 17th BA Inf, Co I; ref: 1, 133, 142
SLINGLUFF, Fielder Cross; Lt; 1st MD Cav, Co F; res: Bt Cty; ref: 1, 2, 19, 21, 23, 36, 56, 64, 68, 70, 94, 233, 412, 469, 507, 684, 700, 881, 904, 1039, 1520, 1523, 1565, 1578
SLINGLUFF, John A.; pvt; 1st MD Cav, Co E; res: Bt Cty; MLCSH; ref: 1, 2, 19, 21, 70, 94, 730, 786, 1562
SLINGLUFF, Josiah H.; sgt; 1st MD Cav, Co F; res: Balt; ref: 1, 2, 19, 21, 23
SLINGLUFF, Truman; pvt; 1st MD Cav, Co C; res: Bt Cty; ref: 1, 19
SLINGLUFF, William H.; sgt; 1st MD Inf, Co D; res: Balt; ref: 1, 2, 19, 21, 23, 412
SLOAN, Charles H.; pvt; 1st MD Inf, Co C; res: Balt; ref: 1, 2, 19, 21, 1540
SLOAN, Edward O.; pvt; 1st MD Lt Arty; res: Balt; ref: 1, 2, 19, 21
SLOAN, John A.; pvt; Davis's MD Cav, Co C; ref: 1, 70
SMALL, Alexander S.; pvt; 12th VA Cav, Co A; res: All Cty; ref: 1, 1035
SMALL, Charles W.; pvt; 1st MD Inf, Co D; res: Balt; ref: 1, 2, 14, 19, 21, 53, 700
SMALL, George, Jr; pvt; 1st VA Cav, Co K; ref: 1, 2, 21, 690, 757
SMALL, James; smn, Navy; Naval Bn; res: Balt; ref: 1
SMALLEY, Anthony; pvt; 19th VA Heavy Arty, Co C; ref: 1, 1580
SMILEY, T. M.; sgt; 5th VA Inf, Co D; res: Frd Cty; ref: 1, 72
SMITH, A. Austin; pvt; 21st VA Inf, Co B; ref: 1, 2, 19, 312, 735
SMITH, Albert; pvt; 9th VA Inf, Co B; res: Sharpsburg, Wash Cty; ref; 1, 1558, 1576
SMITH, Allen P. (M.D.); Asst Surg; 21st FL Cav; ref: 1, 18
SMITH, Andrew J.; pvt; Rhett's 1st SC Heavy Arty; res: Balt; ref: 1, 21, 700, 1549
SMITH, Augustine Jaqualine; Capt; 31st VA Inf, Co C; res: Balt; ref: 1, 2, 19, 21, 93, 684, 700, 758, 866
SMITH, C. W.; pvt; 1st VA Cav, Co K; ref: 2, 19, 21
SMITH, Carroll; pvt; 2nd MD Lt Arty; ref: 1
SMITH, Channing M.; pvt; 4th VA Cav, Co H; res: Highland, How Cty; ref: 1, 71
SMITH, Charles; pvt; Lucas' 15th SC Heavy Arty; res: Balt; ref: 1
SMITH, Charles; pvt; 2nd MD Cav, Co G; ref: 1, 19, 1609
SMITH, Charles W.; pvt; 35th VA Cav, Co B; res: Poolesville, Mont Cyt; ref: 1, 3, 15, 1611, 1677
SMITH, Clay; smn, Navy; ref: 1, 55, 97, 1494
SMITH, Constant Freeman; Lt; 1st Engineer Corps, Co F; ref: 1, 316, 757
SMITH, Daniel; pvt; 1st MD Cav, Co A; res: Downsville, Wash Cty; ref; 1, 2, 19, 21, 1558
SMITH, E. T.; pvt.; 9th VA Cav, Co K; ref: 21, 700
SMITH, Edward; pvt; 2nd MD Cav, Co E; ref: 1, 19, 1609
SMITH, Edward; pvt; Maryland Guerrilla Zouaves; res: Balt; MLCSH; ref: 1, 786

SMITH, Edward T.; pvt; 55th VA, Co A; MLCSH; ref: 1, 786
SMITH, Elhandan Collia; pvt; 2nd VA Inf, Co B; res: Balt; MLCSH; ref: 1, 92, 93,627, 735, 786
SMITH, Elias; pvt; 1st SC Inf, Co G; ref: 1, 800
SMITH, Eugene; sgt; 2nd MD Inf, Co G; res: Princess Anne, Som Cty; ref: 1, 2, 21, 23, 1556
SMITH, Francis; pvt; 3rd MD Lt Arty; ref: 1, 2, 19, 21, 160, 511, 726
SMITH, Frank A.; 23rd VA; res: Balt; ref: 70
SMITH, Frank H.; pvt; 4th MD Lt Arty; ref: 1, 53
SMITH, Frederick H.; Capt; Nitre & Mining Corps, Army of Tennessee; res: Balt; ref: 1, 2, 19, 21, 56, 70, 684, 700
SMITH, George A.; sgt; 4th MD Lt Arty; res: Vienna, Dor Cty; ref: 1, 2, 19, 21, 112, 511, 700, 1547
SMITH, George H.; pvt; 25th VA Inf, Co F; res: St. M. Cty; ref: 1, 19, 21, 700, 1670
SMITH, George W.; pvt; Zarvona's MD Zouaves; ref: 1, 735
SMITH, H. R.; cpl; Stuart's Horse Arty, Breathed's Battery; ref: 1
SMITH, Hamilton Tillard; cpl; 2nd MD Inf, Annapolis, Co A; ref: 1, 2, 19, 21, 23, 92, 93, 470, 511, 650, 685, 1523, 1539
SMITH, Harry; pvt; 2nd MD Cav, Co D; ref: 1, 19, 1609
SMITH, Henry; pvt; Davis's MD Cav, Co A; ref: 735
SMITH, Henry Clay; pvt; 2nd MD Lt Arty; res: Balt; ref: 1, 2, 21, 511
SMITH, Henry M.; pvt; 3rd VA local Defense, Dillin's Co; res: PG Cty; ref: 69, 316
SMITH, J. J.; pvt; 1st MD Inf, Co E; ref: 1
SMITH, J. Louis; Capt; 1st MD Inf, Co F; res: Bt Cty; ref: 1, 2, 19, 21, 23, 38, 44, 64, 70, 240, 456, 511, 559, 693, 724, 753, 757, 791, 1511, 1578
SMITH, J. Nicholas; pvt; Marine Corps, Co F, Mobile Station; res: Doubs, Frd Cty; ref: 1, 90, 1573, 1594
SMITH, J. R.; pvt; 1st SC Inf, Co G; ref: 1
SMITH, J. S.; pvt; 3rd MD Lt Arty; ref; 2, 19, 21, 160, 511, 726
SMITH, J. W.; 3rd MD Lt Arty; ref: 1, 2, 19, 21, 23, 160, 511, 726
SMITH, James; pvt; 3rd MD Lt Arty; ref: 1, 2, 19, 21, 726
SMITH, James; pvt; 1st MD Cav, Co B; res: QA Cty; ref: 1, 2, 19, 21, 785
SMITH, James; gun, Navy; ref: 1, 19, 735, 791
SMITH, James Henley; pvt; 43rd VA Cav (Mosby's), Co D; res: Centreville, QA Cty; ref: 8, 1554, 1571, 1578, 1579, 1654
SMITH, James Henry; sgt; 2nd MD Lt Arty; res: Great Mills, St. M. Cty; ref: 1, 2, 19, 21, 23, 64, 160, 511, 601, 1509, 1555
SMITH, James T.; pvt; Davis's MD Cav, Co B; res: Balt; ref: 1
SMITH, Jeff; Lt; 2nd MD Cav, Co D; ref: 11, 511
SMITH, Jesse Rice; pvt; 35th VA Cav, Co B; res: Poolesville, Mont Cty; ref: 1, 3, 1611, 1677
SMITH, John; pvt; 19th VA Heavy Arty, Co C; res: Annapolis, AA Cty; ref: 1, 1539, 1580
SMITH, John; pvt; Stuart's Horse Arty, Breathed's Battery; ref: 1
SMITH, John; pvt; 2nd MD Cav, Co E; ref: 1, 1523, 1609
SMITH, John C. of Ezra; Lt; 1st MD Inf, Co A; res: Frd Cty; ref: 19, 89, 90, 511, 1635
SMITH, John Donnell; Capt; Lee's Balt Lt Arty; res: Balt; ref: 1, 2, 17, 19, 21, 23, 34, 69, 70, 105, 316, 469, 684, 685, 690, 700, 724, 791, 793, 1131, 1173, 1520, 1580, 1583, 1617, 1620
SMITH, John E.; pvt; 2nd MD Lt Arty; ref: 1, 2, 19, 21, 511, 1523
SMITH, John F.; pvt; Davis's MD Cav, Co A; ref: 1, 72

SMITH, John P.; pvt; 1st VA Cav, Co K; res: PG Cty; ref: 1, 2, 21, 69, 89, 316, 511

SMITH, John T.; pvt; 3rd MD Lt Arty; ref: 1, 2, 19, 21, 160, 511, 726

SMITH, John T.; Lt; Barry's MD Inf Vols; res: Frd Cty; ref: 1, 2, 19, 21, 23, 69, 72, 316, 456, 511

SMITH, Jon H.; pvt; Davis's MD Cav, Co C; ref: 1, 735

SMITH, Joseph; pvt; 1st SC Inf, Co G; ref: 1

SMITH, Joseph D.; pvt; 9th VA Inf, Co B; res: Balt; ref: 1, 1540, 1576

SMITH, Joseph E.; drummer; 2nd MD Inf; res: Cambridge, Dor Cty; ref: 1, 2, 19, 21, 23, 64, 93, 470, 511, 700, 1523, 1547

SMITH, K. B.; pvt; 30th VA Inf, Co C; ref: 1, 2, 19, 21

SMITH, Lewis J.; pvt; Stuart's Horse Arty, Breathed's Battery; res: Bt Cty; ref: 1, 1027, 1541

SMITH, P. D.; pvt; 1st MD Lt Arty; ref: 1, 470, 511

SMITH, Peter; pvt; 1st MD Cav, Co C; ref: 1, 19

SMITH, Peter Pierre, Jr; 2nd MD Inf, Co B; res: St. M. Cty; ref: 1, 2, 19, 21, 1509

SMITH, Pharis; pvt; 3rd MD Lt Arty; ref: 1, 2, 19, 21, 160, 511, 726

SMITH, Richard C.; cpl; 1st MD Cav, Co C; ref: 1, 2, 19, 21

SMITH, Robert Carter; Lt Col; Commanding Prison, Danville; res: Balt; ref: 1, 2, 19, 21, 23, 34, 38, 44, 56, 57, 64, 68, 69, 70, 222, 233, 240, 316, 456, 511, 559, 583, 638, 690, 700, 791, 825, 862, 873, 1037, 1251, 1511, 1523, 1600, 1635

SMITH, Robert Selden; pvt; 7th VA Cav, Co A; res: Balt; MLCSH; ref: 627, 700, 786

SMITH, Robert W.; pvt; ref: 1690

SMITH, S. Clapham; Lt; Asst A.G., Gen T. Rosser's staff; res: Balt; ref: 1, 3, 23

SMITH, S. D.; pvt; Davis's MD Cav, Co B; ref: 1, 2, 21

SMITH, Samuel D., Jr; Capt; Asst I.G., Gen J. Magruder's staff; res: Balt; ref: 1, 2, 19, 70, 793

SMITH, Samuel P.; cpl; 9th VA Inf, Co B; res: Balt; MLCSH; ref: 1, 19, 21, 93, 700, 786, 1576

SMITH, Seabury Dennison; pvt; 17th VA Inf, Co H; ref: 1, 19, 21, 70, 511, 700

SMITH, Simeon A.; pvt; 4th NC Inf Vols, Co K; res: Balt; MLCSH; ref: 1, 21, 700, 786

SMITH, T.; pvt; 1st SC Inf, Co G; ref: 1

SMITH, T. Jefferson; Lt; 7th VA Cav, Co G; res: Bt Cty; ref: 1, 2, 3, 19, 21, 64, 68, 70, 511, 791

SMITH, Thomas; pvt; 1st VA Inf, Co E; ref: 1, 628

SMITH, Thomas; pvt; 3rd MD Lt Arty; ref: 1, 2, 19, 21, 160, 511, 726

SMITH, Thomas B.; pvt; Lee's MD Cav; res: Balt; ref: 1, 21, 700, 735

SMITH, Thomas T.; pvt; 1st MD Cav, Co F; res: Balt; ref: 1, 2, 19, 21

SMITH, Thomas Washington; Lt; Barry's Co, MD Vols; res: Cec Cty; ref: 1

SMITH, Victor; Lt; Engineer Corps; res: Balt; ref: 21, 700, 791

SMITH, Virgil; pvt; 2nd MD Cav, Co D; ref: 1, 19

SMITH, W. J.; 12th TN Cav; ref: 93

SMITH, Walter George; pvt; Stuart's Horse Arty, Breated's Battery; res: Balt; ref: 1, 19, 21, 70, 498, 700, 1613

SMITH, Walter S.; pvt; 2nd MD Inf, Co F; res: Harrison, Dor Cty; ref: 21, 511, 700, 1547

SMITH, William; pvt; 2nd MD Cav, Co B; ref: 1

SMITH, William; pvt; 3rd MD Lt Arty; ref: 1, 2, 19, 21, 160, 511, 726, 1523

SMITH, William; pvt; 4th MD Lt Arty; ref: 1, 2, 19, 21, 511

SMITH, William F.; pvt; 21st VA Inf, Co B; res: Balt; ref: 1, 2, 19, 44, 312, 650, 735, 893, 1520

SMITH, William H.; sgt; 2nd MD Inf, Co A; res: Balt; ref: 1, 2, 19, 21, 23, 511, 650, 685, 700, 793, 1579, 1583
SMITH, William J.; pvt; 1st MD Cav, Co K; res: Queen Ann, AA Cty; ref: 1, 1539
SMITH, William P.; pvt; 2nd MD Lt Arty; res: St. M. Cty; ref: 1, 2, 19, 21, 511, 1509
SMITH, William Sidney; pvt; 2nd MD Inf, Co F; res: Princess Anne, Som Cty; ref; 1, 2, 19, 21, 1556
SMITH, William W.; pvt; 1st MD Inf, Co F; ref: 1, 2, 19, 21
SMITH, Wilson Cary; pvt; 1st MD Cav, Co C; res: Balt; ref: 1, 2, 19, 21, 70, 511, 756
SMOOT, Benjamin F.; pvt; 9th VA Inf, Co B; ref: 1, 1576
SMOOT, J. T.; pvt; 7th VA Cav, Co G; ref: 1
SMOOT, Joseph G.; pvt; 43rd VA Cav (Mosby's), Co F; ref: 1, 2, 8, 21, 1523
SMOOT, Luther Rice; Capt; Quartermaster Dept, Richmond Defense; ref: 1, 19
SMOOT, Samuel; pvt; 9th VA Inf, Co B; ref: 1, 735, 1576
SMOOT, W. F.; pvt; 43rd VA Cav (Mosby's), Co G; ref: 1, 8, 20
SMOOT, William; Henry; pvt; 15th VA Inf, Co H; ref: 1, 19
SMYTH, Thomas; pvt; 1st VA Inf, Co E; ref: 1, 735
SMYTH, William; sgt; 1st MD Inf, Co C; res: Balt; MLCSH; ref: 1, 2, 19, 21, 23, 700, 786
SNEAD, Charles W.; sgt; 19th VA Heavy Arty, Co B; res: Balt; ref: 1, 70
SNEAD, Samuel Wesley; pvt; 13th VA Cav, Co K; res: Balt; MLCSH; ref: 1, 21, 786
SNELLING, Z. H.; pvt; 9th VA Inf, Co B; ref: 1, 1576
SNIPES, R.; pvt; 3rd MD Lt Arty; ref: 2, 19, 21, 160, 726
SNIVELY, George T.; pvt; 2nd MD Cav, Co B; ref: 1, 1609
SNIVELY, Griffin B.; pvt; 2nd MD Cav, Co F; res: Bt Cty; ref: 1, 2, 19, 21, 1609
SNODGRASS, ---; pvt; 2nd MD Cav, Co C; ref: 2, 19, 21, 791
SNOOK, Jarome A.; pvt; 1st MD Cav, Co D; res: Frd Cty; ref: 1, 2, 19, 21, 1601
SNOUT, Klaber Augustus; bugler; 9th VA Cav; res: Balt; ref: 70
SNOVELL, D. M.; Lt; Richmond Local Defense, Maryland Co; ref: 1, 2, 17, 19, 21
SNOWDEN, Arthur Monteith (M.D.); Asst Surg, General Hospital, Staunton; res: Laurel, PG Cty; ref: 1, 18, 34, 69, 316, 511, 687
SNOWDEN, C. H.; Lt; 21st VA Inf, Co B; res: PG Cty; ref: 2, 312, 511, 1520
SNOWDEN, Charles Alexander; Maj; Cosby's Cav Brig; res: Laurel, PG Cty; ref: 34, 69, 316, 511, 687, 791
SNOWDEN, De Wilton (M.D.); Asst Surg; 2nd MD Inf; res: Laurel, PG Cty; ref: 1, 2, 18, 19, 21, 23, 63, 64, 68, 69, 316, 511, 687, 700, 791, 1523, 1533, 1634
SNOWDEN, Edward F.; pvt; 54th VA Inf, Co D; res: Laurel, PG Cty; ref: 1, 69, 511, 316
SNOWDEN, George T.; Capt; Davis's MD Cav, Co D; res: How Cty; ref: 1, 34, 511, 791, 1609
SNOWDEN, Gustavus Warfield; ref: 34, 511
SNOWDEN, John Captron; pvt; 1st MD Cav, Co C; res: PG Cty; MLCSH; ref: 1, 2, 19, 21, 70, 511, 627, 687, 700, 786
SNOWDEN, John Hudson; Lt; Aide de Camp, Gen L. Northrop's staff; res: Balt; ref: 1, 2, 19, 34, 511, 1578
SNOWDEN, Nicholas N.; Lt; 1st MD Inf, Co D; res: Laurel, PG Cty; ref: 1, 2, 13, 18, 19, 21, 23, 34, 64, 69, 93, 240, 316, 456, 501, 511, 559, 560, 687, 711, 791, 1511, 1523, 1553

SNOWDEN, Richard M.; Maj; Adj & Asst I.G., Gen L. Polk's staff; res: PG Cty; ref: 34, 69, 127, 316, 511, 791, 823
SNOWDEN, Thomas Heber; pvt; 13th NC Lt Arty, Co A; res: Balt; MLCSH; ref: 1, 627, 700, 786
SNOWDEN, William; pvt; MD Guerrilla Zouaves; res: Laurel Factory, AA Cty; ref: 1, 1539
SNYDER, Edward; pvt; 14th VA Inf, Co H; ref: 1, 735
SNYDER, J.; 92
SNYDER, Samuel; res: Frederick, Frd Cty; ref: 89
SNYDER, William F.; pvt; 13th VA Inf, Co G; ref: 1, 735
SOIECKE, Isidore A.; pvt; 2nd MD Cav, Co B; res: Balt; ref: 1, 2, 19, 21, 92, 93, 700, 1609
SOLANO, Philip G.; sgt maj; 5th FL Inf, Co C; ref: 1, 21
SOLLERS, Andrew Jackson; pvt; 2nd MD Inf, Co A; res: Balt; ref: 1, 2, 19, 21, 650, 1663
SOLLERS, James H.; pvt; 2nd MD Inf, Co F; res: Cha Cty; ref: 1, 2, 19, 21
SOLLERS, Somerville; pvt; 2nd MD Inf, Co A; res: Cal Cty; ref: 1, 2, 19, 21, 23, 70, 81, 493, 503, 511, 650, 700, 746, 760, 1058, 1663
SOLLERS, William O.; pvt; 1st MD Cav, Co D; res: Balt; MLCSH; ref: 1, 2, 19, 21, 92, 93, 511, 700, 786, 1663
SOLOMON, Samuel Lewis; mast. a., Navy; C. S. North Carolina; res: Balt; MLCSH; ref: 1, 19, 21, 58, 97, 700, 735, 783, 1494
SOMMERS, John; smn, Navy; C.S. Beauregard; res: Som Cty; ref: 1
SOMMERS, Samuel; pvt; Hampton Leg Lt Arty, Co B; ref: 1, 2, 19, 21
SORREL, William G.; pvt; 47th VA Inf, Co H; ref: 1
SOTHORN, M. L.; pvt; ref: 1690
SOTHORON, John H.; pvt; Edelin's MD Heavy Arty; res: St. M. Cty; ref: 1, 7, 511, 1523
SOTHORON, Marshall Lane; Paymaster, Navy; C.S.S. Sampson; res: The Plains, St. M. Cty; ref: 1, 2, 7, 19, 21, 70, 511, 700, 783, 822, 1509, 1523, 1555, 1564, 1583
SOTHORON, Webster H.; Capt; Sothoron's Co, VA Lt Arty; ref: 1, 2, 17, 19, 21, 70, 456, 511, 650, 1520, 1583
SOUTH, F.; pvt; 3rd MD Lt Arty; ref: 2, 19, 21, 160, 726
SOUTH, George; pvt; 2nd MC Inf, Co G; ref: 1, 681
SOUTH, Howard; pvt; 1st MD Inf, Co B; ref: 1, 2, 19, 21
SOUTH, William; ref: 681
SOUTHERD, Hugh Alexander; pvt; 30th VA Sharpshooters, Co E; res: How Cty; MLCSH; ref: 19, 21, 627, 700, 786
SOUTHERLAND, L. M.; pvt; 2nd MD Cav, Co A; res: Cha Cty; ref: 1, 26
SOUTHWORTH, Clinton; Lt; Pollock's Co, VA Lt Arty; res: Balt; ref: 1, 21, 700
SOWERS, James Kerfoot; pvt; 4th VA Cav, Co H; res: Balt; ref: 1, 70
SPALDING, Basil William; McNeill's Rangers; res: Leonardtown, Cha Cty; ref: 18, 19, 26, 605, 1010
SPALDING, Daniel S.; pvt; 2nd MD Inf, Co B; res: St. Clements Bay, St. M. Cty; ref: 1, 1509, 1555, 1662
SPALDING, J., Navy; res: St. M. Cty; ref: 1670
SPALDING, John I. T.; pvt; Barry's Co, MD Vols; res: St. M. Cty; ref: 1, 1670
SPALDING, Samuel E. (M.D.); Lt; 59th VA Inf, Co F; res: Leonardtown, St. M Cty; ref: 1, 18, 69, 316, 791, 1563, 1670
SPANGLER, Samuel M.; pvt; 10th VA Inf, Co F; ref: 1, 700
SPARKS, James H.; pvt; 4th MD Lt Arty; res: QA Cty; ref: 1, 2, 19, 21, 34
SPATES, Thomas J.; pvt; 35th VA Cav, Co A; res: Mtg Cty; ref: 1, 3, 15, 735, 1611, 1677

SPATH, John F.; pvt; MD Guerrilla Zouaves; ref: 1
SPEAKER, John; pvt; 1st Choctan Mounted Rifles, Co D; res: Elk Ridge Landing, AA Cty; ref: 1, 1539
SPEAR, De Wit Clinton; pvt; 1st MD Cav, Co B; res: QA Cty; ref: 1, 2, 19, 21, 785, 1584
SPEAR, Edwin W.; pvt; 1st MD Cav, Co B; res: Kt Cty; ref: 1, 2, 19, 21, 785, 800, 1584
SPEAR, James Jackson; cpl; 1st MD Cav, Co B; res: Kt Cty; ref: 1, 2, 19, 21, 23, 785, 1584
SPEDDEN, John R.; pvt; 2nd MD Cav, Co A; res: Balt; MLCSH; ref: 19, 21, 700, 786
SPEDDEN, Robert; pvt; 19th VA Heavy Arty, Co C; ref: 1, 1580
SPENCE, James R.; 24th VA Cav, Co F; ref: 735
SPENCE, John; pvt; 2nd MD Inf, Co D; ref: 1, 2, 19, 21
SPENCER, Bendenfield Hand; pvt; 4th MD Lt Arty; res: Kt Cty; MLCSH; ref: 1, 2, 19, 21, 470, 627, 700, 786, 1584
SPENCER, D. J.; pvt; Holbrook's Independent MD Lt Arty; ref: 1
SPENCER, Edward N.; pvt; 21st VA Inf, Co B; ref: 1, 2, 19, 21, 700
SPENCER, Frank (M.D.); Surg; Cobb's GA Leg; res: St. M. Cty; ref: 1, 1509, 1670
SPENCER, Jervis, Jr; pvt; 1st MD Cav, Co C; res: Balt; MLCSH: ref: 1, 2, 19, 21, 70, 700, 786
SPENCER, John Chapman; pvt; 1st MD Cav, Co E; res: Snow Hill, Wor Cty; ref: 1, 2, 19, 21, 668, 730, 791, 1559, 1584
SPENCER, Julian Murray; Lt, Navy; C.S. Baltic; ref: 1, 19, 34, 58, 61, 97, 279, 1564
SPENCER, Samuel B.; sgt; 1st VA Inf, Co E; ref: 1, 2, 19, 21, 23, 45, 735, 785, 941
SPENGLING, P.; pvt; 3rd MD Lt Arty; ref: 2, 19, 21, 160, 726
SPICER, Benjamin Bushrod; pvt; 7th VA Cav, Co E; res: Balt; MLCSH; ref: 1, 627, 786
SPIER, Thomas; pvt; 9th GA Lt Arty Bn, Co A; ref: 1, 92
SPINGER, Albert; pvt; Zarvona's MD Zouaves; ref: 1, 735
SPIRL, Michael; pvt; MD American Rifles; ref: 1
SPITTLE, Lewis B.; 15th VA Cav, Co H; res: Point of Rocks; ref: 1, 90
SPOKE, Milford; pvt; 19th VA Inf, Co C; ref: 1, 1580
SPON, Wilford; pvt; 20th VA Cav, Co I; ref: 1, 735
SPOTT, Remelton; pvt; 7th VA Cav, Co G; ref: 1
SPRIGG, J.; sgt; 2nd MD Cav, Co F; ref: 1, 2, 19, 21, 23, 1523, 1609
SPRIGG, Richard Lamar; pvt; 2nd VA Inf, Co G; res: Cumberland, All Cty; ref: 1, 19, 65, 95, 148, 735
SPRINGER, A. G.; pvt; 2nd MD Cav, Co C; ref: 1, 19
SPRINGER, Albert; pvt; 2nd MD Inf, Co E; ref: 1
SPROSTON, John Glendy; Lt, Navy; ref: 68, 97
SPROWL, A. B.; pvt; Stuart's Horse Arty, Breathed's Battery; ref: 1
SPURRIER, Grafton D.; Capt; 1st MD Inf; res: Balt; ref: 1, 2, 19, 63, 64, 559, 703, 791
SPURRIER, Jay; pvt; 1st MD Inf, Co D; ref: 1, 2, 19, 21
SQUIRES, Henry; pvt; 6th NC Cav, Co F; ref: 1, 55
SQUIRES, William; pvt; Davis's MD Cav; res: Annapolis, AA Cty; ref: 1, 1539
STACEY, John; smn, Navy; Wilmington Navy Station; res: Bt Cty; ref: 1
STACLE, John; pvt; 1st MD Cav, Co D; ref: 1601
STACK, Garrett; pvt; 1st VA Inf, Co C; ref: 1, 735
STACK, John P.; pvt; 39th VA Inf, Co D; res: Balt; ref: 1, 1540
STACK, Patrick A.; pvt; 26th VA Inf, Co A; res: Balt; ref: 1, 1540

STAIMAN, J. F.; pvt; 1st MD Cav, Co A; ref: 1, 19
STAINBACK, John M. (M.D.); cpl; 56th VA Inf, Co E; res: Balt; ref: 1, 70
STAKS, Bradley Lyles; Gen B. T. Johnson's staff; ref: 72
STALLINGS, Charles L.; pvt; 1st MD Cav, Co E; ref: 1, 2, 19, 21, 730
STALLINGS, John; pvt; Jacobs Mounted Rifles; res: Millersville, AA Cty; ref: 1, 19, 1539
STALLINGS, Richard S. P.; pvt; 35th VA Cav, Co B; res: Carrollton Manor, Frd Cty; ref: 1, 3, 90, 106, 643, 1611, 1677
STAMBAUGH, J. E.; pvt; 2nd MD Lt Arty; ref: 1, 2, 19, 21
STANDBERG, Samuel; Chew's Battery, VA Lt Arty; ref: 735
STANEY, Edward; pvt; Stuart's Horse Arty, Breathed's Battery; ref: 1
STANGLINGS, George C.; pvt; 2nd MD Inf; res: AA Cty; ref: 1
STANLEY, Alfred; cpl; 2nd MD Cav, Co A; ref: 1, 19
STANLEY, Charles H.; pvt; 1st MD Cav, Co B; res: Collington, PG Cty; ref: 1, 2, 21, 23, 56, 687, 700, 785, 1553, 1622
STANLEY, E. H.; pvt; 1st MD Cav, Co B; res: Balt; ref: 19, 21
STANLEY, Howard; pvt; 43rd VA Cav (Mosby's), Co E; ref: 1, 8, 20
STANLEY, Patrick; pvt; Stuart's Horse Arty, Breathed's Battery; ref: 1, 489
STANSBURY, Edward O. N.; pvt; 4th MD Lt Arty; res: Balt; ref: 1, 2, 19, 93
STANSBURY, John L.; pvt; 2nd MD Inf, Co E; ref: 1, 2, 19, 21
STANSBURY, John L.; pvt; 13th VA Inf, Co G; ref: 1, 2, 19, 21, 160, 689, 726
STANSBURY, John R.; pvt; 9th VA Inf, Co B; res: Balt; ref: 1, 1576
STANSBURY, Joseph W.; sgt; 2nd MD Cav, Co A; res: Balt; ref: 1, 2, 11, 19, 21, 23, 1609
STANSBURG, Smith; Maj; Ordnance Bureau; ref: 1, 19, 735, 787, 791
STANSFIELD, J. M.; pvt; 1st SC Inf, Co G; ref: 1
STANTON, William; pvt; 1st MD Inf, Co E; ref: 1, 2, 19, 21
STAPLES, John M.; pvt; 2nd MD Cav, Co A; ref: 1, 19
STARK, Adam; pvt; 23rd VA Cav, Co I; ref: 1, 93
STARLING, George Columbus; pvt; 2nd MD Inf, Co A; res: AA Cty; ref: 1, 2, 19, 21, 259, 650
STARR, George W., Jr; sgt; Watson's Battery, LA Lt Arty; res: Balt; ref: 1, 720, 735
STAUB, Richard P. H.; Capt; Asst Q.M., Gen B. Robertson's staff; res: Balt; ref: 1, 3, 21, 70, 700
STAYLER, S. J.; pvt; 2nd MD Inf, Co E; ref: 1
STAYLOR, Charles H.; pvt; 5th LA Inf, Co E; res: Balt; ref: 21, 700
STAYLOR, George W.; pvt; 2nd MD Lt Arty; res: Balt; ref: 1, 2, 19, 21, 700, 1540
STAYLOR, Louis P.; cpl; 2nd MD Inf, Co E; res: Balt; ref: 1, 2, 19, 21, 23, 1540
STAYTON, Thomas; cpl; 9th VA Inf, Co B; res: Bt Cty; ref: 1, 1575, 1576
ST. CLAIR, Albert L.; pvt; 3rd MD Lt Arty; ref: 1, 2, 19, 21, 160, 726
STEADMAN, G. C.; Mast. M., Navy; Norfolk Naval Yard; res: Balt; ref: 1
STEDHAM, Richard; cpl; 23rd AL Inf, Co I; ref: 1, 19, 34
STEECE, ---; Midn, Navy; ref: 68
STEELE, Billings; pvt; 43rd VA Cav (Mosby's), Co D; res: Annapolis, AA Cty; ref: 1, 8, 21, 23, 107, 257, 700, 1628
STEELE, Charles Hutchins; pvt; 2nd MD Inf, Co A; res: Annapolis, AA Cty; ref: 1, 2, 19, 21, 81, 259, 486, 650, 681, 715, 757, 1520
STEELE, Frank Key; pvt; 2nd MD Inf, Co C; res: Annapolis, AA Cty; ref: 1, 2, 19, 21, 107, 1520, 1539

STEELE, Henry A.; smn, Navy; Wilmington Navy Yard; res: Annapolis, AA Cty; ref: 1, 1539
STEELE, James of John; res: Cambridge, Dor Cty; ref: 112, 1547
STEELE, John H.; pvt; 1st MD Cav, Co D; res: Carr Cty; MLCSH; ref: 1, 2, 19, 21, 92, 93, 700, 786
STEELE, Thompson B.; pvt; 7th VA Cav, Co G; res: Cambridge, Dor Cty; ref: 1, 1547
STIEGER, Nicholas; pvt; MD Guerrilla Zouaves; ref: 1
STEIN, James A.; pvt; 4th AL Inf, Co A; ref: 1, 693
STEINBACH, John M.; (M.D.); pvt; 56th VA Inf, Co E; res: Balt; ref: 1, 18
STEINCHCOMT, Thomas W.; res: AA Cty; ref: 1539
STEINE, Simon; pvt; 1st VA Inf, Co E; ref: 1, 735
STEINER, Harry H. (M.D.); Surg; Georgia District; ref: 1, 18
STEINMETZ, J. H.; Lt; AL Reserve Bn, Co C; ref: 1, 735
STENET, William J.; pvt; 4th MD Lt Arty; ref: 1
STENO, Joseph A.; pvt; 1st MD Lt Arty; ref: 2, 19, 21
STENSON, R. James; ref: 70, 488
STEPHENS, David; pvt; MD Line, Co B; ref: 1
STEPHENS, James; pvt; 4th MD Lt Arty; ref: 1
STEPHENS, John; pvt; 2nd MD Inf, Co H; ref: 1, 2, 19, 21
STEPHENS, William M.; pvt; 2nd MD Cav, Co D; ref: 1, 19, 1609
STEPHENSON, Thomas H.; pvt; 1st MD Cav, Co D; ref: 2, 19, 21
STEPHENSON, Watkins W.; cpl; 9th VA Inf, Co B; ref: 1, 1576
STERETT, James S.; sgt; 1st MD Inf, Co C; res: Balt; ref: 1, 559
STERETT, Isaac S.; Capt, Navy; Richmond Naval Station; ref: 1, 19, 58, 61, 64, 97, 279, 674, 735, 789, 791, 1297, 1511, 1520, 1523, 1564, 1673
STERLING, Henry; pvt; 19th VA Heavy Arty, Co C; ref: 1, 1580
STERLING, James Randolph; Lt; 2nd NC Inf, Co A; res: Balt; ref: 1, 70
STERLING, Joseph; pvt; 19th VA Heavy Arty, Co C; ref: 1, 1580
STERLING, William H.; pvt; 1st LA Lt Arty; res: Balt; ref: 70
STERN, Samuel; pvt; 1st VA Inf, Co E; ref: 1, 19, 735
STETSON, W. H.; pvt; Davis's MD Cav, Co B; ref: 1, 19
STEUART, George Hume, Jr; Brig Gen; Army of Northern Virginia; res: Balt; ref: 1, 2, 11, 13, 17, 18, 19, 21, 23, 30, 34, 35, 36, 38, 42, 44, 47, 48, 50, 53, 57, 62, 63, 64, 68, 70, 88, 97, 100, 105, 107, 117, 121, 125, 126, 127, 129, 131, 145, 169, 222, 240, 259, 309, 380, 397, 403, 422, 431, 441, 443, 444, 445, 456, 450, 462, 463, 469, 489, 490, 493, 494, 501, 503, 517, 559, 583, 595, 601, 631, 638, 674, 689, 700, 735, 743, 753, 781, 782, 787, 789, 790, 791, 793, 828, 839, 843, 857, 859, 860, 862, 873, 878, 893, 896, 1006, 1015, 1053, 1110, 1168, 1325, 1356, 1365, 1395, 1487, 1511, 1519, 1520, 1523, 1569, 1577, 1578, 1579, 1588, 1609, 1623, 1628, 1633, 1634, 1642, 1652
STEUART, Harry A.; Lt; 3rd MD Lt Arty; res: Balt; ref: 1, 2, 18, 19, 83, 160, 461, 511, 726, 735, 903, 911, 1015, 1153, 1395, 1460, 1519, 1523, 1584
STEUART, James; pvt; 31st VA Inf, Co B; res: Balt; ref: 1, 594, 1540
STEUART, William Frederick, Jr; Lt; Signal Officer, Gen C. Lee's staff; res: AA Cty; ref: ref: 1, 18, 735, 911, 1395
STEUART, William Frederick, Sr. (M.D.); Surg; Examiner of Conscripts, 5th VA Congressional District; res: Balt; ref: 1, 2, 18, 19, 21, 44, 63, 83, 511, 601, 735, 911, 1395, 1533, 1579

STEUART, William James; Lt; Aide de Camp, Gen G. H. Steuart's staff; res: Balt; ref: 1, 70, 611, 753
STEVENS, D. M.; pvt; 1st SC Inf, Co G; ref: 1
STEVENS, James .; pvt; 1st MD Cav, Co B; res: Broad Creek, QA Cty; ref: 1, 2, 19, 21, 785, 1554
STEVENSON, Charles E.; Capt; 16th VA Cav, Co A; ref: 1, 21, 700
STEVENSON, Dawson H.; pvt; 1st MD Cav, Co D; res: Frd Cty; ref: 1, 2, 19, 21, 700, 1601
STEVENSON, Thomas H.; pvt; 1st MD Cav, Co D; ref: 1, 2, 19, 21, 1601
STEVES, Christopher P.; pvt; 1st MD Cav, Co D; res: Frederick, Frd Cty; ref: 1, 2, 19, 21, 90, 643, 1601
STEWART, Benjamin; pvt; Lee's Balt Lt Arty, Alexander's Bn; res: Davidsonville, AA Cty; ref: 1, 1539
STEWART, Columbus J.; cpl; 2nd MD Cav, Co F; res: Balt; ref: 1, 2, 19, 21, 23, 511, 700, 1609
STEWART, Edward Burkley; pvt; 1st MD Inf, Co A; res: Cambridge, Dor Cty; ref: 1, 2, 19, 21, 44, 511, 1547
STEWART, Francis M.; pvt; 4th MD Lt Arty; res: Cambridge, Dor Cty; ref: 1, 2, 19, 21, 112, 511, 1547
STEWART, Frederick Augusta; pvt; McNeill's Rangers; res: Balt; MLCSH; ref: 1, 504, 511, 627, 700, 786, 1010, 1540
STEWART, Henry; pvt; 35th VA Cav, Co B; res: Balt; ref: 1, 2, 3, 19, 21, 1611, 1677
STEWART, James P.; pvt; 4th MD Lt Arty; res: Davidsonville, AA Cty; ref: 1, 2, 19, 21, 511, 1539
STEWART, John Allen; pvt; 1st MD Cav, Co D; res: Davidsonville, AA Cty; ref: 1, 1539
STEWART, Joseph H.; Lt; 1st MD Inf, Co F; res: Cambridge, Dor Cty; ref: 1, 2, 19, 21, 23, 64, 456, 511, 700, 791, 854, 1511, 1547
STEWART, Robert H.; sgt; 1st VA Cav, Co B; res: Bt Cty; ref: 1, 2, 19, 21, 720
STEWART, Septimus H.; Capt; Asst Q.M., MD Line; ref: 1, 2, 19, 21, 23, 64, 93, 456, 511
STEWART, Thomas Richard; Capt; Chief of Passports, Gen J.H. Winder's Detectives; res: Camebridge, Dor Cty; MLCSH; ref: 1, 2, 19, 21, 23, 44, 64, 68, 70, 92, 93, 511, 627, 700, 786, 791
STEWART, Walter; pvt; Rhett's 1st SC Heavy Arty; res: Balt; ref: 1, 735
STEWART, Walter H.; pvt; Zarvona's MD Zouaves; res: Bt Cty; ref: 1, 720, 735, 1575
STEWART, William Eccleston; Maj; 15th AR Inf; res: Easton, Tal Cty; ref: 1, 2, 19, 21, 511, 631, 700, 735, 1612
STEWART, William H.; pvt; Jacobs Mounted Riflemen; res: South River, AA Cty; ref: 1, 1539
STEWART, Wilson M.; pvt; 4th BN LA Washington Lt Arty; ref: 1, 316, 735
STEDHAM, Richard; pvt; Hampton Leg Lt Arty, Co B; ref: 1, 2, 19, 21
STINCHCOMB, Joshua E.; pvt; 1st MD Lt Arty; res: Balt; ref: 1, 2, 19, 21, 700
STINE, Isaac; pvt; 1st MD Cav, Co E; res: Balt; ref: 1, 19
STINE, Joseph A.; sgt; 2nd MD Cav, Co F; res: Balt; ref: 1, 2, 19, 21, 23, 700, 1540, 1609
STINSON, Charles R.; pvt; 1st MD Cav, Co C; res: Balt; ref: 1, 19
STINSON, Robert James; pvt; 2nd MD Lt Arty; res: Balt; MLCSH; ref: 1, 2, 19, 21, 39, 700, 848, 849, 866, 906, 923, 1050
STITH, Donald C.; Col; I.G., Gen S. Lee's staff; ref:1, 735, 787, 791
STITLER, Charles B.; pvt; 1st MD Inf, Co B; ref: 1, 2, 19, 21
STOAKS, Brad; pvt; 7th VA Cav, Co G; res: Frd Cty; ref: 3

STOCKDALE, George W.; pvt; Barbier's Bn, AL Cav, Bowie's Co; res: Balt; ref: 1, 2, 19, 21, 57, 700
STOCKS, Thomas; pvt; 7th VA Cav, Co G; ref: 1, 3
STODDERD, John T.; pvt; Davis's MD Cav, Co A; res: Cha Cty; ref: 1, 19, 735
STOKES, Bradley T.; Lt; Aid de Camp, Gen B. Johnson's staff; res: Frd Cty; ref: 1, 90
STOKES, William B.; pvt; 13th TX Inf, Co B; res: Frederick, Frd Cty; ref: 1, 88, 89, 735
STOMBAKER, J. R.; pvt; 1st MD Cav, Co C; ref: 1, 2, 19, 21
STONE, A.; pvt; 3rd MD Lt Arty; ref: 2, 19, 21, 160, 726
STONE, Carter; pvt; 1st MD Cav, Co A; ref: 1, 2, 19, 21
STONE, Henry; pvt; 1st MD Cav, Co A; res: Rockville, Mont Cty; ref: 1, 2, 19, 21, 1487, 1552, 1574
STONE, J. W.; pvt; 3rd MD Lt Arty; ref: 2, 19, 21, 160, 726
STONE, John A. C.; pvt; 1st MD Cav, Co A; ref: 1
STONE, John H.; Lt; 2nd MD Inf, Co B; res: Port Tobacco, Cha Cty; ref: 1, 2, 19, 21, 23, 64, 68, 1509, 1546, 1665
STONE, Joseph F.; pvt; 1st MD Cav, Co C; res: Leonardtown, St. M. Cty; ref: 1, 2, 7, 19, 21, 69, 316, 1509, 1555, 1627
STONE, William R.; pvt; 7th VA Cav, Co G; ref: 1, 3, 735, 1611, 1677
STONEBRAKER, A. S.; Capt; Q.M., 2nd VA Inf; res: Mont Cty; ref: 1, 827, 1574
STONEBRAKER, Edward L.; 2nd MD Cav; res: Wash Cty; ref: 2, 19, 23
STONEBRAKER, Joseph R.; pvt; 1st MD Cav, Co C; res: Funkstown, Wash Cty; ref: 1, 19, 21, 23, 49, 70, 431, 509, 700, 827, 866
STONER, Henry D.; pvt; 19th VA Heavy Arty, Co C; ref: 1, 93, 1580
STONER, John D.; cpl; 14th NC Inf, Co I; res: Johnsville, Frd Cty; ref: 1, 93, 1548
STONESTREET, Joseph Harris; Lt; 1st MD Lt Arty; res: Port Tobacco, Cha Cty; ref: 1, 2, 19, 21, 23, 64, 69, 316, 791, 1523, 1546
STORM, Francis E.; pvt; 2nd MD Inf, Co C; ref: 1, 2, 19, 21
STORY, Caleb E.; pvt; 9th VA Inf, Co B; ref: 1, 1576
STOUT, William U.; pvt; 2nd MD Lt Arty; res: Balt; ref: 1, 2, 19, 21, 700, 1540, 1613
STOUTSENBUGER, Albert C.; pvt; 35th VA Cav, Co B; res: Frd Cty; ref: 1
STOW, F. E.; pvt; 1st MD Cav, Co C; ref: 1, 19
STRAFFORD, John R.; Asst Q.M.; 43rd NC Inf; ref: 2, 19, 735
STRAHAN, Charles; Lt; Signal Officer, Gen Preston's staff; res: Balt; ref: 1, 2, 19, 21, 312, 700, 735, 1373, 1471
STRAILMAN, Frank T.; sgt; 9th VA Inf, Co A; ref: 1, 735
STRAIN, George; pvt; 18th VA Heavy Arty, Co C; res: Balt; MLCSH; ref: 1, 92, 93, 627, 700, 735, 786
STRASBURG, David E.; musician; 5th VA Inf; res: Balt; ref: 1, 21, 700
STRASBURGER, Albert; pvt; 2nd MD Cav, Co C; ref: 1, 2, 19, 21, 615
STRATTEN, D. W.; pvt; Stuart's Horse Arty, Breathed's Battery; ref: 1
STRAUS, Julius; pvt; 3rd MD Lt Arty; ref: 1
STREET, Charles; pvt; Stuart's Horse Arty, Breathed's Battery; ref: 1, 19
STREET, James; pvt; 1st MD Cav, Co C; res: Har Cty; ref: 1, 2, 19, 21
STREET, John H.; pvt; 1st MD Inf, Co A; res: Balt; ref: 1, 2, 19, 21, 93, 700, 1609
STRIBLE, George A., Jr; pvt; 1st MD Inf, Co G; ref: 1, 2, 19, 21, 53
STRICKER, Herman; cpl; 16th TX Inf, Co E; res: Balt; ref: 1, 1540
STRICKLAND, Jesse; pvt; 1st MD Inf, Co A; ref: 1, 2, 19, 21

STRICKLER, Harrison Monroe (Revd); Lt; 35th VA Cav, Co E; ref: 1, 3, 371, 1326, 1434, 1677
STRINGER, Thomas E.; sgt; 5th VA Inf, Co I; res: Balt; ref: 1, 21, 700
STROACH, William; McPhersons Pack, AA Cty; ref: 1539
STROBEL, R. S.; sgt; 27th SC Inf, Co D; ref: 1, 21, 700
STROEMER, Alphonso, bugler; 2nd GA Lt Arty; ref: 1, 21, 92, 93, 700
STRONG, W. R.; pvt; 1st MD Cav, Co B; ref: 1, 2, 19, 21, 785
STUART, John Nelson; pvt; 31st MS Inf, Co A; ref: 1, 70, 511
STUART, Sept. H.; pvt; 3rd TN Cav, Co C; ref: 1, 38,511
STUART, William Brewer; pvt; 12th LA Inf, Co B; ref: 1, 70, 511
STUART, Wilson Waters; pvt; 39th MS Inf, Co D; ref: 1, 70, 511
STUBBS, Daniel W.; Lt; 18th TN Inf, Co G; res: Balt; ref: 1, 21, 53, 57, 700
STUBBS, Richard Boswell; 18th TN Inf, Co G; res: Balt; MLCSH; ref: 1, 92, 93, 627, 786
STUBBS, William C.; cpl; 40th VA Cav, Co D; ref: 1, 316
STUMP, George C.; pvt; 2nd MD Lt Arty; res: Balt; ref: 1, 2, 19, 21
STUMP, Herman; sgt; 30th TX Cav, Co H; ref: 1, 53
STUNT, Robert; pvt; 3rd MD Lt Arty; ref: 2, 19, 21, 160, 726
STURMAN, John F.; pvt; 2nd MD Cav, Co C; res: Balt; ref: 1, 1609
SUDLER, John Emory; Capt; 2nd MD Cav, Co E; res: Kt Cty; ref: 1, 2, 19, 21, 23, 57, 70, 107, 1584, 1609
SUEAD, S. Wesley; pvt; ref: 700
SUGGART, J. Z.; pvt; 2nd MD Cav, Co D; ref: 1, 19, 1609
SUIT, Michael H.; pvt; 10th NC Heavy Arty, Co D; ref: 1, 2, 19, 21
SUIT, Norris M.; pvt; 4th MD Lt Arty; res: Charlotte Hall, St. M. Cty; ref: 1, 2, 19, 21, 1555
SULIVAN, Thomas; pvt; Davis's MD Cav, Co A; ref: 1
SULLIVAN, Andrews; pvt; 3rd MD Lt Arty; ref: 1, 2, 19, 21, 160, 511, 726
SULLIVAN, Clement; Lt Col; Asst A.G., Gen G. W. C. Lee's staff; res: Cambridge, Dor Cty; ref: 1, 2, 19, 21, 23, 125, 127, 511, 592, 631, 685, 700, 735, 1268, 1520, 1578, 1579, 1620
SULLIVAN, Frank; pvt; 1st MD Cav, Co C; res: Balt; ref: 1, 2, 21, 511, 700, 1523
SULLIVAN, J. Henry; pvt; 53rd VA Inf, Co E; ref: 1, 2, 19, 21, 44, 511, 690, 724
SULLIVAN, James G.; pvt; 42nd GA Inf, Co K; res: Bristol, AA Cty; ref: 1, 1539
SULLIVAN, Jeremiah, pvt; Marine Corps; C.S.S. Virginia II; ref: 1, 1594
SULLIVAN, John; pvt; 2nd MD Cav, Co E; ref: 1, 2, 19, 21
SULLIVAN, John I.; pvt; 3rd MD Lt Arty; ref: 1, 2, 19, 21, 160, 511, 726
SULLIVAN, John II; pvt; 3rd MD Lt Arty; ref: 1, 2, 19, 21, 160, 511, 726
SULLIVAN, John H.; sgt; 21st VA Inf, Co B; res: Balt; ref: 1, 2, 19, 312, 511, 650, 750
SULLIVAN, Joseph; pvt; 13th VA Inf, Co G; ref: 1, 735
SULLIVAN, Joseph D.; pvt; 2nd MD Cav, Co B; res: Bt Cty; ref: 1, 21, 511, 1609
SULLIVAN, M. H.; pvt; Davis's MD Cav, Co C; ref: 1, 628
SULLIVAN, Samuel J; pvt; 3rd KY Cav, Co B; res: Balt; ref: 1, 1014
SULLIVAN, William H.; pvt; 1st VA Inf, Co E; ref: 1, 735
SUMMER, S. H.; pvt; 2nd MD Inf, Co A; ref: 1
SUMMER, T.; pvt; Stuart's Horse Arty, Breathed's Battery; ref: 1
SUMMERFIELD, James; pvt; 19th VA Heavy Arty, Co C; ref: 1, 19, 1580

SUMMERFIELD, Richardson; pvt; Edelin's MD Heavy Arty; res: West River, AA Cty; ref: 1, 1539

SUNDERLAND, Thomas; pvt; 1st MD Lt Arty; res: Bristol, AA Cty; MLCSH; ref: 1, 2, 19, 21, 93, 627, 700, 786, 1539

SUNTON, T. T.; pvt; Lee's MD Cav; ref: 1, 19, 1574

SUPINGER, James; pvt; Stuart's Horse Arty, Breathed's Battery; ref: 1

SURMAN, Gustave; pvt; 1st MD Cav, Co C; ref: 1, 19

SURPELL, G. M.; res: PG Cty; ref: 107

SURRATT, Isaac D.; sgt; 33rd TX Cav, Co A; res: Cha Cty; ref: 1, 17, 21, 70, 700, 1608

SURRATT, John H.; Messenger, Secret Service Bureau; res: Balt; ref: 19, 21, 700, 735, 1560, 1578, 1607, 1608

SURVICK, George W.; pvt; 35th VA Cav, Co A; res: Hyattstown, Mont Cty; ref: 1, 3, 1611, 1677

SUTHERLAND, Joel Barlow; sgt; Fairnholt's VA Reserve, Co C; res: Balt; ref: 1, 18, 71, 81, 85, 700

SUTHERLAND, Leigh M.; pvt; 17th VA Inf, Co H; ref: 1, 2, 19, 21, 133, 142

SUTHERLAND, St. Clair F.; Lt Col; 3rd VA Local Defense; ref: 1, 18, 689, 720, 1345, 1600

SUTTER, William T.; pvt; Crescent LA Lt Arty, Hutton's Co; res: Balt; ref: 1, 2, 312

SUTTON, John C.; cpl; 1st VA Lt Arty, Co I; res: Balt; MLCSH; ref: 1, 21, 700, 786

SUTTON, Robert; pvt; Jacobs' Mounted Riflemen; res: Balt; ref: 1, 70, 1540

SUTTON, Thomas E.; pvt; 55th VA Inf, Co C; res: Balt; ref: 1, 70

SWAMLEY, Frank; pvt; 1st MD Cav, Co D; ref: 1, 791

SWAN, Baynard R.; pvt; 43rd VA Cav (Mosby's), Co F; ref: 1, 8

SWAN, George W.; pvt; 1st MD Inf, Co F; ref: 1, 2, 19, 21

SWAN, James; pvt; 17th VA Inf, Co E; ref: 1, 2, 19, 21, 133, 142, 251

SWAN, John; pvt; 1st MD Inf, Co I; res: St. M. Cty; ref: 1, 2, 19, 21, 1662

SWAN, John N.; pvt; 17th VA Inf, Co A; ref: 1, 133, 142, 251

SWAN, Robert; Maj; 1st VA Cav; res: All Cty; ref: 1, 7, 88, 361, 685, 791, 1600

SWANCOAT, Richard J.; Lt; 13th VA Inf, Co G; ref: 1, 735

SWANCOAT, William; sgt; Stuart's Horse Arty, Breathed's Battery; ref: 1, 498, 735

SWANN, James Monroe; sgt; 14th VA Inf, Co E; res: Balt; MLCSH; ref: 1, 92, 93, 627, 700, 786

SWANN, Thomas; pvt; Barry's Co MD Vols; ref: 1, 724

SWANN, Z. Samuel; pvt; 2nd MD Inf, Co B; ref: 1

SWAUKE, L. S.; pvt; 2nd MD Cav, Co D; ref: 1, 19, 1609

SWEENEY, George W. H.; pvt; 1st MD Cav, Co E; ref: 1, 2, 19, 21, 94

SWEENEY, Sam; Stuart's Cav; res: Balt; ref: 1, 350

SWEETING, Benjamin H.; pvt; 1st MD Inf, Co F; res: Har Cty; MLCSH; ref: 1, 2, 19, 21, 684, 686, 700, 786

SWEETING, Harry B. H. (M.D.); pvt; 43rd VA Cav (Mosby's), Co B; res: Balt; ref: 8, 258, 261, 735

SWINDLER, Marshall; Lt; 12th VA Cav, Co G; ref: 1, 11, 19, 194

SWITZER, John A.; pvt; Davis's MD Cav, Co B; res: Mt. Airy, Carr Cty; ref: 1, 64, 90, 503, 789

SWOMLEY, Frank; res: New Market, Frd Cty; ref: 90

SWOMLEY, Thomas; pvt; 1st MD Cav, Co D; ref: 1601

SYDNOR, Adoninam Judson; Capt; 40th VA Inf, Co B; res: Balt; MLCSH; ref: 1, 21, 93, 700, 786, 791

SYKES, William T.; cpl; 3rd MD Lt Arty; ref: 1, 2, 19, 21, 23, 160, 726, 1460

SYLVESTER, Lewis; sgt; 5th GA Inf, Co E; ref: 1, 81

SYMINGTON, Thomas A.; Capt; Aide de Camp, Gen G. Picket's staff; res: Catonsville, Bt Cty; ref: 1, 2, 19, 21, 23, 56, 511, 690, 700, 1540

SYMINGTON, William H.; pvt; 21st VA Inf, Co B; res: Balt; ref: 1, 2, 19, 312, 511, 681, 735, 1540

SYMINGTON, William Newton; pvt; Barry's Co, MD Vols; ref: 1, 735

SYMINGTON, William Steuart; Maj; Adj & Asst I.G, Gen G. Pickett's staff; res: Balt; ref: 1, 2, 19, 21, 22, 23, 29, 44, 53, 64, 70, 150, 312, 469, 506, 511, 592, 681, 685, 700, 791, 866, 906, 976, 1058, 1311, 1520

SYNTIS, Sylvester; pvt; 18th GA Cav, Bn, Co A; res: Balt; ref: 1, 21, 700

TABB, Harlan Peyton; pvt; McNeill's Rangers; res: Cumberland, All Cty; ref: 19, 65, 95, 148, 504, 519, 1610

TABB, John; pvt; V.M.I. Cadets; res: Balt; ref: 19, 21, 700, 1687

TABLER, John W.; pvt; 35th VA Cav, Co B; res: Urbana, Frd Cty; ref: 1, 3, 67, 90, 1611

TACEY, Hillary; pvt; Davis's MD Cav, Co A; ref: Frd Cty; ref: 1, 19, 735

TALBERT, F.; pvt; 2nd MD Cav, Co F; ref: 1, 2, 19, 21

TALBERT, William; pvt; Jacobs Mounted Riflemen; res: Friendship, AA Cty; ref: 1, 19, 1539

TALBOT, Lewis T.; cpl; 2nd MD Lt Arty; ref: 1, 2, 19, 21, 23

TALBOTT, J. Fred C.; pvt; 2nd MD Cav, Co C; res: Lutherville, Bt Cty; ref: 1, 2, 11, 19, 21, 700, 1056, 1609

TALBOTT, Samuel G.; pvt; 13th VA Lt Arty, Co A; ref: South River, AA Cty; ref: 1, 70

TALBOTT, Thomas J.; pvt; Jeffress Co VA Lt Arty; res: South River, AA Cty; ref: 1, 70

TALBY, George; pvt; 1st MD Cav, Co A; ref: 1, 2, 19, 21

TALIAFERRO, Alexander G.; Capt; 13th VA Inf, Co G; ref: 1, 518, 735, 791

TALIAFERRO, Felix T.; sgt; 12th VA Cav, Co B; res: Balt; ref: 1, 19, 1609

TALIAFERRO, Garvin C.; Lt; 9th VA Cav, Co C; res: Balt; MLCSH; ref: 1, 2, 19, 21, 700, 786

TALIAFERRO, John R.; pvt; Holbrook's Independent MD Lt Arty; res: Balt; ref: 1, 2, 19, 21

TALL, George M.; pvt; 1st Bn, KY Mounted Rifles, Co C; res: West River, AA Cty; ref: 1, 1539

TALLIAFERCO, Charles S.; res: Balt; ref: 1540

TALLIAFERCO, John R.; res: Balt; ref: 1540

TALLIFERRO, W. G.; pvt; Stuart's Horse Arty, Breathed's Battery; ref: 1, 498, 782

TALTON, M. P.; pvt; 3rd MD Lt Arty; ref: 1, 2, 19, 21, 160, 461, 726

TANERA, Frank; pvt; 47th VA Inf, Co H; res: Bt Cty; MLCSH; ref: 21, 93, 700, 735, 786

TARBUTTON, William S.; pvt; 4th MD Lt Arty; res: QA Cty; ref: 1, 2, 19, 21, 470

TARING, James; pvt, Marine Corps, Pensacola, Co B; ref: 1, 1594

TARLETORE, Robert; Lt; 1st AL Inf; res: Balt; ref: 70

TARMAN, Henry A.; pvt; Lee's Balt Lt Arty, Alexander's Bn; res: South River, AA Cty; ref: 1, 1539

TARMAN, John R.; pvt; 26th NC Inf, Co K; res: West River, AA Cty; ref: 1, 1539

TARR, B. A. (M.D.); Physician; Medical Corps; res: Balt; ref. 18, 832

TARR, Charles E.; Capt; Chamber's Independent Lt Arty Bn, Co B; ref: 1, 789

TARR, William J.; pvt; 2nd MD Lt Arty; res: QA Cty; ref: 1, 2, 19, 21

TASKER, H. P.; res: Cumberland; ref: 19, 65, 95, 148
TAVENER, Joseph A.; Lt; 8th VA Inf, Co E; res: Buckeystown, Frd Cty; ref: 1, 1166
TATUM, Samuel; pvt; Zarvona's MD Zouaves; ref: 19, 58, 735, 1520
TAY, J. L.; pvt; 2nd MD Cav, Co A; ref: 1, 19, 1609
TAYMAN, John H.; res: Owensville, AA Cty; ref: 1539
TAYMAN, Joseph; res: Annapolis, AA Cty; ref: 1539
TAYLOE, John; Lt; V.M.I. Cadets; ref: 21, 700, 791, 1687
TAYLOR, ---; cpl; ref: 456
TAYLOR, Algernon S.; Col, Marine Corps; res: Carr Cty: MLCSH; ref: 1, 18, 21, 57, 93, 97, 431, 700, 783, 786, 791, 792, 1349, 1495, 1500, 1501, 1515, 1593, 1594
TAYLOR, B. C.; pvt; 35th VA Cav, Co C; ref: 1, 3
TAYLOR, Charles Henry; pvt; 5th LA Inf, Co E; res: Balt; MLCSH; ref: 1, 19, 627, 786
TAYLOR, Charles J.; pvt; 1st MD Cav, Co D; res: Frd Cty; ref: 1, 2, 19, 21, 90, 1573, 1601
TAYLOR, Charles S.; pvt; Barry's Co, MD Vols; ref: 1
TAYLOR, David Bayley; pvt; 15th VA Cav, Co I; res: Balt; ref: 1, 21, 23, 631, 700
TAYLOR, George B. P.; pvt; Hampton Leg SC Inf, Co A; res: Balt; MLCSH; ref: 1, 93, 700, 786
TAYLOR, George L.; pvt; 2nd MD Inf, Co A; res: Georgetown; ref: 1, 2, 19, 21, 316, 650
TAYLOR, George W.; pvt; 1st VA Inf, Co E; res: Bladensburg, PG Cty; ref: 1, 1622
TAYLOR, George W.; pvt; 43rd VA Cav (Mosby's), Co C; res: Port Tobacco, Cha Cty; ref: 1, 2, 8, 19, 21, 735, 1546
TAYLOR, H. P.; 7th GA, Co E; ref: 92
TAYLOR, Henry G.; pvt; 57th AL Inf, Co K; ref: 1, 2, 19, 21
TAYLOR, J.; pvt; 3rd MD Lt Arty; ref: 1, 2, 19, 21, 160, 726
TAYLOR, J. Vincent; pvt; 1st VA Inf, Co E; res: Georgetown; ref: 1, 735
TAYLOR, James; Pegrams Lt Arty; res: Cumberland, All Cty; ref: 65, 95, 148, 677
TAYLOR, John; pvt; MD Guerrilla Zouaves; ref: 1
TAYLOR, John B.; pvt; 35th VA Cav, Co D; ref: 1, 2, 19, 21, 1677
TAYLOR, John F.; pvt; 47th VA Inf, Co H; ref: 1
TAYLOR, John W.; Gunboat Crew, Navy, Vicksburg Naval Station; res: West River, AA Cty; ref: 1, 1539
TAYLOR, L. T.; Quartermaster Dept; ref: 1
TAYLOR, Martin; pvt; 40th VA Cav, Co A; res: Barnesville, Mont Cty; ref: 1, 3, 15, 1611, 1677
TAYLOR, R. W. W.; ordnance sgt; 10th KY Cav, Co E; ref: 1, 700
TAYLOR, Robert; pvt; Davis's MD Cav, Co C; ref: 1
TAYLOR, W. H. S.; pvt; 3rd VA Inf, Co D; ref: 1
TAYLOR, W. John; pvt; Consoldiated Crescent Regt, LA Inf, Co O; ref: 1, 735
TAYLOR, Walter Hanson Stone; pvt; 3rd Bn, VA Local defense Inf, Co D; ref: 1
TAYLOR, William T.; pvt; 47th VA Inf, Co H; ref: 1
TAYLOR, William W.; pvt; Lee's MD Cav; res: Balt; ref: 1, 1540
TEAGLE, John; pvt; 2nd MD Cav, Co D; ref: 1, 19, 1609
TEARNEY, Leonidas Joseph; pvt; 12th VA Cav, Co B; res: Hagerstown, Wash Cty; MLCSH; ref: 21, 627, 700, 786
TEASDALE, George A.; pvt; 1st MD Inf, Co H; ref: 1
TEEMS, Daniel; pvt; 38th GA Inf, Co G; ref: 1, 92
TELYEA, John; pvt; 3rd MD Lt Arty; ref: 1, 2, 19, 21, 160, 726
TEMPLE, Charles A.; pvt; MD Guerrilla Zouaves; ref: 1
TEMPLE, Thomas Price (M.D.); Surgeon-in-Charge; Howard Grove

Hospital, Richmond; res: Clarksville, How Cty; ref: 1, 18, 71, 1534, 1536

TENNANT, Thomas M.; pvt; 21st VA Inf, Co B; res: Balt; ref: 1, 2, 19, 312, 735

TENNENT, John C. (Revd); Chaplain; 32nd NC Inf; res: Glyndon, Bt Cty; ref: 1, 21, 700, 783

TENNENT, Thomas; pvt; 1st MD Cav, Co C; res: Balt; ref: 1, 2, 19, 21

TENNISON, Bernard Zakariah; pvt; 2nd MD Inf, Co B; res: Newburg, Cha Cty; ref: 1, 2, 19, 21, 23, 1665

TERBMAN, Richard W.; 1st MD Cav, Co C; ref: 70

TERELLY, B. F.; pvt; 2nd MD Inf, Co E; ref: 1

TERRANT, Frank M.; 40th VA Inf, Co B; res: Bt Cty; ref: 735

TERRELL, D.; pvt; 2nd MD Cav, Co D; ref: 1, 19, 1609

TERRELL, George W.; pvt;19th VA Inf, Co B; res: Balt; ref: 1, 21, 700

TERRELL, J. Thomas; pvt; 1st MD Cav, Co B; ref: 1, 92

TERRES, Charles Edward; Lt; 5th NC Cav, Co F; res: Balt; MLCSH; ref: 21, 93, 627, 700, 786

TERRETT, Berry; pvt; 2nd MD Cav, Co D; ref: 1, 19

TERRIBERRY, John S.; pvt; Stuart's Horse Arty, Breathed's Battery; ref: 1, 498

TERRY, George R.; pvt; Stuart's Horse Arty, Breated's Battery; ref: 1, 498

TERRY, J. C.; pvt; 2nd MD Cav, Co B; ref: 1, 19, 1609

TERRY, James Monroe; pvt; Holbrook's Independent MD Lt Arty; res: Annapolis, AA Cty; ref: 1, 19, 70, 1539, 1628

TEXAS, W.; pvt; Edelin's MD Heavy Arty; ref: 1

THARP, James M.; res: Tal Cty; ref: 645

THAXTON, David; pvt; 9th VA Inf, Co B; ref: 1, 1576

THELIN, William T.; pvt; 2nd MD Inf, Co A; res: Balt; ref: 1, 2, 19, 21, 70, 488, 650, 700, 746, 849, 923, 1520, 1540, 1613

THOM, J. Penbroke (M.D.); Capt; Irish BN, VA Inf, Co C; res: Balt; ref: 1, 18, 21, 23, 56, 70, 631, 700

THOMAS, Allen E.; Brig Gen; Trans-Mississippi Department; res: How Cty; ref: 1, 18, 50, 97, 108, 145, 431, 511, 674, 684, 735, 791, 1006, 1578, 1579, 1588, 1622, 1623

THOMAS, Armstrong; ref: 936

THOMAS, Bradley; Lt; 15th NC Inf, Co C; res: Fairlee, Kt Cty; ref: 1584

THOMAS, Charles; pvt; 7th VA Cav, Co G; res: Cha Cty; ref: 1, 3

THOMAS, Charles Byron (M.D.); pvt; 35th VA Cav, Co B; res: Furnace Ford, Frd Cty; ref: 1, 3, 15, 18, 19, 90, 643, 1573, 1611, 1677

THOMAS, Charles C.; pvt; 13th NC Lt Arty, Co F; ref: 1, 21, 700

THOMAS, Charles F.; pvt; 2nd MD Cav, Co A; res: Balt; ref: 1, 19, 1609

THOMAS, Daniel L., Jr; pvt; 43rd Cav (Mosby's); res: Balt; ref: 1, 2, 8, 19, 21, 23, 70, 488, 493, 511, 700, 735, 849, 866, 906, 923, 976, 1058, 1579, 1613

THOMAS, David O.; 35th VA Cav, Co B; res: Frd Cty; ref: 90, 1611

THOMAS, E. H.; pvt; 43rd MS Inf, Co B; ref: 1, 735

THOMAS, Edmond; pvt; 35th VA Cav, Co B; res: Point of Rocks, Frd Cty; ref: 1, 3, 19, 72, 90, 643, 1548, 1677

THOMAS, Edward; pvt; 2nd MD Cav, Co B; ref: 1, 2, 19

THOMAS, Edward of C.; res: Frederick, Frd Cty; ref: 89

THOMAS, Edwin; pvt; 1st MD Cav, Co B; res: St. M. Cty; ref: 1, 2, 19, 21, 45, 46, 511, 650, 700, 785, 1509, 1520

THOMAS, Francis J.; Col; Asst I.G., Gen J. E. Johnston's staff; res: Balt; ref: 1, 2, 18, 34, 44, 53, 68, 82, 86, 126, 127, 129, 735, 787, 791, 1520, 1523

THOMAS, Franklin; pvt; 35th VA Cav, Co B; res: Adamstown, Frd Cty; ref: 3, 19, 86, 89, 1548, 1611, 1677

THOMAS, George; Capt; 2nd MD Inf, Co H; res: Mattapeny, St. M. Cty; ref: 1, 2, 19, 21, 23, 38, 44, 63, 64,68, 456, 469, 511, 615, 631, 650, 674, 700, 791, 822, 843, 1509, 1511, 1520, 1555, 1579, 1627

THOMAS, George E. of John; pvt; Stuart's Horse Arty, Breathed's Battery; res: Hills Point, Dor Cty; ref: 498, 1547

THOMAS, George H.; pvt; 9th VA Inf, Co B; ref: 1, 2, 19, 21, 160, 259, 511, 726, 1523, 1576

THOMAS, J. A.; pvt; Stuart's Horse Arty, Breathed's Battery; ref: 1

THOMAS, J. Henry; sgt; Stuart's Horse Arty, Breathed's Battery; ref: 1, 2, 19, 21, 498

THOMAS, Jacob G. (M.D.); Surg; 39th AL Inf; res: Adamstown, Frd Cty; ref: 1, 18

THOMAS, Jacob N.; pvt; 35th VA Cav, Co B; res: Point of Rocks, Frd Cty; ref: 1, 3, 19, 89, 1548, 1611, 1677

THOMAS, James; pvt; Davis's MD Cav, Co B; ref: 1

THOMAS, James D. (Revd); Chaplain; 19th VA Lt Arty; res: Frd Cty; ref: 1, 23

THOMAS, James E.; pvt; 7th VA Cav, Co G; res: Cha Cty; ref: 1

THOMAS, James G.; pvt; Zarvona's MD Zouaves; ref: 1, 735

THOMAS, James H.; pvt; 7th VA Cav, Co G; res: Merryland Tract, Frd Cty; ref: 1, 3, 90, 1278

THOMAS, James William; sgt; 1st MD Inf, Co H; res: Great Mills, St. M. Cty; ref: 1, 2, 19, 21, 23, 312, 511, 650, 700, 784, 1509, 1520, 1555

THOMAS, John E.; sgt; 43rd VA Cav (Mosby's), Co A; ref: 1, 2, 8, 19, 21

THOMAS, John Hanson, Jr; pvt; 1st MD Cav, Co B; res: PG Cty; ref: 1, 2, 19, 21, 92, 93, 511, 650, 785, 786, 1540

THOMAS, John Roger; pvt; 1st MD Lt Arty; res: Tal Cty; ref: 1, 2, 19, 21, 70, 74, 330, 511, 645

THOMAS, John W.; pvt; 9th VA Inf, Co B; res: Balt; ref: 1, 1576

THOMAS, Joshua; pvt; 17th VA Inf, Co A; res: Balt; ref: 1, 21, 53, 70, 700, 866, 906, 1058

THOMAS, Lawrence R.; cpl; 2nd MD Inf, Co A; ref: 1, 2, 19, 21, 23, 650

THOMAS, Levin; pvt; 35th VA Cav, Co B; res: Point of Rocks, Frd Cty; ref: 1, 3, 19, 90, 1539, 1548, 1611, 1677

THOMAS, Lewis; pvt; 9th VA Inf, Co B; ref: 1, 1576

THOMAS, Lewis D.; pvt; 25th VA Bn, Co G; res: Balt; ref: 1, 56

THOMAS, Oliver H.; Lt; Aid de Camp, Gen J. J. Archer's staff; ref: 1, 689

THOMAS, Paulus; pvt; Stuart's Horse Arty, Breathed's Battery; ref: 1, 498

THOMAS, Philip F.; Asst Engr, Navy; C.S.S. McRae; res: Tal Cty; ref: 1, 82, 1564, 1673

THOMAS, R. H.; sgt; 2nd MD Cav, Co D; ref: 1, 19, 1609

THOMAS, Raleigh, C.; pvt; 1st MD Cav, Co C; ref: 1, 2, 19, 21, 39, 511, 693, 700

THOMAS, Richard; Col; Zarvona's MD Zouaves; res: St. M. Cty; ref: 1, 2, 17, 18, 19, 30, 43, 44, 50, 58, 61, 63, 64, 68, 70, 97, 125, 128, 272, 350, 480, 501, 511, 514, 518, 558, 559, 593, 594, 607, 608, 616, 617, 686, 781, 789, 791, 818, 1113, 1509, 1520, 1523, 1560, 1582, 1583, 1636

THOMAS, Richard T.; ref: 685

THOMAS, Rosbury; res: Bristol, AA Cty; ref: 1539

THOMAS, Samuel Franklin (M.D.); 35th VA Cav, Co B; res: Adamstown, Frd Cty; ref: 1, 18, 72, 86, 90, 873, 880, 1677

THOMAS, Samuel S.; pvt; 1st MD Lt Arty; ref: 1, 2, 19, 21, 68, 511, 782, 791, 1273

THOMAS, Thomas; res: Carrollton Manor; ref: 643

THOMAS, Thomas H. (M.D.); Asst Surg; Wayside Hospital, Richmond; res: Cambridge, Dor Cty; ref: 1, 18, 112

THOMAS, Tobias; res: Frederick, Frd Cty; ref: 89

THOMAS, Wesley; pvt; Lanier's Co, VA Lt Arty; res: St. M. Cty; ref: 1, 7

THOMAS, William; pvt; 18th VA Cav, Co D; res: Davidsonville, AA Cty; ref: 1, 735, 1539

THOMAS, William; pvt; 1st MD Cav, Co D; ref: 1, 2, 19, 21, 55, 511, 1601

THOMAS, William C.; ref: 53

THOMAS, William H.; ref: 53

THOMAS, William P.; 1st MD Inf, Co C; ref: 1, 2, 19, 21, 64, 456, 511

THOMAS, William W.; Navy; res: Balt; ref: 1

THOMPSON, A. C. C.; Maj; 3rd GA; res: Tal Cty; ref: 645, 1152, 1494

THOMPSON, Benjamin William; pvt; 43rd VA Cav (Mosby's), Co A; res: Cha Cty; ref: 1, 2, 8, 19, 21, 730

THOMPSON, C. Gratiot; Capt; Ordnance Dept, McGowan's Brigade; res: Balt; ref: 1, 2, 19, 21, 23, 44, 700, 791

THOMPSON, Charles R.; pvt; 1st MD Cav, Co E; res: Cha Cty; ref: 1, 2, 19, 21, 690, 730, 1577, 1578

THOMPSON, D. Bowly; Capt; Asst Commissary of Supply, Gen J. A. Wharton's staff; res: Balt; ref: 1, 2, 19, 21, 312, 681, 690, 700, 735, 791, 1520

THOMPSON, Dorsey; pvt; 1st MD Cav, Co A; res: Ellicott City, How Cty; ref: 1, 2, 10, 19, 21, 71

THOMPSON, Edward Livingstone; pvt; 43rd VA Cav (Mosby's), Co A; ref: 1, 2, 8, 10, 19, 21, 71, 75

THOMPSON, Francis; res: Balt; ref: 1540

THOMPSON, George; pvt; 2nd MD Cav, Co F; ref: 1, 2, 19, 21, 1523

THOMPSON, Gilbert Livingstone; pvt; 1st MD Cav, Co A; res: Ellicott City, How Cty; ref: 1, 2, 19, 21, 71, 628

THOMPSON, Henry; pvt; Lee's MD Cav; res: Balt; ref: 1, 19

THOMPSON, Ignatius Davis (M.D.); Asst Surg; Ladies Relief Hospital, Lynchburg; res: Balt; ref: 1, 18, 21, 44, 91, 700, 1533, 1534

THOMPSON, James H.; pvt; Davis's MD Cav; res: Balt; ref: 1, 11, 70, 700, 735

THOMPSON, James R.; cpl; 48th VA Inf, Co A; res: Leonardtown, St. M. Cty; ref: 1, 69, 316

THOMPSON, James West; pvt; Searcy's Bn, MO Sharpshooters; ref: 1, 70

THOMPSON, John; pvt; Edelin's MD Heavy Arty; ref: 1

THOMPSON, John; pvt; 19th VA Heavy Arty, Co C; ref: 1, 1580

THOMPSON, John E.; pvt; 17th VA Inf, Co A; res: PG Cty; ref: 1, 2, 21, 133, 142

THOMPSON, John W.; Lt; Ordnance Officer, Gen H. R. Jackson's staff; res: Frederick, Frd Cty; ref: 90, 93

THOMPSON, John W.; pvt; Zarvona's MD Zouaves; res: Leonardtown, St. M. Cty; MLCSH; ref: 1, 2, 19, 21, 627, 700, 735, 786, 1509

THOMPSON, Joseph; cpl; Zarvona's MD Zouaves; ref: 1, 2, 19, 58, 97

THOMPSON, Joseph; pvt; Davis's MD Cav, Co C; res: Frd Cty; ref: 1

THOMPSON, L. G.; pvt; Graham's Co, VA Lt Arty; res: How Cty; ref: 1, 10

THOMPSON, M. King; pvt; 7th VA Cav, Co G; ref: 1, 1621

THOMPSON, Magnus Stribling; pvt; 35th VA Cav, Co C; res: Frd Cty; ref: 1, 3, 677, 992, 1259, 1611, 1677

THOMPSON, Meredith (M.D.); Physician; Medical Corps; ref: 1, 18, 735
THOMPSON, R.; pvt; MD American Rifles; ref: 1, 19
THOMPSON, Robert; pvt; Davis's MD Cav, Co A; ref: 1, 735
THOMPSON, Samuel T.; cpl; 1st MD Lt Arty; res: Balt; ref: 1, 2, 19, 21, 34, 684, 758, 791, 823, 1273, 1523
THOMPSON, Thomas G.; res: St. M. Cty; ref: 1670
THOMPSON, Thomas M.; pvt; 2nd MD Lt Arty; res: Cha Cty; MLCSH; ref: 1, 2, 19, 21, 92, 93, 700, 786
THOMPSON, Thomas Maskins; pvt; 1st MD Inf, Co I; res: Chaptico, St. M. Cty; ref: 1, 19, 627, 1539, 1555
THOMPSON, Tompkins J.; Lmn, Navy; C.S. Webb; res: Ellicott City, How Cty; ref: 1, 10, 1550
THOMPSON, Winfield Scott; Chief Engr, Navy; C.S. Florida; ref: 1, 19, 21, 58, 61, 93, 97, 700, 783, 1564, 1574, 1673
THORBURN, Henry C.; Capt; Fredericksburg Lt Arty; res: Balt; ref: 21, 56, 105, 700
THORNTON, Earnest M.; pvt; 3rd MD Lt Arty; ref: 1, 2, 19, 21, 160, 726
THORNTON, Francis A.; pvt; Stuart's Horse Arty, Breathed's Battery; res: Balt; ref: 1, 2, 19, 21, 498
THRASHER, Thadeus L.; Lt; 35th VA Cav, Co B; res: Merryland Tract, Frd Cty; ref: 1, 3, 11, 64, 90, 291, 791, 1154, 1156, 1278, 1371
THRIFT, Augustus; pvt; 19th VA Heavy Arty, Co C; ref: 1, 1580
THRIFT, James W.; Navy; C.S. Beaufort; res: Balt; ref: 1
THROGMARTIN, Albert; pvt; 19th VA Heavy Arty, Co C; ref: 1, 1580
THURMAN, John R.; Lt; Lee's Balt Lt Arty, Alexander's Bn; ref: 1
THURMOND, Erasmus Stewart; Lt; 15th TN Cav, Co F; ref: 1, 72
THURSTON, James; Lt, Marine Corps; C.S.S. Atlanta; res: Catonsville, Bt Cty; ref: 1, 21, 23, 56, 97, 700, 783, 791, 792, 1495, 1515, 1593, 1594
TIFFANY, Henry, Jr; pvt; 21st VA Inf, Co B; res: Balt; ref: 1, 2, 19, 312, 735
TILGHMAN, James of John; pvt; 1st MD Cav, Co B; res: QA Cty; ref: 1, 19
TILGHMAN, John; pvt; 2nd MD Cav, Co F; ref: 1, 2, 19, 21
TILGHMAN, John Leeds; Lt; Moore's Co, VA Lt Arty; res: Oxford Neck, Tal Cty; ref: 1, 19, 23, 330, 511, 645, 791, 1481, 1523
TILGHMAN, Lloyd, Jr; Lt; Aide de Camp, Gen L. Tilghman's staff; res: Tal Cty; ref: 1, 834
TILGHMAN, Lloyd, Sr.; Brig Gen; Army of Tennessee; res: Tal Cty; ref: 1, 2, 18, 19, 23, 31, 39, 44, 50, 70, 109, 127, 130, 137, 151, 153, 156, 158, 164, 166, 175, 266, 319, 330, 388, 431, 511, 592, 601, 631, 645, 674, 681, 686, 735, 787, 789, 791, 834, 835, 857, 863, 978, 993, 1000, 1006, 1048, 1051, 1094, 1132, 1152, 1279, 1481, 1523, 1526, 1568, 1577, 1578, 1579, 1588, 1623, 1640
TILGHMAN, Ogle S.; Lt; 1st TN Lt Arty; res: Tal Cty; ref: 1, 17, 19, 82, 789, 791, 1523
TILGHMAN, Oswald, Capt; Weller's Co, TN Lt Arty; res: Oxford Neck, Tal Cty; ref: 1, 2, 19, 23, 57, 330, 511, 541, 635, 645, 791, 873, 885, 910, 1001, 1134, 1152, 1162, 1423, 1481, 1523, 1612, 1626
TILGHMAN, Richard Cooke; Pvt; 2nd MD Inf, Co A; res: Easton, Tal Cty; ref: 1, 2, 19, 21, 70, 511, 645, 650, 1510, 1690
TILGHMAN, Tench Francis; Col; Jefferson Davis body guard; res: Oxford Neck, Tal Cty; ref: 19, 23, 60, 330, 511, 592, 613, 645, 791, 1510, 1612
TILLINGHAST, J. H. (Revd); Chaplain; 44th NC Inf, Frd Cty; ref: 1, 72
TILLMAN, Henry; res: Mont Cty; ref: 615

TIMBERLAKE, Philip; pvt; Stuart's Horse Arty, Breathed's Battery; ref: 1

TIMMONS, William E.; pvt; 2nd MD Inf, Co G; ref: 1, 2, 19, 21

TINGAE, Thomas; 39th VA Inf, Co B; ref: 735

TINGES, Charles S.; pvt; 4th MD Lt Arty; res: Balt; ref: 1, 2, 19, 21, 82, 700

TINGLE, David P. B.; pvt; Barry's Co, MD Vols; ref: 1, 2, 19, 21, 628

TINGLE, Thomas N.; cpl; 39th VA Inf, Co B; ref: 1, 735

TINGLE, Thomas N.; pvt; Barry's Co MD Vols; res: Berlin, Wor Cty; ref: 1, 1559

TINGLE, W.; pvt; 2nd MD Inf, Co G; ref: 1

TINGSLEY, Alexander (M.D.); Asst Surg; Williamsburg Hospital; res: Balt; ref: 1, 18, 1534, 1536

TINLEY, John; pvt; 3rd MD Lt Arty; ref: 1, 2, 19, 21, 160, 316, 461, 726, 1460

TIPPETT, George W.; pvt; MD American Rifles; res: St. Clements Bay, St. M. Cty; ref: 1, 2, 19, 21, 1555, 1627

TIPPETT, James B.; pvt; 1st MD Inf, Co H; res: St. M. Cty; ref: 1, 2, 19, 21, 650, 1509, 1662

TIPPETT, Maximillian Alaway Kepler; pvt; 1st MD Cav, Co B; res: St. M. Cty; MLCSH; ref: 1, 2, 19, 21, 93, 627, 700, 785, 786, 1509

TIPPETT, Thomas E.; pvt; 35th VA Cav, Co A; ref: 1, 15, 791, 1611, 1677

TITUS, William; pvt; 35th VA Cav, Co A; ref: 1, 3, 15, 1611, 1677

TRUIT, George; Stuart's Horse Arty, Breathed's Battery; ref: 735

TOBIN, John; pvt; MD Guerrilla Zouaves; ref: 1

TODD, George; pvt; 9th VA Cav, Co B; res: Tal Cty; ref: 1, 19, 645

TODD, Henry S.; Lt; 9th VA Inf, Co B; ref: 1, 735, 1576

TODD, Joseph; Hospital Steward; Medical Dept; res: Bt Cty; MLCSH; ref: 1, 21, 93, 700, 786

TODD, Merryman; sgt; 2nd MD Cav, Co C; res: Bt Cty; ref: 1, 2, 19, 21, 23, 680, 791, 1575

TODD, Richard; pvt; 13th VA Inf, Co G; ref: 1, 735

TODD, Thomas R.; pvt; Edelin's MD Heavy Arty; ref: 1

TODD, William E.; pvt; 30th LA Inf, Co B; ref: 1, 677

TODD, William H.; pvt; 2nd MD Cav, Co C; res: Bt Cty; ref: 1, 2, 19, 21, 39, 680, 700

TOLBY, George W.; pvt; 6th VA Inf, Co I; res: Bty Cty; MLCSH; ref: 1, 21, 93, 700, 786, 881

TOLER, Washington Nelson; Capt; 6th VA Cav, Co K; res: Bt Cty; MLCSH; ref: 1, 786, 791

TOLLY, E. George; pvt; 1st MD Cav, Co A; res: Cambridge, Dor Cty; ref: 1, 1547

TOLSON, Albert; sgt; Barry's Co, MD Vols; res: Hyattsville, PG Cty; ref: 1, 2, 19, 21, 34, 456, 488, 700, 923, 1553, 1622

TOLSON, Alfred C.; pvt; 1st MD Cav, Co B; res: Old Fields, PG Cty; ref: 1, 2, 19, 21, 86, 785, 1553, 1574

TOLSON, Charles E.; pvt; 1st MD Cav, Co B; res: Broad Creek, QA Cty; ref: 1, 2, 19, 21, 785, 1554

TOLSON, Frank A.; pvt; 2nd MD Inf, Co A; res: Balt; ref: 1, 2, 19, 21, 650, 800

TOLSON, Thomas Hill; Lt; 2nd MD Inf, Co C; res: Balt; ref: 1, 2, 19, 21, 23, 68, 70, 674, 700, 1520, 1523

TOMLINSON, T. M.; pvt; 3rd MD Lt Arty; ref: 2, 19, 21, 160, 726, 1460

TOMPKINS, E. A.; pvt; 3rd MD Lt Arty; ref: 1, 2, 19, 21, 160, 726

TOMPKINS, John H. F.; pvt; Parker's VA Lt Arty Battery; res: Balt; ref: 1, 1595

TOMPKINS, William T.; pvt; 19th VA Inf, Co C; res: Balt; ref: 1, 21, 700
TOMS, Anderson Clay; V.M.I. Cadets; res: Balt; ref: 70, 1687
TOMS, Richard H. R.; pvt; 12th VA Inf, Co G; ref: 1, 70
TONGE, W. G. D.; pvt; 2nd MD Cav, Co A; res: Bt Cty; ref: 1, 19
TONGUE, Henry M.; cpl; 39th VA Cav, Co B; res: Bristol, AA Cty; ref: 1, 34, 1539
TONGUE, James; pvt; 1st MD Inf, Co H; ref: 1, 2, 19, 21, 650
TONGUE, Richard H.; cpl; Stuart's Horse Arty, Breathed's Battery; res: Balt; ref: 1, 2, 19, 21, 498, 1609
TONGUE, William; pvt; 43rd VA Cav (Mosby's), Co D; ref: 1, 8, 735
TONTON, M. W.; pvt; 1st MD Cav, Co E; ref: 1, 19, 730
TOOMEY, C. C.; pvt; 1st MD Cav, Co K; res: Balt; ref: 1, 19
TOOMEY, Daniel; sgt; 3rd MD Lt Arty; ref: 1, 2, 19, 21, 23, 160, 454, 461, 726, 1523
TOPPER, Pica; pvt; 6th VA Cav, Co D; res: Frederick, Frd Cty; ref: 1, 89
TORMEY, Thomas A.; Capt; 42nd TN Cav; res: Balt; ref: 1
TORNAY, Sylvester C.; Navy; Naval Bn; res: Towson, Bt Cty; ref: 1, 2, 19, 21, 23, 57, 700, 783, 873, 1541
TORPIE, James; pvt; 2nd MD Cav, Co A; ref: 1, 19
TORRENT, Joseph F.; pvt; 1st SC Inf, Co E; res: Balt; ref: 1, 1352
TORRINGTON, John; pvt; Lucas' 15th SC Heavy Arty; res: Balt; ref: 1
TORSCH, John W.; Capt; 2nd MD Inf, Co E; res: Balt; ref: 1, 2, 19, 21, 23, 61, 63, 64, 68, 240, 488, 511, 647, 700, 703, 735, 791, 848, 849, 860, 862, 923, 1057, 1520, 1523
TOTER, W. Nelson; ref: 700
TOWILL, M. T.; pvt; 48th MS Inf, Co E; ref: 1, 700
TOWLES, E. W.; pvt; 43rd VA Cav (Mosby's), Co F; ref: 8
TOWLES, John Chouning; pvt; 9th VA Cav, Co D; ref: 1, 2, 19, 21, 70
TOY, Joseph L.; pvt; 2nd MD Inf, Co A; res: Balt; ref: 1, 2, 19, 21, 650
TOY, Thomas B.; pvt; 4th MD Lt Arty; res: Balt; ref: 1, 2, 19, 21
TOYSEY, James; pvt; Davis's MD Cav, Co A; ref: 1
TRADER, George; pvt; 9th VA Inf, Co B; res: Balt; ref: 1, 1576
TRAIL, Barton; pvt; 17th VA Cav, Co H; ref: 1, 86
TRAIL, Charles M.; pvt; 2nd MD Inf, Co A; ref: 1, 2, 19, 21, 650, 1577
TRAIL, Lewis William; sgt; 1st MD Cav, Co D; res: Prospect Hill, Frd Cty; ref: 1, 2, 19, 21, 23, 70, 90, 112, 1001, 1312, 1601
TRAINOR, E.; pvt; 2nd MD Cav, Co G; ref: 1, 19
TRAMMILL, John; pvt; 35th VA Cav, Co A; ref: 1, 1677
TRAPIER, Pierre D. G.; pvt; Engineer Corps, Co F; ref: 1, 21, 700
TRAPIER, Theodore D.; pvt; Parker's Co, SC Lt Arty; ref: 1, 21, 700
TRAPNELL, Joseph H.; pvt; 7th VA Cav, Co G; res: Merryland Tract, Frd Cty; ref: 1, 2, 3, 19, 21, 90, 1601
TRAVERS, Alonzo; sgt; 2nd MD Cav, Co A; ref: 1, 2, 19, 21, 23, 614, 695, 1609
TRAVERS, J. H.; pvt; 2nd MD Cav, Co F; ref: 1, 2, 19, 21, 1609, 1631
TRAVERSS, John M.; pvt; Letcher's Co, VA Lt Arty; res: Balt; ref: 1, 2, 19, 21, 700, 735, 1613
TRAVIS, James R.; pvt; 9th VA Inf, Co B; ref: 1, 1576
TRAYNOR, John Henry; pvt; 59th VA Inf, Co D; ref: 1, 70
TRAYWICK, Bryant S. (D.D.S.); sgt; ref: 1690
TREAKLE, Albert; pvt; 1st VA Cav, Co K; res: How Cty; ref: 1, 2, 10, 19, 21

TREAKLE, Emanuel S.; pvt; 1st MD Cav, Co A; res: Cooksville, How Cty;ref: 1, 2, 10, 19, 21, 1550
TREAKLE, Henry W.; cpl; 40th VA Inf, Co H; res: Balt; ref: 1, 1388
TREGOE, John L.; pvt; 4th MD Lt Arty; res: Cornersville, Dor Cty; ref: 1, 2, 19, 21, 112, 259, 1547, 1666
TRIGGER, John; pvt; 4th MD Lt Arty; ref: 1, 2, 19, 21
TRIMBLE, Isaac Ridgeway; Maj Gen; Army of Northern Virginia; res: Balt; ref: 1, 2, 15, 17, 18, 19, 21, 23, 34, 35, 39, 42, 44, 45, 46, 48, 50, 54, 62, 63, 64, 65, 68, 70, 88, 96, 97, 104, 105, 110, 111, 114, 115, 116, 126, 127, 129, 130, 138, 139, 144, 145, 152, 154, 155, 159, 165, 166, 169, 209, 211, 240, 386, 397, 422, 431, 443, 450, 453, 456, 462, 484, 489, 494, 501, 503, 508, 513, 515, 541, 606, 674, 678, 684, 686, 700, 722, 735, 753, 758, 764, 776, 781, 782, 787, 789, 791, 816, 818, 838, 857, 873, 875, 894, 916, 931, 944, 962, 974, 1006, 1029, 1124, 1128, 1140, 1181, 1279, 1282, 1330, 1347, 1379, 1423, 1489, 1523, 1560, 1570, 1577, 1578, 1579, 1583, 1623, 1633, 1642, 1644, 1652, 1673, 1674, 1675
TRIMBLE, John D.; Midn, Navy; C.S.S. Savannah; ref: 1, 2, 21, 58, 97, 282, 1564
TRIPLETT, H. F.; pvt; Stuart's Horse Arty, Breathed's Battery; res: St. M. Cty; ref: 1, 498, 1670
TRIPPE, Charles; pvt; Lee's MD Cav; ref: 1, 19
TRIPPE, Andrew Cross; Lt; Ordnance Officer, Maryland Line; res: Balt; ref: 1, 2, 19, 21, 23, 53, 56, 57, 68, 70, 150, 259, 493, 541, 650, 686, 693, 700, 734, 798, 848, 885, 891, 906, 916, 944, 945, 994, 1001, 1058, 1603
TRIPPLETT, George; pvt; 35th VA Cav, Co B; ref: 1, 1677
TRITAPOE, Samuel E.; cpl; Loudoun Rangers, Co A; res: Petersville; ref: 67
TROUT, William; pvt; 2nd MD Cav, Co C; res: Balt; ref: 1, 19
TRUEHEARD, J. G.; pvt; 2nd MD Cav, Co A; ref: 1, 19, 1609
TRUNDLE, Joseph H.; pvt; 35th VA Cav, Co B; res: Carrollton Manor, Frd Cty; ref: 1, 3, 19, 72, 73, 90, 615, 643, 1405, 1548, 1579, 1611, 1677
TRUNDLE, Samuel; pvt; 35th VA Cav, Co D; res: Carrollton Manor, Frd Cty; ref: 1, 19, 90, 643, 1677
TRUNDLE, William H.; cpl; 43rd VA Cav (Mosby's), Co D; ref: 1, 8, 19, 64, 393, 710
TRUST, George; pvt; Stuart's Horse Arty, Breathed's Battery; res: Balt; MLCSH; ref: 1, 21, 498, 700, 786
TSCHIFFELY, Edgar L.; pvt; 1st MD Cav, Co A; res: Huntings Hill, Mont Cty; ref: 1, 2, 19, 21, 23, 71, 73, 86, 718, 1452, 1463, 1467, 1487, 1574
TUBMAN, Charles; pvt; Ramsey's Battery, TN Lt Arty; res: Church Creek, Dor Cty; ref: 1, 112, 1547
TUBMAN, Richard; pvt; Davis's MD Cav, Co B; ref: 1, 19
TUCK, Richard W.; 2nd MD Cav, Co C; ref: 7
TUCKER, Albert J.; pvt; 19th VA Heavy Arty, Co C; ref: 1, 2, 19, 21, 1580
TUCKER, Enock Brison; pvt; 3rd VA Inf, Co F; res: Balt; ref: 1, 21, 57, 70, 700, 916
TUCKER, Erastus B.; cpl; 12th VA Inf, Co C; res: Balt; MLCSH; ref: 1, 786
TUCKER, Frank E.; pvt; Holbrook's Independent MD Lt Arty; ref: 1
TUCKER, George W.; sgt; 12th VA Cav, Co F; res: Balt; MLcSH; ref: 21, 700, 786
TUCKER, James L.; pvt; 35th VA Cav, Co C; ref: 1677

TUCKER, John W.; pvt; Hampton Leg Lt Arty, Co B; res: Friendship, AA Cty; ref: 1, 2, 19, 21, 1539
TUIT, Michael; pvt; 1st MD Inf, Co G; ref: 1
TULL, Martin L.; Lt; Aide de Camp, Gen A. Thomas's staff; res: Gales Town, Dor Cty; ref: 1, 19, 112, 1547
TULLY, John; pvt; 2nd MD Cav, Co D; ref: 1, 19, 1609
TUNIS, John Oliver; pvt; 1st MD Cav, Co B; res: Broad Creek, QA Cty; ref: 1, 2, 19, 21, 80, 645, 785, 1554
TUNIS, Theophilus; pvt; 1st MD Cav, Co B; res: Broad Creek, QA Cty; MLCSH; ref: 1, 2, 19, 21, 23, 39, 57, 80, 122, 645, 700, 785, 786, 1361, 1383, 1474, 1483, 1554
TURNBULL, S. Graeme; Lt; 1st MD Cav, Co C; ref: 1, 2, 19, 21, 23, 28, 1583
TURNBULL, W. S.; Lt; 1st MD Cav, Co C; ref: 2, 19, 21, 23, 28, 64
TURNER, Alfred; pvt; Davis's MD Cav, Co C; ref: 1
TURNER, Benjamin; sgt; 40th VA Inf, Co C; res: Balt; ref: 1, 21, 700
TURNER, Duncan Manro; sgt; 1st MD Cav, Co B; res: Bachelors Hope, St. M. Cty; ref: 1, 2, 19, 21, 23, 81, 503, 650, 715, 785, 822, 1509, 1555
TURNER, Franklin P.; Captain; 36th VA Inf, Co E; res: Sharpsburg, Wash Cty; ref: 1, 361, 681, 791
TURNER, J. H. (Revd); Lt; 10th VA Cav, Co K; res: Lutherville, Bt Cty; ref: 21, 70, 681, 700
TURNER, James B.; Navy; C.S.S. Gaines; res: Johnsons Store, AA Cty; ref: 1, 1539
TURNER, John A.; pvt; 3rd MD Lt Arty; res: Forge, AA Cty; ref: 2, 19, 21, 160, 461, 726, 1539
TURNER, John Henry; pvt; 2nd MD Inf, Co B; res: Charlotte Hall, St.M. Cty; ref: 1, 2, 19, 21, 1509, 1555, 1627
TURNER, Joseph; pvt; 9th VA Inf, Co B; ref: 1, 800, 1576
TURNER, Richard; Naval Bn, Navy; res: Millersville, AA Cty; ref: 1, 1539
TURNER, Theopilus J.; pvt; MD Guerrilla Zouaves; ref: 1, 1377
TURNER, Thomas; Lt; 43rd VA Cav (Mosby's), Co A; ref: 1, 2, 8, 19, 21, 44, 123, 393, 710, 735, 1523
TURNER, Thomas; pvt; Stuart's Horse Arty, Breathed's Battery; ref: 19, 498
TURNER, Vince Edward; Capt; 23rd NC Inf, Co G; ref: 1, 1529
TURNER, William L.; pvt; 43rd VA Cav (Mosby's); res: Molesville, Bt Cty; ref: 1, 2, 8, 19, 21, 1540, 1541, 1555
TURNER, William Mason (M.D.); Asst Surg; Navy; C.S.S. Chicora; ref: 1, 18, 70, 1534, 1536, 1564
TURNER, Wilson; pvt; Stuart's Horse Arty, Breathed's Battery; res: St. M. Cty; ref: 498, 1670
TURPIN, Henry W. (M.D.) Acting Asst Surg, Bristol, Tennessee Hospital; MLCSH; ref: 1, 18, 316, 786
TUPRIN, Richard; pvt; 2nd MD Cav, Co D; ref: 1, 19, 1609
TURPIN, Thomas L.; pvt; 59th VA Inf, Co D; res: Balt; ref: 1, 2, 19, 21, 700
TURRELL, Barron; pvt; 1st MD Cav, Co D; ref: 1, 19
TURTON, Benjamin F.; cpl; 1st MD Cav, Co E; ref: 1, 2, 19, 21, 23, 730
TURTON, M. W.; pvt; 1st MD Cav, Co E; ref: 1, 2, 19, 21, 730
TUTTLE, Charles; drummer; 1st MD Inf, Co D; ref: 1, 2, 19, 21
TUTWILER, William; pvt; 1st MD Cav, Co A; res: Hyattsville, PG Cty; ref: 1, 1622
TWILLEY, Benjamin F.; cpl; 2nd MD Inf, Co G; res: Salem, Dor Cty; MLCSH;ref: 1, 2, 19, 21, 23, 112, 786
TWILLEY, George H.; pvt; 2nd MD Inf, Co G; res: Salem, Dor Cty; ref: 1, 2, 19, 21, 112

TYDINGS, Richard; res: Annapolis, AA Cty; ref: 1539
TYES, J. M.; pvt; 6th AL Inf, Co G; ref: 1, 92
TYLER, Albert; pvt; 1st MD Cav, Co D; ref: 1, 2, 19, 21, 1601
TYLER, Arthur; 8th LA Inf; ref: 735
TYLER, Charles; pvt; 3rd MD Lt Arty; ref: 1, 2, 19, 21, 160, 726
TYLER, Emmet; ref: 681
TYLER, George; sgt; 1st MD Inf, Co A; res: Frederick, Frd Cty; ref: 1, 2, 19, 21, 23, 90, 456, 488, 923, 1601
TYLER, Grafton, Jr; Lt; Braxton's Bn, Lt Arty; res: Georgetown; ref: 1, 2, 19, 21
TYLER, John Bailey; pvt; 1st MD Cav, Co D; res: Frederick, Frd Cty; ref: 1, 2, 19, 21, 89, 90, 107, 1601
TYLER, Nathaniel; Maj; 20th VA Inf; res: Balt; ref: 1600
TYLER, Robert Charles; Brig Gen; Army of Tennessee; res: Balt; ref: 1, 18, 23, 100, 110, 114, 127, 130, 256, 431, 601, 735, 791, 993, 1006, 1094, 1578, 1579, 1588, 1623
TYLER, Samuel Albert; sgt; 26th VA Inf, Co C; res: Frederick, Frd Cty; ref: 1, 90
TYLER, Walter Bowie; pvt; Carpenter's VA Lt Arty; ref: 1, 316, 700
TYLER, William; pvt; 1st MD Inf, Co B; ref: 1, 2, 19, 21
TYLER, Winfield; pvt; 1st MD Cav, Co F; ref: 1, 2, 19, 21
TYSON, Henry H.; Passed Midn, Navy; C.S.S. Richmond; res: Glenel, How Cty; ref: 1, 19, 58, 59, 97, 279, 1550, 1564
TYSON, Isaac; pvt; 1st FL Cav, Co B; res: Balt; ref: 1, 1540
TYSON, Richard; pvt; 3rd MD Lt Arty; ref: 1, 2, 19, 21, 160, 726

UKHORN, Joseph H. K.; pvt; 2nd MD Cav, Co C; ref: 1, 19
UHLHORN, John H.; sgt; 1st MD Inf, Co C; res: Balt; ref: 1, 2, 19, 21, 23
ULLMAN, Jacob; pvt; 49th VA Inf, Co C; res: Annapolis; ref: 1, 1539, 1628
UNCLE, William F.; cpl; Zarvona's MD Zouaves; ref: 1, 2, 21, 61, 703, 735
UNKLES, William F.; pvt; 2nd MD Inf, Co E; res: Great Mills, St. M. Cty; ref: 1, 2, 19, 21, 23, 470, 1509, 1555
UPSHIRE, Avin; sgt; Davis's MD Cav; res: Wor Cty; ref: 1
UPSHUR, Abel P.; cpl; 1st VA Lt Arty, Co B; ref: 1, 700
UPSHUR, J.; pvt; 13th VA Inf, Co G; ref: 1, 735
UPSHUR, Levin; sgt; 2nd MD Cav, Co E; ref: 2, 21, 700
URLSON, J. H.; Lt; Davis's MD Cav, Co B; ref: 1
USSERY, D.; pvt; 3rd MD Lt Arty; ref: 2, 19, 21, 160, 726
UTTERBACK, John N.; pvt; 35th VA Cav, Co F; res: Burkettsville, Frd Cty; ref: 1, 67, 1611, 1677

VALENTINE, George; pvt; 1st MD Cav, Co C; res: Bt Cty; ref: 1, 2, 19, 21
VALENTINE, John C.; pvt; 4th MD Lt Arty; ref: 1
VALIANT, Thomas Rigby; 1st MD Inf, Co H; res: Tal Cty; ref: 1, 2, 19, 21, 35, 645, 650, 1284
VALK, John M. E.; Capt; 21st NC Inf; ref: 1, 70
VALLANDINGHAM, Irving S. (M.D.); Asst Surg, Davis's MD Cav; res: Eastern Shore of Maryland; ref: 1, 700
VALLANDINGHAM, J. L.; pvt; McNeill's Rangers; res: St. M. Cty; ref: 1, 19, 504, 1670
VALLANDINGHAM, John L.; pvt; 1st MD Cav, Co B; res: Cec Cty; ref: 1, 2, 21, 785
VALLIANT, Edwin S.; pvt; 2nd MD Inf, Co C; res: Tal Cty; ref: 1, 2, 19, 21, 595, 645, 1284, 1612

VALLIANT, George E.; smn, Navy; res: Tal Cty; ref: 1, 645, 1284, 1612
VALLIANT, George E. W.; pvt; 1st MD Inf, Co E; ref: 1, 2, 19, 21
VALLIANT, William W.; Capt; Quartermaster Dept, Gen M. McIntosh's staff; res: Tal Cty; ref: 1, 70, 1284
VAN AMBURG, Charles Jesse; pvt; Davis's MD Cav, Co A; ref: 1, 735, 800
VAN BUSSUM, Phillip; pvt; 35th VA Cav, Co B; res: Balt; ref: 1, 3, 1611, 1677
VANCE, Henry; pvt; MD American Rifles; ref: 1, 70, 735
VANDIVER, George T.; pvt; 1st MD Cav, Co E; res: Havre-de-Grace, Har Cty; ref: 1, 2, 19, 21, 350, 720, 730, 1560
VANHEP, James H.; Balt; ref: 1540
VAN METER, Reasin Bell; pvt; 7th VA Cav, Co F; res: Balt; ref: 1, 21, 700, 1389
VANNOY, Henry S.; pvt; Lee's MD Cav; res: AA Cty; ref: 1, 1628
VANSANT, John B.; pvt; 4th MD Lt Arty; res: QA Cty; ref: 1
VANZANDT, Nicholas H.; Lt, Navy; Charleston Squadron; res: Balt; ref: 1, 735, 1564
VASSER, Franklin; pvt; 9th VA Inf, Co B; ref: 1, 1576
VAUGHAN, James G.; pvt; Holbrook's Independent MD Lt Arty; ref: 1
VAUGHMAN, John M.; Lt; 10th VA Cav, Co D; res: Balt; ref: 21, 70, 700
VAUGLAN, Robert F.; 4th VA Cav; ref: 70
VEIT, Lewis H.; pvt; 2nd MD Inf, Co C; res: Frd Cty; ref: 1, 2, 19, 21, 90
VEITCH, Wilberforce; pvt; V.M.I. Cadets; res: Balt; ref: 1, 1687
VERBAL, C. M.; pvt; Stuart's Horse Arty, Breathed's Battery; ref: 1
VERDIN, William W. (M.D.); Surg; 63rd NC Inf; res: Lapadum, Har Cty; ref: 1, 18, 70
VERNON, John A.; sgt; 13th VA Inf, Co G; res: Chestertown, Kt Cty ref: 1, 735, 1584
VESTLE, Denis A.; pvt; 1st MD Cav, Co A; ref: 1, 19
VIA, Dillard; pvt; 9th VA Inf, Co B; ref: 1, 1576
VIA, James T.; pvt; Davis's MD Cav, Co A; ref: 1, 19, 735
VICENTE, J.; sgt; 1st SC Inf, Co G; ref: 1, 693
VICK, James; pvt; 9th VA Inf, Co B; ref: 1, 1576
VICKERS, Benjamin Clothier; pvt; 4th TN Inf, Co A; res: Kt Cty; ref: 1, 107, 668, 1584
VICKERS, Washington A.; pvt; 2nd MD Inf, Co G; res: East New Market, Dor Cty; ref: 1, 2, 19, 21, 112, 650, 1510
VICKERS, William; pvt; Barry's Co, MD Vols; ref: 1
VIERS, Elijah; pvt; 35th VA Cav, Co B; res: Old Medley's, Mont Cty; ref: 1, 3, 15, 106, 371, 1611, 1677
VIERS, Henry Bollingbroke; pvt; 35th VA Cav, Co B; res: Old Medley's, Mont Cty; ref: 1, 3, 106, 1552, 1611, 1677
VIERS, John Montgomery; pvt; 35th VA Cav, Co B; ref: 735, 1611, 1677
VIERS, William Hezekiah; pvt; 35th VA Cav, Co B; res: Rockville, Mont Cty; MLCSH; ref: 1, 93, 627, 700, 786, 921, 1552, 1611, 1621, 1677
VIERS, William Seneca; pvt; 35th VA Cav, Co B; res: Old Medley's, Mont Cty; ref: 1, 3, 106, 1552, 1611, 1677
VINSON, Joshua A.; pvt; 35th VA Cav, Co B; res: Mont Cty; ref: 1, 3, 1116, 1574, 1611, 1677
VIRDIN, William Ward, Jr (M.D.); Asst Surg; 63rd NC; res: Lapadum, Har Cty; ref: 1, 18, 21, 122, 700, 735, 1536
VOGHT, Frederick E.; sgt; 1st MD Inf, Co F; res: Balt; ref: 1, 2, 19, 21, 700
VOGLE, John A.; pvt; 2nd MD Cav, Co D; res: Smithsburg, Wash Cty; ref: 1, 1558

VOSS, Franklin; pvt; 1st MD Inf, Co C; res: Balt; ref: 1, 2, 19, 21, 38, 536, 628

WADDELL, James A.; sgt; 23rd VA Inf, Co B; res: Balt; MLCSH; ref: 1, 21, 92, 93, 700, 735, 786

WADDELL, James Iredall; Lt Commanding, Navy; C.S.s. Shenandoah; res: Annapolis, AA Cty; ref: 1, 19, 61, 97, 269, 274, 280, 282, 283, 284, 431, 511, 550, 600, 654, 697, 700, 721, 731, 774, 1495, 1499, 1515, 1523, 1578, 1632, 1673, 1676, 1685

WADDELL, John; pvt; Davis's MD Cav, Co C; ref: 1

WADE, A. P.; pvt; 10th VA Cav, Co C; ref: 1, 2, 19, 21, 461, 726

WADE, Charles; Edward; pvt; 2nd MD Inf, Co F; res: Homonky, Cha Cty; ref: 1, 2, 19, 21, 1546

WADE, George A.; pvt; 2nd MD Inf, Co F; res: Homonky, Cha Cty; ref: 1, 2, 19, 21, 1546

WADE, John R.; pvt; Hampton Leg Lt Arty, Co B; ref: Homonky, Cha Cty; MLCSH; ref: 1, 2, 19, 21, 786, 1546

WADE, Joshua Richard; pvt; 9th VA Inf, Co B; res: Homonky, Cha Cty; ref: 1, 1546, 1576

WADE, W. E.; pvt; 2nd MD Cav, Co A; ref: 1, 7, 19, 1609

WADE, William O.; smn, Navy; ref: 1

WAESCHE, William H.; Lt; 10th VA Inf, Co B; res: Old Medleys, Mont Cty; ref: 1, 106, 1611, 1677

WAGGNER, Louis Clinton; pvt; 61st VA Inf, Co E; res: Balt; MLCSH; ref: 21, 627, 700, 786

WAGNER, Charles V.; pvt; 7th VA Cav, Co G; res: Balt; MLCSH; ref: 1, 3, 21, 68, 700, 735, 777, 786

WAGNER, Gustavus; pvt, Marine Corps; C.S.S. Charleston; res: Balt; ref: 1, 1594

WAGNER, Henry; pvt; 1st VA Cav, Co K; res; Frd Cty; ref: 1, 2, 19, 21, 90

WAGNER, Henry C.; pvt; Holbrook's Independent MD Lt Arty; res: Balt; ref: 1, 690, 777

WAGNER, John G.; pvt; 2nd MD Inf, Co A; res: Balt; ref: 1, 2, 19, 21, 92, 93, 259, 650, 1520

WAGNER, John J.; pvt; 2nd MD Inf, Co H; ref: 1, 2, 19, 21

WAGNER, Joseph L.; sgt; 2nd MD Inf, Co F; res: Libertytown, Frd Cty; ref: 1, 2, 19, 21, 23, 90

WAGNER, Richard C.; pvt; 2nd MD Inf, Co F; res: Libertytown, Frd Cty; ref: 1, 2, 19, 90

WAGONER, Henry E.; pvt; 1st TN Inf, Co D; res: Reisterstown, Bt Cty; ref: 21, 700

WAIL, John; pvt; 1st VA Inf, Co E; ref: 1, 735

WAKEFIELD, James; pvt; 3rd MD Lt Arty; ref: 1, 2, 19, 21, 160, 726

WAKENIGHT, John; pvt; Davis's MD Cav, Co A; res: Wash Cty; ref: 1, 3, 735

WALBRACH, John J. Barth; Lt; Stonewall Brigade Lt Arty; MLCSH: ref: 21, 93, 700

WALES, J. C.; pvt; 2nd MD Lt Arty; ref: 1, 2, 19, 21

WALKER, Basil Manly; 8th AL Inf, Co K; res: Balt; ref: 1689

WALKER, Benjamin F.; 59th VA Inf, Co B; ref: 1, 92

WALKER, Charles C.; pvt; 35th VA Cav, Co A; res: Mont Cty; ref: 1, 3, 1677

WALKER, Charles Wilson Patrick; pvt; 3rd AL Inf, Co I; res: Hagerstown, Wash Cty; ref: 1, 1050

WALKER, Edmund Rhett (M.D.); Asst Surg; 8th SC Inf; ref: 1, 18, 1532, 1536

WALKER, George W.; Asst Engr, Navy; C.S. Sea Bird; res: Balt; ref: 1, 21, 57, 97

WALKER, George W.; 23rd VA Inf, Co C; res: Frd Cty; ref: 1, 72, 513, 700

WALKER, Hiram H. (M.D.); Lt Col; 40th VA Inf; ref: 1, 18, 1690

WALKER, James R.; Cpl; 9th VA Inf, Co B; ref: 1, 1576
WALKER, Leonidas D.; Lt; Signal Officer, Gen R. S. Ripley's staff; res: Balt; ref: 1, 70
WALKER, Noah Dixon; Lt; 44th VA Inf, Co E; res: Bt Cty; ref: 1, 19, 720
WALKER, Samuel T.; Lt Col; 10th VA Inf; res: Emmitsburg, Frd Cty; ref: 1, 1600
WALKER, T. J.; pvt; 2nd MD Cav, Co D; ref: 1, 19, 1609
WALKER, Thomas Merriweather; pvt; 55th VA Inf, Co A; res: Carr Cty; MLCSH; ref: 1, 93, 627, 786
WALKER, W. H.; pvt; Barry's Co, MD Vols; ref: 1
WALKINS, Andrew; pvt; MD American Rifles; res: Laurel Factory, AA Cty; ref: 1, 70, 1539
WALKINS, N. J.; ref: 503
WALKINS, Nick W.; pvt; MD American Rifles; MLCSH; ref: 35, 700
WALL, James D.; sgt; 4th MD Lt Arty; ref: 1, 2, 19, 21, 23, 64
WALLACE, Benjamin G.; sgt; 2nd MD Inf, Co D; res: QA Cty; ref: 1, 1612
WALLACE, William; cpl; 2nd MD Lt Arty; ref: 1, 2, 19, 21
WALLACE, William T.; pvt; 1st MD Cav, Co B; res: Kt Cty; ref: 1, 19
WALLACH, Charles; Maj; Quartermaster Dept; ref: 1, 735, 791
WALLACK, Richard L.; pvt; 1st MD Lt Arty; ref: 1, 2, 19, 21
WALLER, John W.; pvt; 9th VA Inf, Co B; ref: 1, 1576
WALLER, Thaddeus W.; cpl; 1st GA Inf, Co K; res: Balt; ref: 1, 21, 700
WALLER, Thomas Conway; Col; 9th VA Cav; ref: 1, 21, 700, 791, 1600
WALLIS, Henry C.; sgt; 1st MD Cav, Co E; MLCSH; res: Kt Cty; ref: 1, 2, 19, 21, 23, 730, 786, 1584
WALLIS, Hugh Maxwell; pvt; 18th SC Inf, Co G; res: Wyatt's Chance, Kt Cty; ref: 1, 1584
WALLIS, James; sgt; Lucas 15th SC Heavy Arty; res: Balt; ref: 1
WALLIS, Teable; ref: 681
WALLIS, Thomas; pvt; 17th GA Inf, Co I; ref: 1, 681
WALLIS, William Thomas; sgt; 1st MD Inf, Co E; res: Kt Cty; ref: 1, 2, 19, 21, 23, 83, 1584
WALLS, J. William (M.D.); Surgeon-in-Charge, Senseney Hospital, Winchester; res: Balt; ref: 1, 2, 18, 21, 700, 1533, 1534, 1536
WALLS, William A.; pvt; 43rd VA Cav (Mosby's), Co A; ref: 1, 8, 20
WALSH, Daniel; pvt; 19th VA Heavy Arty, Co C; res: Balt; ref: 1, 1580
WALSH, Edward; pvt; 2nd MD Inf, Co H; ref: 1, 2, 19, 21
WALSH, James; pvt; 1st MD Inf, Co B; ref: 2, 19, 21
WALSH, John; pvt; Stuart's Horse Arty, Graham's Battery; res: Balt; MLCSH; ref: 1, 21, 700, 786
WALSH, Lawrence; pvt; 3rd MD Lt Arty; ref: 1
WALSH, Robert; pvt; 2nd MD Cav, Co D; ref: 1, 19, 1609
WALSH, Thomas; pvt; 1st VA Cav, Co K; res: Balt; ref: 1, 2, 19, 21
WALSH, Thomas K.; pvt; 1st MD Inf, Co C; ref: 1, 2, 19, 21
WALSLAGER, G. H.; Navy; Richmond Naval Yard; res: Balt; ref: 1
WALTER, Edward H.; Lt; 1st VA Cav, Co A; res: Balt; MLCSH; ref: 1, 2, 19, 21, 700, 786
WALTER, John A.; pvt; 2nd MD Lt Arty; ref: Balt; ref: 1, 2, 19, 21, 55, 693, 700
WALTERS, Charles H. M.; MD American Rifles; res: Balt; ref: 1, 1540, 1613
WALTERS, James D.; Lt; 1st MD Cav, Co C; ref: 1, 2, 19, 21, 23, 791
WALTERS, John; pvt; Davis's MD Cav, Co A; ref: 1, 735
WALTERS, W.; pvt; Barry's Co, MD Vols; ref: 1
WALTERS, William C.; Capt; 47th VA Inf, Co H; res: Balt; ref: 1, 19,

21, 50, 61, 64, 518, 700, 703, 735, 791, 1540
WALTHER, Charles; pvt; MD Guerrilla Zouaves; ref: 1
WAMBERZIE, Jonathan E.; pvt; 21st VA Inf, Co B; res: Balt; ref: 1, 2, 19, 44, 312, 690, 735, 1540
WAMPLER, John Morris; Capt; 8th VA Inf, Co H; res: Balt; ref: 1, 1076
WAMMACH, John F.; Navy; Shreveport Naval Station; res: Balt; ref: 1, 1540
WARD, Archer; pvt; 1st MD Cav, Co E; ref: 1, 2, 19, 21, 730
WARD, Frank X.; Capt; Hdqtrs, Gen A. Elzey' staff; rs: Balt; ref: 1, 2, 19, 21, 23, 44, 50, 53, 63, 64, 69, 312, 316, 456, 494, 503, 511, 631, 643, 681, 690, 700, 735, 757, 791, 893, 1115, 1523
WARD, Jeremiah; pvt; 43rd VA Cav (Mosby's), Co C; res: Frederick, Frd Cty; ref: 1, 89, 511
WARD, John J.; cpl; 2nd MD Inf, Co H; ref: 1, 2, 19, 21
WARD, Joseph; pvt; 1st MD Cav, Co F; ref: 1, 2, 19, 21
WARD, Maurice; pvt; 2nd MD Inf, Co H; ref: 1, 2, 19, 21
WARD, Samuel; pvt; 2nd MD Inf, Co A; res: Friendship, AA Cty; ref: 1, 1539
WARD, Thomas; carpenters mate, Navy; C.S.S. Richmond; res: Balt; MLCSH: ref: 1, 627, 700, 786
WARD, Thomas J. (M.D.); pvt; 2nd MD Lt Arty; res: Balt; ref: 1, 2, 18, 19, 21, 53, 511, 700, 1533
WARD, Thomas P.; pvt; 13th VA Inf, Co G; ref: 1
WARD, Warren W.; sgt; 1st MD Inf, Co I; res: Charlotte Hall, St. M. Cty; ref: 1, 2, 19, 21, 23, 1509, 1555
WARD, William B.; pvt; 2nd MD Cav, Co A; res: Friendship, AA Cty; ref: 1, 19, 1539, 1609
WARD, William Hunter; pvt; Stuart's Horse Arty, Breathed's Battery; res: PG Cty; ref: 1, 2, 19, 21, 69, 316, 511
WARDEN, Arthur W.; pvt; 9th VA Inf, Co B; ref: 1, 1576
WARDEN, William; pvt; 2nd MD Lt Arty; ref: 1, 2, 19, 21
WARE, R.; pvt; 3rd MD Lt Arty; ref: 2, 19, 21, 160, 726
WARFIELD, Abel D.; pvt; 17th VA Inf, Co A; ref: 1, 133, 142, 251
WARFIELD, Adolph; pvt; 2nd MD Cav, Co F; res: Balt; ref: 1, 2, 19, 21, 511
WARFIELD, Albert Gallatin, Jr; pvt; 1st MD Cav, Co A; res: Lisbon, How Cty; ref: 1, 2, 10, 13, 19, 21, 23, 70, 82, 511, 628, 748, 904, 1550
WARFIELD, Charles Alexander; pvt; 1st MD Cav, Co A; ref: 1, 19, 93, 148, 511
WARFIELD, Dorsey; sgt; 43rd VA Cav (Mosby's), Co B; ref: 1, 2, 8, 19, 21, 257, 258
WARFIELD, Edgar; pvt; 17th VA Inf, Co H; ref: 1, 13, 133, 142, 251, 748
WARFIELD, F. W.; pvt; 1st MD Cav, Co D; ref: 1, 2, 19, 21, 1601
WARFIELD, Gassaway Watkins; pvt; 1st MD Cav, Co A; res: How Cty; ref: 1, 2, 10, 13, 19, 21, 23, 70, 511, 748, 904
WARFIELD, George Thomas; cpl; 17th VA Inf, Co E; ref: 13, 133, 142, 251, 748
WARFIELD, Henry Mactier; pvt; 11th TN Inf, Co F; res: 1, 19, 1523
WARFIELD, James H. H. (M.D.); Acting Asst Surg; res: Poplar Lawn Hospital, Petersburg; ref: 1, 18, 86
WARFIELD, Milton W. (M.D.); Lt; Gen J. H. Winder's Detectives; res: Lisbon, How Cty; ref: 1, 13, 18
WARFIELD, William; pvt; 1st MD Cav, Co D; ref: 1, 19
WARING, James, Jr; pvt; 21st VA Inf, Co B; res: Chaptico, St. M. Cty; ref: 1, 2, 7, 12, 19, 21, 69, 70, 316, 1627
WARING, Robert Bowie; pvt; 1st MD Cav, Co B; res: Bald Eagle, PG Cty; ref: 1, 12, 19, 70, 785

WARING, William H.; pvt; 3rd VA Cav, Co F; ref: 1, 21, 700
WARING, William Worthington (M.D.); pvt; 1st MD Cav, Co B; res: Upper Marlboro, PG Cty; ref: 1, 2, 12, 18, 19, 21, 23, 70, 785, 1690
WARKEN, Daniel; pvt; 1st MD Inf, Co C; ref: 2, 19, 21
WARNER, Joseph F.; Lt; Charlmette LA Militia Inf, Co D; res: Balt; ref: 1, 1620
WARNICK, John F.; cpl; Lucas' 15th SC Heavy Arty; res: Balt; MLCSH; ref: 1, 21, 92, 93, 700, 786
WARNICK, Richard; pvt; Holbrook's Independent MD Lt Arty; res: Balt; ref: 1, 1540
WARREN, Edward; pvt; res: St. M. Cty; ref: 1670
WARREN, Edward (M.D.); Surg; Surgeon General of North Carolina; res: Balt; ref: 1, 18, 1367, 1534, 1536, 1561, 1690
WARREN, George W.; pvt; Barry's Co, MD Vols; ref: 1, 19
WARREN, William; pvt; 9th VA Inf, Co B; res: St. M. Cty; ref: 1, 1576, 1670
WARRING, Edwin; pvt; 1st MD Cav, Co B; res: Chaptico, St. M. Cty; ref: 1, 2, 19, 21, 141, 785, 1509, 1555, 1634
WARRING, Henry W., Jr; pvt; 35th VA Cav, Co B; res: Middlebrook, Mont Cty; ref: 1, 2, 19, 21, 69, 316, 1487, 1552, 1574, 1611, 1634, 1677
WARRING, James; pvt; 1st MD Cav, Co B; res: Chaptico, St. M. Cty; ref: 1, 1509, 1555
WARRING, John L.; pvt; Hampton Leg Lt Arty, Co B; res: Nottingham, PG Cty; ref: 1, 1553
WARRING, Thomas G.; pvt; 1st MD Cav, Co E; ref: 1, 2, 19, 21
WARRINGTON, Lewis; pvt; 4th MD Lt Arty; res: Balt; ref: 2, 19, 690
WARRINGTON, Smith; pvt; 4th MD Lt Arty; ref: 1, 2, 19, 21, 34
WARRINGTON, William W.; chief musician; 5th AR Inf; res: Johnsons Store, AA Cty; ref: 1, 1539
WARRO, Joseph; cpl; Stuart's Horse Arty, Breathed's Battery; ref: 1, 19, 498, 1575
WARWICK, James W.; cpl; 40th VA Inf, Co I; res: Balt; ref: 1, 70
WASON, James; pvt; 67th VA Militia, Co B; res: West River, AA Cty; ref: 1, 1539
WASHINGTON, James B.; Lt; Aide de Camp, Gen J. E. Johnston's staff; res: Balt; ref: 1, 44, 53, 1583
WASHINGTON, Robert Wright; pvt; 35th VA Cav, Co A; res: Frederick, Frd Cty; ref: 1, 72, 1677
WATERS, Greenbury Griffith; pvt; 1st VA Cav, Co K; res: New Market, Frd Cty; ref: 1, 2, 19, 21, 73, 90, 93, 827
WATERS, Hugh T.; pvt; 43rd VA Cav (Mosby's), Co A; ref: 8, 20
WATERS, Ignatius H.; Capt; Asst Commissary of Supply, Gen R. C. Tyler's staff; ref: 1, 19
WATERS, James F.; pvt; Hampton Leg Lt Arty, Co B; res: Aquaser, PG Cty; ref: 1, 2, 19, 21, 823, 1553
WATERS, Jesse; pvt; 2nd MD Inf, Co G; res: Balt; ref: 1, 2, 19, 21, 720, 825
WATERS, John H.; pvt; 17th VA Inf, Co E; res: Piney Point, St. M. Cty; MLCSH; ref: 1, 2, 7, 19, 21, 69, 92, 93, 133, 142, 251, 316, 700, 738, 786
WATERS, John W.; sgt; 19th VA Heavy Arty, Co C; ref: 1, 2, 19, 21, 1580
WATERS, Richard; pvt; Jacobs Mounted Riflemen; res: Crownsville, AA Cty; ref: 1, 1539
WATERS, Thomas Jackson; pvt; 1st VA Cav, Co K; res: St. M. Cty; ref: 1, 2, 19, 21, 46, 68, 107, 316, 1289
WATERS, Walter G.; pvt; 1st VA Inf, Co E; ref: 1, 316, 735
WATHEN, Clement; pvt; Wood's Regt, Confederate Cav, Co K; res: St. M. Cty; ref: 1, 1509, 1627

WATHEN, Daniel; pvt; 1st MD Inf, Co C; res: St. M. Cty; ref: 1, 2, 19, 21, 1509, 1627
WATHERHOLT, Jonathan; pvt; 7th VA Cav, Co G; ref: 1
WATKINS, ---; Navy; Merrimac; res: Georgetown; ref: 559
WATKINS, Benjamin; pvt; Lee's MD Cav; res: Davidsonville, AA Cty; ref: 1, 1539
WATKINS, Claiborne; pvt; 5th VA Cav, Co E; res: St. M. Cty; ref: 1670
WATKINS, Charles M.; pvt; Marine Corps; C.S.S. Tallahassee; res: Annapolis, AA Cty; ref: 1, 1539, 1594
WATKINS, E.; pvt; 3rd MD Lt Arty; ref: 1, 2, 19, 21, 726
WATKINS, George G.; pvt; MD American Rifles; res: Annapolis, AA Cty; ref: 1, 70, 1523
WATKINS, John M.; pvt; 3rd MD Lt Arty; ref: 1, 2, 21, 160, 1523
WATKINS, John R.; pvt; 43rd VA Cav (Mosby's), Co E; res: Annapolis, AA Cty; ref: 1, 2, 8, 19, 21, 700, 650, 735, 1579, 16131
WATKINS, Louis J.; pvt; 1st MD Cav, Co A; res: Clarksville, How Cty; ref: 1, 2, 10, 19, 21, 700, 1550, 1563, 1634
WATKINS, Nicholas J.; pvt; 1st MD Inf, Co H; res: Towson, Bt Cty; ref: 1, 2, 19, 21, 23, 650, 1519
WATKINS, Nicholas W.; pvt; 9th GA Inf, Co A; res: Balt; MLCSH; rf: 1, 2, 19, 21, 44, 470, 627, 786
WATKINS, W. C.; sgt; Stuart's Horse Arty, Breathed's Battery; ref: 1
WATKINS, William S.; pvt; Stuart's Horse Arty, Breathed's Battery; ref: 1
WATSON, Charles; pvt; 15th NC Inf, Co G; ref: 1, 735
WATSON, Joseph Edward; pvt; 19th VA Lt Arty, Co C; res: Balt; MLCSH; ref: 1, 93, 627, 700, 786, 1580
WATSON, Oliver; pvt; Barry's Co, MD Vols; res: AA Cty; ref: 1
WATSON, P. S.; pvt; Davis's MD Cav, Co C; ref: 1
WATSON, Samuel; pvt; 2nd MD Cav, Co B; res: Balt; ref: 1
WATSON, Sparton; pvt; Barry's Co, MD Vols; ref: 1
WATTER, John A.; cpl; 2nd MD Lt Arty; ref: 64
WATTERS, Daniel C.; Lt; 6th VA Inf, Co C; ref: 1, 689
WATTERS, James D. (Hon.); Lt; 1st VA Cav; res: Bel Air, Har Cty; ref: 2, 21, 122, 700, 827, 1012, 1634
WATTS, George W.; pvt; Zarvona's MD Zouaves; ref: 1, 19, 58, 97
WATTS, John N.; pvt; 2nd MD Inf, Co C; res: Elk Ridge Landing, AA Cty; ref: 1, 2, 19, 21, 700, 1539
WATTS, Joshua; pvt; 2nd MD Inf, Co C; res: Elk Ridge Landing, AA Cty; ref: 1, 2, 19, 21, 23, 470, 1523, 1539
WATTS, L. D.; 21st GA, Co C; ref: 92
WATTS, Philip; pvt; 35th VA Cav, Co B; res: Pikesville, Bt Cty; ref: 1, 21, 70, 700, 720, 1677
WATTS, Thomas L.; pvt; 14th VA Inf, Co H; res: Bt Cty; ref: 1, 70, 94
WATTS, William; pvt; 2nd MD Inf, Co D; ref: 1, 2, 19, 21
WAYS, James C.; pvt; Edelin's MD Heavy Arty; res: Balt; ref: 1
WEAVER, Benjamin F.; cpl; 3rd MD Lt Arty; ref: 1, 2, 19, 21, 23, 160, 726
WEAVER, Bushrod; res: St. M. Cty; ref: 1670
WEAVER, George W.; pvt; 1st MD Inf, Co B; ref: 1, 2, 19, 21
WEAVER, Hiram S.; pvt; 2nd MD Cav, Co C; res: Funkstown, Wash Cty; ref: 1, 2, 19, 21, 1301, 1558, 1601
WEAVER, John; pvt; 3rd MD Lt Arty; ref: 1, 2, 19, 21, 160, 726
WEAVER, Lawson A.; pvt; 15th VA Cav, Co D; res: Balt; ref: 1, 21, 700
WEAVER, Louis H.; pvt; 2nd MD Inf, Co G; res: Som Cty; ref: 1, 2, 19, 21
WEAVER, Robert Potts; Lt; Adj, 46th Mounted AR Inf; ref: 1, 1146

WEBB, Elisha; Navy; Port Royal Station; res: Balt; ref: 628, 720, 1540
WEBB, Emmett M.; cpl; 2nd MD Inf, Co D; res: Upper Marlboro, PG Cty; ref: 1, 2, 19, 21, 23, 70, 1135, 1542
WEBB, George W., Jr; pvt; 21st VA Inf, Co B; res: Balt; ref: 1, 2, 19, 312, 735
WEBB, H. W.; pvt; 15th VA Cav, Co E; res: Carr Cty; ref: 1, 825
WEBB, James Robinson; pvt; Brooke's Co, VA Lt Arty; res: Georgetown; ref: 1, 70, 1540
WEBB, Lewis S.; pvt; 1st MD Lt Arty; res: Balt; ref: 1, 2, 19, 21, 470
WEBB, Otway G.; pvt; 40th VA Inf, Co I; res: Balt; MLCSH; ref: 1, 21, 700, 786
WEBB, Richard Watson; pvt; 4th MD Lt Arty; res: Dor Cty; ref: 1, 2, 19, 21, 148, 791
WEBB, Thomas J.; pvt; 2nd MD Inf, Co F; res: Dor Cty; ref: 1, 2, 19, 21, 1540
WEBB, William A.; pvt; 9th VA Inf, Co B; res: Lisbon, How Cty; ref: 1, 2, 10, 19, 21, 40, 70, 806, 1550, 1576
WEBBER, William N.; Lt; Quartermaster Dept; res: Uniontown, Carr Cty; ref: 1, 40, 1544
WEBER, Edward; pvt; 1st MD Cav, Co C; ref: 1, 2, 19, 21, 700
WEBER, Philip; pvt; 1st MD Cav, Co F; ref: 1, 2, 19, 21
WEBER, William; cpl; 1st MD Inf, Co D; res: Balt; ref: 1, 2, 19, 21, 23
WEBLE, William G.; pvt; Lee's Balt Lt Arty, Alexander's Bn; res: Balt; ref: 1, 1540
WEBSTER, Charles; pvt; 4th VA Cav, Co F; ref: 1, 40
WEBSTER, George F.; pvt; 1st MD Inf, Co I; ref: 1, 2, 21
WEBSTER, George W.; pvt; 35th VA Cav, Co E; ref: 1, 735, 1677
WEBSTER, James R.; pvt; 30th VA Inf, Co A; ref: 1, 2, 19, 21
WEBSTER, Joshua; pvt; 28th LA Inf, Co B; res: Johnsons Store, AA Cty; ref: 1, 1539
WEBSTER, Thomas J.; pvt; 33rd AR Inf, Co B; res: Princeland, AA Cty; ref: 1, 1539
WEBSTER, William H.; pvt; 1st MD Cav, Co A; ref: 1, 2, 19, 21, 240
WEBSTER, William S.; pvt; 1st VA Cav, Co K; ref: 1, 2, 19, 21
WEDDERBURN, George C.; Lt; 3rd VA Local Defense Inf, Co A; ref: 1, 53
WEDDINGER, Ferdinand; pvt; 1st MD Inf, Co F; ref: 1, 2, 19, 21
WEEKS, Henry; pvt; Stuart's Horse Arty, Breathed's Battery; res: Balt; ref: 1, 2, 19, 21, 56, 57, 498, 700, 1613
WEEKS, Jospeh A.; pvt; 12th VA Cav, Co G; ref: 1, 700
WEEMS, Charles H., Jr; pvt; 2nd MD Inf, Co A; res: Cal Cty; ref: 1, 2, 19, 21, 650, 700, 1542
WEEMS, Eugene V. H.; pvt; 2nd LA Cav, Co G; res: South River, AA Cty; ref: 1, 70
WEEMS, G. W.; pvt; 43rd VA Cav (Mosby's), Co F; 1, 8, 1520
WEEMS, James N.;pvt; 1st MD Lt Arty; res: Balt; ref: 1, 2, 19, 21, 93, 470, 700
WEEMS, Juan Crompton (M.D., Prof.); Acting Asst Surg; Jackson Hospital, Richmond; res: St. M. Cty; ref: 1, 18, 23
WEEMS, Octaurus T.; Capt; 11th VA Cav, Co K; ref: 1, 700
WEGNER, Charles J.; q.m. sgt; Davis's MD Cav; res: Balt; ref: 1, 2, 19, 21, 23
WEGNER, Henry Frederick; pvt; Stuart's Horse Arty, Breathed's Battery; res: Balt; MLCSH; ref: 1, 2, 19, 21, 412, 627, 700, 786
WEIDENKAM, A.; cpl; Barry's Co, MD Vols; ref: 1
WEILS, John; pvt; 1st VA Inf, Co E; ref: 735
WEISESICH, John; pvt; 1st SC Inf, Co G; res: Balt; ref: 735

WEISHEER, Michael; pvt; 39th VA Cav, Co B; res: Uniontown, Carr Cty; ref: 1, 2, 19, 21, 40, 806
WEISIGER, Pawhatan; Lt; Aide de Camp, Gen F. Lee's staff; res: Frd Cty ref: 1, 72
WEISKEER, Ernest; pvt; 1st SC Inf, Co G; res: Balt; ref: 735
WEITZELL, William; pvt; 1st MD Inf, Co F; res: Balt; ref: 1, 2, 19, 21, 1540
WELCH, Andrew J.; pvt; 1st MD Cav, Co E; ref: 1, 2, 19, 21, 730
WELCH, C. Joseph; pvt; 1st MD Cav, Co C; res: Balt; ref: 1, 2, 19, 21
WELCH, Edward; pvt; 35th VA Cav, Co B; res: Hyattstown, Mont Cty; ref: 1, 3, 15, 1611, 1677
WELCH, Edward A.; cpl; 2nd MD Inf, Co C; res: Annapolis, AA Cty; MLCSH: ref: 1, 2, 19, 21, 700, 786, 1539
WELCH, James; pvt; Davis's MD Cav, Co C; ref: 1, 2, 21
WELCH, John L.; pvt; 2nd MD Cav, Co A; res: St. M. Cty; ref: 1, 2, 19, 21
WELCH, Joseph C.; pvt; Stuart's Horse Arty, Breathed's Battery; ref: 1, 19
WELCH, Martin; pvt; 2nd MD Cav, Co E; ref: 1, 2, 19, 21
WELCH, Robert Hamilton; pvt; 2nd MD Inf, Co C; res: Annapolis, AA Cty; ref: 1, 2, 19, 21, 23, 34, 686, 700, 1081, 1539
WELKER, George; pvt; MD American Rifles; ref: 1
WELLANS, John; pvt; 9th VA Inf, Co B; ref: 1, 1576
WELLER, F. F.; pvt; 1st MD Cav, Co A; ref: 1
WELLER, J. C.; pvt; 24th VA Inf, Co I; ref: 1, 92
WELLHAM, N. Wesley; res: AA Cty; ref: 1539
WELLMORE, Edward; pvt; 1st MD Inf, Co E; res: Balt; ref: 1, 2, 19, 21
WELLMORE, Henry; Capt; 1st MD Inf, Co H; res: Balt; ref: 1, 2, 19, 21, 64, 68, 456, 791
WELLS, A. H.; pvt; Davis's MD Cav, Co B; ref: 1, 19
WELLS, Benjamin F.; pvt; 21st VA Inf, Co D; res: Bladensburg, PG Cty; ref: 1, 69, 559, 1511
WELLS, Emmit; pvt; 3rd MD Lt Arty; ref: 1, 2, 19, 21, 160, 726
WELLS, Herschel; pvt; 1st MD Inf, Co D; res: Buena Vista, PG Cty; ref: 1, 2, 19, 21, 1553
WELLS, James M.; Col; 23rd MS Inf; ref: 1, 735, 787
WELLS, John B.; Lt; 2nd MD Cav, Co A; res: Annapolis, AA Cty; ref: 1, 2, 11, 19, 21, 23, 55, 88, 700, 735, 791, 1539, 1609
WELLS, Morris L.; pvt; 1st VA Inf, Co E; ref: 1, 735
WELLS, Plummer L.; pvt; Jacobs Mounted Riflemen; res: Bristol, AA Cty; ref: 1, 1539
WELLS, William; pvt; 3rd MD Lt Arty; ref: 2, 19, 21, 160, 461, 726
WELSH, Daniel; pvt; 3rd MD Lt Arty; ref: 1, 2, 21, 160, 726
WELSH, Edward; pvt; 2nd MD Cav, Co A; ref: 1, 2, 19, 21, 1609
WELSH, Enoch O.; pvt; 2nd MD Cav, Co A; res: Bristol, AA Cty; ref: 1, 1539
WELSH, Luther, Jr; 1st MD Cav, Co D; Libertytown, Frd Cty; ref: 1, 2, 19, 21, 90, 1601, 1620
WELSH, Martin; pvt; 1st MD Inf, Co E; ref: 1, 2, 19, 21
WELSH, Michael L.; cpl; 3rd MD Lt Arty; ref: 1, 2, 19, 21, 23, 160, 461, 726
WELSH, Milton; Lt; 1st MD Cav, Co D; res: Liberytown, Frd Cty; ref: 1, 2, 19, 21, 23, 64, 68, 90, 1601, 1620
WELSH, Warner Griffith; Capt; 1st MD Cav, Co D; res: Libertytown, Frd Cty; ref: 1, 2, 11, 17, 19, 21, 23, 45, 64, 66, 68, 72, 90, 240, 349, 462, 638, 693, 700, 740, 791, 1156, 1301, 1523, 1579, 1601, 1620, 1634

WELTENS, R. P.; 17th NC, Co E; ref: 92
WENTWORTH, George W.; pvt; 2nd MD Inf, Co C; res: Balt; ref: 1, 2, 19, 21, 92, 93, 456, 488, 700, 923, 1663
WENTZ, Louis, Jr; pvt; 1st MD Inf, Co A; res: Frederick, Frd Cty; ref: 1, 2, 19, 21, 72, 90
WERNSING, Henry; pvt; 15th VA Inf, Co E; res: Balt; ref: 1, 21, 700, 735
WESCOTT, Robert; lmn, Navy; Naval Brigade; ref: 1, 735
WESLEY, John; fmn, Navy; C.S.S. Bombshell; res: Laurel Factory, AA Cty; ref: 1, 1539
WESLEY, Watson; pvt; 33rd NC Inf, Co E; res: West River, AA Cty; ref: 1, 1539
WESLEY, Terry; ref: 55
WEST, Benjamin Srawiner; pvt; 9th VA Cav, Co A; res: Laurel, PG Cty; MLCSH; ref: 1, 93, 627, 700, 786
WEST, Charles N.; pvt; 18th GA Inf, Co A; ref: 1, 2, 19, 21, 650, 700
WEST, Clarence C.; 35th VA Cav; ref: 70, 1677
WEST, Edward Lloyd; pvt; 1st MD Inf, Co H; res: PG Cty; ref: 1, 2, 19, 21, 21, 93, 259, 650, 715, 1520
WEST, Eugene; pvt; 7th VA Cav, Co G; res: Merryland Tract, Frd Cty; ref: 1, 3, 90, 1278
WEST, George Franklin; pvt; 1st MD Inf, Co C; ref: 1, 2, 19, 21, 75
WEST, John; cpl; Rhett's 1st SC Heavy Arty; res: Balt; ref: 1, 735
WEST, John Pratt; pvt; 7th VA Cav, Co G; res: Merryland Tract, Frd Cty; MLCSH; ref: 1, 3, 21, 90, 700, 735, 786, 1156, 1278, 1552
WEST, Joseph, Jr; pvt; 1st MD Cav, Co E; ref: 1, 2, 19, 21, 730
WEST, Nelson G. (M.D.); Surg; General Hospital Hospital No. 10, Richmond; res: Frd Cty; ref: 1, 18, 21, 700, 791, 1141, 1534, 1573
WEST, Thomas W.; cpl; 27th MS Inf, Co B; res: Cumberland, All Cty; ref: 1, 19, 65, 95, 148
WEST, William B.; pvt; 13th VA Inf, Co G; ref: 1, 735
WESTFALL, George; q.m. sgt; Lucas' 15th SC Heavy Arty; res: Balt; ref: 1
WESTON, J. Alden; Maj; Weston MD Bn; ref: 1, 18, 34, 38, 63, 68, 789
WESTON, Napoleon Bonaparte; sgt; Armistead's Battery, VA Lt Arty; res: Balt; ref: 1, 21, 70, 700
WETTER, Ludwick; res: Johnsons Store, AA Cty; ref: 1539
WEXTER, George B.; pvt; 9th VA Inf, Co B; res: Balt; ref: 1, 1576, 1613
WHALEN, Charles Augusta; pvt; 35th VA Cav, Co A; ref: 1677
WHALEN, John; pvt; 3rd MD Lt Arty; ref: 1, 2, 19, 21, 160, 726
WHALEN, John W.; pvt; 35th VA Cav, Co B; res: Cooksville, How Cty; ref: 1, 2, 10, 19, 21, 90, 881, 1487, 1550, 1611, 1677
WHALEN, Michael; pvt; Barry's Co, MD Vols; ref: 1
WHALEN, William P.; pvt; 2nd MD Lt Arty; ref: 1, 2, 19, 21
WHARTON, George; pvt; Stuart's Horse Arty, Breathed's Battery; ref: 1
WHARTON, Henry M. (Revd); Signal Corp; res: Balt; ref: 1, 23, 56, 57, 513, 700, 891, 906, 1381, 1420
WHARTON, J. Murray; pvt; 21st VA Inf, Co D; res: Balt; MLCSH; ref: 1, 21, 57, 700, 786
WHARTON, John J.; Capt; Aid de Camp, Gen C. C. Wharton's staff; res: Bt Cty; ref: 1, 361, 677
WHARTON, V. J. M.; ref: 513
WHARTON, William F.; pvt; 1st MD Cav, Co C; ref: PG Cty; ref: 1, 2, 19, 21, 361, 685, 700, 827, 1690
WHEATLEY, Charles; pvt; 1st VA Cav, Co K: res: Georgetown; ref: 1, 2, 19, 21, 497, 505, 511, 677, 700, 947, 952, 1025, 1071, 1492, 1547

WHEATLEY, Francis M.; pvt; 2nd MD Inf, Co C; res: Georgetown; ref: 1, 2, 19, 21, 1492
WHEATLEY, Levin; pvt; 2nd MD Inf, Co G; res: Buck Town, Dor Cty; ref: 1, 2, 19, 21, 1547
WHEATLEY, John Walter; pvt; 43rd VA Cav (Mosby's), Co F; res: Georgetown; ref: 1, 2, 8, 19, 21, 511, 1492
WHEATLEY, William F.; cpl; 2nd MD Inf, Co B; res: Waldorf, Cha Cty; ref: 1, 2, 19, 21, 23, 56, 107, 511, 700, 1509, 1546
WHEATLY, Joseph; pvt; Lucas' 15th SC Heavy Arty; ref: 1
WHEEDEN, James H. fmn, Navy; C.S. Tennessee; res: Balt; ref: 1, 1540
WHEEDEN, Thomas J. (M.D.); Navy; Passed Asst Surg; C. S. Richmond; res: Balt; ref: 1, 18, 58, 97, 279, 1564
WHEELER, Albert; pvt; Letcher's Battery, Lt Arty; res: Balt; ref: 1, 2, 19, 21, 511, 700, 735
WHEELER, Alexander; pvt; 58th VA Inf, Co F; res: Annapolis, AA Cty; ref: 1, 1539
WHEELER, C. G.; pvt; Zarvona's MD Zouaves; res: St. M. Cty; ref: 1, 735, 1509
WHEELER, Charles W.; pvt; 1st MD Inf, Co A; ref: 1, 2, 19, 21
WHEELER, Claudious; pvt; Lee's Balt Lt Arty, Alexander's Bn; res: Forge, AA Cty; ref; 1, 1539
WHEELER, Edward H.; pvt; 2nd MD Inf, Co F; res: AA Cty; ref: 1, 86
WHEELER, Henry; pvt; 13th VA Inf, Co G; ref: 1
WHEELER, J. W.; Navy; Richmond Naval Station; res: Balt; ref: 1
WHEELER, James Russell; pvt; 1st MD Cav, Co E; res: Havre de Grace, Har Cty; ref: 1, 2, 19, 21, 70, 75, 79, 350, 488, 511, 686, 700, 730, 848, 849, 906, 923, 962, 976, 1058, 1350, 1470
WHEELER, Samuel Wilson; pvt; 19th VA Lt Arty, Co B; res: Havre-de-Grace, Har Cty; ref: 1, 2, 19, 21, 70, 79, 511, 700, 735
WHEELER, Thomas; res: Patuxent Forge, res: AA Cty; ref: 1539
WHEELER, W.; pvt; Barry's Co, MD Vols; ref: 1
WHEELEY, John Fountain; 5th VA Inf, Co D; res: PG Cty; MLCSH; ref: 21, 93, 700, 786
WHEELEY, Thomas N.; pvt; 25th VA Inf, Co G; res: Balt; ref: 1, 21, 93, 700
WHILDEN, DeLeon; pvt; Walter's Co, SC Lt Battery; ref: 1, 21, 700
WHISTLER, William McNiel (M.D.); Surg; Libby Prison Hospital; res: Balt; ref: 1, 18, 735
WHITE, Benjamin S.; Maj; Asst I.G., Gen J. E. B. Stuart's staff; res: Poolesville, Mt Cty; ref: 1, 19, 45, 46, 47, 64, 72, 73, 86, 106, 113, 118, 126, 368, 385, 457, 725, 791, 1123, 1552, 1560, 1633
WHITE, David G.; Capt; Ordnance Officer, Gen W. J. Hardee's staff; res: Cec Cty; ref: 1, 2, 19, 21, 350, 735, 791
WHITE, Dennis (M.D.); Contract Surg; res: Wheaton, Mont Cty; ref: 1666
WHITE, Edward C.; pvt; 3rd SC Inf, Co F; res: Annapolis, AA Cty; ref: 1, 1539
WHITE, Elijah Veirs; Lt Col; 35th VA Cav; res: Poolesville, Mont Cty; ref: 1, 3, 7, 11, 15, 18, 19, 35, 37, 42, 45, 46, 47, 50, 64, 66, 67, 73, 88, 105, 111, 113, 118, 125, 126, 129, 168, 169, 215, 256, 371, 385, 421, 422, 517, 518, 559, 560, 643, 693, 718, 725, 765, 778, 791, 912, 921, 992, 1002, 1011, 1032, 1037, 1076, 1086, 1097, 1108, 1122, 1129, 1154, 1259, 1302, 1326, 1346, 1358, 1386, 1405, 1434, 1465, 1486, 1492, 1560, 1577, 1579, 1588, 1600, 1611, 1619, 1620, 1654, 1674, 1677
WHITE, Fisher A.; pvt; 1st MD Inf, Co C; ref: 1, 2, 19, 21
WHITE, George H.; pvt; 35th VA Cav, Co B; ref: 1, 700, 1677

WHITE, Henry N.; pvt; LA Washington Lt Arty; ref: 1, 735
WHITE, J. Collison; pvt; 35th VA Cav, Co B; res: Buck Lodge, Mont Cty; ref: 1, 3, 73, 106, 1552, 1611, 1677
WHITE, James; pvt; LA Washington Lt Arty; ref: 1, 735
WHITE, James H.; pvt; 19th VA Heavy Arty, Co E; res: Balt; ref: 1, 21, 511, 700
WHITE, James McKenney; pvt; 2nd MD Inf, Co A; res: Cambridge, Dor Cty; ref: 1, 2, 19, 21, 23, 53, 112, 493, 503, 511, 650, 685, 700, 711, 1519, 1578, 1579
WHITE, John; pvt; 1st NC Inf, Co F; ref: 1, 735
WHITE, John; pvt; 9th VA Inf, Co B;re f: 1, 1576
WHITE, John Goldsborough; pvt; 2nd MD Inf, Co C; res: Easton, Tal Cty; ref: 1, 2, 19, 21, 595, 645, 1433, 1557, 1612
WHITE, Kevin; pvt; Holbrooks' Independent MD Lt Arty; ref: 1, 559, 1511
WHITE, Levi S.; Master, Navy; Purchasing Agent; res: Balt; ref: 70, 511, 594, 1564
WHITE, Patrick; pvt; Stuart's Horse Arty, Breathed's Battery; ref: 1
WHITE, Richard T.; pvt; 61st VA Inf, Co I; res: Balt; MLCSH; ref: 1, 700, 786
WHITE, Robert Hunter; pvt; 35th VA Cav, Co C; res: Georgetown; ref: 1, 3, 1611
WHITE, S. P.; pvt; 2nd MD Inf, Co A; ref: 1, 628
WHITE, Samuel C.; Lt; 35th VA Cav, Co B; res: Old Medley's, Mont Cty; ref: 1, 3, 15, 73, 106, 371, 1552, 1611, 1677
WHITE, Stephen; pvt; 2nd MD Cav, Co C; ref: 1, 11, 19, 693
WHITE, Thomas B.; pvt; LA Washington Lt Arty; 1, 735
WHITE, Thomas Henry; pvt; 35th VA Cav, Co B; res: Old Medley's, Mont Cty; ref: 1, 3, 73, 74, 106, 1097, 1346, 1465, 1552, 1611
WHITE, Thomas W.; Lt; 35th VA Cav, Co C; res: Mont Cty; ref: 1, 73, 735, 1574, 1611, 1677
WHITE, William C.; pvt; 35th VA Cav, Co B; res: Poolesville, Mont Cty; ref: 1, 3, 73, 1552, 1611, 1677
WHITEHEAD, Augustus; pvt; 4th GA Reserves, Co A; res: Laurel Factory, AA Cty; ref: 1, 1539
WHITEHURST, James O.; pvt; Norfolk Lt Arty Blue; ref: 1, 70
WHITELEY, Robert M.; pvt; 1st MD Inf, Co D; ref: 1, 2, 19, 21
WHITELEY, William; pvt; 17th VA Inf, Co H; res: Balt; MLCSH; ref: 1, 21, 133, 700, 786
WHITELY, William F. cpl; 2nd Cav, Co B; res: Federalsburg, Dor Cty; ref: 1, 19, 1547, 1609
WHITING, Charles C.; sgt; 43rd VA Cav (Mosby's), Co C; ref: 1, 3, 8
WHITING, James; pvt; 3rd MD Lt Arty; ref: 1, 2, 19, 21, 160, 726
WHITLOCK, Charles E.; Lee's Balt Lt Arty, Alexander's Balt; res: Balt; ref: 1
WHITTEN, Alexander; pvt; Davis's MD Cav, Co B; ref: 1, 19
WHITTER, George T.; pvt; 2nd VA Inf, Co C; res: Buckeystown, Frd Cty; ref: 1, 90
WHITTINGTON, George T.; pvt; 17th VA Inf, Co E; ref: 1, 133, 142, 251
WHITTINGTON, John H.; pvt; MD Guerrilla Zouaves; res: Friendship, AA Cty; ref: 1, 1539
WHITZEL, Joseph; pvt; 2nd MD Cav, Co C; ref: 1, 19, 1609
WIBLE, William E.; pvt; VA Inf, res: St. M. Cty; ref: 1670
WICKLIFFE, A. J.; cpl; 2nd Bn, VA Local Defense Inf, Co A; res: Balt; ref: 1, 21, 700
WIEL, George; pvt; 1st MD Cav, Co C; res: Balt; MLCSH; ref: 2, 19, 21, 700, 786
WIER, Benjamin S.; res: West River, AA Cty; ref: 1539
WIESNER, John D.; pvt; 1st MD Cav, Co A; ref: 1, 2, 19, 21
WIGFALL, Francis H.; Maj; Ordnance Dept; Gen J. E. Johnston's staff;

res: Balt; ref: 1, 21, 53, 498, 700, 791

WIGHT, Charles Copland; Capt; Adj; 58th VA Inf; res: Balt; ref: 1, 21, 23, 70, 697, 700, 1613

WILBURN, W. W.; pvt; Stuart's Horse Arty, Breathed's Battery; ref: 1

WILCOME, Casper; pvt; 2nd MD Inf, Co F; res: Frederick Junction, Frd Cty; MLCSH; ref: 1, 2, 19, 21, 89, 90, 786

WILCOX, James; pvt; Davis's MD Cav; res: Forge, AA Cty; ref: 1, 1539

WILCOX, Richard; pvt; 9th VA Inf, Co B; ref: 1, 1576

WILD, George; pvt; 1st MD Cav, Co C; res: Balt; ref: 1, 2, 19, 21

WILDEN, Richard; pvt; 1st MD Inf, Co F; res: Balt; ref: 1

WILDS, Luther Daniel; pvt; Stuart's Horse Arty, Breathed's Battery; ref: 1, 19, 498

WILE, Daniel L.; pvt; Davis's MD Cav, Co B; res: Frederick, Frd Cty; ref: 1, 19, 89

WILE, Henry A.; sgt; 1st MD Cav, Co F; ref: 1, 2, 19, 21, 23, 800

WILEY, Frederick J.; Capt; Warden, Castle Thunder Prison; res: St. M. Cty; ref: 1

WILEY, W. F.; pvt; 1st MD Inf, Co A; ref: 1

WILEY, William; pvt; 9th VA Inf, Co B; ref: 1, 1576

WILEY, Zephaniah K. (M.D.); Acting Asst Surg; 1st MS Cav; ref: 1, 18, 1536

WILFORD, Charles; pvt; Barry's Co, MD Vols; ref: 1

WILHELM, George; pvt; 6th TX Field Arty; ref: 1, 2, 19, 1523

WILHELM, James T. (M.D.); Lt; 2nd MD Lt Arty; res: Leonardtown, St. M. Cty; ref: 1, 2, 18, 21, 23, 1533, 1536, 1627

WILHELM, John B.; res: AA Cty; ref: 1539

WILKERS, G. W.; pvt; Davis's MD Cav, Co C; ref: 1

WILKERSON, Basil Manly (M.D.); 8th AL Inf, Co K; res: Balt; ref: 1, 18, 631, 1529

WILKERSON, Henry; sgt; 9th VA Inf, Co B; ref : 1, 518, 735, 1576

WILKINS, John D.; pvt; 3rd MD Lt Arty; ref: 1, 2, 19, 21, 160, 724, 726

WILKINSON, Daniel A.; bugler; 4th MD Lt Arty; res: St. M. Cty; ref: 1, 2, 19, 21, 23, 64, 1509

WILKINSON, William A.; pvt; Zarvona's MD Zouaves; res: Leonardtown, St. M. Cty; ref: 1, 2, 19, 21, 93, 735, 1509, 1555

WILKS, Thomas M.; Midn, Navy; Richmond Navy Yard; ref: 1, 2, 21

WILLARD, Peter Fulerton; sgt; 2nd Missouri State Guard, Co K; res: Broad Run, Frd Cty; ref: 1, 90

WILLARD, Robert; 3rd NC Inf, Co G; ref: 1, 735

WILLIAMS, Augustus A.; pvt; 1st MD Cav, Co C; res: Balt; ref: 1, 2, 19, 21, 650, 1540

WILLIAMS, B. G.; Gen J.H. Winder's Detectives; ref: 30

WILLIAMS, David Rogerson; pvt; 2nd FL Cav, Co C; ref: 1, 70

WILLIAMS, David W. S.; pvt; 1st MD Cav, Co F; ref: 1, 2, 19, 21

WILLIAMS, Edward; Lt; 19th VA Heavy Arty, Co C; res: Frederick, Frd Cty; ref: 1, 1573, 1580

WILLIAMS, Edward; sgt maj; 2nd MD Cav; res: Georgetown; ref: 1, 2, 11, 19, 21, 23, 316

WILLIAMS, Edward Jones (M.D.); 2nd Lt; 31st NC Inf, Co I; res: Balt; ref: 1, 18, 21, 700, 720, 735, 1536

WILLIAMS, Eldridge; pvt; 9th VA Inf, Co B; ref: 1, 1576

WILLIAMS, Elias; pvt; 9th VA Inf, Co B; ref: 1, 1576

WILLIAMS, Erastus P.; pvt; 9th VA Inf, Co B; ref: 1, 1576

WILLIAMS, Francis T.; cpl; 35th VA Cav, Co B; res: Old Medley's, Mont Cty; ref: 1, 3, 15, 73, 106, 371, 735, 1677

WILLIAMS, G. A.; Lt; Aide de Camp, Gen J. J. Archer's staff; ref: 1, 735

WILLIAMS, George; 12th NC Inf, Co C; ref: 735
WILLIAMS, George; pvt; 2nd MD Inf, Co G; ref: 1, 7, 689
WILLIAMS, George W.; pvt; Lucas' 15th SC Heavy Arty; res: Balt; ref: 1, 19, 1609
WILLIAMS, Henry; pvt; 33rd TX Cav, Co A; res: Frederick, Frd Cty; ref: 1, 67, 72, 89, 90, 1540
WILLIAMS, J. H.; pvt; 9th VA Inf, Co B; ref: 1, 1576
WILLIAMS, James; pvt; 2nd MD Cav, Co E; ref: 1, 19, 1609
WILLIAMS, James B.; pvt; 2nd MD Cav, Co D; ref: 1, 19
WILLIAMS, James J. (D.D.S.); sgt; 43rd VA Cav (Mosby's), Co F; res: Bel Air, Har Cty; ref: 1, 8, 21, 700, 735, 906, 1058, 1578, 1579
WILLIAMS, James P.; pvt; Richmond Howitzers, 1st Co; ref: 1
WILLIAMS, John; Master, Navy; C.S. Mary Virginia; res: Balt; ref: 1, 1564, 1620
WILLIAMS, John; Capt; Chambers' Independent Lt Arty Bn, Co D; ref: 1, 19, 735
WILLIAMS, John M. P.; pvt; 7th VA Cav, Co G; ref: 1
WILLIAMS, John P., Sr; pvt; 9th VA Inf, Co B; res: St. Leonards, Cal Cty; ref: 1, 2, 19, 21, 70, 75, 650, 700, 1542, 1576
WILLIAMS, John Tyler; pvt; 12th VA Inf, Co C; res: Balt; ref: 1, 21, 700
WILLIAMS, John W.; pvt; 1st MD Cav, Co B; res: Aquaser, PG Cty; ref: 1, 2, 19, 21, 785, 800, 1380, 1383, 1509, 1553
WILLIAMS, Patrick H.; pvt; 2nd MD Cav, Co C; ref: 1, 2, 19, 21, 55
WILLIAMS, Peter; pvt; 4th MD Lt Arty; ref: 2, 19, 1523
WILLIAMS, R. A.; Maj; Asst Commissary of Supply, Gen S. R. Gist's staff; res: Balt; ref: 1, 21, 700
WILLIAMS, Samuel; pvt; Castle Pinkney SC Heavy Arty; ref: 1, 735
WILLIAMS, Sewell Turpin; pvt; 43rd VA Cav (Mosby's), Co A; res: Berlin, Wor Cty; MLCSH; ref: 1, 8, 93, 627, 700, 786
WILLIAMS, Taylor; pvt; 20th VA Heavy Arty, Co C; res: Balt; ref: 1, 21, 700
WILLIAMS, Thomas F.; pvt; MD Guerrilla Zouaves; res: Charlotte Hall, St. M. Cty; ref: 1, 2, 19, 21, 1555, 1627
WILLIAMS, Thomas H. (M.D.); Surgeon-in-Charge; Purveyors Dept, Richmond; res: Cambridge, Dor Cty; ref: 1, 18, 1578, 1579
WILLIAMS, Thomas H., Jr; pvt; 3rd MD Lt Arty; res: Church Creek, Dor cty; ref: 1, 2, 19, 21, 160, 685, 726, 1534, 1536, 1547
WILLIAMS, Thomas P., Jr; pvt; Marion Battery, GA Lt Arty; res: Caro Cty; ref: 1, 2, 19, 21, 312, 681, 700, 1523, 1577, 1579
WILLIAMS, William F.; pvt; 4th VA Cav, Co A; res: Georgetown; ref: 1, 316, 700
WILLIAMS, William G. (M.D.); Asst Surg; 12th VA Cav; res: Millersville, AA Cty; ref: 1, 18, 81, 1534
WILLIAMS, William M.; pvt; 4th MD Lt Arty; ref: 1, 2, 19, 21, 34, 470
WILLIAMS, Wilson D.; pvt; 32nd NC Inf, Co I; ref: 1, 57
WILLIAMS, Z. F.; sgt; Stuart's Horse Arty, Breathed's Battery; res: Balt; ref: 1, 21, 498, 700
WILLIAMSON, Benjamin R.; Lt; 59th VA Inf, Co G; res: Millersville, AA Cty; ref: 1, 1539
WILLIAMSON, Charles H.; Lt; 50th VA Inf, Co C; res: Chesterville, Kt cty; ref: 1, 70, 1584
WILLIAMSON, George; Capt; Asst Adj & I.G., Gen C. S. Winder's staff; res: Balt; ref: 1, 2, 19, 21, 35, 44, 70, 93, 259, 309, 501, 650, 674, 690, 753, 754, 791
WILLIAMSON, Hugh; pvt; Holbrook's Independent MD Lt Arty; ref: 1

WILLIAMSON, James J.; pvt; 43rd VA (Mosby's), Co A; ref: 1, 8, 393, 677, 686, 706, 710, 1476, 1620

WILLIAMSON, John B.; pvt; McNeill's Rangers; ref: 21, 148, 504, 519, 700, 735, 1610

WILLIAMSON, Joseph Alleine; pvt; Richmond Howitzers, 1st Co; res: Frederick, Frd Cty; ref: 1, 67, 72

WILLIAMSON, Philip B.; pvt; 19th VA Heavy Arty, Co C; res: Balt; ref: 1, 2, 19, 21, 1580

WILLIAMSON, Swift Augustus; Lt; 21st NC Inf, Co E; res: Balt; MLCSH; ref: 1, 93, 627, 700, 786

WILLIAMSON, William P.; chief engr, Navy; res: Balt; ref: 1, 1564

WILLIS, Albert C.; pvt; 43rd VA Cav (Mosby's), Co C; res: Hoods Mill, How Cty; ref: 8, 10, 19, 1550

WILLIS, Alfred; pvt; 19th VA Heavy Arty; ref: 1, 1580

WILLIS, Bennett; cpl; 54th VA Inf, Co D; res: Myersville, Frd Cty; ref: 1, 67

WILLIS, Carver; smn, Navy; Richmond Naval Station; res: How Cty; ref: 1, 10, 14, 19

WILLIS, Charles N.; pvt; 1st MD Cav, Co C; res: Caro Cty; ref: 1, 2, 19, 21, 645, 1253

WILLIS, Francis W.; pvt; Lee's MD Cav; res: Hoods Mill, How Cty; ref: 1, 10, 19, 1550

WILLIS, Henry C.; Lt; 45th NC Inf, Co B; MLCSH; ref: 1, 700

WILLIS, J. A.; 12th NC Inf, Co G; ref: 735

WILLIS, Robert W.; pvt; 2nd MD Inf, Co C; ref: 1, 2, 19, 21, 1609

WILLIS, Samuel; Stonewall Jackson's Command; res: Myersville, Frd Cty; ref: 67

WILLIS, Thomas E.; bugler; Stuart's Horse Arty, Breathed's Battery; ref: Frederick, Frd Cty; ref: 1, 2, 19, 21, 498, 645

WILLIS, Thomas N.; pvt; 1st MD Cav, Co B; res: Centreville, QA Cty; ref: 1, 2, 19, 21, 785, 1554

WILLIS, William; cpl; 9th VA Inf, Co B; res: Cratchers Ferry, Dor Cty; ref: 1, 735, 1547, 1576

WILLIS, William B.; pvt; 2nd VA Inf, Co G; res: How Cty; ref: 1, 10, 735

WILLIS, Zorobabel L. C.; Capt; 19th VA Heavy Arty, Co B; res: Balt; ref: 1, 21, 70, 700, 791

WILLMORE, Henry; Capt; 1st MD Inf, Co H; ref: 1, 2, 19, 23

WILLS, Angier; pvt; 3rd MD Lt Arty; ref: 1, 2, 19, 21, 160, 461, 726

WILLS, F. Leo; cpl; 1st VA Cav, Co K; res: Cha Cty; ref: 1, 2, 19, 21, 1665

WILLS, James A.; pvt; 2nd MD Inf, Co B; res: Cha Cty; ref: 1, 2, 19, 21, 23, 470, 700, 1665

WILLS, John R.; pvt; Lucas' 15th SC Heavy Arty; res: Bt Cty; ref: 1

WILLS, John W.; pvt; 2nd MD Inf, Co B; res: Church Creek, Dor Cty; ref: 1, 2, 19, 21, 1547, 1665

WILLS, Joseph P.; pvt; 3rd MD Lt Arty; ref: 1, 2, 19, 21, 160, 461, 726, 1267

WILLS, W.; pvt; 3rd MD Lt Arty; ref: 2, 19, 21, 160, 726

WILLS, William A.; pvt; Hampton Leg Lt Arty, Co B; ref: 1, 2, 19, 21

WILLSON, A. M.; pvt; 1st MD Lt Arty; ref: 1, 2, 19, 21

WILLSON, Albert A.; pvt; 1st VA Cav, Co G; res: Balt; MLCSH; ref: 1, 21, 700, 786

WILLSON, Thomas; pvt; 3rd MD Lt Arty; ref: 1, 2, 19, 21, 160, 726

WILMER, Skipwith; Lt; Signal Officer, Gen J. B. Gordon's staff; res: Balt; ref: 1, 19, 21, 23, 53, 56, 700, 791

WILMOTH, Jacob Vanscoy; pvt; 18th VA Inf, Co A; res: How Cty; ref: 1, 71

WILNE, J. S.; pvt; 1st MD Cav, Co F; ref: 2, 19, 21

WILSON, A. S.; pvt; 43rd VA Cav (Mosby's), Co C; ref: 1, 2, 8, 19, 21

WILSON, Albert A.; pvt; 1st VA Cav, Co G; MLCSH; ref: 1, 627

WILSON, Algernon; pvt; Donald's Co, VA Lt Arty; res: Homonky, Cha Cty; ref: 1, 2, 19, 21, 735, 1546
WILSON, Aquila H.; pvt; 1st MD Cav, Co B; res: Nottingham, PG Cty; ref: 1, 2, 19, 21, 785, 1553
WILSON, C. P.; pvt; 7th VA Cav, Co G; res: Merryland Tract, Frd Cty; ref: 1, 3, 19, 90
WILSON, Charles; pvt; 1st MD Cav, Co E; ref: 1, 2, 19, 21, 730
WILSON, Charles A.; pvt; Stuart's Horse Arty, Breathed's Battery; res: Balt; MLCSH; ref: 1, 2, 19, 21, 498, 786
WILSON, Charles George; pvt; 1st MD Inf, Co; ref: 1, 2, 19, 21
WILSON, Cyrus; Archibald's Co, VA Lt Arty; res: Millersville, AA Cty; ref: 1, 735, 1539
WILSON, Edward; St. Margarett, AA Cty; ref: 1539
WILSON, Edward F.; pvt; 1st MD Cav, Co D; res: Bt Cty; ref: 1, 19, 1541
WILSON, Frederick S.; pvt; 1st MD Cav, Co D; res: Frd Cty; ref: 1, 2, 19, 21, 69, 316, 1601
WILSON, George L.; pvt; 2nd MD Cav, Co F; ref: 1, 19
WILSON, George W.; pvt; Davis's MD Cav; res: Forest Home, AA Cty; ref: 1, 1539
WILSON, George Washington; pvt; Lucas' 15th SC Heavy Arty; res: Balt; ref: 1
WILSON, George Washington; pvt; 1st MD Lt Arty; res: Upper Marlboro, PG Cty; ref: 1, 2, 21, 83, 489, 700, 1523
WILSON, Henry; pvt; 4th MD Lt Arty; Queens Town, QA Cty; ref: 1, 2, 19, 34, 1523, 1554
WILSON, J. J.; pvt; 3rd MD Lt Arty; ref: 1, 2, 19, 21, 160, 726
WILSON, J. J. W.; Lt; 23rd VA Inf, Co H; ref: 21, 700
WILSON, James C.; pvt; 18th LA Inf, Co D; res: Carr Cty; ref: 1, 72
WILSON, James Henry; Lt; 2nd MD Inf, Co B; res: Great Mills, St. M. Cty; ref: 1, 2, 19, 21, 23, 64, 68, 312, 674, 735, 791, 1509, 1555, 1584
WILSON, James Henry; pvt; 4th MD Lt Arty; ref: QA Cty; MLCSH; ref: 1, 2, 19, 21, 92, 93, 627, 700
WILSON, James S.; pvt; 3rd MD Lt Arty; res: Cornersville, Dor Cty; ref: 1, 19, 21, 160, 726, 1547
WILSON, James W.; pvt; 21st VA Inf, Co B; res: Balt; MLCSH; ref: 1, 21, 93, 700, 786, 1540
WILSON, John; pvt; 2nd MD Inf, Co A; res: Balt; ref: 1, 2, 19, 21, 650, 1540
WILSON, John A.; Passed Midn, Navy; C.S.S. Richmond; ref: 1, 2 , 19, 21, 58, 97, 279, 700, 750, 1564, 1673
WILSON, John Joseph; pvt; 3rd MD Lt Arty; ref: 1, 2, 19, 21, 160, 726
WILSON, John P., Jr; Capt; 9th VA Inf, Co B; ref: 1, 518, 791, 1576
WILSON, John T. (M.D.); pvt; 1st MD Lt Arty; res: PG Cty; ref: 1, 18, 1052
WILSON, Joseph K.; pvt; 18th VA Cav, Co K; res: PG Cty; MLCSH; ref: 1, 2, 21, 786, 1523
WILSON, Lancelot; pvt; 2nd VA Inf, Co F; res: Balt; ref: 1, 21, 700
WILSON, Luther; pvt; 1st VA Cav, Co K; ref: 2, 19, 21
WILSON, Martin; smn, Navy; C.S. Webb; ref: 1, 735
WILSON, Pierce Butler, Sr (M.D.) Maj; Chemist in Chief of Ordnance; res: Balt; ref: 1, 18, 21, 57, 700, 791, 1533
WILSON, Richard R.; pvt; 1st MD Cav, Co A; ref: 1, 19, 355
WILSON, Robert; pvt; 1st MD Cav, Co D; res: Georgetown; ref: 1, 2, 19, 21, 316, 1601
WILSON, Robert N.; Capt; Asst A.G., Gen J. A. Early's staff; res: Balt; ref: 1, 21, 700, 1540
WILSON, Samuel; Lt; Adj; 10th VA Heavy Arty; res: Balt; ref: 1, 21, 700
WILSON, Thomas J.; pvt; 2nd MD Lt Arty; res: Annapolis, AA Cty; ref: 1, 2, 19, 21, 1539

WILSON, Virgil A.; pvt; 63rd AL Inf, Co H; res: Traceys Landing, AA Cty; ref: 1, 1539
WILSON, W. H.; pvt; Holbrook's Independent MD Lt Arty; ref: 1
WILSON, William Sydney; Lt Col; 48th MS Inf; res: Snow Hill, Wor Cty; ref: 1, 631, 1600
WILSON, William; pvt; 3rd MD Lt Arty; ref: 1, 2, 19, 21, 160, 726
WILSON, William; pvt; 4th MD Lt Arty; ref: 1, 2, 19
WILSON, William Alexander; sgt; 1st MD Cav, Co B; res: Cal Cty; MLCSH; ref: 1, 2, 19, 21, 23, 45, 70, 627, 700, 785, 786
WILSON, William Bowley; pvt; 1st VA Cav, Co K; res: Balt; ref: 2, 19, 21, 70, 700, 777
WILSON, William M.; pvt; 4th MD Lt Arty; ref: 1, 2, 19, 21
WILSON, William T.; pvt; 1st MD Lt Arty; res: Annapolis, AA Cty; ref: 1, 2, 19, 21, 470, 1273
WILSON, William Thomas; pvt; 3rd VA Inf, Co K; res: Balt; ref: 1, 21, 700
WILSON, William W.; pvt; 1st MD Lt Arty; res: Bladensburg, PG Cty; ref: 1, 2, 19, 21, 69, 316, 782, 791, 1553
WILTSHIRE, Charles; pvt; 43rd VA Cav (Mosby's), Co G; res: Hagerstown, Wash Cty; ref: 1, 8, 20, 1418
WILTSHIRE, James B.; pvt; 2nd MD Cav, Co B; ref: 1, 19
WILTSHIRE, James Gerard (M.D); Lt; 43rd VA Cav (Mosby's), Co H; res: Funkstown, Wash Cty; ref: 1, 8, 18, 20, 21, 23, 57, 393, 700, 710, 906, 916, 1001, 1519, 1533, 1536, 1613
WINCHESTER, John P.; pvt; Butler's Co, KY Cav; res: Balt; ref: 1, 70
WINDBIGLER, George H.; pvt; 10th VA Inf, Co I; res: Balt; ref: 21, 700
WINDER, ---; pvt; 43rd VA Cav (Mosby's), Co G; ref: 8, 20
WINDER, Charles Sidney; Brig Gen; Army of Northern Virginia; res: Tal Cty; ref: 1, 2, 11, 13, 18, 19, 23, 32, 34, 39, 42, 44, 48, 50, 62, 63, 64, 68, 70, 88, 100, 104, 105, 117, 121, 125, 126, 127, 129, 130, 138, 140, 145, 240, 266, 344, 345, 350, 397, 404, 409, 422, 431, 456, 501, 592, 635, 645, 674, 684, 686, 695, 735, 753, 754, 757, 787, 791, 838, 857, 873, 965, 993, 1006, 1092, 1094, 1134, 1152, 1164, 1168, 1273, 1279, 1347, 1423, 1486, 1520, 1523, 1560, 1569, 1570, 1579, 1588, 1612, 1623, 1642, 1644, 1683
WINDER, Edward Lloyd; Lt, Navy; C.S.R.S. United States; res: Tal Cty; ref: 1, 19, 58, 61, 97, 279, 1564
WINDER, John Henry; Brig Gen; Department of Henrico and Department of North Caroina; res: Som Cty; ref: 1, 18, 19, 22, 23, 24, 30, 46, 50, 61, 64, 97, 110, 117, 122, 125, 127, 130, 137, 145, 266, 314, 344, 345, 397, 431, 439, 600, 631, 674, 693, 722, 735, 787, 789, 791, 792, 794, 949, 993, 1006, 1124, 1133, 1164, 1489, 1511, 1520, 1523, 1560, 1563, 1571, 1572, 1577, 1578, 1579, 1588, 1623, 1624, 1647, 1654, 1666, 1676
WINDER, Richard Bayley; Capt; Asst Q.M., Gen J. H. Winder's staff; res: Balt; ref: 1, 19, 21, 30, 44, 110, 700, 783, 791, 1529, 1564, 1583, 1623, 1688
WINDER, William Sidney; Capt; Asst A. G., Gen J. H. Winder's staff; res: Annapolis, AA Cty; MLCSH; ref: 1, 2, 18, 19, 21, 23, 44, 110, 592, 627, 645, 700, 727, 753, 786, 791, 826, 1489, 1523, 1609, 1623
WINDOLPH, John H.; pvt; 2nd MD Inf, Co A; res: PG Cty; ref: 19, 259
WINDSOR, Christopher Hall; pvt; Independent Signal Corps, 2nd Co; res: Balt; ref: 1, 21, 56, 79, 93, 700
WINFREE, William H.; pvt; 2nd MD Cav, Co E; ref: 1, 19, 1609

WINGATE, Frederick A.; pvt; 19th VA Heavy Arty, Co C; ref: 1, 2, 19, 21, 1580
WINGATE, Thomas Curran; pvt; 1st MD Lt Arty; ref: 1, 2, 19, 21, 631
WINGFIELD, L. M.; pvt; Stuart's Horse Arty, Breathed's Battery; ref: 1, 628
WINGROVE, Thomas; pvt; 2nd MD Cav, Co E; ref: 1, 19, 1609
WINTERS, ---; res: Cumberland, All Cty; ref: 19, 65, 95, 148
WINTERS, Harry S.; pvt; 1st MD Cav, Co D; ref: 1, 2, 19, 21
WINTLING, George Denis; pvt; LA Zouave Bn, Co B; res: Balt; ref: 1, 1540
WIREK, P.; South Carolina; ref: 693
WISE, Charles B.; Lt; 2nd MD Inf, Co B; res: Great Mills, St. M. Cty; ref: 1, 2, 19, 21, 23, 57, 63, 64, 68, 69, 443, 503, 511, 650, 674, 1509, 1520, 1555
WISE, Felix J.; pvt; 1st MD Cav, Co F; res: Emmitsburg, Frd Cty; ref: 1, 19
WISE, Henry A.; Lt; Lee's Balt Lt Arty, Alexander's Bn; res: Great Mills, St. M. Cty; ref: 1, 2, 7, 19, 21, 53, 70, 511, 700, 1375, 1509, 1555
WISE, Henry Alexander, Jr; Capt; V.M.I. Cadets; res: Balt; ref: 1, 19, 21, 40, 511, 686, 697, 700, 791, 1687
WISE, James Calvert; Maj; 1st LA Inf; res: St. M. Cty; ref: 1600
WISE, John O.; pvt; 35th VA Cav, Co B; res: Boyds, Mont Cty, ref: 1, 1611, 1677
WISE, Samuel H.; pvt; Stuart's Horse Arty, Breathed's Battery; ref: 1
WISE, William H.; pvt; Stuart's Horse Arty, Breathed's Battery; ref: 1
WISEMAN, J. R.; pvt; Stuart's Horse Arty, Breathed's Battery; ref: 1
WISHER, pvt; Lee's MD Cav; res: AA Cty; ref: 1, 19, 1628
WISSMAN, Louis O.; pvt; 1st MD Cav, Co B; res: Beltsville, PG Cty; ref: 1, 2, 19, 21, 700, 1553
WITHERS, Douglas Augustus; pvt; 47th VA Inf, Co G; res: Balt; MLCSH; ref: 1, 21, 92, 93, 627, 700, 786
WITHERS, Henry; pvt; Stuart's Horse Arty, Breathed's Battery; ref: 1
WITHERS, W.; pvt; MD Line, Co C; ref: 1
WITTER, Charles; pvt; MD American Rifles; res: Balt; ref: 1, 1540
WITTS, William; pvt; Castle Pinkney SC Heavy Arty; ref: 1, 735
WITZLEBEN, Theodore A.; pvt; 1st VA Inf, Co E; ref: 1, 2, 19, 21, 735
WOLF, J. R. K. P.; pvtl; 1st MD Cav; Co C; ref: 1, 19
WOLF, Joseph; pvt; 1st MD Inf, Co B; res: Balt; ref: 1, 2 19, 21, 55
WOLF, Michael; pvt; Rhett's 1st SC Heavy Arty; res: Balt; ref: 1, 735
WOLFE, John; pvt; MD Guerrilla Zouaves; ref: 1
WOLFE, Nicholas; sgt; 2nd MD Cav, Co D; ref: 1, 609
WOMBLE, William; pvt; 9th VA Inf, Co B; ref: 1, 1576
WOOD, Benjamin H., Jr; pvt; 59th VA Inf, Co F; res: Johnsons Store, AA Cty; ref: 1, 700, 1539
WOOD, Charles; sgt; 13th VA Inf, Co G; ref: 1
WOOD, Charles E.; musician; 5th VA Inf, Co F; res: Balt; ref: 1, 21, 700
WOOD, Charles S.; pvt; 2nd MD Cav, Co F; ref: 1, 2, 19, 21, 819, 1523
WOOD, Francis M.; cpl; 19th VA Heavy Arty, Co C; ref: 1, 2, 19, 21, 730, 1580
WOOD, Francis Peyton; pvt; 16th TX Inf, Co I; ref: 1, 70
WOOD, George Wisner; pvt; Crescent LA Inf, Co D; res: Balt; ref: 1, 2, 19, 21, 56, 700, 1578
WOOD, Henry W.; pvt; 1st MD Inf, Co I; ref: 1, 2, 19, 21
WOOD, James D.; pvt; 16th MS Cav, Co F; res: Ridge, St. M. Cty; ref: 1, 92, 1555

WOOD, James Luther; Lt; MD Guerrilla Zouaves; res: Millersville, AA Cty; ref: 1, 1539
WOOD, John; smn, Navy; res: Norfolk Naval Station; res: Patuxent Forge, AA Cty; ref: 1, 1539
WOOD, John J.; pvt; 1st MD Cav, Co C; ref: 1, 2, 19, 21, 1523
WOOD, John Taylor; Capt, Navy; C.S.S. Tallahassee; res: AA Cty; ref: 1, 97, 280, 543, 550, 1668, 1673, 1676
WOOD, Thomas; pvt; Stuart's Horse Arty, Breathed's Battery; ref: 1, 1611, 1677
WOOD, W. H.; pvt; 2nd MD Lt Arty; ref: 1, 2, 19, 21
WOOD, Walter; pvt; 2nd MD Inf, Co B; res: St. M. Cty; ref: 1, 2, 19, 21, 23, 470, 1509, 1523, 1627, 1662
WOOD, William Nathaniel; Lt; 19th VA Inf, Co A; res: Balt; ref: 124
WOODALL, Theadore; pvt; 2nd VA State Reserves, Co N; res: Balt; ref: 1, 1540
WOODEN, William T.; pvt; 1st MD Lt Arty; ref: 63, 64, 68
WOODFORD, Arthur; pvt; 2nd MD Inf, Co F; ref: 2, 21
WOODHALL, T.; Gen J. H. Winder's Detectives; ref: 1563
WOODHOUSE, L. Nathan; Telegraph operator; Army of Northern Virginia; res: Havre de Grace; MLCSH; ref: 21, 350, 700, 735, 786
WOODS, Charles; pvt; 1st MD Inf, Co E; ref: 1, 2, 19, 21, 1523
WOODS, James; Lt; MD Guerrilla Zouaves; res: Friendship, AA Cty; ref: 1, 1539
WOODVILLE, ---; ref: 724
WOODVILLE, ---; ref: 724
WOODWARD, Arch; pvt; Davis's MD Cav, Co A; ref: 1
WOODWARD, Charles; pvt; 12th VA Cav, Co G; res: Frederick, Frd cty; ref: 1, 89
WOODWARD, Columbus O.; pvt; 1st MD Cav, Co D; res: How Cty; ref: 1, 2, 19, 21, 1601
WOODWARD, Richard H. (M.D.); Asst Surg, Charleston Prison Hospital; res: Carr Cty; ref: 1, 18, 316, 1534
WOODWARD, W. S.; pvt; 43rd VA Cav (Mosby's), Co C; ref: 1, 8, 20
WOODY, W. R.; pvt; 49th VA Inf, Co H; ref: 1, 53
WOODYARD, J.; pvt; 3rd MD Lt Arty; ref: 1, 2, 19, 21, 160, 726
WOOLDRIDGE, Robert A.; pvt; 9th VA Inf, Co C; res: Balt; ref: 1, 21, 700
WOOLFOLK, A. M. (M.D.); Surg; 2nd MD Cav; res: Tal Cty; ref: 1, 18, 1609
WOOLFOLK, James L.; Capt; Woolfolk's Co, VA Lt Arty; res: Cambridge, Dor Cty; ref: 1, 21, 112, 700, 791
WOOLFORD, Arthur G.; pvt; 1st MD Cav, Co A; res: Princess Anne, Som Cty; ref: 1, 2, 19, 21, 1556
WOOLFORD, James L.; pvt; 1st MD Inf, Co C; res: Milton, Dor Cty; ref: 1, 2, 19, 21, 112, 1547
WOOLLEY, George Sidney; pvt; 1st MD Cav, Co B; res: Centreville, QA Cty; ref: 1, 2, 81, 785, 1554
WOOLSEY, John; pvt; 8th LA Inf, Co D; res: Balt; ref: 1, 21, 700
WOOSTER, Henry; pvt; 13th VA Inf, Co G; ref: 1, 735
WOOTEN, Frank; vol aid, Gen B. J. Hill's staff; ref: 689
WOOTEN, Henry E.; pvt; 18th VA Inf, Co B; res: Rockville, Mont Cty; ref: 1, 316
WOOTEN, Henry E.; pvt; 1st MD Cav, Co A; res: How Cty; ref: 1, 2, 10, 19, 21
WOOTEN, Josesh; pvt; 3rd MD Lt Arty; ref: 1, 2, 19, 21, 160, 726
WOOTEN, William T.; pvt; 21st VA Inf, Co B; res: PG Cty; ref: 1, 2, 12, 19, 21, 34, 69, 215, 312, 316, 782, 800, 791, 1273
WOOTERS, Alexander; pvt; 1st MD Cav, Co E; ref: 1, 2, 21, 730
WOOTON, Edward (M.D.); Asst Surg; 35th VA Cav; res: Poolesville, Mont Cty; ref: 1, 3, 15, 18, 23,

64, 69, 73, 91, 106, 316, 735, 791, 1534, 1611, 1677
WOOTTON, Francis Hall; Capt; Ordnance Dept, Fredericksburg; res: PG Cty; ref: 1, 12
WOOTON, William Turner (M.D.); Contract Surg; Medical Corps, Army of Northern Virginia; res: Frederick, Frd Cty; ref: 1, 18
WORKS, A. P.; ref: 643
WORRALL, Elijah; pvt; 9th VA Inf, Co B; ref: 1, 1576
WORRALL, William; pvt; 3rd MD Lt Arty; ref: 1, 2, 19, 21, 160, 726
WORTH, Frank A.; cpl; Lucas' 15th SC Heavy Arty; ref: Balt; ref: 1
WORTH, John A.; sgt maj; Lucas' 15th SC Heavy Arty; res: Balt; ref: 1
WORTHAM, John B. (M.D.); Surg; 2nd MD Lt Arty; ref:, 1, 2, 18, 19, 21, 68, 740, 1523, 1634
WORTHAM, William G.; com. sgt; 55th VA Inf, Co H; res: Balt; ref: 1, 21, 700
WORTHINGTON, Charles; pvt; 1st MD Cav, Co A; ref: 1, 2, 19, 21, 1634
WORTHINGTON, Eugene; pvt; 1st MD Lt Arty; ref: 1, 2, 19, 21, 23, 34, 81, 470, 690, 700, 844, 850, 852, 1104, 1550, 1579
WORTHINGTON, George E.; pvt; 1st MD Cav, Co D; ref: 1, 2, 19, 21, 1601
WORTHINGTON, Henry T.; pvt; 1st MD Cav, Co E; ref: 1, 2, 19, 21, 930
WORTHINGTON, Joshua; pvt; 1st MD Cav, Co A; res: Frd Cty; ref: 1, 2, 19, 21, 90
WORTHINGTON, Thomas G.; sgt; 1st MD Cav, Co D; res: New Market, Frd Cty; ref: 1, 19, 90, 1523, 1601
WREN, John; pvt; MD American Rifles; ref: 1, 2, 19, 21
WRENCH, John; pvt; 1st VA Cav, Co K; ref: 1, 2, 19, 21
WRENCH, W. Joseph; cpl; 1st MD Inf, Co D; ref: 1, 488, 923
WRENN, A. C.; pvt; 3rd VA Reserves; ref: 1, 685
WRENSHALL, John C.; Lt; Engineers Corps, Army of Tennessee; ref: 57
WRIGHT, Albert; Castle Pinkney SC Heavy Arty; ref: 735
WRIGHT, Clinton; pvt; 1st MD Cav, Co E; res: QA Cty; ref: 1, 2, 19, 21, 730, 1612
WRIGHT, Daniel Girand; Lt; 43rd VA Cav (Mosby's); res: Balt; ref: 1, 2, 8, 19, 20, 21, 23, 29, 35, 44, 272, 312, 503, 601, 650, 681, 690, 700, 735, 1571, 1577, 1578, 1579, 1613, 1654
WRIGHT, Frank (M.D.); mast. m., Navy; res: Centreville, QA Cty; ref: 1, 93, 1554
WRIGHT, George; pvt; 2nd MD Cav, Co B; ref: 1, 19, 1609
WRIGHT, George S.; pvt; Barry's Co MD Vols; ref: 1
WRIGHT, J. J.; Lt; 2nd VA Inf, Co B; ref: 1, 735
WRIGHT, Joel D.; pvt; 2nd MD Inf, Co F; res: Frd Cty; ref: 1, 2, 19, 21, 23, 470, 1573
WRIGHT, John W.; pvt; 1st VA Cav, Co C; res: Har Cty; ref: 1, 720
WRIGHT, Joseph H.; pvt; 36th VA Inf, Co F; res: Williamsport, Wash Cty; ref: 1, 1359
WRIGHT, Lewis; pvt; Davis's MD Cav, Co C; ref: 1
WRIGHT, Nelson; pvt; 7th VA Cav, Co G; ref: 1
WRIGHT, O. H.; pvt; 30th VA Inf, Co F; res: Balt; ref: 1, 21, 700
WRIGHT, Richard B.; pvt; 1st MD Cav, Co B; ref: 1, 2, 19, 21, 785
WRIGHT, Richard W.; pvt; 1st MD Inf, Co A; ref: 1
WRIGHT, Robert; Asst Engr, Navy; C.S.S. Palmetto State; ref: 1, 1564
WRIGHT, Solomon; sgt; 1st MD Cav, Co E; res: Kt Cty; ref: 1, 2, 19, 21, 23, 56, 57, 513, 700, 730, 1584
WRIGHT, Thomas Croft; pvt; 2nd KY Mounted Inf, Co H; res: Georgetown; ref: 1, 316
WRIGHT, W. T.; sgt; 30th VA Inf, Co F; res: Balt; ref: 21, 700
WRIGHT, William Holmes; 43rd VA Cav (Mosby's), Co D; res: Cooksville,

How Cty; MLCSH; ref: 1, 2, 10, 19, 21, 93, 627, 700, 786, 952, 1550
WRIGHTSON, William C.; Lt; 2nd MD Inf, Co G; res: Hicksburg, Dor Cty; ref: 1, 2, 19, 21, 23, 64, 1523, 1547
WROTE, John; res: Balt; ref: 1540
WURSTEN, Henry; pvt; 13th VA Inf, Co G; ref: 1, 2, 19, 21
WYATT, A. Joseph; sgt; 19th VA Heavy Arty, Co C; ref: 1, 1580
WYATT, Charles; pvt; 15th VA Inf, Co I; res: Annapolis, AA Cty; ref: 1, 1539
WYATT, James A.; pvt; 19th VA, Co C; Heavy Arty; ref: 1, 1580
WYATT, Owen; pvt; 3rd TX Cav, Co E; res: Balt; ref: 70
WYATT, R. C.; pvt; 19th VA Heavy Arty, Co C; ref: 1, 1580
WYNN, Edward (M.D.); sgt; 3rd MD Lt Arty; ref: 1, 2, 18, 19, 21, 23, 160, 461, 726
WYNN, James A.; pvt; 19th VA Cav, Co C; res: Balt; ref: 1, 2, 19, 21, 730, 1523, 1563
WYNN, Joseph; pvt; 1st MD Cav, Co E; ref: 1, 2, 19, 21, 730
WYSHAM, William E. (M.D.); Surg; Navy; Gosport Naval Hospital; res: Catonsville, Bt Cty; ref: 1, 18, 21, 58, 61, 279, 700, 735, 783, 1533, 1534, 1564
WYSONG, Henry; pvt; 2nd MD Lt Arty; ref: 1, 2, 19, 21
WYVILLE, Samuel W.; Lt; 19th VA Heavy Arty, Co C; ref: 1, 1580

YATES, Frank; pvt; Zarvona's MD Zouaves; res: Lonardtown, St. M. Cty; ref: 1, 735, 1555, 1627, 1662
YATES, John R., Jr; pvt; Hampton Leg Lt Arty, Co B; ref: 1, 2, 19, 21, 34, 63, 64, 68, 215, 782, 791, 1273
YATES, Thomas Frank; pvt; Stuart's Horse Arty, Breathed's Battery; res: Leonardtown, St. M. Cty; ref: 1, 21, 498, 700, 1509, 1584, 1670
YATES, William F.; pvt; 4th MD Lt Arty; res: St. M. Cty; ref: 1, 2, 19, 21, 470, 1509
YEATES, Henry P. P. (M.D.); Contract Surg; Medical Corps; ref: 1, 18, 1536
YEATMAN, Henry; Acting Master, Navy; res: Catonsville, Bt Cty; ref: 1, 21, 700, 960, 1564, 1613
YELLOTT, George W.; pvt; 43rd VA Cav (Mosby's), Co A; res: Bty Cty; ref: 1, 8, 72, 511, 720, 735
YELLOTT, Washington; 1st MD Inf, Co H; res: Bt cty; ref: 1, 2, 19, 21, 650, 720
YERBY, Albert F.; pvt; 43rd VA Cav (Mosby's), Co G; ref: 1, 70, 800
YERBY, William Henry; cpl; 32nd VA Inf, Co C; res: Balt; MLCSH; ref: 1, 93, 627, 700, 786
YINGER, Lawrence; res: Frederick, Frd Cty; ref: 89
YINGLING, John David; sgt; 8th VA Inf, Co H; res: Park Mills, Frd Cty; MLCSH; ref: 1, 90, 93, 700, 786
YINGLING, Zadoc Adam; pvt; 35th VA Cav, Co B; res: Park Mills, Frd Cty; ref: 1, 3, 90, 1548, 1611, 1677
YOUNG, Alexander; sgt; Hampton Leg Lt Arty, Co B; res: Frd Cty; ref: 1, 2, 19, 21, 23, 34, 72, 90, 511, 823, 830, 873, 1111, 1151, 1405
YOUNG, Benjamin; pvt; 4th MD Lt Arty; res: PG Cty; MLCSH; ref: 1, 2, 19, 21, 93, 511, 627, 700, 786
YOUNG, Edward D.; pvt; 2nd MD Cav, Co B; res: Wash Cty; ref: 1, 19, 1609
YOUNG, George L.; pvt; 2nd MD Cav, Co C; ref: 1, 19, 1609
YOUNG, H. L.; pvt; 3rd MD Lt Arty; ref: 1, 2, 21, 160, 511, 726
YOUNG, John; pvt; 2nd MD Cav, Co B; ref: 1, 19, 1575
YOUNG, John E.; pvt; 11th VA Inf, Co A; res: Rockville, Mont Cty; ref: 1, 69, 316, 511

YOUNG, M. B.; pvt; Stuart's Horse Arty, Breathed's Battery; ref: 1, 498
YOUNG, Mortimer Miller; pvt; 1st VA Inf, Co F; res: Balt; MLCSH; ref: 627, 700, 786
YOUNG, Robert; pvt; 17th VA Inf, Co H; ref: 1, 316
YOUNG, W. Washington; pvt; Baton Rouge Lt Arty, 1st Co; res: Frd Cty; ref: 1, 2, 19, 21, 72, 511, 643
YOUNG, William Proby (M.D.); Asst Surg; 4th GA Inf, res: Middleton, Frd Cty; ref: 1, 18, 1578, 1579
YOUNG, William T.; 7th VA Cav, Co G; res: Poolesville, Mont Cty; ref: 1098, 1552

ZACHARIAS, Granville; pvt; MD Guerrilla Zouaves; res: Frd Cty; ref: 1, 90
ZACHARIAS, John Forney (M.D.); Asst Sur; Shipp Hospital; Army of Tennessee; res: Frederick, Frd Cty; ref: 1, 18, 57, 90, 686, 945, 1536, 1579
ZAMETZER, John; res: Annapolis, AA Cty; ref: 1539
ZELL, James A.; pvt; 7th VA Cav, Co F; res: Balt; ref: 1, 628, 1299
ZELL, Michael E.; pvt; 26th MS, Co E; ref: 1, 92
ZELL, Robert R.; pvt; 7th VA Cav, Co F; res: Balt; ref: 1, 21, 700
ZELLER, John; pvt; 35th VA Cav, Co A; res: Balt; ref: 1, 21, 684, 700, 1611, 1677
ZELLERS, John; cpl; 19th VA Heavy Arty, Co C; ref: 1, 2, 19, 142, 1580
ZEPP, Charles T.; pvt; 1st MD Cav, Co A; res: How Cty; ref: 1, 2, 10, 19, 21, 71, 881
ZIMMERMAN, Archibald M.; pvt; 1st VA Inf, Co E; ref: 1, 735
ZIMMERMAN, Frank A.; Lt; 9th VA Inf, Co B; res: Balt; ref: 1, 2, 21, 167, 700, 735, 1576
ZIMMERMAN, George H. (Revd); Chaplain; 12th VA Cav; res: Easton, Tal Cty; ref: 1, 21, 498, 700, 1541
ZIMMERMAN, Isaac; pvt; 3rd MD Lt Arty; ref: 1, 2, 19, 21, 160, 461, 726, 1460
ZIMMERMAN, William A.; pvt; 2nd MD Cav, Co F; res: Balt; ref: 1, 2, 19, 21, 1540, 1609
ZIMMERMAN, William E.; pvt; Stuart's Horse Arty, Breathed's Battery, ref: 1, 498
ZIMMERS, Louis; Lt; ref: 21, 700
ZOLLINGER, Jacob E.; pvt; 2nd MD Inf, Co A; res: Balt; ref; 1, 2, 19, 21, 70, 511, 650
ZOLLINGER, William P.; Lt; 2nd MD Inf, Co A; res: Balt; ref: 1, 2, 17, 19, 21, 23, 58, 64, 68, 70, 412, 441, 501, 511, 650, 685, 700, 791, 1520, 1523, 1540, 1577
ZOMBRO, John L.; pvt; 6th VA Cav, Co F; res: Wash Cty; ref: 1, 74

APPENDIX B: REFERENCES

The following is a list of the sources of Marylanders who served in the Confederacy as listed in Appendix A. These items are numbered to correspond to the numbers given in Appendix A at the end of each entry, following the abbreviation, "ref." Included are published and unpublished items: books, manuscripts, periodicals, pamphlets; names contained in collections of memorabilia; inscriptions on monuments; public speeches; official documents; personal handwritten lists; personal correspondence; scrapbooks; and diaries. The location of unique material is given except when anonymity has been requested by the owner. The reader may obtain assistance from the author in learning more about the content of these individual holdings.

1. National Archives, Military Records, Washington, D.C.

2. GOLDSBORUGH, W.W. The Maryland Line in the Confederate Army. Baltimore: Guggenheimer, Weil and Company, 1900.

3. McDonald, William N. A History of the Laurel Brigade. Baltimore: Sun Job Printing Office, 1907.

4. OWENS, Cpl. James William, 1st MD Arty. List of Fellow Confederate Veterans of Anne Arundel County, 1925. Private collection of Carroll Brice, Baltimore, MD.

5. CHILDS, Pvt. Nathan Soper, 1st MD Cav Co. A roster of brother Confederate soldiers from Anne Arundel County, 1925. Private collection of Carroll Brice, Baltimore, MD.

6. Duke, Mrs. John, comp. List of Confederate Soldiers of St. Mary's County. 1915. Unpublished. In a private collection.

7. Beitell, Edwin W. List of Confederate prisoners at Point Lookout Prison Camp for Confederates. 1972. Unpublished. In a private collection, Abell, MD.

8. WILLIAMSON, James J. Mosby's Rangers. New York: Sturgis and Walton Company, 1909.

9. Henderson, Judge George. Maryland Confederate Soldiers Who Resided in Allegany County. 1957. Unpublished. In a private collection, Cumberland, MD.

10. The Howard County Confederate Monument Association. Howard County Court House Plaque, "In Honor of These Brave Men Who Fought So Courageously in the Confederate Army."

11. GILMOR, Harry. Four Years in the Saddle. New York: Harper and Brother, 1866.

12. Bowie, Effie Gwynn. Across the Years in Prince George's County. Richmond, VA: Garrett and Massie, 1947.

APPENDIX B: REFERENCES

13. Warfield, J.D. The Founders of Anne Arundel and Howard Counties, Maryland. Baltimore: Kohn and Pollock, 1905.

14. Gaddy, David Winfred, comp. Marylanders in the Confederate Signal Service. Unpublished. In a private collection, New Carrollton, MD.

15. Myers, Frank M. The Comanches; A History of WHITE's Battallion, Virginia Cavalry. Baltimore, MD: Kelly, Piet and Company, 1871.

16. Donnelly, Ralph W. Marylanders Among the District of Columbia Confederates. Unpublished. In a private collection, New Carrollton, MD.

17. Hartzler, Daniel D. Arms Makers of Maryland. York, PA: George Shumway Publisher, Longrifle Series, 1977.

18. Hartzer, Daniel D. Medical Doctors of Maryland in the C.S.A. Funkstown, MD: Tri-State Printing Inc., 1979.

19. Newman, Harry Wright, comp. Maryland Soldiers, Sailors and Marines Who Served in the Confederate States of America. Unpublished. In the private collection of the compiler (deceased).

20. Brice, Carroll, comp. Maryland C.S.A. veterans' dates of birth and death from cemeteries. Unpublished. In the private collection of the compiler, Baltimore, MD.

21. BOOTH, George W. Society of the C.S.A. Army and Navy of Maryland. Illustrated Souvenir - Maryland Line Confederate Soldiers Home. 1894.

22. Harrison, Mrs. Burton. Recollections Grave and Gay. New York: Charles Scribner's Sons, 1916.

23. Distinguished Men of the South. Confederate Military History, 12 vols. Atlanta, GA: Confederate Publishing Company, 1899.

24. Chesnut, Mary Botkin. A Diary from Dixie. Boston: Houghton Mifflin Company, 1905.

25. Victor, Orville J. The History, Civil, Political, and Military, of the Southern Rebellion. New York: J.D. Torrey, 1961.

26. Klaphor, Margaret B. and Brown, Paul D. The History of Charles County, Maryland. La Plata, MD: Charles County Tercentenary Inc.

27. LITTLE, Brig. Gen Henry. Unpublished diaries, held in a private collection.

28. Gay, Mary A.H. Life in Dixie During the War. Atlanta, GA: Foote & Davies Company, 1894.

APPENDIX B: REFERENCES

29. Wright, Mrs. D. Giraud. A Southern Girl in '61. New York: Doubleday, Page and Company, 1905.

30. Jones, John Beauchamp. A Rebel War Clerk's Diary, 2 vols. New York: Old Hickory Bookshop, 1935.

31. Wood, William. Captains of the Civil War. New Haven, CT: Yale University Press, 1921.

32. Hassler, William. A.P. Hill: Lee's Forgotten General. Richmond, VA: Garrett and Massie, 1957.

33. Kirwan, A.D., ed. Johnny Green of the Orphan Brigade. Lexington, KY: University of Kentucky Press, 1956.

34. ANDREWS Richard Snowden. A Memoir. Baltimore: The Sun Job Printing Office, 1910.

35. MCKIM, Randolph H. A Soldier's Recollections. Baltimore: Longmans, Green and Company, 1910.

36. Summers, Festus P., ed. A Borderland Confederate - Diaries of William L. Wilson. Pittsburg, PA: University of Pittsburgh Press, 1962.

37. HOPKINS Luther W. From Bull Run to Appomattox. Baltimore: Fleet-McGinley Company, 1908.

38. HOWARD James McHenry. Recollections and Opinions of James McHenry HOWARD.

39. Shipley, Charles L. The Old Confederate Soldiers Home. n.p.

40. Klein, Frederick Shriver. Just South of Gettysburg. Westminster, MD: Newman Press, 1963.

41. Wild, Frederick W. Memoirs and History of Captain F.W. Alexander's Baltimore Battery. Baltimore, 1912. n.p.

42. DOUGLAS, Henry Kyd. I Rode With Stonewall. Chapel Hill, NC: Univ. of North Carolina Press, 1940.

43. Jones Katherine M. Heroines of Dixie. New York: Bobbs-Merrill Company, 1955.

44. HOWARD, McHenry. Recollections of a Maryland Confederate Soldier. Baltimore: Williams and Williams Company, 1914.

45. McCellan H.B. I Rode with Jeb Stuart. Bloomington, IN: Indiana University Press, 1958.

46. Davis, Burke. Jeb Stuart: The Last Cavalier. New York: Holt, Rinehardt and Winston, 1957.

APPENDIX B: REFERENCES

47. Stackpole, Edward J. Sheridan in the Shenandoah. Harrisburg, PA: Stackpole Company, 1961.

48. Esten, John. Stonewall Jackson: A Military Biography. New York: D. Appleton and Company, 1876.

49. Stonebraker, J. Clarence. The Unwritten South. Hagerstown: Hagerstown Bookbinding and Printing Company, 1903.

50. Manakee Harold R. Maryland in the Civil War. Baltimore: Garamond Press, 1961.

51. Letters of Pvt. John C. CARROLL, 1st Maryland Cav. Co F. Private collection.

52. National Archives, Washington, D. C. John Snowden Pleasents Trial Records. Collection of Daniel D. Hartzler, New Windsor, MD.

53. JOHNSON Bradley T. A Memoir of Joseph E. Johnston. Baltimore: R.H. Woodward and Company, 1891.

54. Brown, George William. Baltimore and the 19th of April, 1861. Baltimore: Johns Hopkins Press, 1887.

55. Diaries of George Pielest, 3rd VA Arty, 2nd MD Arty, Confederate Navy. A copy held in the private collection of Daniel D. Hartzler, New Windsor, MD.

56. Roster of Franklin Buchanan United Confederate Veterans Camp No. 747 of Baltimore, 1896 Roster.

57. Roster of Isaac R. Trimble United Confederate Veterans Camp No. 1025 of Baltimore, 1900.

58. Lewis, Louise Quarles. Records of Marylanders in Confederate Navy. Baltimore: Maryland U.D.C., 1944. Handwritten biographies compiled by a member of U.D.C. Copy held by Maryland Historical Society, Baltimore, MD.

59. Semmes, Raphael. Service Afloat. Baltimore: The Baltimore Publishing Company, 1887.

60. TILGHMAN, Tench Francis. The Confederate Baggage and Treasure Train. Publisher unknown. Copy available at the State Archives, Annapolis, MD.

61. SCHARF, J. Thomas. Confederate States Navy. New York: Rogers and Sherwood, 1887.

62. Andrews, Matthew P. History of Maryland. New York: Andrews, Doubleday, Doran and Company, 1929.

63. SCHARF, J. Thomas. Chronicles of Baltimore. Baltimore, Maryland: Turnball Brothers, 1874.

64. ----------. History of Western Maryland Vol. 1. Philadelphia: Everts, 1882.

65. ----------. History of Western Maryland Vol. 2. Philadelphia: Everts, 1882.

66. Williams T.J.C. History of Frederick County, Vol 1. Hagerstown: L.R. Titsworth and Company, 1910.

67. ----------. History of Frederick County, Vol 2. Hagerstown: L.R. Titsworth and Company, 1910.

68. SCHARF J. Thomas. History of Maryland Vol. 3. Hatboro, PA: Tradition Press, 1879.

69. Georgetown University Alumni Men from Maryland in the Confederate Forces. Collection of Georgetown University Library, Washington, D.C.

- - - - - - -

The following items, 70 through 86, are collections of certificates of eligibility, which give evidences of the descendancy of the applicant from a Confederate veteran. These files are held either in the local chapter or at the Maryland Historical Society, Baltimore, MD.

70. United Daughters of the Confederacy, Baltimore Chapter #8, Baltimore.
71. United Daughters of the Confederacy, Co. A. 1st Maryland Cavalry Chapter #1858, Ellicott City.
72. United Daughters of the Confederacy, Fitzhugh Lee Chapter #279, Frederick.
73. United Daughters of the Confederacy, E.V. WHITE Chapter #1360, Poolsville.
74. United Daughters of the Confederacy, Henry Kyd DOUGLAS Chapter # 1720, Hagerstown.
75. United Daughters of the Confederacy, C.S.S. Shenandoah Chapter #2328, Annapolis.
76. United Daughters of the Confederacy, John F. HICKEY Chapter #1677, Hyattsville.
77. United Daughters of the Confederacy, Harford Chapter #114, Bel Air.
78. United Daughters of the Confederacy, President Jefferson Davis Chapter, Boonesboro.
79. United Daughters of the Confederacy, James R. WHEELER Chapter #1859, Baltimore.
80. United Daughters of the Confederacy, Gen. Bradley T. Johnson Chapter #1940, Baltimore.
81. United Daughters of the Confederacy, Jeff Davis Chapter #2168, Dundalk.
82. United Daughters of the Confederacy, Gen. Robert E. Lee Chapter #2043, Baltimore.

APPENDIX B: REFERENCES

83. United Daughters of the Confederacy, Andrew Jackson GWYNN Chapter #2059, Upper Marlboro.
84. United Daughters of the Confederacy, Stonewall Jackson Chapter #2062, Baltimore.
85. United Daughters of the Confederacy, William RISIN Chapter #2063, Baltimore.
86. United Daughters of the Confederacy, Ridgely BROWN Chapter #1347, Rockville.

- - - - - - -

87. The Bel Air Aegis Newspaper - June 21, 1923.

88. Valley News Echo Newspaper - April 1961 - April 1965. Special monthly issues, published by Potomac Edison Company, Hagerstown, MD, during the bicentennial of the Civil War.

89. Frederick Examiner Newspaper - 1861-1862. Frederick, MD. Copies held by Burr Arts Library, Frederick, MD.

90. A Souvenir of the Unveiling of the Confederate Monument, June 4, 1933, Mt. Olivet Cemetery, Frederick, Confederate Soldiers from Frederick County. A pamphlet giving names of some who served in the Civil War.

91. Diary of Katherine Susannah Markell of Frederick. Unpublished. Held in a private collection.

92. Parr, Margaret Sutherland, comp. Loudon Park Cemetery, Baltimore - Confederate Hill. United Daughters of the Confederacy Magazine Nov. 1954. A listing of interments.

93. Miller, Samuel H., comp. Confederate Hill - Loudon Park Cemetery Baltimore. 1962. Typescript listing of veterans buried in Loudon Park Cemetery.

94. METTAM, Henry Clay. Memoirs of the First Maryland Cavalry C.S.A. Written in November of 1912. Unpublished. Held in a private collection.

95. Lowdermilk William H. History of Cumberland. Baltimore: Regional Publishing Company, 1971.

96. Radcliffe, George L.P. Governor Thomas H. Hicks of Maryland. Baltimore: Johns Hopkins Press.

97. Knox, Dudley W. Official Records of the Union and Confederate Navies in the War of the Rebellion. (Series 2, 3 vols.) U.S. Government Printing Office, Washington D.C., 1927.

98. Truitt, Charles J. Historic Salisbury, Maryland Garden City, NY: Country Life Press, 1932.

APPENDIX B: REFERENCES

99. Helper, Hinton Rowan. The Impending Crisis of the South. South Carolina, 1860.

100. Sorrel, G. Moxley. Recollections of a Confederate Staff Officer. Jackson, Tennessee: McCowat-Mercer Press, 1950.

101. DAME, William Meade. From the Rapidan to Richmond. Baltimore: Green-Lucas Company, 1920.

102. Welch, Spencer Glasgow. A Confederate Surgeon's Letters to his Wife. Washington, D.C.: Neale Publishing Company, 1911.

103. Young, Bennett H. Confederate Wizards of the Saddle. Boston: Chapple Publishing Company, 1914.

104. Ham Chamberiayne - Virginian, Letters and Papers of an Artillery Officer. Richmond, VA: Dietz Printing Company, 1932.

105. Longstreet, James. From Manassas to Appomattox. Philadelphia: J.B. Lipincott Company, 1896.

106. Tablet at Monocacy Cemetery - "This tablet is created by the Ladies of Old Medley's district, Montgomery County, Maryland. To the memory and the valor and self-sacrifice of Maryland soldiers in the Confederate Army whose names are inscribed hereon. War of 1861-1865."

107. Hull, Susan R. Boy Soldiers of the Confederacy Washington, D.C.: Neale Publishing Company, 1905.

108. Martin, Bessie. Desertion of Alabama Troops from the Confederate Army. New York: Columbia University Press, 1932.

109. Fiske, John. The Mississippi Valley in the Civil War. New York: Houghton, Mifflin, and Company, 1900.

110. Rowland, Dunbar. Jefferson Davis Constitutionalist, His Letters, Papers and Speeches. New York: J.J. Little and Ives Company, 1923.

111. Freeman, Douglas Soauthall. R.E. Lee, A Biography. New York: Charles Scribner's Sons, 1935.

112. Jones, Elias. Revised History of Dorchester County, Maryland Baltimore: Read Taylor Press, 1925.

113. White, Henry Alexander. Stonewall Jackson. 1908.

114. MARSHALL Charles. An Aide-de-Camp of Lee. Boston: Little, Brown, and Company, 1927.

115. Haskell, John Cheves. The Haskell Memoirs. New York: G.P. Putnam's Sons, 1960.

APPENDIX B: REFERENCES

116. Durkin, Joseph T., ed. John Dooley Confederate Soldier - His War Journal. Indiana: University of Notre Dame Press, 1963.

117. Worsham, John H. One of Jackson's Foot Cavalry. Jackson, TN: McCowat-Mercer Press, 1964.

118. Bakeless, John. Spies of the Confederacy. Philadelphia: J.B. Lippincott Company, 1970.

119. Blessington, J.P. Walkers Texas Division. Austin, TX: Pemberton Press, 1968.

120. Reagan, John H. Memoirs of John H. Reagan. Austin, TX: Pemberton Press, 1968.

121. Bean, W.G. The Liberty Hall Volunteers. Charlottesville, VA: University Press of Virginia, 1964.

122. Portrait and Biographical Records of Harford and Cecil Counties, Maryland. New York: Chapman Publishing Company, 1897.

123. Russell Charles W., ed. Memoirs of Colonel John S. Mosby Bloomington: Indiana University Press, 1959.

124. Richey, Homer., ed. Memorial History of the John Bowie Strange Camp, U.C.V. Charlottesville, VA: Michie Company, 1920.

125. Maryland Remembers. Hagerstown, MD: Maryland Civil War Centennial Commission, 1961.

126. Freeman, Douglas S. Lee's Lieutenants. 2 vols. New York: Charles Scribner's Sons, 1943.

127. Battles and Leaders of the Civil War. 4 vols. New York: The Century Company, 1888.

128. Horan, James D. Confederate Agent. New York: Crown Publishers Inc., 1954.

129. Early, Jubal A. Jubal A. Early (autobiography). Philadelphia: J.D. Lippincott Company, 1912.

130. Davis, Jefferson. The Rise and Fall of the Confederate Government. 2 vols. New York: D. Appleton and Company, 1881.

131. Richardson, Hester D. Side-Lights on Maryland History, Baltimore: Williams and Wilkins Company, 1903.

132. Pinkerton, Allan. The Spy of the Rebellion. Hartford, CT: M.A. Winter and Company, 1883.

APPENDIX B: REFERENCES

133. Warfield, Edgar. A Confederate Soldier's Memoirs. Richmond, VA: Masonic Home Press, 1936.

134. Manarin, Louis H. A Guide to Military Organizations and Installations of North Carolina. Raleigh, NC, 1961.

135. Coulter, E. Merton. The Confederate States of America, A History of the True South, Vol. VII. 1950.

136. Maurice, Frederick. Robert E. Lee, The Soldier. New York: Houghton Mifflin Company, 1925.

137. Richardson, James D. Messages and Papers of the Confederacy, Vol. I, II. Nashville, TN: United States Publishing Company, 1906.

138. Taylor, Walter H. Four Years with General Lee. Bloomington: Indiana University Press, 1962.

139. Hall, Harry H. A Johnny Reb Band from Salem. North Carolina Confederate Centennial Commission, Raleigh, NC, 1963.

140. Sheppard, E. W. The Campaign in Virginia and Maryland, June 26th to September 20th, 1862. London, England: George Allen and Company, 1911.

141. Kurtz, Lucy F. and Benny Ritter. A Roster of Confederate Soldier Buried in Stonewall Cemetery, Winchester, VA. 1962.

142. Delancy, Wayne R. and Marie E Bowery. The Seventeenth Virginia Volunteer Infantry Regiment C.S.A. Washington, D.C.: American Printing Company, 1961.

143. Sevanberg, W. A. First Blood. New York: Charles Scribner's Sons, 1957.

144. Young, James C. Marse Robert. New York: Rae-D-Henkle Company, 1929.

145. Casler, John O. Four Years in the Stonewall Brigade. Girade, KS: Appeal Publishing Company, 1906.

146. Pember, Phoebe Y. A Southern Woman's Story. Jackson, Tennessee: McCowat-Mercer Press, 1959.

147. Page, Thomas Nelson. Robert E. Lee, The Southerner. New York: Charles Scribner's Sons, 1909.

148. Thomas, James W. and T.J.C. Williams. History of Allegany County, Maryland, 2 vols. Cumberland, 1923.

149. Wesley, Charles H. The Collapse of the Confederacy. Washington, D.C.: Associated Publishers, 1937.

APPENDIX B: REFERENCES

150. Military records of Brig. Gen. Bradley T. JOHNSON 1861-1865. Held by Duke University Library and Confederate Museum.

151. Henry, Robert S. First with the Most. New York: Bobbs-Merrill Company, 1944.

152. Dyer, John P. The Gallant Hood. New York: Bobbs-Merrill Company, 1950.

153. Johnston, William Preston. The Life of Gen. Albert Sidney Johnston. New York: D. Appleton and Company, 1878.

154. Parks, Joseph Howard. Gen. Edmund Kirby Smith C.S.A. Baton Rouge: Louisiana State Press, 1954.

155. Eckenrode, H.J. James Longstreet Lee's War Horse. University of North Carolina Press, 1936.

156. Matkes, J. Harvey. General Forrest. D. Appleton and Company, 1902.

157. Swiggett, Howard. The Rebel Raider. New York: Bobbs-Merrill Company, 1934.

158. Polk, William M. Leonidas Polk Bishop and General. 2 vols. New York: Longmans, Green and Company, 1893.

159. Pickett, LaSalle Corbell. Pickett and His Men. Atlanta, Georgia: Foote and Davis Company, 1899.

160. RITTER, William L. Biographical Memoir and Sketch of the Third Battery of Maryland Artillery. Baltimore: John S. Bridges and Company, 1902.

161. Avary, Myrta L. Dixie After the War. New York: Doubleday, Page and Company, 1906.

162. Castel, Albert. General Sterling Price. Baton Rouge: Louisiana State University Press, 1968.

163. Dyer, John P. Fightin' Joe Wheeler. Louisiana State University Press, 1941.

164. Hartje, Robert G. Van Dorn. Vanderbilt University Press, 1967.

165. Derry, Joseph T. Story of the Confederate States. Richmond, VA: B.F. Johnson Publishing Company, 1895.

166. Greeley, Horace. The American Conflict. 2 vols. Hartford, CT: O.D. Case and Company, 1867.

167. Memorandum of Artillery Officers in the Confederate States Service. U.S. War Records, Washington, 1889. Published by U. S. Government.

APPENDIX B: REFERENCES

168. McKim, Randolph H. The Numerical Strength of the Confederate Army. New York: The Neale Publishing Company, 1912.

169. Jones, J. William. Army of Northern Virginia Memorial Volume. Richmond, Virginia: J.W. Randolph and English, 1880.

170. Hagood, Johnson. Memoirs of the War of Seccession. Columbia, South Carolina: The State Company, 1910.

171. Early, Jubal A. A Memoir of the Last Year of the War for Independence. Lynchburg, VA: Charles W. Button, 1867.

172. Jones, Charles C. Jr. A Roster of General Officers C.S.A. Richmond, VA: Southern Historical Society, 1876.

173. Kaessmann, Beta and Harold R. Manakee and Joseph L. Wheeler. My Maryland. Boston, MA: Ginn and Company, 1934.

174. Roman, Alfred. The Military Operations of General Beauregard. 2 vols. New York: Harper and Brother, 1883.

175. Nichols, James L. Confederate Engineers. Tuscaloosa, AL: Confederate Publishing Company, 1957.

176. List of Staff Officers of the Confederate States Army. Washington, D.C.: Government Printing Office, 1891.

177. Memorandum of Field Officers and Regiments in the Confederate Army. The U.S. War Recording Office, Washington D.C.

178. The General Officers Appointed by the President in the Armies of the Confederate States, The U.S. War Department, Washington, D.C.

179. Henderson, Lillian. Roster of the Confederate Soldiers of Georgia, 1861-1865. 2vols. Hopeville, GA: Longino and Porter, 1958.

180. Woodruff, W.E. With the Light Gun in '61 '65. Little Rock, AR: Central Printing Co., 1903.

181. Saver, Lewellyn A. A History of the Sixtieth Alabama Regiment. Montgomery, AL: Barrett and Brown, 1867.

182. Botsford, T.F. A Sketch of the 47th Alabama Regiment Volunteers, C.S.A. Copy held by Army War College, Carlisle, PA.

183. Willett, E.D. History of Company B, 40th Alabama Regiment. Alabama: Norway Anuiston, 1902.

184. Roll and History of Company C, 19th Alabama Regiment, Department of Archives, State of Alabama. Copy held by the Army War College, Carlisle, PA.

APPENDIX B: REFERENCES

185. Newman, Harry Wright. Charles County Gentry. Washington D.C., 1940. Repr. Baltimore: Genealogical Publishing Co., 1971.

186. Smith, Daniel P. Company K. First Alabama Regiment. Philadelphia: Burk and McFetridge, 1885.

187. McMorries, Edward Y. History of the First Regiment Alabama Volunteer Infantry C.S.A. Brown: Montgomery, AL, 1904.

188. Thomas, Henry W. History of the Doles-Cook Brigade. Atlanta, GA: Franklin Printing and Publishing Company, 1903.

189. Olmstead, Charles H. First Volunteer Reigiment of Georgia Charleston Harbor in 1863. Savannah, GA: J.H. Estill, 1879.

190. Austin, Aurelia. Georgia Boys with Stonewall Jackson. Athens, GA: University of Georgia Press, 1967.

191. W.H. Andrews Diary. 1st Georgia Inf. Com. Unpublished. Copy held at Army War College, Carlisle, PA.

192. Jones, Charles Edgeworth. Georgia in the War 1861-1865. Alanta, GA: Foote & Davies Co. 1909.

193. Croom, Wendell D. The War-History of Company C Sixth Georgia Regiment Infantry. Fort Valley, GA: Advertiser, 1879.

194. Passano, L. Magruder. Maryland. Baltimore: Williams and Wilkins Company, 1905.

195. Nichols, G.W. A Soldier's Story of His Regiment. Kennesaw, GA: Continental Book Co, (1898) 1961.

196. Mayer, Brante. The Emancipation Problem in Maryland. Baltimore: 1862. Pamphlet, originally contained in The Baltimore American, newpaper.

197. Thompson, Ed Porter. History of the First Kentucky Brigade. Cincinnati, OH: Coxton, 1868.

198. George, Henry. History of the 3rd, 7th, 8th, and 12th Kentucky C.S.A. Louisville, KY: C.T. Dearing, 1911.

199. Report of the Adjutant General of the State of Kentucky, Confederate Volunteers. Frankfurt, KY: State Journal Company, 1902.

200. Carter, Howell. A Cavalryman's Reminiscences of the Civil War. New Orleans: American Printing Company.

201. Bradley James. The Confederate Mail Carrier. Mexico, MO, 1894.

APPENDIX B: REFERENCES

202. Bevier, R.S. History of the First and Second Missouri Confederate Brigades. St. Louis, MO: Bryan Brand and Company, 1879.

203. Owen, William M. In Camp and Battle with the Washington Artillery of New Orleans. Boston: Ticknor and Company, 1885.

204. Hall, Winchester. The Story of the 26th Louisiana Infantry.

205. Booth, Andrew B. Records of Louisiana Confederate Soldiers. New Orleans, LA: 1920.

206. Bragg, Jefferson Davis. Louisiana in the Confederacy. Baton Rouge, LA: Louisiana State University Press, 1941.

207. Journal of the Proceedings of the Maryland House of Delegates in Extra Session, Frederick, 1861. Printed by Elehus Riley.

208. Journal of the Proceedings of the Senate of Maryland in Extra Session, Frederick, MD, 1861. Printed by Beale H. Richardson.

209. Nisbet, James Cooper. Four Years on the Firing Line. Jackson, TN: McCowat-Mercer Press, 1963.

210. Sloan, John A. Reminiscences of the Guilford Grays. Washington, D.C.: R.O. Polkinhorn, 1883.

211. Clark, Walter. History of the Several Regiments and Battalions from North Carolina. 5 vols. Goldsboro, NC: Nash Brothers, 1901.

212. Wall, H.C. Historical Sketch of the Pee Dee Guards. Raleigh, NC: Edward Broughton and Company, 1876.

213. Moore, John W. Roster of North Carolina Troops in the War Between the States. 4 vols. Raleigh, NC: Ashe and Gatling, 1882.

214. Dobst, Richard W. The Bloody Sixth. Durham, NC: Christian Printing Company, 1965.

215. Post war scrapbook of Pvt. Augustus James ALBERT, Jr., 1st Md Arty. In a private collection of the family.

216. Brooks, U.R. Butler and His Cavalry in the War of Secession. Columbia, SC: The State Company.

217. Salley, A.S. Jr. South Carolina Troops in Confederate Service. Columbia, SC: R.L. Bryan Company, 1913.

218. Caldwell, J.F.J. History of a Brigade of South Carolinians - McGowan's Brigade. Philadelphia: King and Baird, 1866.

219. Walker, C.I. 10th Regiment S.C. Vols Confederate States Army. Charleston, SC: Walker, Evans and Cocswell, 1881.

APPENDIX B: REFERENCES

220. Reid, J.W. History of the Fourth Regiment of South Carolina Volunteers. Greenville, SC: Shannon and Company, 1892.

221. Walkins, Sam. R. Company Aytch. Nashville, TN: Cumberland Presbyterian Publishing House, 1882.

222. Address of Spence C. JONES, Unveiling of the Monument of Maryland Confederate Dead at Winchester, Virginia. June 5, 1880. Pamphlet. Copy held by the Library of Winchester, VA.

223. Lindsley, John Berien. The Military Annals of Tennessee. Nashville: TN: Lindsley and Company, 1886.

224. Vaughan, Alfred J. Personal Record of the Thirteenth Regiment Tennessee Infantry. Memphis, TN: Press of South Carolina Toof and Company, 1897.

225. Head, Thomas A. Campaigns and Battles of the Sixteenth Regiment in the War Between the States. Nashville, TN: Cumberland Presbyterian Publishing House, 1885.

226. Diary of Captain J.J. Womach, 16th TN Inf., Co. E. Held by Army War College, Carlisle, PA.

227. Worsham, W.J. The Old Nineteenth Tennessee Regiment C.S.A. Knoxville, TN: Press of Paragon Company, 1902.

228. McMurray, W.J. History of the Twentieth Tennessee Regiment Volunteer Infantry C.S.A. Nashville, TN: The Publication Committee, 1904.

229. Hancock, R.R. Hancock's Diary: A History of the Second Tennessee Confederate Cavalry. 2 vols. Nashville, TN: Brandon Publishing Company, 1887.

230. Young, J.P. The Seventh Tennessee Cavalry. Nashville, TN: Barbee and Smith, 1890.

231. Davis, Nicholas A. The Campaign from Texas to Maryland. Richmond, VA: Presbyterian Committee of Publication, 1863.

232. Johnson, Sid S. Texans Who Wore the Gray Suit - Autobiography of Pvt. Hamilton Lefevre of Harford County, 1st Va. Cav. Co. L. Erick Davis Collection, Baltimore, MD.

233. Wilson, Isabella George. A Stray Leaf from Oak Hill. Pikesville: 1864. Erick Davis Collection, Baltimore, MD.

234. Winkler, Mrs. A.V. The Confederates Capital and Hood's Texas Brigade. Austin, TX: Eugene Von Boeckmann, 1894.

235. Wright Marcus J. Texas in the War 1861-1865. Hillsboro, TX: Hill Junior College Press, 1965.

236. Fitzhugh, Lester N. Texas Batteries, Battalions, Regiments, Commanders and Field Officers, Confederate States Army. Midlothian, TX: Mirror Press, 1959.

237. Everett, Donald E. Chaplain Davis and Hood's Texas Brigade. San Antonio, TX: Principia Press, 1962.

238. Barron, S.B. The Lone Star Defenders. Washington, D.C.: The Neale Publishing Company, 1908.

239. Simpson, Harold B. Gaines Mill to Appomattox. Waco, TX: Texian Press, 1963.

240. BOOTH George W. Personal Reminiscence of a Maryland Soldier in the War Between the States. Baltimore: Fleet McGinley and Company, 1898.

241. Rose, Victor M. Ross Texas Brigade. Louisville, KY: Courier-Journal Book and Job Rooms, 1881.

242. Debray, Xavier B. A Sketch of the History of Debray's 26th Regiment of Texas Cavalry. Austin, TX: Eugene Von Boeckmann, 1881.

243. Anderson, John Q., edit. Campaigning with Parson's Texas Cavalry Brigade C.S.A. Hillsboro, TX: Hill Junior College: Hillsboro, 1967.

244. Clark, Charles B., "Politics in Maryland During the Civil War. Chestertown, Maryland," 1952. A collection of articles appearing in Md. Hist. Mag., Sept 1941 to June 1946.

245. Hamilton, D.H. History of Company M. First Texas Volunteer Infantry. Waco, TX: W.M. Morrison, 1925.

246. Todd, George T. First Texas Regiment. Waco, TX: Texian Press, 1964.

247. Wood, W.D. A Partial Roster of Officers and Men Raised in Leon County Texas. 1899. Copy held by Army War College, Carlisle, PA.

248. Blessington, J.P. The Campaign of Walker's Texas Division. New York: Lange, Little and Company, 1875.

249. Simpson, Harold B. Hood's Texas Brigade. Waco, TX: Texian Press, 1970.

250. Loehr, Charles T. War History of the Old First Virginia Infantry Regiment. Richmond, VA: William Ellis Jones, 1884.

251. Wise, George. History of the Seventeenth Virginia Infantry C.S.A. Baltimore: Kelly, Piet and Company, 1870.

252. Irby, Richard. Historical Sketch of the Nottoway Grays. Richmond, VA: Fergusson and Sons, 1878.

APPENDIX B: REFERENCES

253. Edwards, John E. The Confederate Soldiers, Being a Memorial Sketch of George N. and Bushrod W. Harris. New York: Blelock and Company, 1868.

254. Hackley, Woodford B. The Little Fork Rangers. Richmond, VA: Press of the Dietz Printing Company, 1927.

255. Baylor, George. Bull Run to Bull Run. Richmond, VA: B.F. Johnson Publishing Company, 1900.

256. Scrapbook of Major George W. Brown of Baltimore. Held by Maryland Historical Society, Baltimore, MD.

257. Monteriro, Aristides. War Reminiscences by the Surgeon of Mosby's Command Richmond: E. Waddey, 1890.

258. Munson, John W. Reminiscences of a Mosby Guerilla. New York: Moffat, Yard and Company, 1906.

259. Addresses- Dedication of the Monument Loudon Park Cemetery to Captain William H. MURRAY. Baltimore: Innes and Company, 1875. Pamphlet.

260. Fonerden, C.A. A Brief History of the Military Career of Carpenter's Battery. New Market, VA: Henkel and Company, 1911.

261. Scott, John. Partisan Life with Colonel John S. Mosby. New York: Harper Brothers Publishers, 1867.

262. Jones, B.W. Under the Stars and Bars. Richmond, VA: Everett Waddey Company, 1909.

263. Moore, Richard C. The Heroic Dead of the Morris Artillery. New York: Thomas Smetzer, 1885.

264. Figg, Royall W. Where Men Only Dare to Go. Richmond, VA: Whittet and Shepperson, 1885.

265. Daniel, F.S. Richmond Howitzers in the War. Richmond, VA: "published anonymously," 1891.

266. Eliot, Ellsworth Jr. West Point in the Confederacy. New York: Baker and Company, 1941.

267. Contributions to a History of the Richmond Howitzer Battalion. Richmond, VA: Carlton McCarthy and Company, 1883.

268. Walker, Charles D. Memorial Virginia Military Institute. Philadelphia: J.B. Lippincott and Company, 1875.

269. Boynton, Charles B. The History of the Navy During the Rebellion. New York: D. Appleton and Company, 1868.

APPENDIX B: REFERENCES

270. Carrison David J. The Navy from Wood to Steel. New York: Franklin Watts, 1965.

271. Wise, Jennings C. The Military History of the Virginia Military Institute. Lynchburg: VA: J.P. Bell Company, 1915.

272. Davidson, Laura Lee. The Services of the Women of Maryland to the Confederate States. Typescript copy held by Maryland Historical Society, Baltimore, MD.

273. Taylor, Thomas E. Running the Blockade. New York: Charles Scribner's Sons, 1896.

274. Bigelow, John. France and the Confederate Navy 1862-1868. New York: Harper and Brothers, 1888.

275. Merli, Frank J. Great Britain and the Confederate Navy 1861-1865. Bloomington: Indiana University Press, 1970.

276. Robinson, William Morrison Jr. The Confederate Privateers. New Haven, CT: Yale University Press, 1928.

277. Still, William N. Jr. Iron Afloat. Nashville, TN: Vanderbilt University Press: 1971.

278. Sinclair, Arthur. Two Years on the Alabama. Boston: Lee and Shepard, 1895.

279. Officers in the Confederate Navy 1861-1865. Washington, D.C.: Office of Naval War Records, Government Printing Office, 1898.

280. A collection of naval correspondence during the Civil War of Lt. Col. and C. Eng. Henry Ashton RAMSEY - Naval Records Library, History and Museums Division, Washington, D.C.

281. Kell, John M. Recollections of a Naval Life. Washington, D.C.: The Neale Company, 1900.

282. Trial of the Officers amd Crew of the Privateer Savannah. New York: Baker and Godwin, 1862.

283. Hunt, Cornelius E. The Shenandoah - Last Confederate Cruiser. New York: G.W. Carleton and Company, 1867.

284. Wilkinson J. A Narrative of a Blockade Runner. New York: Sheldon and Company, 1877.

285. Goodrich, Albert M. Cruise and Capture of the Alabama. Minneapolis, Minnesota: The H.W. Wilson Company, 1906.

286. Cross, Joseph. Camp and Field Papers from the Portfolio of an Army Chaplain.

APPENDIX B: REFERENCES

287. Casler, John O. Four Years in the Stonewall Brigade. Guthrie, OK: State Capital Printing Company, 1893.

288. Bowman, T.H. Reminiscence of and Ex-Confederate Soldier. Austin, TX: Gammel-Statesman.

289. Blackford, Susan L. Letters from Lee's Army. New York: Charles Scribner's Sons, 1947.

290. Runge, William H., ed. Four Years in the Confederate Artilley. Chapel Hill, NC: University of North Carolina Press, 1961.

291. Burial Places of the Remains of Confederate Soldiers Who Fell in the Battle in Washington and Frederick Counties. Hagerstown, MD: Free Press.

292. Ford, Arthur P. Life in the Confederate Army Washington, D.C.: The Neale Publishing Company, 1905.

293. Dunlop, W.S. Lee's Sharpshooters. Little Rock, AR: Tunnah and Pittard, 1899.

294. Dinkins, James. 1861 - 1865, by an Old Johnnie ... Personal Recollections and Experiences in the Confederate Army. Cincinnati, OH: The Robert Clarke Company, 1897.

295. Dawson, Francis W. Reminiscences of Confederate Service 1861-1865. Charleston, SC: The News And Couries Book Presses, 1882.

296. Goodloe, Albert T. Some Rebel Relics from the Seat of the War. Nashville, TX: Barbee and Smith, 1893.

297. Hague, Parthenia A. A Blockaded Family. Boston: Houghton, Mifflin and Company, 1888.

298. Houghton, W.R. and M.B. Two Boys in the Civil War and After. Montgomery, AL: The Paragon Press, 1912.

299. Hubbard, John M. Notes of a Private. Memphis, TN: E.H. Clarke and Brother: Memphis, 1909.

300. Humphreys, David. Heroes and Spies of the Civil War. Washington D.C.: The Neale Publishing Company.

301. Johnson, Adam R. The Partisan Rangers of the Confederate States Army. Louisville, KY: George C. Fetler Company, 1904.

302. Jordan, William C. Some Events and Incidents During the Civil War. Montgomery, AL: The Paragon Press, 1909.

303. Lawrence, George Alfred. Border and Bastille. New York: W.I. Pooley and Company.

304. Ledford, P.L. Reminiscences of the Civil War. Thomasville, NC: News Printing House, 1909.

305. McCarthy, Carlton. Detailed Minutes of Soldiers Life in the A.N.V. Richmond, VA: Carlton McCarthey and Company, 1882.

306. McGuire, Judith W. Diary of a Southern Refugee During the War. New York: E.J. Hale and Son, 1868.

307. Mixson, Frank M. Reminiscences of a Private. Columbia, SC: The Slate Company: Columbia, 1910.

308. Montgomery, Frank A. Reminiscences of a Mississippian in Peace and War. Cincinnati, OH: The Robert Clarke Company, 1901.

309. Civil War papers of Brig. Gen. George Hume, Stewart Jr. Held by Maryland Historical Society, Baltimore MD.

310. Opie, John Newton. A Rebel Cavalryman with Lee, Stewart, and Jackson. Chicago: W.B. Conkey Company, 1899.

311. Neese, George M. Three Years in the Confederate Horse Artillery. Washington, D.C.: The Neale Publishing Company, 1911.

312. Description Rolls of Company B, Maryland Guard, Maryland Line. Maryland Historical Society.

313. Ridley, Bromfield L. Battles and Sketches of the Army of Tennessee. Mexico, MO: Missouri Printing and Publishing Company, 1906.

314. Noll, Arthur Howard, edit. Doctor Quintard. Sewanee, TN: The University Press, 1905.

315. Pryor, Mrs. Roger A. Reminiscences of Peace and War. London: The MacMillan Company, 1904.

316. Georgetown University Alumni. Blue and Gray - Georgetown University and the Civil War. 1961.

317. Pember, Phoebe Yates. A Southern Woman's Story. New York: G.W. Carleton and Company, 1879.

318. O'Ferrall, Charles T. Forty Years of Active Service Washington, D.C.: The Neale Publishing Company, 1904.

319. Wiley, Bill I., ed. Kentucky Cavaliers in Dixie. Jackson, TN: McCowat-Mercer Press, 1957.

320. Morgan, William H. Personal Reminiscences of the War of 1861-1865. Lynchburg, VA: J.P. Bell Company, 1911.

APPENDIX B: REFERENCES

321. Silver, James W. A Life for the Confederacy. Jackson, TN: McCowat-Mercer Press, 1959.

322. Moore, Edward A. The Story of a Cannoneer Under Stonewall Jackson. Lynchburg, VA: J.P. Bell Company, 1910.

323. Letters of Pvt. Frank L. Hering, 1st Md Cav Co. Private collection of Margaret Hering, Westminster, MD.

324. Sorrel, G. Moxley. Recollections of a Confederate Staff Officer. Washington, D.C.: The Neale Publishing Company, 1905.

325. Smith, Ralph J. Reminiscences of the Civil War and Other Sketches. Waco, TX: W. M. Morrison, 1911, 1962.

326. Robson, Johns S. How a One-Legged Rebel Lives. Richmond, VA: W.H. Wade and Company, 1876.

327. Toney, Marcus B. The Privations of a Private. Nashville, TN, 1905.

328. Worthington, C.J., ed. The Woman in Battle. Hartford, CT: T. Belk-nap, 1876.

329. Watson, William. Life in the Confederate Army. New York: Scribner and Welford, 1888.

330. Tilghman, Oswald. History of Talbot County, Maryland. 2 vols. Easton, 1915.

331. WILEY, Bell I. The Life of Johnny Reb. New York: The Bobbs-Merrill Company, 1943.

332. West, John C. A Texan in Search of a Fight. Waco, TX: J.S. Hill and Company, 1901.

333. Stevenson, William G. Thirteen Months in the Rebel Army. London: Sampson, Low, and Son and Company, 1862.

334. Williams, R.H. With the Border Ruffians. London: John Murray, 1908.

335. Wood, James H. The War. Cumberland, MD: Eddy Press Corporation, 1910.

336. Young, L.D. Reminiscneces of a Soldier of the Orphan Brigade. Paris, Kentucky. Louisville, KY: Courier journal job Printing Co, 1918.

337. Wood, William N. Reminiscences of Big I. Jackson, TN: McCowat-Mercer Press, 1956.

338. Zettler, B.M. War Stories. New York: The Neale Publishing Company, 1912.

APPENDIX B: REFERENCES

339. Officers and Enlisted Men Who Served on Signal Duty C.S.A., 1891. Author and publisher unknown. Copy held by Army War College, Carlisle, PA.

340. Sigand, Louis A. Belle Boyd: Confederate Spy. Richmond, VA: The Dietz Press, 1944.

341. Headley, John W. Confederate Operations in Canada and New York. Washington, D.C.: The Neale Publishing Company, 1906.

342. Dowling, Morgan E. Southern Prisons. Detroit, MI: William Graham, 1870.

343. Thompson, J.T. (secret agent). A Leaf from History ... dated Richmond, Nov. 16, 1864. Report madc to J. P. Benjamin, Secretary of State. Copies held by Library of Congress and Army War College, Carlisle, PA.

344. Jones, J. William. Confederate View of the Treatment of Prisoners of War. Richmond, VA: Southern Historical Society, 1876. Copy held by Army War College, Carlisle, PA.

345. Stevenson, R. Randolph. The Southern Side of Andersonville Prison. Baltimore: Turnbull Brothers, 1876.

346. Various Southern Prisoners in Lafayette. Fort-La-Fayette Life in 1863-1864. Liverpool, England: Simpkin, Marshall and Company, 1865.

347. JOHNSON, Bradley T. The First Maryland Campaign - Association of the Maryland Line. Baltimore: Andrew J. Conlon, 1886.

348. Cumming, Kate. A Journal of Hospital Life in the Confederate Army of Tennessee. Louisville, KY: John P. Morton and Company, 1866.

349. The Jones Brothers. The Grayjackets. Richmond, VA, 1867.

350. WOODHOUSE, Pvt. L. Nathan. The Cause that Was Lost and the Home that Was Found. Erick Davis Collection, Baltimore, MD.

351. Lamax, Virginia. The Old Capitol and Its Inmates. New York: E.J. Hale and Son, 1867.

352. Knauss, William H. The Story of Camp Chase. Nashville, TN: Smith and Lamar, 1906.

353. Keiley, A.M. In Vinculis or The Prisoner of War. New York: Blelock and Company, 1866.

354. Hundley, Daniel R. Prison Echoes of the Great Rebellion. New York: S.W. Green, 1874.

APPENDIX B: REFERENCES

355. Holmes, Clay W. The Elmira Prison Camp. New York: G.P. Putnam's Sons, 1912.

356. Confederate Soldiers, Sailors and Civilians Who Died as Prisoners of War at Camp Douglas, Chicago, IL, 1862-1865. Edgar Gray Publication.

357. Praus, Alexis. Confederate Soldiers Who Died as Prisoners of War at Camp Butler, Illinois, 1862-1865. Kalamazoo, MI: Edgar Gray Publication, [1968?].

358. Jones, William. Christ in the Camp. Richmond, VA: B.F. Johnson and Company, 1887.

359. Sheeran, James B. Confederate Chaplain. Milwaukee, WI: The Bruce Publishing Company, 1960.

360. Randall, James G. The Confiscation of Property During the Civil War. Indianapolis: Mutual Printing, 1913.

361. Williams Thomas J.C. History of Washington County. 2 vols. Hagerstown, Maryland, 1906.

362. Underwood, J.C. Report of Proceedings Incidental to the Erection and Dedication of the Confederate Monument. Chicago: William Johnston Printing Co., 1896.

363. The Flags of the Confederate Armies Returned to the Men Who Bore Them. 1905. U.S. Government Printing Office, Washington, D.C.

364. Christian Commission Report of the Committee of Maryland. Baltimore: MD: Sherwood and Company, 1862.

365. Christian Commission - Second Report of the Committee of Maryland. Baltimore: Sherwood and Company, 1863.

366. Cooke, John Esten. Hammer and Rapier. New York: Carleton Publishers, 1870.

367. Wharton, H.M. War Songs and Poems of the Southern Confederacy. Philadelphia, PA: The John C. Winston Co., [1904?].

368. Love, Edmund G. An End to Bugling. New York: Harper and Row, 1963.

369. Gilbert, R.R. High Private's Confederate Letters. Austin, TX: Eugene Von Boeckmann, 1894.

370. DeFontaine, Felix G. Marginalea or Gleanings from an Army Notebook. Columbia, SC: F.G. DeFontaine and Company, 1864.

371. Diehl, George West. A True Confederate Soldier - Col. Elijah Viers White. Typescript, published by author, [circa 1976]. A copy held in private collection of Daniel D. Hartzler, New Windsor, MD.

372. Honor Men. The Story of American Heroism. New Haven, CT: Butler and Alger, 1896.

373. MCKIM, Randolph Harrison. The Motives and Aims of the Soldiers of the South in the Civil War. Nashville, TN, 1904.

374. DeLeon, T.C. Four Years in Rebel Capitals. Mobile, AL: The Gossip Printing Company, 1890.

375. Eggleston, George Cary. A Rebel's Recollections. New York: G.P. Putnam's Sons, 1905.

376. Eggleston, George Cary. Southern Soldiers Stories. New York: The Macmillan Company, 1898.

377. Estvan, B. War Pictures from the South. New York: D. Appleton and Company, 1863.

378. Personal memorabilia of Major Mason Morfit, Quarter Master. Held by Duke University Library.

379. Lord, Walter, ed. The Fremantle Diary. Boston: Little, Brown and Company, 1954.

380. Gordon, John B. Reminiscences of the Civil War. New York: Charles Scribner's Sons 1904.

381. Lonn, Ella. Salt as a Factor in the Confederacy. New York: Walter Neale, 1933.

382. Hanna, Alfred J. Flight into Oblivion. Richmond, VA: Johnson Publishing Company, 1938.

383. ALLEN, William. Jackson's Valley Campaign. Richmond, VA: G.W. Gary and Company, 1878.

384. Abbot, Willis J. Battlefields of '61. New York: Dodd, Mead and Company, 1889.

385. Blackford, W.W. War Years with Jeb Stuart. New York: Charles Scribner's Sons, 1945.

386. Radoll, Morris L., ed. The Old Line State - A History of Maryland. Baltimore: Twentieth Century Printing Company, 1971.

387. Boggs, William R. Military Reminiscences By William R. Boggs, C.S.A. Durham, North Carolina: The Seeman Printery, 1913.

388. Reports of Fall of Forts Henry and Donelson. Richmond, VA: Enquirer Book and Job Press, 1862.

389. Cox, William V. The Defenses of Washington. Typescript held by Army War College, Carlisle, PA.

390. Connelly, William Elsey. Quantrill and the Border War. Cedar Rapids, IA: The Torch Press, 1910.

391. Dodson, W.C., ed. Campaigns of Wheeler and His Cavalry. Atlanta, GA: Hudgins Publishing Company, 1899.

392. Edwards, John N. Shelby and His Men. Cincinnati, OH: Miami Printing and Publishing Company, 1867.

393. Civil War scrapbook of Pvt. James J. Williamson, 43rd Va Cav, Co. A. Held by Maryland Historical Society, Baltimore, MD.

394. Duke, Basil W. Reminiscences of General Basil W. Duke C.S.A. New York: Doubleday, Page and Company, 1911.

395. DuPont, Henry A. The Campaign of 1864 in the Valley of Virginia. New York: National American Society, 1925.

396. Fiske, John. The Mississippi Valley in the Civil War. New York: Houghton, Mifflin, and Company, 1900.

397. Fiebeger, G.J. Campaigns of the American Civil War. West Point, New York: U.S. Military Printing Office, 1914.

398. Estvan, B. War Pictures from the South. New York: D. Appleton and Company, 1863.

399. Ellis, Edward S. The Camp Fires of General Lee. Philadelphia: Henry Harrison and Company, 1886.

400. Brig. Gen. Mansfield Lovell - Civil War Papers. Library of Congress. (Beginning with shelf number E472.8.C74)

401. Hale, Edward E., ed. Stories of War. Boston: Roberts Brothers, 1879.

402. Corman, J.C. Lee's Last Campaign. Raleigh, NC: William B. Smith and Company, 1866.

403. Gordon, John B. Reminiscences of the Civil War. New York: Charles Scribner's Sons, 1904.

404. Gerrish, Theodore and Hutchinson, John S. The Blue and the Gray. Portland, OR: Hoyt, Fogg and Donkam, 1883.

405. General H.W. Halleck's Report. NY: Anson D.F. Randolph, 1862.

406. Geer, Walter. Campaigns of the Civil War. NY: Brentano's, 1926.

APPENDIX B: REFERENCES

407. Fuller, B.H. A Study of the Antietam Campaign. 1913. Typescript held by Army War College, Carlisle, PA.

408. Fenton. Earl's Raid on Washington. 1916. Typescript held by Army War College, Carlisle, PA.

409. Hess, George. Battlefield Guide of the Battles South Mountain and Antietam, Maryland. Hagerstown, MD: Globe jobs room Printing Co., 1890.

410. Lewaas, Jay, ed. The Civil War - A Soldier's View Chicago: University of Chicago Press, 1958.

411. Hall, Granville D. Lee's Invasion of Northwest Virginia. Chicago, IL: Mayer and Miller Company, 1911.

412. Gunz, Dieter. The Maryland Germans. Princeton, NJ: Princeton University Press, 1948.

413. Johnson, W.T. Wilson's Raid South of Petersburg, 1916. Typescript held by Army War College, Carlisle, PA.

414. Johnston, Joseph E. Narration of Military Operations. NY: D. Appleton and Company, 1874.

415. Howe, Daniel W. Civil War Times - 1861-1865. Indianapolis: The Bowen-Merrill Company, 1902.

416. Hodd, J.R. Advance and Retreat. Phildelphia: Press of Burk and M'Fetridge, 1880.

417. Hickersmith, L.D. Morgan's Escape. Madisonville, KY: Glenn's Graphic Print, 1903.

418. Hinton, C.R.J. Rebel Invasion of Missouri and Kansas. Leavenworth, TX: Church and Goodman, 1865.

419. Heysinger, Isaac W. Antietam. NY: The Neal Publishing Company, 1912.

420. Kerbey, J.O. On the War Path. Chicago: Donohue, Henneberry and Company, 1890.

421. Kellogg, Sanford C. The Shenandoah Valley and Virginia 1861-1865. Washington, D.C.: The Neale Publishing Company, 1903.

422. Freeman, Douglas S., ed. Lee's Dispatches. NY: G.P. Putnam's Sons, 1915.

423. Marks, James J. The Peninsula Campaign in Virginia. Philadelphia: J.B. Lippincott and Company, 1864.

APPENDIX B: REFERENCES

424. Buchholz, Heinrich E. Governors of Maryland. Baltimore, MD: Williams and Wilkins Company, 1908.

425. Maguire, T. Miller. The Campaigns in Virginia. London: W.H. Allen and Company, 1891.

426. Barnes, A.S. A Critical History of the Late American War NY: A.S. Barnes and Company, 1877.

427. Magruder's Report of His Operations on the Peninsula. Richmond, VA: Charles H. Wynne, 1862.

428. Patterson, Robert. A Narrative of the Campaign in the Valley of the Shenandoah in 1861. Philadelphia: John C. Campbell, 1865.

429. Sloan, Benjamin. The Merrimac and the Monitor. Columbia, SC: University of South Carolina, 1926.

430. Correspondence of Brig. Gen. Joseph L. BRENT during the Civil War. A divided collection with some portions held by Louisiana Historical Association and other portions held by Howard Tilton Memorial Library, Tulane University.

431. *Civil War Times Illus. Mag.*, Vol. 1, No. 1 thru Vol. 20, No. 3.

432. Cunningham, Frank. General Stand Waties Confederate Indians. San Antonio, TX: Naylor Company, 1959.

433. Early, Jubal. The Campaigns of General Robert E. Lee. Baltimore, MD: J. Murphy, 1872.

434. Gibson, John Mendinghall. Those 163 Days. New York: Coward-McCann, 1961.

435. Letters of Pvt. Zabedee Beall, 1st MS Cav C.C. Erick Davis Collection, Baltimore, MD.

436. Hay, Thomas Robson. Hood's Tennessee Campaign. New York, 1929.

437. McIntosh, David Gregg. Review of the Gettysburg Campaign.

438. Mosby, John S. Stuart's Cavalry in the Gettysburg Campaign. New York, 1908.

439. Seddon, James A., "Defense of General J.H. WINDER," South. Hist. Soc. Papers, Vol. 1, 1875.

440. RITTER, William L., "Account of the Death of Sergeant Langley," South. *Hist. Soc. Papers*, Vol. 1, 1875.

441. "General G.H. STEWART's Brigade at the Battle of Gettysburg," *South. Hist. Soc. Papers*, Vol. 2, 1876.

APPENDIX B: REFERENCES

442. "Defense of Fort Gregg by CHEW's Maryland Artillery," *South. Hist. Soc. Papers*, Vol. 3, 1877.

443. HOLLYDAY, Lamar, "Maryland Troops in the Confederate Service," *South. Hist. Soc. Papers*, Vol. 3, 1877.

444. MCKIM, Randolph H., "Stewart's Brigade of the Battle of Gettysburg," *South. Hist. Soc. Papers*, Vol. 5, 1879.

445. HAYDEN, Horace Edwin, "The First Maryland Cavalry C.S.A.," *South. Hist. Soc. Papers*, Vol. 6, 1879.

446. "Battle of Mobile Bay Report of Adm. Franklin BUCHANAN," *South. Hist. Soc. Papers*, Vol. 6, 1879.

447. CURRY, Jaby Lamar Monroe, "Did Lee Violate His Oath in Siding with the Confederacy?," *South. Hist. Soc. Papers*, Vol. 6, 1879.

448. Early, J.A., "Barbara Fritchie - Refutation of Whittier's Myth," *South. Hist. Soc. Papers*, Vol. 7, 1879.

449. Lyon, James W., "Foreign Recognition of the Confederacy," *South. Hist. Soc. Papers*, Vol. 7, 1879.

450. Munford, T.T., "Reminiscences of Jackson's Valley Campaigns," *South. Hist. Soc. Papers*, Vol. 7, 1879.

451. RITTER, W. L., "Operations of a Section of Third Maryland Battery on the Mississippi in the Spring of 1863," *South. Hist. Soc. Papers*, Vol. VII, 1879.

452. Witherspoon, T. D., "Prison Life at Fort McHenry," *South. Hist. Soc. Papers*, Vol VIII, 1880.

453. "Report of General TRIMBLE Operation 14-29, August, 1862," *South. Hist. Soc. Papers*, Vol. VIII, 1880.

454. RITTER, W. L., "An Incident of the Deer Creek Expedition of 1863," *South. Hist. Soc. Papers*, Vol. IX, 1881.

455. Early J. A., "Advance on Washington in 1864," South. Hist. Soc *Papers*, Vol. IX, 1881.

456. JOHNSON, B. T., "Memoir of First Maryland Regiment," *South. Hist. Soc. Papers*, Vol. IX, 1881.

457. HAYDEN, Horace Edwin, "The Maryland Line," *South. Hist. Soc. Papers*, Vol. IX, 1881.

458. "Report of General G. H. STEUART, Winchester, 1863," *South. Hist. Soc. Papers*, Vol. IX, 1881.

APPENDIX B: REFERENCES

459. "Report of Col. Snowden ANDREWS, Gettysburg, 1863," *South. Hist. Soc. Papers,* Vol. X, 1882.

460. McINTOSH, Davis Gregg, "The Artillery on the Gettsburgh Campaign," *South. Hist. Soc. Papers,* Vol. X, 1882.

461. RITTER, William L., "Sketch of Third Battery of Maryland Artillery," *South. Hist. Soc. Papers,* Vol. X, XI, XII.

462. JOHNSON, B. T., "The Maryland Line in the Confederate Army," *South. Hist. Soc. Papers,* Vol. X, XI.

463. -----, "Maryland Campaign," *South. Hist. Soc. Papers,* Vol XII, 1883.

464. "Capture of a Flag by Maryland Confederates," *South. Hist. Soc. Papers,* Vol. XIII, 1884.

465. JOHNSON, B. T. and Waldhauer, David, "Affair at Frederick City," *South. Hist. Soc. Papers,* Vol. XIII, 1884.

466. "Report of B. T. JOHNSON," *South. Hist. Soc. Papers,* XIII, 1884.

467. HILL, D. H., "Lost Dispatch at Frederick City," *South. Hist. Soc. Papers,* XIII, 1884.

468. BLACKFORD, Eugene, "Official Report of Gettysburg," *South. Hist. Soc. Papers,* XIII, 1884.

469. "Maryland Confederate Monument Unveiling at Gettysburg," *South. Hist. Soc. Papers,* Vol. XIV, 1885.

470. "Paroles of the Army of Northern Virginia at Appomatox, April 9, 1865," *South. Hist. Soc. Papers,* Vol. XV, 1886.

471. Brady, Lewis, "Chew's Battery," *South. Hist. Soc. Papers,* Vol. XVI, 1887.

472. BUCHANAN, Franklin, "Official Report of the Battle of Hampton Roads," *South. Hist. Soc. Papers,* Vol. XVII, 1885.

473. "Capture of General Crook and Kelly at Cumberland, Maryland," *South. Hist. Soc. Papers,* Vol. XIX, 1891.

474. BRENT, Joseph L., "Artillery of the Army of Western Louisiana," *South. Hist. Soc. Papers,* Vol. XIX., 1891.

475. DOUGLAS, Henry Kyd, "A Ride For Stonewall," *South. Hist. Soc. Papers,* Vol. XXI, 1893.

476. GOLDSBOROUGH, W. W., "How General Turner Ashby was Killed," *South. Hist. Soc. Papers,* Vol. XXI, 1893.

APPENDIX B: REFERENCES

477. MARSHALL, Charles, "Appomattox Courthouse Address," *South. Hist. Soc. Papers,* Vol. XXI, 1893.

478. CARTER, Thomas Henry, "The Bloody Angle," *South. Hist. Soc. Papers,* Vol. XXI, 1893.

479. RITTER, W. L., "Brief History of Third Battery Maryland Artillery," *South. Hist. Soc. Papers,* Vol. XXII, 1894.

480. HOLLINS, George N., Sr., "A Daring Exploit - The Capture of the Steamer Saint Nicholas," *South. Hist. Soc. Papers,* Vol. XXIV, 1896.

481. Donohoe, John C., "The Capture of the Federal Garrison at Front Royal, May 23, 1862," *South. Hist. Soc. Papers,* Vol. XXIV, 1896.

482. Wise Henry A., "A Tribute to James Murray Mason," *South. Hist. Soc. Papers,* Vol. XXV, 1897.

483. "Boonsboro Flight of the Maryland Campaign," *South. Hist. Soc. Papers,* Vol. XXV, 1897.

484. Trimble, I. R., "The Battle and Campaign of Gettysburg," *South. Hist. Soc. Papers,* Vol. XXVI, 1898.

485. Moore, J. Scott, "A Southern Account of the Burning of Chambersburg," *South. Hist. Soc. Papers,* Vol. XXVI, 1898.

486. Gaines, J. M., "Sick and Wounded Confederate Soldiers at Hagerstown and Williamsport," *South. Hist. Soc. Papers,* Vol. XXVII, 1899.

487. "How Lt. Walter BOWIE of Mosby's Command Met His End," *South. Hist. Soc. Papers,* Vol. XXVII, 1900.

488. "Memoir of Jane Claudia Johnson," *South. Hist. Soc. Papers,* Vol. XXIX, 1901.

489. PETERS, Winfield, "Monument to Maryland Confederates," *South. Hist. Soc. Papers,* Vol. XXIX, 1901.

490. McDONALD, E. H., "How Virginia Supplied Maryland with Arms," *South. Hist. Soc. Papers,* Vol. XXIX, 1901.

491. Von Phul, Frank, "General LITTLE's Burial," *South. Hist. Soc. Papers,* Vol. XXIX, 1901.

492. JOHNSON, B. T., "How General Jeb Stuart Lost His Life in Recapturing a Borrowed Maryland Battery," *South. Hist. Soc. Papers,* Vol. XXIX, 1901.

493. "A Maryland Warrior and Hero," *South. Hist. Soc. Papers,* Vol. XXIX, 1901.

APPENDIX B: REFERENCES

494. "April 19, 1861, A Record of the Events in Baltimore," *South. Hist. Soc. Papers*, Vol., XXIX, 1901.

495. MARSHALL, Charles, "The Sword of Lee," *South. Hist. Soc. Papers*, Vol. XXIX, 1901.

496. JOHNSON, B. T., "My Ride Around Baltimore in Eighteen Hundred and Sixty-Four," *South. Hist. Soc. Papers*, Vol. XXX, 1902.

497. DORSEY, G. W., "Fatal Wounding of General J. E. B. Stuart," *South. Hist. Soc. Papers*, Vol. XXX, 1902.

498. Matthews, H. H., "Recollections of Major James BREATHED - A Maryland Confederate," *South. Hist. Soc. Papers*, Vol. XXX, 1902.

499. "Inboden's Dash into Charlestown," *South. Hist. Soc. Papers*, Vol. XXXI, 1903.

500. HOWARD, McHenry, "Closing Scenes of the War," *South. Hist. Soc. Papers*, Vol. XXXI, 1903.

501. Wright, Mrs. D. G., "Maryland and the South," *South. Hist. Soc. Papers*, Vol. XXXI, 1903.

502. McCausland, J., "Burning of Chambersburg, Pennsylvania," *South. Hist. Soc. Papers*, Vol. XXXI, 1903.

503. PETERS, Winfield, "First Battle of Manassas," *South. Hist. Soc. Papers*, Vol. XXXIV, 1906.

504. "Roster of McNeill's Rangers," *South. Hist. Soc. Papers*, Vol. XXXV, 1907.

505. Burgess, W. W., "Soldier's Story of J. E. B. Stuart's Death," *South. Hist. Soc. Papers*, Vol. XXXVI, 1908.

506. Jeffreys, Thomas D., "The Red Bade Explained," South. Hist. Soc. Papers, Vol. XXX VI, 1908.

507. SLINGLUFF, Fielder, "The Burning of Chambersburg," *South. Hist. Soc. Papers*, Vol. XXX VII, 1909.

508. "Marylanders in the Confederate Army," *South. Hist. Soc. Papers*, Vol. XXXVII, 1909.

509. Stonebraker, John R., "Munford's Marylanders Never Surrendered to Foe," *South. Hist. Soc. Papers*, Vol. XXXVII, 1909.

510. COLSTON, Frederick M., "Recollections of the Last Months in the Army of Northern Virginia," *South. Hist. Soc. Papers*, Vol. XXX VIII, 1910.

APPENDIX B: REFERENCES

511. Shepherd, Harry E., "Centennial of Birth of Admiral Raphael SEMMES," *South. Hist. Soc. Papers,* Vol. XXXVIII, 1910.

512. PETERS, Winfield, "Confederates Who Fell in Battle Re-interred in Maryland," *South. Hist. Soc. Papers,* Vol. XXX VIII, 1910.

513. "Maryland Line Confederate Soldiers Home," *South. Hist. Soc. Papers,* Vol. XXXVIII, 1910.

514. "United Confederate Veterans - Isaac R. TRIMBLE Camp," *South. Hist. Soc. Papers,* Vol. XXX VIII, 1910.

515. "Baltimore in 1861," *South. Hist. Soc. Papers,* Vol. XXX VIII, 1910.

516. Semmes, S. Spencer, "Admiral Raphael SEMMES - A Monograph," *South. Hist. Soc. Papers,* Vol., XXXVIII, 1910.

517. Avirett, James B. The Memoirs of General Turner Ashby and His Compeers. Baltimore, Maryland: Selby and Dulany, 1867.

518. Wallace, Lee A., Jr. A Guide to Virginia Military Organizations, 1861-1865. Richmond, VA: Virginia Civil War Commission, 1964.

519. DUFFEY, J. W. Two Generals Kidnapped. Washington, D. C., 1927. Pamphlet. A copy available at Allegany County Library, Cumberland, MD.

520. Richardson, William. Roster of Warren County Veterans, C.S.A. Camp U. C. V., No. 804., 1907.

521. Porter, John W. History of Norfolk County, Virginia, 1861-1865. Portsmouth, VA: W.A. Fishe, 1892.

522. Graves, Joseph A. The History of the Bedford Light Artillery. Bedford City, VA: Bedford Democrat, 1903.

523. Lt. Col. Jabez L.M. Curry 5th Al Cav - Civil War Correspondent. Library of Congress, University of North Carolina, and Virginia Baptist Historical Society.

524. Young, Charles P. A History of Crenshaw Battery. Richmond, VA: William Ellis Jones, 1904.

525. Headspeth, W. Carroll. Halifax Volunteers in the Confederate Army. 1939.

526. The Right of Recognition, A Sketch of the Present Policy of the Confederate States. London: R. Hardwicke, 1862.

527. Caroline County Schools. History of Caroline County, Maryland From Its Beginning. Federalsburg, MD: J.W. Strowell Printers, 1920.

APPENDIX B: REFERENCES

528. Some Historical Facts About Sussex County. Copy available at Army War College, Carlisle, PA.

529. Evans, Mrs. O.W. Craig's Share in the War Between the States. New Castle, VA.

530. Crawford, Charles A. The First Virginia Regiment. Richmond, VA, 1916.

531. Fontaine, C.R. 57th Virginia Regiment of Infantry. Typescript copy at Army War College, Carlisle, PA.

532. Herbert, Arthur. Sketches and Incidents of Movements of the Seventeenth Virginia Infantry. Washington, D.C. Typescript copy at Army War College, Carlisle, PA.

533. Myers, Clifford R. Biennial Report of the Department of Archives and History - West Virginia. Charleston, WV: Jarrett Printing Company, 1933.

534. Bylaws and Regulations of the Warrenton Rifle Company. Warrenton, VA: Whig Printing Office, 1860.

535. Jones, William Ellis. Annual Reunion of Pegram Battalion, May 21, 1886. Richmond, VA, 1886.

536. Johnson, John Lipscomb. The University Memorial. Baltimore: Turnbull Brothers, 1871.

537. Blackford, C.M. Annals of the Lynchburg Home Guard. Lynchburg, VA: John W. Rohr, 1891.

538. Strode, Hudson. Jefferson Davis - American Patriot. New York: Harcourt, Brace, 1955.

539. Jones, B.W. Battle Roll of Surry County, Virginia. Richmond, VA: Everett Waddey Company, 1913.

540. Page, R.C.M. Sketch of Page's Battery, of Morris Artillery, 2d Corps, Army of Northern Virginia By One of the Company. New York, NY: Thomas Smeltzer, 1885.

541. Mickle, William E. Well Known Confederate Veterans and Their War Records. New Orleans, LA, 1907.

542. Moore, Alison. The Louisiana Tigers. Baton Rouge, LA: Ortlieb Press, 1961.

543. Admiral Franklin BUCHANAN Civil War Papers. Held by University of North Carolina Library.

APPENDIX B: REFERENCES

544. Washington Artillery Souvenir, 1896. Pamphlet. A copy is held by Louisiana Historical Association, Confederate Memorial Hall, New Orleans, LA.

545. Tunnard, W. H. A Southern Record. The History of the Third Regiment Louisiana Infantry. Baton Rouge, LA, 1866. Repr. Dayton, OH: Morngingside Bookshop, 1970.

546. Bartlett, Napier. Military Record of Louisiana. New Orleans, LA: L. Graham and Company, 1875.

547. Soldiers of Florida by Board of State Institutions. Live Oak, FL: Democrat Book and Job Print.

548. Dickison, Mary E. Dickison and His Men. Louisville, KY: Courier-Journal Job Printing Company, 1890.

549. Barnard, Harry Vollie. Tattered Volunteers. Northport, Alabama: Hermitage Press, 1965.

550. Personal memorabilia of Cmdr. Joseph N. BARNEY, U.S. Navy. Office of Naval Records, History and Museums Division, Washington, D.C.

551. Roll of Officers and Members of the Georgia Hussars. Savannah, GA: The Morning News.

552. Clark, Walter O. Under the Stars and Bars. Augusta, GA: Chronicle Printing Company, 1900.

553. Hodge, G.B. Sketch of the First Kentucky Brigade. Frankfurt, KY: Majors and Johnston, 1874.

554. Nichols, G.W. A Soldier's Story of His Regiment. Jessup, GA, 1898. Repr. Kennesaw, GA: Continental Book Co., 1961.

555. Schrantz, Ward L. Jasper County Missouri in the Civil War. Carthage Press, MO: The Carthage Press, 1923.

556. Mathes, J. Harvey. The Old Guard in Gray. Memphis, TN: S.C. Toof and Company, 1897.

557. Sellman, Mrs. F. May of Frederick, Maryland, comp. A calendar presented to the Maryland Room, Confederate Museum, Richmond, VA, December, 1937. A typed manuscript.

558. Gresham, Bessie E. Memories of the Confederacy. Baltimore, Maryland, 1898 - Copy held by Confederate Museum, Richmond VA.

559. Scrapbook of Lt. James Innis Randolph, Engr. Held by White House of the Confederacy, Richmond, VA.

APPENDIX B: REFERENCES

560. Farquhar, Roger Brooke. Historic Montgomery County, Maryland. Baltimore: Monumental Printing Company, 1952.

561. Rains, George W. History of the Confederate Power Works. Augusta, GA: Chronicle and Constitutionalist Print, 1882.

562. Summers, Festus P. The Baltimore and Ohio in the Civil War. New York: G.P. Putnam's Sons, 1939.

563. Thompson Samuel Bernard. Confederate Purchasing Operations Abroad. Chapel Hill, NC: University of North Carolina Press, 1935.

564. Vandiver, Frank E. Ploughshares into Swords. Austin, Texas: University of Texas Press, 1952.

565. Bates, Samuel P. The Battle of Chancellorville. Meadville, PA, 1882.

566. Battine, Cecil. The Crisis of the Confederacy. London: Longmans, Green and Company, 1905.

567. Baxter, William. Pea Ridge and Prairie Grove. Cincinnatti, OH: Poe and Hitchcock, 1864.

568. Boykin, Edward Carrington. Beefsteak Raid. New York: Funk and Wagnalls, 1960.

569. Britton, Wiley. The Civil War on the Border. New York: G.P. Putnam's Sons, 1899.

570. Confederate papers of Major Wells J. Hawks, C.C.S. Held by Duke University Library.

571. Colton, Ray Charles. The Civil War in the Western Territories. Norman, OK: University of Oklahoma Press, 1959.

572. Confederate War Department. Southern History of the War. Richmond, VA: C.B. Richardson, 1863.

573. Hagood, Johnson. Memoirs of the War of Secession. Columbia, SC: The State Company, 1910.

574. Macon, T.J. Life Gleanings. Richmond, VA, 1913.

575. Holland, Celia M. Ellicott City, Maryland. Chicago, IL: Adams Press, 1970.

576. Cannon, J.P. Inside of Rebellion. Washington, D.C.: National Tribune, 1900.

577. Iglar, William Valmore. A Sketch of the War Record of the Edisto Rifles 1861-1865. Columbia, SC: The State Company, 1914.

578. Wells, Edward L. A Sketch of the Charleston Light Dragoons. Charleston, SC: Lucas, Richards and Company, 1888.

579. Noel, T. A Campaign from Santa Fe to the Mississippi. Raleigh, NC: C.R. Sanders, Jr., 1961.

580. Private and offical records of Lieut. Henry Kyd Douglas of the Civil War. Held by University of Virginia, Library.

581. Allen, V.C. Rhea and Meigs Counties in the Confederate War. 1908.

582. Rennolds, Edwin H. A History of the Henry County Commands. Jacksonville, FL: Sun Publishing Company, 1904.

583. SMITH, Tunstall. James McHenry HOWARD - A Memoir. Baltimore, 1916. n.p.

584. Wagandt, Charles L. The Army Versus Maryland Slavery 1862-1864.

585. Pitts, Charles Frank. Chaplains in Gray. Nashville, TN: Broadman Press, 1957.

586. Nichols, James L. The Confederate Quartermaster in the Trans-Mississippi. Austin, TX: University of Texas Press, 1964.

587. Lovermore, Thomas L. Numbers and Losses in the Civil War in America. New York: Houghton, Mifflin and Company, 1901.

588. Hayden, Frederick Stanbury. Aeronautics in the Union and Confederate Armies. Baltimore, MD: Johns Hopkins Press, 1941.

589. Fox, William Freeman. Regimental Loss in the American Civil War 1861-1865. Albany, NY: Albany Publishing Company, 1889.

590. Cunningham, Horace Herndon. Doctors in Gray. Baton Rouge: LA: Louisiana State University Press, 1953.

591. Black, Robert C. The Railroads of the Confederacy. Chapel Hill, NC: University of North Carolina Press, 1952.

592. Dulaney, Carroll. Day by Day. Baltimore, Maryland, 1939. Vertical File, Maryland Historical Society, Baltimore, MD.

593. Thomas, James William. Col. Richard Thomas ZARVONA, A Maryland Hero. Pamphlet. A copy held by Daniel D. Hartzler, New Windsor, MD

594. WHITE, Levi S. Running the Blockade on the Chesapeake Bay. Baltimore Sun Newspaper, Dec. 15, 1907.

595. WHITE, John Goldsborough. A Rebel's Memoirs of the Civil War. Baltimore Sun Newspaper, May 7, 1929.

APPENDIX B: REFERENCES

596. Kramer, Samuel. Letter to Governor Augustus Bradford dated July 21, 1864. Erick Davis Collection, Baltimore, MD.

597. Chevalier, M.M. France, Mexico and the Confederate States. New York: C.B. Richardson, 1863.

598. Head, Thomas A. Campaigns and Battles of the Sixteenth Regiment. Nashville, TN: Cumberland Presbyterian Publishing House, 1885.

599. Guild, George B. A Brief Narrative of the Fourth Tennessee Cavalry Regiment. Nashville, TN, 1913.

600. Civil War memorabilia of Brig. Gen. John H. Winder. Held by University of North Carolina.

601. Albaugh, William A., III. Confederate Faces. Solana Beach, CA: Verde Publishers, 1970.

602. Albaugh, William A., III. More Confederate Faces. Washington, D.C.: A.B.S. Printers, 1973.

603. Goddard, Henry P. Some Distinguished Marylanders I Have Known. *Md. Hist. Mag.*, Vol. IV, 1909.

604. Culver, Francis B. War Romance of John Thomas SCHARF. *Md. Hist. Mag.*, Vol. XXI, 1926.

605. Spalding, Basil William. The Confederate Raid on Cumberland. *Md. Hist. Mag.*, Vol. XXVII, 1927.

606. Russ, William A., Jr. Disfranchisement in Maryland 1861-1867. *Md. Hist. Mag.*, Vol. XXVIII, 1933.

607. Kelly, William J. Baltimore Steamboats in the Civil War. *Md. Hist. Mag.*, Vol. XXIII, 1942.

608. HOLLINS, George Nicholas. Autobiography of Commodore George Nicholas Hollins, C.S.A., *Md. Hist. Mag.*, Vol. XXXIV.

609. Clark, Charles B. Politics in Maryland During the Civil War. *Md. Hist. Mag.*, Vol. XXVI, 1941 and Vol. XLI, 1946.

610. Cunz, Dieter. The Maryland Germans in the Civil War. *Md. Hist. Mag.*, Vol. XXXVI, 1941.

611. Matthews, Sidney T. Control of the Baltimore Press During the Civil War. *Md. Hist. Mag.*, Vol. XXXVI, 1941

612. Green, Fletcher M. A People at War - Hagerstown June 15 - Aug 31, 1863. *Md. Hist. Mag.*, Vol. XL, 1945.

APPENDIX B: REFERENCES

613. Tilghman, Tench Francis, "The College Green Barracks - St. John's During the Civil War," *Md. Hist. Mag.*, Vol. XLIV, 1949.

614. Fielding, Geoffrey W., ed., "GILMOR'S Field Report of His Raid in Baltimore County," *Md. Hist. Mag.*, Vol. XLVII, 1952.

615. Memphill, John M. "Gettysburg Described in Two Letters From a Maryland Confederate - Joseph H. TRUNDLE," *Md. Hist. Mag.*, Vol. LII, 1959.

616. Clark, Charles B., "Suppression and Control of Maryland 1861-1865," *Md. Hist. Mag.*, Vol. LVI, 1961.

617. Wychoff, V.J., "The Amazing Colonel Zarvona," *Md. Hist. Mag.*, Vol. LIV, 1961.

618. Duncan, Richard R., "Maryland Methodists and the Civil War," *Md. Hist. Mag.*, Vol. LIX, 1964.

619. Wagandt, Charles L., "The Opinion of Maryland on the Emancipation Proclamation - Bernal to Russell, September 23, 1862," *Md. Hist. Mag.*, Vol. LVIII, 1963.

620. Wagandt, Charles L., "Election by Sword and Ballot - The Emancipation Victory of 1863," *Md. Hist. Mag.*, Vol. LIX, 1964.

621. Briggs, Herbert Whittaker. The Doctrine of Continuous Voyage. Baltimore, MD: The Johns Hopkins Press, 1926.

622. Beale, R.L.T. History of the Ninth Virginia Cavalry. Richmond, VA: B.F. Johnson Publishing Company, 1899.

623. Dinkens, James. 1861 to 1865 by an Old Johnnie. Cincinnati, OH: Robert Clark Company, 1897.

624. Henry, Robert S. Story of the Confederacy. Garden City, NJ, 1931.

625. Adams Douglass Ephraim. Great Britain and the American Civil War. New York: Russell and Russell, 1958.

626. Von Boeckman, F.E. Daniel. Recollections of a Rebel Surgeon. Austin, Texas: Schutze and Company, 1899.

627. Biographical Sketches of the Members of Maryland Line Confederate Soldiers Home, January, 1900. Erick Davis Collection, Baltimore, MD.

628. A listing of members of Company A, 1st Maryland Cavalry United Confederate Veterans Camp. Held by Edward St. C. Buckler, Jr., Annapolis, MD.

629. Castleman, John B. Active Service. Louisville, KY: Courier-Journal Job Printing Company, 1917.

APPENDIX B: REFERENCES

630. Bruce, Philip Alexander. Brave Deeds of Confederate Soldiers. Philadelphia: G.W. Jacobs and Company, 1916.

631. Biographical Cyclopedia of Representative Men of Maryland. Baltimore: National Biographical Publishing Company, 1879.

632. Henderson G.F.R. Stonewall Jackson and the American Civil War, Vol. I, II. 1906.

633. Chapman, R.D. A Georgia Soldier in the Civil War. Little Rock, AR: General T.J. Churchill Chapter, United Daughters of the Confederacy, 1932.

634. Huffman, James. Up and Down of a Confederate Soldier. New York: W.E. Rudge's Sons, 1940.

635. Ingraham, Prentiss. Land of Legendary Lore. Easton, MD: The Gazette Publishing House, 1898.

636. McDaniel, Ruth B., comp. Confederate War Correspondence of James Michael Barr. n.p., 1963. Typescript held by Army War College, Carlisle, PA.

637. Bernard, George S., ed. War Talks of Confederate Veterans. Petersburg, VA: Fenn and Owen, 1892.

638. Guide Book and Descriptive Manual of Battle Flags in the Flag Room of State House at Annapolis. State of Maryland, 1907.

639. Boggs, William R. Military Reminiscence of General William R. Boggs C.S.A. Durham, NC: Seeman Printery: Durham, 1913.

640. Moffett, Mary C., ed. Letters of General James Conner C.S.A. Columbia, SC: The State Company, 1933.

641. Brown, Varina D. A Colonel at Gettysburg and Spotsylvania. Columbia, SC: The State Company, 1931.

642. Ford, Arthur P. Life in the Confederate Army. Washington, D.C.: Neale Publishing Company, 1905.

643. Grove, William J. History of Carrollton Manor, Frederick County, Maryland. Frederick, Maryland, 1922.

644. Knott, A. Leo. A Biographical Sketch of Hon. A. Leo Knott with a Relation - Some Political Transactions in Maryland 1861-1867. Being the History of the Redemption of a State. Baltimore, MD: S.B. Nelson, 1898.

645. Talbot County Court House Monument to the Talbot Boys 1861-1865, C.S.A.

APPENDIX B: REFERENCES

646. Henderson, Henry E. Yankee in Gray - The Civil War Memoirs of Henry E. Henderson. Cleveland: Press of Western Reserve University, 1962.

647. Ridley, Bromfield L. Battles and Sketches of the Army of Tennessee. Mexico, MO: Missouri Printing and Publishing Company, 1906.

648. Addey, Markinfield. Old Jack and His Foot Cavalry. New York: J. Bradburn, 1864.

649. Barlett, Napier. A Soldier's Story of the War. New Orleans, LA: Clark and Hofeline, 1874.

650. The Murray Confederate Association of Maryland Composed of the Surviving Members. Baltimore, MD: Lucas Brothers, 1885. Pamphlet.

651. Crocker, James F. Gettysburg. Portsmouth, VA: W.A. Fiske, 1915.

652. Henderson, E. Prioleau. Autobiography of Arab. Columbia, SC: R.L. Bryan Company, 1901.

653. Ellicott, James Carson. The Southern Soldier Boy. Raleigh, NC: Edward and Broughton, 1901.

654. Civil War scrapbook and papers of Colonel William Norris, Chief Signal Corps and Secret Service. Portions held by the University of Virginia Library and Tufts College Library.

655. Claiborne, Jane E. War History of Charles H. CLAIBORNE of Baltimore. 1900. Typescript copy held by Daniel D. Hartzler, New Windsor, MD.

656. Ferguson, John L. With Honor Untarnished. Little Rock, AR: Pioneer Press, 1961.

657. Hermann, I. Memoirs of a Veteran Who Served as a Private in the 60's in the War Between the States. Atlanta, GA: Byrd Printing Company, 1911.

658. Clark, Charles B. The Eastern Shore of Maryland and Virginia, 3 vols. New York: Lewis Historical Publishing Company, 1950.

659. Fleming, Seton. Memoir of Captain Seton Fleming of the Second Florida Infantry C.S.A. Jacksonville, FL: Times-Union Publishing House, 1884.

660. Griggs, Earle E., ed. Army Life of Frank Edwards - Confederate Veteran, Army of Northern Virginia. n.p., 1911.

661. Emory, Frederick. Queen Anne's County. Centreville Observer, 1886.

662. Hamlin, Percy G., ed. The Making of a Soldier. Richmond, VA: Whittet and Shepperson, 1935.

APPENDIX B: REFERENCES

663. Duncan, Thomas D. Recollections of Thomas D. Duncan - A Confederate Soldier. Nashville, TN: McQuiddy Printing Company, 1922.

664. Montgomery, Horace. Johnny Cobb Confederate Aristocrat. University of Georgia Press, 1964.

665. Callahan, James Morton. The Diplomatic History of the Southern Confederacy. Baltimore: The Johns Hopkins Press, 1901.

666. Maddox, George T. Hard Trials and Tribulations of an Old Confederate Soldier. Van Buren, AR: Printed at Argus Office.

667. Memorabilia of Lt. Col. William Allan, Ordnance Dept. Held by University of North Carolina Library.

668. Usilton, Fred G. History of Kent County, Maryland. 1916.

669. McGavock, Randal W. Pen and Sword. Nashville, TN: Tennessee Historical Commission, 1959.

670. Staff letters of Captain William K. Bradford. Erick Davis Collection.

671. LeConte, Joseph. Ware Sherman. Berkeley, CA: University of California Press, 1937.

672. Brown, Phillip R. Brown. Reminiscences of the War of 1861-1865. Roanoke, VA: Union Printing Company, 1912.

673. Benson, Susan Williams. Memoirs of a Confederate Scout and Sharpshooter. Athens, GA: University of Georgia Press, 1962.

674. MCKIM, Randolph H. The Second Maryland Infantry. 1909. Copy held by Daniel D. Hartzler, New Windsor, MD.

675. Paxton, Elisha Franklin, arr. by his son, John G. Paxton. Memoirs and Memorials. n.p., 1905. Typescript held by Army War College, Carlisle, PA.

676. Lee, Robert E., Jr. Recollections and Letters of General Robert E. Lee. New York: Doubleday, Page and Company, 1904.

677. Constitution and Roll of Members of the Confederate Veterans' Association of the District of Columbia. Age Printing Company: Washington, D.C. Pamphlet.

678. Personal documents of Major General Isaac R. TRIMBLE, C.S.A. Held by Maryland Historical Society, Baltimore, MD.

679. McIlwaine, Richard. Memories of Three Score Years and Ten. Washington, D.C.: Neale Publishing Company, 1908.

APPENDIX B: REFERENCES

680. With Thirty-Five Men Harry Gilmor Captured a Regiment. November 19, 1913. Handwritten account, Erick Davis Collection, Baltimore, MD.

681. Personal letters of Col. Robert Lemmon 21st VA Inf, Co B. Held by Maryland Historical Society, Baltimore, MD.

682. Boykin, Edward C. Sea Devil of the Confederacy. New York: Funk and Wagnalls, 1959.

683. LaBree, Benjamin. Camp Fires of the Confederacy. Louisville, KY: Courier-Journal Job Printing Company, 1898.

684. Relics from the Confederate Maryland Line Soldiers Home, Pikesville, Maryland. A listing compiled by Daniel D. Hartzler from inventory of relics of the Home, showing the owners (the veterans). The inventory is held by Maryland Historical Society, Baltimore, MD.

685. Taken from a listing of veterans' relics in the Maryland Room of the White House of the Confederacy, Richmond, Virginia, compiled by Daniel D. Hartzler.

686. Taken from a listing of veterans' relics in the Confederate Room of the Maryland Historical Society, Baltimore, MD. Compiled by Daniel D. Hartzler.

687. Address of Charles H. Stanley of Laurel to the Confederate Veterans of Prince George's County, Laurel, Maryland, 1903. Pamphlet. A copy is held by Daniel D. Hartzler, New Windsor, MD.

688. Hunton, Eppa. Autobiography of Eppa Hunton. Richmond, VA: The William Boyd Press, 1933.

689. Letters of Brig. Gen. James J. ARCHER, 1861-1865. Held by Maryland Historical Society, Baltimore, MD.

690. Members of the Pre-War Baltimore Maryland Guard 53rd Militia Infantry, Who Served in the Maryland Line C.S.A., compiled by Daniel D. Hartzler from manuscript collection held by Maryland Historical Society, Baltimore, MD.

691. Ross, Fitzgerald. A Visit to the Cities and Camps of the Confederate States. London: W. Blackwood and Sons, 1865.

692. Beale, G.W. A Lieutenant of Cavalry in Lee's Army. Boston: Gorham Press, 1918.

693. Personal memorabilia of Lt. Col. Harry W GILMOR, 2nd MD Cav. Held by Maryland Historical Society, Baltimore, MD.

694. Jackson, Alfred, Hanna and Kathryn Abbey. Confederate Exiles in Venezuela. Tuscaloosa, AL: Hanna Confederate Publishing Company, 1960.

APPENDIX B: REFERENCES

695. Patterson, William Warden. Some Reminiscences of the Civil War by William Warden Patterson, 43rd Virginia Cavalry Company C. Baltimore, MD: Maryland Historical Society, 1919.

696. Jefferson Davis Confederate President. Author and publisher unknown.

697. Civil War scrapbook of Emily Graves. Held by Maryland Historical Society, Baltimore, MD.

698. Logan, Mrs. India W.P. Kelion Franklin Peddicord of Quirks Scouts - Morgans' Kentucky Cavalry C.S.A. Washington, D.C.: Neale Publishing Company, 1908.

699. Letters of Maj. Eugene BLACKFORD 5th Alabama Infantry. Held by Maryland Historical Society, Baltimore, MD.

700. Roster of the Society of the Army and Navy of the Confederate States, in the State of Maryland. Held by Maryland Historical Society, Baltimore, MD.

701. Vandiver, Frank E. Confederate Blockade Running Through Bermuda 1861-1865. Austin, Texas: University of Texas Press, 1947.

702. Brady, Cyrus Townsend. Three Daughters of the Confederacy. New York: G.W. Dillingham Co., 1905.

703. Civil War clippings of Charles Bishop Hitchcock. Held by Maryland Historical Society, Baltimore, MD.

704. Governor Thomas Holliday Hicks of Maryland, Civil War Papers. Held by Maryland Historical Society, Baltimore, MD.

705. Governor Augustus W. Bradford of Maryland, Civil War Papers. Held by Maryland Historical Society, Baltimore, MD.

706. Confederate Veteran Camp of New York. A pamphlet listing names of members. Location unknown.

707. Yates, Bowling C. History of the Georgia Military Military Institute. Marietta, GA: n.p., 1968.

708. Civil War scrapbook of Pvt. John William KING, 1st MD Inf., Co C. Held by Maryland Historical Society, Baltimore, MD.

709. Alfriend, Frank H. The Life of Jefferson Davis. 1868.

710. WILLIAMSON, James J. Leaves from the Diary of One of Mosby's Men. Copy held by Daniel D. Hartzler, New Windsor, MD.

711. Letter of Capt. John Eager HOWARD Post, 1st MD Cav. Held by Maryland Historical Society, Baltimore, MD.

APPENDIX B: REFERENCES

712. Tate, Allen. Stonewall Jackson, the Good Soldier. New York: Minton, Balch & Co., 1928.

713. Boykin, Edward. Ghost Ship of the Confederacy. New York: Funk and Wagnalls Company, 1957.

714. Besse, S.B. U.S. Ironclad Monitor with Data and References for a Scale Model. Newport News, VA: The Mariners Museum, 1936.

715. Letters of Capt. William H. MURRAY, 1st MD Inf, Co. H. Maryland Historical Society, Baltimore, MD.

716. Horn, Stanley F. Gallant Rebel. New Brunswick, NJ: Rutgers University Press, 1947.

717. Meriwether, Colyn. Raphael Semmes. Philadelphia: George Jacobs and Company, 1913.

718. Sellman, Miss F. May. War History of John P. SELLMAN. 1908.

719. Nuun, W.C., ed. Ten Texans in Gray. Hillsboro, TX: Hill Junior College Press, 1968.

720. Genealogy and Biography of the Leading Families of the City of Baltimore and Baltimore County. Chicago, IL, 1897.

721. Roberts, W. Adolphe. Semmes of the Alabama. New York: The Bobbs-Merrill Company, 1938.

722. Papers of Major Charles Howard, staff officer of the cavalry corps of General Lomax. Includes war correspondence of General Lomax. Held by Maryland Historical Society, Baltimore, MD.

723. Jackson, Elmer Martin. Annapolis. The Capital Gazette Press: Annapolis, 1936.

724. Letters of Capt. John Donnell Smith, Lee's Baltimore Light Arty. Held by Maryland Historical Society, Baltimore, MD.

725. Keidal, George C. J.E.B. Stuart in Maryland. Maryland Historical Society, Baltimore, MD.

726. Diary of Capt William L. Ritter and Third Battery Maryland Artillery C.S.A. Roll Book. Held by Maryland Historical Society, Baltimore, MD.

727. Scrapbook of Dr. Samuel Theobald 1860 1865, Baltimore. Held by Maryland Historical Society, Baltimore, MD.

728. Confederate scrapbook of Mary A. King. Held by Maryland Historical Society, Baltimore, MD.

729. Randall, Prof. James Ryder. Southern Poems of the late 1860's.

APPENDIX B: REFERENCES

730. Muster roll of Capt William I. RASIN, 1st MD Cav, Co C. Held by Maryland Historical Society, Baltimore, MD.

731. Memo book of Miss Fannie V. Morphit of Baltimore. Held by Maryland Historical Society, Baltimore, MD.

732. Thom, Helen Hopkins. Johns Hopkins - A Silhouette. Johns Hopkins Press, 1929.

733. Autographs of Confederate Officers on Johnson Island - Belonging to Capt. John D. Kline, Chief of Ordnance. Held by Maryland Historical Society, Baltimore, MD.

734. Autographs of Confederate Soldiers in the Hospital of Fort McHenry - Belonging to Elizabeth C. Lee. Held by Maryland Historical Society, Baltimore, MD.

735. Confederate Record Book - Marylanders Who Were in the Confederate Services Outside of Maryland Commands. Held by Maryland Historical Society, Baltimore, MD.

736. Morgan, Mrs. Irby. How It Was. Nashville, TN: Barbee and Smith, 1892.

737. Montgomerys Grey's Sixth Infantry Regiment Alabama Volunteers A copy of this book is held by Army War College, Carlisle, PA.

738. Letters of Pvt. R. Stuart LATROBE, 1st MD Cav, Co C. Held by Maryland Historical Society, Baltimore, MD.

739. Diary and letters of Lt. Col. Osman LATROBE, A.A.G. Held by Maryland Historical Society, Baltimore, MD.

740. Military correspondence of Lt. Gen. Jubal Early and Gen. L.L. Lomax, 1861-1865. Maryland Historical Society, Baltimore, MD.

741. Lonn, Ella. Salt as a Factor in the Confederacy. University of Alabama Press, 1965.

742. Letters of Dr. R. Samuel Ringgold, Asst. Surgeon, Charpentiers Battery. Held by Maryland Historical Society, Baltimore, MD.

743. Polk, J.M. Memories of the Lost Cause. Stories and Adventures of a Confederate Soldier in R. E. Lee's Army, 1861-1865. Austin, TX, 1905.

744. Two Months in Fort La-Fayette by a Prisoner. "Authorship has been attributed to Mr. Wm. Gilchrist." New York: printed for the author, 1862.

745. Civil War scrapbook of Edward H. Rider. Held by Maryland Historical Society, Baltimore, MD

APPENDIX B: REFERENCES

746. Letters of Pvt. Somerville SOLLERS, 2nd MD Inf Co. A. Held by Maryland Historical Society, Baltimore, MD.

747. Giles, L.B. Terry's Texas Rangers. Austin, TX: Von Boeckmon-Jones Co., printers, 1911.

748. Stein, Charles Francis, Jr. Origin and History of Howard County, Maryland. Baltimore, MD: Howard County Historical Society, 1972.

749. Fell, Thomas. St. John's College. Annapolis, Maryland.

750. Austin, J.P. The Blue and Gray. Atlanta, GA, 1899.

751. Breckinridge, William C.P. The Ex-Confederate and What He Has Done in Peace. Richmond, VA: J.L. Hill Printing Co., 1892.

752. Winters, John D. Life in the Confederate Army. Louisiana State University Press, 1963.

753. Staff diaries and letters of Capt. McHenry HOWARD, 1861-1865. Held by Maryland Historical Society, Baltimore, MD.

754. Civil War campaign reports of Brig. Gen. Charles S. Winder. Held by Maryland Historical Society, Baltimore, MD.

755. Nichelson, B.C. Brief Sketch of the Life of a Confederate Soldier. Dallas, Texas, 1928.

756. Diary of Pvt. Wilson C. Smith, 1st MD Cav, Co. C. Held by Maryland Historical Society, Baltimore, MD.

757. Diary of Major Wilson Mile CARY, Quarter Master. Held by Maryland Historical Society, Baltimore, MD.

758. Confederate documents from the Maryland Line Confederate Soldiers' Home. Held by Maryland Historical Society, Baltimore, MD.

759. Johnson John. Defense of Charleston Harbor. Charleston, SC: Evans & Cogswell Co., 1890.

760. Stein, Charles Francis, Jr. A History of Calvert County, Maryland. Calvert County Historical Society, 1960.

761. Personal papers of Pvt. James M. Monroe CONRAD, 12th VA Cav Co B. Held by Maryland Historical Society, Baltimore, MD.

762. Ann Schaeffer Records of the Past. September, 1862. Maryland Historical Society, Baltimore, MD.

763. Brand, W.F. The Capture of the Indianola. Maryland Historical Society, Baltimore, MD.

APPENDIX B: REFERENCES

764. Family letters concerning death of Major William Duncan MCKIM, Staff Officer. Held by Maryland Historical Society, Baltimore, MD.

765. Williams, William. Narrative of My Arrest in the Civil War and Imprisonment. Held by Maryland Historical Society, Baltimore, MD.

766. Letters of Dr. George W. Archer, Asst. Surgeon, during the Civil War. Held by Maryland Historical Society, Baltimore, MD.

767. Diary of Margaret Mehring, New Windsor. Held by Maryland Historical Society, Baltimore, MD.

768. Papers of Pvt. Herman Henry Radecke, Simkin's South Carolina Infantry Company E. Held by Maryland Historical Historical Society, Baltimore, MD.

769. Proceedings of the Trial of Pvt. Charles McDowell, 1st MD Cav, Co. A - Confederate Spy. Held by Maryland Historical Society, Baltimore, MD.

770. Memorabilia of Dr. Edmund K. Goldsborough, Naval Surgeon, 1861-1865. Held by Maryland Historical Society, Baltimore, MD.

771. Personal papers of Pvt. R. Stewart LATROBE, 1st MD Cav, Co. C. during the Civil War. Held by Maryland Historical Society, Baltimore, MD.

772. Civil War correspondence of Major William L. Bailey, Staff. Held by Maryland Historical Society, Baltimore, MD.

773. Civil War letters of Pvt. Simeon KOINER, 5th VA Inf, Co. H. Held by Maryland Historical Society, Baltimore, MD.

774. C. Eng and Lt. Col. H. Ashton Ramsay - Fragment of a Journal, Ordnance Dept. and Naval Battalion. Held by Maryland Historical Society, Baltimore, MD.

775. Douns, Pvt. James S. and J. Leeds Barroll. The Lincoln Rule in Maryland. May, 1863.

776. Statement Written by Isaac R. TRIMBLE, while in federal prison concerning his action in Baltimore during the month of April, 1861. Held by Maryland Historical Society, Baltimore, MD.

777. Andrews, Matthew Page. Baltimore in War Times. 1911.

778. Brice, Marshall Moore. Conquest of a Valley. Charlottesville, VA: The University Press of Virginia, 1965.

779. Battey, George M. A History of Rome and Floyd County, Georgia. Atlanta, GA: Webb & Vary Co., 1922.

780. Fauquier County Bicentennial Committee. Fauquier County, VA. War-Warrington, VA, 1959.

APPENDIX B: REFERENCES

781. Diary of David Creamer, April 19, 1861. Held by Maryland Historical Society, Baltimore, MD.

782. Memoirs of Pvt. Augustus James ALBERT, Jr., 1st MD Arty, 1861-1865. Held by Maryland Historical Society, Baltimore, MD.

783. Fickus, Charles. Maryland in the Confederate Navy. Held by Maryland Historical Society, Baltimore, MD.

784. List of the Confederate Wounded in the College Hospital Near Gettysburg. Held by Maryland Historical Society, Baltimore, MD.

785. Roster of Capt. George M. EMACK, 1st MD Cav, Co B. Held by Maryland Historical Society, Baltimore, MD.

786. Listing of residents of the Maryland Line Confederate Soldiers Home. Held by Maryland Historical Society, Baltimore, MD.

787. Ross, Ishbel. Rebel Rose. New York: Harper Brothers, 1954.

788. Huse, Caleb. The Supplies for the Confederate Army. Boston: Press of T.R. Marvin & Son, 1904.

789. Civil War scrapbook of Ridgely Family. Held by Maryland Historical Society, Baltimore, MD,

790. Scrapbook of Steveson Newspaper. Held by Maryland Historical Society, Baltimore, MD.

791. The War of the Rebellion - Official Records of the Union and Confederate Armies, Series I, II, III, IV. Washington, D.C.: Government Printing Office, 1897.

792. Donnelly, Ralph W. Biographical Sketches of the Commissioned Officers of the Confederate States Marine Corps. Alexandria, VA, 1973.

793. Samuel Smith's Three Sons in the Confederate Army. Author and publisher unknown.

794. Letters of Capt. Eugene DIGGS, 2nd MD Cav, Co B. Erick Davis Collection, Baltimore, MD.

795. Weddle, Robert S. Plowhorse Cavalry: The Caney Creek Boys of the 34th Texas. Austin, TX: Madrona Press, 1974.

796. Murfin, James V. The Gleam of Bayonets. New York: T. Yoseloff, 1965.

797. Schildt, John W. Drums Along the Antietam. Parsons, WV: McClain Printing Company, [1972?].

APPENDIX B: REFERENCES

798. Johnston, Christopher, ed. Society of Colonial Wars in the State of Maryland: Genealogies of the Members. Baltimore, MD: Friednwold Company, 1905.

799. Rutherford, Mildred Lewis. Truths of History. Athens, GA: n.p., 1920.

800. A listing of members of Company C, 1st Maryland Calvary, United Confederate Veterans Camp

801. Kinchen, Oscar A. Women Who Spied for the Blue and the Gray. Philadelphia: Dorrance and Company, 1972.

802. Summersell, Charles G., ed. The Journal of George Townley Fullam: Boarding Officer of the Confederate Sea Raider Alabama. University of Alabama Press, 1973.

803. Gaddy, David Winfred. William Norris and the Confederate Signal and the Secret Service. Maryland Historical Society, Baltimore, MD.

804. Frassanito, William A. Gettysburg: A Journey in Time. New York: Charles Scribner's Sons, 1975.

805. Wiley, Bell Irvin. Confederate Women. Westport, CT: Greenwood Press, 1975.

806. Warner, Nancy M. Carroll County, Maryland, A History 1837-1976. Haddon Craftsman, Inc., 1976.

807. Ray, Frederic E. Alfred R. Waeed, Civil War Artist. New York: The Viking Press, 1974.

808. Sword, Wiley. Shiloh: Bloody April. New York: William Morrow and Company, 1975.

809. Public Duty Is My Only Master. New York, 1888.

810. Dall, Caroline H. Barbara Fritchie, A Study. Boston, 1892.

811. Memoirs of the War of Secession fron the Original Manuscripts of Johnson Hagood. Columbia, SC: Dorn Busch, 1910.

812. Hill, Daniel Harvey. Bethel to Sharpsburg, Vol. I, II. Raleigh, NC: Edwards & Broughton Company, 1926.

813. BRENT, Joseph L. Capture of the Ironclad Indianola. Searcy and Pfaff: New Orleans, LA, 1926.

814. Edwards, John N. Noted Guerillas: Or, The Warfare of the Border... Morningside Bookshop, 1976.

815. MARSHALL, Charles. Address Delivered Before the Lee Monument Association at Richmond, Virginia, October 27, 1887. Baltimore, MD: John Murphy and Company, 1888.

816. SHEPHERD, Henry E. Narrative of Prison Life at Baltimore and Johnson's Island, Ohio. Baltimore, MD: Commercial Printing and Sta. Company, 1917.

817. Myers, Williams Starr. The Self-Reconstruction of Maryland 1864-1867. The Johns Hopkins Press, 1909.

818. Wills, Mary Alice. The Confederate Blockade of Washington, D.C., 1861-1862. Parsons, WV: McClain Printing Company: Parsons, 1975.

819. Hale, Laura. Virginia. VA: Warren Press: Front Royal, 1956.

820. Seabrook, William L.W. Maryland's Great Part in Saving the Union. Westminster, MD: The American Sentinel Company, 1913.

821. Smith, James Power. With Stonewall Jackson in the Army of North Virginia. Richmond, VA: Old Dominion Press.

822. Pogue, Robert E. T. Yesterday in Old St. Mary's County. New York: Carlton Press, 1968.

823. JENKINS, Williams K. A Memoir of Comrades and Campaigns in the 1st Maryland Artillery C.S.A. Baltimore, Maryland 1903. Erick Davis Collection, Baltimore, MD.

824. Davis, Erick F. "The Baltimore County Horse Guard." *History Trails*. Baltimore County Historical Society, Vol. 10, 1975.

825. RICH, Edward. R. Comrades Four. New York and Washington, D.C.: The Neale Publishing Company, 1907.

826. Howard, Frank Key. Fourteen Months in American Bastilles. Baltimore, Maryland: Kelly, Hedian, and Piet, 1863.

827. STONEBRAKER, Joseph R. A Rebel of '61. New York: Wynkoop Hallinbeck Crawford Company, 1899.

828. Cochran, Hamilton. Blockade Runners of the Confederacy. New York: The Bobbs-Merrill Company, 1958.

829. "Cause of Confederates in Maryland," *Conf. Vet. Mag.*, Vol. I, February, 1893.

830. "Confederate Association in Maryland," *Conf. Vet. Mag.*, Vol. I, March, 1893.

831. Burrows, F.M., "Harper's Ferry in 1861," *Conf. Vet. Mag.*, Vol. I, April, 1893.

APPENDIX B: REFERENCES

832. "Tarr, Dr. B.A.," *Conf. Vet. Mag.*, Vol. I, June, 1893.

833. "Miscellaneous Correspondence," *Conf. Vet. Mag.*, Vol. I, September, 1893.

834. "Career and Fate of General Lloyd TILGHMAN," *Conf. Vet. Mag.*, Vol. I, September, 1893.

835. Eggleston, E.T., "Scenes Where General TILGHMAN was Killed," *Conf. Vet. Mag.*, Vol. I, October, 1893.

836. POPE, William H., "Memorial Day," *Conf. Vet. Mag.*, Vol. I, Nov I, November, 1893.

837. BUCK, Samuel D., "Burning a Bridge Over the Rappahannock," *Conf. Vet. Mag.*, Vol. I, December, 1893.

838. "The Confederate Cause in Maryland," *Conf. Vet. Mag.*, Vol. II, January, 1894.

839. "Confederate Generals Yet Living," *Conf. Vet. Mag.*, Vol. II, January, 1894.

840. "Maryland Line Confederate Soldiers Home," *Conf. Vet. Mag.*, Vol. II, February, 1894.

841. DICKINSON, L.T., "Service of a Maryland Command, *Conf. Vet. Mag.*, Vol. II, June, 1894.

842. Brown, Joshua, "Killed Two Artillerymen With His Sabre," *Conf. Vet. Mag.*, Vol. II, June, 1894.

843. "Heroic and Patriotic Marylanders," *Conf. Vet. Mag.*, Vol. II, September, 1894.

844. "Eugene WORTHINGTON of Annapolis," *Conf. Vet. Mag.*, Vol. II, November, 1894.

845. BUCK, S.D., "Battle of Fishers Hill," *Conf. Vet. Mag.*, Vol. II, November, 1894.

846. "The Late Colonel Augustus M. Foute," *Conf. Vet. Mag.*, Vol. II, November, 1894.

847. Haskins, Benjamin, "General James ARCHER," *Conf. Vet. Mag.*, Vol. II, December, 1894.

848. "Board of Governors, Maryland Confederate Home," *Conf. Vet. Mag.*, Vol. II, December, 1894.

849. "Mrs. Bradley T. Johnson Honored," *Conf. Vet. Mag.*, Vol. II, December, 1894.

APPENDIX B: REFERENCES

850. "Eugene WORTHINGTON, Esquire," *Conf. Vet. Mag.*, Vol. III, January, 1895.

851. Harris, F.S., "General James J. ARCHER," *Conf. Vet. Mag.*, Vol. III, January, 1895.

852. "To the Veteran Annapolis, Maryland," *Conf. Vet. Mag.*, Vol. III, February, 1895.

853. "The Cavalry at Fisher's Hill," *Conf. Vet. Mag.*, Vol. III, February, 1895.

854. "Members of the Confederate Veteran Camp of New York," *Conf. Vet. Mag.*, Vol. III, April, 1895.

855. "Captain W.H. POPE, Superintendent of the Maryland Line Confederate Home," *Conf. Vet. Mag.*, Vol. III, May 1895.

856. "Baltimore Wants the Reunion in '97," *Conf. Vet. Mag.*, Vol. III, June, 1895.

857. "Memorial Day in Maryland," *Conf. Vet. Mag.*, Vol. III, July, 1895.

858. "General Sherman on Bishop Polk's Death," *Conf. Vet. Mag.*, Vol. III, September, 1895.

859. "National Confederate Memorial," *Conf. Vet. Mag.*, Vol. III, September, 1895.

860. "Maryland Confederate Veterans Camps," *Conf. Vet. Mag.*, Vol. IV, March, 1896.

861. Rowland, Kate Mason, "Tribute to the Carrolls of Carrollton," *Conf. Vet. Mag.*, Vol. IV, June, 1896.

862. "Maryland Confederate Veterans Camps," *Conf. Vet. Mag.*, Vol. IV, August, 1896.

863. "General Lloyd TILGHMAN," *Conf. Vet. Mag.*, Vol. IV, September, 1896.

864. Dudley, C.W., "Battle of Iuka," *Conf. Vet. Mag.*, Vol. IV, October, 1896.

865. BUCK, S.D., "Unjust History Refuted," *Conf. Vet. Mag.*, Vol. IV, December, 1896.

866. "Confederate Society of Army and Navy in Maryland," *Conf. Vet. Mag.*, Vol. V, January, 1897.

867. "Birthday of Lee in Baltimore," *Conf. Vet. Mag.*, Vol. V, 1897.

APPENDIX B: REFERENCES

868. JOHNSON, Mrs. Bradley T., "Confederate Home in Maryland," *Conf. Vet. Mag.,* Vol. V, March, 1897.

869. "Confederate Flag Not Infamous," *Conf. Vet. Mag.,* Vol. V, April, 1897.

870. "One of Mosby's Bravest Men," *Conf. Vet. Mag.,* Vol. V, May, 1897.

871. Lunsford, Abner, "Rescuing Graves in Maryland," *Conf. Vet. Mag.,* May 1897.

872. "Captain William Hunter GRIFFIN," *Conf. Vet. Mag.,* Vol. V, May 1897.

873. "Maryland Division U.C.V.," *Conf. Vet. Mag.,* Vol. V, July, 1897.

874. "Maryland Line Confederate Soldiers Home, Pikesville, Maryland," *Conf. Vet. Mag.,* Vol. V, September, 1897.

875. Farinholt, B.L., "Escape from Johnson's Island," *Conf. Vet. Mag.,* Vol. V, October, 1897.

876. ----------. "Escape from Johnson's Island," *Conf. Vet. Mag.,* Vol. V, November, 1897.

877. COLSTON, F.M., "Gettysburg as I Saw It,' *Conf. Vet. Mag.,* Vol. V, November, 1897.

878. HEWES, M. Warner," Turner Ashby's Courage," *Conf. Vet. Mag.,* Vol. V, December, 1897.

879. "Honor-Roll of Confederate Dead in Ohio," *Conf. Vet. Mag.,* Vol. VI, January, 1898.

880. "S.F. THOMAS, Commander of Alexander Young Camp, Frederick, Maryland," *Conf. Vet. Mag.,* Vol. VI, January, 1898.

881. BOND, Frank A., "Company A, First Maryland Cavalry, *Conf. Vet. Mag.,* Vol. VI, February, 1898.

882. "General Bradley T. JOHNSON, on the Main Disaster," *Conf. Vet. Mag.,* Vol. VI, March, 1898.

883. "Dr. George HAMMOND," *Conf. Vet. Mag.,* Vol. VI, March, 1898.

884. "A Baltimore Daughter of the Confederacy," *Conf. Vet. Mag.,* Vol. VI, March, 1898.

885. "List of Officials Corrected to Date," *Conf. Vet. Mag.,* Vol. VI, July, 1898.

886. "First Virginia in the Great War," *Conf. Vet. Mag.,* Vol. VI, August, 1898.

APPENDIX B: REFERENCES

887. BOND, Frank A., "Fitz Lee in the Army of Northern Virginia," *Conf. Vet. Mag.*, Vol VI, September, 1898.

888. "Confederate Officers Buried in Hollywood Cemetery Richmond," *Conf. Vet. Mag.*, Vol. VI, September, 1898.

889. Connor, W.O., "Sixteen Faithful Confederates," *Conf. Vet. Mag.*, Vol. VI, November, 1898.

890. HANDS, Washington, "Baltimore Light Artillery Maryland Line, A.N.V.," *Conf. Vet. Mag.*, Vol. VI, December, 1898.

891. "Isaac R. TRIMBLE, Camp No. 1052," *Conf. Vet. Mag.*, Vol. VII, January, 1899.

892. "James F. BROWN Memorial," *Conf. Vet. Mag.*, Vol. VII, January, 1899.

893. Hands, Washington, "From Baltimore to First Bull Run," Conf. Vet. Mag., Vol. VII, February, 1899.

894. "Isaac R. TRIMBLE Camp, No. 1053," *Conf. Vet. Mag.*, Vol. VII, February, 1899.

895. "Blucher of the Day at Manassas," *Conf. Vet. Mag.*, Vol. VII, March, 1899.

896. "Surviving Generals," *Conf. Vet. Mag.*, Vol. VII, March, 1899.

897. "Distinguished Soldier for Whom It Was Named," *Conf. Vet. Mag.*, *Conf.* VII, 1899.

898. "In An Appreciated Letter," *Conf. Vet. Mag.*, Vol. VII, April, 1899.

899. "Chris J. CONRADT," Conf. Vet. Mag., Vol. VII, June, 1899.

900. "Blucher of the Day at Manassas, T.O. CHESTNEY. *Conf. Vet. Mag.*, Vol. VII, July, 1899.

901. "The Six Hundred Confederate Officers Placed Under Fire of Confederate Cannon in Retaliation," *Conf. Vet. Mag.*, Vol. VII, July, 1899.

902. Rostall, John E., "Union Soldiers Slave Owners," *Conf. Vet. Mag.*, Vol. VII, August, 1899.

903. "R.D. STUART Preparing a Sketch," *Conf. Vet. Mag.*, Vol. VII, October, 1899.

904. "Company A of the 1st Maryland Cavalry," *Conf. Vet. Mag.*, Vol. VII, October, 1899.

905. "H.H. MATTHEWS Memorial," *Conf. Vet. Mag.*, Vol. VII, November, 1899.

APPENDIX B: REFERENCES

906. "Confederate Society in Baltimore," *Conf. Vet. Mag.*, Vol. VIII, January, 1900.

907. Pendleton, S.H., "Colonel John Thompson Brown," *Conf. Vet. Mag.*, Vol. VIII, January, 1900.

908. "Brig. Gen. James J. ARCHER," *Conf. Vet. Mag.*, Vol. VIII, February, 1900.

909. Doran, Charles, "Franklin BUCHANAN," *Conf. Vet. Mag.*, Vol. VIII, Febraury, 1900.

910. TILGHMAN Oswald, "Membership of a Famous Escort Company," *Conf. Vet. Mag.*, Vol. VIII, May, 1900.

911. "William Frederick STEUART Memorial," *Conf. Vet. Mag.*, Vol. VIII, May, 1900.

912. French, Marcellus, "Second Dispatch from Grant to Lee," *Conf. Vet. Mag.*, Vol. VIII, June, 1900.

913. Barton, Randolph, "Stonewall Brigade at Louisville," *Conf. Vet. Mag.*, Vol. VIII, November, 1900.

914. JOHNSON, Bradley T., "Confederate Muster Rolls," *Conf. Vet. Mag.*, Vol. VIII, November, 1900.

915. JOHNSTON, B.S., "Battle of Sailor's Creek," *Conf. Vet. Mag.*, Vol. VIII, December, 1900.

916. "The Isaac R. TRIMBLE Camp," *Conf. Vet. Mag.*, Vol. IX, January, 1901.

917. "Admiral Raphael SEMMES," *Conf. Vet. Mag.*, Vol. IX, January, 1901.

918. "Flags Captured by New Hampshire Troops," *Conf. Vet. Mag.*, Vol. IX, Febraury, 1901.

919. "H.B. BAYLOR of Cumberland," *Conf. Vet. Mag.*, Vol. IX, February, 1901.

920. "Reburial of Confederates in Maryland," *Conf. Vet. Mag.*, Vol. IX, March, 1901.

921. "Letter from Colonel E.V. WHITE," *Conf. Vet. Mag.*, Vol. IX, April, 1901.

922. "Benjamin Gough-Pikesville," *Conf. Vet. Mag.*, Vol. IX, June, 1901.

923. Johnson, Mrs. Jane Claudia, "Work of a Confederate Woman," *Conf. Vet. Mag.*, Vol. IX, July, 1901.

924. BAYLOR, H.B., "Concerning the Execution of Captain J. Yeates," *Conf. Vet. Mag.*, Vol. X, January, 1902.

APPENDIX B: REFERENCES

925. BUCK, S.D., "Vigilant Regard for His Commander," *Conf. Vet. Mag.*, Vol. X, January, 1902.

926. "Comrad C.R. POLLARD who was Adjutant of the 13th Virginia Regiment Infantry, " *Conf. Vet. Mag.*,Vol. X, January, 1902.

927. BUCK, S.D., "General Joseph A. Walker," *Conf. Vet. Mag.*, Vol. X, January, 1902.

928. Bobbitt, John H., "That Moorefield Surprise," *Conf. Vet. Mag.*, Vol. X, February, 1902.

929. "Amos BENSON Memorial," *Conf. Vet. Mag.*, Vol. X, February, 1902.

930. "Dr. William H. JOHNSON Memorial," *Conf. Vet. Mag.*, Vol. X, March, 1902.

931. "History of Confederates in Maryland," *Conf. Vet. Mag.*, Vol. X, April, 1902.

932. "Two Georgia Martyrs of Sharpsburg," *Conf. Vet. Mag.*, Vol. X, May, 1902.

933. "E.S. ANDERSON," *Conf. Vet. Mag.*, Vol. X, June, 1902.

934. "Richard Davis MURPHY Memorial," *Conf. Vet. Mag.*, Vol. X, June, 1902.

935. RITTER, W.L., "Those Present at the Burial of Latame," *Conf. Vet. Mag.*, Vol. X, July, 1902.

936. ANDERSON, W.M., "Harry GILMOR Camp, U.C.V.," *Conf. Vet. Mag.*, August, 1902.

937. "Trusten POLK Memorial," *Conf. Vet. Mag.*, Vol. X, August, 1902.

938. "William W. GOLDSBOROUGH Memorial," *Conf. Vet. Mag.*, Vol. X, August, 1902.

939. "J.W. BREEDLOVE," *Conf. Vet. Mag.*, Vol. X, September, 1902.

940. "Captain Joseph Nicholas BARNEY Memorial," *Conf. Vet. Mag.*, Vol. X, September, 1902.

941. HICKEY, John F., "With Colonel William S. Hawkin in Camp Chase," *Conf. Vet. Mag.*, Vol. XI, January, 1903.

942. "Maryland Monument at Chickamauga," *Conf. Vet. Mag.*, Vol. XI, March, 1903.

943. Ruckstull. "Baltimore Monument," *Conf. Vet. Mag.*, Vol. XI, March, 1903.

944. "Unveiling of Maryland Monument," *Conf. Vet. Mag.*, Vol. XI, June, 1903.

945. "Maryland Confederate Veterans," *Conf. Vet. Mag.*, Vol. XI, July, 1903.

946. "Captain J.W. BENNETT Memorial," *Conf. Vet. Mag.*, Vol XI, July, 1903.

947. DORSEY, Frank, "Fatal Shot of Jeb Stuart," *Conf. Vet. Mag.*, Vol. XI, August, 1903.

948. "A Sword of Admiral Raphael SEMMES," *Conf. Vet. Mag.*, Vol. XI, September, 1903.

949. Kerr, W.J.W., "Execution of Captain Henry Wirz," *Conf. Vet. Mag.*, Vol. XI, September, 1903.

950. "The Burning of the Chambersburg," *Conf. Vet. Mag.*, Vol. XI, October, 1903.

951. "Dr. Arthur R. BARRY Memorial," *Conf. Vet. Mag.*, Vol. XI, October, 1903.

952. Watson, Thomas Jackson, "I Was with Jeb Stuart When He Was Shot," *Conf. Vet. Mag.*, Vol. XI, October, 1903.

953. BUCK, S.D., "General Early in the Valley," *Conf. Vet. Mag.*, Vol. XII, January, 1904.

954. "General H. Kyd DOUGLAS Memorial," *Conf. Vet. Mag.*, Vol. XII, March, 1904.

955. Harris, John. W., "Confederate Naval Cadets," *Conf. Vet. Mag.*, Vol. XII, April, 1904.

956. "Captain John Taylor PERRIN Memorial," *Conf. Vet. Mag.*, Vol. XII, April, 1904.

957. RITTER, William L., "Noted Landmarks in Baltimore," *Conf. Vet. Mag.*, Vol. XII, April, 1904.

958. "Sheppard Pictures for the Jefferson Davis Monument Fund," *Conf. Vet. Mag.*, Vol. XII, April, 1904.

959. "Signal Corps of the Confederate Army," *Conf. Vet. Mag.*, Vol XII, May, 1904.

960. "Henry YEATMAN Memorial," *Conf. Vet. Mag.*, Vol. XII, June, 1904.

961. "L.B. PENDLETON Memorial," *Conf. Vet. Mag.*, Vol. XII, August, 1904.

962. "Col. Paul Francis DE GOURNAY Memorial," *Conf. Vet. Mag.*, Vol. XII, August, 1904.

APPENDIX B: REFERENCES

963. Cunningham, E.S., "Capture of Two Federal Generals," *Conf. Vet. Mag.*, Vol. XII, September, 1904.

964. Whittle, W.C., "The Cruise of the Shenandoah," *Conf. Vet. Mag.*, Vol. XII, October, 1904.

965. "Col. Prentiss INGRAHAM Memorial," *Conf. Vet. Mag.*, Vol. XII, November, 1904.

966. "L.B. Pendleton Memorial," *Conf. Vet. Mag.*, Vol. XII, November, 1904.

967. BUCK, S.D., "Thirteenth Virginia at Fredericksburg," Conf. Vet. Mag., Vol. XIII, January, 1905.

968. Given, Maggie Mohler, "A Successful Blockade Runner," *Conf. Vet. Mag.*, Vol. XIII, January, 1905.

969. DE GOURNAY, P.F., "DE GOURNAY'S Battalion of Artillery," *Conf. Vet. Mag.*, 1905.

970. "Father and Son Confederate Veterans," *Conf. Vet. Mag.*, Vol. XIII, February, 1905.

971. "James R. Randalls Tribute to Col. Krauss," *Conf. Vet. Mag.*, Vol. XIII, February, 1905.

972. MCKIM, R.H.,"The Confederate Soldier," *Conf. Vet. Mag.*, Vol. XIII, March, 1905.

973. "Thomas Nelson CONRAD, The Rebel Scout," *Conf. Vet. Mag.*, Vol. XIII, May, 1905.

974. "Captain W.H. FARINHOLT Memorial," *Conf. Vet. Mag.*, Vol. XIII, May, 1905.

975. "Mrs. Sarah Lloyd Bennett Memorial," *Conf. Vet. Mag.*, Vol. XIII, June, 1905.

976. "Memorial Day Services in Baltimore," Conf. Vet. Mag., Vol. XIII, August, 1905.

977. Moffett, George H., "The Jones Raid Through West Virginia," *Conf. Vet. Mag.*, Vol. XIII, October, 1905.

978. "Illustrative Incident Under Lloyd TILGHMAN," *Conf. Vet. Mag.*, Vol. XIII, October, 1905.

979. BUCK, S.D., "General Early and His Campaigns," *Conf. Vet. Mag.*, Vol. XIII, November, 1905.

980. "Thomas Leiper PATTERSON Memorial," *Conf. Vet. Mag.*, Vol. XIV, January, 1906.

APPENDIX B: REFERENCES

981. "Lt. E.H.D. PUE Memorial," *Conf. Vet. Mag.*, Vol. XIV, February, 1906.

982. Floyd, N.J., "Moses and Stonewall Jackson," *Conf. Vet. Mag.*, Vol. XIV, March, 1906.

983. "Lt. Arthur BRYDE Memorial," *Conf. Vet. Mag.*, Vol. XIV, March, 1906.

984. "Major Charles Morgan PEARCE Memorial," *Conf. Vet. Mag.*, Vol. XIV, March, 1906.

985. "Cool Bravery of a Virginian," *Conf. Vet. Mag.*, Vol. XIV, April. 1906.

986. "Norvel E FOARD Memorial," *Conf. Vet. Mag.*, Vol. XIV, May, 1906.

987. "William Henry HERBERT Memorial," *Conf. Vet. Mag.*, Vol. XIV, June, 1906.

988. "Portrait of General Robert Edward Lee," *Conf. Vet. Mag.*, Vol. XIV, August, 1906.

989. McNeill, Jesse C., "Capture of Generals Kelly and Crook," *Conf. Vet. Mag.*, Vol. XIV, September, 1906.

990. PETERS, Winfield, "Maryland Confederates at First Manassas," *Conf. Vet. Mag.*, Vol. XV, January, 1907.

991. "Maryland Confederate Daughters," *Conf. Vet. Mag.*, Vol. XV, February, 1907.

992. THOMPSON, Magnus S., "Col. Elijah V. WHITE," *Conf. Vet. Mag.*, Vol. XV, April, 1907.

993. "C.S.A. Generals Killed or Died of Wounds," *Conf. Vet. Mag.*, Vol. XV, May 1907.

994. "Thomas Edward HAMBLETON Memorial," *Conf. Vet. Mag.*, Vol. XV, June, 1907.

995. "John Mifflin HILL Memorial," *Conf. Vet. Mag.*, Vol. XV, June, 1907.

996. "Robert Edward GARRETT Memorial," *Conf. Vet. Mag.*, Vol. XV, July, 1907.

997. HICKEY, John M., "Confederate Shaft at Arlington Cemetery," *Conf. Vet. Mag.*, Vol. XV, August, 1907.

998. "Loudon Park Cemetery," *Conf. Vet. Mag.*, Vol. XV, August, 1907.

999. Eggleston, J.R., "The Navy of the Confederate States," *Conf. Vet. Mag.*, Vol. XV, October, 1907.

APPENDIX B: REFERENCES

1000. "Monument to General Lloyd TILGHMAN," *Conf. Vet. Mag.*, Vol. XV, October.

1001. "Strong Staff Officials of Maryland Line," *Conf. Vet. Mag.*, Vol. XV, November, 1907.

1002. NOUSE, Charles H., "Walter Gibson Peter Executed at Franklin," *Conf. Vet. Mag.*, Vol. XV, December, 1907.

1003. CARY, Miles, "How Richmond Was Defended," *Conf. Vet. Mag.*, Vol. XV, December, 1907.

1004. COOKE, Rev. Giles B., "The V.M.I. Cadets at New Market, Virginia," *Conf. Vet. Mag.*, Vol. XVI, January, 1908.

1005. NOUSE, Charles H., "Captain W.G. Peter Executed at Franklin," *Conf. Vet. Mag.*, Vol. XVI, January, 1908.

1006. "Confederate Officers of the Regular C.S. Army," *Conf. Vet. Mag.*, Vol. XVI, January, 1908.

1007. ODENHEIMER, Cordelia Powell, "Report of the Maryland Division U.D.C.," *Conf. Vet. Mag.*, Vol XVI, Febraury, 1908.

1008. "Townsend N. CONRAD Memorial," *Conf. Vet. Mag.*, Vol. XVI, February, 1908.

1009. "Great War Song Was Cheap," *Conf. Vet. Mag.*, Vol. XVI, May, 1908.

1010. FAY, J.B., "Capture of Generals Crook and Kelley, U.S.A.," *Conf. Vet. Mag.*, Vol. XVI, June, 1908.

1011. "John Mortimer KILGOUR Memorial," *Conf. Vet. Mag.*, Vol. XVI, June, 1908.

1012. "Judge James D. WATTERS Memorial," *Conf. Vet. Mag.*, Vol. XVI, June, 1908.

1013. "Col. Robert HOUGH Memorial," *Conf. Vet. Mag.*, Vol. XVI, June, 1908.

1014. "Samuel J. SULLIVAN Memorial," *Conf. Vet. Mag.*, Vol. XVI, June, 1908.

1015. STEUART, Richard D., "Henry A. Stewart - Rebel Spy," *Conf. Vet. Mag.*, Vol. XVI, July, 1908.

1016. MATTHEWS, H.H., "Major William M. McGregor - A Tribute," *Conf. Vet. Mag.*, Vol. XVI, July, 1908.

1017. SULIVAN, Clement, "Miles CARY's Report Criticised," *Conf. Vet. Mag.*, Vol. XVI, August, 1908.

APPENDIX B: REFERENCES

1018. "Col. Robert HOUGH Memorial," *Conf. Vet. Mag.*, Vol. XVI, August, 1908.

1019. "Col. Clarence DERRICK Memorial," *Conf. Vet. Mag.*, Vol. XVI, August, 1908.

1020. "William Penn COMPTON Memorial," *Conf. Vet. Mag.*, Vol. XVI, August, 1908.

1021. "The Gallant Pelham," *Conf. Vet. Mag.*, Vol. XVI, September, 1908.

1022. Harris, Jasper W., "Sixty-Second Virginia at New Market," *Conf. Vet. Mag.*. Vol. XVI, September, 1908.

1023. "My Maryland and Other Poems," *Conf. Vet. Mag.*, Vol. XVI, October, 1908.

1024. Breathed, Frank, "In Memoriam of Major James BREATHED," *Conf. Vet. Mag.*, Vol. XVI, November, 1908.

1025. DORSEY, Frank, "General J.E.B Steuart's Last Battle," *Conf. Vet. Mag.*, Vol. XVII, February, 1909.

1026. DORSEY, Frank, "Grant as the South's Friend," *Conf. Vet. Mag.*, Vol. XVII, February, 1909.

1027. "James LUSLY Memorial," *Conf. Vet. Mag.*, Vol. XVII, March, 1909.

1028. HOPKINS, Luther W., "Bull Run to Appomattox," *Conf. Vet. Mag.*, Vol. XVII, April, 1909.

1029. "Marylanders in Confederate Army," *Conf. Vet. Mag.*, Vol. XVII, June, 1909.

1030. "To Honor Admiral SEMMES," *Conf. Vet. Mag.*, Vol. XVII, July, 1909.

1031. "Career of General Joseph Lancaster BRENT," *Conf. Vet. Mag.*, Vol. XVII, July, 1909.

1032. "Captain William B. LYNCH Memorial," *Conf. Vet. Mag.*, Vol. XVII, August, 1909.

1033. "Raphael SEMMES - Centenary of His Birth," *Conf. Vet. Mag.*, Vol. XVII, September, 1909.

1034. "Flag of the Maryland Infantry," *Conf. Vet. Mag.*, Vol. XVII, September, 1909.

1035. "Alexander S. SMALL Memorial," *Conf. Vet. Mag.*, Vol. XVII, September, 1909.

APPENDIX B: REFERENCES

1036. "In Honor of Admiral SEMMES," *Conf. Vet. Mag.*, Vol. XVII, October, 1909.

1037. BOND, Frank A., "Storming Blockhouse in Greenland Gap," *Conf. Vet. Mag.*, Vol. XVII, October, 1909.

1038. "Grandson of Francis Scott Key," *Conf. Vet. Mag.*, Vol. XVII, Nov, 1909.

1039. SLINGLUFF, Fielder C., "Burning of Chambersburg - Retaliatory," *Conf. Vet. Mag.*, Vol. XVI, November, 1909.

1040. Steuart, R.D., "Rare Confederate Relics," *Conf. Vet. Mag.*, Vol. XVI, November, 1909.

1041. Saussy, Clement, "Relics of Admiral SEMMES at Savannah," *Conf. Vet. Mag.*, Vol. XVI, December, 1909.

1042. "Henry Frederick WEGNER Memorial," *Conf. Vet. Mag.*, Vol. XVI, December, 1909.

1043. "Randall's Inspiration to Write 'Maryland, My Maryland,'" *Conf. Vet. Mag.*, Vol. XVIII, January, 1910.

1044. "Maryland Daughters in Convention," *Conf. Vet. Mag.*, Vol. XVIII, February, 1910.

1045. "Baltimore Celebrates Lee's Birthday," *Conf. Vet. Mag.*, Vol. XVIII, March, 1910.

1046. "Grandson of Francis Scott Key," *Conf. Vet. Mag.*, Vol. XVIII, May, 1910.

1047. Keane, Mrs. B.A., "Petitions to Have Barbara Fritchie Banned from Schools," *Conf. Vet. Mag.*, Vol. XVIII, May, 1910.

1048. "General Lloyd TILGHMAN," *Conf. Vet. Mag.*, Vol. XVIII, July, 1910.

1049. "Confederate Cemetery at Frederick, Maryland," *Conf. Vet. Mag.*, Vol. XVIII, July, 1910.

1050. "Charles Wilson Patrick WALKER Memorial," *Conf. Vet. Mag.*, Vol. XVIII, August, 1910.

1051. Flatan, L.S., "Tribute to General Lloyd TILGHMAN," *Conf. Vet. Mag.*, Vol. XVIII, September, 1910.

1052. "Dr. J.T. WILSON Memorial," *Conf. Vet. Mag.*, Vol. XVIII, September, 1910.

1053. "Dr. Benjamin Rush JENNINGS Memorial," *Conf. Vet. Mag.*, Vol. XVIII, September, 1910.

APPENDIX B: REFERENCES

1054. MCKIM, Randolph H., "Confederate Soldier's Recollections," Conf. Vet. Mag., Vol. XVIII, November, 1910.

1055. "The Maryland Division," Conf. Vet. Mag., Vol. XIX, January, 1911.

1056. "Confederate in Congress," Conf. Vet. Mag., Vol. XIX, January, 1911.

1057. "Lt. William BYERS Memorial," Conf. Vet. Mag., Vol. XIX, January, 1911.

1058. "Maryland Line Officers," Conf. Vet. Mag., Vol. XIX, February, 1911.

1059. "Monument at Point Lookout, Maryland," Conf. Vet. Mag., Vol. XIX, March, 1911.

1060. "Marylanders Fought at Chichanauga," Conf. Vet. Mag., Vol. XIX, May, 1911.

1061. Key, Clarence, "Fun in Camp," Conf. Vet. Mag., Vol. XIX, June, 1911.

1062. MCKIM, Randolph H., "Men Who Wore the Gray," Conf. Vet. Mag., Vol. XIX, July, 1911.

1063. Hawks, A.W.S., "Major Wells J, HAWKS," Conf. Vet. Mag., Vol. XIX, August, 1911.

1064. "Col. Levin LAKE Memorial," Conf. Vet. Mag., Vol. XIX, August, 1911.

1065. "McINTOSH's Battery at Sharpsburg," Conf. Vet. Mag., Vol. XIX, September, 1911.

1066. Barger, Rev. W.D., "The Field of Sharpsburg," Conf. Vet. Mag., Vol. XIX, October, 1911.

1067. Woodson, W.H., "Tribute to Admiral Raphael SEMMES," Conf. Vet. Mag., Vol. XIX, November, 1911.

1068. "Lt. Col. G.W. DORSEY Memorial," Conf. Vet. Mag., Vol. XIX, November, 1911.

1069. "Clarence KEY Memorial," Conf. Vet. Mag., Vol. XIX, November, 1911.

1070. Johnston, David E., "MCINTOSH'S Battery at Sharpsburg," Conf. Vet. Mag., Vol. XIX, December, 1911.

1071 "Colonel Gus W. DORSEY Memorial," Conf. Vet. Mag., Vol. XIX, December, 1911.

1072. Thompson, Magnus S., "Plan to Release Our Men at Point Lookout," Conf. Vet. Mag., Vol. XX, February, 1912.

APPENDIX B: REFERENCES

1073. "Comus Maryland Chapter offers a Calendar," *Conf. Vet. Mag.*, Vol. XX, March, 1912.

1074. MCINTOSH, D.G., "MCINTOSH'S Battery at Sharpsburg," *Conf. Vet. Mag.*, Vol. XX, May, 1912.

1075. "Rev Dr. James B. Avisett Memorial," *Conf. Vet. Mag.*, Vol. XX, May, 1912.

1076. "Mrs. Annie E. Oxley Memorial," *Conf. Vet. Mag.*, Vol. XX, May, 1912.

1077. "Dr. MCKIM Writes the Veteran," *Conf. Vet. Mag.*, Vol. XX, June, 1912.

1078. "Richard Poole HAYS Memorial," *Conf. Vet. Mag.*, Vol. XX, June, 1912.

1079. "To Honor Barbara Frietchie for What?," *Conf. Vet. Mag.*, Vol. XX, July, 1912.

1080. "Rev. James Battle Avisett Memorial," *Conf. Vet. Mag.*, Vol. XX, July, 1912.

1081. "Robert Hamilton WELCH Memorial," *Conf. Vet. Mag.*, Vol. XX, August, 1912.

1082. "Care of the Wounded Prisoners in Baltimore," *Conf. Vet. Mag.*, Vol. XX, September, 1912.

1083. "Monument to Maryland Women," *Conf. Vet. Mag.*, Vol. XX, November, 1912.

1084. "George Smith NORRIS Memorial," *Conf. Vet. Mag.*, Vol. XX, November 1912.

1085. Barger, Rev. W.D., "Over the Field of Gettysburg," *Conf. Vet. Mag.*, Vol. XX, December, 1912.

1086. Kohlein, C.F., "The Shelling of Leesburg, Virginia," *Conf. Vet. Mag.*, Vol. XXI, January, 1913.

1087. Semmes, O.J., "The First Confederate Battery an Orphan," *Conf. Vet. Mag.*, Vol. XXI, February, 1913.

1088. Beale, C.H.," Service of 26th North Carolina Regiment," *Conf. Vet. Mag.*, Vol. XXI, February, 1913.

1089. Booth, Roowell V., "Poetic Tribute to John Wilkes Booth," *Conf. Vet. Mag.*, Vol. XXI, April, 1913.

1090. "Col. L.T. BRIEN Memorial," *Conf. Vet. Mag.*, Vol. XXI, April, 1913.

1091. "Dr. A.T. BELL Memorial," *Conf. Vet. Mag.*, Vol. XXI, May, 1913.

1092. Wright, Marcus J., "General Officers of the Confederate Army Killed," *Conf. Vet. Mag.,* Vol. XXI, June, 1913.

1093. "Daniel M. KEY Memorial," *Conf. Vet. Mag.,* Vol. XXI, July, 1913.

1094. Wright, Marcus J., "General Officers of the Confederate Army Killed," *Conf. Vet. Mag.,* Vol. XXI, September, 1913.

1095. "Major General L.L. Lomax," *Conf. Vet. Mag.,* Vol. XXI, September, 1913.

1096. "Monument at Rockville, Maryland," *Conf. Vet. Mag.,* Vol. XXI, December, 1913.

1097. WHITE, Thomas H., "About the Shelling of Leesburg," *Conf. Vet. Mag.,* Vol. XXI, 1913.

1098. Young, T.Y., "More About the Capture of Beverly," *Conf. Vet. Mag.,* Vol. XXI, December, 1913.

1099. DYSER, L.J., "Comrades of the 41st Virginia," *Conf. Vet. Mag..* Vol. XXI, December, 1913.

1100. "Sumner Archibald Cunningham," *Conf. Vet. Mag.,* Vol. XXII, January, 1914.

1101. "Adolphus FEARHAKE Memorial," *Conf. Vet. Mag.,* Vol. XXII, January, 1914.

1102. "Robert T. HEMPSTONE Memorial," *Conf. Vet. Mag.,* Vol. XXII, January, 1914.

1103. "To Southern Women in Baltimore," *Conf. Vet. Mag.,* Vol. XXII, February, 1914.

1104. "Eugene WORTHINGTON Memorial," *Conf. Vet. Mag.,* Vol. XXII, March, 1914.

1105. "Major Alexander HUNTER Memorial," *Conf. Vet. Mag.,* Vol. XXII, April, 1914.

1106. "Captain William L. RITTER of Maryland," *Conf. Vet. Mag.,* Vol. XXII, April, 1914.

1107. Young, Bennett H., A.E. Richards and Thomas D. Osborn, "Necrologic Report of Kentuckians," *Conf. Vet. Mag.,* Vol. XXII, May, 1914.

1108. "Confederate Monument at Rockville, Maryland," *Conf. Vet. Mag.,* Vol. XXII, May, 1911.

1109. "The Confederate Monument at Arlington," *Conf. Vet. Mag.,* Vol. XXII, July, 1914.

1110. Denahoe, John C., "The Fight Near Front Royal, Virginia," *Conf. Vet. Mag.*, Vol. XXII, July, 1914.

1111. "James M. MULL Memorial," *Conf. Vet. Mag.*, Vol. XXII, July, 1914.

1112. LeMonnier, Dr. Y.R., "Who Lost Shiloh to the Confederacy," *Conf. Vet. Mag.*, Vol. XXII, September, 1914.

1113. Letcher, John," Col. Richard Thomas ZARVONA," *Conf. Vet. Mag.*, Vol. XXII, September, 1914.

1114. DOUGLAS, Henry Kyd, "Capture of Harper's Ferry," *Conf. Vet. Mag.*, Vol. XXII, October, 1914.

1115. "Col. Francis X. WARD Memorial," *Conf. Vet. Mag.*, Vol. XXII, November, 1914.

1116. "J.A. VINSON Memorial," *Conf. Vet. Mag.*, Vol. XXII, Decmber, 1914.

1117. "Origin of Maryland My Maryland," *Conf. Vet. Mag.*, Vol. XXIII, February, 1915.

1118. "Preparation for the War - Virginia in the Army & Navy of the Confederacy," *Conf. Vet. Mag.*, Vol. XXIII, February, 1915.

1119. "S.L. LAMKIN Memorial," *Conf. Vet. Mag.*, Vol. XXIII, February, 1915.

1120. PEGRAM, William M., "Credit to Whom Credit is Due," *Conf. Vet. Mag.*, Vol. XXIII, March, 1915.

1121. McComb, William, "The Battles in Front of Richmond, 1862," *Conf. Vet. Mag.*, Vol. XXIII, March, 1915.

1122. Young, T.J., "Battle of Brandy Station," *Conf. Vet. Mag.*, Vol. XXIII, March, 1915.

1123. Weller, B., "Last Orders of Great Generals," *Conf. Vet. Mag.*, Vol. XXIII, March, 1915.

1124. Davis, Samuel Boyer and Kate Mason, "A Hero of the Sixties," *Conf. Vet. Mag.*, Vol. XXIII, March, 1915.

1125. "Mrs. Harry S. Davis," *Conf. Vet. Mag.*, Vol. XXIII, March, 1915.

1126. Porter, John W.H., "Origin of an Ironclad," *Conf. Vet. Mag.*, Vol. XXIII, May, 1915.

1127. Porter, John W.H., "The Battle of Hampton Roads," *Conf. Vet. Mag.*, Vol. XXIII, May, 1915.

1128. Thompson, Will H., "Who Lost Gettysburg," *Conf. Vet. Mag.*, Vol. XXIII, June, 1915.

APPENDIX B: REFERENCES

1129. Davis, Leslie, "General T.L. Rosser in Rockbridge County, Virginia in 1864," *Conf. Vet. Mag.*, Vol. XXIII, June, 1915.

1130. FAY, J.B., "Cavalry Fight at Second Manassas," *Conf. Vet. Mag.*, Vol. XXIII, June, 1915.

1131. Jarrett, D.W., "Who Fired That Shot," *Conf. Vet. Mag.*, Vol. XXIII, June, 1915.

1132. Cobb, Virginia, "Commander of the Famous Cobb's Battery," *Conf. Vet. Mag.*, Vol. XXIII, July, 1915.

1133. Kerr, W.J.W., "Sad Ending of a Wedding Trip," *Conf. Vet. Mag.*, Vol. XXIII, July, 1915.

1134. "Aaron B. HARDCASTLE Memorial," *Conf. Vet. Mag.*, Vol. XXIII, July, 1915.

1135. "Edwin P. GOVER Memorial," *Conf. Vet. Mag.*, Vol. XXIII, July, 1915.

1136. STILES, John C., "The Career of the Confederate States Cruiser Shenandoah," *Conf. Vet. Mag.*, Vol. XXIII, August, 1915.

1137. DAVIS, Leslie H., "General T. L. Rosser in Rockbridge County, Virginia in 1864," *Conf. Vet. Mag.*, Vol. XXIII, August, 1915.

1138. STILES, John C., "The Confederate States Naval Academy," *Conf. Vet. Mag.*, Vol. XXIII, September, 1915.

1139. MUDD, Joseph A., "The Confederate Negro," *Conf. Vet. Mag.*, Vol. XXIII, September, 1915.

1140. "An Unsung Hero, John C. Stiles," *Conf. Vet. Mag.*, Vol. XXIII, October, 1915.

1141. "Dr. Nelson G. WEST Memorial," *Conf. Vet. Mag.*, Vol. XXIII, October, 1915.

1142. "The Oldest Confederate Mother," *Conf. Vet. Mag.*, Vol. XXIII, October, 1915.

1143. "Valuable Works on Confederate History," *Conf. Vet. Mag.*, Vol. XXIII, October, 1915.

1144. "Henry W. RIDDER Memorial," *Conf. Vet. Mag.*, Vol. XXIII, November, 1915.

1145. "James HEWES of Baltimore," *Conf. Vet. Mag.*, Vol. XXIII, November, 1915.

1146. "Robert Potts WEAVER Memorial," *Conf. Vet. Mag.*, Vol. XXIV, February, 1916.

1147. "Thomas H. HAIGHTON Memorial," *Conf. Vet. Mag.*, Vol. XXIV, February, 1916.

1148. "James A. CARLISLE Memorial," *Conf. Vet. Mag.*, Vol. XXIV, February, 1916.

1149. "Confederate Mothers a Centenarian," *Conf. Vet. Mag.*, Vol. XXIV, February, 1916.

1150. "James Dickson POLLOCK Memorial," *Conf. Vet. Mag.*, Vol. XXIV, April, 1916.

1151. "William G. DELASHMUTT Memorial," *Conf. Vet. Mag.*, Vol. XXIV, April, 1916.

1152. SETH, Joseph B., "Sons of Maryland," *Conf. Vet. Mag.*, Vol. XXIV, April, 1916.

1153. Steuart, Richard D., "Truth in Mighty," *Conf. Vet. Mag.*, Vol. XXIV, June, 1916.

1154. "Thomas HILLARY Memorial," *Conf. Vet. Mag.*, Vol. XXIV, June, 1916.

1155. Kern, Albert, "Bullets Used in the Civil War," *Conf. Vet. Mag.*, Vol. XXIV, July, 1916.

1156. PHILPOT, G.B., "A Maryland Boy in the Confederate Army," *Conf. Vet. Mag.*, Vol. XXIV, July, 1916.

1157. "James Mercer GARNETT Memorial," *Conf. Vet. Mag.*, Vol. XXIV, July, 1916.

1158. "Luke J. DYSER Memorial," *Conf. Vet. Mag.*, Vol. XXIV, July, 1916.

1159. PHILPOT, G.B., "A Maryland Boy in the Confederate Army," *Conf. Vet. Mag.*, Vol. XXIV, August, 1916.

1160. PEGRAM, William M., "In Christian Charity," *Conf. Vet. Mag.*, Vol. XXIV, September, 1916.

1161. WILKINS, E.L., "The Fighting at Sharpsburg," *Conf. Vet. Mag.*, Vol. XXIV, September, 1916.

1162. "Confederate Monument at Easton, Maryland," *Conf. Vet. Mag.*, Vol. XXIV, September, 1916.

1163. "John H.K. SHANNAHAN Memorial," *Conf. Vet. Mag.*, Vol. XXIV, September, 1916.

1164. Hallock, Charles, "The Hidden Way to Dixie," *Conf. Vet. Mag.*, Vol. XXIV, November, 1916.

APPENDIX B: REFERENCES

1165. "The Sumter Runs the Mississippi Blockade," *Conf. Vet. Mag.*, Vol. XXIV, November, 1916.

1166. "Joseph E. TAVENNER Memorial," *Conf. Vet. Mag.*, Vol. XXIV, November, 1916.

1167. "Defenders of Fort Gregg," *Conf. Vet. Mag.*, Vol. XXV, January, 1917.

1168. Pile, George C., "Capture of General Prince," *Conf. Vet. Mag.*, Vol. XXV, January, 1917.

1169. "Comrades at Savannah, Georgia," *Conf. Vet. Mag.*, Vol. XXV, January, 1917.

1170. "Edward Alexander MOORE Memorial," *Conf. Vet. Mag.*, Vol. XXV, January, 1917.

1171. BUCK, S.D., "Where Pegram Was Killed," *Conf. Vet. Mag.*, Vol. XXV, January, 1917.

1172. SHEPHERD, Henry E., "Miss Kate Mason Rowland," *Conf. Vet. Mag.*, 1917.

1173. Reed, J.C., "That Apple Tree at Appomattox," *Conf. Vet. Mag.*, Vol. XXV, February, 1917.

1174. McCabe, W. Gordon, "A Noted Law Class of the University of Virginia," *Conf. Vet. Mag.*, Vol. XXV, February, 1917.

1175. Barton, Randolph, "The Battle of Hatcher's Run," *Conf. Vet. Mag.*, Vol. XXV, March, 1917.

1176. HOLLYDAY, Henry, "Organized in Maryland," *Conf. Vet. Mag.*, Vol. XXV, March, 1917.

1177. Berkeley, F. Carter, "Imboden's Dash into Charlestown," *Conf. Vet. Mag.*, Vol. XXV, April, 1917.

1178. "A Young Virginia Hero," *Conf. Vet. Mag.*, Vol. XXV, April, 1917.

1179. "Col. David Gregg MCINTOSH Memorial," *Conf. Vet. Mag.*, Vol. XXV, April, 1917.

1180. "The Character and Motives of General Robert E. Lee," *Conf. Vet. Mag.*, Vol. XV, May, 1917.

1181. TRIMBLE, Isaac. R., "The Campaign and Battle of Gettysburg," *Conf. Vet. Mag.*, Vol. XXV, May, 1917.

1182. SHEPHERD, Henry E., "Gettysburg: A Critical Review," *Conf. Vet. Mag.*, Vol. XXV, May, 1917.

APPENDIX B: REFERENCES

1183. "Last Colonel of Artillery, A.N.V.," *Conf. Vet. Mag.*, Vol. XXV, May 1917.

1184. SHEPHERD, Henry E., "Jefferson Davis: A Character Study," *Conf. Vet. Mag.*, Vol. XXV, June, 1917.

1185. "Jacob Mead JENNINGS Memorial," *Conf. Vet. Mag.*, Vol. XXV, June, 1917.

1186. SHEPHERD, Henry E., "General D.H. Hill: A Character Study," *Conf. Vet. Mag.*, Vol. XXV, July, 1917.

1187. COLSTON, Frederick M., "General Lee's Sentiment," *Conf. Vet. Mag.*, Vol. XXV, July, 1917.

1188. "Captain S.H. DENT Memorial," *Conf. Vet. Mag.*, Vol. XXV, July, 1917.

1189. SHEPHERD, Henry E., "General D.H. Hill: A Character Study," *Conf. Vet. Mag.*, Vol. XXV, August, 1917.

1190. "Dr. B.M. CROMWELL Memorial," *Conf. Vet. Mag.*, Vol. XXV, August, 1917.

1191. SHEPHERD, Henry E., "General D.H. Hill: A Character Study," *Conf. Vet. Mag.*, Vol. XXV, September, 1917.

1192. "Bishop G.W. PETERKIN, D.D., L.L.D. Memorial," Conf. Vet. Mag., Vol. XXV, September, 1917.

1193. Fletcher, R.V., "The Iuka Battle Field," *Conf. Vet. Mag.*, Vol. XXV, September, 1917.

1194. "Stephen B. ROLLINS Memorial," *Conf. Vet. Mag.*, Vol. XXV, October, 1917.

1195. SHEPHERD, Henry E., "Characteristic Features of the Old South," *Conf. Vet. Mag.*, Vol. XXV, November, 1971.

1196. SHEPHERD, Henry E., "The Genius of Lanier," *Conf. Vet. Mag.*, Vol. XXV, December, 1917.

1197. PEARCE, James A., "Memorial to the Soldiers of Kent County, Maryland," *Conf. Vet. Mag.*, Vol. XXV, December, 1917.

1198. "Rev. Horace E. HAYDEN Memorial," *Conf. Vet. Mag.*, Vol. XXV, December, 1917.

1199. "Deaths in Washington Camp," *Conf. Vet. Mag.*, Vol. XXV, December, 1917.

1200. "Samuel B. HEARN Memorial," *Conf. Vet. Mag.*, Vol. XXV, December, 1917.

APPENDIX B: REFERENCES

1201. McChesney, James Z., "Hard Fighting in West Virginia," *Conf. Vet. Mag.*, Vol. XXVI, January, 1918.

1202. "Major James Du Gue GERGUSON Memorial," *Conf. Vet. Mag.*, Vol. XXVi, January, 1918.

1203. SHEPHERD, Dr. Henry E., "D.H. Hill at Sharpsburg," *Conf. Vet. Mag.*, Vol. XXVI, February, 1918.

1204. Gordon, W.A., "An Association of Famous Membership," *Conf. Vet. Mag.*, Vol. XXVI, March, 1918.

1205. Andrews, Matthew Page, "The Treatment of Prisoners in the Confederacy." *Conf. Vet. Mag.*, Vol. XXVI, April, 1918.

1206. Pegram, William, "A Pleasant Reminder," *Conf. Vet. Mag.*, Vol. XXVI, May, 1918.

1207. SHEPHERD, Dr. Henry E., "Southern Leadership," *Conf. Vet. Mag.*, Vol. XXVI, May, 1918.

1208. Andrews, Matthew Page, "The Treatment of Prisoners in the Confederacy," *Conf. Vet. Mag.*, Vol. XXVI, May, 1918.

1209. SHOWER, George T., "Another If," *Conf. Vet. Mag.*, Vol. XXVI, June, 1918.

1210. Andrews, Matthew Page, "Review of Fighting for the Same Principle," *Conf. Vet. Mag.*, Vol. XXVI, June, 1918.

1211. SHEPHERD, Dr. Henry E., "Studies in Southern History," *Conf. Vet. Mag.*, Vol. XXVI, July, 1918.

1212. "Robert Castleman PAUL Memorial," *Conf. Vet. Mag.*, Vol. XXVI, July, 1918.

1213. "Captain William Stewart POLK Memorial," *Conf. Vet. Mag.*, Vol. XXVI, July, 1918.

1214. Andrews, Matthew Page, "Review of Sectional Predjudice at Present," *Conf. Vet. Mag.*,, Vol. XXVI.

1215. DUFFEY, J.W., "Daring Capture, McNeill's Rangers," *Conf. Vet. Mag.*, Vol. XXVI, August, 1918.

1216. SHEPHERD, Dr. Henry E., "Southern Poets - Edgar Allan Poe," *Conf. Vet. Mag.*, Vol. XXVI, August, 1918.

1217. "Captain Nicholas Jackson FLOYD Memorial," *Conf. Vet. Mag.*, Vol. XXVI, August, 1918.

APPENDIX B: REFERENCES

1218. SHEPHERD, Henry E., "Southern Poets - Sidney Lamier," *Conf. Vet. Mag.*, Vol. XXVI, September, 1918.

1219. "General A.C. TRIPPE Memorial," *Conf. Vet. Mag.*, Vol. XXVI, September.

1220. "Col. Winfield PETERS Memorial," *Conf. Vet. Mag.*, Vol. XXVI, September, 1918.

1221. Davis, Rev. L.H., "Famous Cattle Raid," *Conf. Vet. Mag.*, Vol. XXVI, October, 1918.

1222. SHEPHERD, Henry E., "Southern Poets - James Ryder Randall," *Conf. Vet. Mag.*, Vol. XXVI, December, 1918.

1223. Cardwell, David., "A Horse Battery," *Conf. Vet. Mag.*, Vol. XXVII, January, 1919.

1224. SHEPHERD, Dr. Henry E., "Henry Timrod - A Critical Study," *Conf. Vet. Mag.*, Vol. XXVII, January, 1919.

1225. "Col. Otho S., LEE Memorial," *Conf. Vet. Mag.*, Vol. XXVII, January, 1919.

1226. BOND, Frank A., "Butler Not Friendly to Davis," *Conf. Vet. Mag.*, Vol. XXVII, February, 1919.

1227. "Maryland Confederate Woman's Monument," *Conf. Vet. Mag.*, Vol. XXVII, February, 1919.

1228. "Prisoners of War," *Conf. Vet. Mag.*, Vol. XXVII, February, 1919.

1229. SHEPHERD, Dr. Henry E., "Division and Reunion," *Conf. Vet. Mag.*, Vol. XXVII, March, 1919.

1230. SHEPHERD, Dr. Henry E., "Southern Poets - John Williamson Palmer," *Conf. Vet. Mag.*, Vol. XXVII, April, 1919.

1231. SHEPHERD, Dr. Henry E., "Recollections of Frederick, Maryland," *Conf. Vet. Mag.*, Vol. XXVII, May, 1919.

1232. Andrews, Matthew Page, "Review of Desecration of the Wirz Monument," *Conf. Vet. Mag.*, Vol. XXVII, June, 1919.

1233. "In Memoriam - Col. Hilary A. Herbert," *Conf. Vet. Mag.*, Vol. XXVII, June, 1919.

1234. SHEPHERD, Dr. Henry E., "Southern Poets - Henry Timrod," *Conf. Vet. Mag.*, Vol. XXVII, June, 1919.

1235. "Col. Otho S. LEE Memorial," *Conf. Vet. Mag.*, Vol. XXVII, June, 1919.

1236. "Gallant Captain RIDGELY," *Conf. Vet. Mag.*, Vol. XXVII, June, 1919.

1237. DORSEY, Frank, "Last Days of the First Maryland Cavalry," *Conf. Vet. Mag.*, Vol. XXVII, July, 1919.

1238. SHEPHERD, Dr. Henry E., "Southern Poets - Henry Timrod," *Conf. Vet. Mag.*, Vol. XXVII, July, 1919.

1239. "Someone Has Blundered," *Conf. Vet. Mag.*, Vol. XXVII, August, 1919.

1240. SHEPHERD, Dr. Henry E., "The Realm of Contract," *Conf. Vet. Mag.*, Vol. XXVII, August, 1919.

1241. MCKIM, Rev Randolph H., "Injustice to the South," *Conf. Vet. Mag.*, Vol. XXVII, August, 1919.

1242. Smith, Miss Kinnie E., "A Sassy Little Rebel," *Conf. Vet. Mag.*, Vol. XXVII, September, 1919.

1243. SHEPHERD, Dr. Henry E., "The Mutation of Words," *Conf. Vet. Mag.*, Vol. XXVII, October, 1919.

1244. "Heroes of the Confederate Navy," *Conf. Vet. Mag.*, Vol. XXVII, October, 1919.

1245. Andrews, Matthew Page, "Review of Sons of the Confederate Veterans," *Conf. Vet. Mag.*, Vol. XXVII, November, 1919.

1246. SHEPHERD, Dr. Henry E., "Gallant Sons of North Carolina," *Conf. Vet. Mag.*, Vol. XXVII, November, 1919.

1247. SHEPHERD, Dr. Henry E., "Southern Poets - Sidney Lanier," *Conf. Vet. Mag.*, Vol. XXVII, December, 1919.

1248. "The Late Bishop PINKNEY of Maryland," *Conf. Vet. Mag.*, Vol. XXVII, December, 1919.

1249. SHEPHERD, Dr. Henry E., "The Great American Myth," *Conf. Vet. Mag.*, Vol. XXVIII, January, 1920.

1250. SHEPHERD, Henry E. "Comment on Gordon's Biography of Jefferson Davis," *Conf. Vet. Mag.*, Vol. XXVIII, March, 1920.

1251. "The Fight at Greenland Gap, West Virginia," *Conf. Vet. Mag.*, Vol. XXVIII, April, 1920.

1252. SHEPHERD, Dr. Henry E., "A Tribute to Wife and Daughter," *Conf. Vet. Mag.*, Vol. XXVIII, April, 1920.

1253. "C.N. WILLIS Memorial," *Conf. Vet. Mag.*, Vol. XXVIII, May, 1920.

APPENDIX B: REFERENCES

1254. Blake, Thomas B., "The Artillery Brigade at Sailor's Creek," *Conf. Vet. Mag.*, Vol. XXVIII, June, 1920.

1255. "List of Confederate Officers Captured at Sailor's Creek, Virginia," *Conf. Vet. Mag.*, Vol. XXVIII, June, 1920.

1256. SHEPHERD, Dr. Henry E., "Influence of Personality in War - The Lost Dispatch," *Conf. Vet. Mag.*, Vol. XXVIIII, June, 1920.

1257. "Soldiers of the War Between the States," *Conf. Vet. Mag.*, Vol. XXVIII, June, 1920.

1258. Zell, Robert R., "The Raid into Pennsylvania - The First Armored Train," *Conf. Vet. Mag.*, Vol. XXVIII, July, 1920.

1259. "Prince of Dare-Devils, Col. M.S. THOMPSON," *Conf. Vet. Mag.*, Vol. XXVIII, Conf. Vet. Mag., Vol. XXVIII, August, 1920.

1260. Smith, Miss Kinnie E., "How I Took a Lein on a Yankee General," *Conf. Vet. Mag.*, Vol. XXVIII, August, 1920.

1261. SHEPHERD, Dr. Henry E., "The University of Virginia, October, 1860 to April, 1861," *Conf. Vet. Mag.*, Vol. XXVIII, August, 1920.

1262. RITTER, Captain William L., "Fighting in the Sunflower Country," *Conf. Vet. Mag.*, Vol. XXVIII, August, 1920.

1263. RITTER, Captain William L., "The Capture of the Steamer Minnesota," *Conf. Vet. Mag.*, Vol. XXVIII, September, 1920.

1264. SHEPHERD, Dr. Henry E., "Spartanburg and Converse College," *Conf. Vet. Mag.*, Vol. XXVIII, September, 1920.

1265. RITTER, Captain William L., "Retreat From the Sunflower Country," *Conf. Vet. Mag.*, Vol. XXVIII, October, 1920.

1266. "Captain S.D. BUCK Memorial," *Conf. Vet. Mag.*, Vol. XVIII, 1920, November, 1920.

1267. RITTER, Captain William L., "The Battle of Jackson," *Conf. Vet. Mag.*, Vol. XXVIII, December, 1920.

1268. SULIVAN, Col. Clement, "Last Meeting with General R.E. Lee," *Conf. Vet. Mag.*, Vol. XXVIII, December, 1920.

1269. "Going South in 1861," *Conf. Vet. Mag.*, Vol. XXIX, January, 1921.

1270. SHEPHERD, Dr. Henry E., "In Defence of Southern Poets," *Conf. Vet. Mag.*, Vol. XXIX, January, 1921.

1271. "Col. Clement SULIVAN Memorial," *Conf. Vet. Mag.*, Vol. XXIX, January, 1921.

APPENDIX B: REFERENCES

1272. Andrews, Matthew Page, "Review of Women of the South in War Times," *Conf. Vet. Mag.*, Vol. XXIX, January, 1921.

1273. "Heroic Defense of a Bridge at Stephenson Depot, Virginia," *Conf. Vet. Mag.*, Vol. XXIX, February, 1921.

1274. "General Lee's Staff," *Conf. Vet. Mag.*, Vol. XXIX, March, 1921.

1275. HOLLYDAY, Henry, "Running the Blockade," *Conf. Vet. Mag.*, Vol. XXIX, March, 1921.

1276. Campbell, Mrs. A.A., "Sidney Lanier," *Conf. Vet. Mag.*, Vol. XXIX, April, 1921.

1277. "Major Randolph BARTON Memorial," *Conf. Vet. Mag.*, Vol. XXIX, 1921.

1278. "John Pratt WEST Memorial," *Conf. Vet. Mag.*, Vol. XXIX, April, 1921.

1279. COYLE, Wilbur F., "The Confederate Home of Maryland," *Conf. Vet. Mag.*, Vol. XXIX, May, 1921.

1280. Campbell, Mrs. A.A., "Father RYAN," *Conf. Vet. Mag.*, Vol. XXIX, June, 1921.

1281. "William E. LOWE Memorial," *Conf. Vet. Mag.*, Vol. XXIX, 1921.

1282. "Confederate Generals Buried in Baltimore," *Conf. Vet. Mag.*, Vol. XXIX, June, 1921.

1283. "Memorial to Dr. Randolph MCKIM," *Conf. Vet. Mag.*, Vol. XXIX, August, 1921.

1284. "Edwin S. VALLIANT Memorial," *Conf. Vet. Mag.*, Vol. XXIX, September, 1921.

1285. "Henry HOLLYDAY Memorial," *Conf. Vet. Mag.*, Vol. XXIX, October, 1921.

1286. "A Maryland Princess, Miss Blacke Taylor," *Conf. Vet. Mag.*, Vol. XXX, January, 1922.

1287. "The Sword of Lee," *Conf. Vet. Mag.*, Vol. XXX, February, 1922.

1288. "William H. FORSYHE Memorial," *Conf. Vet. Mag.*, Vol. XXX, February, 1922.

1289. Campbell, Mrs. A.A., "Boy Soldiers of the Confederacy," *Conf. Vet. Mag.*, Vol. XXX, 1922.

1290. "George A. LAMAR Memorial," *Conf. Vet. Mag.*, Vol. XXX, April, 1922.

1291. Ellerbe, Mrs. J.E., "Raphael SEMMES," *Conf. Vet. Mag.*, Vol. XXX, May, 1922.

1292. "Rev. C.R. PAGE Memorial," *Conf. Vet. Mag.*, Vol. XXX, May, 1922.

1293. COLSTON, F.M., "General Lee on States Rights," *Conf. Vet. Mag.*, Vol. XXX, June, 1922.

1294. "Frederick M. COLSTON Memorial," *Conf. Vet. Mag.*, Vol. XXX, July, 1922.

1295. "Memorial Day in Baltimore," *Conf. Vet. Mag.*, Vol. XXX, August, 1922.

1296. Morton, G. Nash, "And Their Works Do Follow Them," *Conf. Vet. Mag.*, Vol. XXX, September, 1922.

1297. HOLLYDAY, Lamar, "The Virginia and the Monitor," *Conf. Vet. Mag.*, Vol. XXX, October, 1922.

1298. REDWOOD, Allen C., "A Thanksgiving Turkey," *Conf. Vet. Mag.*, Vol XXX, November, 1922.

1299. "James A. ZELL Memorial," *Conf. Vet. Mag.*, Vol. XXX, November, 1922.

1300. COOKE, Rev. Giles B., "Indorsement of Committee," *Conf. Vet. Mag.*, Vol. XXX, November, 1922.

1301. SELVAGE, Edwin, "Reunited at Gettysburg," *Conf. Vet. Mag.*, Vol. XXX, 1922.

1302. Copeland, J.E., "The Fighting at Brandy Station," *Conf. Vet. Mag.*, Vol. XXX, December, 1922.

1303. Purifoy, John, "With Ewell and Rodes in Pennsylvania," *Conf. Vet. Mag.*, Vol. XXX, December, 1922.

1304. "The Barbara Frietchie Myth," *Conf. Vet. Mag.*, Vol. XXXI, January, 1923.

1305. "Captain A.F. MARNELSTEIN Memorial," *Conf. Vet. Mag.*, Vol. XXXI, January, 1923.

1306. "Major Mason MORFIT Memorial," January, *Conf. Vet. Mag.*, Vol. XXXI, 1923.

1307. "Captain John C. APPLER Memorial," *Conf. Vet. Mag.*, Vol. XXXI, January, 1923.

1308. "Allen Christian REDWOOD Memorial," *Conf. Vet. Mag.*, Vol. XXXI, February, 1923.

1309. Goode, Mrs. Elizabeth Redwood, "I Knew Barbara Frietchie," *Conf. Vet. Mag.*, Vol. XXI, February, 1923.

1310. Tomb, James H., "Confederate Torpedo Boats," *Conf. Vet. Mag.*, Vol. XXI, March, 1923.

1311. Gochnaner, P.B., "With the Eighth Virginia A.N.V.," *Conf. Vet. Mag.*, Vol. XXXI, April, 1923.

1312. "Louis Williams TRAIL Memorial," *Conf. Vet. Mag.*, Vol. XXXI, May, 1923.

1313. "George M. SLATER Memorial," *Conf. Vet. Mag.*, Vol. XXXI, May, 1923.

1314. "William Pinckney MASON Memorial," *Conf. Vet. Mag.*, Vol. XXXI, 1923.

1315. Ellerbe, Mrs. J.E., "Sidnet LANIER," *Conf. Vet. Mag.*, Vol. XXXI, June, 1923.

1316. FAY, J.B., "The Last Winter of the War," *Conf. Vet. Mag.*, Vol. XXXI, June, 1923.

1317. Thornberry, Miss Ruby S., "The Alabama," *Conf. Vet. Mag.*, Vol. XXXi, July, 1923.

1318. "George T. SHOWER, M.D. Memorial," *Conf. Vet. Mag.*, Vol. XXXI, July, 1923.

1319. Fulton, W.F., "Archer's Brigade at Cold Harbor," *Conf. Vet. Mag.*, Vol. XXXI, August, 1923.

1320. "General Edward Lloyd Thomas of Georgia," *Conf. Vet. Mag.*, Vol. XXXI, 1923.

1321. "Lawrence Thompson DICKINSON Memorial," *Conf. Vet. Mag.*, Vol. XXXI, September, 1923.

1322. "Incidents of the Surrender," *Conf. Vet. Mag.*, Vol. XXXI, October, 1923.

1323. "General Lee's Proclamation to the People of Maryland," *Conf. Vet. Mag.*, Vol. XXXI, December, 1923.

1324. Myus, Henry, "Cruising with the Sumter," *Conf. Vet. Mag.*, Vol. XXXI, 1923.

1325. Purifoy, John, "Ewell's Attack at Gettysburg, July 2, 1863," *Conf. Vet. Mag.*, Vol. XXXI, December, 1923.

1326. STRICKLER, H.M., "Some Experiences with the Cavalry," *Conf. Vet. Mag.*, Vol. XXXII, February, 1924.

1327. "Dr. Basil Lanneau GILDERSLEEVE Memorial," *Conf. Vet. Mag.*, Vol. XXXII, March, 1924.

APPENDIX B: REFERENCES

1328. "Henry REDWOOD Memorial," *Conf. Vet. Mag.*, Vol. XXXII, March, 1924.

1329. Andrews, Matthew Page, "Review of Historical Ignorance," Conf. Vet. *Mag.*, Vol. XXXII, April, 1924.

1330. "Autographs from an Old Album," *Conf. Vet. Mag.*, Vol. XXXII, April, 1924.

1331. "Autographs from an Old Album," *Conf. Vet. Mag.*, Vol. XXXII, May, 1924.

1332. "John J. CONROY Memorial," *Conf. Vet. Mag.*, Vol. XXXII, May, 1924.

1333. Morton, G. Nash, "From the Rapidan to Richmond," *Conf. Vet. Mag.*, Vol. XXXII, June, 1924.

1334. "John H. SCHOPPERT Memorial," *Conf. Vet. Mag.*, Vol. XXXII, July, 1924.

1335. Sitler, John C., "The Signal Corps," *Conf. Vet. Mag.*, Vol. XXXII, July, 1924.

1336. Jones, John Ashley, "Some Childhood Recollections of Admiral Raphael SEMMES, The Confederate Naval Hero and Father RYAN, The Poet of the Confederacy," *Conf. Vet. Mag.*, Vol. XXXII, 1924.

1337. Venable, M.W., "On the Way to Appomattox - War Memories," *Conf. Vet. Mag.*, Vol. XXXII, August, 1924.

1338. "Promotions in the Army and Navy of the Confederacy for Distinguished Valor and Skill," *Conf. Vet. Mag.*, Vol. XXXII, August, 1924.

1339. Agnew, N.J., "With the Virginia Cavalry," *Conf. Vet. Mag.*, Vol. XXXII, September, 1924.

1340. Siles, John C., "For Distinguisned Valor and Skill," *Conf. Vet. Mag.*, Vol. XXXII, 1924.

1341. "William H.H. RALEIGH Memorial," *Conf. Vet. Mag.*, Vol. XXXII, September, 1924.

1342. Purifoy, John, "The Artillery at Gettysburg," *Conf. Vet. Mag.*, Vol. XXXII, November, 1924.

1343. "Rev. William Meade DAME D.D. Memorial," *Conf. Vet. Mag.*, Vol. XXXII, November, 1924.

1344. Andrews, Matthew Page, "Review of Women of the South in War Times," *Conf. Vet. Mag.*, Vol. XXXIII, February, 1925.

1345. Siles, John C., "Shock Officers," *Conf. Vet. Mag.*, Vol. XXXIII, February, 1925.

APPENDIX B: REFERENCES

1346. "One of the Oldest Confederate Veterans," *Conf. Vet. Mag.*, Vol. XXXIII, April, 1925.

1347. PETERKIN, W.G., "Stonewall Jackson's Corps," *Conf. Vet. Mag.*, Vol. XXXIII, 1925.

1348. "John B. FAY Memorial," *Conf. Vet. Mag.*, Vol. XXXIII, April, 1925.

1349. Siles, John C., "Some Marines," *Conf. Vet. Mag.*, Vol. XXXIII, May, 1925.

1350. "General James R. WHEELER Memorial," *Conf. Vet. Mag.*, Vol. XXXIII, May, 1925.

1351. "Mrs. G. Smith Norris Memorial," *Conf. Vet. Mag.*, Vol. XXXIII, May, 1925.

1352. TORRENT, Captain Joseph F., "With the Blockade Runners," Conf. Vet. Mag., Vol. XXXIII, June, 1925.

1353. "Alexander MURRAY Memorial," *Conf. Vet. Mag.*, Vol. XXXIII, June, 1925.

1354. Barney, Judge Saffold, "Personal Recollections of Admiral SEMMES," *Conf. Vet. Mag.*, Vol. XXXIII, July, 1925.

1355. "Claphan MURRAY Memorial," *Conf. Vet. Mag.*, Vol. XXXIII, September, 1925.

1356. "Lost Survivor of the Battle Abby Committee," *Conf. Vet. Mag.*, Vol. XXXIII, October, 1925.

1357. DUFFEY, J.W., "Capture of Generals Crook and Kelly," *Conf. Vet. Mag.*, Vol. XXXIII, November, 1925.

1358. "John Ogilvie ELGIN Memorial," *Conf. Vet. Mag.*, Vol. XXXIII, November, 1925.

1359. "Comrades of Hagerstown, Maryland," *Conf. Vet. Mag.*, Vol. XXXIII, December, 1925.

1360. Tomb, Captain James H., "When Farragut Passed the Forts," *Conf. Vet. Mag.*, Vol. XXXIV, February, 1926.

1361. AISQUITH, Hobart, "The Confederate Home of Maryland," *Conf. Vet. Mag.*, Vol. XXXIV, March, 1926.

1362. Brunson, Mattie M., "The Flag of Pee Dee Battery," *Conf. Vet. Mag.*, Vol. XXXIV, March, 1926.

1363. "Rev. William B. EVERETT Memorial," *Conf. Vet. Mag.*, Vol. XXXIV, March, 1926.

1364. Siles, John C., "General Pemberton's Staff Officers," *Conf. Vet. Mag.*, Vol. XXXIV, April, 1926.

1365. "Major T.O. CHESTNEY Memorial," *Conf. Vet. Mag.*, Vol. XXXIV, April, 1926.

1366. "Samuel P. MENDEZ Memorial," *Conf. Vet. Mag.*, Vol. XXXIV, April, 1926.

1367. Baxley, Dr. Haughton, "Surgeons of the Confederacy," *Conf. Vet. Mag.*, Vol. XXXIV, 1926.

1368. "Major Thomas B. BEALL Memorial," *Conf. Vet. Mag.*, Vol. XXXIV, May, 1926.

1369. Kuykendall, Rhea, "Surgeons of the Confederacy," *Conf. Vet. Mag.*, Vol. XXXIV, June, 1926.

1370. Seth, Judge Joseph B., "Dr. Edward N. COVEY of Maryland," *Conf. Vet. Mag.*, Vol. XXXIV, June, 1926.

1371. GATCH, Thomas B., "Recollections of New Market," *Conf. Vet. Mag.*, Vol. XXXIV, June, 1926.

1372. Hite, Cornelius B., "Bravery of Southern Women," *Conf. Vet. Mag.*, Vol. XXXIV, June, 1926.

1373. Straham, Charles, "Jackson's Grim Humor," *Conf. Vet. Mag.*, Vol. XXXIV, June, 1926.

1374. Andrews, Matthew Page, "Review of A Popular Myth," *Conf. Vet. Mag.*, Vol. XXXIV, June, 1926.

1375. SHEPHERD, Dr. Henry E., "Heroic Leader of the Boys at New Market," *Conf. Vet. Mag.*, Vol. XXXIV, July, 1926.

1376. "Stonewall's Commissary General Major Wells J. HAWKS," *Conf. Vet. Mag.*, Vol. XXXIV, August, 1926.

1377. "Maryland Confederate Home," *Conf. Vet. Mag.*, Vol. XXXIV, August, 1926.

1378. "West Virginia Battle Ground," *Conf. Vet. Mag.*, Vol. XXXIV, September, 1926.

1379. "Henry Monfort GRAVES Memorial," *Conf. Vet. Mag.*, Vol. XXXIV, September, 1926.

1380. "John WILLIAMS Memorial," *Conf. Vet. Mag.*, Vol. XXXIV, November, 1926.

1381. "Maryland Division U.C.V.," *Conf. Vet. Mag.*, Vol. XXXIV, December, 1926.

1382. "Charles E. BIEDLER Memorial," *Conf. Vet. Mag.*, Vol. XXXIV, December, 1926.

1383. "John W. WILLIAMS Memorial," *Conf. Vet. Mag.*, Vol. XXXIV, December, 1926.

1384. Stewart, Richard D., "A Woman of the Sixties," *Conf. Vet. Mag.*, Vol. XXXIV, December, 1926.

1385. Haw, Joseph R., "Last of C.S. Ordnance Department," *Conf. Vet. Mag.*, Vol. XXXV, January, 1927.

1386. Sellman, Mrs. John P., "Experiences of a War-Time Girl," *Conf. Vet. Mag.*, Vol. XXXV, January, 1927.

1387. AISQUITH, Col. Hobart., "A Confederate Mother," *Conf. Vet. Mag.*, Vol. XXXV, February, 1927.

1388. "Henry W. TREAKLE Memorial," *Conf. Vet. Mag.*, Vol. XXXV, March, 1927.

1389. "Reasin Beall VAN METER Memorial," *Conf. Vet. Mag.*, Vol. XXXV, March, 1927.

1390. WORTHINGTON, Glenn H., "A Young Maryland Confederate," *Conf. Vet. Mag.*, Vol. XXXV, March, 1927.

1391. HAWKS, A.W., "Old War Stories - Ever New," *Conf. Vet. Mag.*, Vol. XXXV, April, 1927.

1392. Andrews, Matthew Page, "Review of An Old Book Re-Reviewed," *Conf. Vet. Mag.*, Vol. XXXV, May, 1927.

1393. Miller, C.M., "Sixty-Two Years From Appomattox," *Conf. Vet. Mag.*, Vol. XXXV, May, 1927.

1394. Andrews, Matthew Page, "Review of An Aide-De-Camp of Lee Reviewed," *Conf. Vet. Mag.*, Vol. XXXV, June, 1927.

1395. Steuart, R.D., "Surgeon of the Confederacy, Dr. William F. STEUART," *Conf. Vet. Mag.*, Vol. XXXV, June, 1927.

1396. "Louisiana in Confederate Congresses," *Conf. Vet. Mag.*, Vol. XXXV, June, 1927.

1397. "Better Than Riches," *Conf. Vet. Mag.*, Vol. XXXV, July, 1927.

1398. Hite, Cornelius B., "Truth Crushed to Earth," *Conf. Vet. Mag.*, Vol. XXXV, July, 1927.

APPENDIX B: REFERENCES

1399. Andrews, Matthew Page, "Review of The Military Genius of Abraham Lincoln," *Conf. Vet. Mag.*, Vol. XXXV, July, 1927.

1400. STEAURT, Richard D., "The Long Arm of the Confederacy," *Conf. Vet. Mag.*, Vol. XXXV, July, 1927.

1401. POWELL, H.F., "Maryland and Religious Freedom," *Conf. Vet. Mag.*, Vol. XXXV, August, 1927.

1402. Andrews, Matthew Page, "Review of The 'Peacemakers of 1864,'' *Conf. Vet. Mag.*, Vol. XXXV, August, 1927.

1403. "Chapman MAUPIN," *Conf. Vet. Mag.*, Vol. XXXV, August, 1927.

1404. Newman, Mrs. S.H., "Admiral Raphael SEMMES: His Service to the Southern Confederacy," *Conf. Vet. Mag.*, Vol. XXXV, 1927.

1405. "Maryland Comrades," *Conf. Vet. Mag.*, Vol. XXXV, September, 1927.

1406. Owen, Annie R. Chalmers, "James Chalmers of Virginia," *Conf. Vet. Mag.*, Vol. XXXV, December, 1927.

1407. "Captain John M. HICKEY Memorial," *Conf. Vet. Mag.*, Vol. XXXV, December, 1927.

1408. Worthington, Judge Glenn H., "The Battle of Monocacy," *Conf. Vet. Mag.*, Vol. XXXVI, January, 1928.

1409. Bradwell, I.G., "In the Battle of Monocacy, Maryland," *Conf. Vet. Mag.*, Vol. XXXVI, February, 1928.

1410. Andrews, Matthes Page, "Review of 'Matthew Fontaine Maury,'" *Conf. Vet. Mag.*, Vol. XXXVI, March, 1928.

1411. Brantley, I.G., "On to Washington," *Conf. Vet. Mag.*, Vol. XXXVI, March, 1928.

1412. "William B. MINOR Memorial," *Conf. Vet. Mag.*, Vol. XXXVI, April, 1928.

1413. "Col. James M. MORGAN Memorial," *Conf. Vet. Mag.*, Vol. XXXVI, June, 1928.

1414. "John R. Kenly Memorial," *Conf. Vet. Mag.*, Vol. XXXVI, June, 1928.

1415. "C.R. HOLLAR Memorial," *Conf. Vet. Mag.*, Vol. XXXVI, June, 1928.

1416. Andrews, Matthew Page, "Review of 'Essays - Historical and Critical,'" *Conf. Vet. Mag.*, Vol. XXXVI, July, 1928.

1417. Tinsley, Alexander L., "Jeb Stuart's Tribute to His Horse," *Conf. Vet. Mag.*, Vol. XXXVI, July, 1928.

APPENDIX B: REFERENCES

1418. Beale, H.D., "An All-Night Ride and Its Reward," *Conf. Vet. Mag.*, Vol. XXXVI, July, 1928.

1419. "John M. HEIGHE Memorial," *Conf. Vet. Mag.*, Vol. XXXVI, July, 1928.

1420. "Commander of the Maryland Division, U.C.V.," *Conf. Vet. Mag.*, Vol. XXXVI, August, 1928.

1421. "Charles M. MILLER Memorial," *Conf. Vet. Mag.*, Vol. XXXVI, August, 1928.

1422. "Captain William L. RITTER Memorial," *Conf. Vet. Mag.*, Vol. XXXVI, September, 1928.

1423. "Maryland Veterans," *Conf. Vet. Mag.*, Vol. XXXVI, September, 1928.

1424. Minnick, J.W., "With the Louisiana Zouaves," *Conf. Vet. Mag.*, Vol. XXXVi, November, 1928.

1425. "William H. MALONEY Memorial," *Conf. Vet. Mag.*, Vol. XXXVI, November, 1928.

1426. DUFFEY, Rev. J.W., "The Blue and the Gray in Reunion," *Conf. Vet. Mag.*, Vol. XXXVII, January, 1929.

1427. Andrews, Matthew Page, "Review of 'Yale University Honors a Southern States Man,'" *Conf. Vet. Mag.*, Vol. XXXVII, 1929.

1428. "John F. LYNNS Memorial," *Conf. Vet. Mag.*, Vol. XXXVII, January, 1929.

1429. "Tablet to Sydney LANIER," *Conf. Vet. Mag.*, Vol. XXXVII, 1929.

1430. Andrews, Matthew Page, "Review of 'The Pageant of America,'" *Conf. Vet. Mag.*, Vol. XXXVII, 1929.

1431. Wickham, Julia Poscher, "Commanders of the Confederate Navy," *Conf. Vet. Mag.*, Vol. XXXVII, February, 1929.

1432. "A Confederate from Arkansas," *Conf. Vet. Mag.*, Vol. XXXVII, February, 1929.

1433. "John Goldsborough WHITE Memorial," *Conf. Vet. Mag.*, Vol. XXXVII, February, 1929.

1434. "Rev. H.M. STRICKLER Memorial," *Conf. Vet. Mag.*, Vol. XXXVII, February, 1929.

1435. "Father RYAN as a Confederate Chaplain," *Conf. Vet. Mag.*, Vol. XXXVII, March, 1929.

APPENDIX B: REFERENCES

1436. Andrews, Matthew Page, "Review of 'John Wilkes Booth,'" *Conf. Vet. Mag.*, Vol. XXXVII, April, 1929.

1437. "General Lee's Staff Officers," *Conf. Vet. Mag.*, Vol. XXXVII, May, 1929.

1438. COOKE, Major Giles B., "When With General Lee," *Conf. Vet. Mag.*, Vol. XXXVII, 1929.

1439. Tilghman, Mary M., "Running the Blockade," *Conf. Vet. Mag.*, Vol. XXXVII, 1929.

1440. TINSLEY, Alexander L., "General Stuart's Spurs," *Conf. Vet. Mag.*, Vol. XXXVII, May, 1929.

1441. Andrews, Matthew Page, "History of Maryland," *Conf. Vet. Mag.*, Vol. XXXVII, May, 1929

1442. "Biography of Admiral BUCHANAN," *Conf. Vet. Mag.*, Vol. XXXVII, June, 1929.

1443. Tinsley, Mrs. R.W., "The Mason and Dixon Line," *Conf. Vet. Mag.*, Vol. XXXVII, 1929.

1444. "Col. Charles S. AMMELL Memorial," *Conf. Vet. Mag.*, Vol. XXXVII, June, 1929.

1445. Maupin, Sally Washington, "In Memoriam Dr. Henry E. SHEPHERD," *Conf. Vet. Mag.*, Vol. XXXVII, July, 1929.

1446. Hunneberger, Mrs. Maude B., "Findings in Maryland History," *Conf. Vet. Mag.*, ol. XXXVII, July, 1929.

1447. "A Reunion at a Reunion," *Conf. Vet. Mag.*, Vol. XXXVII, August, 1929.

1448. Bouldin, Mrs. Charles N., "The Maryland Flag," *Conf. Vet. Mag.*, Vol. XXXVII, September, 1929.

1449. Winter, Mrs. Mary Carter, "Honored at Stratford," *Conf. Vet. Mag.*, Vol. XXXVII, October, 1929.

1450. Andrews, Matthew Page, "Review of 'The Tragic Era,'" *Conf. Vet. Mag.*, Vol. XXXVII, October, 1929.

1451. Lewis, Charles Lee, "Admiral Franklin BUCHANAN," *Conf. Vet. Mag.*, Vol. XXXVII, November, 1929.

1452. "Last of a Maryland Company," *Conf. Vet. Mag.*, Vol. XXXVII, November, 1929.

1453. Ashe, Captain S.A., "Trained in the Old Naval School," *Conf. Vet. Mag.*, Vol. XXXVIII, January, 1930.

APPENDIX B: REFERENCES

1454. Andrews, Matthew Page, "Review of 'Admiral Franklin BUCHANAN,'" *Conf. Vet. Mag.*, Vol. XXXVIII, 1930.

1455. "Mason and Dixon Line," *Conf. Vet. Mag.*, Vol. XXXVIII, February, 1930.

1456. Andrews, Matthew Page, "Review of 'Thomas Jefferson, the Apostle of Americanism,'" *Conf. Vet. Mag.*, Vol. XXXVIII, March, 1930.

1457. Floyd, Mrs. J.W., "Southern Sentiment in Maryland," *Conf. Vet. Mag.*, Vol. XXXVIII, April, 1930.

1458. Andrews, Matthew Page, "Review of John Brown: The Making of a Martyr,'" *Conf. Vet. Mag.*, Vol. XXXVIII, May, 1930.

1459. "Jefferson Waite DUFFEY Memorial," *Conf. Vet. Mag.*, Vol. XXXVIII, June, 1930.

1460. "Tennesseans with a Maryland Battery," *Conf. Vet. Mag.*, Vol. XXXVIII, June, 1930.

1461. "George C. JENKINS Memorial," *Conf. Vet. Mag.*, Vol. XXXVIII, July, 1930.

1462. Andrews, Matthew Page, "Review of 'Sons of the Old South,'" *Conf. Vet. Mag.*, Vol. XXXVIII, August, 1930.

1463. "Edgar L. TSCHIFFELY Memorial," *Conf. Vet. Mag.*, Vol. XXXVIII, August, 1930.

1464. Clift, Brooks, "The Confederate Navy," *Conf. Vet. Mag.*, VOl. XXXVIII, September, 1930.

1465. "Thomas H. WHITE Memorial," *Conf. Vet. Mag.*, Vol. XXXVIII, October, 1930.

1466. "Thomas K. NAYLOR Memorial," *Conf. Vet. Mag.*, Vol. XXXVIII, October, 1930.

1467. "E.L. TSCHIFFELY Memorial," *Conf. Vet. Mag.*, Vol. XXXVIII, October, 1930.

1468. Andrews, Matthew Page, "Review of 'Award of the Simon Baruch University Prize,'" *Conf. Vet. Mag.*, CVol. XXXVIII, December, 1930.

1469. Andrews, Matthew Page, "Review of 'The Age of Hate,'" *Conf. Vet. Mag.*, Vol. XXXIX, February, 1931.

1470. "From the President General - U.D.C.," *Conf. Vet. Mag.*, Vol. XXXIX, July, 1931.

1471. "Comrades Passing," *Conf. Vet. Mag.*, Vol. XXXIX, August, 1931.

APPENDIX B: REFERENCES

1472. Collier, Mrs. Bryan Wills, "Raphael SEMMES C.S. Navy," *Conf. Vet. Mag.*, Vol. XXXIX, September, 1931.

1473. Anderson, Mrs. John H., "Mrs. Rose Greenhow, Confederate Spy," Conf. *Vet. Mag.*, Vol. XXXIX, November, 1931.

1474. "U.D.C. Notes, Maryland," *Conf. Vet. Mag.*, Vol. XXXIX, 1931.

1475. "A Confederate Surgeon's Story," *Conf. Vet. Mag.*, Vol. XXXIX, December, 1931.

1476. Contes, Mrs. C.F., "Mosby's Rangers," *Conf. Vet. Mag.*, Vol. XL, March, 1932.

1477. Maupin, Sally Washington, "Battles Fought on Maryland Soil," *Conf.* Vet. Mag., Vol. XL, March, 1932.

1478. Dulaney, Carroll, "Mrs. Greenhow, Confederate Spy," *Conf. Vet. Mag.*, XL, May, 1932.

1479. Andrews, Matthew Page, "Review of 'Another Lee Biography,'" *Conf. Vet. Mag.*, Vol. XL, June, 1932.

1480. Taylor, Dr. Charles, "The Signal and Secret Service of the Confederate States," *Conf. Vet. Mag.*, Vol. XL, 1932.

1481. "Col. Oswald TILGHMAN of Maryland," *Conf. Vet. Mag.*, Vol. XL, September, 1932.

1482. Taylor, Charles E., "The Signal and Secret Service of the Confederate States," *Conf. Vet. Mag.*, Vol. XL, September, 1932.

1483. "Captain Theopilus TUNIS Memorial," *Conf. Vet. Mag.*, Vol. XL, November, 1932.

1484. Walkins, Mattie A., "Sidney LANIER, Poet, Musician, Soldier of the Confederacy," *Conf. Vet. Mag.*, Vol. XL, December, 1932.

1485. Davis, William C., "The Battle of New Market, Garden City, NY: Doubleday & Co., 1975.

1486. Hale, Laura Virginia, Four Valiant Years in Lower Shenandoah Valley. Strasburg, VA: Shenandoah Publishing House, 1968.

1487. Diary of Pvt. Edgar L. TSCHIFFELY, 1st Md Cav, Co A Erick Davis Collection, Baltimore, MD.

1488. Schilichter, Harvey G. Two Centuries of Grace and Growth in Manches*ter*. Wesminster, MD: The Times, 1961.

1489. DAVIS, Samuel B. Escape of a Confederate Officer from Prison. Norfolk, VA: The Landmark Publishing Company, 1892.

APPENDIX B: REFERENCES

1490. History of the Confederate Memorial Association of the South. Washington, D.C., 1904.

1491. LATIMER, Thomas S. Memoir of Professor Edward Lloyd HOWARD, M.D. Baltimore, MD, 1882.

1492. Mitchell, Mary. Divided Town. MA: Barre, 1968.

1493. CONRAD, Thomas Nelson. The Rebel Scout. Washington, D.C.: The National Publishing Co., 1904.

1494. Diary of an Unknown Member of the 2nd Maryland Artillery. Erick Davis Collection, Baltimore, MD.

1495. Captain Julius Ernast MEIRE, Marine Corps Papers. Held by Probate Court, Mobile County, AL.

1496. Confiscation of Rebel Property. Washington, D.C.

1497. Davis, Andrew Jackson. Defeats and Victories. Dodworth's Hall: New York, 1863.

1498. Bill, Alfred Hoyt. The Beleaguered City, Richmond 1861-1865. New York, 1964.

1499. Civil War Memorabilia of Captain French FORREST, Navy. Held by Virginia State Archives.

1500. Gasser, Charles. A typescript listing of Confederate Marines in the Civil War. Held By U.S. Naval Academy Museum, Annapolis, MD.

1501. Gardner, Philip. The Confederate States Marine Corps 1861-1865. A typescript held by U.S. Naval Academy Museum, Annapolis, MD.

1502. WARREN, Edeward. An Epitome of Practical Surgery for Field & Hospital. Richmond, VA: West & Johnston, 1863.

1503. CHISOLM, John Julius. A Manual of Military Surgery for the Use of Surgeons in the Confederate Army. Richmond, VA: West & Johnston, 1861.

1504. Speech on the Joint Resolution Explanatory of the Confederate Act, Washington, 1864. Pamphlet.

1505. Dorris, Jonathan Truman. Pardon & Amnesty Under Lincoln and Johnson. Chapel Hill, NC: University of North Carolina Press, 1953.

1506. Craven, Avery. Civil War in the Making. Baton Rouge, LA: Louisiana University Press, 1959.

1507. Barney, William L. The Secessionists Impulse. Princeton, NJ: Princeton University Press, 1974.

APPENDIX B: REFERENCES

1508. Alevander, Thomas B. and Richard E. Beringer. The Anatomy of the Confederate Congress. Nashville, TN: Vanderbilt University Press, 1972.

1509. Hammett, Regina Combs. St. Mary's County, MD. Ridg MD: St. Mary's County Bicentennial Commission, 1977.

1510. Diary of Col. Tench Francis TILGHMAN. Held by Hall of Records, Annapolis, MD.

1511. Civil War scrapbook of Mary Clara Hebb. Held by Hall of Records, Annapolis, MD.

1512. Thomas, John P. Career and Character of General Micah Jenkins, C.S.A. Columbia, SC: The State Company, 1903.

1513. Lewis, Samuel E. The Treatment of Prisoners of War 1861-1865. Washington, D.C., 1910.

1514. Tribute to Valor, Senator Wood. 1901.

1515. Personal papers and letters of Major Richard Taylor Allison, Marines. Private collection.

1516. Jenkins, Brian. Feniams and Anglo-American Relations During Reconstruction. Ithaca, NY: Cornell University Press, 1969.

1517. Johnston, James Angus. Virginia Railroads in the Civil War. Chapel Hill, NC: University of North Carolina Press, 1961.

1518. Carven, John J. Prison Life of Jefferson Davis. New York: Carlton, 1866.

1519. Gill, John. Reminiscences of Four Years as a Private Soldier in the Confederate Army. Baltimore, MD: Baltimore Sun Printing, 1904.

1520. Thomas, Armstrong. The Thomas Brothers of Mattapany. Washington, 1963.

1521. Jones, Katherine M. Ladies of Richmond, Confederate Capitol. Indianapolis, IN: Bobbs-Merrill, 1962.

1522. McWhiney, Grady. Southerners and Other Americans. New York, 1973.

1523. Newman, Harry Wright. Maryland and the Confederacy. Annapolis, MD: publ. by author, 1976.

1524. Collins, Clarence Eugene. Brief History of Somerset County Physicians. Crisfield, MD, 1959.

1525. ARCHER, George W. Some Doctors of Ye Olden Times. Emmorten, MD, 1892.

APPENDIX B: REFERENCES

1526. Steiner, Paul E. and Charles C. Thomas. Disease in the Civil War. Springfield, IL: [C.C. Thomas?], 1968.

1527. Brooks, Stewart and Charles C. Thomas. Civil War Medicine. Springfield, IL: [C.C. Thomas?], 1966.

1528. Harwell, Richard Barksdale, ed. Kate: The Journal of a Confederate Nurse. Baton Rouge, LA: Louisiana State University Press, 1959.

1529. Foley, Gerdner P.H. Proceedings of the 125th Anniversary Celebration of the Baltimore College of Dental Surgery. Baltimore, MD: Horn-Shafer Co., 1966.

1530. Platt, Samuel Joseph and Mary Louise Ogden. Medical Men and Institutions of Knox County, Tennessee 1789-1957. Knoxville, TN: S.B. Newman Printing Co., 1969.

1531. Ellis, John H. Medicine in Kentucky. The University Press of Kentucky, 1977.

1532. Waring, Joseph Ioor. A History of Medicine in South Carolina 1825-1900. South Carolina Medical Association, 1967.

1533. Quinan, John B. and Isaac Friedenwald. Medical Annals of Baltimore. Baltimore, MD, 1884.

1534. Blanton, Wyndham B. Medicine in Virginia in the Nineteenth Century. n.p.

1535. Diary of Dr. Robert R. GIBBES, Asst Surgeon. Private collection.

1536. Fauntleroy, Eugene. The Medical Annals of Maryland 1799-1899. Baltimore, MD: Williams and Williams, 1903.

1537. Atkinson, William B. and Charles Robson, ed. The Physicians and Surgeons of the United States. Philadlephia, PA, 1878.

1538. 1862-1864 U.S. Enrollment Records - Allegany County, Hall of Records, Annapolis, MD. Civilians designated as "gone south" or "serving in the C.S.A."

1539. 1862-1864 U.S. Enrollment Records - Anne Arundel County, Hall of Records, Annapolis, MD. Civilians designated as "gone south" or "serving in the C.S.A."

1540. 1862-1864 U.S. Enrollment Records - Baltimore, Hall of Records, Annapolis, MD. Civilians designated as "gone south" or "serving in the C.S.A."

1541. 1862-1864 U.S. Enrollment Records - Baltimore County, Hall of Records, Annapolis, MD. Civilians designated as "gone south" or "serving in the C.S.A."

APPENDIX B: REFERENCES

1542. 1862-1864 U.S. Enrollment Records - Calvert County, Hall of Records, Annapolis, MD. Civilians designated as "gone south" or "serving in the C.S.A."

1543. 1862-1864 U.S. Enrollment Records - Caroline County, Hall of Records, Annapolis, MD. Civilians designated as "gone south" or "serving in the C.S.A."

1544. 1862-1864 U.S. Enrollment Records - Carroll County, Hall of Records, Annapolis, MD. Civilians designated as "gone south" or "serving in the C.S.A."

1545. 1862-1864 U.S. Enrollment Records - Cecil County, Hall of Records, Annapolis, MD. Civilians designated as "gone south" or "serving in the C.S.A."

1546. 1862-1864 U.S.Enrollment Records - Charles County, Hall of Records, Annapolis, MD. Civilians designated as "gone south" or "serving in the C.S.A."

1547. 1862-1864 U.S. Enrollment Records - Dorchester County, Hall of Records, Annapolis, MD. Civilians designated as "gone south" or "serving in the C.S.A."

1548. 1862-1864 U.S. Enrollment Records - Frederick County, Hall of Records, Annapolis, MD. Civilians designated as "gone south" or "serving in the C.S.A."

1549. 1862-1864 U.S. Enrollment Records - Harford County, Hall of Records, Annapolis, MD. Civilians designated as "gone south" or "serving in the C.S.A."

1550. 1862-1864 U.S. Enrollment Record - Howard County, Hall of Records, Annapolis, MD. Civilians designated as "gone south" or "serving in the C.S.A."

1551. 1862-1864 U.S. Enrollment Reocords - Kent County, Hall of Records, Annapolis, MD. Civilians designated as "gone south" or "serving in the C.S.A."

1552. 1862-1864 U.S. Enrollment Records - Montgomery County, Hall of Records, Annapolis, MD. Civilians designated as "gone south" or "serving in the C.S.A."

1553. 1862-1843 U.S. Enrollment Records - Prince George's County, Hall of Records, Annapolis, MD. Civilians designated as "gone south" or "serving in the C.S.A."

1554. 1864 U.S. Enrollment Records - Queen Anne's County, Hall of Records, Annapolis, MD. Civilians designated as "gone south" or "serving in the C.S.A."

APPENDIX B: REFERENCES

1555. 1862-1864 U.S. Enrollment Records - St. Mary's County, Hall of Records, Annapolis, MD. Civilians designated as "gone south" or "serving in the C.S.A."

1556. 1862-1864 U.S. Enrollment Records - Somerset County, Hall of Records, Annapolis, MD. Civilians designated as "gone south" or "serving in the C.S.A."

1557. 1862-1864 U.S. Enrollment Records - Talbot County, Hall of Records, Annapolis, MD. Civilians designated as "gone south" or "serving in the C.S.A."

1558. 1862-1864 U.S. Enrollment Records - Washington County, Hall of Records, Annapolis, MD. Civilians designated as "gone south" or "serving in the C.S.A."

1559. 1862-1864 U.S. Enrollment Records - Worcester County, Hall of Records, Annapolis, Md. Civilians designated as "gone south" or "serving in the C.S.A."

1560. Toomey, Daniel Carroll. The Civil War in Maryland. Baltimore, MD: Toomey Press, 1983.

1561. WARREN, Edward. A Doctor's Experiences in Three Continents. Baltimore, MD: Cushings and Bailey, 1885.

1562. Brooks, Neal A. and Eric G. Rockel. A History of Baltimore County. Towson, MD: Friends of the Towson Library, 1979.

1563. Smith, H.B. Between the Lines, Secret Service Stories. New York: Booz Brothers, 1911.

1564. Register of Offices of the Confederate States Navy 1861-1865. U.S. Government Printing Office, 1931.

1565. Davis, Erick F., "A Pikesville Diary of 1864," *History Trails* Baltimore County Historical Society. Vol. 13, No. 3.

1566. Davis, Erick F., "A Counterspy Reports," *History Trails* Baltimore County Historical Society. Vol. 13, No. 3.

1567. Hollifield, William, "Confederates at Chestnut Ridge," *History Trails* Baltimore County Historical Society. Vol. 13, No. 3.

1568. The National Historical Society, "Shadows of the Storm," *The Image of War 1861-1865,* Vol. I, Garden City, NY: Doubleday and Co., 1981.

1569. -----"The Guns of '62," *The Image of War 1861-1865,* Vol. II, Garden City, NY: Doubleday and Co., 1982.

1570. -----"The Embattled Confederacy," *The Image of War 1861-1865,* Vol. III, Garden City, NY: Doubleday and Co., 1982.

APPENDIX B: REFERENCES

1571. -----"Fighting For Time," The Image of War 1861-1865, Vol. IV, Garden City, NY: Doubleday and Co., 1983.

1572. -----"The South Besieged," The Image of War 1861-1865, Vol. V, Garden City, NY: Doubleday and Co., 1983.

1573. A listing of members of Alexander YOUNG United Confederate Veterans Camp No. 500 of Frederick.

1574. A listing of members of Ridgely BROWN United Confederate Veterans Camp No. 518 of Gaithersburg.

1575. A listing of members of Harry GILMOR United Confederate Veterans Camp No. 673 of Towson.

1576. Diary of Lt. Frank A ZIMMERMAN, 9th Va Inf Co B. Private collection.

1577. Tintypes - Ambrotypes - Cartes Devisites and Albumens of Maryland Confederates. Collection of Dave Mark, Linthicum, MD.

1578. Portraits of Maryland Confederates from the Collection of Erick F. Davis, Baltimore, MD.

1579. Photographs of Uniformed Maryland Confederate Soldiers, Sailors and Marines from the Collection of Daniel D. Hartzler, New Windsor, MD.

1580. Field, Sgt. George W. Roster of the Baltimore Artillery Company C, 19th Virginia Heavy Artillery.

1581. NORRIS, William. The Story of the Confederate States Ship Virginia. Baltimore, MD: John B. Piet, 1879.

1582. A Rebel Came Home, Diary of Floride Clemson. Private collection.

1583. Between North and South - A Maryland Journalist Views of the Civil War Narrative of William Wilkins Glenn 1861-1869. London, England: Associated University Press, 1976.

1584. Kirby, Walter J. Roll Call - The Civil War in Kent County, Maryland. Silver Spring, MD: Family Line, 1985.

1585. Hewitt, John H. Shadows on the Wall. Baltimore, MD: Turnbull Brothers, 1877.

1586. Gaede, Frederick C. The Independent Greys - Co. A, 53rd Regiment M.V.I. 1980.

1587. Gaede, Frederick C. The Militia of Baltimore 1792-1861. Johns Hopkins University, 1979.

1588. Virginia County Civil War, 4 vols. Middleburg, VA: The County Publishers, 1983.

APPENDIX B: REFERENCES

1589. Tyler, Lyon G. Encyclopedia of Virginia, 4 vols. New York: Lewis Historical Publshing Co., 1915.

1590. Biography, Virginia. History of Virginia, 6 vols. New York: The American Historical Society, 1924.

1591. Owen, Thomas McAdory. History of Alabama and Dictionary of Alabama, 4 vols. Spartanburg, South Carolina: The Reprint Co., 1978.

1592. Douglas, Henry Kyd. The Douglas Diary. Franklin and Marshall College, Lancaster, Pennsylvania, 1973.

1593. Donnelly, Ralph W. The History of the Confedeate States Marine Corps. New Bern, NC: Owen G. Dunn & Co., 1976.

1594. Connelly, Ralph W. Service Records of Confederate Enlisted Marines. New Bern, NC: Owen G. Dunn & Co., 1979.

1595. Krich, Robert K. Parker's Virginia Battery C.S.A. Barryville, VA: Virginia Book Co., 1975.

1596. The Alumni Register of Civil War People from the University of Pennsylvania Medical School.

1597. Browne, Bennet B., Jr., comp. Browne Family Civil War Genealogy. Typescript held by Daniel D. Hartzler.

1598. Listing of members of James R. Herbert United Confederate Veterans Camp No. 657 of Baltimore. Private collection.

1599. Listing of members of Arnold ELZEY United Confederate Veterans Camp No. 1015 of Baltimore. Private collection.

1600. Krich, Robert K. Lee's Colonels - A Biographical Register of the Field Officers of the A.N.V. Dayton, OH: Morningside Bookshop, 1979.

1601. Capt. Warner G. Welsh, 1st Md Cav Co. D, - Heirlooms of the War for Southern Independence. Collection of Mrs. Oscar Joy, Libertytown, MD

1602. Buckler, Edward St. C., Jr., comp. Hough Family. Private collection of compiler, Annapolis, MD.

1603. TRIPPE, James McC. Address Delivered at the Dedication of the Confederate Women's Monument, Baltimore, MD, November 2, 1918.

1604. Jones, G.W. In Prison at Point Lookout. Martinsville, MD: Bulletin Printing and Publishing Company.

1605. The 1st Maryland Campaign. An Address by General Bradley T. John of Maryland before the Virginia Division of the Association of the Army of Northern Virginia. Richmond, VA: William Ellis Jones, 1884.

APPENDIX B: REFERENCES

1606. Address by S.T. Wallis delivered at the Academy of Music in Baltimore, April 10, 1875 on behalf of the Lee Memorial Association. Baltimore, MD: John Murphy and Company, 1875.

1607. Brenson, John C. "Gen. Bradley T. JOHNSON's Plan to Abduct President Lincoln." Chronicles of St. Mary's, Vol. 22, No. 11, November, 1974.

1608. Brenson, John C. "Gen. Bradley T. JOHNSON's Plan to Abduct President Lincoln." Chronicles of St. Mary's, Vol. 22, No. 12, December, 1974.

1609. Michel, Robert E. Colonel Harry GILMOR's Raid Around Baltimore. Baltimore, MD: Erbe Publishers, 1976.

1610. A listing of members of James BREATHED United Confederate Veterans Camp No. 1046 of Cumberland.

1611. Civil War memorabilia of Capt. J. Mortiner KILGOUR, Quartermaster, 35th Va Cav.

1612. A listing of members of Charles S. Winder United Confederate Veterans Camp No. 989 of Easton.

1613. A listing of members of John S. Mosby United Confederate Veterans Camp No. 821 of Baltimore.

1614. Albaugh, William A., III and Richard D. Stewart. The Original Confederate Colt. New York: Greenberg Publisher, 1953.

1615. Albaugh, William A., III and Edward N. Simmons. Confederate Arms. Harrisburg, PA: Stackpole Company, 1957.

1616. Albaugh, William A., III. Confederate Edged Weapons. New York: Harper and Brothers, 1960.

1617. Albaugh, WIlliam A., III, Hugh Benet Jr. and Edward N. Simmons. Confederate Handguns. York, PA: George Shumway, 1967.

1618. Hill, Richard T. and William E. Anthony. Confederate Longarms and Pistols. Dallas, TX: Taylor Publishing Company, 1978.

1619. Albaugh, William A., III. A Photographic Supplement of Confederate Swords. Orange, VA: Moss Publications, 1979.

1620. Hartzler, Daniel D. Confederate Presentation and Inscribed Swords and Revolvers. Unpublished manuscript.

1621. A listing of members of Mansfield Lovell United Confederate Veterans Camp No. 843 of Rockville.

1622. A listing of members of Allen THOMAS United Confederate Veterans Camp No. 918. of Hyattsville.

APPENDIX B: REFERENCES

1623. Blue and Gray Magazine - Vol. I, Issue 1, and Vol. II, Issue 4.

1624. Personal Civil War papers of Capt. Vincent CAVALIER - Signal Corps. Held by Maryland Hall of Records, Annapolis, MD.

1625. Ankrum, Freeman. Maryland and Pennsylvania Historical Sketches. West Newton, PA: The Times Sun, 1947.

1626. Truitt, Reginald V. and Millard G. Les Callete. Worcester County Maryland's Arcadia. Snow Hill, MD: Worcester County Historical Society, 1977.

1627. A listing of members of Bradley T. Johnson United Confederate Veterans Camp No. 1110 of Leonardtown.

1628. A listing of members of George H. Stewart United Confederate Veterans Camp No. 775 of Annapolis.

1629. Murphy, Dr. John M. Confederate Carbines & Musketoons. Dallas, TX: Taylor Publishing Company, 1986.

1630. Civil War letters written by Eugene C. Belden to relatives, 1862-1864.

1631. Bichy, H. Ellsworth. The Last Link. Copy held by Enoch Pratt Free Library, Baltimore, MD.

1632. Parker, William Harwar. Recollections of A Naval Officer 1841-1865. New York: Charles Scribner's & Sons, 1883.

1633. BUCK, Samuel D. With the Old Confeds. Baltimore, MD: H.E. Houck & Co., 1925.

1634. Diary of Pvt. Louis J. Watkins, 1st Md Cav Co. Dave Mark Collection.

1635. Diary of Pvt Fetter S. Hoblitzell, 1st Maryland Inf. Co. H. Dave Mark Collection.

1636. The McCraig Journal - A Confederate Family of Cumberland. Cumberland, MD: Allegany Co. Historical Society, 1984.

1637. Davis, William C., "The Civil War - Brother Against Brother," Alexandria, VA: *Time-Life Books*

1638. ------"The Civil War - First Blood," Alexandria, VA: *Time-Life Books*

1639. "The Civil War - The Blockade," Alexandria, VA: *Time-Life Books*

1640. Nevin, David, "The Civil War - The Road to Shiloh," Alexandria, VA: *Time-Life Books*.

APPENDIX B: REFERENCES

1641. Bailey, Ronald H., "The Civil War - Forward to Richmond," Alexandria, VA: *Time-Life Books*.

1642. Clark, Champ, "The Civil War - Decoying the Yanks," Alexandria, VA: *Time-Life Books*.

1643. Channing, Steven A.. "The Civil War - Confederate Ordeal," Alexandria, VA: *Time-Life Books*

1644. "The Civil War - Lee Takes Command," Alexandria, VA: *Time-Life Books*.

1645. Korn, Jerry, "The Civil War - The Fight for Chattonoog," Alexandria, VA: *Time-Life Books*

1646. Chaitin, Peter M., "The Civil War - The Coastal War," Alexandria, VA: *Time-Life Books*

1647. Robertson, James I., "The Civil War - Tenting Tonight," Alexandria, VA: *Time-Life Books*.

1648. Bailey, Ronald H., "The Civil War - The Bloodiest Day," Alexandria, VA: *Time-Life Books*

1649. Korn, Jerry, "The Civil War - War on the Mississippi," Alexandria, VA: *Time-Life Books*

1650. Goobrick, William K., "The Civil War - Rebels Resurgent," Alexandria, VA: *Time-Life Books*.

1651. Jackson, Donald Dale, "The Civil War - Twenty Million Yankees," Alexandria, VA: *Time-Life Books*

1652. Clark, Champ, "The Civil War - Gettysburg," Alexandria, VA: *Time-Life Books*.

1653. Korn, Jerry, "The Civil War - The Struggle for Tennessee," Alexandria, VA: *Time-Life Books* .

1654. Marphy, Wendv, "The Civil War - Spies, Scouts and Raiders," Alexandria, VA: *Time-Life Books* .

1655. Bailey, Ronald H.: "The Civil War - Battle for Atlanta," Alexandria, VA: *Time-Life Books* .

1656. Jaynes, G., "The Civil War - The Killing Ground," Alexandria, VA: *Time-Life Books*.

1657. Nevin, David, "The Civil War - Sherman's March," Alexandria, VA: *Time-Life Books*.

1658. "The Civil War - Death in the Trenches," Alexandria, VA: *Time-Life Books*.

APPENDIX B: REFERENCES

1659. Joseph, H., "The Civil War - War on the Frontier," Alexandria, VA: Time-Life Books.

1660. Osbornet, C., "The Civil War - Scourging the Rebels," Alexandria, VA: Time-Life Books.

1661. "The Civil War - Pursuit to Appomattox," Alexandria, VA: Time-Life Books.

1662. A listing of members of Captain Vincent CAMALIER Sons of Confederate Veterans Camp 1359 of Lenonardtown.

1663. A listing of members of Colonel Harry W. Gilmor Sons of Confederate Veterans Camp 1388 of Pikesville.

1664. A listing of members of Colonel William NORRIS Sons of Confederate Veterans Camp 1398 of Laurel.

1665. A listing of members of Private Wallace BOWLING Sons of Confederate Veterans Camp 1400 of La Plata.

1666. A listing of members of General John H. Winder Sons of Veterans Camp 1416 of Salisbury.

1667. Williams, T. Harry. The Life History of the United States, Volume V 1849-1865 -The Union Sandered.

1668. John Taylor Wood. Sea Ghost of the Confederacy. Athens, GA: The University of Georgia Press.

1669. Buck, Irving A. Cleburn & His Command. Washington, D.C.: Neale Publishing Company, 1908.

1670. Beitzell, Edwin W., comp. St. Mary's Countians in the Confederacy Who Were Not in Maryland Command:

1671. LYNCH, William F. Naval Life: Observations Afloat and On Shore. 1851.

1672. Mackall, William W. A Son's Recollections of His Father. New York: E.P. Dulton & Co., 1930.

1673. FORREST, Douglas Franch. Odyssey In Gray: A Diary of Confedertae Service, 1863-1865. Richmond, VA: Virginia State Library, 1979.

1674. Turner, William A. Even More Confederate Faces. Orange, VA: Turner, Moss Publications, 1983.

1675. Evidence of the Contested Election In the Case of Ridgely Vs. Grason to the General Assembly. Annapolis, MD: Richard P. Bayly Printers, 1865.

APPENDIX B: REFERENCES

1676. Horan, James D., ed. C.S.S. Shenandoah: The Memoirs of Lieutenant Commanding James I. WADDELL. New York: Crown Publishers, 1960.

1677. Divine, John E. 35th Battalion Virginia Cavalry. Lynchburgh, VA: H.E. Howard, 1985.

1678. Daniel, Larry J. and Gunter, Riley W. Confederate Cannon Foundries. Union City, TN: Pioneer Press, 1977.

1679. Holzman, Robert S. Adapt or Perish. Hamden, CT: The Shoe String Press, 1976.

1780. Burns, Zed H. Confederate Forts. Natchez, MS: Southern Historical Publications, 1977.

1681. Whitley, Edythe John Rucker. Sam Davis, Hero of the Confederacy. Nashville, TN, 1971.

1682. Goff, Richard D. Confederate Supply. Durham, NC: Duke University Press, 1969.

1683. Breeden, James O. Joseph Jones, M.D., Scientist of the Old South. University Press of Kentucky, 1975.

1684. Chance, Franklin N., Paul C. Chance and David L. Topper. Tangled Machinery and Charred Relics. Orangeburg, SC: Sun Printing, 1985.

1685. Dalaney, Caldwell. Confederate Mobile. Mobile, AL: The Haunted Book Shop, 1971.

1686. Gaddy, David Winfred. John William "Altamont" Palmer, Confederate Agent.

1687. Couper, Wm. The V.M.I. New Market Cadets. Charlottesville, VA: The Michie Co., 1933.

1688. Jones, Laddie L. Dentristry Under the Stars and Bars. Typescript held by Dental College Library, University of Maryland.

1689. The Alumni of of the Baltimore College of Dental Surgery, Maryland Dental College of the University of Maryland who Served in the Civil War. Typescript held by Dental College Library, University of Maryland.

1690. Callcott, George H. A History of the University of Maryland. Baltimore, MD: Maryland Historical Socity, 1966.

INDEX to narrative section (does not include Roster of Appendix A)

INDEX to narrative section (does not include Roster of Appendix A)

INDEX to narrative section (does not include Roster of Appendix A)

INDEX to narrative section (does not include Roster of Appendix A)